A+ Certification Troubleshooting and Repair, Third Edition

Gail Sandler
Rozanne Murphy Whalen

A+ Certification Troubleshooting and Repair, Third Edition

Part Number: ACS21140
Course Edition: 1.0

Acknowledgments

Project Team

Curriculum Developer and Technical Writer: Gail Sandler and Rozanne Murphy Whalen • **Development Assistance:** Lorraine Vachon, Nancy Curtis, Judith A. Kling, Andrew LaPage, Taryn Manuele and Sue San Filippo • **Content Manager:** Tina Maria Nelson and Clare Dygert • **Copy Editors:** Angie J. French, Christy D. Johnson, Elizabeth M. Swank and Laura Thomas • **Material Editors:** Lance Anderson and Frank Wosnick • **Print Designer:** Isolina Salgado Toner • **Cover Designer:** Vanessa Boehmke • **Photography:** Greg Gefell • **Project Technical Specialist:** Michael Toscano

NOTICES

DISCLAIMER: While Element K Courseware LLC takes care to ensure the accuracy and quality of these materials, we cannot guarantee their accuracy, and all materials are provided without any warranty whatsoever, including, but not limited to, the implied warranties of merchantability or fitness for a particular purpose. The name used in the data files for this course is that of a fictitious company. Any resemblance to current or future companies is purely coincidental. We do not believe we have used anyone's name in creating this course, but if we have, please notify us and we will change the name in the next revision of the course. Element K is an independent provider of integrated training solutions for individuals, businesses, educational institutions, and government agencies. Use of screenshots, photographs of another entity's product, or another entity's product name or service in this book is for editorial purposes only. No such use should be construed to imply sponsorship or endorsement of the book by, nor any affiliation of such entity with Element K.

TRADEMARK NOTICES Element K and the Element K logo are trademarks of Element K LLC.

A+ Certification is a registered trademark of CompTIA in the U.S. and other countries; the CompTIA products and services discussed or described may be trademarks of CompTIA .

All other product names and services used throughout this book may be common law or registered trademarks of their respective proprietors.

Copyright © 2003 Element K Content LLC. All rights reserved. Screenshots used for illustrative purposes are the property of the software proprietor. This publication, or any part thereof, may not be reproduced or transmitted in any form or by any means, electronic or mechanical, including photocopying, recording, storage in an information retrieval system, or otherwise, without express written permission of Element K, 500 Canal View Boulevard, Rochester, NY 14623, (585) 240-7500, (800) 434-3466. Element K Courseware LLC's World Wide Web site is located at www.elementkcourseware.com.

This book conveys no rights in the software or other products about which it was written; all use or licensing of such software or other products is the responsibility of the user according to terms and conditions of the owner. Do not make illegal copies of books or software. If you believe that this book, related materials, or any other Element K materials are being reproduced or transmitted without permission, please call 1-800-478-7788.

The logo of the CompTIA Authorized Curriculum Program and the status of this or other training material as "Authorized" under the CompTIA Authorized Curriculum Program signifies that, in CompTIA's opinion, such training material covers the content of the CompTIA's related certification exam. CompTIA has not reviewed or approved the accuracy of the contents of this training material and specifically disclaims any warranties of merchantability or fitness for a particular purpose. CompTIA makes no guarantee concerning the success of persons using any such "Authorized" or other training material in order to prepare for any CompTIA certification exam. The contents of this training material were created for the CompTIA A+ exam covering CompTIA certification exam objectives that were current as of April, 2003.

How to Become CompTIA Certified: This training material can help you prepare for and pass a related CompTIA certification exam or exams. In order to achieve CompTIA certification, you must register for and pass a CompTIA certification exam or exams. In order to become CompTIA certified, you must:

1. Select a certification exam provider. For more information please visit http://www.comptia.org/certification/genral_information/test_locations.asp.
2. Register for and schedule a time to take the CompTIA certification exam(s) at a convenient location.
3. Read and sign the Candidate Agreement, which will be presented at the time of the exam(s). The text of the Candidate Agreement can be found at http://www.comptia.org/certification/general_information/candidate_agreement.asp.
4. Take and pass the CompTIA certification exam(s).

For more information about CompTIA's certifications, such as their industry acceptance, benefits, or program news, please visit http://www.comptia.org/certification/default.asp. CompTIA is a non-profit information technology (IT) trade association. CompTIA's certifications are designed by subject matter experts from across the IT industry. Each CompTIA certification is vendor-neutral, covers multiple technologies, and requires demonstration of skills and knowledge widely sought after by the IT industry. To contact CompTIA with any questions or comments: Please call + 1 630 268 1818 questions@comptia.org.

A+ Certification Troubleshooting and Repair, Third Edition

Chapter 1: Introduction to Computers

A. A Brief History of Computers 2
    Evolution of Mechanical Computers 2
    Electronic Computers 4
    Vacuum Tubes 4
    Transistors and Magnetic Memory 5
    Integrated Circuits 5

B. Desktop Computer System Components and Their Functions 8
    Input/Output Devices 8
    System Board 9
    Processor 11
    Memory 12
    Storage Media 12

C. Software and Firmware 14
    System Software 14
    Application Software 15
    Driver Software 15

D. Numbering Systems	**17**
The Decimal Number System	17
The Binary Number System	19
The Hexadecimal Number System	22

Chapter 2: Setting Up a Personal Computer

A. Install Video Output Devices	**30**
Peripheral Devices	30
Video Output Devices	31
Ports	34
Display Characteristics	35
B. Install PS/2 Devices	**41**
PS/2 Interface	41
PS/2 Devices	43
Device Drivers	44
C. Install Parallel Devices	**46**
Parallel Interfaces	47
Parallel Devices	51
D. Install Serial Devices	**52**
Bits and Bytes	52
Serial Communications	53
Serial Interfaces	53
Device Manager	58
Serial Port Settings	58
Registered Jacks	61
Modem	62
Modem Commands	66
E. Install Game and Sound Devices	**68**
Sound Card Interfaces	68
Sound Devices	70

F. Install USB Devices	74
USB	74
Touch Screen Input Devices	77
USB Power	78
G. Install FireWire Devices	79
FireWire	79
H. Connect Wireless Devices	82
Wireless Connections	82

CHAPTER 3: INSTALLING OR REMOVING INTERNAL HARDWARE

A. Establish an ESD-free Work Area	90
The Electrical Flow Process	90
Electrical Terms	91
ESD	92
ESD Safety Equipment	93
Electrical Safety Hazards Inside the PC	94
Optimal Operating Environment	95
B. Install or Remove Adapter Cards	96
Internal PC Components	96
Adapter Cards	97
Bus Types	98
Number Systems	105
Hex Numbers in Addresses	106
Hardware Resources	106
Technician's Toolkit	110

C. Install a Network Adapter and Cable 112

Networks 113
Network Cables and Connectors 114
Twisted Pair Cable 115
Coaxial Cables 117
Coaxial Cable Connectors 118
Backbone Cables 119
PVC and Plenum Cables 120
Network Protocols 121
IP Address 121
Subnet Mask 122
TCP/IP 123
Name Servers 124
Automatic TCP/IP Configuration Methods 125
Network Architectures 125
Internet Connections 127
LAN Internet Connection 128
DSL Internet Connections 130
Cable Internet Connections 131
ISDN Internet Connections 131
Dial-up Internet Connections 132
Satellite Internet Connections 132
A Wireless Internet Connection 133

D. Install or Remove IDE Drives 134

Drives 134
Drive Bay 139
Disk Drive Architecture 140
Disk Drive Geometry 141
Drive Interfaces 143
Drive Controller 146
IDE Drives 146

| E. Install or Remove Internal SCSI Drives **149**
            SCSI 150
            SCSI Addresses 151
            SCSI Signaling Techniques 152
            SCSI Termination 153
            SCSI Types 154
            SCSI Interface 155

       F. Install External SCSI Devices **157**

       G. RAID **158**

CHAPTER 4: UPGRADING SYSTEM COMPONENTS

       A. Add Memory **166**
            Memory 166
            Types of RAM 167
            Types of ROM 170
            Memory Packages 170

       B. Upgrade the CPU **174**
            CPU 174
            Factors that Affect CPU Performance 177
            Intel Processors 179
            CPU Speeds 180
            Socket and Slot Types 181
            CPU Package Types 184
            Instruction Sets 186

       C. Add a CPU **188**

       D. Upgrade the System BIOS **189**
            Basic Input Output System (BIOS) 189
            Methods for Accessing the System BIOS 189
            BIOS Settings 190
            Firmware 191

E. Upgrade the Power Supply	**192**
Power Supply	192
Internal Power Connections	193
System Board Power Supply Connections	194
Drive Power Connectors	195
How to Calculate Your Power Needs	196
F. Upgrade the System Board	**198**
System Board	199
Form Factors	202
Computer Cases	205
ATX System Board Components	206
G. Decide When to Upgrade	**209**
Indications You Need to Upgrade	210

Chapter 5: Supporting Portable Computing Devices

A. Connect External Peripherals to a Portable Computer	**218**
Portable Computing Devices	218
Notebook Computers	221
Integrated Peripherals	223
Docking Solutions	226
Portable Device Power Sources	229
Types of Batteries	231
Power a Portable Device	232
B. Install or Remove Portable Computing Device Drives	**233**
Portable Computer Drives	233
C. Install or Remove PCMCIA Cards	**235**
PC Cards	236
Card and Socket Services	237
PC Card Uses	237
D. Install or Remove Mini-PCI Cards	**239**
Mini-PCI Card	239

E. Install or Add Memory to a Portable Computing Device	242
Portable Device Memory Options	242
Flash Memory	242
F. Connect PDAs to Computers	248
PDA	248

Chapter 6: Performing Preventative Maintenance

A. Hard Disk Maintenance	258
Fragmentation	258
Hard Disk Maintenance Tools	258
B. Perform Printer Maintenance	**262**
Laser Printers	262
Dot-matrix Printers	264
Inkjet Printers	268
Solid Ink Printers	270
Dye Sublimation Printers	270
C. Use a UPS	**273**
UPS	273
D. Clean Peripheral Components	**276**
Cleaning Compounds and Materials	276
E. Clean Internal System Components	**279**
F. Dispose of Computer Equipment	**280**
Material Safety Data Sheets	280
Hazardous Materials	280

CHAPTER 7: TROUBLESHOOTING DEVICE PROBLEMS

A. Correct Monitor Problems 290
    The Troubleshooting Process 290
    Troubleshooting Tips 291
    How CRTs Produce Images 292
    Electron Beam Positioning Technologies Used in Monitors 294
    Monitor Safety 295
    Power Management 295
    Common Monitor Problems 295

B. Correct Input Device Problems 300
    How Keyboards Work 300
    Common Keyboard Problems 302
    Keyboard Troubleshooting Techniques 303
    How Pointing Devices Work 304
    Common Pointing Device Problems 306
    How Touch Screen Devices Work 308
    Common Touch Screen Device Problems 309

C. Correct Adapter Card and PC Card Problems 311
    How Adapter Cards Work 311
    Common Problems with Adapter Cards 312
    Common USB Problems 313

D. Correct Hard Drive Problems 317
    How Hard Drives Work 317
    Common Problems with Hard Drives 318
    Troubleshooting SCSI Drive Problems 319
    Slow Drives 320
    Hard Drive Maintenance Tools 320

E. Correct Internal Removable Media Drive Problems **325**
    Removable Cartridge Drive Utility Software 325
    How Floppy Drives Work 326
    How Removable Cartridge Drives Work 326
    How Tape Drives Work 327
    Common Problems with Internal Removable Media Devices 328

F. Correct CD or DVD Drive Problems **331**
    Common Problems with CD and DVD Drives 331

G. Correct Printer Problems **335**
    Common Problems with Printers 335
    Environmental Effects on Printing 335
    Windows Print Process 336
    The Laser Printing Process 337
    Common Laser Printer Problems 338
    How an Inkjet Printer Works 339
    Common Inkjet Problems 340
    How a Dot-matrix Printer Works 340
    Common Dot-matrix Printer Problems 341

CHAPTER 8: TROUBLESHOOTING SYSTEM PROBLEMS

A. Correct Network Connection Problems **350**
    Common Problems with Network Connections 350
    Network Troubleshooting Utilities 351

B. Correct Modem Problems **352**
    Common Problems with Modems 352

C. Correct Power Problems **356**
    Common Power Problems 356
    Electrical Safety 357
    How Surge Protectors Protect Computer Equipment 358

D. Correct Boot Problems ... 361
   The Boot Process ... 361
   Common Boot Problems ... 363

E. Correct Memory Problems ... 364
   Symptoms of Memory Problems ... 364

F. Correct System Board Problems ... 366
   Symptoms of System Board Problems ... 366

G. Correct Portable System Problems ... 367
   Common Portable System Problems ... 368

H. Diagnose System Problems ... 370
   Collect, Isolate, and Correct Troubleshooting Model ... 370
   Collecting Troubleshooting Information ... 370
   Isolating the Problem ... 372
   Troubleshooting Resources ... 373
   Correcting the Problem ... 374

CHAPTER 9: WINDOWS TOOLS

A. Windows Graphical Tools ... 380
   Graphical Tools ... 380
   Taskbar ... 381
   Start Menu ... 382
   Windows Explorer ... 384
   My Computer ... 385
   Control Panel ... 385
   Computer Management in Windows 2000/XP ... 387
   Network Neighborhood and My Network Places ... 388
   Device Manager ... 390
   Disk Management Tools ... 391
   System Monitoring Tools ... 391

B. Windows Command-line Tools	392
Command-line Tool	392
Popular Command-line Tools	393

CHAPTER 10: MANAGING APPLICATIONS

A. Install a Windows Application	402
Installation Types	402
The Background Logon Authentication Process	403
Registry	404
Registry Entries	406
Editing the Registry	407
Installation Changes	409
User Profiles	409
User Profile Folder Locations	411
B. Configure Virtual Memory	**415**
Virtual Memory	415
C. Install a Non-Windows Application	**419**
Non-Windows Applications	419
D. Configure a Non-Windows Application	**422**
Operating System Startup Files	422
DOS Memory Segments	422
Environment Variables	424
Files and Buffers	424
E. Remove an Application	**428**

CHAPTER 11: INSTALLING NETWORK COMPONENTS

A. Update a Network Card Driver	434
Hardware Driver	434
Plug and Play	435
How to Use Device Manager	435

B. Configure TCP/IP **440**
    Network Protocols 441
    IP Address.. 441
    Subnet Mask 442
    TCP/IP 443
    Name Servers 444
    Automatic TCP/IP Configuration Methods 445
    The TCP/IP Configuration Process 445
    The IPConfig Command.. 446
    The Ping Command.. 447
    Internet Service Provider (ISP) 448

C. Troubleshoot TCP/IP Connectivity **452**
    The Troubleshooting Process 452
    The TCP/IP Connectivity Process 453
    Common Connectivity Problems 454
    Troubleshooting Tools 455

D. Install or Remove NetBEUI **458**
    The NetBEUI Protocol 459

E. Install or Remove NWLink IPX/SPX **461**
    The NWLink IPX/SPX Protocol 461
    NWLink IPX/SPX Configuration Settings 462

F. Install a NetWare Client **466**
    Network Client 467
    NetWare Client Properties 468

G. Configure a Network Connection in Windows 9x..................... **472**
    Primary Network Logon Types 472

CHAPTER 12: IMPLEMENTING LOCAL SECURITY IN WINDOWS 2000/NT/XP

A. Create or Delete Local User Accounts **482**
    Local Security 482
    The Built-in User and Group Accounts 483

B. Modify User Account Properties **489**
    User Account Properties 489

C. Set Workgroup or Domain Membership **493**
    Workgroup 494
    Domain 494

D. Configure File and Folder Security **499**
    File Systems 499
    NTFS Permissions 501
    Attributes 502

E. Encrypt Files and Folders **505**
    Encryption 506

CHAPTER 13: MANAGING FILE AND PRINT RESOURCES IN WINDOWS 2000/NT/XP

A. Share Folders **512**
    Share Permissions 512
    The Effective Permissions Process 513

B. Connect to a Network Printer **516**
    Network Printer 516
    Print Driver 516
    Device Settings 516

C. Capture a Printer Port **522**
    Printer Ports 522
    Port Capture 523

D. Install a Local Printer **524**
    Print Permissions 524

E. Troubleshoot Printing **529**
    Print Components 529
    Print Process 530
    Common Print Problems 530

Chapter 14: Managing File and Print Resources in Windows 9x

- **A. Set Workgroup or Domain Membership** 540
  - NetBIOS Names 540
- **B. Configure the Security Level** 542
  - Security Levels 542
- **C. Share Folders** 543
  - Share Permissions in Windows 9x 543
- **D. Install a Printer** 546
- **E. Troubleshoot a Printer in Windows 9x** 549
- **F. Enable User Profiles** 552
  - Windows 9x User Profile Folders 553
  - Windows 9x Users 553

Chapter 15: Managing Disk Resources in Windows 2000/NT/XP

- **A. Create or Delete a Partition** 560
  - Partitions 560
  - Other Names for Partitions 561
  - Basic Disks 562
  - Dynamic Disks 562
- **B. Convert a FAT Partition to NTFS** 571
  - File System Conversion 571
- **C. Compress Files and Folders** 572
  - Compression 572
- **D. Defragment a Hard Disk in Windows 2000/XP** 574
  - Fragmentation 574

Chapter 16: Managing Disk Resources in Windows 9x

- **A. Create or Delete a Partition** 580
  - Large Disk Support 580
  - MS-DOS Mode 581

B. Compress a Hard Disk.	**584**
C. Convert a FAT Partition to FAT32.	**586**
The Conversion Process.	586
Cluster Size.	587
D. Defragment a Hard Disk.	**589**

CHAPTER 17: CONNECTING TO INTERNET AND INTRANET RESOURCES

A. Create a Dial-up Connection.	**594**
Outbound Connection.	594
Dial-Up Connection.	597
B. Create a VPN Connection.	**608**
Virtual Private Network Connection.	608
C. Configure a Web Browser.	**613**
Web Browser.	613
Web Protocols.	614
D. Configure an Email Client.	**624**
Email Protocol.	624
Email Clients.	625
E. Troubleshoot Internet and Intranet Connections.	**629**
Common Internet/Intranet Problems.	629

CHAPTER 18: IMPLEMENTING VIRUS PROTECTION

A. Install Virus Protection Software.	**638**
Malicious Code Attacks.	638
Virus Protection Software.	640
System Requirements.	640
B. Configure Virus Protection Software.	**644**
Common Virus Protection Software Configuration Properties.	645
C. Create a Clean Boot Disk.	**650**
Boot Disk.	650

D. Manually Update Virus Definitions 654

E. Remove a Virus 655

    Virus Removal Options 655

CHAPTER 19: PREPARING FOR DISASTER RECOVERY

A. Create a Boot Disk 664

    DOS Boot Files 664

    DOS Boot Process 665

    Windows 9x Boot Files 666

    Windows 9x Boot Process 666

    Windows 2000/NT/XP Boot Files 667

    Windows 2000/NT/XP Boot Process 668

    Windows 2000/NT/XP Partition Terminology 669

    The Boot.ini File 670

B. Create an Emergency Repair Disk 675

    Emergency Repair Disk 675

    The Emergency Repair Process 676

    Creating Installation Boot Disks 676

C. Install the Recovery Console 678

    Recovery Console 679

D. Back Up Data 680

    The Archive File Attribute 680

    Backup Types 681

    Backup Media 682

    Batch/Script Files 682

E. Back Up System State Data 693

    System State Data 693

F. Back Up the Registry 696

G. Prepare for an Automated System Recovery 698

    Automated System Recovery Process 698

Chapter 20: Recovering from Disaster

- **A. Troubleshoot an Application** **706**
  - Common Problems 706
  - Troubleshooting Tools 707
  - Web Sites for Troubleshooting Information 710
- **B. Troubleshoot Hard Disks** **714**
  - Common Error Messages 714
  - Windows 2000/NT/XP Boot Troubleshooting Tools 715
- **C. Restore Data** **728**
- **D. Restore the Registry** **731**
- **E. Restore System State Data** **734**
- **F. Recover Boot Sector Files** **735**
- **G. Perform an Automated System Recovery** **739**

Chapter 21: Installing Client Operating Systems

- **A. Install a Windows Client Operating System** **746**
  - Windows Operating Systems Features 746
  - Installation Requirements 749
  - Multiple Boot Computer 750
  - Windows Setup Programs 750
  - Windows Upgrade Paths 751
  - Windows Update 751
- **B. Upgrade a Windows Client Operating System** **766**
- **C. Troubleshoot Operating System Installations** **770**
  - Common Problems 770
- **D. Add or Remove Operating System Components** **772**
  - Operating System Components 772

Chapter 22: Automating Client Operating System Installations

- A. Perform an Unattended Installation **778**
  - Answer File 778
  - Setup Command Syntax for Unattended Installations 780
  - Setup Batch Files 780
- B. Create a Computer Image **785**
  - Computer Image 785
  - The Computer Image Deployment Process 785
- C. Install a Computer Image **792**

Appendix A:

A+ Certification Exam Objectives **799**

Appendix B:

Basics of Electricity **829**

Appendix C:

Peripherals and Connector Types **835**

Appendix D:

Upgrade From Windows 95 to Windows 98 .... **837**

Appendix E:

Upgrade From Windows NT to Windows 2000 or Windows XP **841**

Appendix F:

Dynamic Disks **847**

Glossary **851**

Index **867**

ABOUT THIS COURSE

This course is the primary course of study for the CompTIA A+ certification program. The course consists of two different volumes: a textbook, containing all the technical information and reference material you will need during class and for later study and review; and a lab manual, containing all the hands-on and discussion activities you will perform during your study.

You should take this course if your job responsibilities include entry-level computer service technician support duties, or if you support computers running any of the Windows client operating systems, such as Windows 98, Windows 2000 Professional, or Windows XP. In this course, you'll build on your experience as a computer user as you acquire the specific skills required to install, configure, maintain, upgrade, and troubleshoot personal computer hardware components and Windows operating systems.

This course can benefit you in two ways. If you want to prepare for the CompTIA A+ Technician certification examinations, this course will provide you with the information you need. But certification alone does not guarantee professional success. So, this course also provides you with the hands-on skills you need to be successful as an A+ technician.

A+ Certification Troubleshooting and Repair, in combination with A+ Certification Troubleshooting and Repair Lab Guide is an effective and comprehensive tool for those seeking preparation for CompTIA's 2003 A+ certification exams. More importantly, with a uniquely performance-based approach, these tools are designed to be the most effective available in preparing you to support personal computers and their operating systems.

The choice and organization of topics shows the emphasis on results—what you will do as a result of instruction rather than a focus on features and functionality. The content is structured around job-based tasks to enable you to learn most effectively—enabling you to retain the material and transfer the information to the job.

The focused, clear presentation of information and the real-world examples make it easy to use this book as a learning tool and as a reference. Each chapter presents one broad topic or group of related topics. Chapters are arranged in order of increasing proficiency; skills covered in one chapter are used and developed in subsequent chapters. You'll notice a progression in your comprehension, application, and integration of skills throughout the course.

Target Student

This course is designed for persons with basic end-user skills with Windows-based personal computers, who wish to begin a career in information technology by becoming personal computer service technicians, or who wish to prepare to take the CompTIA A+ Core Hardware and Operating Systems examinations.

Course Prerequisites

End-user skills with Windows-based personal computers, including the ability to:
- Start up and shut down the computer.
- Log on to a computer or computer network.

- Run programs.
- Move, copy, delete, and rename files in Windows Explorer.
- Browse and search for information on the Internet.

Basic knowledge of computing concepts including:

- The difference between hardware and software.
- The functions of software components such as the operating system, applications, and file system.
- The function of a computer network.

You can obtain this level of skills and knowledge by taking any of the following Element K courses:

- *Introduction to Personal Computers Using Windows 95*
- *Introduction to Personal Computers Using Windows 98*
- *Introduction to Personal Computers Using Windows 2000*
- *Introduction to Personal Computers Using Windows XP*
- *Introduction to Networks and the Internet*

And also:

- *Hard Disk Management for DOS 6.22*

Course Objectives

In this course, you will install, remove, upgrade, maintain, and troubleshoot computer hardware, and support Windows 9x, Windows NT 4.0, Windows 2000, and Windows XP computers.

You will:

- explore foundational information about computers.
- install or remove devices on standard ports.
- install and remove internal hardware.
- upgrade system components.
- install, configure, and work with various portable computing devices.
- perform preventative maintenance procedures.
- troubleshoot and correct device problems.
- troubleshoot system problems.
- list Windows and command-line tools.
- manage applications.
- install network components.
- implement local security in Windows 2000/NT/XP.
- manage file and print resources in Windows 2000/NT/XP.

- manage file and print resources in Windows 9x.
- manage disk resources in Windows 2000/NT/XP.
- manage disk resources in Windows 9x.
- connect to Internet and intranet resources.
- implement virus protection.
- prepare for disaster recovery.
- recover from disaster.
- install client operating systems.
- automate client operating system installations.

Course Requirements

Hardware

For Chapters 1 through 7:

For each lab station, you will need the following hardware. It is recommended that the documentation and driver disks for each device be included for use by students as needed. For some of the more expensive items, or less common devices, you might perform an instructor demonstration, have one lab station install the item and others watch, or pass the device from one lab station to the next with each station installing then removing the device.

- An ATX-based system with PCI and ISA slots. Whenever possible, have enough components for each lab station to install each device. If the systems you are using have only PCI slots, have at least one other system that contains both ISA and PCI slots. The computer also needs at least one of each of the following ports: parallel, VGA, keyboard and mouse PS/2 ports, serial, USB, FireWire, and sound including Line In, Line Out, Mic, and Game ports. If Windows XP cannot be installed on this additional system, you can install Windows 98 or Windows 2000 on it.
- PCI Cards.
- ISA Cards.
- Printer with a Parallel port.
- Printer with a Serial port.
- Printer with an Infrared port.
- Printer with a USB port.
- Internal and external modems.
- USB hub.
- USB devices.
- Network cards (and any required networking equipment for students to reach the Internet).
- PDA with serial, USB, and/or Infrared ports.

Introduction

- Extra RAM to install.
- Additional IDE Hard Drive, CD-ROM, CD-RW, DVD, or DVD-R Drive to install.
- Additional SCSI Hard Drive or CD/DVD drive to install.
- External SCSI device.
- Additional parallel port devices.
- FireWire port.
- FireWire devices.
- FireWire hub.
- Speakers.
- Microphone.
- Joystick or other game controller that connects to the 15-pin game port.
- MIDI device.
- Other quarter-inch mini-jack device (cassette player, musical keyboard, and so on).
- Digital camera.
- Laptop with docking station and/or port replicator.
- External SCSI devices.
- PC Cards (Type I, II, and III if possible).
- UPS.
- ESD protection devices such as workbench mats with wrist strap and grounding cord, or floor mat with grounding cord and shoe straps.
- PC cleaning supplies such as compressed air canisters, mini-vacuum suitable for laser printers, swabs, alcohol, monitor wipes, and other PC cleaning solutions.
- Audio CD.
- AGP video card.
- RAID controller and drives.
- Wireless devices including mouse and/or keyboard and networking devices.
- Cartridge drive and cables (Iomega Zip or Jaz, SuperDisk, or similar drives).
- At least one system with dual processors.
- Cables for all devices. In addition, you also need the following cables: Null modem, RJ-45, RJ-11, RG 6, RG 8, RG 58, RG 59, STP, Fiber Optic.

Optional Hardware for Chapters 1 through 7:

Some topics describe hardware that you are less likely to have. However, if you do have access to the hardware, it will enhance the learning experience for the students. Any of the following items will be of benefit to students in installing, configuring, working with, and troubleshooting.

- Digital flat panel monitor with DVI connection.
- DVI port.

- CPU cooling systems including temperature sensors, liquid cooling systems, thermal compounds, heat sinks, and fans.
- Riser cards for audio and communications (also known as daughter boards).
- Mini PCI adapters for notebook computers.
- Different kinds of memory packages.
- Different kinds of CPU packages.
- Touchscreen monitor or panel to attach to a monitor.
- External tape drive.
- CAD/CAM devices.
- Cable modem.
- DSL modem.
- Special function video card such as those with TV tuner or TV connection capabilities.
- Various types of RAM.
- Solid Ink printer.
- Thermal printer.
- Dye sublimation printer.
- Printers with features such as the ability to add memory, hard drives, NICs, operational trays and feeders, finishers such as staplers, and/or functions such as scanning, fax, and copier built into the printer.
- Battery operated printer.

Non-working Devices for Chapters 1 through 7:

For the troubleshooting chapters, if you have access to any non-working devices, the devices can be installed for students to troubleshoot.

- Any of the devices students have worked with (from the hardware list for the course) that are not working are suitable for this purpose.
- Some suggestions for simulating problems are included as Instructor Notes in the activities, but actual non-working devices can often be beneficial in helping students identify when something is broken as opposed to not correctly configured.
- Damaged CD-ROM.
- Broken or damaged cables.
- Any non-working items which can be broken open to show students the internal workings of devices.

For Chapters 8 through 21:

Except where noted, the requirements listed are for the student and instructor computers.

- 300 MHz Pentium processor or higher.
- 10 GB hard disk or larger for the student and instructor computers.

Introduction

- 12 GB hard disk or larger for the classroom domain controller. (You will need an even larger hard disk if you want each student to use Ghost to create a computer image.) You will need approximately 2 GB of disk space per computer image stored on the server.
- 128 MB of RAM or more. For the classroom domain controller, 256 MB of RAM or more.
- 800 x 600-capable display adapter and monitor.
- Floppy disk drive and bootable CD-ROM drive.
- One computer installed as a Windows 2000-based classroom domain controller. This computer's hardware must be on the Windows 2000 Hardware Compatibility List (HCL).
- Network adapter and cabling connecting each classroom computer.
- A projector system to display the instructor's screen output.
- 17 3.5" floppy disks for each student and the instructor.
- Bootable Windows XP Professional CD-ROMs for the ASR recovery topic.
- Internet access.

Software

For Chapters 1 through 7:
- Windows XP.
- Device drivers for any cards and devices students will install.
- A MIDI sequencer. You can download one of the many MIDI sequencers listed at **www.hitsquad.com/smm/win95/MIDI_SEQUENCERS/**. Several are Freeware, some are Shareware, and some are demos.

For Chapters 8 through 21:
- For the classroom domain controller, you can use either Windows 2000 Server or Windows 2000 Advanced Server. Make sure you have enough per-server licenses for the classroom.
- Windows XP Professional for each student and instructor computer. Be sure you have met the licensing or activation requirements for your situation.
- Windows 2000 Professional for each student and instructor computer. Be sure you have met the licensing or activation requirements for your situation.
- Service Pack 2 or later for Windows 2000.
- Bootable Windows 98 Second Edition CD-ROM for each student and instructor computer. Be sure you have met the licensing or activation requirements for your situation.
- Norton AntiVirus 2002 Professional Edition or McAfee VirusScan Professional Edition. If you choose to use McAfee VirusScan, students will not be able to manually update their virus definitions unless they register their software.
- Norton Ghost.
- PowerQuest Partition Magic or Norton Disk Commander.

- If you want to teach students how to install and configure Netscape Navigator instead of Internet Explorer, you will need Netscape Navigator 7.01 or later. You can download Netscape Navigator at **http://channels.netscape.com/ns/borwsers/download.asp**.
- There are additional requirements for some of the chapter-level lab activities. Please see the setup procedures for each lab activity for these requirements.
- You will need an email account for each student. Obtain these accounts either by installing Microsoft Exchange Server on the classroom domain controller and creating the necessary accounts, or by creating the accounts with one of the free email services that support Outlook Express, such as Hotmail. You can create one account for each student or create a single account and have students share this account.

Class Setup

For Chapters 1 through 7:

1. A working PC for each lab station is configured for the class. The computer has the following ports configured at the start of class:
   - Parallel
   - Serial
   - USB
   - VGA
   - Sound card with line in, line out, mic, and game port
   - FireWire
   - PS/2 Keyboard and Mouse

   It is recommended that each lab station have no more than two students. Having two students per lab station boosts confidence for those who have never worked with hardware previously. The computers have Internet access; default DHCP configuration for network access is assumed for the course. If your network requires different settings, configure accordingly.
   - Install Windows XP Professional using the entire hard disk as an NTFS partition.
   - When prompted, use Typical Settings.
   - When prompted to add the system to be a member of the domain, select No, and then continue with the installation.
   - All other settings should be as appropriate to your system and location.
2. Additional hardware is located in bins in a central location.
3. Any equipment that is to be shared (such as laptops, dual processor systems, printers, or other more expensive items that you don't have enough of for each lab station) should be accessible by all lab stations.

4. One or more systems are connected to the Internet to be used as reference stations if students need to access documentation for a particular card or device, for troubleshooting help, or for other system information.
5. To test the network components installation, students will need to connect to a network. Internet access via DHCP is assumed. If your location uses static IP addresses, or needs additional TCP/IP settings, assign accordingly.
6. For any devices that you do not have the original drivers disk for, download the drivers to student systems in a folder named C:\Drivers.
7. The class should start with the computers turned off and the monitor unplugged.
8. Monitors that students will be installing should have the image slightly messed up. Change the brightness so it is very dim, and lower the contrast. Also, adjust the settings so that the image is not centered on the screen. If the monitor buttons or menu allow it, adjust the monitor so that the lines displayed on screen appear to not be straight. This could be pincushion, trapezoid/parallel, hourglass/hooking, tilt, or a combination. However, be sure that students will be able to see the screen well enough to log on.

For the Classroom Domain Controller (for Chapters 8 through 21):

1. Perform a clean installation of Windows 2000 Server or Advanced Server on the C drive in the default installation location. To start the Windows 2000 Server Setup program, you can either boot the computer from the Windows 2000 Server installation CD-ROM, create Setup boot disks by using the appropriate command (Makeboot.exe or Makebt32.exe) and then boot from the Setup boot disks, or create a network boot disk and install from a network share. Use the following installation parameters:

    - Create a single C partition using the entire disk.
    - Format the C partition to use NTFS.
    - Set the appropriate regional settings for your country.
    - Enter the appropriate user name and organization for your environment.
    - Enter the product key.
    - Configure enough per-server licenses so that all classroom computers can connect.
    - Use a computer name of 2000SRV.
    - Set the administrator's password to password.
    - Install the Domain Name System (DNS), Dynamic Host Configuration Protocol (DHCP), and Windows Internet Name Service (WINS) networking services.
    - Configure the date and time settings that are appropriate for your locale.
    - Select Custom networking settings. Assign a static IP address of 192.168.200.200 and a subnet mask of 255.255.255.0. Enter this IP address as the Preferred DNS Server address and also the WINS server address.
    - Accept the default workgroup membership.
    - When installation is complete, log on as Administrator.

- Uncheck Show This Screen At Startup and close the Windows 2000 Configure Your Server window.

2. Configure the DNS domain name properties for this computer to be class.com.
    - Open the Properties for My Computer.
    - Select the Network Identification tab.
    - Click Properties, and then click More.
    - In the Primary DNS Suffix Of This Computer text box, type class.com and click OK.
    - Click OK to close all open windows.
    - Restart the computer when prompted and log on as Administrator.

3. Using the DNS console, create a standard primary forward lookup zone and a reverse lookup zone for the class.com domain.
    - From the Start menu, choose Programs→Administrative Tools→DNS.
    - In the console tree, expand and select your 2000SRV computer.
    - Choose Action→Configure the Server.
    - Click Next.
    - Make sure that Yes, Create A Forward Lookup Zone is selected and click Next.
    - In the Zone Type portion of the wizard, verify that Standard Primary is selected and click Next.
    - In the Zone Name portion of the wizard, in the Name text box, type class.com and click Next.
    - In the Zone File portion of the wizard, verify that Create A New File With This File Name is selected along with a file name of class.com.dns, and then click Next.
    - Verify that Yes, Create A Reverse Lookup Zone is selected and click Next.
    - In the Zone Type portion of the wizard, verify that Standard Primary is selected and click Next.
    - In the Network ID text box, type 192.168.200 and click Next.
    - On the Zone File Page, click Next to accept the default file name of 200.168.192.in-addr.arpa.dns.
    - Click Finish.

4. Configure the class.com forward lookup zone and the 200.168.192 reverse lookup zone to accept dynamic updates.
    - Select and right-click each zone and choose Properties.
    - On the General page, from the Allow Dynamic Updates drop-down list, choose Yes.
    - Click OK to configure the zone to accept dynamic updates.
    - Close the DNS console.

5. Promote this computer to Active Directory domain controller status for the class.com domain.
    - From the Start menu, choose Run. Enter dcpromo and click OK.

- Click Next to advance through the Welcome To The Active Directory Installation Wizard page.
- Create a domain controller for a new domain.
- Create a new domain tree.
- Create a new forest of domain trees.
- In the Full DNS Name For New Domain text box, type class.com.
- Accept the default NetBIOS name, database, and log locations.
- Accept the default location for the Shared System Volume.
- Set the permissions to be compatible with only Windows 2000 servers.
- Enter password for the Directory Services Restore Mode password.
- When prompted, restart the computer and log on as Administrator.
- If necessary, close the Windows 2000 Configure Your Server window.
- If desired, configure the W32Time Service.

6. Configure DHCP so that this server can assign IP addresses to the instructor and student computers.
    - From the Start menu, choose Programs→Administrative Tools→DHCP.
    - Select and right-click 2000srv.class.com and choose New Scope.
    - On the Welcome page, click Next.
    - In the Name text box, type Class Scope and click Next.
    - In the Start IP Address text box, type 192.168.200.1.
    - In the End IP Address text box, type 192.168.200.199.
    - Verify that the Length is 24 and the Subnet Mask is 255.255.255.0, and then click Next.
    - Do not create any exclusions (unless required by your network).
    - Accept the default lease duration of eight days.
    - When prompted as to whether you want to define options, verify that Yes, I Want To Configure These Options Now is selected, and then click Next.
    - If you're using a router to access the Internet from the classroom, on the Router page, enter the IP address of the router and click Add. Click Next to continue.
    - On the Domain Name And DNS Servers page, in the Parent Domain text box, type class.com. In the IP Address text box, type 192.168.200.200 and click Add. Click Next.
    - On the WINS Servers page, in the IP Address text box, type 192.168.200.200 and click Add. Click Next to continue.
    - Verify that Yes, I Want To Activate This Scope Now is selected and click Next.
    - Click Finish.
    - Right-click 2000srv.class.com and choose Authorize to authorize the DHCP server in the Active Directory.
    - Close DHCP.

7. In Active Directory Users And Computers, create two users for each student. Name the first user Admin#, where # is a unique number for each student. Assign each user the password of password. Add these users to the Domain Admins group. Grant the Dial-In Permission to each of these users. Name the second user User#, where # is a unique number for each student. Assign each user the password of password.
8. Install an HP Laser Jet 5si MX printer on this server. Share the printer as NetPrint.
9. Install the server as a VPN server.
   - Configuring the server as a VPN server requires the server to have two network cards. You can install the Microsoft Loopback Adapter to simulate a second network card if your server doesn't have two network cards. (You're going to use this network card to simulate a connection to the Internet.)
     - In Control Panel, double-click Add/Remove Hardware.
     - Click Next.
     - Verify that Add/Troubleshoot A Device is selected and click Next.
     - Select Add A New Device and click Next.
     - Select No, I Want To Select The Hardware From A List and click Next.
     - Select Network Adapters and click Next.
     - Below Manufacturers, select Microsoft.
     - Below Network Adapter, verify that Microsoft Loopback Adapter is selected and click Next.
     - Click Next.
     - Click Finish.
     - On the desktop, right-click My Network Places and choose Properties.
     - Right-click Local Area Connection 2 and choose Properties.
     - Select Internet Protocol (TCP/IP) and click Properties.
     - Choose Use The Following IP Address. In the IP Address text box, type 10.0.0.1. Verify that the Subnet Mask is 255.0.0.0. Click OK.
     - Click OK to close the Local Area Connection 2 Properties dialog box.
     - Close Network And Dial-Up Connections and Control Panel.
   - From the Start menu, choose Programs→Administrative Tools→Routing And Remote Access.
   - In the console tree, right-click 2000SRV and choose Configure And Enable Routing And Remote Access.
   - Click Next.
   - On the Common Configurations page, select Virtual Private Network (VPN) Server and click Next.
   - On the Remote Client Protocols page, verify that TCP/IP is selected and click Next.
   - Below Internet Connections, select Local Area Connection 2 (the one with Microsoft Loopback Adapter in the Description column) and click Next.

- On the IP Address Assignment page, verify that Automatically is selected and click Next.
- Do not specify that you have a RADIUS server. Click Next.
- Click Finish.
- Click OK to close the message box about the DHCP Relay Agent.
- In Routing And Remote Access, configure the DHCP Relay Agent.
  - In the console tree, expand the 2000SRV (local) object.
  - Right-click DHCP Relay Agent and choose Properties.
  - In the Server Address text box, type 192.168.200.200.
  - Click Add.
  - Click OK.
- Close Routing And Remote Access.

10. Install the latest Service Pack for Windows 2000.
11. Create a directory named C:\Support and share it as Support. Copy the contents of the \Support\Tools folder from the Windows 2000 Professional CD-ROM to the C:\Support folder.
12. Create a directory named C:\AntiVirus and share it as AntiVirus. Copy the installation files for Norton AntiVirus to this share.
13. Create a directory named C:\VirusScan and share it as VirusScan. Copy the installation files for Norton AntiVirus to this share.
14. Create a directory named C:\Ghost and share it as Ghost. Copy the installation files for Norton Ghost to this share.
15. Create a directory named C:\Images and share it as Images. Copy C:\Ghost\Ghost.exe and C:\Ghost\Ghost.env to C:\Images.
16. Create at least one email account for students to use in Exercise 8-4. Create these accounts on your own mail server (such as Microsoft Exchange Server) or by using a free email service such as Hotmail.
17. Create a directory named C:\Win2000 and share it as Win2000. Copy the contents of the \i386 folder from the Windows 2000 installation CD-ROM to this folder.
18. Create a directory named C:\WinXP and share it as WinXP. Copy the contents of the \i386 folder from the Windows XP installation CD-ROM to this folder.

For the Student and Instructor Computers (for Chapters 8 through 21):

1. Delete all partitions on the computers' hard disks.

   ⚠ Do not use all of the available disk space when you install Windows 98.

2. Perform a clean installation of Windows 98 using the following parameters:
   - Create a C partition of 2 GB in size. Do not enable large disk support on this partition or Setup will use all available disk space.

- Install Windows 98 Second Edition to the default C:\Windows folder.
- Perform a Typical installation.
- Select the Install The Most Common Components (Recommended) option.
- Name the computer WIN98-#, where # is a unique number for each student (such as 1, 2, 3, and so on). Install the computer into the default workgroup (named Workgroup).
- Select the appropriate country or region for your location.
- When prompted, restart the computer.
- On the User Information page, enter the appropriate Name and Company information.
- Accept the Windows 98 license agreement.
- If necessary, type your Windows 98 product key. After copying some additional files, Setup will restart your computer again.
- Select your time zone.
- After configuring the startup environment, Setup will restart your computer again.
- Log on to the computer as Admin# (where # is the same number you assigned to the computer) with a password of password. When prompted, re-enter the password.
- In the Welcome To Windows 98 dialog box, uncheck Show This Screen Each Time Windows 98 Starts. Close the dialog box.
- Close the Channels bar. Click No to configure Windows 98 to no longer display the Channels bar when Windows 98 starts.
- Rename the My Computer icon to WIN98-#, where # is the number you assigned to the computer.
- In the Network dialog box, enable File and Printer Sharing for Microsoft Networks.

3. In Windows 98, create a folder named C:\WIN98. Copy the contents of the \WIN98 folder from the Windows 98 CD-ROM to the C:\WIN98 folder.

4. Configure Windows 98 so that the computer can connect to the Internet. Open Internet Explorer and configure it to use this connection.

 You must use Partition Magic or Norton Disk Commander to create these partitions. If you create the partitions during the installation of Windows 2000 and Windows XP, setup will create a single extended partition using all of the remaining free space on the disk. A single extended partition will prevent students from creating partitions later on in the course.

5. Use Partition Magic or Norton Disk Commander to create two additional 2 GB primary partitions on the hard disk.

Do not upgrade Windows 98 to Windows 2000 Professional. Perform a clean install instead.

6. After you've successfully installed Windows 98 and created the two additional primary partitions, insert the Windows 2000 Professional CD-ROM. When you're prompted to upgrade to Windows 2000, click No. Click Install Windows 2000 to install Windows 2000 Professional with the following parameters:

Introduction

- Choose Install A New Copy Of Windows 2000 (Clean Install).
- Enter the appropriate product key.
- If you need to install additional languages for your location, click Language Options and make the appropriate selections.
- On the Windows Setup page, click Advanced Options. Check I Want To Choose The Installation Partition During Setup so that you can create a new partition on which you can install Windows 2000.
- If you need to install Accessibility Options, click Accessibility Options and make the appropriate selections.
- Install Windows 2000 into the D primary partition. Format this partition to use the NTFS file system.
- Configure the regional settings that are appropriate for your country.
- Enter the appropriate user name and organization for your environment.
- Name the computer WIN2000-#, where # is the same number you chose for this computer when installing Windows 98.
- Set the Administrator's password to password.
- If the computer on which you're installing Windows 2000 has a modem, you'll be prompted to configure the modem dialing options. Enter the appropriate area code and number for accessing an outside line for your environment.
- Configure the date and time settings that are appropriate for your locale.
- Select Typical Settings for the network configuration.
- Install the computer into the default workgroup.
- When the installation is complete, restart the computer. In the Network Identification Wizard, on the Users Of This Computer page, select Users Must Enter A User Name And Password To Use This Computer.
- Rename the My Computer icon to WIN2000-#, where # is the number you assigned to this computer.
- In Computer Management, create a user account named Admin#, where # is the computer's assigned number. Assign a password of password to this user. Configure the password so that it never expires. Add the Admin# account to the Administrators group.

> If you find that you need to load hardware drivers from the manufacturers' disks instead of the Windows 2000 Professional installation CD-ROM, students will need these drivers when they install Windows 2000.

7. Configure Windows 2000 so that the computer can connect to the Internet. Open Internet Explorer and configure it to use this connection.

8. After you've completed the installation of Windows 2000, install Windows XP Professional with the following parameters:
    - Select New Installation (Advanced) as the installation type.
    - Enter the appropriate product key.

- On the Setup Options page, click Advanced Options. Check I Want To Choose The Install Drive Letter And Partition During Setup so that you can create a new partition on which you can install Windows XP.
- Configure the Accessibility Options and Language as appropriate for your environment.
- Do not upgrade the Windows 98 FAT partition to NTFS.
- Do not download updated Setup files.
- Install Windows XP into the E primary partition. Format this partition to use the NTFS file system.
- Configure the regional and language options that are appropriate for your locale.
- Enter the appropriate user and organization names.
- Name the computer WINXP-#, where # is the same number you assigned to this computer for the other operating system installations.
- Set the Administrator's password to password.
- If necessary, enter the appropriate area code and number for accessing an outside line for your environment.
- Configure the date and time settings that are appropriate for your locale.
- Select Typical Settings for the network configuration.
- Install the computer into the default workgroup.
- After the computer restarts, use the Setup program to create a user account named Admin#, where # matches the computer number. Set the password to password. (This account should become a member of the local Administrators group by default.) Use the following steps to set the password:
    - Open Control Panel.
    - Click User Accounts.
    - Click the Admin# user account.
    - Click Create A Password.

 If you find that you need to load hardware drivers from the manufacturers' disks instead of the Windows XP Professional installation CD-ROM, students will need these drivers when they install Windows XP.

9. Configure Windows 2000 Professional as the default operating system.
    - In Windows XP, from the Start menu, choose Control Panel.
    - Click Performance And Maintenance.
    - Below Or Pick A Control Panel Icon, click System.
    - In the System Properties dialog box, select the Advanced tab.
    - Below Startup And Recovery, click Settings.
    - From the Default Operating System drop-down list, select Windows 2000 Professional.
10. Configure the C, D, and E drives with the following drive labels:

- In Windows 2000, open Computer Management. In the console tree, select the Disk Management tool.
- In the right pane, right-click C: and choose Properties. In the Label text box, type Win98. Click OK to save your changes.
- In the right pane, right-click D: and choose Properties. In the Label text box, type Win2000. Click OK to save your changes.
- In the right pane, right-click E: and choose Properties. In the Label text box, type WinXP. Click OK to save your changes.

11. Configure Windows XP so that the computer can connect to the Internet. Open Internet Explorer and configure it to use this connection.
12. Extract the data files to both the C and D drives on each student and instructor computer prior to class. Remove the Read-only attribute from the data files after extracting them.

For the Instructor's Computer Only (for Chapters 8 through 21):

1. If you've chosen to use McAfee VirusScan and you want to be able to demonstrate manually updating virus definitions during the class, install McAfee VirusScan on the instructor's computer.
2. Register the McAfee VirusScan software.

To Provide Data File and Overhead Access Throughout the Course:

1. Keep the courseware CD-ROM available at the instructor computer to display PowerPoint slides. The CD-ROM includes the PowerPoint viewer.

CHAPTER 1
Introduction to Computers

Chapter Objectives:

In this chapter, you will explore foundational information about computers.

You will:
- Describe the evolution of today's computers.
- List important computer components.
- List types of software and firmware.
- Convert numbers from one number system to another.

Introduction

Before you begin to learn how to install and configure computer hardware, you need the basics of what computers are and where they come from. In this chapter, we'll introduce you to computers by tracing their history and showing you some of what makes them work.

While it might seem like a good idea to jump right into the specifics of computer support and maintenance, it's a better idea to first ground yourself in some basics, such as the history of computers, a description of some of their components, and an explanation of the number systems they use. With the proper foundation, you'll be ready to tackle the more complex subjects in the rest of the course.

TOPIC A
A Brief History of Computers

The best place to start is at the beginning. So before you learn about the computers of today, you'll learn about the computers of yesterday, both mechanical and electronic. In this chapter, you'll learn how the computer evolved into the machine it is today.

Knowing a little about the history of computers can help you appreciate the current industry situation and prepare you for future developments. And understanding how computers evolved can help you appreciate how they're built and help you better understand why they work the way they do, which makes troubleshooting and repair that much easier.

Evolution of Mechanical Computers

The *abacus* is usually listed as the first mechanical computation device. Created 2,000 or more years ago in India or the Far East, an abacus consists of columns of beads that can slide up and down on rods that are held together in a frame. The position of the beads represents a number. Skilled users could perform calculations more quickly than early electronic computers.

Figure 1-1: *An abacus.*

The written number for zero appeared around 650 A.D. in India and made written calculations much easier. A Persian scholar wrote the first textbook on algebra in 830 A.D. During the 1100s, Europeans learned the written form of math used by the Arabs and wrote down multiplication tables to help merchants. Five hundred years later, John Napier, a Scotsman, carved a set of multiplication tables on ivory sticks that could slide back and forth to indicate certain results. The use of logarithms on *Napier's Bones* in 1617 led to the development of the slide rule. Today's mature engineers can still remember using slide rules in their college days.

The Frenchman Blaise Pascal is usually given credit for the first calculating machine. In 1642, to help his father—a tax collector—with his work, Pascal invented a machine with eight metal dials that could be turned to add and subtract numbers. Leonardo da Vinci and Wilhelm Schickard, a German, designed calculating machines before Pascal, but Pascal receives the recognition because he produced 50 models of his *Pascaline machine*, not just a prototype or description. In 1673, Gottfried von Leibniz, a German mathematician, improved on Pascal's design to create a *Stepped Reckoner* that could do addition, subtraction, multiplication, and division. Only two prototypes were produced.

A Frenchman, Thomas de Colmar, created an Arithmometer in 1820 that was produced in large numbers over the ensuing 100 years. The Swedish inventor Willgodt T. Odhner improved on the Arithmometer, and his calculating mechanism was used by dozens of companies in the calculating machines they produced.

Punched cards first appeared in 1801. Joseph Marie Jacquard used the holes placed in the card to control the patterns woven into cloth by power looms. In 1832, Charles Babbage was working on a Difference Engine when he realized Jacquard's punched cards could be used in computations. The *Analytical Engine*, the machine Babbage designed but never manufactured, introduced the idea of using memory for storing results and the idea of printed output. His drawings described a general-purpose, fully program-controlled, automatic mechanical digital computer. Lady Ada Augusta Lovelace worked with Babbage on his machine. She became the first computer programmer when she wrote out a series of instructions for the Analytical Engine.

Charles Babbage's Difference Engine No. 1 was the first successful automatic calculator. Although the 12,000 parts were never assembled into a finished engine, the parts that were completed functioned perfectly.

Punched cards were used in the United States census of 1890, and a data-processing machine created by Herman Hollerith tabulated the census results in only 2.5 years—much shorter than the predicted 10 years. Punched cards provided input, memory, and output on an unlimited scale for business calculating machines for the next 50 years. The company Hollerith founded to manufacture his card-operated data processors, which used electrical contacts to detect the pattern of holes in each card, eventually became IBM.

Electronic Computers

With the beginning of World War II, electronic computers took on national importance. The accurate calculation of projectile trajectories became a life-and-death concern for the military. The calculations needed to develop the atomic bomb also required more calculating power than was available before the war. Between 1939 and 1944, Howard H. Aiken developed the Harvard *Mark I*—also known as the IBM Automatic Sequence-Controlled Calculator (ASCC). The Mark I was made out of mechanical switches, electrical relays, rotating shafts, and clutches totalling 750,000 components weighing 5 tons. Programming instructions were fed to the Mark I on paper tape, and data was fed in on paper punched cards. Grace Hopper worked at Harvard on the Mark I, II, and III, and discovered the first computer "bug" when she removed a moth that had flown into a mechanical relay, causing it to malfunction. Also, during the war, Konrad Zuse was working secretly on his Z3 computer in Germany. Because so little was known about the Z3 for so long, most people describe the Mark I as the first modern (but not electronic) digital computer.

Vacuum Tubes

Dr. John Vincent Atanasoff was an associate professor at Iowa State College when he designed an Electronic Digital Computer (EDC) that would use base two (binary) numbers. In 1939, with his assistant Clifford Berry, he built the world's first electronic digital computer using *vacuum tubes*. After a lecture, Dr. John W. Mauchly asked to see Atanasoff's computer and later used so many of Atanasoff's ideas in the ENIAC that it took a lawsuit to declare that Atanasoff was the first to use vacuum tubes in an electronic digital computer.

Dr. Mauchly and J. Presper Eckert were at the University of Pennsylvania in 1942 when they built the *Electronic Numerical Integrator And Computer (ENIAC)* to aid the United States military during World War II. ENIAC used 18,000 vacuum tubes, had 500,000 hand-soldered connections, was 1,000 times faster than the Mark I, and had to be rewired to change its program. ENIAC was used from 1946 to 1955, and because of its reliability, it is commonly accepted as the first successful high-speed electronic digital computer. Eckert and Mauchly also designed the Electronic Discrete Variable Automatic Computer (EDVAC), which contained 4,000 vacuum tubes and 10,000 crystal *diodes*. After their success with ENIAC, Eckert and Mauchly proposed to build a *Universal Automatic Computer (UNIVAC)* machine to help the Census Bureau handle all its data. After four years of delays and cost overruns, Remington Rand Inc. worked with the Eckert-Mauchly Computer Corporation to develop UNIVAC, the first commercially successful computer. The computer used magnetic tape to store data, a major change from IBM's punched cards, and introduced many other features that are common today. Starting in 1951, 46 UNIVAC I computers were made for the government and businesses, although some experts at the time thought that five computers would be enough to handle all the computational needs of the world.

John von Neumann did not design the electronics in computers, but he is credited with the theoretical work that all modern computers are based on. Von Neumann recommended that a computer program should be able to stop under certain conditions and start again at another point. He also recommended storing both the data and instructions in memory so both could be changed as needed. He realized that physically rewiring a computer to change the program, or feeding in another paper tape to meet different conditions, was not practical for successful high-speed computing. The *Electronic Delay Storage Automatic Computer (EDSAC)* at Cambridge University, England, and Eckert and Mauchly's *Electronic Discrete Variable Automatic Computer (EDVAC)* were among the first to use von Neumann's ideas. Combining von Neumann's stored program concept with a 1,000-word main memory, magnetic tape for secondary memory, printer and typewriter output, and a 2.25 MHz clock rate, UNIVAC set the standard for computers in the 1950s.

Transistors and Magnetic Memory

The progress of electronic computing was limited by technology. Vacuum tubes, which were used to control the flow of electricity in digital computer circuits, were large (several inches high), red-hot to touch, and unreliable. Dr. William Shockley worked at Bell Telephone Laboratories as co-head of a solid-state research group that developed the *transistor*. Transistors performed the same function but were the size of a pencil eraser, generated almost no heat, and were extremely reliable. The replacement of vacuum tubes with transistors opened up new possibilities.

Another important innovation was *magnetic core memory*, which allowed information to be stored in the magnetic orientation of tiny magnetic rings strung together on fine wire. Using magnetic core memory, the huge mainframes increased their memory from 8,000 to 64,000 words. Combining the computational capability made available through transistors with expanded magnetic core memory gave computers so much power that they had to be used in new ways to justify the cost. Some mainframes used batch processing, where a series of programs and data was stored on magnetic drums and fed to the computer one after the other so no computing time was wasted. Other computers used time sharing, where the computing power was shifted among several different programs running at the same time so no power was wasted waiting for an individual program's results to print or for more input to arrive.

At this time, the United States and the former Soviet Union were involved in a race to see who would be first in space. The complex rockets demanded sophisticated computers to control them. The Soviet Union concentrated on designing bigger rockets to carry larger computers into space, while the United States worked on making smaller, more powerful computers that fit into the smaller rockets they had. The millions spent on research to miniaturize computer components used in the space race produced the technology needed for current computers.

Integrated Circuits

Transistors were great, but combining several transistors and the *resistors* needed to connect them on a single semiconductor chip in an *integrated circuit* was even better. In 1958, Jack Kilby at Texas Instruments made several components on a single-piece semiconductor. By 1961, Fairchild and Texas Instruments were mass-producing integrated circuits on a single chip. In 1967, Fairchild introduced the Micromosaic, which contained a few hundred transistors. The transistors could be connected into specific circuits for an application using computer-aided design. The Micromosaic was an Application-Specific Integrated Circuit (ASIC).

Now usually called just a chip, the first integrated circuit was fabricated in 1958 by Texas Instruments inventor Jack Kilby.

Figure 1-2: *Integrated circuit.*

In 1970, Fairchild introduced the first 256-bit static *RAM chip*, while Intel announced the first 1,024-bit dynamic RAM. Computers that could make use of this memory were still monsters to maintain. Handheld calculators, on the other hand, appealed to everyone from scientists to school kids. Marcian "Ted" Hoff at Intel designed a general-purpose integrated circuit that could be used in calculators, as well as other devices. Using ideas from this circuit, Intel introduced, in 1972, the *8008*, which contained approximately 3,300 transistors and was the first *microprocessor* to be supported by a high-level language compiler called PL/M.

A major breakthrough occurred in 1974 when Intel presented the 8080, the first general-purpose microprocessor. The 8080 microprocessor had a single chip that contained an entire programmable computing device on it. The 8080 was an 8-bit device that contained around 4,500 transistors and could perform 200,000 operations per second. Other companies besides Intel designed and produced microprocessors in the mid-1970s, including Motorola (6800), Rockwell (6502), and Zilog (Z80). As more chips appeared and the prices dropped, personal desktop computers became a possibility.

Personal Computers

About a dozen computers claim to be the first *Personal Computer (PC)*. Credit for the first popular personal computer often goes to Ed Roberts whose company, MITS, designed a computer called the Altair 8800 and marketed a kit for about $400 in 1974. The Altair 8800 used Intel's 8080 microprocessor, contained 256 bytes of RAM, and was programmed by means of a panel of toggle switches. In 1975, Bill Gates and Paul Allen founded Microsoft and wrote a BASIC interpreter for the Altair. More than 2,000 systems were sold in 1975.

Figure 1-3: *An early PC.*

In 1975, MOS Technology announced its 6502-based KIM-1 desktop computer, and Sphere Corporation introduced its Sphere 1 kit. Both kits were strictly for computer fanatics. In 1976, Steve Wozniak and Steve Jobs formed the Apple Computer Inc. company and modified the Apple I to create the Apple II (with a 6502 microprocessor). In 1977, the Apple II cost $1,300, came with 16 KB of ROM, 4 KB of RAM, a keyboard, and color output. The Apple II is usually listed as the first personal computer that was available for the general public. The Commodore PET (6502) and Radio Shack's TRS-80 (Z80) were also popular. In 1979, VisiCalc, a spreadsheet program for the Apple II, made desktop computers attractive to businesses. As more businesses bought Apples, demand appeared for word-processing applications, and the software development industry took off. In 1981, IBM joined the party with its first PC. Dozens of other models and companies followed IBM's lead, but in 1984, Apple broke from the pack and produced the Macintosh computer with a mouse and graphical user interface that opened the computer world to artists and publishers. Of all the computers designed during this period, only the IBM PC and Apple Macintosh have withstood the test of time.

Today there are several types of personal computers:

- Desktop: A type of computer that's more broad than tall. Designed to sit on top of a desk and support a monitor. Probably the most common type of computer in offices today.
- Minitower: As its name implies, this type of computer is tall and narrow. It can sit on top of the desk or on the floor or shelf beneath the desk. Common in offices and in homes.
- Laptop: A small computer that can be transported anywhere. Usually weighs less than ten pounds; in fact, many weigh under five pounds. Used by travelers and those that need to easily carry their work with them to multiple locations.

- Tablet: Designed to look like a writing tablet, these computers are often mostly screen on which users can write or type in data using their fingers or more likely a special pen called a stylus. Some tablet computers have a keyboard that folds out of the way.
- Handheld/Personal Digital Assistant (PDA): A small computer about the size of a large calculator, these computers can have much of the same functionality that desktops and laptops have, although they're often slower and have less storage space, and there are fewer programs that can be used on them. Highly mobile, PDAs are generally used to manage contacts and calendars, and access email and the Internet through wireless radio connections. Users can input data using a small attachable or attached keyboard or a stylus.

Topic B
Desktop Computer System Components and Their Functions

Computers are made up of thousands of pieces that all work together. Before you move on to examine these parts in greater detail later in the course, in this topic, to get your feet wet, you will begin to investigate some of the parts that you will find in practically every personal computer.

If you don't understand the main components inside a computer, when you open it up, it'll seem like the most elaborate puzzle you've ever seen. Like most puzzles, the inner workings of a computer all have a specific place they need to be, but unlike jigsaw puzzles, for the most part in all kinds of different computers, you'll find that the pieces fit together almost exactly the same way. To help you put the puzzle together, you need to understand what the pieces look like and where they go.

Input/Output Devices

There are several types of devices used to enter data into a computer and receive data back from the computer. They are listed in Table 1-1.

Figure 1-4: *Input/Output devices.*

Table 1-1: *Input/Output Devices*

Name	Type of Device	Description
Keyboard	Input	A device that looks like a typewriter that plugs into a computer. Allows you to enter commands, create documents, add numbers, and write emails, among other tasks.
Mouse	Input	Another device that you can use to point to and "touch" and select items on a computer screen.
Monitor	Output	Displays the output from the computer, the operating system, and any software you use.
Speaker	Output	Allows you to hear warnings and other notifications from the computer and plays music, although not very well.
Printer	Output	Allows you to transfer to paper data you see on the monitor or data stored on the computer.

System Board

 This topic is meant to provide you with only an overview of the major system components. You will investigate many of these components in much greater depth throughout the remainder of the course.

The *system board* is the main circuit board in a computer. It is a very thin plate that has chips and other electrical components on it that make up the Central Processing Unit (CPU), the computer memory, and basic controllers for the system. Sometimes called the *motherboard*, the system board has some electrical components *soldered* directly to it, as well as slots and sockets where other components can be added and removed easily. The wires that connect the soldered components, the slots, and the sockets are all permanently built into the system board. Usually the microprocessor, or CPU, is on a large chip that is held in a socket on the system board so you can upgrade the chip when a compatible, newer chip comes out. The chips that control the flow of information to and from the CPU are usually soldered to the system board and are not replaceable. The jacks where you plug in the mouse and keyboard are usually soldered to the system board, but the network and modem connections are usually on interface cards that are easily inserted and removed from slots on the system board.

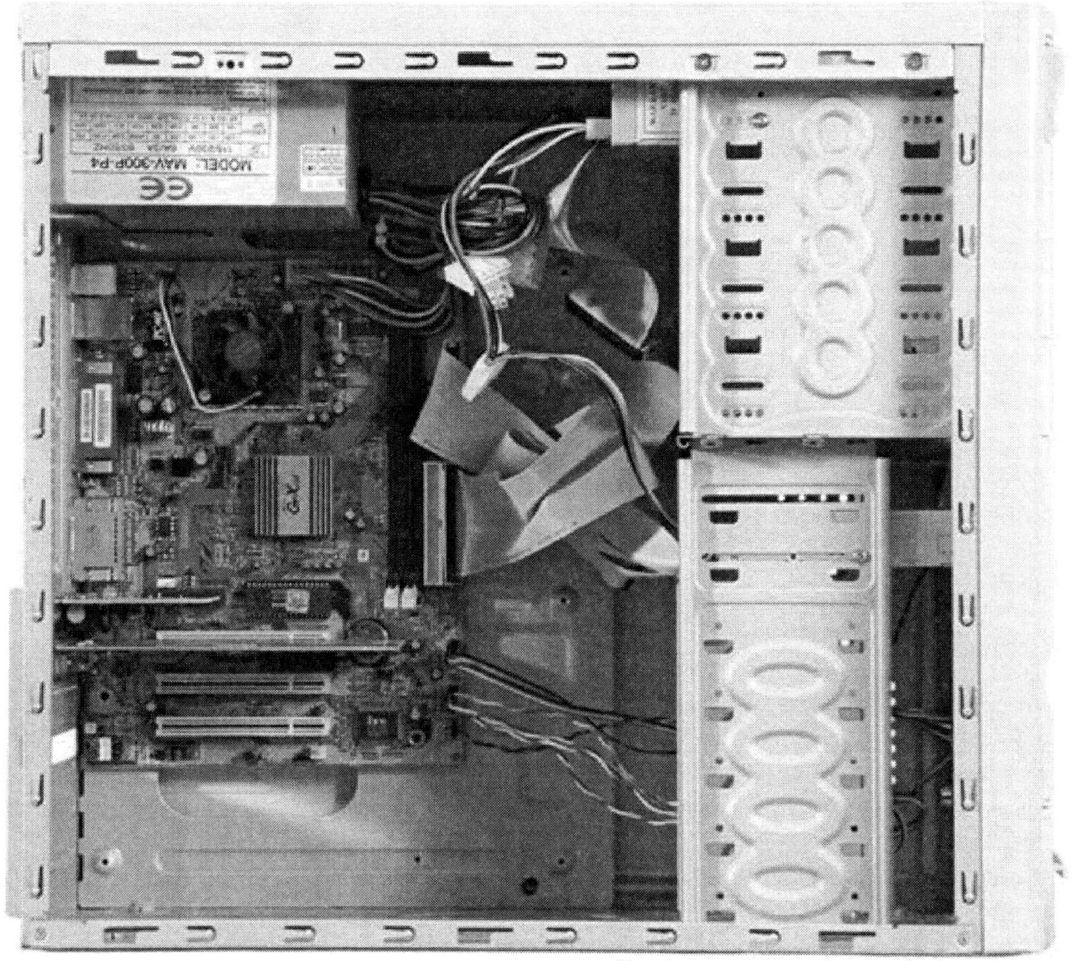

Figure 1-5: *System components.*

 Some of these complete systems include special BIOS settings that you can use to disable the built-in components. Then, you can upgrade or customize these systems by adding expansion cards, just as you would do with a regular system board.

Because features that are built into the design of the system board cannot be changed without replacing the whole system board, most system boards include only the standard features that most users want—those that will not change much in the near future. Not incorporating features that many users do not use, like SCSI and network connections, helps manufacturers keep the cost of the board low. By allowing users to buy modems with the speed and features they want, and letting the users attach the card to the motherboard, the designers build in flexibility that most users appreciate.

Sometimes computer makers who sell complete systems find it is cheaper to build a system board with the modem, sound card, video, and all other features built-in, rather than add interface cards to a standard system board. The buyers of these complete systems get a low price but give up the freedom of easily upgrading and customizing the computer.

Because system boards must be replaceable, they all come with certain standard features. Unfortunately, the standards for these features change over time. For example, the system board usually has slots that hold cards full of memory chips, rather than having the chips soldered directly to the board. You can increase the memory of your computer by replacing the memory cards with cards with more capacity. Every few years, though, a completely new style of memory card will appear that will not fit into the old-style slots. At that point, you either need to buy a new system board or miss out on the advantages of the new-style memory cards.

System boards are often described by their general physical characteristics. The original motherboard design was the AT, which was 12 inches wide. A smaller Baby AT board, 9 inches wide by 10 inches long, became popular after 1989 when the demand for small computers increased. New processor chips required a redesigned system board, and in 1996 the ATX design was introduced. This system board was 12 inches wide by 9.6 inches long, while the Baby ATX was about an inch shorter in both width and length. The ATX board design took into account the need to cool the CPU and memory chips, and the need to move high-speed components as close together as possible to reduce errors as the extremely high-speed signals move across the system board.

Another way to classify system boards is by the *chipset* it uses. The chipset is a group of chips on the system board that support the CPU and each of the other subsystems. When buying or working on a computer, you must know the general design of the system board, the make and model of the processor on the board, *and* the kind of chipset that is on the board.

Processor

The microprocessor, sometimes called just the *processor* or the Central Processing Unit (CPU) is the real brains of the computer where most of the calculations take place. On very large computers, the CPU may consist of many chips mounted on a series of printed circuit boards, but on personal computers, the CPU is housed in a single microprocessor chip. The microprocessor is divided into areas, the first of which retrieves programmed instructions from the computer's memory, decodes, and executes the instructions. The second area is the Arithmetic and Logic Unit (ALU) that does the math operations when needed. The third area sends the results back out to the rest of the computer.

Many companies make microprocessors for IBM-compatible Personal Computers (PCs), but Intel CPUs are the ones against which the other companies' CPUs are compared and rated. The original IBM PCs were based on Intel's 8086 CPU. Other models followed over the years, including 80286 (commonly called the 286), the 386, and the 486. Each of these processors came in a variety of configurations. Because Intel couldn't own the name 486 for a processor, it used a name it could trademark, Pentium, for its 586 processor and Pentium Pro for its 686 equivalent processor.

Today, microprocessors are available in a variety of configurations, including different clock speeds, bus speeds, and cache levels and amounts. Most have backward-compatibility so that they can still run older programs, as well as meet the demands of more current software. Older processors aren't capable of running newer software programs that take advantage of CPU technology advancements that were introduced after their release.

Memory

Memory refers to the internal storage areas in the computer. In common usage, memory refers to actual chips that keep track of computer data and not the information stored on tape or hard drives. Memory chips contain millions of transistors etched on one sliver of a semiconductor. These transistors either conduct electricity and represent the binary number 1, or they don't conduct electricity and represent the binary number 0.

Random Access Memory (RAM) is the main memory. The computer can both read the data stored in RAM memory and write different data into the same RAM memory. Any byte of data can be accessed without disturbing other data, so the computer has random access to the data in RAM memory. RAM memory requires a constant source of electricity to keep track of the data it is storing. If the electricity is cut off, RAM forgets everything. Because of this, RAM memory is described as volatile memory. *Dynamic RAM (DRAM)* is the most common type of RAM. DRAM must be refreshed thousands of times per second. *Static RAM (SRAM)* does not need to be refreshed. SRAM is faster, but more expensive, than DRAM, but both forms of RAM are volatile.

Read-Only Memory (ROM) refers to special permanent memory used to store programs that boot the computer and perform diagnostics. ROM also allows the computer random access to data in its memory. More importantly, the computer cannot change any of the data stored on the ROM, so ROM is read-only memory.

In the early personal computers, you added more memory by filling empty sockets on the motherboard with more memory chips. A *Single In-line Memory Module (SIMM)* made adding memory easier because all the chips were soldered to a single, small, printed circuit board that you inserted into a slot on the system board of your computer. SIMMs transfer information 32 bits at a time, while *Dual In-line Memory Modules (DIMMs)* transfer data 64 bits at a time. Pentium processors require a 64-bit path, so you must add either two SIMMs at a time or one DIMM to a Pentium computer.

Complementary Metal Oxide Semiconductor RAM (CMOS RAM) is special memory that has its own battery to help it keep track of its data even when the power is turned off. CMOS RAM stores information about the computer setup that the computer refers to each time it starts. Because you can write new information to CMOS RAM, you can store information about new disk drives that you add to your system. The computer will remember to look for the drive each time it is turned on.

Storage Media

In addition to memory, there are other ways to store data on different media. These media are listed in Table 1-2.

Table 1-2: *Storage media.*

Device	Description
Hard disk	A fixed unit inside a computer that magnetically stores data on rigid circular platters. The hard disk typically holds all the data on a computer, and usually a computer is run from the hard disk itself. There can be multiple hard disks in a single computer depending on its the internal configuration.

Device	Description
Floppy disk	Like a hard disk, a floppy disk magnetically stores data, but on a flexible circular medium. Although housed in a rigid case for protection, floppy disks are actually made of a pliable material that you could actually bend or tear. Floppy disks are not fixed inside a computer and can be transported from one computer to another to exchange data.
Compact Disc-Read Only Memory (CD-ROM)	A rigid, plastic platter on which data is pressed, much like records used to be.
Compact Disc-Recordable (CD-R)	A CD on which you can write information. Data is written by a laser beam, which modifies a light-sensitive layer on the CD-ROM. Once the information is "burned" onto the CD-R disc, it can't be modified or deleted.
Compact Disc-Re-writeable (CD-RW)	Another CD on which you can burn data, but unlike a CD-R disc, you can delete and modify (depending on the software and hardware you're using) data on a CD-RW disc.

Interfaces

An *interface* on a computer is a place where you can connect another device like a disk drive, keyboard, modem, or mouse. Sometimes the interface connection is built into the system board, like the mouse port and keyboard port. Sometimes the actual connector is on a printed circuit card that adapts the signals to and from the attached device so it can communicate with the computer. Modems are generally on an *interface card*.

Interface cards are inserted into a slot on the system board that connects to the microprocessor. The collection of wires that make the connection, and the rules that describe how the data should flow through the wires, is called a *bus*. The Industry Standard Architecture (ISA) bus connects to ISA slots that accept only ISA cards. The ISA slots were used on early IBM computers and became the industry standard. As computers became faster, they needed buses that could transfer more data, more quickly, than the ISA bus could handle. The development of the Peripheral Component Interconnect (PCI) local bus helped to solve this problem. Unfortunately, PCI and ISA cards and slots are *not* interchangeable. PCI cards must go into PCI slots, and ISA cards must go into ISA slots. Most computers have a combination of ISA and PCI slots on the system board.

A slot cover is a thin strip of metal, held in place by a screw or a tab, that protects an opening (in the system case) for an interface card. When you want to add an interface card into a slot on the system board, you need to remove the corresponding slot cover before you can install the card. If you remove a card and don't replace it with another one, you should replace it with a slot cover that's designed to be held in place by a screw. Doing so will help protect the computer from dust and maintain proper airflow currents within the chassis.

Parallel and Serial Interfaces

There are two important types of computer interfaces that are commonly used to connect peripheral devices, including printers and pointing devices, such as a mouse, to a computer.

- Parallel interface, which transmits data across multiple channels at once.
- Serial interface, which transmits data in a single stream.

TOPIC C
Software and Firmware

Now that you know a little about how computers evolved and what their basic components are, it's time to learn how to make computers run. All computers function because of some type of software, and in this topic, you'll learn about the different types of software and the different tasks they perform.

Even the most modern and sophisticated computers are just lumps of metal, plastic, and glass if you can't get them to do what you need them to do. This is where software and firmware come into the picture. Software provides the interface between the user and the hardware, as well as among the various hardware components. Knowing about software and how a computer uses it is vital to a computer support technician.

System Software

System software is the low-level program that interacts with the computer at a very basic level. An *Operating System (OS)* is a type of system software found on every personal computer. The operating system is the most important software that runs on the computer, because it is the master control program that determines what the computer will do and how it will do it. Examples of operating systems include Windows 2000 Professional, Windows ME, Windows 98, UNIX, Linux, Macintosh OS, IBM OS/2, and DOS. A computer's OS performs many functions. It recognizes input from the keyboard and mouse, sends output to the display screen, keeps track of files and directories on the disk, and controls peripheral devices such as disk drives, CD-ROM drives, and printers. Some operating systems allow more than one user to use the computer at a time, and more than one application to run on the computer at a time. Multi-user operating systems keep users from interfering with each other, and provide security for their work. Multi-user operating systems can also keep track of who uses the computer and determine which programs they can run and which data they can access.

Operating systems are a common base for *application software*. Applications like word processing and graphics programs are written for specific operating systems, not make and model of each computer. The applications communicate with the computer through the operating system. For this reason, Macintosh programs cannot be run on a straight Windows machine, and Windows programs will not run on a pure Linux machine. The operating system does all the hardware communication for the application.

Operating systems have one to two types of interfaces for interacting with users. Operating systems like DOS and UNIX are command-driven interfaces—users type commands in by hand from the keyboard. Operating systems like Windows and the Mac OS are *Graphical User Interfaces (GUIs)*. In a GUI, the user uses a mouse to point, click, and drag graphic elements on the screen. The early Windows programs were DOS programs that translated clicks into DOS commands that were sent to DOS, which actually still had complete control of the computer. Newer versions of Windows are complete operating systems that bypass DOS.

Application Software

Application software is a program designed to help the end-user accomplish a task. An application sits on top of the operating system and uses the operating system to communicate with the computer hardware. The following list shows some of the categories of application software and example applications:

- Word processing—Microsoft Word, Corel WordPerfect
- Spreadsheets—Microsoft Excel, Lotus 1-2-3, Quattro Pro
- Communications and email—Microsoft Outlook, Eudora
- Web browsers—Netscape Navigator, Internet Explorer

Sometimes several programs are bundled together and sold as a suite. Examples of bundled programs are Microsoft Office and Corel WordPerfect Suite. When several applications are combined into a single program, like Microsoft Works or ClarisWorks, the package is called integrated software. Utilities that perform a function for the computer, like disk compression or virus protection, are sometimes listed separately from applications. Computer languages may also be given their own software category. There is really no right or wrong way to categorize software.

Driver Software

Driver software is often called a device driver or just a driver. A driver is considered part of the system software by some experts. A *driver* is a program that lets the operating system and a peripheral device talk to each other. The driver takes generalized commands from the system software or application—like Print This Page—and translates them into unique programming commands that the device can understand. When you install a new CD-ROM drive, printer, disk drive, or any other peripheral, part of the installation process is setting up a driver and letting the operating system know to use the driver to make the peripheral function as needed. New operating systems include thousands of drivers that let them work with all current, popular devices. Peripherals that are designed after the operating system comes out have to supply their own drivers on a CD-ROM or floppy disk, otherwise the device will not function with that operating system.

Firmware

Firmware is software that is stored in memory chips. These chips retain their data even when the power is turned off. Firmware can be stored in Read-Only Memory (ROM) chips, as well as in several other types of chips. Programs stored on a ROM chip cannot be changed, so if they become outdated, the whole chip must be replaced. Usually the only programs stored in ROM are those that will not become outdated, as long as you use the same system board. Firmware is usually a small program that knows how to read a small part of the hard drive into memory. The program that the firmware reads into memory from the hard drive then instructs the computer on how to load the operating system.

There are several types of memory chips.

- ROM is memory that can be read but not changed, as you learned earlier. ROM is non-volatile because its contents stay unchanged even when the power is turned off. ROMs store the firmware that is essential for a computer to have access to when the power is first turned on. The firmware in ROM is usually specific for the hardware on the system board, which will not change. The program in the ROM chip is manufactured into the chip, not added later, so ROM chips are usually mass produced. ROM chips are mainly used for storing control routines (such as ROM BIOS, which you'll investigate later in the course) and other programs that aren't likely to change. The computer chips in cars, small electronic devices, and appliances are often ROM chips. Other types of chips are non-volatile like ROMs, but use a slightly different technology to make them more economical to use if the firmware is needed in small quantities.

- *Programmable Read-Only Memory (PROM)* is a memory chip that can be programmed only once by a user who has access to the right equipment. Once it is programmed, the PROM chip behaves just like a ROM chip. The difference is that the ROM chips have the program etched into the silicon chip by the manufacturer, while the PROM chip can have a program added later.

  A PROM chip is programmed by applying high voltages that permanently alter the circuits so they store the desired program. The voltages are higher than those used in the computer, so the program remains on the chip. PROMs are used as ROM prototypes—to test programs before the final ROM chip is designed and manufactured. A somewhat older technology, PROMs are giving way to EPROMs and other reprogrammable memory chips.

- *Erasable Programmable Read-Only Memory (EPROM)* is a re-usable memory chip that can be programmed electrically and erased by exposure to ultraviolet light. Once the EPROM is programmed, it behaves just like a ROM chip. However, if ultraviolet light is shined through a quartz crystal window over the silicon chip on the integrated circuit package, it will erase the program; the user can then store a different program on the same chip. When the chip is in use, the crystal window is always covered to prevent unwanted ultraviolet light from destroying the program on it.

  EPROMs have a lifespan of a few hundred rewrites and are widely used in PCs because of this versatility. Computer manufacturers can test for and correct program errors throughout the manufacturing process, right up to the time the computer is ready for shipping.

- *Electrically Erasable Programmable Read-Only Memory (EEPROM)* is a memory chip that can be recorded or erased electrically, but that does not lose its content when electrical power is removed. Once it is programmed, the EEPROM behaves just like a ROM chip. Instead of using ultraviolet light like the EPROM, the EEPROM is erased by using an electrical charge. In addition, you can reprogram portions of an EEPROM, while the EPROM is completely erased. EEPROMs have a longer lifespan than EPROMs—from 10,000 to 100,000 write cycles.

- *Flash memory*, also known as *flash EEPROM*, is a special type of EEPROM that enables you to erase and write data more quickly than with standard EEPROMs. With EEPROMs, you can erase and write data one byte at a time, while with flash memory, you can erase and write data in fixed blocks, usually ranging in size from 512 bytes to up to 256 KB. Flash memory also has a significantly longer lifespan than other types of PROMs—from 100,000 to 300,000 write cycles. Often used for storing BIOS information and in modems, flash memory is also used in digital cameras and home video games.

Topic D
Numbering Systems

Computers process data internally using numbers, so to begin to understand how computers work, you must know how they store and process numerical information. But computers use numbers other than the decimal numbers that we're familiar with. In this topic, you'll learn about all the number systems computers use.

What would you do one day if you saw the number 3E0H? If you're like most people, you probably don't even recognize that as a number. However, computers do, and that's just one example of a number other than a decimal number you might encounter when working with computers. When you see a number like that, you need to be able to recognize what number system it's from and the value it represents.

The Decimal Number System

Imagine this: You are given a large pail that will hold exactly 1,000 marbles, a can that will hold exactly 100 marbles, and a small cup that holds only 10 marbles. You are asked to report how many pails, cans, and cups of marbles are stored in a large jar as quickly as possible. You could fill the cup over and over until you run out of marbles, but that takes too long. To save time, you put all the marbles in the pail, which is only partly filled. You pour the marbles from the pail into the can, which you can fill up only two times. You pour the remaining marbles into the cup, which you can fill three times. There are seven marbles left in the bottom of the pail. Your report on the number of marbles might be zero pails, two cans, three cups, and seven left over. This report will make little sense to people who do not know the number of marbles that can fit into the pail, can, and cup. A table can make things clearer.

 10^0 equals 1. Why? Division in exponential notation involves subtracting exponents. Follow these examples if you are unsure. $1000/100=10$ is the same as $10^3/10^2=10^{3-2}=10^1=10$. Along the same line, $1000/1000=1$ is the same as $10^3/10^3=10^{3-3}=10^0=1$. Any number raised to the power of zero is one. This is the same as saying $n^0=1$.

Number in Container	1,000 (10^3)	100 (10^2)	10 (10^1)	1 (10^0)
Times Filled	0	2	3	7

Chapter 1: Introduction to Computers

Using the number in a container as a place value, you could say that you counted no thousands, two hundreds, three tens, and seven individual marbles in the jar. This report leaves no room for misunderstanding, but it could be shorter. Stating that 237 marbles were in the jar is just as precise if everyone agrees that the 7 on the right tells how many individual marbles you had, the 3 in the second place from the right tells how many tens of marbles you had, and the 2 in the third place from the right tells how many hundreds of marbles you had. If you only dealt with humans, 237 would be fine, but now you are also working with computers that use other number systems. For a computer, the answer must be 237 Base 10.

 The asterisk (*) indicates multiplication and is a valid alternative to the times sign (which, because it so closely resembles the letter x, can cause confusion). When you are working with computers, you should always use the asterisk to ensure that the computer correctly interprets the mathematical statement you are making.

A computer would analyze your report this way: Base 10 tells the computer that the place value of each digit in your number is based on some power of 10. The digit in the first place on the right tells how many individuals (ones) you had. Another way of expressing one using exponents is 10^0. The second place from the right tells how many tens (10^1) you had. The third place tells how many hundreds (10^2, or 10*10) you counted, and the fourth place tells how many thousands (10^3, or 10*10*10) you had. Knowing you had 0*1000 plus 2*100 plus 3*10 plus 7 marbles, the computer could then translate the value into its own number system.

Exponential notation is just an extension of this idea. The number 237 could be written as $2*10^2+3*10^1+7*10^0$. Going from right to left, the place value of the digits are 10^0, 10^1, 10^2, 10^3, 10^4, and so on. The following table is a summary of Base 10 information.

Items to Count	Result	Exponential Notation	Decimal Equivalent
	0	$0*10^0$	0=0
|	1	$1*10^0$	1=1
||	2	$2*10^0$	2=2
|||	3	$3*10^0$	3=3
||||	4	$4*10^0$	4=4
|||||	5	$5*10^0$	5=5
||||||	6	$6*10^0$	6=6
|||||||	7	$7*10^0$	7=7
||||||||	8	$8*10^0$	8=8
|||||||||	9	$9*10^0$	9=9
||||||||||	10	$1*10^1+ 0*10^0$	10+0=10
|||||||||| + |	11	$1*10^1+ 1*10^0$	10+1=11
|||||||||| + ||	12	$1*10^1+ 2*10^0$	10+2=12

Items to Count	Result	Exponential Notation	Decimal Equivalent
||||||||||+|||	13	$1*10^1 + 3*10^0$	10+3=13
||||||||||+||||	14	$1*10^1 + 4*10^0$	10+4=14
||||||||||+|||||	15	$1*10^1 + 5*10^0$	10+5=15
||||||||||+||||||	16	$1*10^1 + 6*10^0$	10+6=16
||||||||||+|||||||	17	$1*10^1 + 7*10^0$	10+7=17
||||||||||+||||||||	18	$1*10^1 + 8*10^0$	10+8=18
||||||||||+|||||||||	19	$1*10^1 + 9*10^0$	10+9=19
||||||||||+||||||||||	20	$2*10^1 + 0*10^0$	20+0=20
||||||||||+||||||||||+|	21	$2*10^1 + 1*10^0$	20+1=21

The Binary Number System

Computers are electronic devices that use electrical patterns to represent numbers. Modern digital computers recognize only two electrical states—ON and OFF—but their memories contain millions of transistors that can be either on or off. Working with numbers in computers is like making numbers out of a row of lights that can be switched on and off independently. Because there are only two ways to represent a number, computers use the *binary number system* (Base 2). The same concepts that you know work for the decimal system also work for the binary system.

Imagine this: You are given the same jar of 237 marbles to count, but this time you have a series of measuring cups that can hold 256, 128, 64, 32, 16, 8, 4, and 2 marbles. The largest cup holds 256 marbles, so it is not filled. The next cup is filled and takes 128 marbles from the total, leaving 109 marbles. You can't fill the 128 cup a second time, so you move down the row to the cup that holds 64, which you fill, leaving 45. This will not fill the 64 cup again, but it will fill the 32 cup, leaving you 13 marbles. You don't have enough to fill the 32 or the 16 cup, so you fill the 8 cup, leaving you 5 marbles. You fill the 4 cup, cannot fill the 2 cup, and have 1 marble left over. Because there are so many cups, it is easiest to report your results in a table.

Number in Cup	256 (2^8)	128 (2^7)	64 (2^6)	32 (2^5)	16 (2^4)	8 (2^3)	4 (2^2)	2 (2^1)	1 (2^0)
Times Filled	0	1	1	1	0	1	1	0	1

Remember, 2^0 equals 1. This is an important idea, so follow along. 256/32=8 is the same as $2^8 / 2^5 = 2^{8-5} = 2^3 = 8$. Along the same line, 128/128=1 is the same as $2^7 / 2^7 = 2^{7-7} = 2^0 = 1$. Any number raised to the power of 0 is 1.

Chapter 1: Introduction to Computers

A report that you counted 1110 1101 (Base 2) marbles would make little sense to most humans, but would be crystal clear to a computer. A human would have to look at the table and figure you counted $1*128 + 1*64 + 1*32 + 1*8 + 1*4 + 1*1$ marbles or 237 (Base 10) marbles. Using exponential notation, the same result would be: $1*2^7 + 1*2^6 + 1*2^5 + 1*2^3 + 1*2^2 + 1*2^0$ marbles or 237 (Base 10) marbles.

Items to Count	Result	Exponential Notation	Decimal Value
	0	$0*2^0$	$0*1=0$
|	1	$1*2^0$	$1*1=1$
||	10	$1*2^1 + 0*2^0$	$1*2+0*1=2$
||+|	11	$1*2^1 + 1*2^0$	$1*2+1*1=3$
||||	100	$1*2^2 + 0*2^1 + 0*2^0$	$1*4+0*2+0*1=4$
||||+|	101	$1*2^2 + 0*2^1 + 1*2^0$	$1*4+0*2+1*1=5$
||||+||	110	$1*2^2 + 1*2^1 + 0*2^0$	$1*4+1*2+0*1=6$
||||+||+|	111	$1*2^2 + 1*2^1 + 1*2^0$	$1*4+1*2+1*1=7$
||||||||	1000	$1*2^3 + 0*2^2 + 0*2^1 + 0*2^0$	$1*8+0*4+0*2+0*1=8$
||||||||+|	1001	$1*2^3 + 0*2^2 + 0*2^1 + 1*2^0$	$1*8+0*4+0*2+1*1=9$
||||||||+||	1010	$1*2^3 + 0*2^2 + 1*2^1 + 0*2^0$	$1*8+0*4+1*2+0*1=10$
||||||||+||+|	1011	$1*2^3 + 0*2^2 + 1*2^1 + 1*2^0$	$1*8+0*4+1*2+1*1=11$
||||||||+||||	1100	$1*2^3 + 1*2^2 + 0*2^1 + 0*2^0$	$1*8+1*4+0*2+0*1=12$
||||||||+||||+|	1101	$1*2^3 + 1*2^2 + 0*2^1 + 1*2^0$	$1*8+1*4+0*2+1*1=13$
||||||||+||||+||	1110	$1*2^3 + 1*2^2 + 1*2^1 + 0*2^0$	$1*8+1*4+1*2+0*1=14$
||||||||+||||+||+|	1111	$1*2^3 + 1*2^2 + 1*2^1 + 1*2^0$	$1*8+1*4+1*2+1*1=15$
||||||||||||||||	1 0000	$1*2^4 + 0*2^3 + 0*2^2 + 0*2^1 + 0*2^0$	$1*16+0*8+0*4+0*2+0*1=16$
||||||||||||||||+|	1 0001	$1*2^4 + 0*2^3 + 0*2^2 + 0*2^1 + 1*2^0$	$1*16+0*8+0*4+0*2+1*1=17$
||||||||||||||||+||	1 0010	$1*2^4 + 0*2^3 + 0*2^2 + 1*2^1 + 0*2^0$	$1*16+0*8+0*4+1*2+0*1=18$
||||||||||||||||+||+|	1 0011	$1*2^4 + 0*2^3 + 0*2^2 + 1*2^1 + 1*2^0$	$1*16+0*8+0*4+1*2+1*1=19$
||||||||||||||||+||||	1 0100	$1*2^4 + 0*2^3 + 1*2^2 + 0*2^1 + 0*2^0$	$1*16+0*8+1*4+0*2+0*1=20$
||||||||||||||||+||||+|	1 0101	$1*2^4 + 0*2^3 + 1*2^2 + 0*2^1 + 1*1^0$	$1*16+0*8+1*4+0*2+1*1=21$

The process of converting binary (Base 2) numbers you get from the computer into decimal (Base 10) numbers for yourself is much easier if you make a table. In the top right-most column, put in 2^0 or 1. In the second column from the right, place 2^1 or 2. In the third column, place 2^2 or 4, fourth column 2^3 or 8, and continue until you have a column for every digit in the binary number. Place the binary number in the second row. In the third row, if the binary digit in the column is 1, copy the decimal number (place value) above it into the third row. If the binary number is 0, leave that cell in the third row blank. Add up all the numbers in the third row and you will have the decimal equivalent of the binary number. For example, to convert 1010 0010 (Base 2) to its decimal value (Base 10), look at the following table where 1010 0010 (Base 2) is equal to 128 + 32 + 2 = 162 (Base 10).

Place Value	128	64	32	16	8	4	2	1
Binary Number	1	0	1	0	0	0	1	0
Decimal Value	128		32				2	

Converting decimal to binary uses a similar table. In the top row, enter the place values for the binary number system—(1, 2, 4, 8, and so on) going from right to left until you reach a power of 2 that is bigger than the decimal number. In the second row, enter the decimal number in the left-most column. Working from left to right, try to subtract the place value for a column from the decimal number. If the result is positive, put a 1 in the third row of that column and place the remainder of the subtraction in the second row of the next column. If the result is negative, put a 0 in the third row of that column and copy the same number over into the second row of the next column. Keep subtracting binary place values from the decimal number until there is no remainder. For example, to convert 213 (Base 10) into a binary number (Base 2), look at the example in this table, where 213 (Base 10) is equal to 1101 0101 (Base 2).

Place Value	128	64	32	16	8	4	2	1
Decimal Number/ Decimal Remainder	213-128=85	85-64=21	21-32<1	21-16=5	5-8<1	5-4=1	1-2<1	1-1=0
Binary Number	1	1	0	1	0	1	0	1

To check your work, convert the binary number 1101 0101 back to decimal. The values you subtracted from the decimal number until you had nothing left should add up to equal the original decimal number.

Place Value	128	64	32	16	8	4	2	1
Binary Number	1	1	0	1	0	1	0	1
Decimal Value	128	64	0	16	0	4	0	1

The binary number 1101 0101 (Base 2) is equal to 128 + 64 + 16 + 4 + 1 = 213 (Base 10). Your answer checks. Notice that, to convert from binary to decimal, we are adding values, and to convert from decimal to binary, we subtract values. Other techniques for converting numbers work just as well, but this one is the most direct.

The Hexadecimal Number System

The *hexadecimal number system* is a compromise by the computer world for humans. Binary numbers tend to be very long and, with only 0s and 1s, tend to all look alike. Humans need a way to communicate with the computer in a number system related to the binary system, but easier to read and understand. The hexadecimal system (Base 16) is the solution.

Imagine this: You are given the same jar of 237 marbles to count, but this time you have a large pail that will hold exactly 256 marbles and a can that will hold exactly 16 marbles. You don't have enough marbles to fill the pail, but you can fill the can 14 times and have 13 marbles left in the bottom of the pail. Your report on the number of marbles might be zero pails, 14 cans, and 13 left over. This report will make little sense to people who do not know the number of marbles that can fit into the pail and can. A table can make things clearer.

Number in Container	256 (16^2)	16 (16^1)	1 (16^0)
Times Filled	0	14	13

Now the trouble starts. Reporting 1413 (Base 16) is too confusing. Did you fill the pail one time, the can 41 times, and have three left over? Computers do not like any doubt in the numbers they are given, so another way of writing hexadecimal values greater than 9 was agreed upon. The letter A (Base 16) is equal to 10 (Base 10), the letter B (Base 16) is equal to 11 (Base 10), C (Base 16) = 12 (Base 10), D (Base 16) = 13 (Base 10), E (Base 16) = 14 (Base 10), and F (Base 16) = 15 (Base 10). Using this notation, you could report you counted ED (Base 16) marbles.

Using exponential notation, the same result would be: $E*16^1 + D*16^0 = 14 * 16 + 13 = 224 + 13$ marbles or 237 (Base 10) marbles.

Items to Count	Result	Exponential Notation	Decimal Value
	0	$0*16^0$	0

Items to Count	Result	Exponential Notation	Decimal Value
|	1	$1*16^0$	1=1
||	2	$2*16^0$	2=2
|||	3	$3*16^0$	3=3
||||	4	$4*16^0$	4=4
|||||	5	$5*16^0$	5=5
||||||	6	$6*16^0$	6=6
|||||||	7	$7*16^0$	7=7
||||||||	8	$8*16^0$	8=8
|||||||||	9	$9*16^0$	9=9
||||||||||	A	$A*16^0$	A=10
|||||||||||	B	$B*16^0$	B=11
||||||||||||	C	$C*16^0$	C=12
|||||||||||||	D	$D*16^0$	D=13
||||||||||||||	E	$E*16^0$	E=14
|||||||||||||||	F	$F*16^0$	F=15
||||||||||||||||	10	$1*16^1 + 0*16^0$	16+0=16
||||||||||||||||+|	11	$1*16^1 + 1*16^0$	16+1=17
||||||||||||||||+||	12	$1*16^1 + 2*16^0$	16+2=18
||||||||||||||||+|||	13	$1*16^1 + 3*16^0$	16+3=19
||||||||||||||||+||||	14	$1*16^1 + 4*16^0$	16+4=20
||||||||||||||||+|||||	15	$1*16^1 + 5*16^0$	16+5=21

The process of converting hexadecimal (Base 16) numbers from the computer into decimal (Base 10) numbers for yourself is much easier if you make a table. In the top right-most column, put in 16^0 or 1. In the second column from the right, put 16^1 or 16. In the third column, place 16^2 or 256, fourth column 16^3 or 4,096, and continue until you have a column for every digit in the hexadecimal number. These numbers are the place values for the hexadecimal digits. Place the hexadecimal number in the second row. In the third row, multiply the hexadecimal digit in the second row times the place value of the column in the first row, and write the product in the third row. Add all the numbers in the third row, and you will have the decimal equivalent of the hexadecimal number. For example, to convert A4 B6 (Base 16) to its decimal value (Base 10), take a look at the following table. A4B6 (Base 16) is equal to 40,960 + 1,024 + 176 + 6 = 42,166 (Base 10).

Chapter 1: Introduction to Computers

Place Value	4,096	256	16	1
Hexadecimal Number	A	4	B	6
Decimal Value	10*4,096=40,960	4*256=1,024	11*16=176	6*1=6

Converting decimal to hexadecimal uses a similar table. In the top row, enter the place values for the hexadecimal number system—(1, 16, 256, 4,096, and so on) going from right to left until you reach a power of 16 that is greater than the decimal number. In the second row, enter the decimal number in the left-most column. Working from left to right, try to divide the place value for a column into the decimal number. If the result is greater than 1, put the number of times the place value went into the decimal number in row three of that column, and place the remainder of the division into row two of the next column to the right. If the result is less than 1, put a 0 in the row three of the column and copy the same number over into row two of the next column to the right. Keep dividing hexadecimal place values into the remaining decimal number until the remainder is less than 16. Place that remainder into the 1s column. For example, to convert 59,660 (Base 10) into a hexadecimal number (Base 16), look at the example in the following table where 59,660 (Base 10) is equal to E90C (Base 16).

Place Value	4,096	256	16	1
Decimal Number/Decimal Remainder	59,660/4,096=E (14) rem. 2,316	2,316/256=9 rem. 12	12/16<1	12/1=C (12)
Hexadecimal Number	E	9	0	C

To check your work, convert the hexadecimal number E90C back to decimal. This is shown in the following table.

Place Value	4,096	256	16	1
Hexadecimal Number	E	9	0	C
Decimal Value	14*4,096=57,344	9*256=2,304	0*16=0	12*1=12

The hexadecimal number E90C (Base 16) is equal to 57,344 + 2,304 + 0 + 12 = 59,660 (Base 10). Your answer checks. Notice that, to convert from hexadecimal to decimal, you are multiplying values, and to convert from decimal to hexadecimal, you divide values. Other techniques for converting numbers work just as well, but this one is the most direct. Hexadecimal values are often identified by a preceding dollar sign or the letter H (upper or lower case). For instance, $3E0, 3E0h, 3E0H, and 3E0 (Base 16) are all equivalent to the decimal number 992.

Computer Values

Many of the values you see on your computer screen are based on numbers converted from the binary number system to decimal or hexadecimal numbers. For example, many addresses, such as memory and network addresses, are often represented in hexadecimal notation. You'll work more with these addresses later in the course. Those numbers may have seemed rather odd before, but with your new knowledge of number theory, you will be able to explain where the numbers came from.

A *bit* is a single binary digit. A bit may have a value of 0 or 1. In a computer, a switch or transistor that is off represents a 0, and a switch or transistor that is on represents a 1. Most computers work with groups of 8 bits, which is called a *byte*. To make it easier to read, the 8 binary digits in a byte are divided into two groups of four, called *nibbles*, when they are written.

A kilobyte is often referred to as 1,000 bytes, but this is not totally accurate. In computer terms, a *kilobyte* is 1,024 bytes. K is used as shorthand for 2^{10}, which equals 1,024. A file listed as having a size of 67 KB may show a more accurate size of 66.5 KB in the Properties dialog box, or 68,096 bytes. The file hasn't changed size (66.5 KB = 66.5 * 1,024 bytes = 68,096 bytes).

Likewise, a *megabyte* is not exactly 1,000,000 bytes, but 1,024 KB, or 2^{20} bytes, or 1,048,576 bytes. A 200 MB drive can store 204,800 KB or 209,715,200 bytes.

Following the trend, a *gigabyte* is not 1 billion bytes, but 1,024 MB, or 2^{30} bytes or 1,073,741,824 bytes. Several years ago, a drive manufacturer promoted its new drive as being a better value than other 3 gigabyte drives, because on their drive you had room to store 3 billion bytes, plus room for another 221,225,472 bytes thrown in for free. A quick check of the math shows the drive maker was misleading but numerically accurate. 3 GB is the same as 3,221,225,472 bytes, no matter what type of drive you're using!

CHAPTER 1 FOLLOW-UP
Introduction to Computers

You have learned some basics about computers, including how they evolved and some of their common components. This background is important as you begin to work through this course. The knowledge in this chapter gives you the foundation you need to complete all the remaining chapters.

Essential Terms

- abacus
- binary
- bus
- CD-ROM
- chipset
- CPU
- decimal

- desktop
- DIMM
- diode
- DRAM
- driver
- EDSAC
- EDVAC

- EEPROM
- ENIAC
- EPROM
- firmware
- flash memory
- floppy disk
- GUI

- hard drive
- hexadecimal
- integrated circuit
- interface
- keyboard
- laptop
- memory
- microprocessor
- minitower
- monitor
- motherboard
- mouse
- operating system
- PC
- PDA
- processor
- PROM
- RAM
- resistor
- ROM
- software
- SIMM
- SRAM
- tablet computer
- transistor
- UNIVAC
- vacuum tube

Review Questions

1. What is the earliest known mechanical computational device?
2. Who invented the first calculating machine?
3. Which machine, invented by Charles Babbage, introduced the idea of using memory to store results?
4. Who was the first to use vacuum tubes in an electronic digital computer?
5. What's the name of the device that contains semiconductor material that can amplify a signal or open and close a circuit?
6. What was the first general purpose processor that Intel introduced in 1974?
7. What's another name for a computer's system board?
8. How are electronic components secured to a circuit board?
9. Original IBM PCs were build on which Intel CPU?
10. Which type of RAM doesn't need to be refreshed?
11. What's the name for a group of memory chips that transfer information 64 bits at a time?
12. What's the special type of memory that stores information about the computer's setup?
13. Windows XP is an example of which type of software?
14. What type of software enables the operating system and a peripheral device to communicate with each other?
15. What type of memory chip can be programmed only once?
16. Which type of memory chip can be erased using ultraviolet light?
17. Which special type of EEPROM enables you to write data more quickly and has a long life span?
18. What's the life span of EEPROM chips?
19. Which numbering system is based on ten discrete states?
20. What is the decimal value of the binary number 10011100010?
21. What is the binary value of the decimal number 5777?

22. Which number system is based on two discrete states?
23. Which number system is based on 16 discrete states?
24. What's the decimal value of the hexadecimal number 3E8?
25. What's the hexadecimal value of the decimal number 3,256?

Review Projects

Project #1: Tracing the History of Computers

The history of computational devices stretches back in time more than 2,000 years. During that time, men and women have made enormous contributions to the technology that would eventually result in the computers we know today.

The Computer History Museum on the Web at http://www.computerhistory.org/ provides a wealth of information about the evolution of the modern electronic computer. Explore the Web site and investigate the timelines, documents, and photographs it has made available.

Which stages in the development of computers do you think were most important? Which computational machines most interest you? Which documents did you find particularly interesting?

Project #2: Exploring Computer Hardware

While some computers have specialized components that are installed to perform a specific function, for the most part, all computers have the same basic parts inside. While some might look a little different from one computer to the next, you can generally recognize the main system components just by looking at them.

Shut down and unplug your computer. Remove the computer's cover. Identify the main system components inside your computer, including the hard disk, processor, interface cards, and RAM. Determine the manufacturer of each of these components and visit each manufacturer's Web site. What information is available for each component? What type of support does each Web site offer? Do any of the manufacturers offer drivers or other software to manage the devices? If so, how new are the drivers? What type of other software can you download?

Project #3: Investigating Popular Operating Systems

While there are several mainstream operating systems in use today on a variety of computer types, when it comes right down to it, most people are familiar with just one of three: Windows, Linux, and Mac OS. Explore the links to these operating systems:

- http://www.microsoft.com/windowsxp/default.asp
- http://www.apple.com/macosx/
- http://www.linux.org/

Which operating system do you have most experience with? Which operating system seems to offer the most features? Which do you think might be easiest to use? Do you prefer one over the other? If so, why?

Reflective Questions

1. What do you think was the most important development in the history of computers?

2. What is the most important component inside a computer?

CHAPTER 2
Setting Up a Personal Computer

Chapter Objectives:

In this chapter, you will install or remove devices on standard ports.

You will:

- Connect a video output device to the monitor port on a computer.
- Install PS/2 devices.
- Connect parallel devices to the parallel port on a computer.
- Connect a serial device to a serial port.
- Connect game and sound devices to the appropriate ports.
- Install USB devices.
- Install FireWire devices.
- Establish a wireless connection between a wireless device and a computer.

Introduction

Your users are all excited—they just received brand new PCs. You have been asked to unpack and set them up. In this chapter, you will learn how to recognize the ports and connectors for basic system components. You will connect these components and, if necessary, configure them for use.

As a computer technician, it is your job to set up PCs. Putting together a PC is similar to putting together a puzzle. If you don't put the PC together correctly, the user downtime and your rework will be expensive.

Topic A
Install Video Output Devices

To make the system usable, you still need to provide a device so that users can see their input. In this topic, you will install a video display monitor.

A monitor can be thought of as the eyes of a system. You will need to provide your users with a way to see their work, so installing the monitor is an important step in assembling a computer system.

Peripheral Devices

Definition:

> A *peripheral* is any computing device besides the CPU and memory. Peripherals expand what you can do with a computer. They all have connectors of some sort to connect to the computer. Peripherals can be internal or external to the computer system case. Internal peripherals are also called integrated peripherals. Most peripherals have a cable to connect it to the computer, but others are able to use various wireless connection methods. Some peripherals are powered by the computer, but others need their own power supply.

This is just one definition that is commonly used for peripheral devices. Other definitions for this word (including something on the edge, something of less importance, or an accessory) define peripherals as any device connected externally to the system case. Still others define it as anything other than the CPU, memory, monitor, and keyboard. For this course, we will use the first definition.

Example:

Examples of peripheral devices include monitor, keyboard, pointing device, printer, scanner, and any other device you can connect to one of the system connectors. Additional components, which never were connected to computers in the past, are being added routinely these days. These include mobile phones, televisions, and other consumer devices. Figure 2-1 shows an example of a computer with several external peripherals attached.

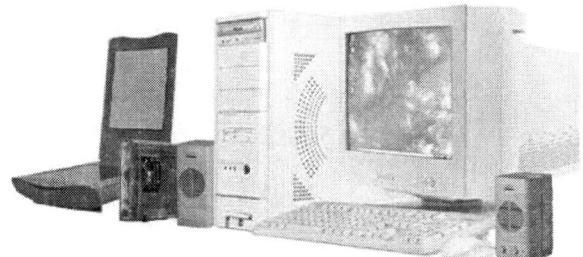

Figure 2-1: *A computer with peripherals attached.*

Video Output Devices

Definition:

A *video output device* is a computer peripheral that enables users to view information on a computer system. Similarities between video output devices include:

- All video output devices display an image of some type.
- They all have controls to change the settings for the device.
- They connect to the computer system using a cable.

Differences between video output devices include:

- The size and shape of the display. Monitors are measured diagonally across the glass screen.
- The location and type of controls. Controls could be separate buttons for each function, or they could be grouped together and use an on-screen menu that is super-imposed over the Windows display.
- Some have a curved screen and others have a flat screen.
- Some use analog signals and some use digital signals. Analog signals are carried on 15-pin VGA cables to the video port on the computer. Digital signals are carried on digital-only or digital-analog cables to a digital or analog port on the computer. These digital cables vary in the number of pins and types of connections used.

- Some use *Cathode Ray Tube (CRT)* technology and others use *Liquid Crystal Display (LCD)* technology. CRTs are at least as deep as the screen size to enable the image to be created. LCD screens are very thin—often only 2 or 3 inches thick.
- The way they produce the image varies:
  - CRTs use a phosphorous coating inside a glass screen.
  - LCD monitors use different colored crystals sandwiched between two sheets of plastic.
  - Projection systems display the image on a wall or movie screen, rather than showing the image on the video output device itself.

Example:

Examples of video display devices include:

- CRT monitors. These can have curved or flat screens. They should not be confused with flat-panel monitors. An example of a CRT monitor is shown in Figure 2-2.
- LCD flat-panel monitors. An example of an LCD flat panel monitor is shown in Figure 2-3.
- Personal display devices such as goggles or glasses monitors.
- Video display systems range from those used to display one image to several monitors (often used in training situations) to those used at trade shows to display an image covering a huge screen.
- Video projectors. These are often used to display the contents of a monitor onto a white board or other surface so that an audience can see the output on a computer screen. An example of an image being displayed on a white board using a video projector is shown in Figure 2-4.
- Touchscreen monitors. These monitors enable input through the screen. This technology is used in bank ATM machines, some point-of-sale terminals at fast food restaurants, and other situations where a separate keyboard for input is not appropriate.

Figure 2-2: *A CRT monitor.*

Figure 2-3: *An LCD flat-panel monitor.*

Figure 2-4: *An image on the monitor is also displayed on the white board using a video projector.*

Digital and Analog Signals

Most information within a computer system is transmitted as a digital electronic signal, but some needs to be converted to an analog signal. Digital signal data is composed of discrete values. Analog signal data is composed of a signal that varies in frequency. An everyday digital device you have encountered is a digital clock. A clock with hands that move around the clock face is an analog clock.

Computers deal in discrete values. It uses on/off or 1/0 for everything it does. CRT monitors use analog signals to produce an image. So, the computer has to convert the digital data to an analog signal that the monitor can display. Digital flat-panel monitors can use the digital data without needing to convert it first.

DVI-I is a digital and analog connection that uses 3 rows of 6 pins each and a flat blade. DVI-A is analog only and uses one row of 5 pins, one row of 3 pins and 1 row of 4 pins and two contacts above and below a flat blade. DVD-D 3 is a digital only connection using 3 rows of 6 pins and a flat blade. DVI-I is a dual link, analog and digital connection that uses three rows of 8 pins each and 2 contacts above and below a flat blade. P&D is an analog and digital connection of three rows of 10 pins each and two contacts above and below a flat blade. DVI-D is a digital only connection composed of 3 rows of 8 pins each and no contacts above or below a flat blade. More information about these can be found at **www.datapro.net/dvi.html**.

Ports

Definition:

A *port* is a hardware connection interface on a computer system that enables devices to be connected to the system. All ports:

- Connect a device that uses a cable that matches the configuration of the port.
- Carry the signals from a device to the computer system.
- Carry the signals from the computer system to a device.
- Are composed of wires, plugs, and sockets that enable two devices to be connected. The plugs will be either on the port or the cable and the sockets will be on the other.

Ports vary by:

- The number of pins or connectors it contains.
- The layout of the pins.
- The signals they carry.
- The devices that can be connected to the port.
- The location. Some connect internal devices and others connect external devices.

Example:

A monitor port is a 15-pin female connector. The monitor cable ends in a matching 15-pin male connector which plugs into the port on the system. An example of a monitor port and cable is shown in Figure 2-5.

 Some systems contain specialized video cards that contain a second 15-pin port so that you can connect two monitors to one system. Other video cards might contain additional ports for connecting a TV to the computer.

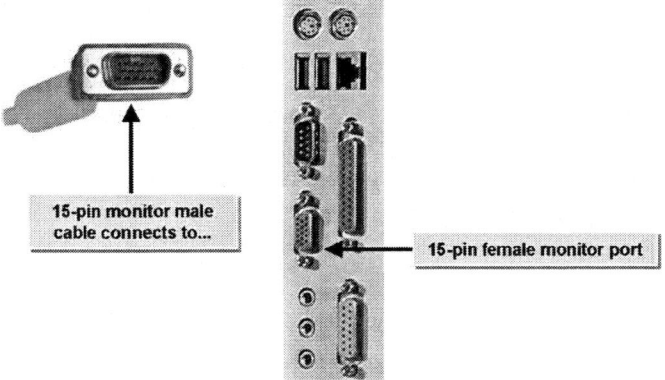

Figure 2-5: *A monitor port and cable.*

Gender

Cables and ports have genders. For example, if the port has plugs, the matching cable will have sockets. The port in this case would be considered female and the cable would be considered male. An example of male and female connectors is shown in Figure 2-6.

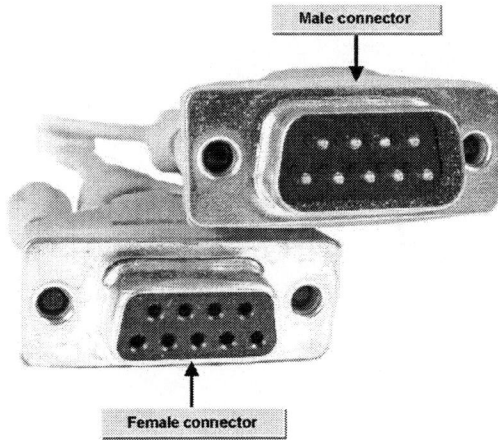

Figure 2-6: *Male and female connections.*

Display Characteristics

Some of the display characteristics are controlled through a dialog box in Windows and others are adjusted through controls on the physical monitor. This first table describes the settings you can control through Windows.

Characteristic	Description
Dot pitch	The distance between the same color dots on the screen. The closer the dots are together, the smoother the image will be and the finer the detail that can be shown.
Resolution	The maximum number of *pixels* on a monitor. A pixel is the smallest discrete element on a video display. This is listed as horizontal pixels x vertical pixels. This is usually in the ratio 4:3. Common resolutions are 640 x 480, 800 x 600, 1024 x 768, and 1600 x 1200. The higher the resolution, the more objects or information you can fit on the screen at once.
Refresh rate	The number of times per second that the entire monitor is scanned (pixels are illuminated). Each time it is scanned is referred to as a frame. The rate is expressed in Hertz (Hz). Typical refresh rates are 60-70 Hz or 60-70 times per second. Any setting lower than 60 Hz usually produces noticeable flickering.
Color depth (also known as color quality)	The number of bits used to store the color of a pixel determines how many colors can be displayed. The following are the color depths you will likely encounter: • 4-bit color depth requires 0.5 bytes per pixel and can display 16 colors. This is standard VGA mode. At 640 x 480 resolution, this requires 0.5 MB of memory. • 8-bit color depth requires 1 byte per pixel and can display 256 colors. This is 256-color mode. At 800 x 600 resolution, this requires 2 MB of memory. • 16-bit color depth requires 2 bytes per pixel and can display 65,536 colors. This is High Color mode. At 1024 x 768 resolution, this requires 4 MB of memory. • 24-bit color depth requires 3 bytes per pixel and can display 16,777,216 colors. This is True Color mode. At 1600 x 1200 resolution, this requires 8 MB of memory.
Font	Changing to another font requires that the fonts be installed on the system and the system to be restarted before they can be used.

Physical monitor adjustments are usually located on the front of the monitor just below the screen. There might be separate buttons for each control and function, or there might be one or a few buttons which display on-screen menus to access each adjustable parameter. For brightness and contrast, there might be a knob you turn, a button you press, or you might need to access the settings through a menu that is super-imposed on the screen over your Windows images. Settings you can control might include those shown in the following table.

The location of buttons or how to access menus varies from monitor to monitor. Refer to your physical monitor or to the monitor documentation for instructions on how to adjust the settings for the particular monitor you are working with.

Setting	Description
Brightness	If the brightness is set too high, you might get an "aura" effect displayed on the screen. If it is set too low, you might not see anything on the screen.
Contrast	If the contrast is not set correctly for the monitor and the lighting conditions in the room (for example, a really bright or really dark room), you might not be able to see anything on the screen, or you might get strange results.
Image position	This is the location of the display in relation to the physical monitor. Sometimes the image is not centered on the monitor. Other times the image doesn't fill the screen, leaving a black band around the edge. Another positioning issue you might need to address is if part of the image is off the screen. There are usually separate buttons or menu options to adjust each of these issues.
Distortions	If lines don't appear straight on the monitor, you might need to adjust settings. Refer to the monitor documentation for how to resolve such issues.

How to Connect a Video Output Device

Procedure Reference: Install a Monitor

To install a monitor:

1. Turn off the computer.
2. Locate the monitor port on the computer:
   - 15-pin VGA adapter. An example is shown in Figure 2-7.

- 29-pin DVI adapter. An example is shown in Figure 2-8.

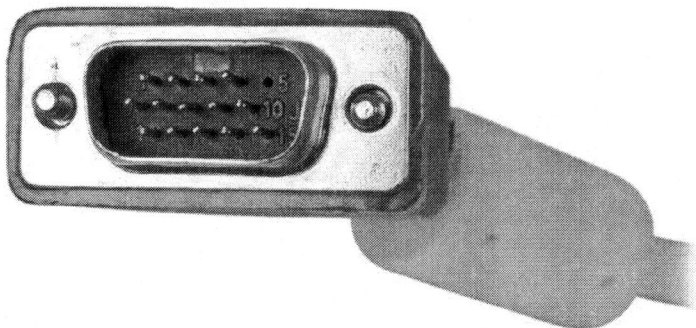

Figure 2-7: *A VGA connector.*

DVI-I receptacle connector

Figure 2-8: *A DVI port.*

3. Align the pins on the monitor cable with the holes in the adapter port and plug in the monitor. An example is shown in Figure 2-9.

Figure 2-9: *A CRT monitor cable.*

4. Secure the monitor to the port by tightening the screws on each side of the port.
5. Plug in the monitor power cord.
6. Turn on the computer.

7. Turn on the monitor.
8. Verify that the monitor works.
   - Check that the power light is on, that it is green, and that it is not blinking.
   - Make sure the colors display correctly (they are not washed out or the wrong colors).
   - Make sure there are no lines or distortion in the image displayed on the monitor.
   - There should be no waviness to the display.

Procedure Reference: Adjust Video Settings

To adjust the video settings for a monitor:

1. Use the control buttons located on the physical monitor to adjust the display size and location. Through these buttons you can change the:
   - Vertical display position.
   - Horizontal display position.
   - Display height.
   - Display width.
2. Use the control buttons located on the physical monitor to adjust brightness and contrast.
3. Use the Windows Display Properties dialog box to adjust user preference for screen resolution.
   a. Right-click the Desktop and choose Properties to display the Display Properties dialog box.
   b. Click Settings.
   c. Drag the Screen Resolution slider to the desired setting. If your video card and monitor only support one resolution, you won't be able to change it. If the video card only supports two resolutions, instead of dragging the indicator, click above the desired resolution to change it.
   d. Click Apply.
   e. Click OK.
   f. If prompted, click Yes. If you don't click within the allotted time, the setting reverts to the previous setting.
4. Use the Windows Display Properties dialog box to adjust user preference for font size. There are a couple of methods to do this. The first is usually sufficient for most needs.
   a. Right-click the Desktop and choose Properties.
   b. From the Display Properties dialog box, display the Appearance page.
   c. Display the Font Size drop-down list.
   d. Choose the desired font size. Choices include Normal, Large, and Extra Large.

e. Click OK.

The second method gives you more precise control as you can customize the DPI (dots per inch) to one of the preset sizes that correspond to the sizes in the first method (Normal (96 DPI) and Large (120 DPI)). Or you can customize the size using the Scale To This Percentage Of Normal Size option under Custom Setting.

a. From the Display Properties dialog box, on the Settings tab, click Advanced.

b. Choose the desired DPI Setting size.

c. Click OK.

d. Click Yes.

e. Click Close, and then click Yes.

Plug and Play

Plug and Play (also written as PnP) is a standard that enables a PnP-compatible computer and a PnP-compatible operating system to work together to automatically configure settings when PnP-compatible hardware is connected to the system. After you install a component into a Plug and Play computer, the system detects the new component and configures the settings. Figure 2-10 shows how the PnP process works.

 Plug and Play, in its early days, was often also called Plug and Pray. This is because, especially in older systems, both PnP and legacy (non-PnP) components were often found in the same system, opening up the potential for conflicts and improper configuration. Systems on the market today are all PnP-compliant as are the current operating systems. Problems are much less likely in such systems. In general, the fewer legacy devices you have installed in your system, the less likely you will be to encounter problems.

1. Install hardware such as a printer.
2. Cards enter PnP configuration mode.
3. Handles assigned to each card.
4. Resources are allocated to prevent conflicts.
5. All PnP cards are activated and exit configuration mode.

Figure 2-10: *The Plug and Play process.*

When you install hardware, this is a very high-level overview of what happens:

1. You connect a piece of hardware to a PnP-compatible system running a PnP- aware operating system.
2. All PnP cards enter Configuration mode by enabling PnP code built into the card.
3. One at a time, PnP cards are isolated and a handle is assigned to the card. The handle is used to identify that card.
4. Resources are allocated to each card that don't conflict with resources allocated to any other card.
5. All PnP cards are activated and exit Configuration mode.

If you install a new device and Windows doesn't automatically detect it, you can also use the Add New Hardware Wizard to install and configure PnP devices. You will find the Add New Hardware Wizard in the Control Panel. When using the wizard, you should initially let Windows try to scan for new hardware (this is the default selection). If Windows can find the new device, it will identify and install the driver for the device. If Windows can't find the device, you can then either choose the device from a list of devices offered by Windows and Windows will install the appropriate driver, or you can click Have Disk to point to a driver you've been provided with by the manufacturer on floppy disk or CD-ROM.

TOPIC B
Install PS/2 Devices

This chapter focuses on setting up a personal computer. One of the required components is the keyboard. Another component on almost every system is a mouse. In this topic, you will connect these devices to the appropriate ports.

One of the most common peripherals you will install is a keyboard or a mouse. Plugging them in to the wrong port won't damage anything but you won't be able to interact with your system if you do.

PS/2 Interface

Definition:

A *PS/2 interface* is how PS/2 devices are connected to the computer. The interface is composed of a PS/2 port on the computer, a device, and a cable to connect the two together. An example of the PS/2 interface is shown in Figure 2-11. PS/2 ports are ports that are used to connect the keyboard and mouse to the computer. PS/2 ports are also referred to as a mini-DIN port. They are 6-pin round ports that are built in to the system. The keyboard and mouse ports look identical, but plugging the mouse into the keyboard port and vice versa does not work.

 PS/2 stands for Personal System 2 which was an IBM computer. The keyboard and mouse connectors used on those systems became the standard for connecting those devices on computer systems.

Most systems mark which port is the keyboard and which is the mouse, because they appear identical when you look at them. The port usually will either be color-coded to match the end of the cable that came with the system or there will be a picture of a mouse and keyboard near the connectors. On some systems, the sticker is under the connectors and perpendicular to the actual ports. Just imagine sliding it up the wall of the computer so that it would be next to the ports to determine which device goes in which port. If the ports are color-coded, the keyboard port is purple and the mouse port is green.

> Color-coded ports were defined by Microsoft, Intel, and Toshiba, to help users connect devices to the computer. It was adopted in 1999 and has slowly been adopted by most manufacturers. Some older systems used color-coded ports which might not match the colors defined by this group. A list of the colors can be found at **www.microlanduk.com/support/external%20connections.htm#colours**.

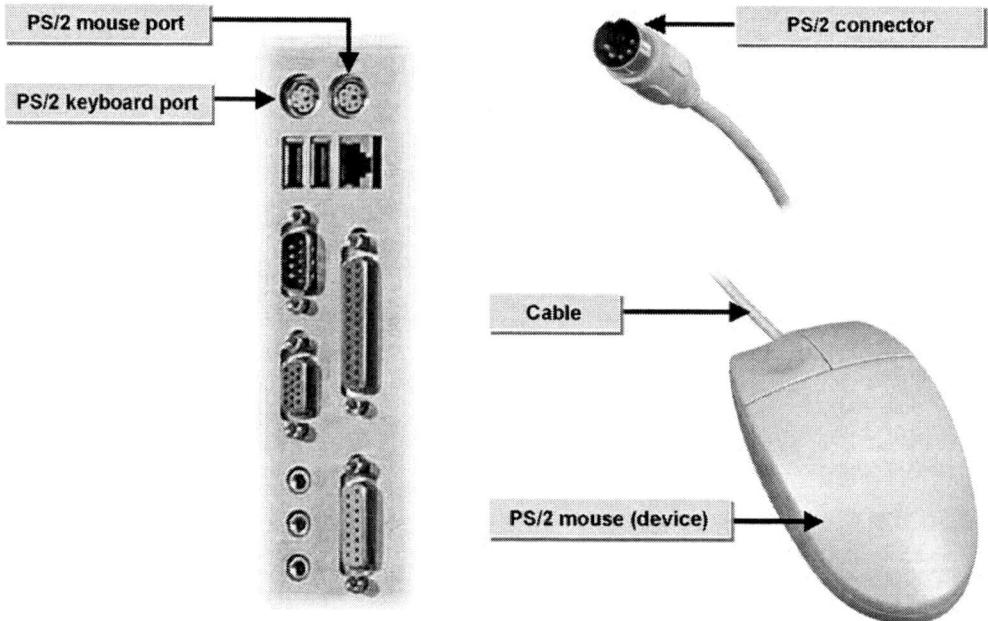

Figure 2-11: *A PS/2 interface.*

The pinouts for a port describe the signal carried on each pin and connection for a port. The signal is carried from the device to the computer through the cable. Each of the pins is connected to a wire in the cable that performs a specific purpose. The pinouts for the PS/2 connector are shown in the following table.

Pin	Direction	Used For	Referred to As
1	Bidirectional	Carrying key data	DATA
2		Nothing; not connected	

Pin	Direction	Used For	Referred to As
3	Through	Ground	GND
4	Computer to keyboard or mouse	Carrying +5 volts of direct current	VCC
5	Computer to keyboard or mouse	Clocking	CLK
6		Nothing; not connected	

Example: PS/2 Keyboard and Mouse Ports

Figure 2-12 shows an example of the keyboard and mouse ports found on the back of a computer system. These are 6-pin round ports. They are usually one above the other as shown here, but could be side-by-side.

Figure 2-12: *PS/2 keyboard and mouse ports.*

PS/2 Devices

Keyboards and mice (and variations of the two) are the devices that can be connected through PS/2 ports on a computer. Keyboards and mice are packaged with computers since they are required components for getting a system up and running. The following table lists the variations of keyboards and pointing devices you are likely to encounter.

PS/2 Device	Variations	Description
Keyboard	Standard Windows keyboard	Contains standard QWERTY keyboard layout in straight rows with Function keys across the top, separate insertion point movement keys, and a numeric keypad.
	Natural keyboard	Contains the same keys as the standard keyboard, but the keys are positioned at an angle in an attempt to reduce stress on users' wrists.
	Dvorak	Alphabetic keys are laid out in a different pattern than the QWERTY layout. More information can be found at **www.mwbrooks.com/dvorak/**.
Pointing devices	2-button Microsoft mouse	The standard-style mouse included with most computers.
	3-button mouse	A mouse with an additional button. The third button (the middle one) is only used in applications that specifically write calls to it. Two-button mice emulate this third button by users pressing both mouse buttons simultaneously.
	Trackball	A pointing device in which the user rolls the ball directly, rather than moving the device to move the ball. It is like an upside-down mouse.
	Tablet and/or pen	A tablet that you use a finger or pen to draw on.
	Touch pad	A sensitive pad that the user moves their finger on to move the insertion point. Button action is accomplished by tapping the pad or by using physical buttons next to the touch pad.
Keyboard and pointing device	Integrated keyboard and pointing device	A keyboard in which a pointing device has been added, usually to the bottom of the keyboard. A split cable connects the keyboard to both the mouse and keyboard ports on the computer.

 QWERTY keyboards are named for the first six letters in the top row of a standard keyboard.

Device Drivers

Definition:

A *device driver* is a piece of software that enables the operating system and a peripheral device to communicate with each other. A device driver:

- Takes generalized commands from the system software or an application and translates them into unique programming commands that the device can understand.
- Provides the code that allows the device to function with the operating system.
- Is installed as part of the installation process for a new piece of hardware.

A device driver may be:

- Included with the Windows XP operating system or supplied with the device on a CD-ROM or floppy disk when you purchase it. Peripherals that are designed after the operating system comes out must supply their own drivers.

> New operating systems include thousands of drivers that let them work with all current, popular devices.

- Downloaded from the Internet from each manufacturer's Web site.
- Considered to be a part of the system software by some experts.
- Generic for a class of device or specific to a particular device.

> A device driver is also known as driver software or just plain driver.

Example: Print Driver

A print driver is an example of a device driver. When you install an HP LaserJet 4si printer, Windows XP also installs a driver specific to that printer. The HP LaserJet 4si driver takes the generalized command, File→Print from a user's application, and translates the instructions to print into code that is specific to the HP LaserJet 4si printer. Since the printer is being installed on a Windows XP system, the driver must be written for XP (and not some other operating system). Otherwise, the printer driver will not be installed.

In most cases, as soon as you connect the printer to the computer, the printer driver will be installed. However, if XP can't find the driver, you will be prompted to specify the location the driver can be installed from. If XP doesn't have the driver for the printer, you will need to either locate it on a CD-ROM, floppy disk, or other source, or download it from the Internet. This particular printer requires a specific driver in order to print documents properly. A device driver example is shown in Figure 2-13.

Figure 2-13: *A device driver.*

How to Install PS/2 Devices

Procedure Reference: Install a PS/2 Device

To install a PS/2 device:

1. Verify that the computer is turned off.
2. Locate the PS/2 keyboard and PS/2 mouse ports on the computer.
3. Align the pins on the cable with the openings in the PS/2 port on the computer and plug the device into the port, being sure to plug the keyboard in to the keyboard port and the mouse in to the mouse port. The rectangular plastic piece in the cable helps you align the pins.
4. Verify that the PS/2 devices are working correctly.
    a. Boot the computer.
    b. Check for error messages when the system boots. If a message about not having a keyboard is displayed, power down the system and switch the cables, and then try powering on again.
    c. Enter text from the keyboard.
    d. Move the mouse to different parts of the screen and click an icon or text to verify that the mouse pointer moves where you point it and that the buttons work properly.

If the mouse and keyboard connections are switched, you won't be able to successfully boot the computer. A keyboard error message would be displayed on the monitor.

TOPIC C
Install Parallel Devices

You have input devices attached to your computer (your keyboard and mouse) and you have an output device connected to your computer (your monitor). That's a fully functional computer system, but what if you want to output your information to a more portable medium? You will need a printer that outputs to paper and provides a portable output medium for your users. You will need to install the printer for your users so that they can output their information to this medium.

Nothing irritates people more than not being able to print that important report for a meeting. In most cases, this involves a parallel port connection. Installing devices on parallel ports correctly averts user dismay when they can't print. It is your responsibility to connect this parallel port device so that you can make sure the users are satisfied and have the resources available to print their reports.

Parallel Interfaces

Definition:

A parallel interface is the hardware interface that enables a parallel device to be connected to the computer. It is composed of the parallel port on the computer, a cable with parallel connectors on it, and a device with a parallel connection. A parallel port is an input/output port on a computer that is commonly used to connect printers to the computer. A PC can have up to three parallel ports. They are referred to as LPT1, LPT2, and LPT3. LPT is short for line printer. Other devices can also be connected through the parallel port such as scanners and some drives. The original parallel ports were unidirectional—they could send but not receive data. As parallel devices increased in their capabilities, the need to send data back to the computer arose. Now, the parallel port is bidirectional by default. The parallel port is a DB-25 female port. The parallel cable has a 25-pin male DB-25 connector that connects to the 25-pin female port. The other end of the parallel cable either ends in a 25-pin connector to the device or in a 36-pin Centronics connector. If it is color-coded, the parallel port is burgundy or dark pink.

The *IEEE* 1284 (Institute of Electrical and Electronic Engineers) standard describes the bidirectional communication between the computer and peripherals over a parallel port connection. The IEEE 1284 standard identifies three different types of connectors. Examples of the connectors are shown in Figure 2-14. These include the:

- 1284 Type A connector which uses a 25-pin DB-25 connector.
- 1284 Type B connector which uses a 36-conductor, 0.085 centerline Champ connector with bale locks.
- 1284 Type C connector which uses a 36-conductor, 0.050 centerline mini-connector with clip latches.

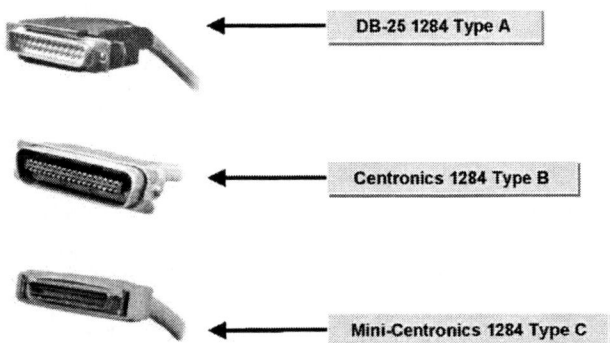

Figure 2-14: *IEEE 1284 Types A, B, and C cable ends.*

The pinouts for the parallel port are shown in the following table. Figure 2-15 shows the pins referred to in the table.

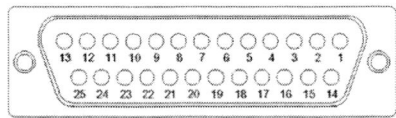

Figure 2-15: *Parallel port pinouts.*

Pin	Signal	Pin	Signal
1	- Strobe	14	- Auto feed
2	+ Data bit 0	15	- Error
3	+ Data bit 1	16	- Initialize printer
4	+ Data bit 2	17	- Select input
5	+ Data bit 3	18	Ground
6	+ Data bit 4	19	Ground
7	+ Data bit 5	20	Ground
8	+ Data bit 6	21	Ground
9	+ Data bit 7	22	Ground
10	- Acknowledge	23	Ground
11	+ Busy	24	Ground
12	+ P.End (out of paper)	25	Ground
13	+ Select		

The Centronics standard is a type of parallel port used to connect printers. It is named after the company that designed the original interface. The Centronics standard uses a 36-pin Centronics connector to connect to the printer, and a DB-25 (25-pin) connector to connect to the PC.

As time has gone on, needs have gone beyond those provided by the original parallel port. In the original, data only flowed in one direction—to the printer (or other device), but the printer couldn't send any information back to the CPU. Designers needed a way to make the port faster, allow communication back and forth, and other features. Newer bidirectional ports are available and are known as Enhanced Parallel Port (EPP) and Extended Capability Port (ECP). *EPP* is used primarily by non-printer parallel port peripherals, whereas *ECP* is used by newer-generation printers.

Both ECP and EPP provide *throughput* that is many times faster than the Centronics standard provides. The ECP and EPP standards are defined in the IEEE 1284 standard. Windows operating systems beginning with Windows 95 have built-in support for IEEE 1284. Both the parallel port and the device must support IEEE 1284 for the higher speeds to be achieved

Type	Standard	Description
Unidirectional	SPP	Standard Parallel Port.
Bidirectional	ECP (IEEE 1284)	Extended Capability Port. Provides faster throughput than Centronics. Used by newer-generation printers and scanners.
Bidirectional	EPP (IEEE 1284)	Enhanced Parallel Port. Also known as a fast parallel port. Provides faster throughput than Centronics. Used by non-printer devices such as drives, network adapters, and scanners.

Example: Parallel Connections

Figure 2-16 shows an example of a Centronics parallel cable.

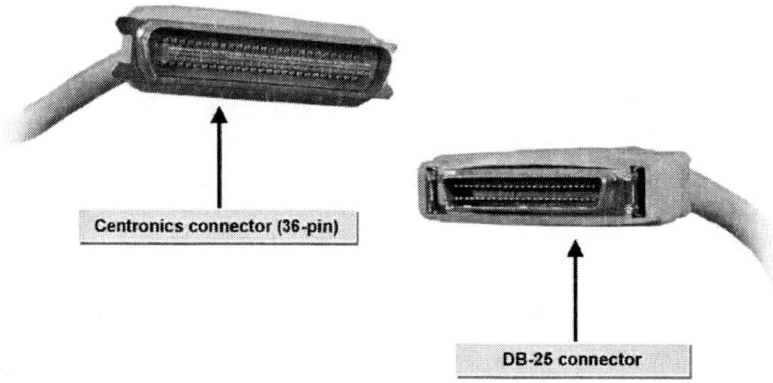

Figure 2-16: *A Centronics parallel cable with a Centronics and a DB-25 connector.*

Figure 2-17 shows an example of the cable that would be used for a parallel connection between the parallel port on the computer and a parallel port Zip drive.

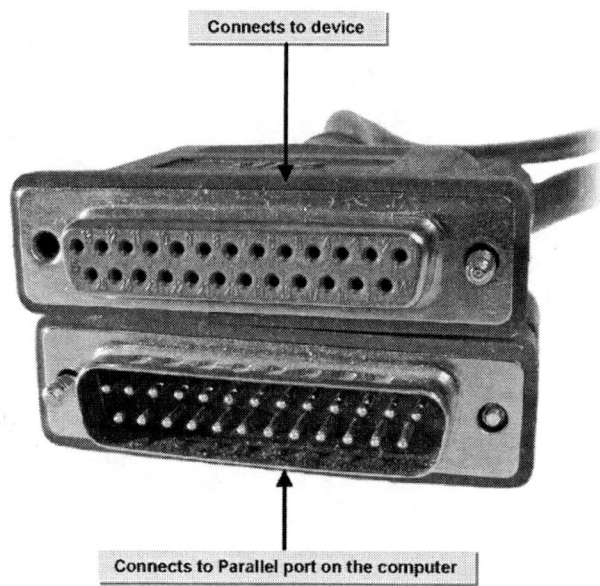

Figure 2-17: *A parallel cable for connecting a non-printer parallel port device.*

Figure 2-18 shows the parallel interface.

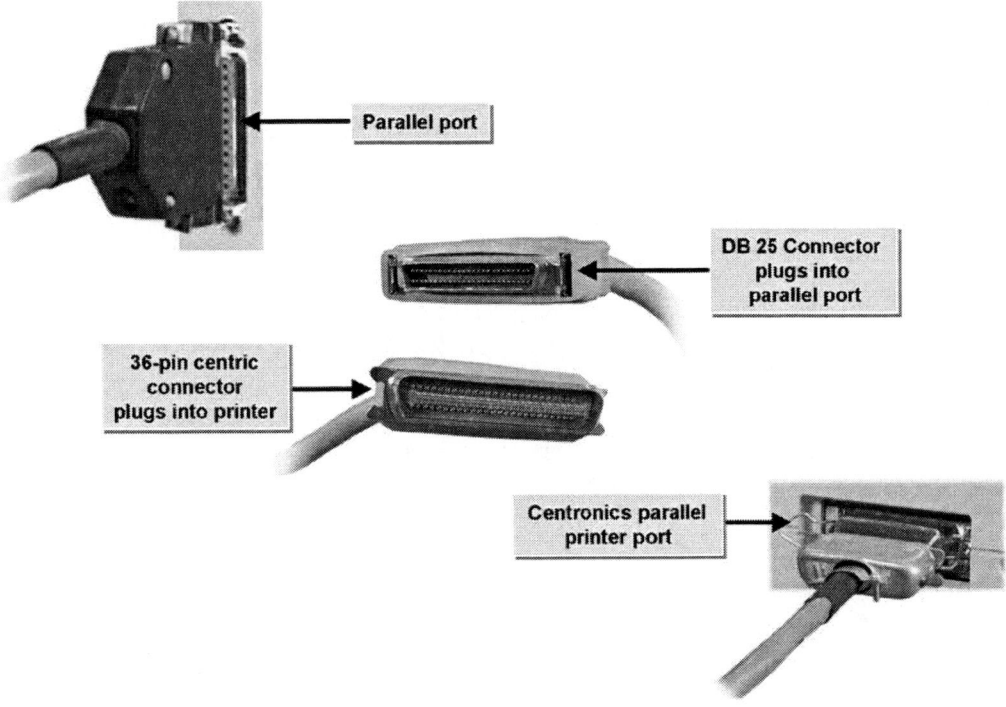

Figure 2-18: *A parallel interface.*

Parallel Devices

Definition:
Parallel devices are peripherals that connect to the computer through the parallel port. The cable end that connects to the parallel port is a DB-25 male connector. The other end is either a DB-25 connector or a 36-pin Centronics connector.

Example:
Printers are the prime example of a parallel port device. This is the traditional method for connecting printers to a computer. Examples of non-printer devices include CD-ROM drives, network adapters, scanners, and other drives such as removable cartridge and tape drives.

How to Connect Parallel Devices

Procedure Reference: Connect a Device to a Parallel Port

To install a device on a parallel port:

1. With the computer and device turned off, connect the parallel cable between the device and the system.

2. If necessary, connect the AC adapter to the device and plug it into an electrical outlet.

3. Turn on the device and computer.
4. Install appropriate drivers for the device.
5. Verify that the device functions properly.

Topic D
Install Serial Devices

You have now installed several required peripherals to create a functional computer system. Users usually want more functionality than this, though, so you will be asked to connect additional peripherals. In this topic, you will add a serial device to the computer.

Most users require more than the basic monitor, keyboard, and mouse peripherals connected to their system. As the computer support technician for the company, users will be asking you to add equipment to their systems to increase functionality. Some of these will be serial devices. You will need to be able to quickly and efficiently install the devices so users can complete their work.

Bits and Bytes

Computers use electrical patterns to represent numbers. Modern digital computers recognize only two electrical states—ON and OFF—but their memories contain millions of transistors that can be either on or off. All characters (numbers, letters, punctuation, and symbols) are represented by a numerical value. The value indicates the number of transistors that are turned on. Computers use the binary number system (base 2) since the on and off states of the transistors can be represented by 1 and 0, respectively. Computers commonly use the values 0 to 255 (base 10) or 0 to 11111111 (base 2). To give you an idea of what binary values would look like, the following table displays the decimal (base 10) numbers from 0 to 10 represented in binary.

Base 10 Decimal Notation	Base 2 Binary Notation
0	0
1	1
2	10
3	11
4	100
5	101
6	110
7	111
8	1000
9	1001

Base 10 Decimal Notation	Base 2 Binary Notation
10	1010

Each binary digit represents a bit (binary digit). To make it easier to work with base 2 numbers, computer scientists have grouped the binary digits into more manageable sizes. The following table shows what these include.

Number of Bits	Referred to as A
1	bit
4	nibble
8	byte
16	word
32	double word

For this course, you will be most interested in bits and bytes. This is how data is typically carried over connections and is used to refer to the settings for hardware devices.

 For more information on the binary number system, you can refer to **www.danbbs.dk/~erikoest/binary.htm** or any number of Web sites.

Serial Communications

In a serial transmission, data is sent and received one bit at a time over a single wire. This process is shown in Figure 2-19. To accomplish this, the serial communication process:

1. Disassembles bytes into bits on the sending end of the communication.
2. Sends the bits across the communication wires.
3. Reassembles the bits into bytes at the receiving end.

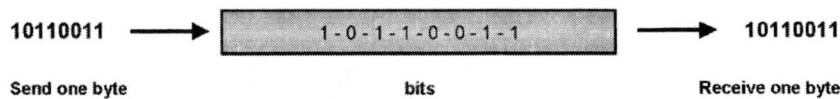

Figure 2-19: *Serial transmission sends one bit at a time.*

Serial Interfaces

Definition:
> A serial interface is a computer hardware interface that enables a serial device to connect to a computer. It is composed of a serial port, serial cable, and a device with a serial connection.

All serial connections are the same in that:
- A serial port is a port on a computer that enables you to connect devices that are capable of two-way communication.
- There can be up to four serial ports on a system, but only two of them can be in use simultaneously.
- Serial ports are referred to as COM1, COM2, COM3, or COM4. COM is short for communications port.
- A serial cable will end with a female connector to plug in to the male connector on the system.
- If serial ports are color-coded, they will be teal colored.

Serial connections vary in that:
- Serial ports can be DB-9 or DB-25 male ports.
- Twisted pair network and phone cables are also serial cables.
- Most systems today only include one or two 9-pin serial ports.
- The serial cable usually does not have all of the wires connected, so that made it possible to reduce serial ports from 25 pins down to nine pins.
- The cable will have the wires connected that are needed for a particular purpose. Pinouts vary based on the purpose of the connection. If a cable other than a standard serial cable is needed, it is usually shipped with the device.
- Wires in the cable can be connected straight through, jumpered, or mirrored. A straight through cable has the same color wire connected to the same pin number on each end of the cable. A jumpered cable combines the output of one or more wires to a single wire on the other end or it can take the output of one pin and send it to multiple pins on the other end. A mirrored or roll-over cable reverses the order of the wires. This is used on flat cables that use a phone-type clip connector.
- Serial connections are typically used for modems. They can also be used for direct PC-to-PC connections, and to connect some mice, printers, and Personal Digital Assistant (PDA) devices.

 Typically only one or two serial ports will be installed on a system. This port is being phased out in favor of other standards, so you might find some systems with no serial ports at all.

Example: Straight Through Cables

Figure 2-20 shows an example of a straight through serial interface. A straight through cable connects the same wire within the cable to the same pin number on each end of the cable.

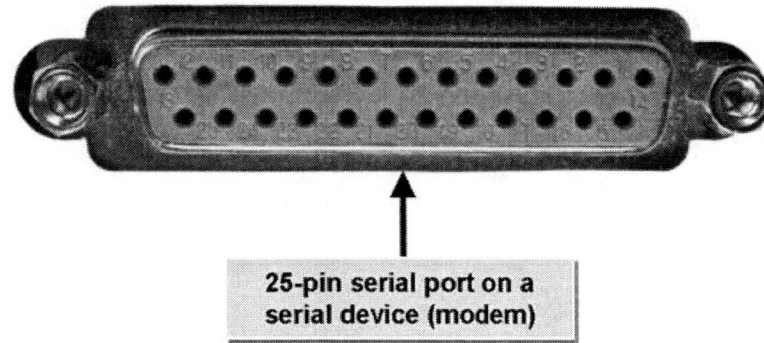

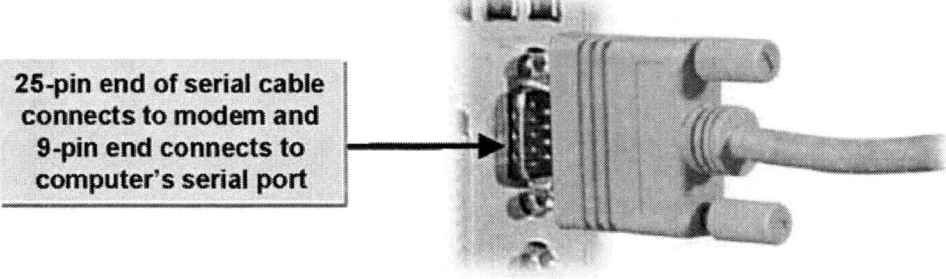

Figure 2-20: *A serial interface.*

The pinouts for a standard 25-pin serial cable are shown in Table 2-1.

 The graphic in the figure shows the female parallel port on the PC and the table below it shows the pinouts for the male cable that would connect to that port.

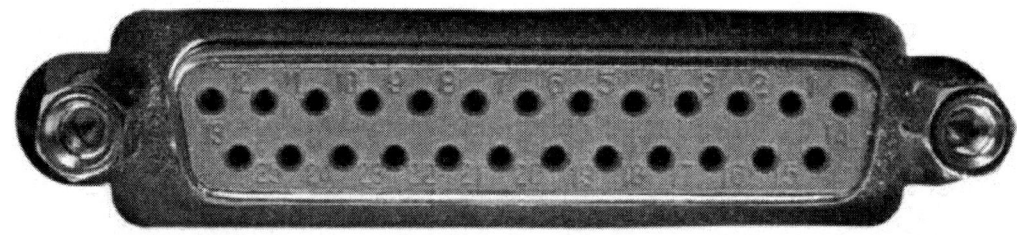

Pin	Signal	Pin	Signal
1	Protected ground	14	Secondary transmitted data
2	Transmitted data	15	Transmit timing signal
3	Received data	16	Secondary received data
4	Request to send	17	Receive timing signal
5	Clear to send	18	Unassigned
6	Data set ready	19	Secondary request to send
7	Signal ground	20	Data terminal ready
8	Data carrier detector	21	Signal quality detector
9	Reserved for data set testing	22	Ring indicator
10	Reserved for data set testing	23	Data rate selector
11	Unassigned	24	External timing signal
12	Secondary carrier detector	25	Unassigned
13	Secondary clear to send		

Figure 2-21: *Serial DB-25 connector pins.*

Table 2-1: *Serial DB-25 Connector Pins*

Pin	Signal	Pin	Signal
1	Protected ground	14	Secondary transmitted data
2	Transmitted data	15	Transmit timing signal
3	Received data	16	Secondary received data
4	Request to send	17	Receive timing signal
5	Clear to send	18	Unassigned
6	Data set ready	19	Secondary request to send
7	Signal ground	20	Data terminal ready
8	Data carrier detector	21	Signal quality detector

Pin	Signal	Pin	Signal
9	Reserved for data set testing	22	Ring indicator
10	Reserved for data set testing	23	Data rate selector
11	Unassigned	24	External timing signal
12	Secondary carrier detector	25	Unassigned
13	Secondary clear to send		

Most implementations do not use all of the pins shown in Figure 2-22. In fact, it is possible to use nine or fewer pins to provide a functional two-way serial connection. For this reason, many computers provide a 9-pin rather than a 25-pin connector for their serial ports. The pinouts for a 9-pin connector are shown in Figure 2-22. This is the female end of a serial cable that would connect to the male serial port on the PC.

Figure 2-22: *Serial port pinouts for a 9-pin connector.*

Table 2-2: *Serial Port Pinout for a 9-pin Connector*

Pin	Signal
1	Received line signal detector
2	Received data
3	Transmitted data
4	Data terminal ready
5	Signal ground
6	Data set ready
7	Request to send
8	Clear to send
9	Ring indicator

Example: Null Modem Cables

Another serial cable you might encounter is a null modem cable. This cable crosses the wires so that the receiving pin on one end is connected to a transmitting pin on the other end. If two devices need to connect and are within tens of meters of each other, a cable wired in a null-modem or "dumb" configuration can be used in place of a modem.

Figure 2-23 shows an example of the pinouts for a null-modem cable. This is a 9-pin null-modem cable. In some cases, such as from Pin 4 on the left to Pins 6 and 1 on the right, a single pin will be jumpered to two or more pins on the other end. If you require a null-modem cable with a different configuration, you will need to refer to the documentation for establishing the connection to figure out which wires need to be jumpered or crossed. This cable has female connectors on both ends to connect to the male serial ports on the PC.

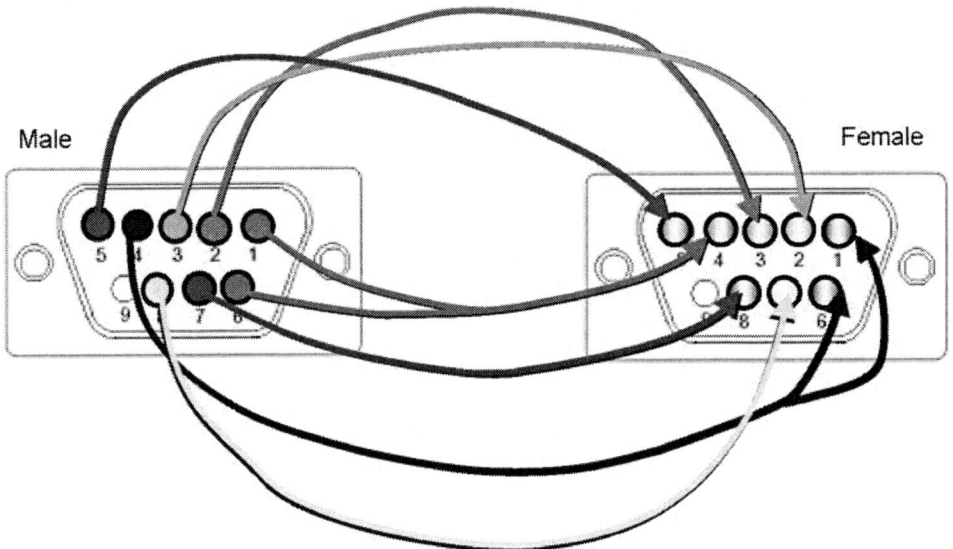

Figure 2-23: *Null-modem pinouts.*

Device Manager

Device Manager is a software tool built in to Windows that enables you to configure settings for hardware devices installed in or connected to your system. A list of all of the hardware devices installed on your system is displayed in Device Manager. You can select a specific device and then set the properties for the device.

Serial Port Settings

Definition:

Serial port settings are the property settings needed for two serial devices to communicate. The settings need to match on the systems that are communicating to each other.

In Device Manager, you can select the serial communications port, and on the Port Settings sheet of the Properties dialog box, you can set the settings. These settings are shown in the following table.

Setting	Description
Bits per second	This is the maximum communication speed at which data will pass through the port. The default is 9600. You will want to set it to the maximum speed at which the sending and receiving devices can communicate.
Data bits	This value is usually 8 for PC-based systems and 7 for Macintosh-based systems. The value specifies how many data bits are used for each character that is exchanged.
Parity	The error-checking method is set in this field. Your choices are: • None—This disables error-checking and is the default value. No parity bit is added to the data bits when transmitting data. • Even—This error-checking method is when a parity bit is added to the data bits when transmitting data, if needed, to have an even number of data bits. • Odd—This error-checking method is when a parity bit is added to the data bits when transmitting data, if needed, to have an odd number of data bits. • Mark—This error-checking method always adds a parity bit that is set to 0. • Space—This error-checking method always adds a parity bit that is set to 1.
Stop bits	The value of this property specifies the time (in bits per second) between the transmission of each character that is sent. The default is 1.

Setting	Description
Flow control	Specifies how the flow of data is controlled and acknowledged. Just as when two people are talking, electronic devices need to know when one device has finished talking so that the other device can talk. Devices also need a way to confirm that they have received data that was sent to them. Handshaking is a flow-control method that can be implemented through hardware or software. • None is the default value. • Hardware handshaking uses a separate wire for flow control. The receiving device sends a signal over this wire to inform the sending device that it is ready to receive data. • Xon/Xoff or software handshaking reserves special characters for the receiving device to send control signals to the sending device. The Xon/Xoff (transmit on/transmit off) protocol is an example of this. The receiving device sends a Control-S character (ASCII value 19) to request that the sending device stop sending data. The receiving device sends a Control-Q character (ASCII value 17) to request that the sending device resume sending data.

Example:

Figure 2-24 shows the default settings for COM1.

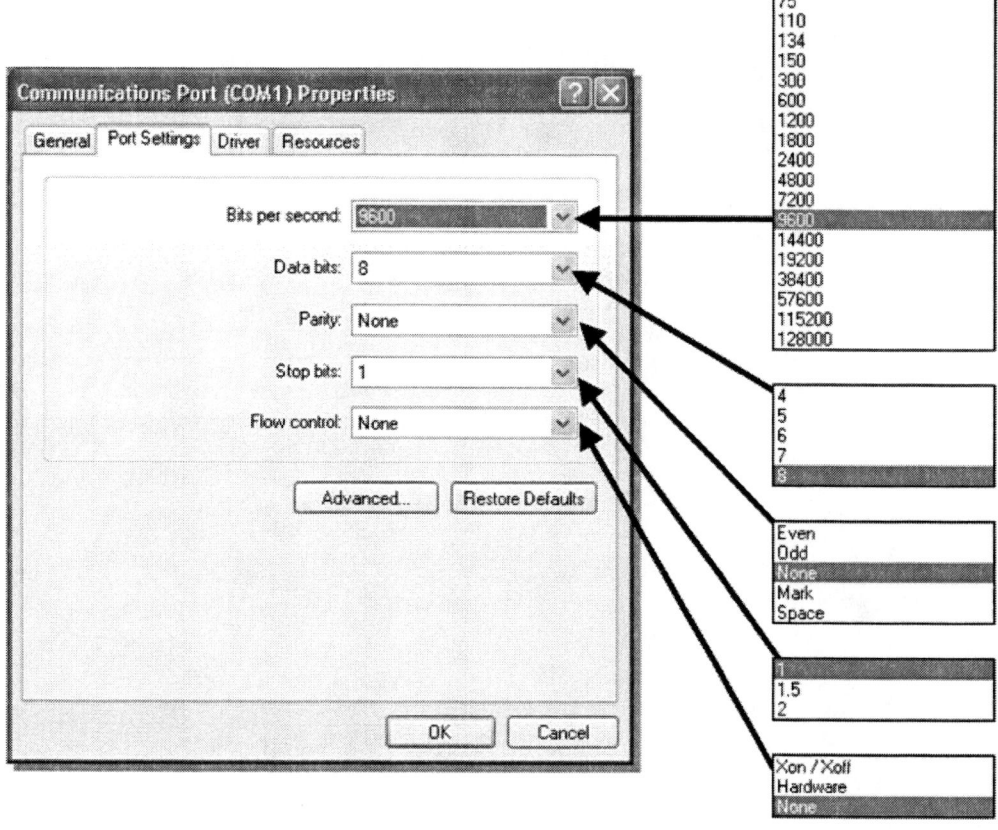

Figure 2-24: *Default settings for a serial port.*

Registered Jacks

Definition:

A registered jack is a flat connector that connects a computer to a network. The network could be a computer network or the telephone public data network. The cable can be 4, 6, or 8 wires. The wires can be connected straight through or be mirrored on each end. The RJ types are defined by the FCC (Federal Communications Commission). RJ communications are serial communications.

Example: RJ-11

RJ-11 cables are used to connect phones to the public telephone network. They are also used to connect between the modem and the phone outlet. It contains 6 wires that are connected straight through. An example of an RJ-11 connector is shown in Figure 2-25.

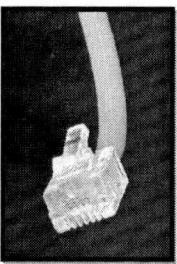

Figure 2-25: *An RJ-11 jack.*

Example: RJ-45

RJ-45 cables are used to connect between a network card and a transceiver or other network device. It contains 8 wires that are usually connected straight through. In some configurations such as when you are connecting two network devices, the wires might be mirrored or rolled over. An example of an RJ-45 connector is shown in Figure 2-26.

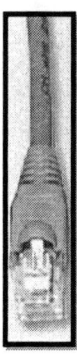

Figure 2-26: *An RJ-45 jack.*

Modem

Definition:

A *modem* is a serial communications device that enables computers to communicate with one another over standard telephone lines. A modem converts digital signals to analog so it can go across the phone line. When it reaches the other system, it is converted back into a digital signal. The process of converting from digital to analog is referred to as modulation and the reverse is referred to as demodulation; hence the term modem (*mod*ulate/*dem*odulate). Modern modems contain support for fax and voice capabilities, in addition to sending data. This allows you to use your PC to send documents as faxes and to use your PC as a phone and answering machine. All modems have an RJ-11 phone jack to which you connect the phone line from the wall jack. Some also have a second phone jack to enable you to connect a telephone so that you can use the same phone line for voice communications when the line is not being used with the modem to communicate.

Some modems are hardware-based and some are software-based (also known as controller-less modems or Win-modems). The following table compares them.

Hardware-based Modems	Software-based Modems
Contains a built-in controller to process the data from digital to analog and back.	Uses the computer's processing power to convert data from digital to analog and back.
Faster because processing occurs at the modem.	Slower because it sends data out for processing and shares processing power with other processes in the system.
More expensive since it contains additional circuitry.	Less expensive.

Modems can operate in *asynchronous* or *synchronous* modes. Some modems can switch between these modes and others are one or the other. Asynchronous modems are more commonly found. The following table describes these modes.

Asynchronous	Synchronous
Data transmissions include stop and start bits to indicate the beginning and end of each character being sent.	Data is sent in frames that contain synch characters before each frame. A frame is a group of characters.
Data flow is controlled by the slower of the two systems between which communication is occurring. The slower system interrupts the transmission whenever its buffers are full and it needs time to catch up.	A timing mechanism is used to regulate data flow between systems.
A parity bit is used for control. If the transmission is incomplete, it must be resent.	Frames only need to be resent if the synch character sent before the frame isn't received as specified.
More prone to errors.	Less prone to errors.
Typically configured with 8 data bits, None for parity, and one stop bit. This is commonly referred to as 8-none-and-one.	Typically configured as High-level Data Link Control (HDLC). It supports variable length frames.

Modem standards, or V dot modem standards, are another way modems vary. These standards are defined by the International Telecommunications Union (ITU). Some standards have the **bis** version suffix; this is French for second. A modem might meet one or more of the standards. The following table lists some of the most popular ITU standards.

ITU Standard	bps	Notes
V.32	9,600	Synchronous to 9,600; Asynchronous is 4,800
V.32 bis	14,400 (14.4 K)	Synchronous and Asynchronous
V.34	28,800 (28.8 K)	
V.34 bis	33,600 (33.6 K)	
V.42	57,600	Specifies standards for error-checking
V.42 bis	33.6 K sending rate 56,000 (56 K) receiving rate	Specifies standards for compression
V.90	56 K	This is the most recent standard. It includes technology that enables receiving data faster than 56 Kbps by not modulating the data. However, when sending data, it must be modulated, resulting in a slower 33.6 Kbps data rate.

All modern modems use the class 5 MNP (Microcom Networking Protocol) standard. *MNP class 5* includes all of the features of classes 1 through 4 in addition to the data compression introduced in class 5. The MNP standards afford the user increased levels of error correction and compression. They are described in the following table.

MNP Class	Offers
1	The ability to send data in one direction at a time. This is referred to as *half-duplex.*
2	The ability to send and receive data simultaneously. This is referred to as full-duplex.
3	Improved throughput by having the sender strip start and stop bits prior to sending data and the receiver to add them back in.
4	Increased error correction through adjustable block sizes for the data based on the quality of the phone lines so that there is less need for retransmission of blocks of data.

MNP Class	Offers
5	Data compression to increase throughput. Redundant data is recoded by the sending modem into fewer bits to increase throughput. Data is uncompressed by the receiving modem prior to handing the data over to the receiving computer.

Example: Modem

A modem is connected to the phone line using an RJ-11 jack. An RJ-11 jack is shown in Figure 2-27. It is also connected to the serial port on the computer.

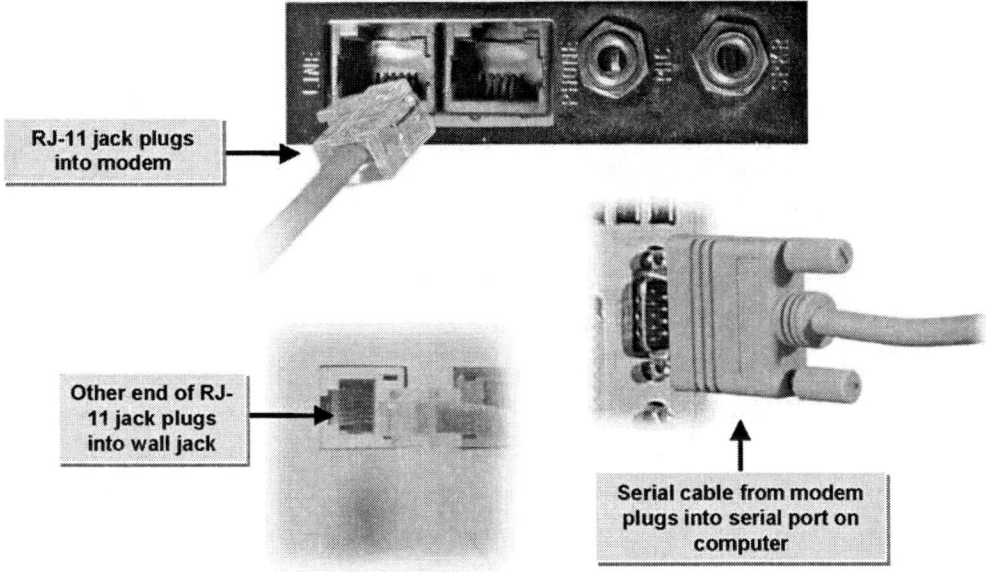

Figure 2-27: *A modem connects to a serial port and a phone line with an RJ-11 jack.*

Non-Example: DSL or Cable Modem

A DSL or cable modem is not truly a modem. It is actually a *transceiver*—a device which is both a receiver and a transmitter. Unlike a modem, a cable modem does not connect to the serial port or use a 9- or 25-pin serial cable. It connects to a network card in the computer or sometimes to a USB port. The data is digital end to end, so there is no modulation or demodulation which needs to occur either. An example of a transceiver is shown in Figure 2-28.

Figure 2-28: *A cable modem which is a transceiver.*

Modem Commands

The *AT*, or Attention, commands are the modem commands set used on most modems. Hayes originally developed it for its line of modems. Since other companies wanted to be Hayes-compatible, they developed their modems to use this command set.

The most basic command is AT, which alerts the modem that you want to communicate with your modem. The following table lists some of the most common commands. Each command begins with the AT command followed by the command.

 For more information on the Extended AT command sets, visit **www.modems.com/general/extendat.html**.

Command	Description
AT	Attention used at the start of modem command lines.
DT	Dial using touchtone.
H	Hang up or disconnect.
A	Answer.
DP	Dial using pulse (rotary dial).
,	Pause (each comma is roughly 3 seconds by default). Often used when you need to dial an access code for an outside line so that you wait for the dial tone. For example, 9,,,5855557300.
*70	Disable call waiting.
Z	Reset.
A/	Repeat. Repeats the last command. Often used to redial.
+++	Escape character sequence. Returns you to the command mode. You can then adjust modem configuration, or hang up. The modem responds with OK to indicate that you are in Command mode.

Command	Description
0	Online. Often used after the escape character sequence to continue communication.

How to Connect a Serial Device

Procedure Reference: Install Serial Devices

To install a serial device:

1. Turn off the computer power.
2. Determine if it is a 9-pin or 25-pin serial port and serial connection.
3. If necessary, locate an appropriate serial cable to connect the device to the computer. Some devices (such as mice) come with the cable already attached, so you don't need to locate an appropriate serial cable.
4. If necessary, connect the male end of the cable to the device.
5. Connect the female end of the cable to the system serial port, carefully aligning the pins.
6. If necessary, connect the AC adapter to the device and plug it into an electrical outlet.
7. Boot the computer.
8. Install the device driver as described in device documentation.
9. Verify that the device works correctly.

Procedure Reference: Configure a Serial Port

To configure serial port settings:

1. From the Start menu, choose Control Panel.
2. In the Control Panel window, click Performance And Maintenance.
3. In the Performance And Maintenance window, click System.
4. Click the Hardware tab, and then click Device Manager.
5. Expand Ports (COM & LPT).
6. Right-click the COM port and choose Properties.
7. Display the Port Settings page.
8. Through the Communications Port (COM#) Properties dialog box, match the settings to those required for the device to function properly as given in the documentation or another source.
   - Port Settings:

- Bits Per Second
- Data Bits
- Parity
- Stop Bits
- Flow Control

9. Click OK.
10. Close Device Manager.
11. Close Control Panel.
12. In the System Properties dialog box, click OK.

Topic E
Install Game and Sound Devices

You have installed the devices most commonly found on business computers. In some computers, you will also have sound cards which usually also include a game port. In this topic, you will connect the external speakers, microphone, and a game controller to the ports on the sound card.

Some of your users, such as marketing or sales reps, will need to use game and sound devices in their presentations. It is your job to connect the speakers and microphone; the ports are often poorly marked and users get frustrated when they cannot get the devices hooked up correctly.

Sound Card Interfaces

Definition:

Sound card interfaces are ports on a *sound card* that enable you to connect sound devices to a computer. The circuitry on a sound card converts digital signals to sound waves. SoundBlaster from Creative Labs is the default standard to which other sound cards are usually designed. All sound cards have at least a Line In and Line Out port along with a microphone port. Most also have a 15-pin female game port. Some also have additional ports specifically for headphones and speakers in addition to the Line Out port.

Sound cards include several connections. These connections are shown in Figure 2-29. The following table describes typical sound card connections.

Port or Interface	Description
Mic In	Receive signal from an external microphone.
Speaker Out or Line Out	Sends signals to a speaker set or headphones. Sends signals from the sound card to an external sound source that can be connected through an eighth-inch jack.

Port or Interface	Description
Line In	Receives signals from the output of an external sound source that can be connected through an eighth-inch jack.
Game Port	Enables you to attach a joystick or similar game controller to the sound card. MIDI devices are also often connected to the computer through the game port. Some sound cards do not include the game port.

There are also internal connections on the sound card. One is a CD audio connection that enables you to play audio CDs on the computer and output the sound through the sound card. Some cards also include an interface to connect CD-ROM drives or hard drives.

Today's sound cards are configured through software, but some of the older cards you might encounter might use jumpers. On some systems, the functions of a sound card are built into the system, rather than on a separate expansion card.

Example:

The typical sound card interface is shown in Figure 2-29.

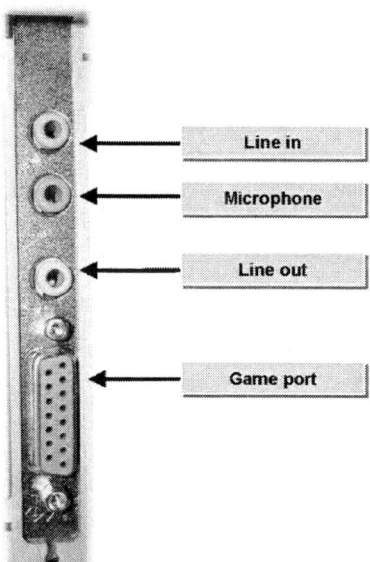

Figure 2-29: *Sound card interfaces.*

Chapter 2: Setting Up a Personal Computer

Sound Devices

The devices you can connect to the sound card are shown in Figure 2-30. The following table describes typical sound card connections.

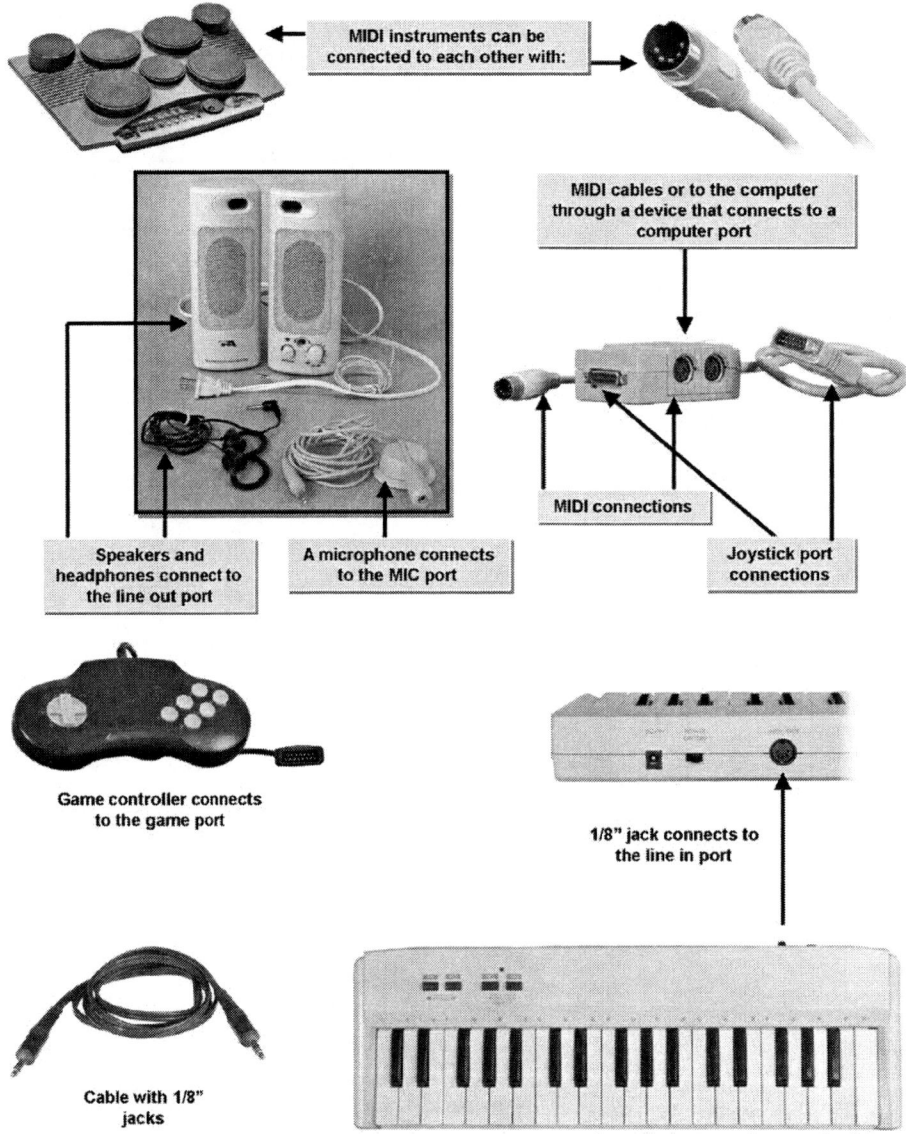

Figure 2-30: *Devices to connect to a sound card.*

Device	Description
Speakers	Speakers are connected to the Line Out port on the sound card. Some speaker sets are permanently connected to each other. Other speaker sets are connected by the user to each other. A cable runs from one of the speakers to the Line Out port to connect both speakers to the computer. If it is color-coded, it will be green or lime. The port might be marked with Line Out, Spkr, Speaker, or have a marking indicating the direction of the audio (out).
Non-MIDI electronic instruments, tape players/recorders, or radios	Any device that can be connected using a eighth-inch jack can be connected to the Line In port. It is often light blue if color-coded. Otherwise, it will be marked Line In or have a marking indicating the direction of the audio (in).
Microphone	A computer microphone can be connected to the MIC port. If color-coded, it will be pink. Otherwise, it will be marked MIC or have a picture of a microphone.
Game devices including controller pads, joysticks, steering wheels, and flight controllers. MIDI devices.	Game controllers can be connected to the game port. If it is color-coded, it will be goldenrod. It is a 15-pin female port composed of one row of eight pins and one row of seven pins. It is usually found on the sound card, but it can be built into the system board or found on a separate adapter card in some systems. Game devices are peripherals that connect to the computer through the game port. Musical Instrument Digital Interface (MIDI) cables are also sometimes connected to this port. Devices that can be connected to the Game port are shown in Figure 2-31. Examples of MIDI cables are shown in Figure 2-32.

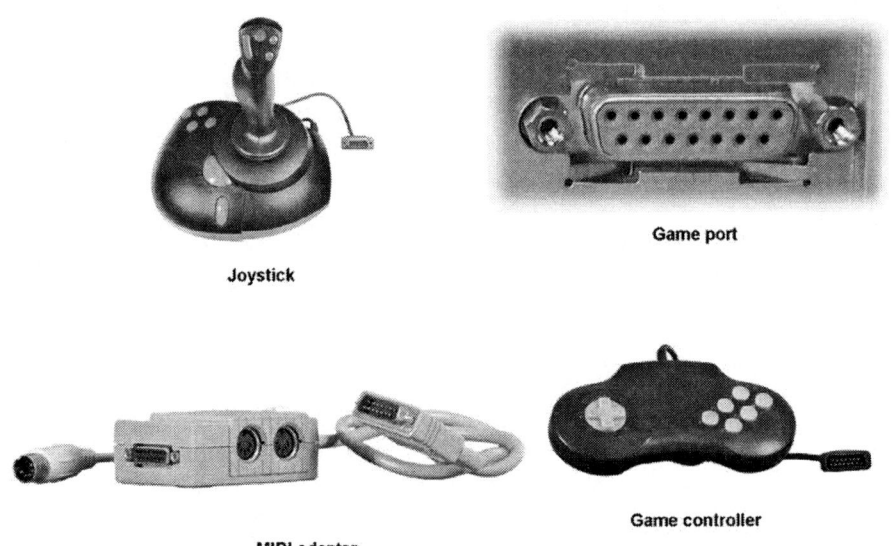

Figure 2-31: *Devices that connect to the game port.*

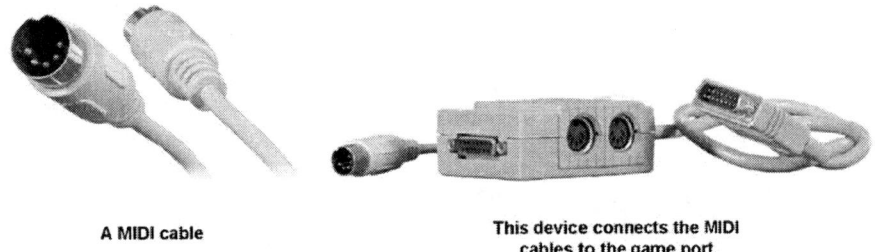

Figure 2-32: *MIDI cables.*

MIDI

The Musical Instrument Digital Interface or *MIDI* connection allows you to connect and control musical devices such as electric keyboards (also known as electric pianos), synthesizers, guitars, and drum kits. Sound cards usually include built-in synthesizers as well, to produce MIDI sounds. If the MIDI connection is made through the game port, then the MIDI cable usually includes an additional port on the cable so that a game controller can still be added to the system. MIDI connections can also be made via other ports other than the game port. MIDI devices can be connected to each other and then to the computer. Examples of MIDI devices are shown in Figure 2-33.

The MIDI connectors are also kown as AT DIN5 connectors. These connectors were originally used on older AT style computers for the keyboard connector. MIDI connectors now use this AT (DIN5) connectors.

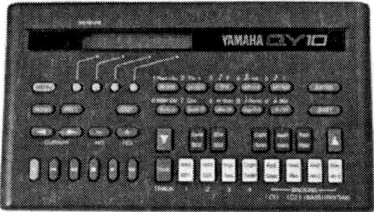

Figure 2-33: *MIDI instruments.*

How to Connect Game and Sound Devices

Procedure Reference: Connect Sound Devices to a Sound Card

To connect sound devices to a sound card:

1. Connect the speakers to the jack on the sound card marked for speakers. Some speakers use an external AC adapter for power, some are powered by the computer, some use batteries, and some contain a standard electrical plug. If necessary, connect the speakers to their power source.

2. Connect any external devices to the Line In jack.

3. Connect a microphone to the MIC jack.

4. Connect MIDI devices or game controllers through the game port. If necessary, connect the AC adapter to the device and to an electrical outlet.

5. If necessary, use Device Manager to configure MIDI device or game controller settings.

6. Test the components by powering on the system and using each device. Verify that Mute is not checked in the Volume Controls. If Microphone is not listed, choose Options→ Properties. Select Recording, and then check Mic Volume. You can then adjust the sound levels for it.

Topic F
Install USB Devices

This chapter focuses on installing and removing devices from the computer system. One of the most common ports used to connect peripherals is the USB port. In this topic, you will connect USB peripheral devices to USB ports.

USB is one of the most common ports you will encounter on a new system. It can be used to connect devices from keyboards to digital cameras, to printers and scanners, and other devices yet to be dreamed up. USB enables you to have all of these devices connected at once and working, as opposed to traditional serial ports where you can only have four devices connected and are limited to only using two of them at the same time.

USB

Definition:

The *Universal Serial Bus (USB)* standard is a hardware interface that enables you to connect peripherals. Compaq, Digital, IBM, Intel, Microsoft, NEC, and Northern Telecom worked together to develop the USB standard. It offers a single-port connector standard to connect to common input/output devices.

PCs typically come with one to four USB ports installed. You can add more devices by connecting a USB hub, which usually contains between four and seven USB ports, to connect additional devices. You can daisy-chain hubs and other devices. Up to five hubs can be connected in the daisy chain. USB ports can also be found on some devices including monitors and keyboards. These ports enable you to daisy-chain more USB devices. Up to 127 USB devices can be connected. Any hubs used in the USB chain count towards the 127 device maximum. USB cables, ports, and connectors are shown in Figure 2-34.

Many devices receive power through the USB connection, rather than requiring an external power transformer or power cord.

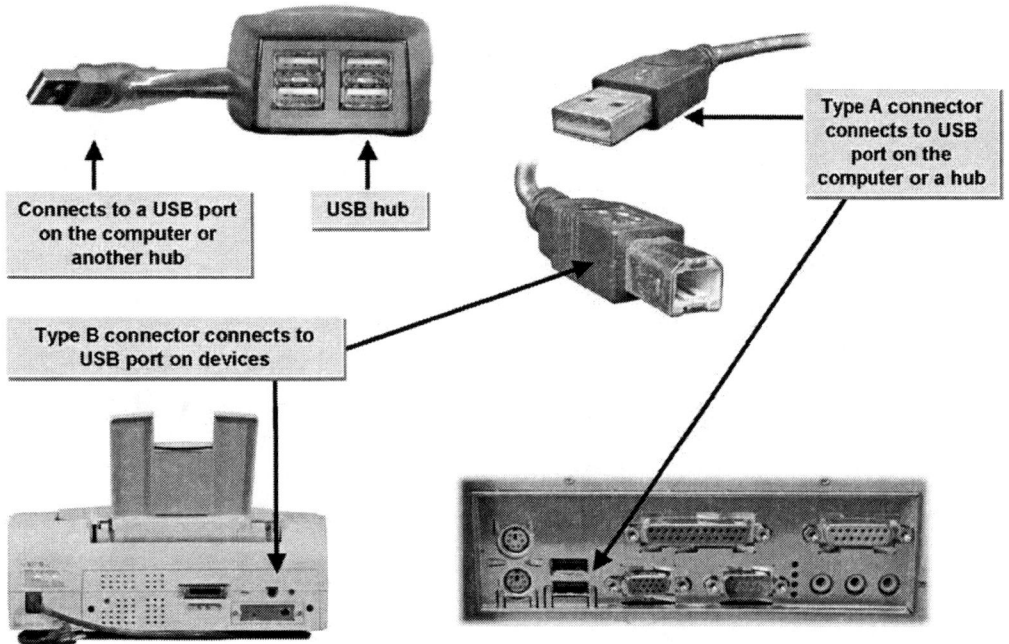

Figure 2-34: *USB ports, cables, and connectors.*

The USB standard defines three classes:

- USB devices. These are further divided into:
  - Functions: Devices that can send, receive, or control data sent over a USB connection. This would include any peripherals that are connected to the computer through a USB interface.
  - Hubs: Devices that provide the ability to attach USB functions to the USB bus.
- USB host. There is only one host per system. It is also known as the USB interface, and can be implemented as hardware, software, or firmware. The host is responsible for managing:
  - The attachment or removal of devices.
  - Power to devices.
  - The flow control of data between the host and devices.
  - The gathering of statistics about device activity.
- USB interconnect. This defines how devices communicate with and connect to the host.

USB devices belong to classes. Examples are shown in the following table.

Class	Devices in that Class
Human Interface	Mouse, keyboard, tablet, game controller
Imaging	Scanner, printer, digital camera
Mass Storage	Including CD-ROM, DVD, and floppy drives

A USB cable usually has two different connectors. The connector from the cable to the computer, or upstream from the device, ends in a Type A connector. The connector from the cable to the device, or downstream from the device, ends in a Type B connector. The cable can be up to 3 meters long for low-speed devices and up to 5 meters long for full- or high-speed devices.

USB 2.0 is the current standard. It can communicate at up to 480 Mbps. USB 1.1 is still commonly found in devices and systems. It can communicate at up to 12 Mbps. A USB 2.0 device connected to a USB 1.1 hub or port will only communicate at USB 1.1 speeds, even though it might be capable of faster speeds.

USB 2.0 defines three data rates. The following table lists the maximum speeds and typical devices for each.

Speed	Maximum Data Rate	Typical Devices
Low speed	1.5 Mbps	Keyboard, mouse, stylus, game peripherals, virtual reality peripherals
Full speed	12 Mbps	Telephone service, broadband service, audio, microphone
High speed	480 Mbps	Video, storage, imaging, broadband

 For more information on the USB standard, visit **http://usb.org/**.

Example:

Examples of devices you can connect to a USB port include modems, digital cameras, printers, scanners, network adapters, CD/RW drives, touch screens, external hard drives, external floppy drives, keyboards, mice, and many other devices. A typical USB interface is shown in Figure 2-35.

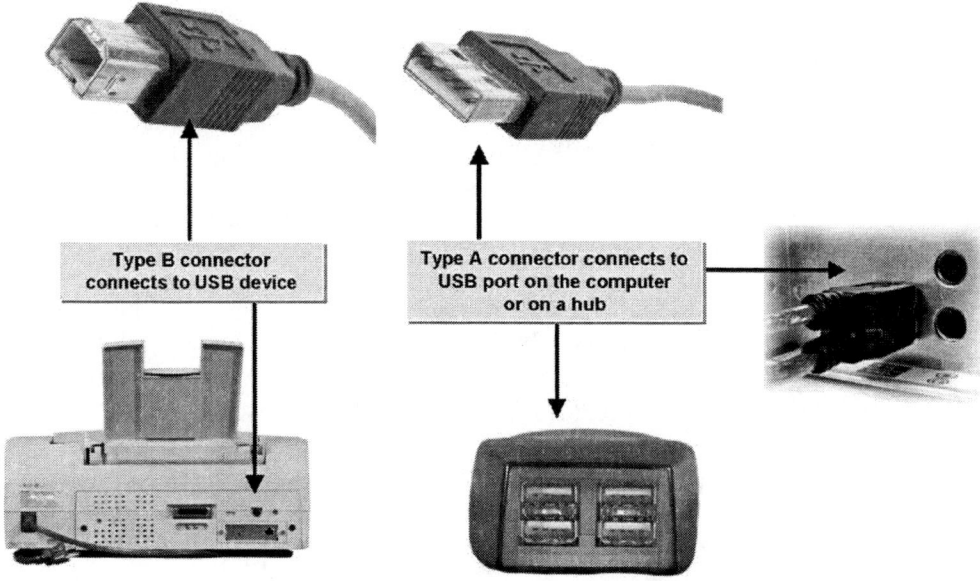

Figure 2-35: *USB interface.*

Touch Screen Input Devices

Definition:

A touch screen input device is a monitor device that enables users to enter input by touching areas on the screen. All touch screens enable you to enter information by pressing the monitor surface rather than needing to use a keyboard or mouse for entering input. Touch screens are composed of:

- Touch sensors—The sensors can be a panel that lays over a standard monitor or can be built into a special touch screen monitor where the user actually touches the glass on the monitor.

- Controller—If using an overlay panel, the controller connects to the panel and then to a PC port such as a COM or USB port, although there are special instances where it connects to a drive or other device or port. For built-in touch screens, the controller is built into the monitor. In this case, the monitor contains two cables—one to the monitor port and one to the COM or USB port (or other port).

- Device driver or specialized software—This enables the operating system to receive and interpret information from the touch screen device.

Touch screens vary in the following ways:

- They can be built into monitors or they can be implemented as screens that lay over regular monitors.

- The interfaces through which they are connected. Many use the USB interface if they are implemented as overlays on regular monitors.

- How the screens gather input. This might include technologies such as:
  — Infrared
  — Capacitive touch
  — Resistive touch
  — Surface acoustic wave
- Whether it is finger touch or stylus touch. Some touch screen surfaces must be touched with a bare finger in order to work. Others can be touched with gloved hands or a pointer or stylus of some type.

Example:

The example shown in Figure 2-36 shows a touch screen input device. It is implemented as a screen overlay and connects to the computer through the USB port. Users interact with it using their fingers to touch active areas on the Web page.

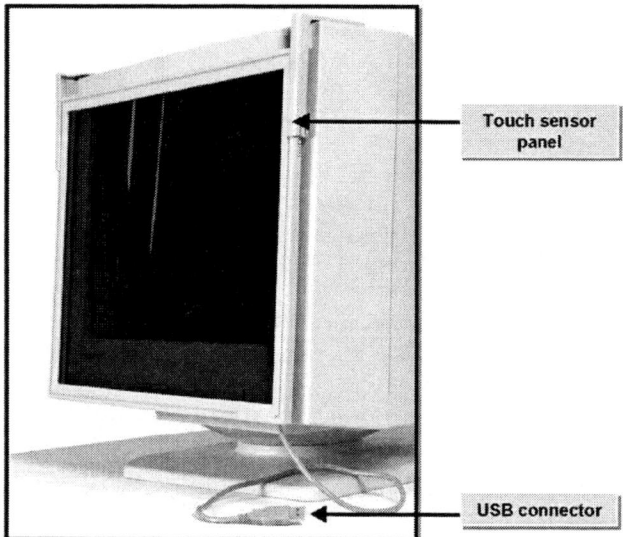

Figure 2-36: *A touch screen input device.*

USB Power

A 5-volt power supply is carried along with the USB signal. This allows small devices, such as hand-held scanners or speakers, to use power from the PC, rather than requiring their own power cables. Devices are plugged directly into 4-pin sockets on PCs or hubs using a rectangular Type A socket.

The USB bus distributes power through each port. This allows low-power devices that normally need their own power adapters to be powered through the cable. Through USB, the PC automatically senses the power that is required and delivers it to the device. Hubs may get all of their power from the USB bus (bus-powered), or they may be powered from their own AC adapter. Powered hubs provide the most flexibility for other downstream devices.

Upstream devices are those between a device and the USB port on the computer, going towards the computer. Downstream devices are those between a device and the end of the daisy chain, going away from the computer.

How to Install USB Devices

Procedure Reference: Connect USB Devices to a System

To connect a USB device to your system:

1. Connect the USB Type B end of the USB cable into the device.
2. Connect the USB Type A end of the USB cable into the computer or the USB hub.
3. If necessary, connect the AC adapter to the device and to an electrical outlet.
4. If required, install any device drivers. You might be presented with a wizard that prompts you to install the driver or you might not be prompted. If you are installing an unsigned device (a device that Microsoft has not given its approval for and provided a signed signature for), you might be prompted several times to install the same device.
5. Test that the device connected through the USB port works properly.

TOPIC G
Install FireWire Devices

In the previous topic, you connected a USB device to your system. Another similar port you might have on your system is a FireWire port. In this topic, you will connect a FireWire device to your system.

Another port you might encounter on a new system is the FireWire port. It can be used to connect devices such as digital video cameras and external hard drives. Members of the marketing department would be very excited to have such a system, so that they could incorporate streaming video into their presentations for trade shows. You will need to be able to support them in this effort.

FireWire

Definition:

A *FireWire* interface is a hardware interface that enables up to 63 FireWire devices to be connected to the computer at the same time. The FireWire interface is a high-speed interface. FireWire is the name given by Apple to the IEEE 1394 standard. Another name coined by Sony for this standard is iLink. FireWire was pioneered by Apple, who was later joined by Microsoft, Philips, National Semiconductor, and Texas Instruments in the 1394 Trade Association. FireWire connectors are 6-pin bullet-shaped or 4-pin square connectors. You might need to upgrade your operating system in order to use FireWire. It works with Windows 98 SE and above. It doesn't work with Windows 95 or the original Windows 98.

 Apple currently receives a $1 royalty per FireWire port.

FireWire is a hot-swappable serial interface. *Hotswap* means that you can change out a device without needing to power down the PC during installation or removal of the device.

FireWire can transmit data at up to 400 Mbps. IEEE 1394 speeds make it a good solution for connecting digital cameras, digital video cameras, printers, TVs, network cards, and mass-storage devices to PCs.

IEEE 1394 can transfer data in two ways. If data can be interrupted (such as when the buffer is full), it uses asynchronous transfer methods. If the data needs to flow at a specific rate so that there are no interruptions, then isochronous transfer methods are used. This is often used for multimedia presentations where buffering and pauses would interrupt the presentation to the user.

Electrical contacts are inside the structure of the connector of an IEEE 1394 cable. This helps prevent shock to the user or contamination of the contacts by the user's hands. These connectors are derived from the Nintendo GameBoy connector. Field-tested by children of all ages, this small and flexible connector is very durable. These connectors are easy to use even when the user must blindly insert them into the backs of machines.

IEEE 1394 uses a six-conductor cable which contains two pairs of wires for data transport, and one pair for device power. In most cases, the cable can be up to 4.5 meters long. In some cases the cable can be up to 14 meters long, but if there are powered devices the voltage could drop too low at these longer lengths. There is also a small square four-wire cable connector which connects to the device. Some systems also include a port for this connection on the system. Examples of the FireWire connectors are shown in Figure 2-37.

Figure 2-37: *FireWire connectors.*

Example:

Figure 2-38 shows a FireWire interface.

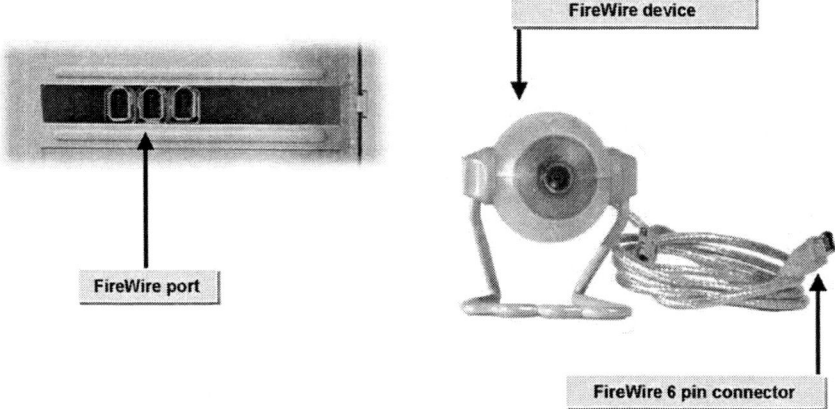

Figure 2-38: *FireWire connections.*

Device Bay

Compaq, Intel, and Microsoft proposed an industry standard called Device Bay. It combines the fast interface of IEEE 1394 and the USB interface. It offers a bay slot to slide in peripherals such as hard disks or DVD-ROM players. Other devices that use IEEE 1394 include ZIP drives, scanners, and CD-RW drives.

How to Install FireWire Devices

Procedure Reference: Connect FireWire Devices

To connect a FireWire device to your system:

 The steps listed here should work for most devices. However, check the documentation for your device. In some instances, you might need to install software prior to connecting the device.

1. Connect the FireWire cable to the device.
2. Connect the FireWire cable to the FireWire port on your computer.
3. If necessary, connect the AC adapter to the device and to an electrical outlet.
4. If necessary, install any required FireWire device drivers.
5. Verify that the device works properly.

Topic H
Connect Wireless Devices

You have installed devices with hard, physical connections to the computer so far. There are also wireless connections you can make between devices and some computers. If your computer is equipped with an infrared port and you have an infrared device, you can communicate between the two. Another wireless method your device might use is digital radio signals, which can be used on any system. In this topic, you will establish a wireless connection.

Infrared devices for a computer use the same technology as the remote control devices you use every day to control things like your TV and DVD player. You will need to be able to help users connect devices; otherwise, the wireless functionality offered by infrared won't be available to your users. Devices using digital radio can be added to any system, giving you more flexibility in adding wireless devices.

Wireless Connections

Definition:

A wireless connection is a method for a device to communicate with the computer without a physical connection between the device and the computer. Some wireless devices must have a direct line of sight to the wireless port on the computer. Others can communicate around corners and over piles of paper and other equipment. There are several wireless communications standards. These include infrared, digital radio, and those that use Bluetooth profiles.

Infrared devices use infrared transceivers that are compliant with the Infrared Data Association's (IrDA) standards. With infrared communications, there is no physical connection between the devices that communicate over the infrared link. Instead, data is sent over a beam of light. Most commonly, infrared technology is used to connect printers to computers (typically portable computers, such as laptops or palmtops), but it can also be used to connect workstations in a network. Figure 2-39 shows how data is transferred over an infrared connection.

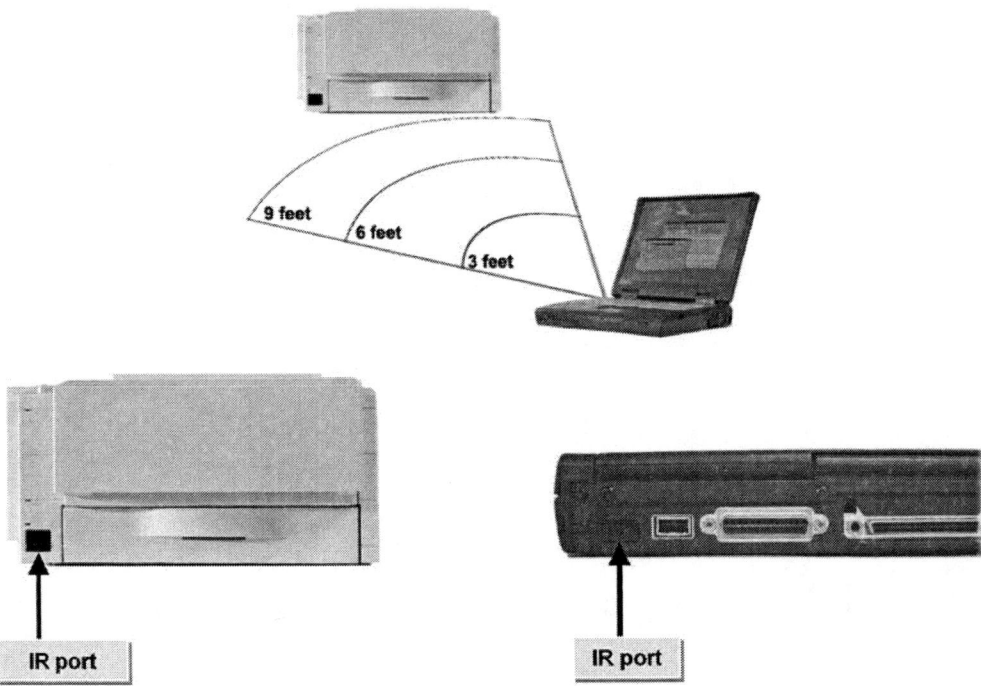

Figure 2-39: *Transferring information over an infrared connection.*

Data transfer speed ranges from 9.6 Kbps (*slow IrDA*) to 4 Mbps on newer devices (*fast IrDA*). Infrared communication uses line-of-sight technology, and the distance between the devices must be minimal (no more than approximately 3 to 9 feet). With the example of a printer, the computer's infrared port must be in the line of sight of the printer's infrared port and the two must be positioned relatively close to each other. Having the devices' infrared ports facing each other head-on is best, but most devices will still connect when placed at a slight angle to each other. An angle of less than 45 degrees is usually required.

Digital radio devices enable you to connect devices to your computer without wires. It eliminates the problem that infrared has in that this requires a direct line of sight between the device and the computer. Cordless keyboards and mice typically use digital radio frequency technologies.

Example:
An example of a digital radio frequency mouse is shown in Figure 2-40. The receiver plugs into a USB or PS/2 port on the computer and receives radio signals from the mouse which acts as a transmitter.

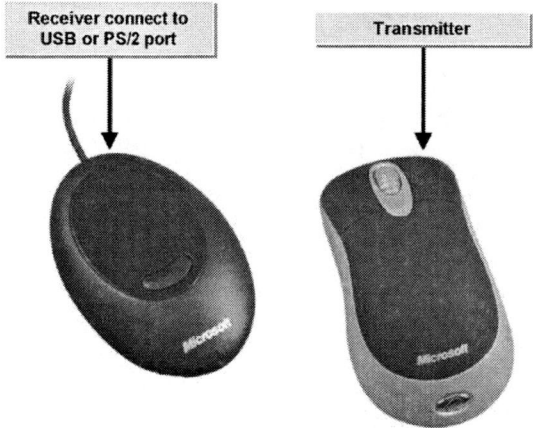

Figure 2-40: *A digital radio frequency mouse.*

How to Establish Wireless Connection

Procedure Reference: Connect Digital Radio Wireless Devices

To connect a device that uses digital radio wireless connections:

1. If necessary, install the wireless device software.

2. Connect the receiver device. Depending on the device, there might be power connections you need to plug in. Other devices can be powered directly from the PC.

3. Connect the transmitter devices. If necessary, install batteries in the remote devices. You can now test whether the devices are communicating with each other.

4. Disconnect hardwired connection devices. In most cases, you will want to disconnect the hardwired devices; however, it is not a requirement that you do so in all cases. For example, if you have a child-sized mouse and a normal-sized mouse, you could leave both connected and use whichever one is more comfortable for the user.

Procedure Reference: Connect Infrared Devices

To connect a device containing an infrared port to a system that has an infrared port:

1. Establish a clear line of sight between the infrared peripheral port on the device and the infrared port on the computer.

2. If necessary, connect the AC adapter for the device and connect it to an electrical outlet.

3. If the device is connected through USB, PCMCIA, or any device that is Plug and Play standard compatible, the appropriate driver should be installed automatically. However, if you are installing the device through a serial port, some USB devices, or any device which was not automatically detected and installed, you will need to configure the device for your system. This might include installing drivers, enabling the IR port on your system or on the device, or other such steps as documented in the device manual.

4. With the infrared ports aimed at each other, transfer data between the peripheral and the system. For example, if you have a printer, send a file to print.

CHAPTER 2 FOLLOW-UP
Setting Up a Personal Computer

In this chapter, you installed and removed devices connected to standard ports. You connected a video output device to the monitor port, connected keyboard and pointing devices to the PS/2 ports, connected parallel and serial devices to the relevant ports, connected game and sound devices to the ports on the sound card, connected USB and FireWire devices, and established wireless connections. In the same way that the jigsaw pieces made a complete picture, the peripherals connected to your computer have created a complete computer system.

Essential Terms

- binary number system
- cables
- connectors
- device drivers
- FireWire
- infrared
- keyboards
- modems
- mouse
- network adapters
- null modem cables
- parallel ports
- peripheral devices
- pinouts
- Plug and Play
- ports
- print drivers
- PS/2 interfaces
- serial devices
- serial ports
- sound cards
- throughput
- USB
- video output devices
- wireless

Review Questions

1. What kind of signal is carried over a 15-pin VGA cable to the video port on a computer?
2. How is a monitor measured?
3. Which DVI connection is a dual link, analog and digital connection?
4. What is a pixel?
5. If a display image is flickering, what should you check?
6. What should you check if part of an image is off the screen?
7. If Plug and Play fails to detect a new device, what Control Panel applet should you use to install the device?
8. What is another name used to identify a PS/2 port?
9. How many pins does a PS/2 connector have??
10. What is the purpose of a device driver?

11. What is the maximum number of parallel ports a computer can host?
12. What are the two bi-directional parallel ports available on a computer?
13. What is the numbering system used by computers?
14. How many bits are in a byte?
15. How many bits are in a word?
16. What three elements comprise a serial interface?
17. What is the purpose of null modem cables?
18. What is the maximum communication speed at which data will pass through a serial port?
19. What is Device Manager?
20. What is a registered jack?
21. What kind of connector is used to connect a phone line to a modem?
22. Which modem operating mode is more prone to errors: asynchronous or synchronous?
23. What is the most recent modem standard?
24. What is a transceiver?
25. What modem command disables call waiting?
26. What modem command do you use to disconnect a connection?
27. On a sound card, what port is used to connect the speakers?
28. What is another name for an AT DIN5 connector?
29. How many USB devices can be connected to one USB port when daisy chaining the maximum number of hubs?
30. What is the maximum length of a USB cable for full- or high-speed devices?
31. What is the maximum number of devices that can be connected to a FireWire interface at the same time?
32. What does it mean to say that FireWire is a hot-swappable serial interface?
33. What is the data transfer speed of fast IrDA?

Review Projects

Project #1 The New V.92 Standard

Cable and xDSL enable computer users to access the Internet and office networks at significantly higher speeds than what is possible from standard 56K modems. However, fast Internet access is not available in many places and even when it is available, not everyone can afford the monthly access fee. The majority of people connecting to the Internet or to office networks use a dial-up 56K modem.

The latest modem standard is V.92. Modems using this standard are still 56K but new features have been added to provide faster, better connections.

Using the Curt's High Speed Modem FAQ Web site, you'll explore the new V.92 standard. To access the Web site, enter the following address in your browser: **http://www.net-boy.com**. Scroll down the list of hyperlinks and click the one titled "the new V.92 standard." What are the features of the new V.92 standard? At the end of the section, click the V.92 FAQ link. What features make a V.92 modem faster than a V.90 modem? Explain how the feature works.

Project #2 Understanding Serial Communication

The objective of this activity is to gain a deeper understanding of serial communication. Most desktop PCs have one or two serial ports which can be identified by the number of pins and whether the port is male of female. Originally, serial ports are also referred to as COM ports and conform to the standard interface referred to as RS-w232c, or just RS-232.

In serial transmissions, data is sent sequentially, one bit at a time, over a wire. Although serial mice and keyboards are still available, modems are probably the most popular serial device. Most PC serial devices use asynchronous data transmission. In the case of modems, this means that data is sent from one modem to another as blocks of data at timed intervals. Clocks on modems synchronize the transmissions and asynchronous transmission refers to how the transfer of data occurs between the two devices based on bits that are sent before and after data (called start and stop bits).

Using Quatech's Web site, located at **http://www.quatech.com/support/comm-over-asyncserial.php#fig8** you'll explore asynchronous communication in some depth. For additional information on synchronous and isochronous serial communication as well as port specifications, there are links at the bottom of the page.

Project #3 USB-ON-THE-GO

Universal Serial Bus, or USB, enables you to add and remove peripherals easily. You can plug a peripheral into a port and the operating system will recognize new hardware and, in most cases, install the necessary software without user intervention.

In this activity, you'll learn about a specification called USB-ON-THE-GO, which is an enhancement to USB 2.0 (also called high speed USB). USB-ON-THE-GO enables devices to communicate without a PC. Not only does the technology give users the ability to bypass a computer and transfer information between mobile devices, but it segments markets and increases business opportunities.

Read more about USB-ON-THE-GO in a PDF article produced by Philips, one of the manufacturers involved in developing the specification, at **www.semiconductors.philips.com/acrobat/literature/9397/75009316.pdf**

What do you consider some of the main advantages of the specification for businesses? For individual consumers? Do you see any disadvantages to either of these groups?

Reflective Questions

1. Which peripherals will you need to install most often?

2. Which peripherals do you feel you will need to practice installing before you are comfortable with quickly and easily installing them to work right the first time?

CHAPTER 3
Installing or Removing Internal Hardware

Chapter Objectives:

In this chapter, you will install and remove internal hardware.

You will:

- Establish an ESD-free work area.
- Open the computer and install an adapter card.
- Install a network card into the computer and attach the network cable.
- Install an IDE drive.
- Install a SCSI drive.
- Connect external SCSI devices.
- Identify RAID levels.

Introduction

So far, you have connected peripherals to the system without needing to open the cover of the computer system. To add functionality to users' systems, you will also need to open the cover and add, remove, or replace internal hardware. In this chapter, you will install internal hardware.

No matter how new a system is and how many features it includes, it often seems that as soon as you buy it, there is another piece of hardware that needs to be added to it. This often requires that you open the cover and install the component directly into the system board. Being able to safely and efficiently install internal components will help keep your users satisfied with your performance as their hardware support technician.

TOPIC A
Establish an ESD-free Work Area

In this chapter, you will be installing components inside systems. Before you begin doing so, you need to make sure your work area is safe for the components and for you. In this topic, you will establish an electrostatic-discharge-free work area.

While you needed to carefully handle the external peripherals you added to the system so far, you need to be even more careful of handling internal components. These components can easily be damaged through electrostatic discharge (ESD). By establishing an ESD-free work area, you can help prevent damage to components from electrostatic discharge.

The Electrical Flow Process

Electricity is an energy form resulting from the movement of electrons and protons. Electrons revolve around the nucleus of an atom in either direction. Applying an electric current to the atoms causes the electrons to leave orbit and follow a path or circuit. The moving electrons create electricity.

Figure 3-1 shows the nucleus and one electron and the path they take with and without an electrical current applied. There are also protons (positively charged particles) and neutrons (particles carrying no charge) revolving around the atom. Only the electrons (negatively charged particles) are involved in the electrical process.

Atoms without electrical current applied

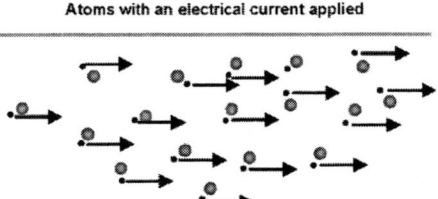
Atoms with an electrical current applied

Figure 3-1: *The electrical process.*

Stage	What Happens
1	Electrons move randomly.
2	A current is applied.
3	Electrons all move in the same direction.

Electrical Terms

The following table lists some of the terms used to describe electricity and the flow of electricity.

Term	Symbol	Unit	Measures
Voltage	V	*Volt*	Push behind electrons; indicates the energy of electrons.
Current	A	*Ampere (Amp)*	The number of electrons per second flowing past a point.
Resistance	Ω	*Ohm*	Opposition to the flow of electrons.
Power	W	*Watt*	Energy per second delivered by electric current.

ESD

ESD can damage sensitive computer equipment. ESD occurs when electrons rush from one body to another that are unequally charged. The path of least resistance is followed between two objects, so it can also occur between a charged body (for example, you) and an electrical circuit ground (a door knob or a computer component). The static electricity process is illustrated in Figure 3-2.

1. Electrons are moved when two objects come together, especially if the objects are moved against each other, thus increasing the contact.
2. Electrons are transferred from one object to the other causing one object to have too many electrons. This imbalance of positive and negative charges is referred to as static electricity.
3. Positive particles repel other positive particles just as negative particles repel other negative particles. Positive particles attract negative particles. So, when an excess of electrons is built up in you and you touch a conductor such as a metal door knob or a computer component, the extra electrons move to the conductive object you touch and you receive a shock.

This is no big deal if it is a door knob, but it can easily damage computer equipment.

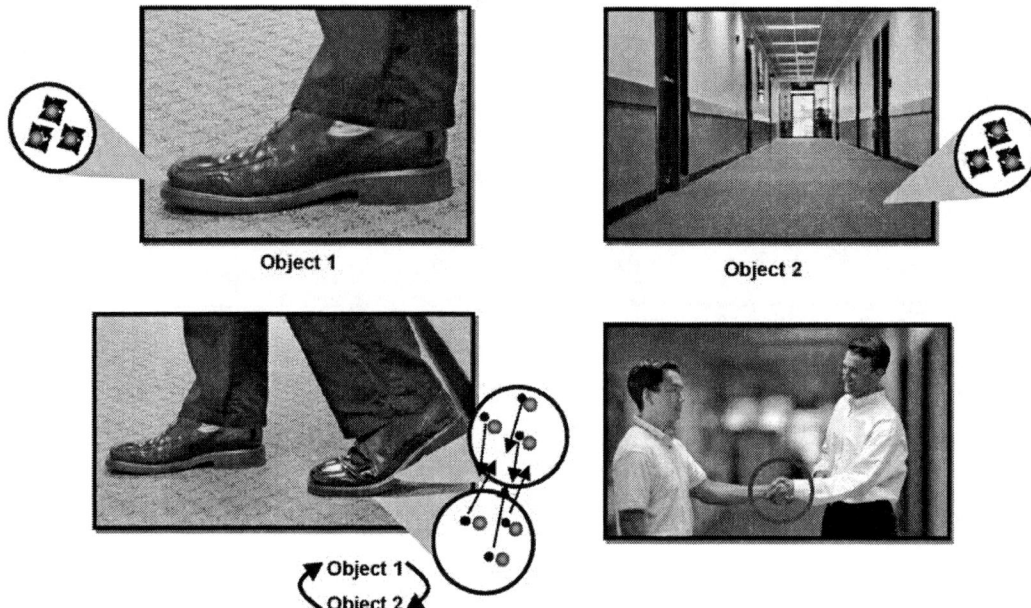

Figure 3-2: *The static electricity process.*

Let's put this all together in an example to see how the ESD process works.
1. You walk across a carpeted area.
2. A large number of electrons are gathered on your body as you walk across the carpet.
3. You touch a door knob.
4. You see and/or feel the shock as the excess electrons jump between your finger and the doorknob.

Insulators and Conductors

Some materials hold their electrons tightly to the nucleus of the atom. These materials make good insulators. Rubber is an example of an insulator. In other materials, the electrons can move very freely. These materials make good conductors. Metals are effective conductors. The metals used in computers are used precisely because they are good conductors.

ESD Safety Equipment

There are lots of people who work on computer equipment and never use a single piece of ESD safety equipment. They discharge themselves by touching an unpainted metal part of the computer case before touching any components.

In other instances, the company policy might require that you use a properly equipped ESD-free work area. An example is shown in Figure 3-3. The minimum equipment in this case would be a grounded wrist strap. Examples of grounded wrist and foot straps are shown in Figure 3-4. Other ESD-protection equipment includes grounded mats to cover the work surface, grounded floor mats to stand on, and leg straps. The mats contain a snap that you connect the wrist or leg strap to. If the technician's clothing has the potential to produce static charges, an ESD smock which covers from the waist up should be worn.

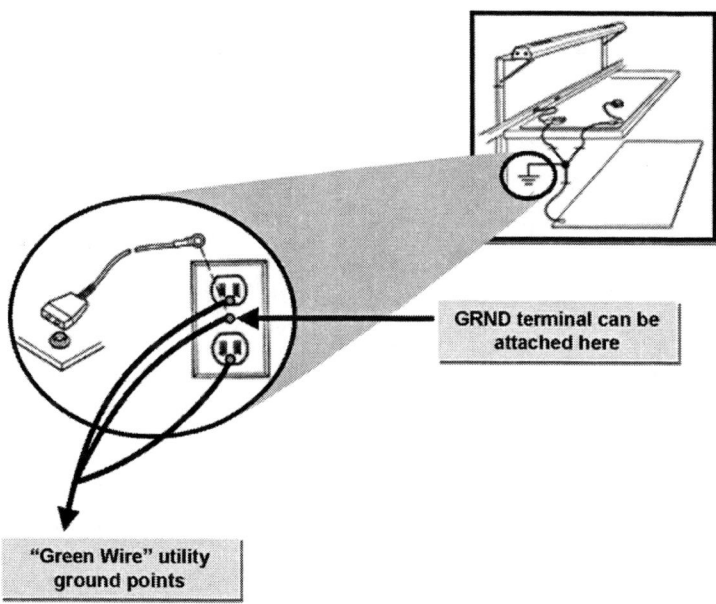

Figure 3-3: *ESD-safe work area.*

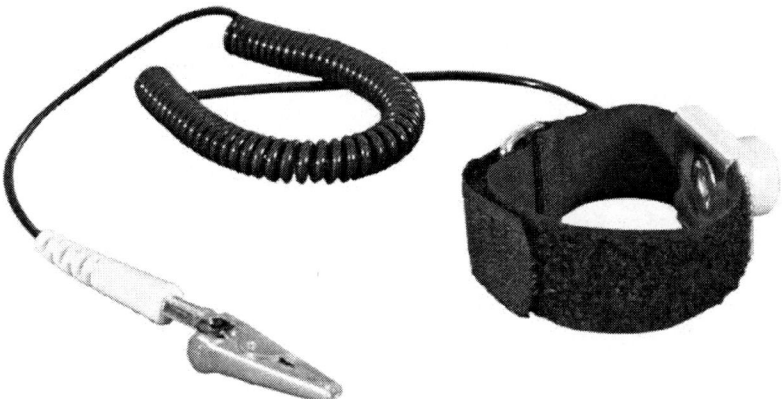

Figure 3-4: *Anti-static wrist strap and foot strap.*

To ensure that the ESD equipment remains effective, you should test it frequently. Even though you may not feel a shock, one strong enough to compromise the ESD safety equipment might be experienced.

In addition to the physical ESD safety equipment, there are ways to limit the production of static electricity by maintaining the atmosphere. An air ionizer might be used. It releases negative ions into the air which attract positive charges to make particles balanced in charges. If the air is extremely dry, more static is likely to be produced. A humidity rate of 50 to 60 percent is most desired.

 The EIA produced a document that covers recommendations for safely handling ESD-sensitive equipment. It is EIA-625 Requirements for Handling Electrostatic Discharge Sensitive Devices. A summary of the contents can be found at **http://.bytemark.com/static/building.html**.

Electrical Safety Hazards Inside the PC

Most internal circuits on a computer use voltages between 3.3 and 12 volts. These voltages do not present a great threat to your personal safety; however, the power supply in the computer takes the electricity from the wall—115 volts—and this voltage could cause you injury or death.

Power supplies have a high voltage in them any time the computer is plugged in, even if the computer power is turned off. Disconnect the power cord before you start work on a power supply and leave it off until you are done. Computer monitors contain circuits that require 35,000 volts with a high current. The voltage and current are stored on components called capacitors that do not discharge when the monitor is turned off or unplugged. Even after months of inactivity, the capacitors may have enough stored electrical energy to kill you. For this reason, leave the internal workings of power supplies and monitors to specialists who have the extra training and special equipment that are required to safely make repairs to those components.

Working on a computer can be safe if you protect yourself from electrical hazards. This includes:

- Perform only the work for which you have sufficient training.
- Don't attempt repair work when you are tired; you may make careless mistakes, and your primary diagnostic tool, deductive reasoning, will not be operating at full capacity.

- Avoid wearing jewelry or other articles that could accidentally contact computer circuits and conduct current.
- Suspend work during an electrical storm.
- Work only with dry hands and feet on a dry surface.
- When removing circuit boards, place them on a dissipative ground mat or put them in an anti-static bag.
- Use proper ESD-safety equipment.

Optimal Operating Environment

Keeping the ESD down can be difficult if your equipment has to run in less than optimal operating environments. Factors that you should try to control include:

- Ventilation
- Dust
- Moisture

All systems tend to accumulate dust. The fan that runs to cool the system pulls dust and debris into the interior of the computer. This can lead to shorts and other electrical damage if it is allowed to accumulate. Having the system in a crowded area without enough room around it for adequate air flow can lead to overheating problems. Computers function best in relative humidity of 50 to 60 percent. Computers being run outdoors such as cash registers at an outdoor plant nursery could easily run into all of these problems. Computers on a factory floor are also prone to problems from these issues.

When possible, control the humidity with air conditioning or dehumidifiers to keep the moisture level from being too high. Be sure to leave adequate room around the air intake and fan area of the computer to prevent overheating. If possible, keep the computer away from areas that collect excessive dust and dirt.

How to Establish an ESD-free Work Area

Procedure Reference: Establish an ESD-free Work Area

You will be opening the case and working inside the computer soon, so you need to protect yourself and the equipment before doing so. To establish an ESD-free work area:

1. Install a grounded anti-static work surface mat on your table.
2. Place a grounded anti-static floor mat at your work area.
3. Connect a grounded wrist or foot strap to your work area.
4. Have a can of anti-static spray available in case you notice any static electricity in your clothes.

Topic B
Install or Remove Adapter Cards

You have now established an ESD-free work area. Since you have done this, you should now be able to safely work with internal computer components. In this topic, you will open the system cover and install an internal adapter card.

As you have seen, much of the work you will be asked to do can be done without the need to remove the cover from the system. You will also be asked to work on internal system components, though. One of the most common internal components you will be asked to install is an adapter card. These adapter cards expand the functionality of the system, bringing greater benefit to users by enabling them to do additional things with their systems.

Internal PC Components

Definition:

An internal PC component is any computing device that resides inside the computer system case. Components are composed of *integrated circuits* and *transistors,* in addition to specific materials for various device functions. All computers must contain the following internal components:

- Motherboard
- Power supply
- Central Processing Unit (CPU)
- RAM
- ROM BIOS

Other internal components can be added to the system to increase functionality of the system. These include adapter cards and drives. Adapter cards can add additional ports or functions. The devices are powered at either 3.3, 5, or 12 volts. Internal devices receive their power either directly from the power supply or through the power supplied to the system board, and thus to the slots in which the components are connected.

Example: Internal PC Components

Figure 3-5 shows the internal components in a computer. The short white slots in the upper left corner of the picture are PCI slots that can hold adapter cards. These slots are powered through the motherboard from the power supply. Each slot receives 3.3 volts of electricity. The cards inserted into the PCI slots in the example provide FireWire ports, network connectivity, and sound support.

Figure 3-5: *Internal computer components.*

Adapter Cards

Definition:

An *adapter card* is a printed circuit board that you install into a slot on the computer's system board to expand the functionality of the computer. It is also known as an expansion card, add-ins, add-ons, or a board.

All adapter cards:

- Must have a connector that matches the slot they are installed in.
- Contain circuitry to connect a specific device to the computer.
- Increase capabilities of the computer.

Almost every card you get now will be a PCI card. ISA has been replaced by PCI. Adapter cards include the following:

- Video cards
- Sound cards
- Network cards
- SCSI host bus adapters
- Internal modems
- USB cards
- IEEE 1394/FireWire cards

Chapter 3: Installing or Removing Internal Hardware

Adapter cards vary by:

- Whether they use local bus.
- The slot type they use.
- Whether it is built into the system circuitry or an actual separate physical board.
- The functionality they provide.

Example: A PCI Modem Adapter Card

The example shown in Figure 3-6 is of a PCI modem card. It uses a PCI connector which fits into the PCI slot in the motherboard. It uses 3.3 volts of electricity powered through the power supply. The circuitry on the adapter card enables this card to be used to connect the computer to a network or another computer through the phone lines.

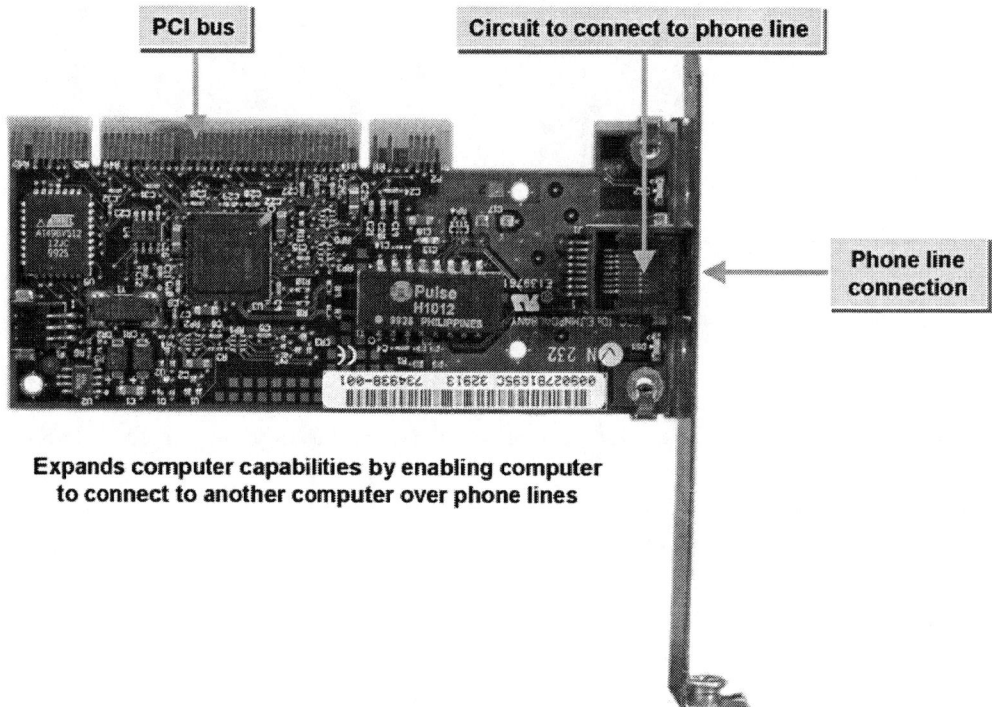

Figure 3-6: *An example of an adapter card.*

Bus Types

Definition:

A *bus* is the collection of wires that connect an interface card and the microprocessor, and it contains the rules that describe how data should be transferred through the connection. Each bus has a specific set of parameters that describe its physical and electrical characteristics.

Example: ISA

The following table describes the *ISA bus*. Devices using this legacy bus usually need to be manually configured and are not configured through Plug and Play.

ISA	Description
Physical characteristic of cards	Card size varies, but must have ISA edge connectors. Slot on the motherboard is black. Can be an 8-bit (short) or 16-bit (long) slot.
Configuration	Configured through jumpers, dip switches, or software. PnP ISA cards are automatically configured by the operating system.
Used for	Most 8-bit boards fit in 16-bit slots. Originally designed for the IBM PC/XT and PC/AT. Many systems still include some ISA slots along with PCI slots. Can access up to 16 MB of RAM.
Number of data lines	8-bit or 16-bit. 16 or 24 data address lines.
Communication method	Signal that they are ready to transfer data, and then send one byte, and repeat this process until all data has been sent.
Pronounced	Eye-sah

Figure 3-7 shows an example of ISA.

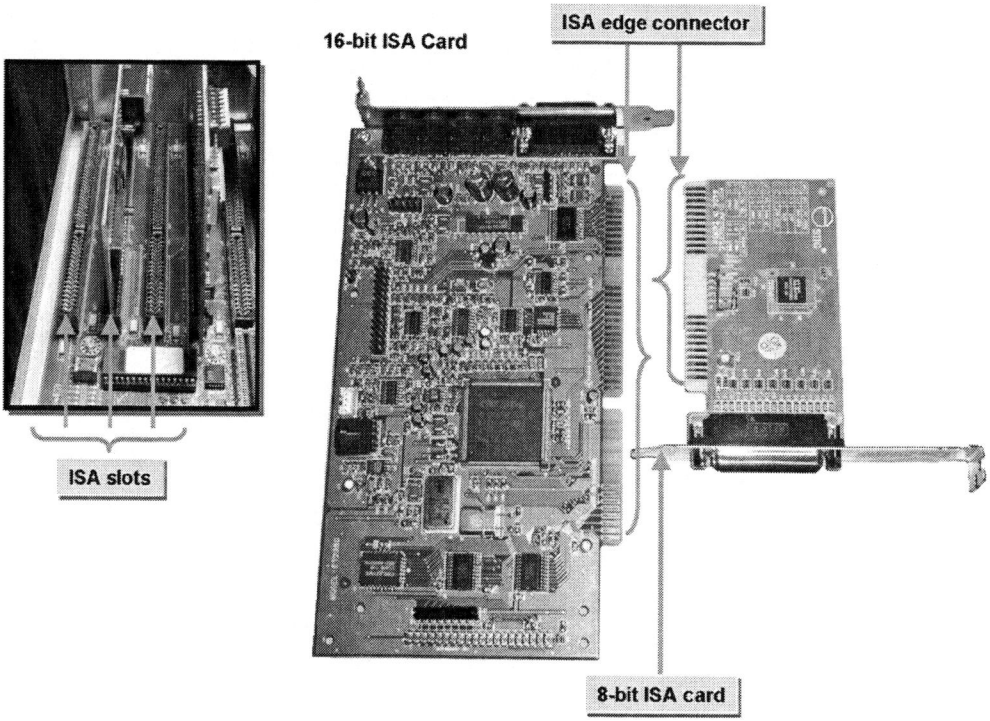

Figure 3-7: *ISA*.

Example: EISA

The following table describes the *EISA bus*.

EISA	Description
Physical characteristic of cards	Most cards are 5 inches high. They contain an additional row of connectors as compared to ISA cards and additional guide notches. They run at 8 or 10 MHz.
Configuration	Software configurable through an EISA configuration disk. Configuration is saved in CMOS, in System Configuration Information (SCI) files, and in onboard non-volatile memory.
Used for	EISA and ISA cards. Can access up to 4 GB RAM. Used in older servers.

EISA	Description
Number of data lines	32 bit. 32 address lines and 32 data lines. If it is really just a ported ISA card, it uses 24 address lines instead so it can access only 16 MB of RAM.
Communication method	Uses the same signaling techniques as ISA. In addition, it can use bus mastering which enables one adapter to occasionally take control of the bus during a data transfer.
Pronounced	E-sah

An example of an EISA card is shown in Figure 3-8. Notice that the EISA card has a double row of pins on the connector edge. This card is not frequently encountered and usually only in older server class machines.

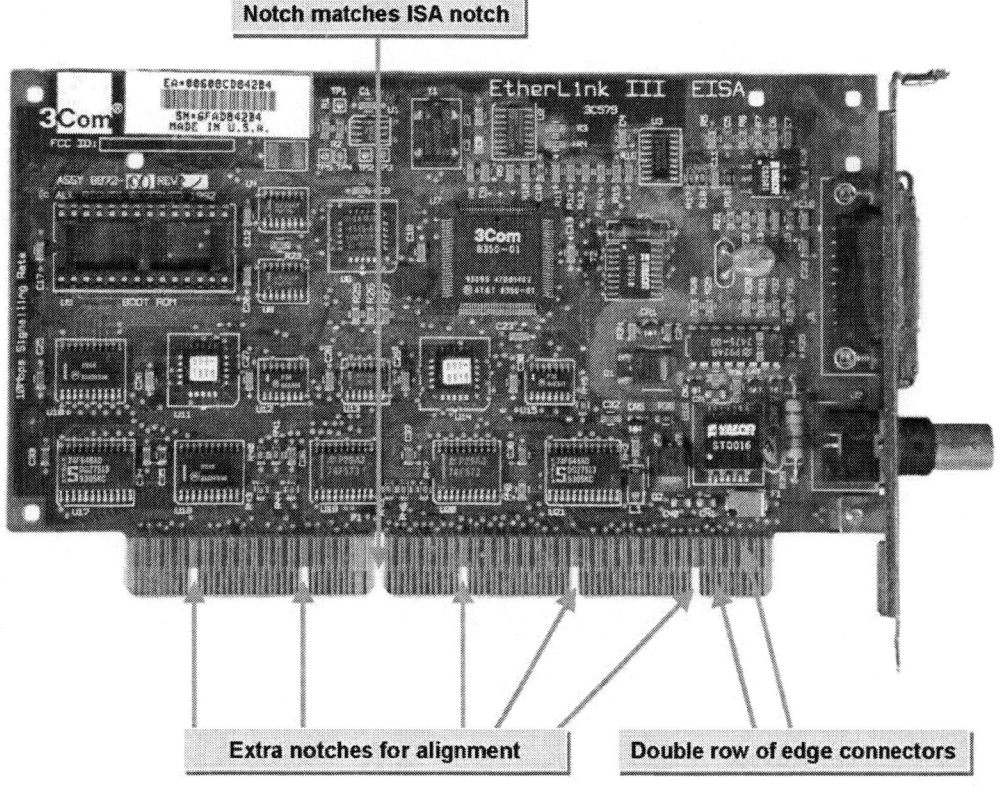

Figure 3-8: *EISA cards.*

Chapter 3: Installing or Removing Internal Hardware

Example: PCI

The following table describes the *PCI bus*.

PCI	Description
Physical characteristic of cards	33 or 66 MHz. 133 MBps throughput at 33 MHz. Up to eight functions can be integrated on one board. Card size varies, but must have a PCI edge connector. Slot on the motherboard is white.
Configuration	Supports 10 devices. Can share IRQs. Uses PnP.
Used for	All current adapters in client and server systems.
Number of data lines	64-bit bus often implemented as a 32-bit bus.
Communication method	Local bus standard. 32-bit bus mastering. Each bus uses 10 *loads*. A load refers to the amount of power consumed by a device. PCI chipset uses three loads. Integrated PCI controllers use one load. Controllers installed in a slot use 1.5 loads.
Pronounced	P C I

A PCI slot and a PCI card are shown in Figure 3-9. Notice that the connector pins on the PCI card are very close together. The connector and slot are much shorter than previous busses even though there are more pins and faster communication rates.

 The PCI slots in Figure 3-9 are shared PCI/ISA slots. They share a single opening on the back of the case, so if an ISA card is in one of the slots, the PCI slot cannot be used unless the ISA card is removed.

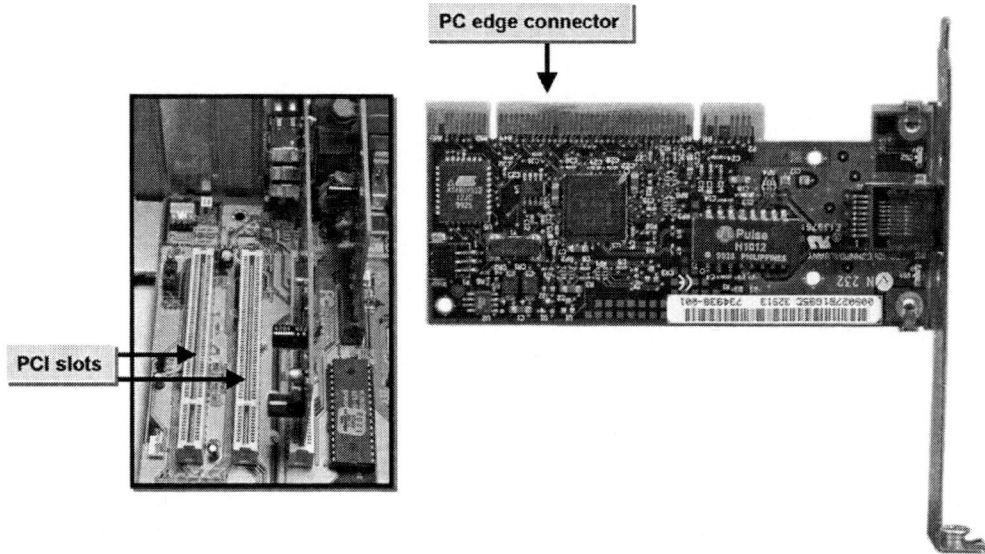

Figure 3-9: *PCI.*

Example: AGP

An example of an AGP slot and an AGP video card are shown in Figure 3-10. The following table describes the *AGP bus*.

AGP	Description
Physical characteristic of cards	Brown slot on the motherboard. AGP 1.0 is a 1x/2x slot. This is the shortest of the AGP slots with a small separator that divides it into two sections. AGP 2.0 is a 2x/4x slot that has extra pins at one end. There is also an AGP Pro Slot. See **www17.tomshardware.com/graphic/20000922/agppro-01.html** for a complete description of the AGP Pro slot.
Used for	Video cards in systems that support the AGP chipset. The system board needs an AGP bus slot or an integrated AGP chip.
Number of data lines	32 bits wide with a throughput of 266 MBps for AGP 1.0. Faster modes with throughput of 533 MBps are available on AGP 2.0 and 1.07 GBps for AGP Pro.
Communication method	Directly accesses RAM rather than needing to transfer data-to-video RAM first.

AGP	Description
Pronounced	A G P

AGP comes in several versions with 3.0 being the most recent. each version runs in several modes as described in the following table.

AGP Version	Mode	Speed	Bytes/Clock Cycle(s)
1.0, 2.0, Pro, 3.0	1x	266 Mbps	8 bytes per 2 clock cycles
1.0, 2.0, Pro, 3.0	2x	533 Mbps	8 bytes per clock cycle
2.0, Pro, 3.0	4x	1.07 Gbps	16 bytes per clock cycle
3.0	8x	2.1 Gbps	32 bits per clock cycle using isochronous communications

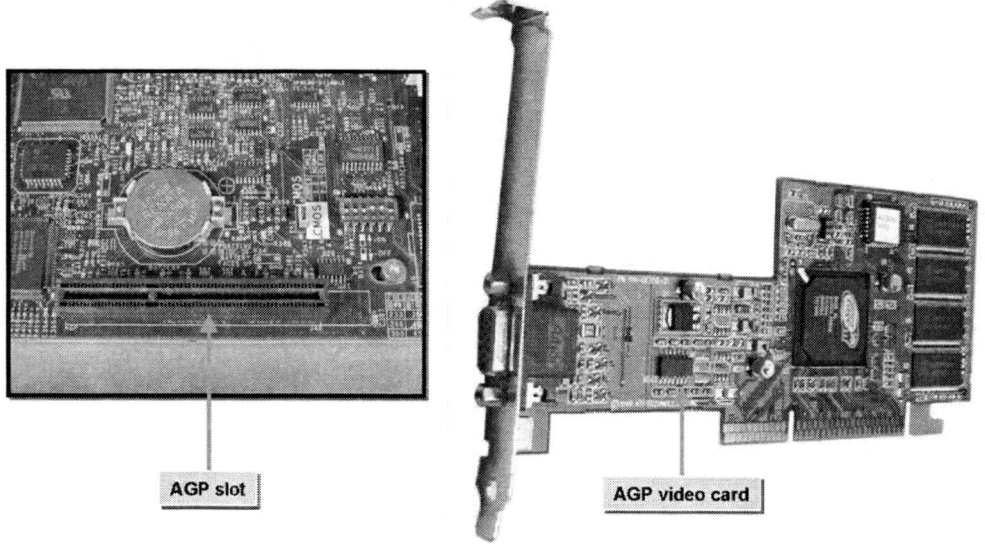

Figure 3-10: *AGP.*

Specialized Video Cards

AGP cards are optimized for speed. This makes them great for game play. They have 3D capabilities in most cases.

More and more users are using dual monitors so that they can see more information at once. Some AGP cards have a dual head—one card has two monitor ports so that you can connect dual monitors to a system. In other cases, you can use two PCI video cards to implement dual monitors. It works best if the cards are the same model.

Other specialized video cards include those with the ability to connect to television or other consumer video sources. This enables you to transfer data from the television or video device to store on the computer. You can also send data out to be displayed on the television screen.

Number Systems

Definition:

A number system is a system that represents numerical values. All number systems use some set of characters to represent values. They vary in the characters used.

Just as in the decimal number system, when you reach the last symbol in the number system, you add another **place** in the number value. For example, when you reach 9 counting in base 10, then you add another character in the **tens** column to create the number 10. Using the same pattern counting in hex, when you reach F, the next number would be 10H (equivalent to 16_{10}).

The most common place you will encounter hexadecimal numbers is in memory addresses. Each hardware resource requires a separate memory area to write to. These are identified by the hexadecimal range that has been assigned to them.

Example:

The decimal or base 10 number system is used in everyday calculations. Computers deal in binary or the base 2 number system. The decimal number 1024_{10} would be 10000000000_2. Since that is hard to read and takes a lot of room to write or store, computer scientists also use the hexadecimal (also known as hex) or base 16 number system. In this case, 1024_{10} would be 400_{16}. Rather than using the subscript 16, you might also see a hex number written as 400H.

 To avoid confusion, a subscripted number denoting the number system being used can be included with numbers. The computer knows which number system it is using, so doesn't need to add such a notation.

The following table shows the characters used in each number system.

Binary	Decimal	Hexadecimal
0	0	0
1	1	1
	2	2
	3	3
	4	4
	5	5
	6	6

Binary	Decimal	Hexadecimal
	7	7
	8	8
	9	9
		A
		B
		C
		D
		E
		F

Hex Numbers in Addresses

The following table shows the memory addresses for parallel and serial ports.

Port	Memory Address
LPT1	378h
LPT2	278h
COM1	3F8h
COM2	2F8h
COM3	3E8h
COM4	2E8h

Hardware Resources

Definition:

Hardware resources are unique system resources assigned to a device installed in a system that enable it to communicate with the operating system. The hardware resources, which include Direct Memory Access (DMA), Input/Output (I/O) Addresses, Interrupt Requests (IRQ), and Memory Addresses, can be assigned manually for a non-PnP device or by the operating system for a PnP device at the time it is installed. No two devices can operate simultaneously with the same hardware resources. The hardware resources assigned to a particular device can be viewed using Device Manager.

The hardware resources that are configured are shown in the following table.

Resource	Description
Direct Memory Access (DMA)	Path set up directly between a device and the computer's main memory. By bypassing the computer's processor, it speeds up the data transfer.
Input/Output (I/O) Port	A *port* or *channel* that appears as a memory address or range that a device can use to transfer data back and forth between a device and the computer's processor.
Interrupt Request Line (IRQ)	When a device needs to request the attention of the computer processor, it sends a signal over the hardware line that was assigned to the device. A unique IRQ is required for each device.
Memory (*Memory Address*)	An area of computer memory assigned to a device.

 Hardware resources are also referred to as system resources.

Most resources cannot be shared. If more than one device is configured to use a resource, a *device conflict* occurs. When this happens, neither device can function properly. Some resources can be shared; this depends on the hardware, operating system, and device drivers being able to support shared resources.

If the device you install is not PnP compatible, you will need to manually set the resources through Device Manager or with software included with the device. Resources are usually set on these devices through software, but in some cases might be set manually by moving *DIP switches* which are usually implemented as rocker switches or *jumpers* which are caps placed over pins to complete a circuit. The resources set on the hardware must match those specified in the operating system or device driver in order for the device to function properly.

The following figures show typical hardware resource settings for DMA, I/O Port, IRQ, and Memory Addresses. These are illustrated in Figure 3-11, Figure 3-12, Figure 3-13, and Figure 3-14.

```
Direct memory access (DMA)
    2  Standard floppy disk controller
    3  ECP Printer Port (LPT1)
    4  Direct memory access controller
```

Figure 3-11: *Typical DMA settings.*

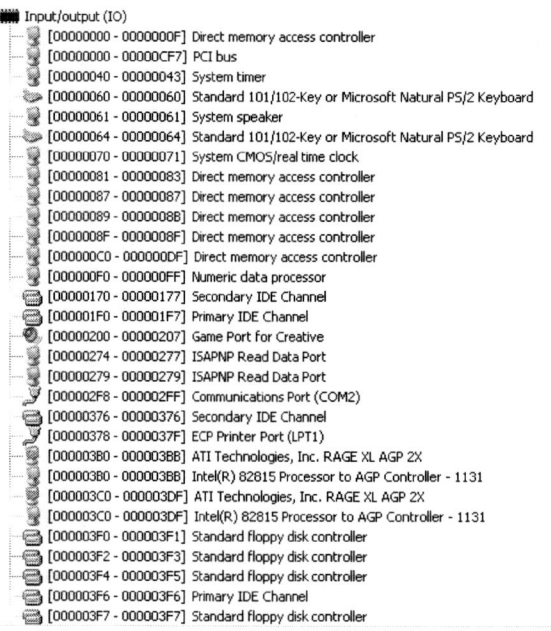

Figure 3-12: *Typical I/O Port settings.*

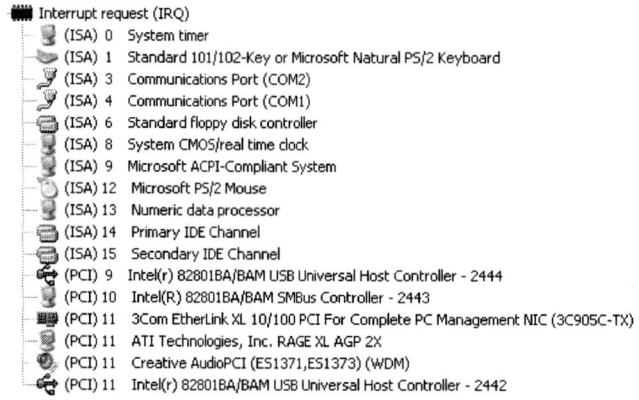

Figure 3-13: *Typical IRQ settings.*

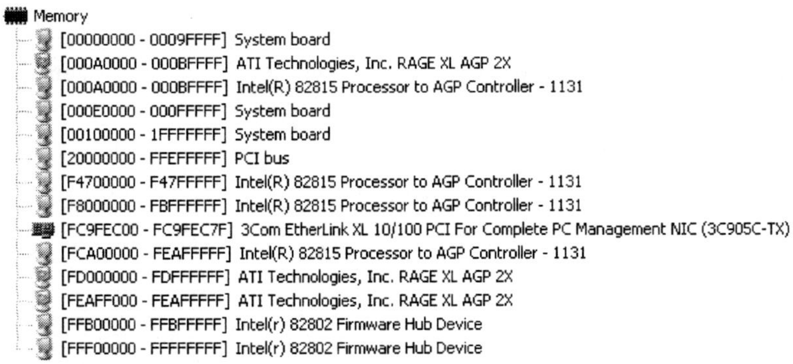

Memory
[00000000 - 0009FFFF] System board
[000A0000 - 000BFFFF] ATI Technologies, Inc. RAGE XL AGP 2X
[000A0000 - 000BFFFF] Intel(R) 82815 Processor to AGP Controller - 1131
[000E0000 - 000FFFFF] System board
[00100000 - 1FFFFFFF] System board
[20000000 - FFEFFFFF] PCI bus
[F4700000 - F47FFFFF] Intel(R) 82815 Processor to AGP Controller - 1131
[F8000000 - FBFFFFFF] Intel(R) 82815 Processor to AGP Controller - 1131
[FC9FEC00 - FC9FEC7F] 3Com EtherLink XL 10/100 PCI For Complete PC Management NIC (3C905C-TX)
[FCA00000 - FEAFFFFF] Intel(R) 82815 Processor to AGP Controller - 1131
[FD000000 - FDFFFFFF] ATI Technologies, Inc. RAGE XL AGP 2X
[FEAFF000 - FEAFFFFF] ATI Technologies, Inc. RAGE XL AGP 2X
[FFB00000 - FFBFFFFF] Intel(r) 82802 Firmware Hub Device
[FFF00000 - FFFFFFFF] Intel(r) 82802 Firmware Hub Device

Figure 3-14: *Typical Memory settings.*

Example: Resource Settings for COM1

Figure 3-15 shows the default resource settings for COM1. These include the IRQ, I/O Address and Memory Address. This device does not use DMA.

Communications Port (COM1) Properties
General
Port Settings
Driver
Resources
Communications Port (COM1)
Resource settings:
Resource type
Setting
I/O Range
03F8 - 03FF
IRQ
04
I/O Address
IRQ
Setting based on:
Current configuration
Use automatic settings
Change Setting...
Conflicting device list:
No conflicts.
OK
Cancel

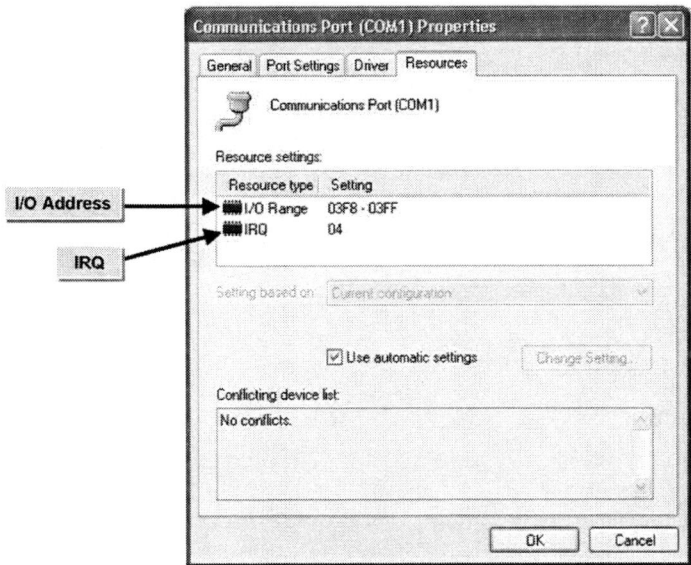

Figure 3-15: *Resource settings for COM1.*

Technician's Toolkit

Definition:

A technician's toolkit is a set of tools that the technician is likely to need to work on hardware. The tools should be demagnetized. Some sort of case for holding all of the hardware should be used.

All toolkits should include the following tools:

- Phillips screwdrivers (small and large, #0 and #1)
- Flat-blade screwdrivers (small and large, eighth inch and three-sixteenth inch)
- Torx driver (size T15)
- Tweezers
- Container for screws
- Nut driver
- Three-prong retriever

Some toolkits might also contain:

- Chip extractor
- Additional sizes of drivers and screwdrivers
- Ratchets
- Chip inserter
- Allen wrenches
- Cotton swabs
- Batteries
- Multimeter
- Anti-static cleaning wipes
- Canister of compressed air
- Anti-static wrist band
- Flashlight
- Mini vacuum
- Pen knife
- Clamp
- Soldering iron and related supplies
- Spare parts container
- Pen and/or pencil
- Notepaper or sticky-notes

Example: A Basic Toolkit

Figure 3-16 shows an example of the minimum tools you should include in your toolkit.

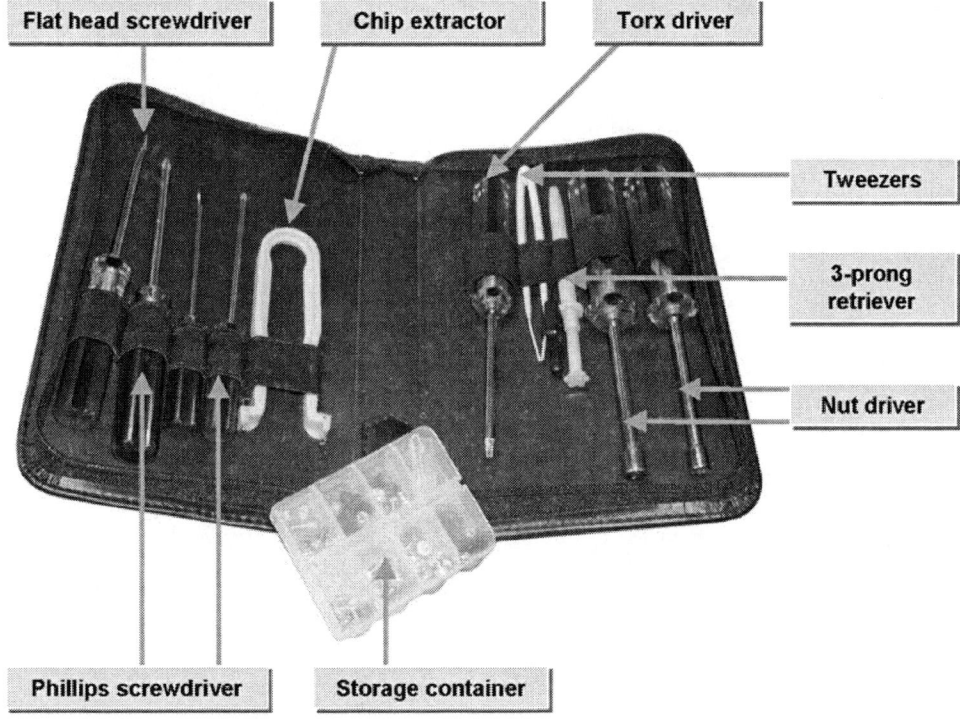

Figure 3-16: *A basic toolkit.*

How to Install an Adapter Card

Procedure Reference: Install an Internal Adapter Card

To install an internal adapter card:

1. Determine unused IRQ, DMA, and I/O Addresses that can be assigned to the card if needed. You can use the Device Manager in Control Panel to print a list of the resources by choosing ViewResources By Type.

     After printing out this report, you can use it when you need to configure system components so that you can avoid conflicts with other components already in the system.

2. Referring to your system documentation for the procedure, remove the system cover and access the slots on the system board.

3. Remove the slot cover from an empty slot. Traditionally, slot covers are secured by a screw to the chassis, but some newer ones slide out or are punched out of the metal case. Save the slot cover so that if you decide to remove the adapter card later, you can replace the slot cover. This will help keep dust and dirt out of the computer and help with regulation of the operating temperature.

   You should consider installing the card in the slot furthest from the opening. This will make it easier to install additional cards in the future.

4. If card resources are set with DIP switches or jumpers, configure the card prior to installing it into the system.

5. Holding the card where there are no metal contacts (by the upper edge), firmly press the card into the slot. ISA slots are black with two areas of gold contacts, about 5.5 inches long. PCI slots are white and about 3.5 inches long. In some instances, it might help to align the bottom tab of the card before inserting the card into the slot.

6. Secure the card to the chassis with the screw from the slot cover (or another screw if the slot cover was not screwed to the case). Normally, you would now secure the cover back on to the system, but since we will be working inside the system for the rest of the chapter, we will leave it off.

7. Configure the card for the system by installing any drivers required for operation. If the card resources are configured through software, configure DMA, I/O Addresses, or interrupts as required.

8. Verify that the card is functioning properly. You can use Device Manager to view the properties for the port or device. You can also check for IRQ, I/O Addresses, or DMA conflicts as well.

TOPIC C
Install a Network Adapter and Cable

You have now installed internal adapter cards in systems. One of the cards you will frequently be asked to install is a network card. In this topic, you will install a network adapter and connect the appropriate cable to it.

Today most business systems are networked. In more and more homes, users want to connect multiple systems into home networks and connect to the Internet through broadband. In all of these cases, the connection is made through a network card and cable. Users who can't quickly and easily connect to the network or Internet will be placing service calls to you, so you need to know how to get users connected as quickly as possible.

Networks

Definition:

A network is a collection of hardware and software that enables computers in a group to communicate with each other. It enables users to share resources. The hardware needed to network computers includes the components found in the following table.

Component	Definition
Server	Any computer that makes resources available to other computers on the network.
Client	Any computer that uses the resources of a server.
Media	The physical means of communication between network computers. This is often a special cable, infrared transmission, or radio signals.
Network adapter	A network adapter card installed in each of the computers on the network to enable the computers to send and receive data over the network medium. Each network adapter card has an address burned into the card which is referred to as the MAC address. It uniquely identifies that network card from any other network card.

The media and network adapter vary based on the physical network. They must be compatible with each other and with the computer. The server and client can each be dedicated machines or the computers can act as either a client or a server or both. The network adapter can have an interface to a specific media, or it might have interfaces to connect to several network medias.

The software needed to network computers includes server and client software. The network adapter requires drivers. *Network protocols* configure how the network computers communicate. All of the software and hardware working together provides users with network access. Some operating systems require separate client software and others have built-in client commands used to access network resources. Each of the required components varies based on the equipment used and the needs of the users.

 Another term you might encounter when talking about networks is node. This refers to any of the devices that can be accessed on the network.

Example: Components of a Basic Network

The most basic network is composed of two computers, two network adapter cards, and a cable between them. The Windows XP operating system software can act as both the client and the server software. This is shown in Figure 3-17.

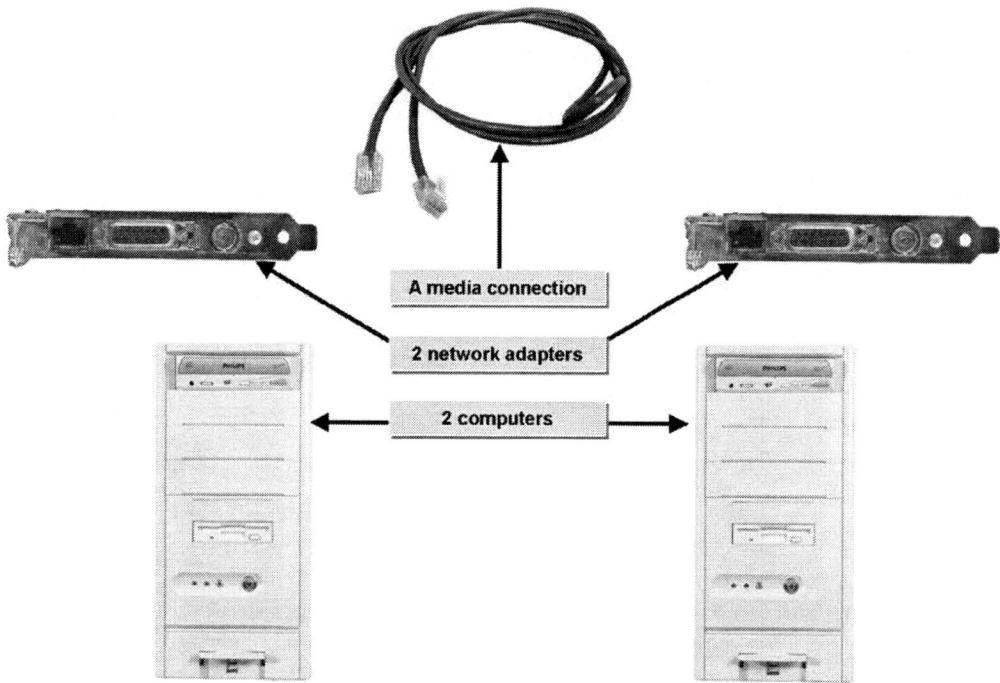

Figure 3-17: *Components of a basic network.*

Network Cables and Connectors

Definition:

Network cables and connectors are the media that are used to establish bounded media connections between clients and servers or Internet resources. Bounded media is any cable and connector system that is not a wireless connection method.

Network cables and connectors vary by:

- The gauge of the wires used in the cable.
- The number of wires used in the cable.
- The relationship of the wires to each other and the rest of the cable construction.
- Whether shielding is used in the cable to prevent or limit interference.
- The connectors used on the cable.
- The maximum length a cable segment can be.
- The cost of the cable.

Example: Twisted Pair Cables

> *Twisted-pair cable* consists of two independently insulated 22- to 26-gauge wires twisted around one another. Examples of RJ45 connectors on twisted pair cables are shown in Figure 3-18. Twisted-pair is the least expensive type of LAN cable, and has a maximum cable length of 100 meters. The twisted pair cables end with an RJ-45 connector.

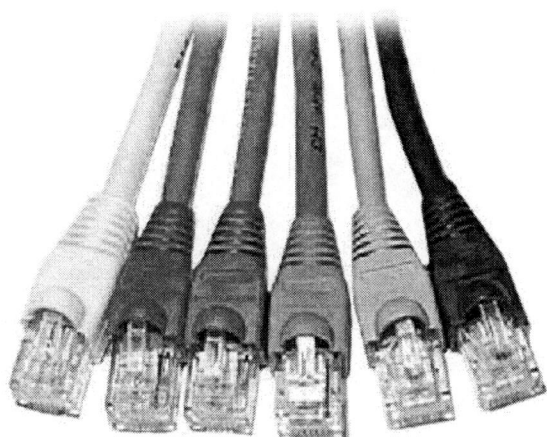

> **Figure 3-18:** *RJ-45 connectors on twisted-pair cables.*

Twisted Pair Cable

Definition:

> Twisted pair cable is a LAN cable that can be used to connect computers into a network. One wire carries the signal while the other wire is grounded and absorbs signal interference. In LAN cables, several sets of twisted-pair wires are wrapped in one protective outer layer. There are two types of twisted pair cabling:
>
> - *UTP* (unshielded twisted-pair) cable has two unshielded wires twisted around each other. Because shielding is omitted, the price is low, but electrical interference can cause a problem.
> - *STP* (shielded twisted-pair) cable is a twisted-pair cable that is wrapped in a metal sheath to provide extra protection from external interfering signals. This is commonly used in Token Ring networks. STP uses specialized connectors, including the IBM Data Connector (IDC) and the Universal Data Connector (UDC).

Example:

> Unshielded twisted-pair cable is what is most commonly used in LANs and home networks. It is composed of four sets of two wires each.
>
> Figure 3-19 shows the wires inside a UTP cable. Notice that each pair of wires is twisted around each other. One is a solid color wire and the other has a stripe of that same color. The connector has not yet been installed on this cable. It will have an RJ-45 connector crimped onto it before it is ready for use.

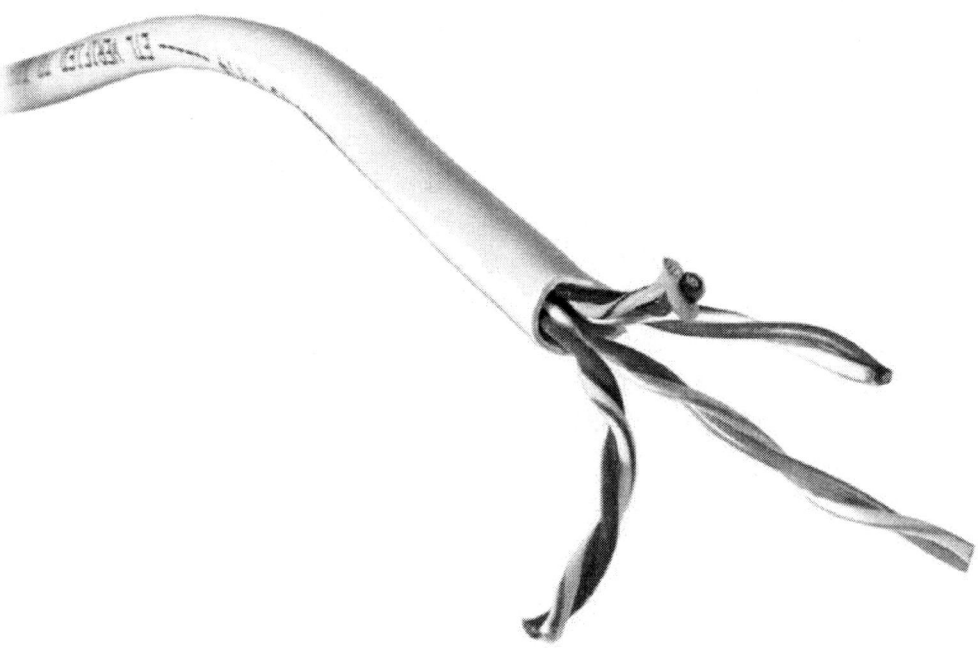

Figure 3-19: *UTP cable.*

Categories of Twisted Pair Cabling

Cable categories with lower numbers have a lower data transmission rate, while cable categories with a higher number support a higher transmission rate. The following table briefly describes the different cable categories.

 As standards for twisted-pair cabling developed, they were given category numbers. Category 5 is the most recent standard for high-quality, reliable cable.

Category	Usage	Speed	Description
1	Voice only	Not applicable	Traditional telephone cable.
2	Voice and data	Up to 4 Mbps	Usually includes four twisted-pair wires.
3	Voice and data	Up to 10 Mbps	Usually includes four twisted-pair wires, at three twists per foot.
4	Voice and data	Up to 16 Mbps	Usually includes four twisted-pair wires.

Category	Usage	Speed	Description
5	Voice and data	Up to 100 Mbps	Usually includes four twisted-pair copper wires.
5e	Voice and data	Up to 1 Gbps	Usually includes four twisted-pair copper wires.
6	Voice and data	Up to 1.2 Gbps (possible theoretical speeds of up to 2.5 Gbps)	Usually includes four twisted-pair copper wires.
7	Voice and data	Projected up to 4 to 10 Gbps	Under development, but expected to include four shielded twisted-pair copper wires.

Cat-5 (Category 5) describes network cabling that consists of four twisted-pairs of copper wire terminated by RJ-45 connectors. Cat-5 can be used for Token Ring, 1000BaseT, 100BaseT, and 10BaseT networking.

Coaxial Cables

Definition:

Coaxial cable is a network cable that consists of a single conductor which is surrounded by insulation and a conductive shield, with a heavy protective covering over the shield. The shield is usually a braided wire that is connected to an electrical ground and prevents the cable from picking up or emitting electrical noise. Coax cable is more expensive than standard phone wires, but it can carry much more data and is more resistant to interference. Cable TV companies now use the same coax cable that brings cable stations into a home to bring in a high-speed Internet connection.

Example:

Figure 3-20 shows a coaxial RG58 cable with a solid core.

Figure 3-20: *Coaxial cable.*

Coaxial Cable Grades

There are several grades of coaxial cables. These are referred to as Radio Guide or RG. The following table describes some of the common grades you might encounter.

Chapter 3: Installing or Removing Internal Hardware

Radio Grade	Description
RG6	Used for surveillance cameras and other video devices.
RG8	52 ohm cable used for thicknet Ethernet networks.
RG58	50 ohm cable used for thinnet Ethernet networks. RG58/U uses a stranded copper wire core. RG58A/U uses a solid copper core wire.
RG59	75 ohm cable used for cable television (CATV).
RG62	93 ohm cable used for ARCNET networks.

Coaxial Cable Connectors

Definition:

Coaxial cable connectors are connectors that are designed specifically for connecting coaxial cables to computers and other network devices to create a network. The connectors need to be able to reach through the plastic sheathing, the shielding, and any other layers to reach the core in order to make the connection to the network. The type of connector varies based on which type of coaxial cable is in use. The connector connects to the cable in various ways depending on which connector is needed. All coax cable requires termination at each end to prevent signal bounce.

Example: BNC Connectors

BNC connectors (British Naval Connector or Bayonet Nut Connector) are used to join coaxial cables like RG58 A/U into a network. This connector is also used for cable TV and cable modem connections. Each cable end has a male BNC connector with a center pin connected to the center cable conductor and a metal tube connected to the outer cable shield. A rotating ring outside the tube locks the cable to any female connector. T-connectors are female devices for connecting two cables to a network interface card (NIC), and a BNC barrel connector allows two cables to be connected. Figure 3-21 shows BNC connectors used connecting coaxial cables. The object on the left is the barrel connector, the object in the center is the BNC connector, and the object on the right is the T-connector. If the T-connector is at the end of a cable segment, then a terminator is needed on the end that doesn't connect to another cable.

Figure 3-21: *BNC connectors.*

Example: AUI Connectors

RG8 or thicknet cables connect using Attachment Unit Interface connectors (AUI). This is a 15-pin female connector. The network card shown in Figure 3-22 shows an AUI connection (along with twisted pair and BNC connections).

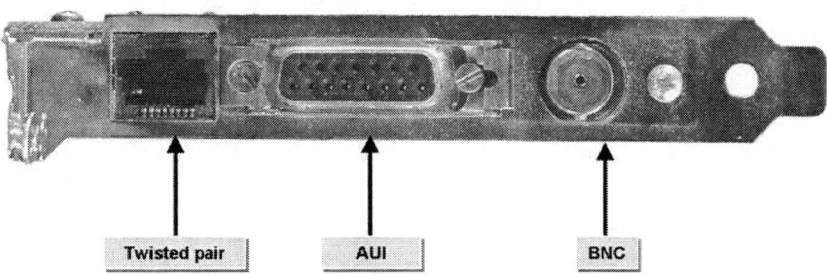

Figure 3-22: *Twisted pair, AUI, and BNC network connections.*

Backbone Cables

The portion of the network that links all of the other portions of the network together is referred to as the backbone. This is usually a more robust and more expensive cable solution that can carry more data.

An example of cable used in backbones is shown in Figure 3-23. All *fiber-optic cable* consists of a number of substructures including:

- A core of glass, ranging from 50 micrometers (m) to 1,000 m in diameter, which carries the light.
- Cladding surrounds the core, bends the light, and confines it to the core.
- Substrate layer of glass (in some fibers) surrounds the cladding, does not carry light, and adds to the diameter and strength of the fiber.
- Primary buffer coating surrounds all the other layers and provides the first layer of mechanical protection.

Chapter 3: Installing or Removing Internal Hardware

- Secondary buffer coating surrounds the primary buffer coating, while protecting the relatively fragile primary coating and the underlying fiber.

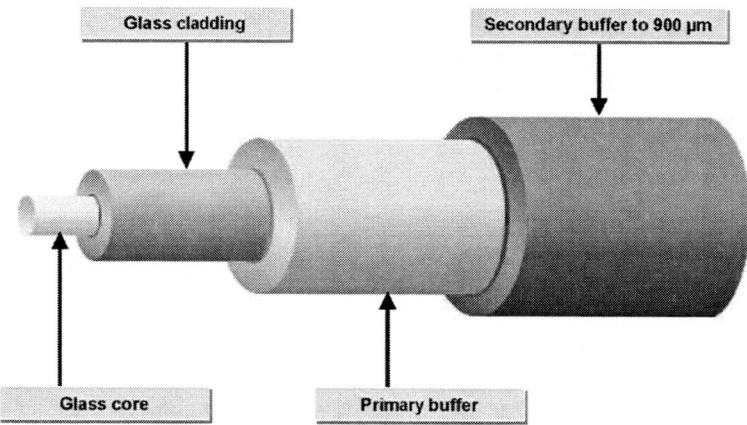

Figure 3-23: *A single fiber-optic strand.*

Fiber optic cables can be single-mode. This is shown in Figure 3-23. Fiber optic cables can also be multi-mode in which several 50-micron to 100-micron strands make up the cable and carry multiple paths through the cable.

Fiber optic cables are connected to the network using either ST or SC connectors. ST connectors are of a similar construction to BNC connectors and SC connectors are similar construction to RJ-45 connectors.

PVC and Plenum Cables

Many cables contain polyvinyl chloride (PVC), a plastic used to make the insulation in cables. PVC is flexible, making cable made with it easy to install. However, when PVC burns, it creates poisonous gases. National and local fire codes regulate where PVC cables can exist in a building. One place they cannot run is within the plenum. A *plenum* is an air-handling space (part of the heating/cooling system) and is often a convenient place to run cables. Figure 3-24 shows examples of where PVC and plenum cables should be used.

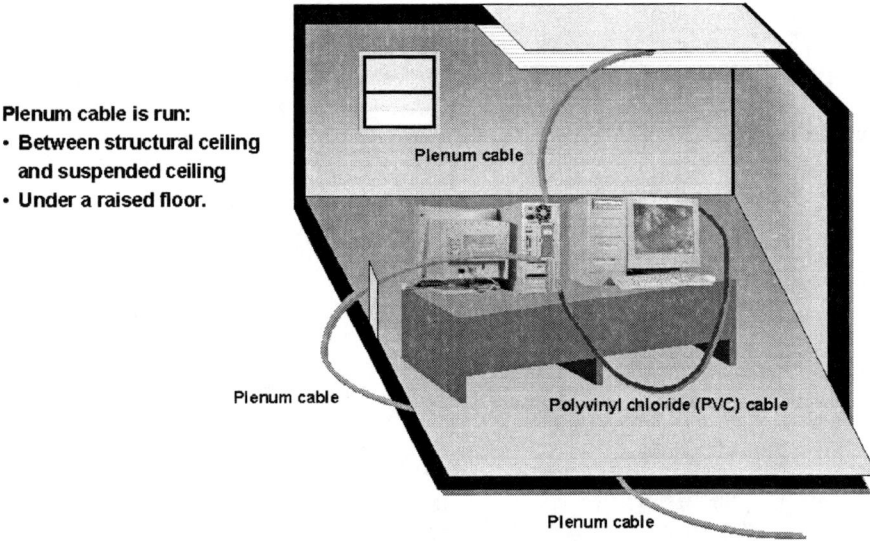

Plenum cable is run:
- Between structural ceiling and suspended ceiling
- Under a raised floor.

Figure 3-24: *Examples of locations for PVC and plenum cables.*

Because poisonous gases and flames can spread quickly throughout the building via the plenum, a special cable must be used. *Plenum cable*, which gets its name from the plenum space, has special materials in the insulation layers that make it fire resistant. When plenum cable burns, it produces a minimal amount of smoke and chemical fumes.

Network Protocols

A network protocol is responsible for formatting the data packets that are sent between computers on a network. In order for two computers to communicate over a network, they must have a network protocol in common. Windows 9x, Windows NT, and Windows 2000 support the TCP/IP, NWLink IPX/SPX, and NetBEUI network protocols. Windows XP supports the TCP/IP and NWLink IPX/SPX network protocols. Macintosh networks use the AppleTalk protocol.

IP Address

Definition:
> An IP Address is a series of four numbers that you assign to a computer on a TCP/IP network. These four numbers will look something like this: 192.168.200.200. The IP address must consist of four numbers, separated by periods. Each number can be from 0 to 255, with the exception that the first number in the series cannot be 0. In addition, all four numbers cannot be 0 (0.0.0.0) or 255 (255.255.255.255).

Analogy:

An IP address is like a mailing address. A portion of the numbers in the IP address identifies the network on which a computer resides, just as a person's mailing address uses a street name to identify the street on which they live. The other portion of the numbers in the IP address uniquely identify the computer on the network, just as the house number uniquely identifies a specific house on a street. So, just as your mailing address consists of both a street name and a house number, so does an IP address consist of numbers to identify the network and numbers to identify the computer on the network.

Example:

In Figure 3-25, you see an example of an IP address with the network and computer portions of the address labeled.

Figure 3-25: *An IP Address.*

 You can think of the street as being 192.168.200 and the last octet is the house number. In this case, house number 200.

Subnet Mask

Definition:

A subnet mask is a series of four numbers that the computer uses to determine how many of the four numbers in the IP address are being used to specify the computer's network address. A subnet mask typically looks like this: 255.255.0.0. The first number of the subnet mask must be 255; the remaining three numbers can be any of the following numbers:

- 255
- 252
- 248
- 240
- 224
- 192
- 128
- 0

Where you see a number other than zero in the subnet mask, you can determine that the number in the same position in the IP address is part of the computer's network address. For example, if the computer's IP address is 192.168.200.200 and the subnet mask is 255.255.255.0, the numbers in the subnet mask tell you that the first three numbers in the IP address are being used to identify the network on which the computer resides. Likewise, where you see a zero in the subnet mask, this tells you that the number in the same position in the IP address is being used to identify the computer itself.

Example:

In Figure 3-26, you see an example of a subnet mask. The subnet mask is 255.255.255.0, which means that the first three numbers in the computer's IP address are being used to identify the network on which the computer resides.

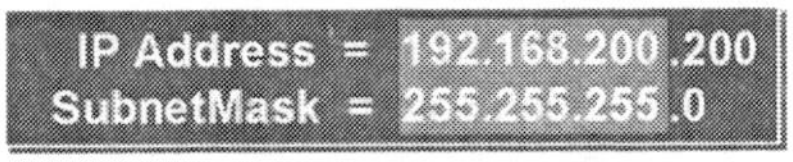

```
IP Address  = 192.168.200.200
SubnetMask  = 255.255.255.0
```
The network address is 192.168.200

Figure 3-26: *A subnet mask.*

TCP/IP

Definition:

TCP/IP is a non-proprietary, routable network protocol suite that enables computers to communicate over a network, including the Internet. (A protocol is called routable if it is able to communicate across routers.) The TCP/IP protocol is the foundation for the Internet. When you install TCP/IP, you must configure the following properties:

- *IP address*—A number composed of four octets that uniquely identify the network on which the computer is installed and the computer itself. The octets are separated by decimals which makes the number known as decimal dotted notation.
- *Subnet mask*—Four numbers used to identify how much of the IP address is being used to identify the network on which the computer is installed.

You might optionally be called upon to configure the following properties for TCP/IP:

- *Default gateway* address—This is the IP address of a router on the network. The computer uses this address to access computers on the other side of the router.

- Preferred and alternate DNS server addresses—Computers use the DNS server address(es) to enable users to access network or Internet resources by name instead of IP address.
- One or more Windows Internet Naming System (WINS) server addresses—Computers use the WINS server address to access Microsoft Windows network resources by name.

Example:

In Figure 3-27, you find an example of the required and some of the optional TCP/IP configuration properties.

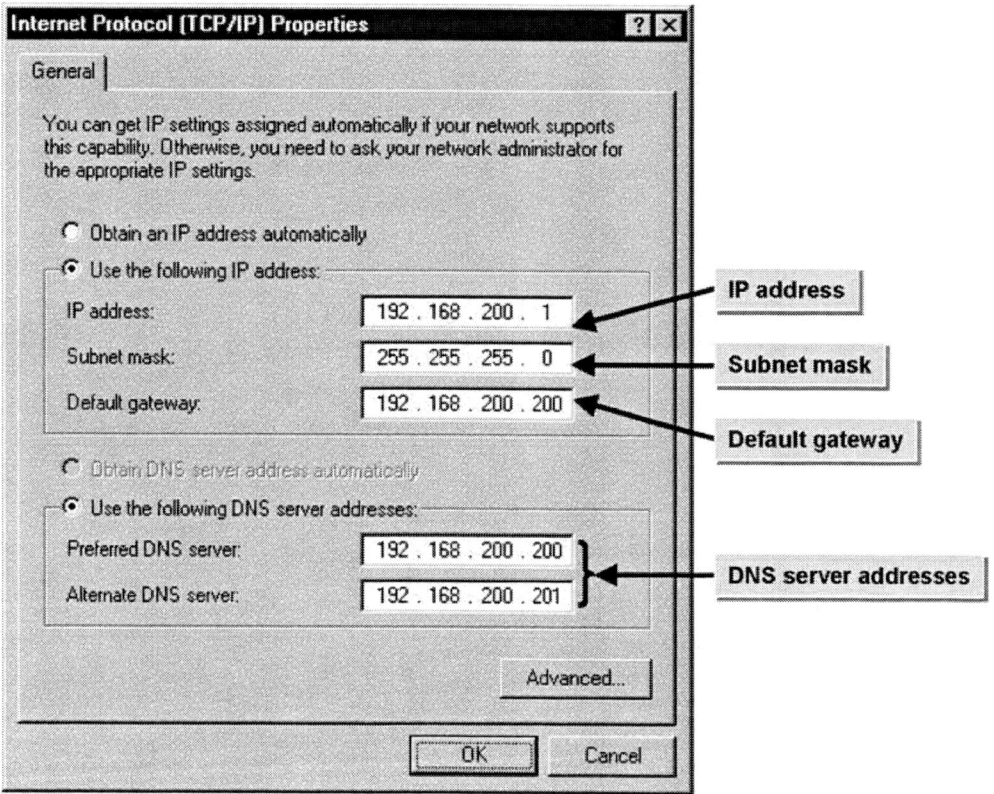

Figure 3-27: *TCP/IP configuration properties.*

Name Servers

On a TCP/IP-based network and even the Internet, you connect to computers by using their names, not their IP addresses. For example, you connect to a computer on your network by using a name such as 2000srv; on the Internet, you connect to computers by using names such as **www.cnn.com**. In order for you to communicate with another computer, however, your computer must know that computer's IP address. There are two ways computers find the IP addresses for specific computer names: *Domain Name System (DNS)* and *Windows Internet Naming System (WINS)* servers. These servers contain databases that consist of computer names and their associated IP addresses.

You'll sometimes hear computer names referred to as host names. This terminology is used with DNS. With WINS, finding computer resources by name is referred to as LMHosts.

Automatic TCP/IP Configuration Methods

Windows 2000 and Windows XP support two methods for automatically assigning IP addresses to computers: by using a *Dynamic Host Configuration Protocol (DHCP)* server or by using *Automatic Private IP Addressing*. Windows NT supports automatic IP address assignment only through a DHCP server. Table 3-1 describes each of these configuration methods. Using an automatic TCP/IP configuration method reduces your workload because you won't have to manually assign an IP address and subnet mask to each computer you configure with TCP/IP.

Table 3-1: *Automatic TCP/IP Configuration Methods*

Method	Description
DHCP Server	A server that a network administrator configures with a pool of IP addresses (along with other IP addressing information such as the subnet mask, default gateway, and so on) to assign to clients.
APIPA (Automatic Private IP Addressing)	A service that automatically configures a computer with an IP address on the 169.254.0.0 network. For example, this service might configure a computer with the IP address of 169.254.217.5.

Network Architectures

Definition:

Network architecture is the resource access model that determines how networked computers are used. The architecture specifies which computers can provide resources to other computers on the network. Resources that can be accessed include printers, drives, and any other shared resources. The networked computers can be a client, a server, or both. Some architectures are better for small groups of computers. The architecture specifies whether network control is centralized or not. The network architecture can be implemented using the following physical layout or *physical topologies*.

Physical Topology	Description
Star	All nodes individually connect to a central device.
Bus	A single main cable called the bus or backbone carries all network data. Nodes connect directly to the bus.

Chapter 3: Installing or Removing Internal Hardware

Physical Topology	Description
Ring	All nodes are connected in a continuous loop. Nodes relay information around the loop in a round-robin manner.
Mesh	Each node has a direct connection to all other nodes on the network, providing dedicated, permanent, point-to-point communication paths.
Hybrid	Two or more of the other basic physical topologies are combined.

Example: Peer-to-Peer Network Architecture

In a *peer-to-peer network*, any computer can act as both a server and a client. Any computer can share resources with another, and any computer can use the resources of another if given access rights to the resource. This architecture is best suited for less than 10 computers. It is commonly used for small offices, home offices, or departmental workgroup needs. A peer-to-peer network is depicted in Figure 3-28. In this example, they are using a star topology.

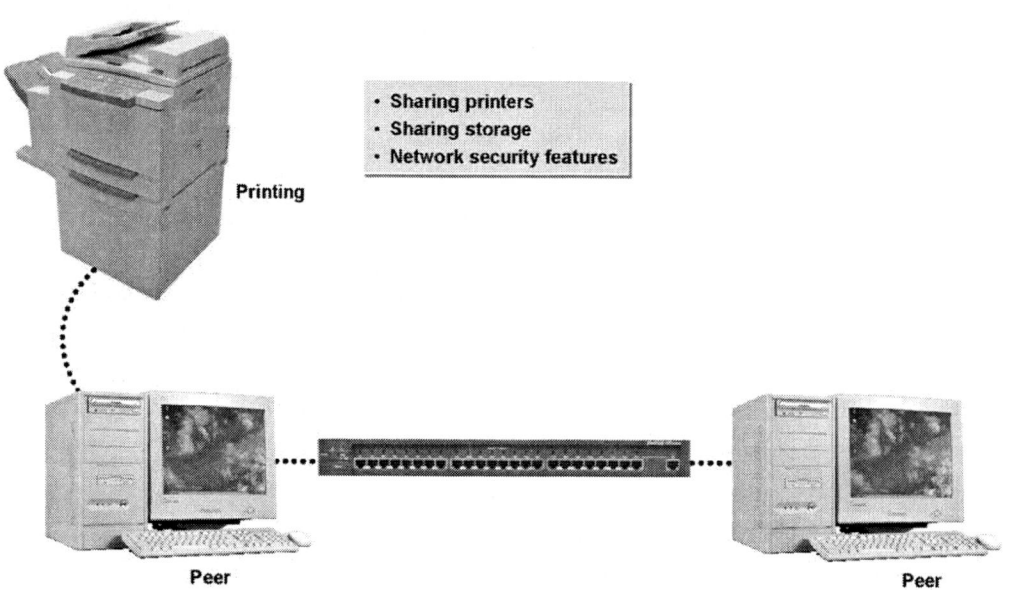

Figure 3-28: *A peer-to-peer network.*

Example: Client-server Network Architecture

In a *client-server network*, at least one centralized server manages shared resources and security for the other network users and computers. Generally, the network servers are not used as clients; they are dedicated to their network services and are usually physically secured by being locked in a server room to prevent casual access. A client-server network is depicted in Figure 3-29. In this example, they are using a star topology.

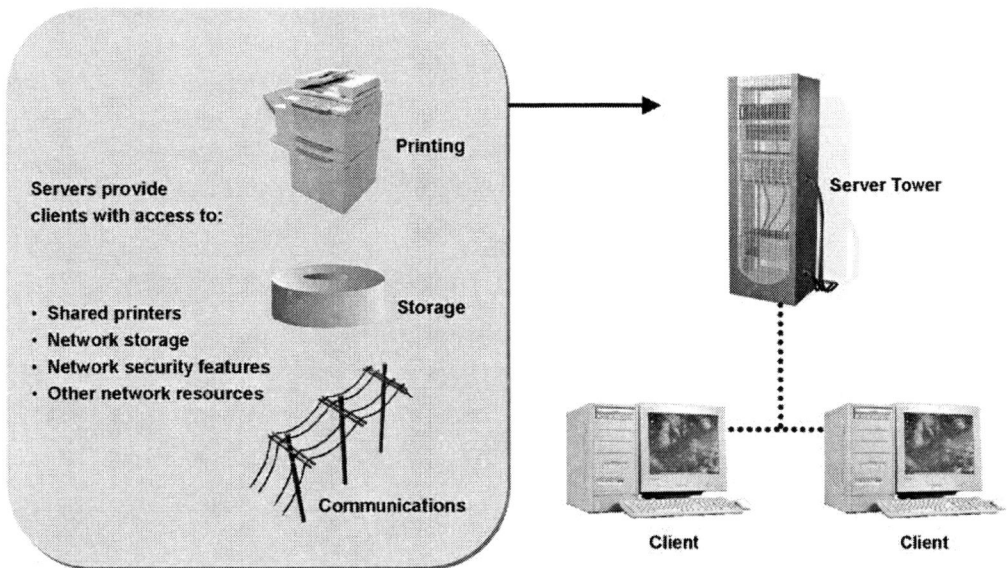

Figure 3-29: *A client-server network.*

Internet Connections

Definition:

An Internet connection is a connection between a client computer and servers that enable users to access services on computers throughout the world. All Internet connections:

- Use the TCP/IP network protocol.
- Require a unique IP address for each node.
- Require an Internet Service Provider (ISP) to connect to the Internet.

Internet connections vary in that:

- They can be established using different connection methods. These include:
    — Local Area Network (LAN)
    — Digital Subscriber Link (DSL)
    — Cable
    — Integrated Services Digital Network (ISDN)
    — Dial-up
    — Satellite

- Wireless
- Require different hardware based on which connection method is being used.
- The speed at which files are transferred. This also varies between files being uploaded and downloaded in some connection methods.
- How many computers can be connected through a single ISP connection. On the customer end of the connection, in some cases additional networking hardware can be used to share the connection to the ISP.

Example:

In Figure 3-30, the user is connecting to the Internet through a cable connection to their ISP. The ISP they are using provides both the Web hosting, mail, and Internet access as well as the physical connection to the Internet.

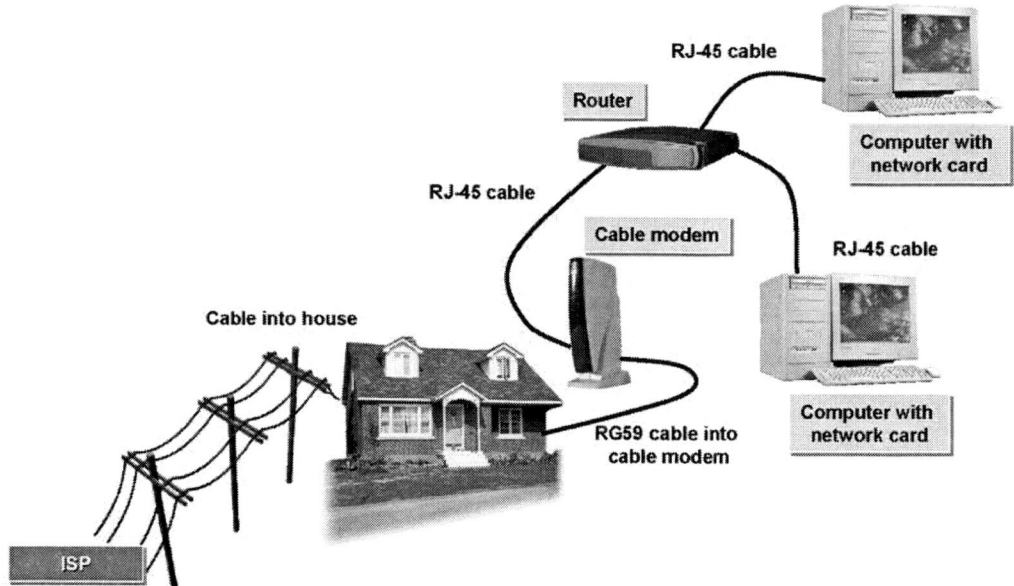

Figure 3-30: *A cable-based Internet connection.*

LAN Internet Connection

Definition:

A LAN Internet connection is an Internet connection that utilizes network hardware (server, media, and other necessary hardware), a router, and the TCP/IP protocol to establish a connection between a client and the Internet. LAN Internet connections are always on and available for use (unless the router goes down) and are relatively fast.

LAN Internet connections vary by:

- The network media used on the LAN.
- The servers on the LAN.

- The speed of the connection between the LAN and the Internet. Connections might be:
  - Dedicated 56 K digital connections. These older connections are being phased out, but in some areas they are still in use.
  - T1, T2, T3, or T4 connections. These are the four standard digital voice systems developed by AT&T. T1 is composed of 24 multiplexed voice channels for a bandwidth of 1.54 Mbps, T2 uses 96 channels for 6.312 Mbps, T3 uses 672 channels for 44.736 Mbps, and T4 uses 4,032 channels for 274.1 Mbps. These lines are leased from a telecommunications company. You can also subscribe to a portion of a T line; this is referred to as fractional T service.
  - Microwave satellite based. Uses a stationary satellite dish, usually placed on top of a building or other high area, that communicates with a satellite in outer space in a *geosynchronous* orbit with the planet.

Example:

Figure 3-31 shows an example of a LAN-based Internet connection. This example includes a T3 line for the Internet backbone. Big Co uses a T1 line to connect from its company Internet hardware to the Internet backbone. Employees also connect at their second location through a dedicated 56 K digital connection. Both of these locations are using the LAN to establish employees' connections from their desktop to the Internet.

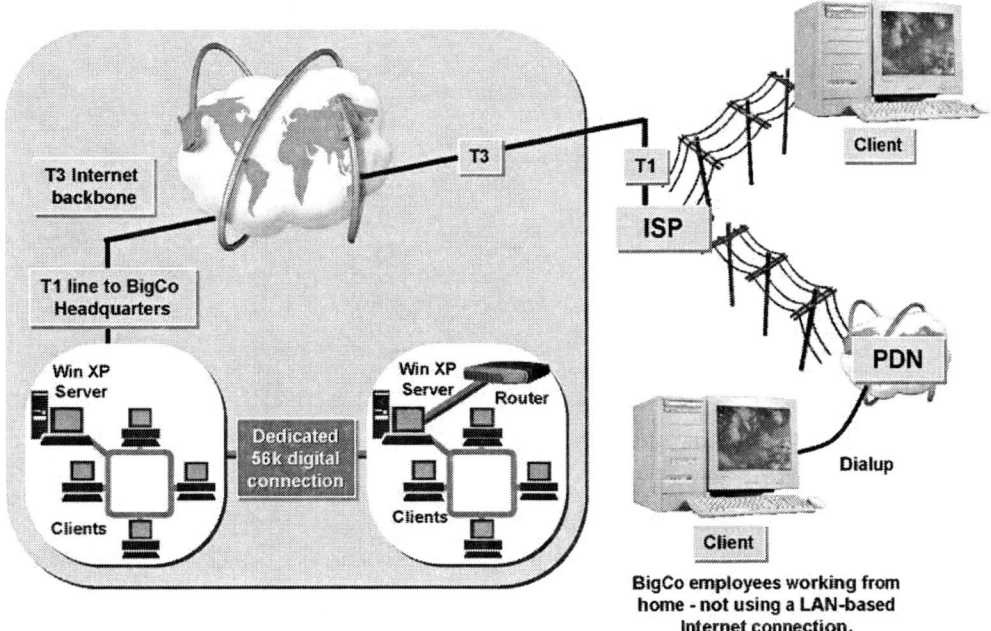

Figure 3-31: *Big Co's Internet connections.*

Non-Example:
> Employees can also dial in or connect to the Internet from home through their dial-up or cable connections, but they would not be using the LAN connection in that case. Figure 3-31 shows the employees' connections outside the LAN to the Internet.

DSL Internet Connections

Definition:
> Digital Subscriber Link (DSL) is an Internet connection method that uses standard copper phone wires and a transceiver. It carries voice and data traffic simultaneously over standard phone lines. The data portion remains connected all of the time. To use DSL, the customer must be within 5.5 km of the phone company central office where the DSL equipment is located unless a router or fiber optic cable is used to extend the distance.
>
> DSL varies by:
>
> - Splitter—A splitter may or may not be required at the customer location. The splitter is what enables the line to carry voice and data simultaneously. Several splitterless technologies have evolved. In splitterless technologies, the splitting is performed at the phone company central office. Splitterless is also known as G.Lite, DSL Lite, and Universal ADSL.
>
> - Data Rate—The closer the customer is to the phone company central office, the faster the data rate. Also a heavier gauge wire improves data rates.
>
> - Modulation Technologies—These vary based on the type of DSL in use. Discrete Multitone Modulation (DMT) is most commonly used. It divides the frequency range of the phone line into 256 different 4.3125 kHz channels. Other modulation techniques are Carrierless Amplitude Modulation (CAP) and Multiple Virtual Line (MVL) techniques.
>
> For a description of the modulation techniques, you can refer to **www.nextep.com.au/pdf/DSL_Modulation_Techniques.PDF**.
>
> - Upstream and downstream speeds—Some DSL connections are up to twice as fast at receiving information as they are at sending information. Other connections vary, but by a smaller degree. When the speeds vary like this, it is referred to as asymmetric since the speeds are not symmetrical to each other.

Example:
> Figure 3-32 shows a DSL Internet connection. This is a DSL connection that uses splitters in front of each phone that is used for voice communications. The location is within 5.5 km of the phone company central office, so the customer is able to use DSL. A DSL modem is placed between the phone outlet on the wall and the computer. Even though it is called a modem, it is really a transceiver since the signal is digital from end to end and needs no conversion from analog to digital and back.

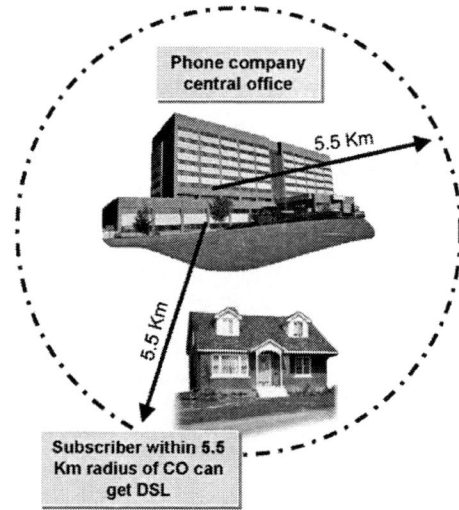

Figure 3-32: *DSL Internet connections.*

Cable Internet Connections

An Internet connection through a cable modem takes advantage of the cable television cable running through most neighborhoods. A splitter is installed on the cable line running into the house to split the TV channel traffic from the data traffic. A cable modem connects via an RG59 coaxial cable from the splitter to the cable modem on one side. The RJ-45 cable connects from the cable modem to the network card in the computer to complete the connections.

 For more information about how cable Internet connections work, refer to www.cabledatacomnews.com/cmic/cmic2.html.

ISDN Internet Connections

Integrated Services Digital Network (ISDN) connections were popular in some major metropolitan areas, but they have largely been replaced by cable and DSL connections. ISDN uses a single wire or fiber optic line to carry voice, data, and video signals. It uses existing phone company switches and wiring, which are upgraded to make a 64 Kbps end-to-end digital channel. Japan and North America use one standard; Europe uses another.

Basic Rate Interface (BRI) is most commonly used in residential ISDN connections. It is composed of two bearer (B) channels at 64 Kbps (used for voice and data) and one delta (D) channel at 16 Kbps (used for controlling the B channels and signal transmission). The total bandwidth is up to 144 Kbps. The two B channels can be bonded together at the phone company central office to provide 128 Kbps bandwidth. Frequently six channels are bonded for a 384 Kbps bandwidth.

Primary Rate Interface (PRI) is most commonly used between a Private Branch Exchange (PBX) at the customer's site and the phone company central office. It is composed of 23 B channels at 64 Kbps and one D channel at 64 Kbps. The total bandwidth is up to 1,536 Kbps. In both BRI and PRI, the D channel is used to reassign channels for voice, fax, and data as required.

In Europe, the BRI is the same as above, but the PRI is composed of 30 B channels and one D channel. The total bandwidth is up to 1,984 Kbps. A Network Terminal Interface (NT1) device is needed to connect your data or telephone equipment to the ISDN line. It provides connection terminal equipment (TE) and terminal adapter (TA) equipment to the phone company local loop. This is a coding and decoding device. It takes the place of a modem in an analog situation.

The TA replaces a modem. It is used to adapt ISDN BRI channels to RS-232 and V.35 standards. it can be a standalone device or an interface card that is installed in the computer, router, or PBX. You might also need other ISDN interfaces and ISDN LAN topology bridges.

Dial-up Internet Connections

A dial-up connection to the Internet is usually the least expensive method available. It uses an analog modem connected to a serial port on your computer and connects to the analog phone line. When the modem is in use, you cannot use that phone line for voice communications. It is limited to 56 Kbps.

Satellite Internet Connections

Definition:

> A satellite Internet connection is a connection to the Internet that uses satellite technology to establish and maintain the connection. All satellite connections require a satellite dish at your location as well as a service contract with a company that provides access to a satellite in geosynchronous orbit. The equipment required for a satellite connection is the satellite dish antennae which is placed outside, facing a southerly direction (for the United States). It also requires a satellite modem or transceiver and standard cable to connect between the modem and the PC's network card or USB port.
>
> Sending data, also known as uplink or upstream data, is slower than receiving data. It is usually in the 50 to 150 Kbps range. Receiving data is also referred to as downlink or downstream data. Downstream data is usually received in the 150 to 1,200 Kbps range. Speed can be affected by server limitations, the amount of traffic the satellite is handling, and file sizes. Heavy rain or snow can cause a poor signal. Solar interference in early spring and early fall when the sun and satellites align with each other briefly each day can also interfere with transmission.
>
> There is a certain degree of delay when using satellite transmissions. You have to wait while data is being transferred between your computer and the satellite. You also have an additional wait as the satellite provider receives your transmission at their network operations center (NOC) and then sends the request on to the Web site you are trying to access. This delay is referred to as *latency*.
>
> Satellite connections can be one-way or two-way. One-way satellite connections receive data via satellite but send data through a standard phone line. Two-way satellite connections receive and send data through the satellite connection and do not require a phone line. The FCC requires that two-way satellite systems be installed by a trained professional because they are transmitter devices. One-way systems can be installed by anyone.

Example:
> Figure 3-33 shows a two-way satellite Internet connection. The connection uses a small dish on the user's roof to both send and receive transmissions. The satellite provider's network operation center receives the requests and passes them on to the requested Web site servers.

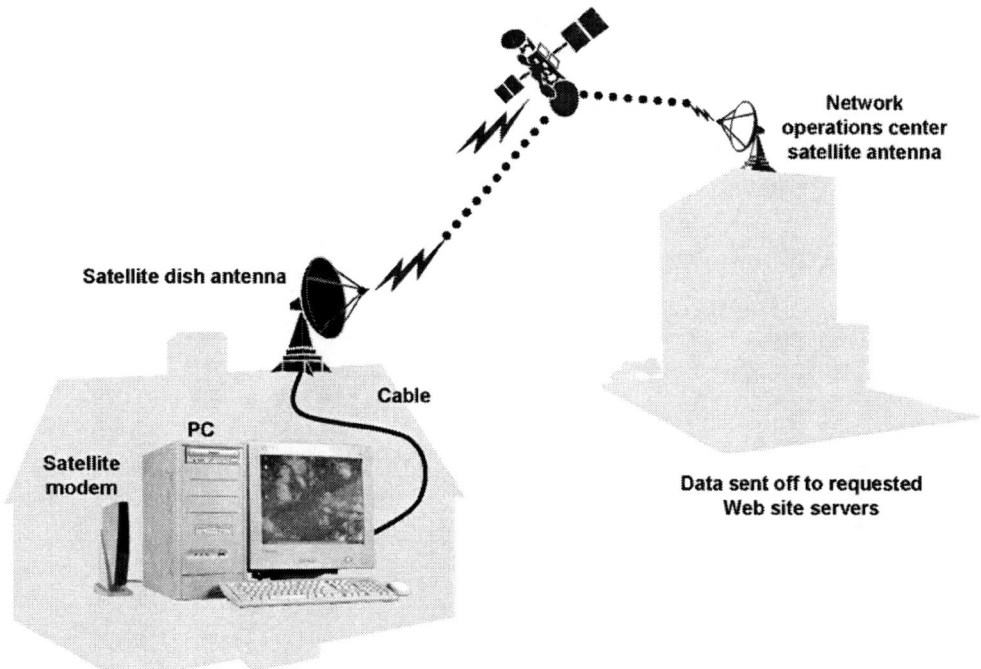

Figure 3-33: *A satellite Internet connection.*

A Wireless Internet Connection

A wireless Internet connection uses an antenna on a tower that broadcasts Internet signals. It is set up by a wireless ISP, or WISP. To access the signal, customers need to be within the range of the antenna—usually between 3 and 35 miles in circumference.

Customers place an antenna on their roof and connect a special wireless transceiver or modem to their PC to access the signal. Data rates of between 1.5 and 128 Mbps are available based on what the WISP has to offer. Obstructions between the two antennas degrade the signal strength and quality.

How to Install a Network Adapter

Procedure Reference: Install a Network Adapter

To install a network card:

1. Install the network card into the system.
2. If prompted, install drivers for the network card.

3. Connect the network cable from the wall or the hub to the network card.

4. Test the network card. You can open an Internet browser and access a Web site, or you can use the ping command to test connectivity to a host.

 A working network adapter will have two status indicator lights. One light will be on steadily, showing that the card is connected to the network. The other light will flash to indicate network activity.

Network Commands

Several command-line commands are available in Windows for testing and troubleshooting network connections. Some of the commands that you might find useful are shown in the following table.

Command	Syntax Examples	Description
ipconfig	`ipconfig /all`	Displays statistics about your network connection including IP address, subnet mask, and default gateway.
ping	`ping host`	A command that can be used to check connectivity between two IP-based devices.

TOPIC D
Install or Remove IDE Drives

You have installed several adapter cards at this point. Your system is equipped with a hard drive, but given the size of applications and the amount of data many users need to store, they might need additional disk space. In this topic, you will install an IDE drive into the system.

Users will often feel very comfortable installing and removing external peripherals. However, there are few users who are comfortable installing and removing internal components, especially drives. In most companies, you don't want users getting inside of their computers either. In many cases, this would void the warranty if unauthorized individuals do work on internal components. Therefore, it is important that you become proficient in working on internal devices such as drives.

Drives

Definition:

A drive is a computer component that stores data for the long term. Data is retained even if the power is turned off. All drives read data. The device can be read-only or have the ability to read and write data. All disk drives rotate very fast. All drives store data on some type of media. The drive media can be fixed or removable. There could be one or more surfaces that data can be stored on. There can be one or more read/write heads. The drive can be internal or external. The data can be stored magnetically or optically. Drives can be connected through different interfaces. Most devices enable you to randomly access a specific location, but others require sequential access to reach a specific location. The size or form factor of the drive is either 3.5 inches or 5.25 inches. The capacity of a drive is measured in the measurements shown in the following table.

Drives are also referred to as mass storage devices since they can store large amounts of data.

Measurement	Contains	Usually Used for Measuring Size Of
KB (kilobytes)	1,024 bytes	Floppy drives
MB (megabytes)	1,024 KB	CD and DVD, small hard drives, cartridge drives, small tape drives
GB (gigabytes)	1,024 MB	Hard drives, large-capacity cartridge drives, some tape drives
TB (terrabytes)	1,024 GB	Very large hard drives and some tape drives

Example: Floppy Drive

A floppy drive connects to the motherboard through a floppy-disk controller. It uses removable media. Data is stored magnetically. Data can be accessed directly rather than sequentially. These are read/write drives. These are internal drives. The form factor of this drive is usually 3.5 inches. Examples of a floppy drive and media are shown in Figure 3-34.

Front view 3.5 inch Floppy Drive

3.5 inch Floppy Disk

Figure 3-34: *Floppy drive.*

Chapter 3: Installing or Removing Internal Hardware

Example: Hard Drives

Hard drives connect to the motherboard through either an IDE or SCSI interface. These are fixed media that are not removed from the computer unless you are performing an upgrade or a repair. These are read/write drives and data is stored magnetically. Data can be accessed directly rather than sequentially. Traditionally, these are internal drives. You might encounter some that are external as well. These drives are usually 3.5 inches, but you might encounter some older 5.25-inch drives. Examples of hard drives are shown in Figure 3-35.

Figure 3-35: *A hard drive.*

Example: Optical Drives

Optical drives include CD-ROM, DVD-ROM, CD-R, CD-RW, and DVD-R. These can be connected via IDE, SCSI, USB, FireWire, or parallel interfaces. Data is stored optically. It is written using a laser to create pits in the reflective surface of the disk. The media is removable. CD-ROM and DVD-ROM drives are read-only. CD-R, CD-RW, and DVD-R drives are read/write. Data can be accessed directly rather than sequentially. These can be internal or external drives. These drives have a 5.25-inch form factor. Examples of optical drives and media are shown in Figure 3-36.

An external DVD drive

A CD-R disc

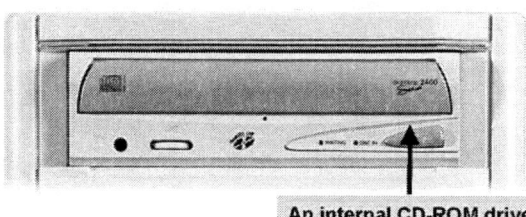
An internal CD-ROM drive

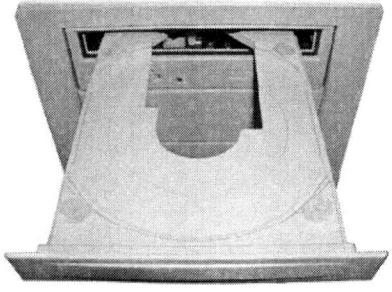

Figure 3-36: *Optical drives.*

Example: Cartridge Drives

Cartridge drives can be internal or external drives. They store data magnetically. They can be connected via IDE, SCSI, USB, FireWire, or parallel interfaces. The media is removable. These are read/write drives. Data can be accessed directly rather than sequentially. The form factor on these drives varies, but is usually a 5.25-inch form factor. Examples of cartridge drives and media are shown in Figure 3-37.

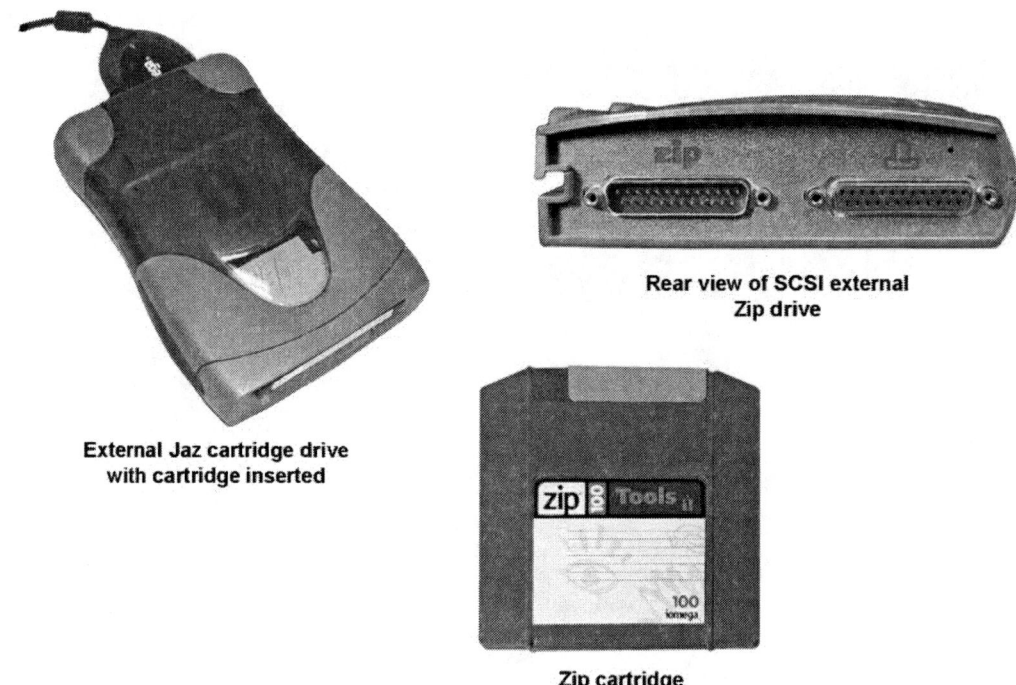

Figure 3-37: *Cartridge drives.*

Example: Tape Drives

Tape drives can be internal or external drives. They store data magnetically. They can be connected via IDE, SCSI, USB, FireWire, or parallel interfaces. The media is removable. These are read/write drives. Data must be read sequentially. The size of these drives varies, but is often a 5.25-inch form factor. Examples of a tape drive and media are shown in Figure 3-38.

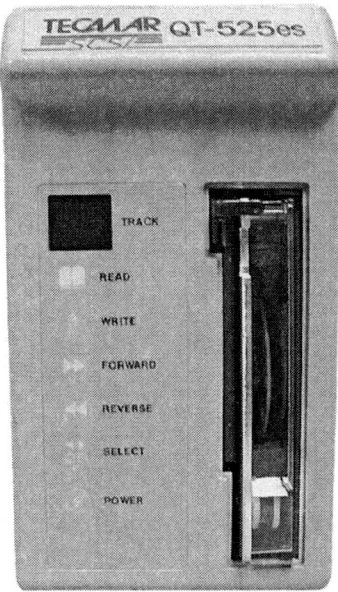

Figure 3-38: *Tape drive.*

Non-Example: RAM

RAM is not an example of a disk drive. The data is not retained if power is removed from the device.

Drive Bay

The location inside a system where drives are placed is referred to as a drive bay. These are either 3.5-inch or 5.25-inch wide openings that are tall enough to hold a drive. If you have a 3.5-inch drive and only have a 5.25-inch drive bay open, you can add rails to the drive to adapt it to fit the larger drive bay. Rails are usually included with the drive, but might need to be purchased separately in some instances. The drive slides into the bay and is secured to the chassis with screws. Align the holes in the side of the drive with one or more of the holes in the rail of the drive bay to secure the drive to the chassis.

Drives can be 3.5-inch or 5.25-inch drives. The top drive in Figure 3-39 is a 3.5-inch drive and the bottom drive is a 5.25-inch drive.

Figure 3-39: *Form factor.*

Disk Drive Architecture

The architecture of a hard drive is hidden from view behind the case of the drive. All of the components inside of a hard drive together are called the Head Disk Assembly (HDA). On the outside of the drive is the logic board that controls movement of internal components as well as controlling the flow of data to and from the drive. You should never open a drive, because any contamination from the air or dust would render the drive useless. We have opened a hard drive to show you the contents. Figure 3-40 shows the internal components of a hard drive.

The architecture includes the components displayed in the following table.

Component	Description
Platter	The disks on a spindle in the drive.
Read/write heads	The magnetic heads on the actuator arms that float just above and just below the platter.
Actuator arms	Arms from the drive motor that hold the read/write heads. The entire arm assembly moves together so all read/write heads move together.
Voice coil actuator	Actuator is a voice coil motor that moves the actuator arms that hold the read/write heads.
Spindle	Spindle holds the platters.
Spindle motor	Spins the platters.

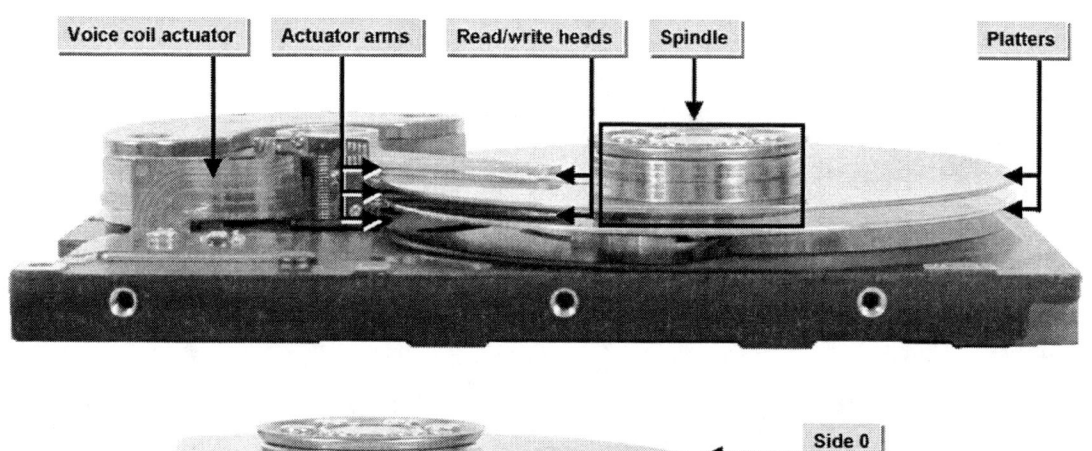
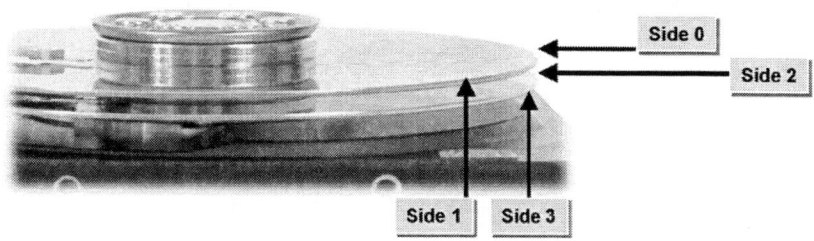

Figure 3-40: *Hard drive architecture.*

Disk Drive Geometry

The drive is divided up into sections so that data can be read and written as efficiently as possible. A drive with the geometry labeled is shown in Figure 3-41. The components that make up the disk geometry as this is referred to are shown in the following table.

Disk Drive Geometry Term	Description
Cylinder	The tracks that can be accessed on all platters without moving the read/write head. The tracks that make up a cylinder are all the same distance from the spindle.
Track	Concentric circles on a platter. Tracks are numbered from the outer edge in, beginning with Track 0.
Sector	Tracks are divided into smaller units. A sector is the smallest unit that can be written to. Traditionally these were pie-shaped units with the outer tracks able to hold more data per sector since they were bigger. This is shown in Figure 3-42. Zoned-bit recording is used on modern drives and divides the outer tracks into smaller segments so that they contain more sectors than inner tracks contain. This is shown in Figure 3-43.

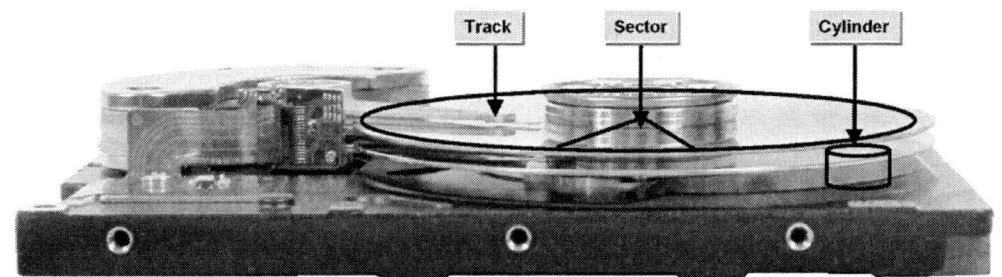

Figure 3-41: *Disk drive geometry.*

Figure 3-42: *Traditional sectors.*

Figure 3-43: *Zoned-bit recording sectors.*

Drive Interfaces

Definition:

A *drive interface* is the connection type between a drive and the computer system. There are two types of interfaces, but each has many variations. They are IDE and SCSI. The following table lists the features of each.

Interface	Features
Integrated Drive Electronics (IDE), also known as Advanced Technology Attachment (ATA)	Controller is built into the drive. Supports master and slave devices. Limited to two channels, each with up to two devices. Less expensive. If not automatically detected, must set drive type in system BIOS. Many updates with improvements in speed and reliability. ATA is the formal name chosen for the ANSI group X3T10. It specifies the interface specifications for the power and data signals between the motherboard, the drive controller, and the drive. The manufacturer can use any physical interface, but must have an embedded controller that uses the ATA interface controller to connect the drive directly to the ISA bus.
Small Computer System Interface (SCSI)	No controller, but is actually a separate bus within the computer system. Supports up to seven devices (15 devices in more recent versions). Must configure separate ID settings for each device. More expensive. May need to set system BIOS to no drive, and then configure SCSI software to recognize drive to boot from. Several variations on the interface.

Example: IDE or ATA

Figure 3-44 shows the IDE interface. The controller is built into the drive. The jumpers determine whether it is a master or slave drive.

IDE interface

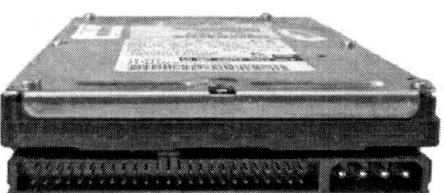
SCSI interface

Figure 3-44: *Drive interfaces.*

IDE was the original name for what became the ATA standard when ANSI standardized the specification. The following table describes the variations on the ATA standard. An example of a drive IDE interface is shown in Figure 3-44

IDE or ATA Standard Variations	Description
ATA-2	Also known as the Advanced Technology Interface with Extensions. Western Digital's implementation was called Enhanced IDE (EIDE). Seagate's implementation was called Fast ATA or Fast ATA-2. Faster data rate than ATA. Support for 32-bit transactions. Some drives supported DMA. Could implement power-saving mode features if desired. Specification also covered removable drives.
ATA-3	Minor enhancement to ATA-2. Improved reliability for high-speed data transfer modes. Self Monitoring Analysis And Reporting Technology (SMART) was introduced. This is logic in the drives that warns of impending drive problems. Password protection available as a security feature of the drives.
ATA-4	Also known as Ultra-DMA, UDMA, Ultra-ATA, and Ultra DMA/33. Doubled data transfer rates.
ATAPI	AT Attachment Packet Interface is an EIDE interface component that includes commands used to control tape and CD-ROM drives.
PIO	Programmed Input/Output is a data transfer method that includes the CPU in the datapath. Has been replaced by DMA and Ultra DMA.
DMA	Direct Memory Access is a data transfer method that moves data directly from the drive to main memory.
Ultra DMA	Transfers data in burst mode at a rate of 33.3 MB per second. The speed is two times faster than DMA.
Serial ATA	An emerging storage-interface standard that uses serial instead of parallel signaling technology for internal ATA and ATAPI devices. Serial ATA employs serial connectors and serial cables, which are smaller, thinner, and more flexible than traditional parallel ATA cables. Data transfer rates are 150 MB per second or greater.

Drive Controller

Definition:

The *drive controller* is the circuitry that enables the drive and CPU to communicate with each other. The controller circuitry is built onto the drive, and other drives are controlled by the host bus adapter.

Example:

An IDE drive includes the circuitry to control the drive. Figure 3-45 shows the controller circuitry on an IDE drive.

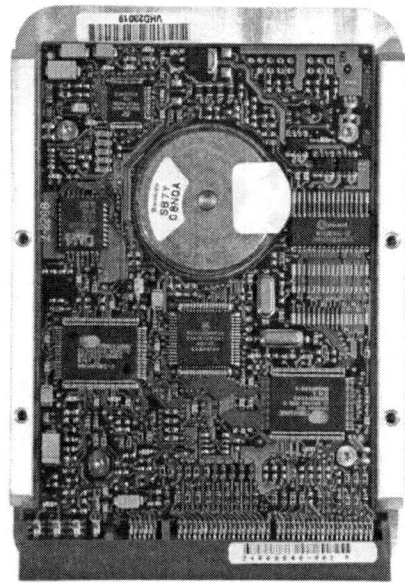

Figure 3-45: *IDE drive controller circuitry.*

IDE Drives

Definition:

An IDE drive is a mass storage device that connects to the motherboard through an IDE interface. These are internal drives. The IDE connection is on the motherboard. There are usually two IDE connections which can each connect two devices. You might need to set the drive type in CMOS. You will need to configure the first drive on each IDE channel as a master, and the other drive as a slave unless you use cable select. If you have IDE hard drives and other IDE drives, the hard drives should be on the first or primary channel and the other slower devices on the secondary channel.

The IDE hard drive uses jumpers to set whether the drive is the master, slave, or you are using cable select. The IDE interface cable connects to the drive on one end and to the IDE controller on the motherboard on the other end. Pin 1 of the data cable is marked with a colored stripe and is usually located closest to the power connection. The Berg power connector connects to the drive to power the drive. An example of an IDE hard drive is shown in Figure 3-46.

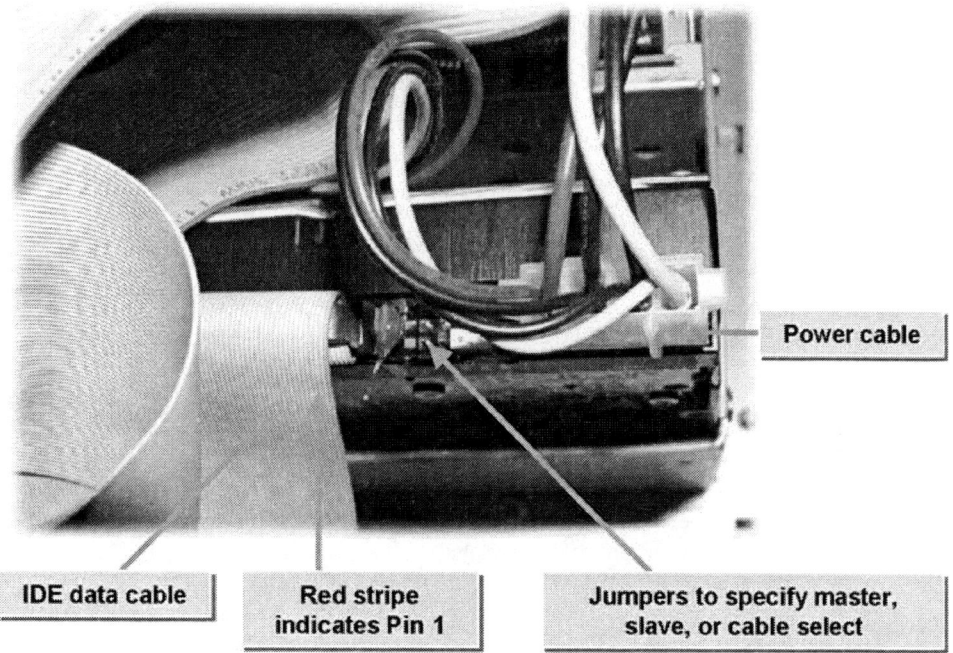

Figure 3-46: *An IDE hard drive.*

Example:

The hard drive is connected to the primary IDE controller on the motherboard. A second hard drive installed in the computer is connected as the second device on the primary channel. The first drive, HD0, is set as the master device and the second drive, HD1, is set as the slave device. HD0 is the drive from which the computer boots.

The secondary IDE controller on the motherboard has slower optical drives connected to it. The first device is the CD-RW drive which is set to be the master and the second device on the secondary IDE channel is the DVD drive which is set to be the slave. Primary and secondary IDE drives are shown in Figure 3-47.

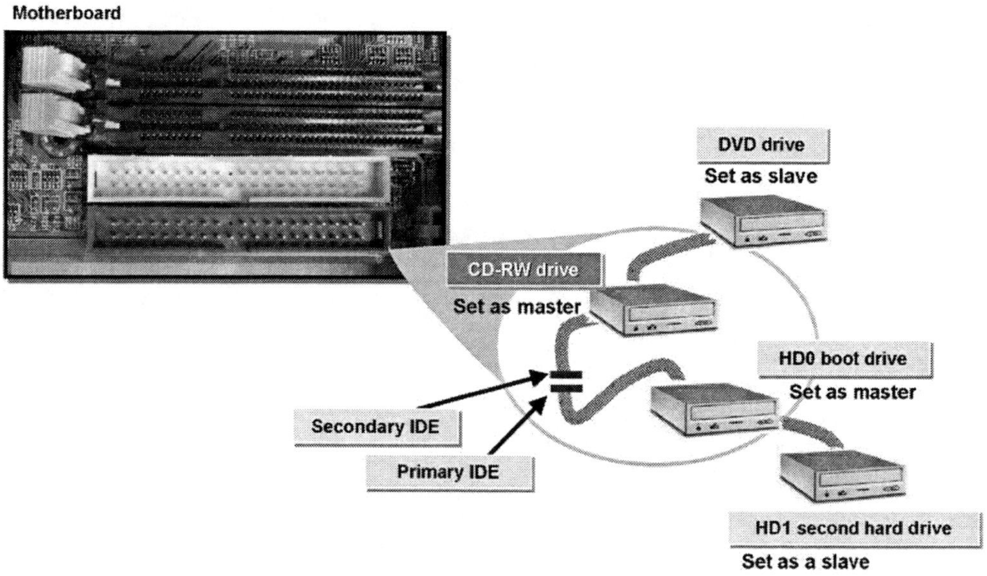

Figure 3-47: *Primary and secondary IDE drives.*

Cable Select

To use cable select, you need to set the jumpers on both drives to cable select. You also need a special cable select cable rather than the normal IDE cable. It has pin 28 configured differently to determine whether the drive should be treated as master or slave. The master and slave determination is made by which connector on the cable the drive is connected to. The connector in the center of the cable is the master and the end connector is the slave. If only one drive is connected, it is recommended that you use the end connector.

How to Install or Remove an IDE Drive

Procedure Reference: Install an IDE Drive

To install an IDE drive:

1. Locate an available drive bay, IDE data connection on the IDE data cable, and a power connector.

2. Set the jumpers for cable select, master, or slave, as appropriate to your needs. There is usually a sticker on the top of the drive that specifies the jumper settings for each of these settings. If there is not a sticker, then the documentation for the drive will include this information.

    - If the drive is the first drive on the channel, it should be configured as cable select or the master.
    - If the drive is the second drive on the channel, it should be configured as cable select or the slave.
    - If cable select is not available on your system, you should use the Slave setting.

3. If necessary, attach rails to the drive to fit in the drive bay.

4. Slide the drive into the bay, and then connect the data and power cables.

5. Restart the system, and if necessary, access CMOS setup to specify the drive type. You might need to know the number of cylinders, heads (tracks), and sectors on the disk as part of the CMOS setup procedure. You can usually find this information printed on a label on the drive or in the documentation that came with the drive.

Procedure Reference: Remove an IDE Drive

To remove an IDE drive:

1. Shut down the system.

2. Disconnect the data and power cables from the drive.

3. Unscrew the drive from the bay and slide it out of the bay.

4. If you are removing the master drive, reset the jumpers on other drives if necessary.

Procedure Reference: Format a Hard Drive

To partition and format a hard drive using Windows XP:

1. In the Computer Management utility, click Disk Management.

2. Right-click the newly installed disk, and choose New Partition.

3. Follow the New Partition Wizard prompts to partition and format the new drive.

Drive Partitions

A partition is an isolated section of a drive that functions like a separate physical drive. It is a logical disk structure used to organize hard drives. The entire disk can be one partition, or you can have up to four partitions. You can partition a drive through the operating system software.

Drive Formatting

Formatting is an operating system function that prepares a mass storage medium for holding data. It tests disk sectors to verify that they can be reliably used to hold data. It marks any unreliable sectors as bad sectors which cannot be used.

Topic E
Install or Remove Internal SCSI Drives

You have installed one type of drive, an IDE drive. Another type of drive you might encounter is a SCSI drive. In this topic, you will install a SCSI drive.

Just as you saw earlier that there are different connection standards for adapter cards such as ISA and PCI, there are different standards for drives. Being able to determine if the appropriate connections are available within the system, and knowing how to install and configure a SCSI internal drive will be essential if you are asked to install one.

SCSI

Definition:

SCSI is a parallel bus standard that connects internal and external peripherals. The following characteristics apply to all SCSI devices.

- It is a hardware interface, as well as a logical interface.
- It moves data in parallel mode a chunk at a time rather than a bit at a time.
- SCSI is technically not a controller, but is an adapter. It converts messages between the system bus and the SCSI bus. The Host Bus Adapter (HBA) is the card or component in the system that connects the SCSI bus to the system bus. This is usually on a separate card, but could be built into the chipset of the computer.
- All SCSI devices have a device ID.
- All devices are connected to the SCSI bus as a device on the daisy chain.
- Both ends of the SCSI chain must be terminated.

SCSI devices vary, with some devices not being compatible with other SCSI devices. Some of the ways they vary include:

- The SCSI type.
- The length of the SCSI chain's cabling.
- The connectors on the devices and the cabling.
- The signal type used to put data on the cable.
- The number of devices that can be on the chain. This depends on the SCSI type and the available device IDs on the devices.
- Depending on the SCSI type, it can be an 8-bit or 16-bit bus.

Example:

The SCSI chain shown here has two external devices connected to the HBA and one internal drive. It is a 16-bit SCSI 2 HBA with a 68-pin internal connection.

SCSI is commonly used to connect internal drives. In addition, it is also used to connect external devices including drives, scanners, network adapters, and monitors, and has been used as a network topology. Figure 3-48 shows an example of a SCSI chain.

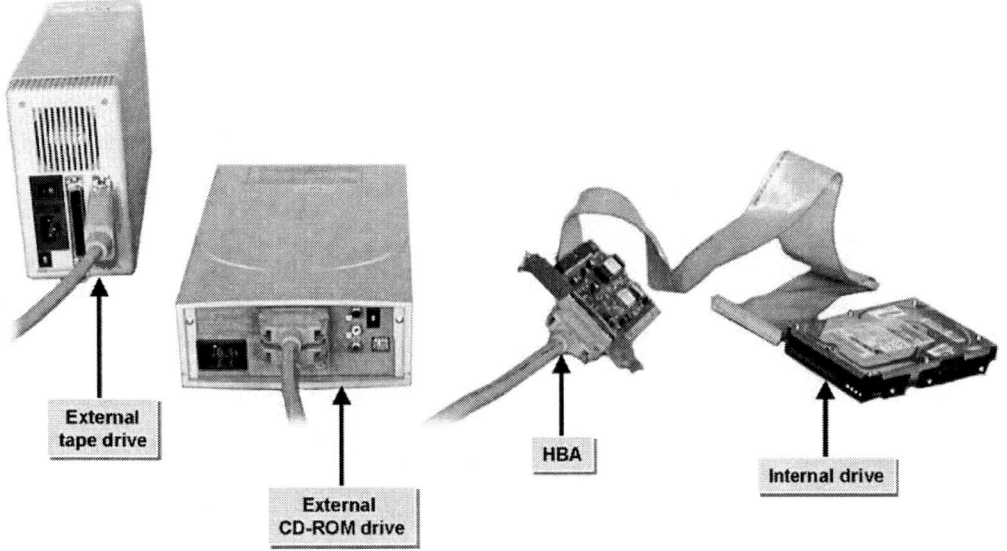

Figure 3-48: *A SCSI chain.*

SCSI Addresses

SCSI device IDs are also known as SCSI addresses. Each device has a SCSI ID number. The ID uniquely identifies the device on the SCSI bus. IDs are 0 to 7 for narrow SCSI or 0 to 15 for wide SCSI. Priority is given based on the drive ID, with 7 being the highest priority. For this reason, the HBA is usually assigned ID 7. Slower devices should have higher priority IDs so that faster devices don't monopolize the bus. So, the primary hard drive should be assigned a lower number and a slow device such as a tape drive would be assigned a higher ID number. Priority for narrow SCSI is 7, 6, 5, 4, 3, 2, 1, 0 and for wide SCSI it is 7, 6, 5, 4, 3, 2, 1, 0, 15, 14, 13, 12, 11, 10, 9, 8. SCSI IDs are set using jumpers or DIP switches on the SCSI device.

 Some versions of UNIX require specific SCSI IDs be set for specific devices.

The devices shown here show two different methods for selecting the device ID. One shows using jumpers and the other two examples use a switch. One switch has two choices, so the manufacturer chose to use a slide switch. The other device has choices from 0 to 6, so the switch is pressed to move from one device ID to the next until you have selected an unused device ID in the SCSI chain. SCSI device IDs are depicted in Figure 3-49

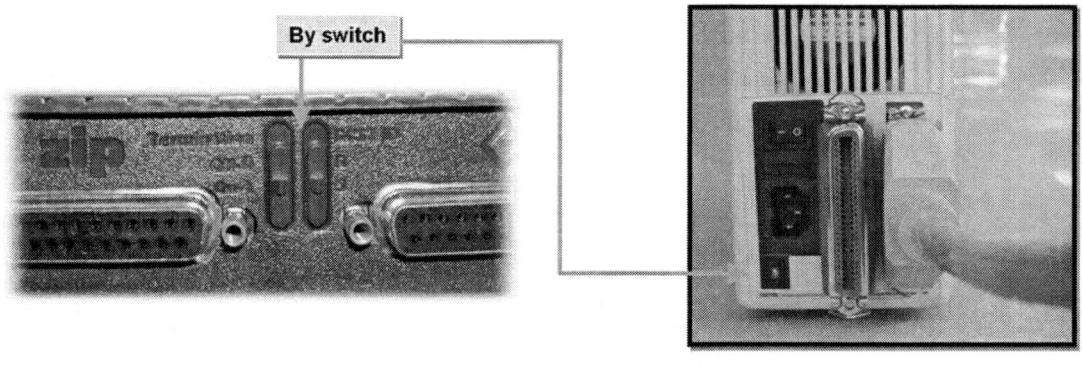

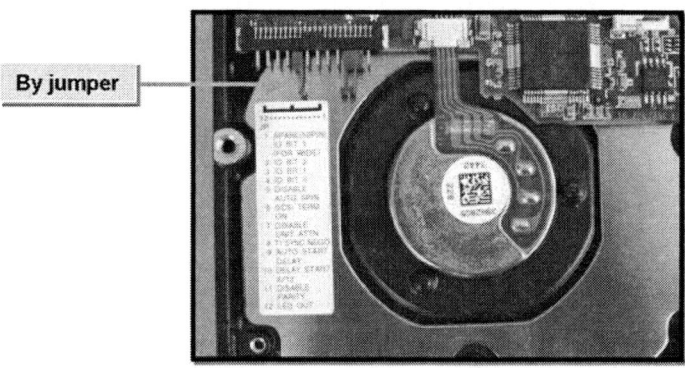

Figure 3-49: *SCSI device IDs.*

The jumpers used to set SCSI IDs each have a binary value assigned to them. The values are 1, 2, and 4, but the assignment of those values to which pins varies by manufacturer. Adding up the value of the jumpered pins gives you the SCSI ID. If it is the pins with the values 4 and 2 that are jumpered, then the SCSI ID will be 6.

SCSI Signaling Techniques

SCSI signaling techniques are the methods used by the SCSI interface to place signals on the SCSI cable. SCSI devices use one of the following techniques.

- *Single Ended (SE)*—Uses a single wire for each bit of data. Cable length is limited to 6 meters due to noise.

- *High Voltage Differential (HVD) Signaling*—Also known as differential signaling. Uses two wires for each data bit—one for the actual data and one for the inverse of the data. By comparing the data and its inverse, noise can be identified and rejected. Cable length can be up to 25 meters. Connecting an HVD device in an SE chain damages SE devices and sometimes also the HVD devices.

- *Low Voltage Differential (LVD) Signaling*—Use less power than HVD devices and can be chained with SE devices without damaging any devices. An LVD device on an SE chain will function like an SE device, so you lose the advantages of differential signaling. LVD cabling is limited to 12 meters.

 SCSI cable length is the total of all cabling in the SCSI chain.

SCSI Termination

Definition:

SCSI termination is the way that reflections (data bouncing back from the end of the cable that can cause errors) from the ends of SCSI chain are prevented. The SCSI chain uses termination on each end of the chain. The SCSI bus requires that both ends of the bus are terminated. This prevents signal reflection and makes the cable appear to be of infinite length. The host bus adapter (HBA) is terminated at one end of the bus by default. The last device on the SCSI chain must also be terminated. No other devices in the chain can be terminated. Termination can be accomplished by:

- Setting switches on the device if the device uses switches.
- Setting jumpers on the device if the device uses jumpers.
- Connecting a terminating resistor or terminating connector to the SCSI port on the device.

Termination varies in that it can be active, passive, or automatic.

- Active termination—Uses a voltage regulator so that the proper termination voltage is used.
- Passive termination—Uses resistors to terminate the SCSI chain. It can only be used for low performance SCSI devices on short SCSI chains.
- Automatic termination—The correct voltage is automatically set if it is determined that the device is at the end of the SCSI chain.

Example:

Each of the devices shown here has a different method of terminating the chain. If the device is not at the end of the chain, termination should be off. If it is at the end of the chain, termination should be enabled. Examples of SCSI termination are shown in Figure 3-50.

Chapter 3: Installing or Removing Internal Hardware   **153**

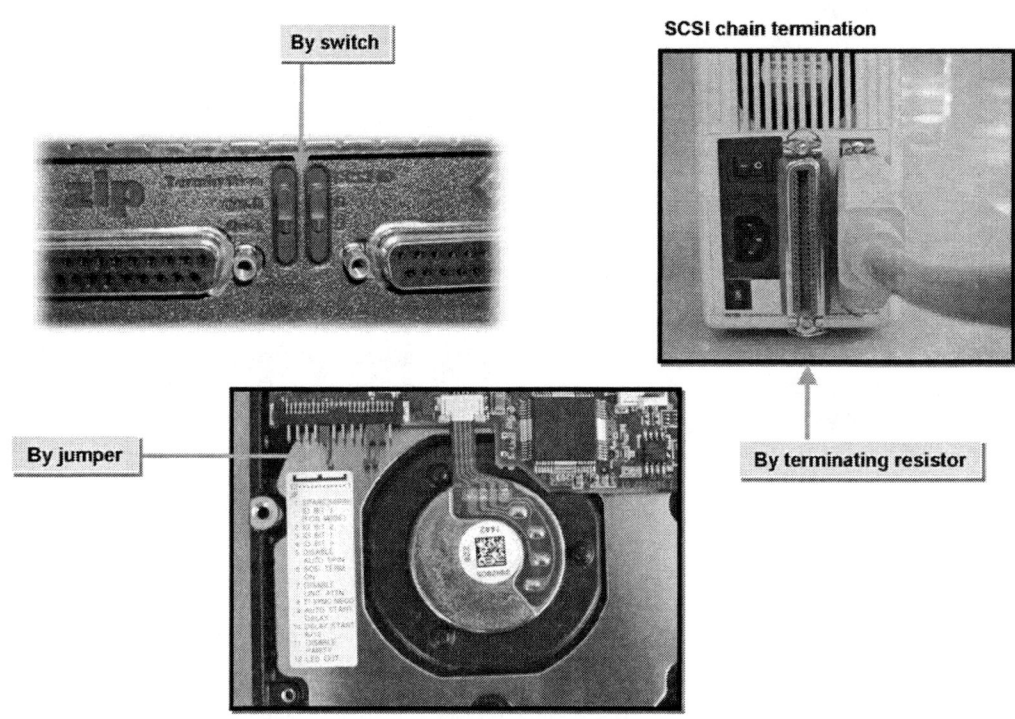

Figure 3-50: *SCSI termination.*

SCSI Types

Over the years, the speed of SCSI has increased greatly. There have been many SCSI types, each with their own specifications. The following is a list of the most popular SCSI types.

- SCSI-1 is 8 bits wide and is also known as narrow SCSI. It supports up to eight devices (seven devices plus the HBA). It uses a 50-pin connector and transfers data at up to 10 MB per second.
- Wide SCSI is 16 bits wide and supports up to 16 devices (15 devices plus the HBA). It transfers data at up to 20 MB per second.
- Ultra Wide SCSI is 16 bits wide. The 50-pin (or lower) connections carry one byte at a time. Ultra Wide connections carry two bytes at a time. It transfers data at up to 40 MB per second.
- Fast SCSI is 8 bits wide and it transfers data at up to 10 MB per second.
- Fast Wide SCSI is 16 bits wide and it transfers data at up to 20 MB per second.
- Ultra SCSI is 16 bits wide and it transfers data at up to 40 MB per second. If implemented on an 8-bit bus, data is transferred at up to 20 MB per second.
- Ultra2 SCSI is 16 bits wide and it transfers data at up to 80 MB per second. If implemented on an 8-bit bus, data is transferred at up to 40 MB per second.
- Ultra3 SCSI is 16 bits wide and it transfers data at up to 160 MB per second. If implemented on an 8-bit bus, data is transferred at up to 80 MB per second.

- Ultra 320 SCSI is 16 bits wide and it transfers data at up to 320 MB per second. If implemented on an 8-bit bus, data is transferred at up to 160 MB per second.

 For a complete list of the SCSI types, refer to the SCSI Trade Association Web site at **www.scsita.org**, and then follow the links About SCSI and Terms & Terminology. A chart listing the terms, bus speeds, bus widths, cable lengths, and number of supported devices is listed.

SCSI Interface

Definition:

The SCSI interface is a hardware interface that is used to connect internal and external peripherals to the SCSI bus. It is composed of the HBA, one or more SCSI devices, and cables to connect devices to the SCSI bus. Cables vary based on the connection type on the devices. They also vary based on whether it is an 8-bit or 16-bit SCSI bus.

SCSI cables vary, as shown in the following table.

SCSI Cable	Description
SCSI 1 Internal	Internal 50-pin flat cable, standard cable, used for 8-bit SCSI chain.
SCSI 3 Internal	Internal 68-pin flat cable, high-density cable, used for 16-bit SCSI chain.
SCSI 1 External A	Centronics external 50-pin connector.
SCSI 2 External A	50-pin high-density connector, 36 mm across.
SCSI 3 External P	68-pin high-density connector, 47 mm across.
DB25 SCSI	25-pin DB 25 connector commonly used for scanners and SCSI Zip drives.
VHDCI	Used for connecting RAID drives.

 Visit **www.ramelectronics.net/html/scsi_connectors.html** for pictures and descriptions of these and other SCSI connectors.

Example:

Examples of SCSI connectors are shown in Figure 3-51 and Figure 3-52.

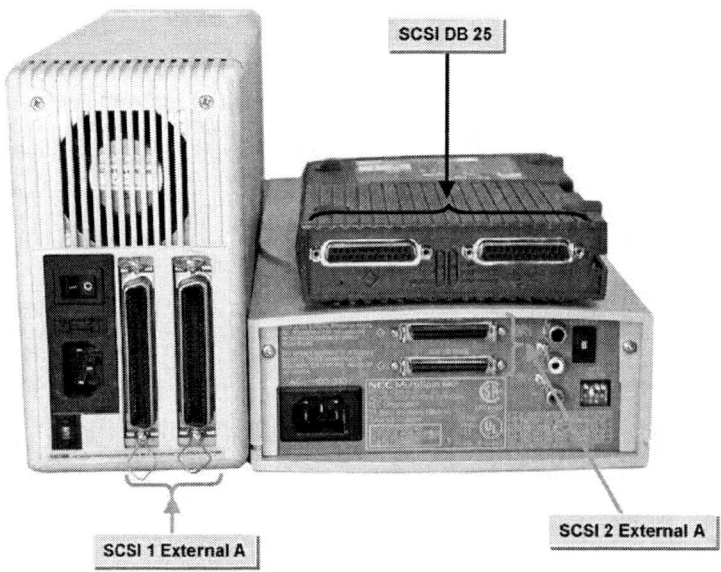

Figure 3-51: *External SCSI connectors.*

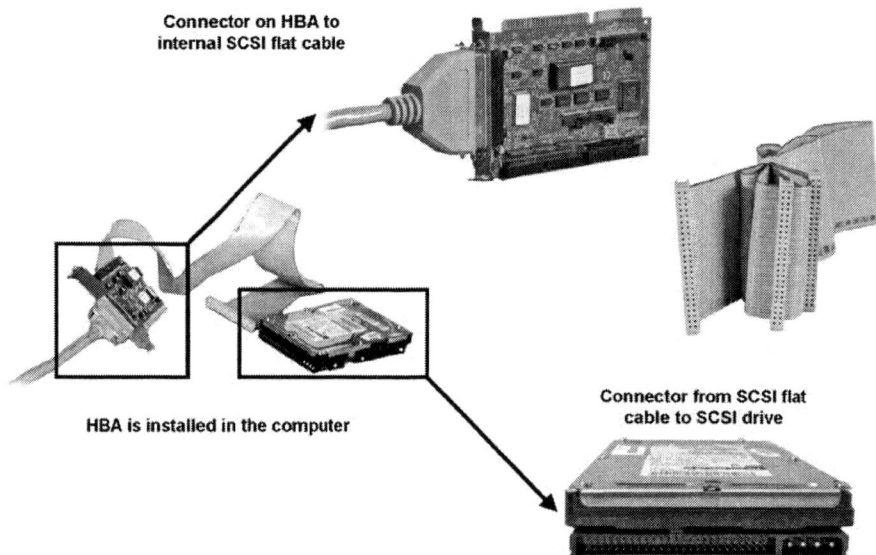

Figure 3-52: *Internal SCSI connectors.*

How to Install a SCSI Drive

Procedure Reference: Install an Internal SCSI Drive

To install an internal SCSI drive.

1. Set the drive ID on the drive. A sticker on the drive or the drive documentation will show how to set the ID and any other settings required to successfully install the drive.

2. Determine which device is at the end of the chain and terminate each end of the chain and remove termination from any other devices in the SCSI chain. Termination is accomplished by changing jumper settings, switches, or by physically inserting a termination plug into the port. Refer to the documentation for the device to determine how termination is accomplished on the particular device you are working with.

3. Insert the drive in an available drive bay. If you are using a 5.25-inch drive bay and a 3.5-inch drive, you will need to install the drive using rails to adapt the drive to the larger bay.

4. Connect the SCSI cable from the host bus adapter to the drive.

5. Connect the power cable to the drive. Most modern systems have plenty of power connectors for all of the internal devices you might install. Some systems might run out of connectors, though. If this happens, you can purchase splitters to enable two (or more) devices to be connected to one existing power connection to the power supply.

6. Restart the system, and if prompted, access CMOS setup and set the disk type, and then exit CMOS and save the settings.

TOPIC F
Install External SCSI Devices

You have installed several devices now through a variety of connections. Now that you have added a SCSI adapter card to your system, one more external connection you have is a SCSI port. In this topic, you will connect a SCSI device to a SCSI port.

Improperly installing a SCSI device can not only be frustrating to the user when it doesn't work, it can also damage the device. To eliminate end-user frustration and costly repairs and replacements, you will want to install SCSI port devices correctly.

How to Connect External SCSI Devices

Procedure Reference: Connect an External SCSI Device

To connect an external SCSI device to your system:

1. Connect the SCSI cable to the device and the other end of the cable to the SCSI port on the computer, being sure not to confuse the SCSI port with the parallel port. SCSI devices might include Jaz drives, external hard drives, printers, tape drives, scanners, and other devices with a SCSI interface.

2. If the SCSI device is the last device in the SCSI chain, terminate the device; if it is not the last device in the chain, remove termination from the device.

3. If you are adding additional SCSI devices to the chain, repeat steps 1 and 2, being sure to only terminate the last device in the chain.

4. Test that all devices in the chain function properly.

TOPIC G
RAID

You have already installed drives in a system. A special arrangement of disks can be installed to improve performance, fault tolerance, or both. In this topic, you will learn about a disk arrangement that provides these features.

What if a drive failed and you never knew the difference because another drive just took over? What if you could replace that failed drive without needing to power down the system? Both of these things can be a reality if you implement RAID on the computer system.

RAID

Definition:

Redundant Array of Inexpensive Disks (RAID) is an arrangement of multiple disk drives and a sophisticated controller that provides higher performance or reliability, or both, than a single disk drive. RAID is more expensive to implement than standard disk implementations. Some versions of RAID implementation are more expensive than others. RAID comes in several levels, each with specific goals and requirements. All implementations of RAID require:

- Multiple disk drives.
- An operating system that supports RAID.

 In some places you will see RAID defined as Redundant Array of Independent Disks

RAID varies by:
- Level. Different levels have been defined that have specific hardware and operating system requirements to meet specific needs.
- The number of drives required for the RAID level.
- Whether additional drive controllers are required.
- Whether specific RAID controllers are required or whether regular drive controllers can be used.
- Whether it improves reliability or performance or both.
- How data is written to the disks.
- It can be implemented using IDE or SCSI drives and controllers.

Example: RAID Level 0

RAID level 0 is also referred to as striping. In this RAID implementation, data is spread in small chunks across multiple drives. This is illustrated in Figure 3-53. Features of RAID level 0 include:

- It requires Windows NT or 2000.
- It requires at least two physical drives and can use up to 32 physical drives.
- Improved read and write performance. Since there are multiple heads and read/write heads, data can be read and written more quickly.
- It includes no provisions for recovering or rebuilding data. Because data is spread across multiple drives, if any drive fails, the risk of losing data is increased. This level provides no fault tolerance.
- It uses a single controller which can be a regular drive controller or a special RAID controller.

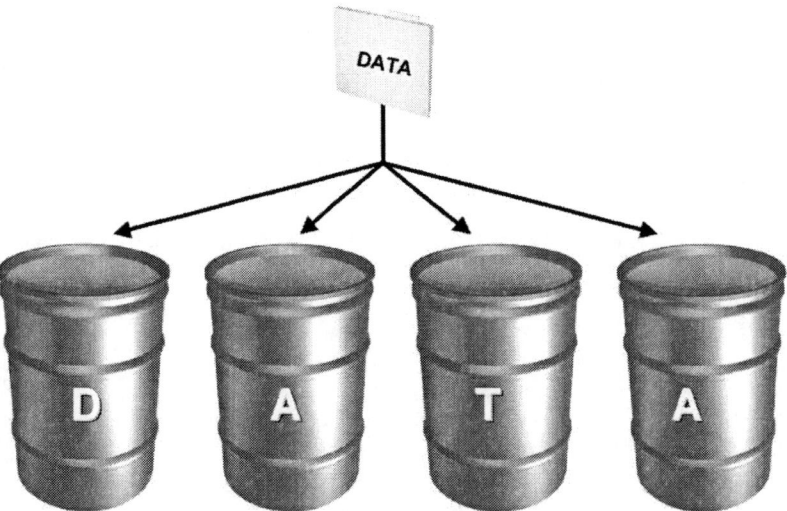

Data is divided across all drives.

Figure 3-53: *Striping with RAID level 0.*

Example: RAID Level 1

RAID level 1 duplicates an entire partition on another partition. All data and drive information is duplicated on the second partition. Drive information that can be duplicated includes the system and boot partitions. It can be implemented in two ways. Both are shown in Figure 3-54.

- As mirroring—This uses two physical disks and one disk drive controller for both disks.
- As duplexing—This uses two physical disks and two disk drive controllers, each drive connected to a separate controller.

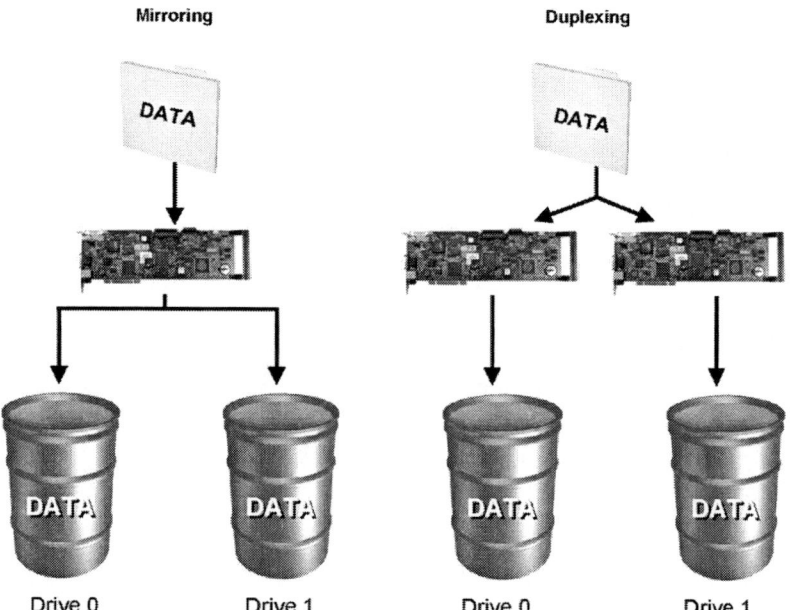

Figure 3-54: *RAID level 1.*

RAID level 1 can be implemented on Windows NT or 2000 operating systems. Even though it is the most expensive RAID level since all equipment is duplicated without any gain in productivity or capacity, it is the only method that can protect the boot disk.

Example: RAID Level 5

RAID level 5 is also known as striping with parity. It is implemented as three to 32 separate physical disk drives over which the data is written. Parity data is also spread across the drives. Because both data and parity are spread across the drives, more than one read and write can occur simultaneously. Hardware-based RAID Level 5 systems offer features such as continuous operation, the ability to schedule failed-drive replacement, and even the ability to hot-swap failed drives. The system and boot partitions cannot be part of a stripe set with parity across multiple drives. They must be stored on a separate partition. It requires a Windows NT or 2000 operating system.

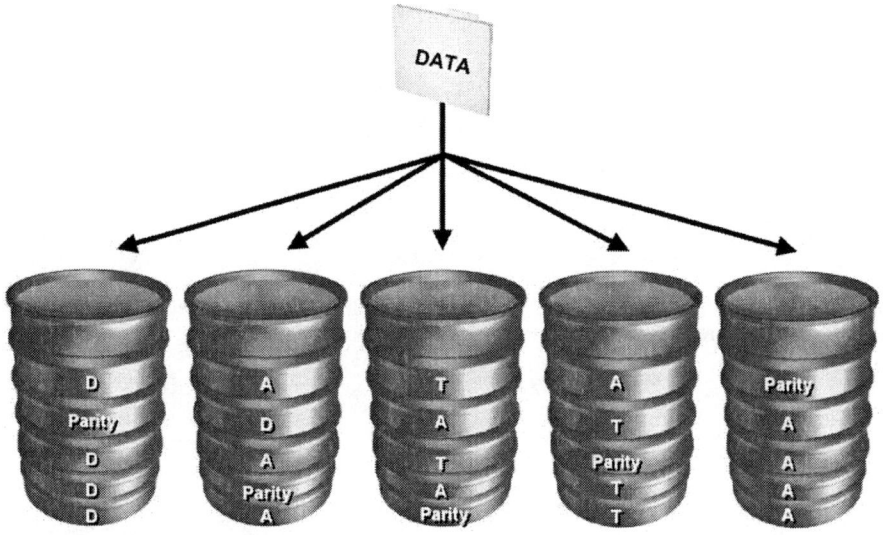

Figure 3-55: *RAID level 5.*

Chapter 3 Follow-up
Installing or Removing Internal Hardware

In this chapter, you established an ESD-free work area so that you can safely work with computer components. Next, you opened the case and installed adapter cards including a network card and connected it to the network. Finally, you installed IDE and SCSI drives.

Essential Terms

- adapter cards
- buses
- device conflicts
- drive bays
- drive controllers
- drive interfaces
- ESD
- hardware resources
- hexadecimal number system

- IDE drives
- internal PC components
- IP addresses
- network adapters
- network cables
- network connectors
- networks
- Plug and Play
- RAID
- safety equipment

- safety hazards
- SCSI
- SCSI drives
- SCSI interfaces
- SCSI termination
- sound cards
- subnet masks
- TCP/IP
- video cards

Review Questions

1. To reduce static electricity in the atmosphere, what is the desired humidity rate?
2. Computer monitors contain circuits that require 35,000 volts with a high current. What are the components that store the voltage and current?
3. What happens when computers are operated in cramped areas with insufficient airflow?
4. What are the five internal compnents that all computers must contain?
5. What is bus mastering?
6. What is a load?
7. Motherboard expansion slots are color-coded. What type of expansion card uses a white slot? What type uses a brown slot? What type uses a black slot?
8. What is the speed of an AGP 3.0 8x video card?
9. What is the function of an IRQ?
10. What is a Media Access Control address?
11. What are the two types of twisted-pair cables?
12. What category of twisted pair has a speed of up to 100 Mbps?
13. What is the Radio Grade (RG) of coaxial cable used on thinnet ethernet networks?
14. What is a BNC connector?
15. What kind of connector is used to connect RG8 cable segments?
16. What are the two modes of fiber optic cables and what are the two types of connectors used to connect fiber optic cables to the network?
17. How many bytes make up an IP address?
18. What is the purpose of the subnet mask?
19. What is TCP/IP and what is its purpose?
20. What are the minimum properties you must configure when you install TCP/IP on a computer?
21. What are the two types of name servers you could run on a TCP/IP-based network?
22. Windows 2000 and Windows XP support two methods for assigning IP addresses to a computer automatically. What are those two methods?
23. What physical network topology uses a single main called a backbone that carries all network data?
24. In what kind of network can any computer act as both a client and a server?
25. What network uses one or more computers that are dedicated to providing network services?
26. What is the bandwidth of a T1 line?
27. What is the purpose of a splitter for DSL?
28. What is a hard drive sector?
29. What is a drive interface and what are the two types of interfaces?
30. How many devices can you attach to one IDE channel?

31. Which ATA specification introduced Self Monitoring Analysis and Reporting Technology (SMART)?
32. What do you have to do to set a drive to either master or slave?
33. What is a partition?
34. After you partition a drive, what is the next step?
35. What is the drive controller?

Review Projects

Project #1: Documenting Hardware Specs

As an A+ technician, you'll need to keep detailed records about the equipment in your computer systems. You'll be able to plan upgrades and troubleshoot hardware problems more easily if you document the hardware configurations of each machine.

In this exercise you'll gather information about the network card in a machine running Windows XP (the same steps apply to Windows 2000).

On a Windows XP machine, right-click My Network Places and select Properties to display network connections. Right-click the Local Area Connection to display the Local Area Connection Properties box. Under the General tab is the name of your network adapter card. Click the Configure box. Examine the information located under each tab. Record the following:

- The card's manufacturer
- The type of bus the card uses and the location of the card on the bus
- The resources the card is using

You may write down the information, but you may find it easier to build your documentation by taking screen images. To take a screenshot of the network adapter information, press the PrtSc key on your PC's keyboard (this is usually located on the right side at the top of the keyboard). Open a word processing program such as Microsoft word, click an area where you want to place the screenshot and press Ctrl+V to paste the image.

Create a folder on the C drive and name it Hardware Documentation. Save the file to the folder.

Project #2 Using Common Network Command-line Utilities

On a machine running Windows 2000 or Windows XP, open a command prompt. From Start, choose run and type cmd in the Open: box. At the command prompt, type Ipconfig. Record the IP address and subnet mask (and default gateway if listed). Next, use the same command and add the /all switch (Ipconfig /all). What new information is listed?

If your machine has more than one adapter card installed, write down the information for each card (or take screenshots using PrtSc). If you are running a Windows 9x machine, you must enter the command winipcfg at the run command to see network configuration information.

To verify that the TCP stack installed properly and is functioning, test the stack using the loopback address of 127.0.0.1. At the command prompt, type ping 127.0.0.1. Write down the message(s) that appear on the screen (you should receive 4 replies if the TCP stack is functioning correctly).

Project #3 Troubleshooting the Hard Drive

Unplug your computer and remove the cover from your machine (you do not have to remove all the peripheral connectors from the back of the computer). Locate the data cable that connects your hard drive to the driver interface on the motherboard. Remove the cable from the hard drive. Plug in your machine and start the computer. What error message do you receive? Turn off the computer and unplug it. Re-attach the data cable to the hard drive (be sure to align the red stripe on the cable with pin one on the drive). If you have a slave device attached to the master, repeat the same steps as above. Did you receive an error message when you booted the machine? Why or why not?

Document the steps you performed in this exercise along with the error message(s) you received. Create a subfolder under Hardware Documentation on drive C. Name the folder Hardware Troubeshooting. Save your file to the subfolder.

Project #4 About ESD

Electrostatic discharge can destroy the sensitive components in your computer. It is crucial to remove static build-up from your body before working inside a computer. A common practice is to wear a wrist strap that includes a metal clip on the end that you can connect to a metal part of the computer case.

To understand ESD and its implications, read the information at the following Web site: **http://www.midwestesd.org/aboutesd.html**. Once you complete the readings, use a search engine such as Google (**http://www.google.com**) to locate Web sites that specialize in ESD accessories. You'll find that Web stores specializing in ESD products carry items ranging from small field kits (usually includes a wrist pad, dissipative mat, and grounding wire) to elaborate ESD workstations that cost thousands of dollars.

Reflective Questions

1. What types of adapter cards do you think you will need to install most often?

2. Would you recommend IDE or SCSI drives to your customers if they were to ask for your opinion?

CHAPTER 4
Upgrading System Components

Chapter Objectives:

In this chapter, you will upgrade system components.

You will:

- Add memory to the computer.
- Replace the CPU.
- Add a CPU to the computer.
- Upgrade the system BIOS.
- Upgrade the power supply.
- Remove the existing system board and install a system board.
- Decide when to upgrade system hardware.

Introduction

You have set up a PC and added both internal and external components. While this is an extensive part of the job of a service technician, another aspect of the job is upgrading system components. In this chapter, you will upgrade memory, the CPU, the BIOS, and the system board.

You should now have most of the skills you need to upgrade system components; you can remove components and you can install them. The additional piece of information you will need is to make sure that the upgrade is compatible with the rest of the system. This will save you hours of aggravation when you try to install a component only to find it either won't fit or the system won't boot after all your hard work.

TOPIC A
Add Memory

You have now successfully set up and configured a working computer system. It won't be long before someone asks you to install more memory in their system. In this topic, you will add memory to a system.

Just as some people say you can never be too rich or too thin, you can never have too much memory. With today's applications and operating systems, it is not unusual for users to install additional memory as soon as they purchase a new system. If they are using an older system, they will definitely need more memory. Since you, as the service technician, are the one they will be calling on, you need to know how to determine what memory modules the user needs and how to install them.

Memory

Definition:

Memory is a chip or set of chips used to store information. Some memory is volatile. This means the information it contains is lost when the system is powered off. Other memory is non-volatile. This means the information is retained even when the system is powered off. Memory is included on the system board and on some expansion cards.

Example:

The following table lists some of the types of memory you will encounter. These types of memory hold their data electronically.

Type of Memory	Volatile?	Used For
Complimentary Metal Oxide Semiconductor (CMOS)	No, because it is maintained by a battery even when the system is off.	Holding the system configuration information.

Type of Memory	Volatile?	Used For
Read Only Memory (ROM)	No, because the information is permanently stored on the chip.	Holding system or card startup information.
Random Access Memory (RAM)	Yes.	Holding program instructions and data so they can be processed by the CPU while you are using the system.
SAM	Yes.	Holding data in a sequential order. When accessing data, each storage cell is checked until the desired information is found. Often used for memory buffers where data is stored in the order it will be used.

Non-Example:

Hard drives and floppy disks are not examples of memory because these devices hold their data magnetically. CD-ROM discs and DVD discs are also not examples of memory because these devices hold their data in pits on the surface of the disc.

Types of RAM

Definition:

RAM is memory that is the main memory in the computer. It is used to hold programs and data while you are working on them. It is volatile. Some RAM is more volatile than other RAM and must be refreshed more often.

RAM is often described as a scratchpad or whiteboard area. This temporary memory area is wiped clean when the system is powered off or rebooted. The following is a list of the characteristics of RAM:

- Data can be accessed in any order.
- When the memory is full, data is purged. It is written to disk.
- Each memory chip is composed of millions of transistors and capacitors which have been paired to create memory cells.

Example:

Over the years, many different RAM specifications have been developed. Most of these changes have been to improve performance. The following table describes the RAM types you might encounter.

 You can find additional information about Rambus and DDR SDRAM at **http://crucial.com/library/ddr_vs_rdram.asp**.

RAM Type	Description
FPM	Fast Page Mode memory is used in older 32-pin SIMMs. Faster than previous RAM types because it reads an entire row rather than reading a row and column address at a time.
EDO	Extended Data Output memory is faster than FPM memory because it doesn't require the wait states required for FPM. It is often found on SIMMs and in Video RAM.
SRAM	Used for cache memory. It does not need to be refreshed to retain information. It does not use assigned memory addresses. It can use synchronous, asynchronous, burst, or pipeline burst technologies.
DRAM	Used on SIMMs and DIMMs. It needs to be refreshed every few milliseconds. Uses assigned memory addresses. Can be implemented using FPM, EDO, BEDO, SDRAM, Direct Rambus DRAM, or Double Data Rate SDRAM.
RDRAM and *DDR SDRAM*	Direct Rambus DRAM is implemented on a RIMM memory module. Double Data Rate SDRAM is a replacement for SDRAM.
VRAM	A special type of DRAM used on video cards that can be written to and read from at the same time. It also requires less refreshing than normal DRAM.
WRAM	Windows RAM is a special type of video memory that can be simultaneously read from and written to in blocks. The Windows in the title of this RAM type does not indicate Microsoft Windows.

RAM Speed

RAM speed is the time needed to read and recharge a memory cell. It's measured in nanoseconds (ns). A nanosecond is one-billionth of a second. The smaller the number, the faster the RAM. For example, 10 ns RAM is faster than 60 ns RAM.

 One of the popular memory manufacturers has an article on the speed of SDRAM at **http://crucial.com/library/sfiles4.asp**. They also have another article on the PC100 Standard, including a discussion on the speed of memory, at **http://crucial.com/library/sfiles5.asp**.

RAM comes in ever-increasing speeds. The RAM on sale at the local computer store might work just fine in your system, or it might be older, slower RAM they are trying to move out of stock.

The SDRAM used in 168-pin DIMMs has access times in the 6 to 12 nanosecond range.

Older EDO RAM was often 60- to 70-ns speed RAM. Modern RAM that you are likely to find runs at clock speeds of 100 MHz and 133 MHz. The 100 MHz RAM has a RAM speed of 10 ns. The 133 MHz RAM has a RAM speed of 6 ns.

You need to check what RAM speed is currently installed. All of the RAM in the system runs at the lowest common speed. It is backward-compatible, so it can run at the lower speed if it finds slower RAM. Some systems will not run with mixed RAM speeds, but these are not common. Either way, the RAM will not run any faster than the motherboard's bus speed.

Cache

When the CPU executes instructions, it stores the temporary results in *registers*, which are storage locations found directly within the CPU, for faster access to the results. But the vast majority of instructions and data are stored in RAM, so when the CPU needs more instructions to process, it has to stop to wait for two distinct system-bus operations (request instructions from RAM, and receive instructions from RAM) before it can proceed. To resolve this bottleneck, CPU design engineers developed a special type of RAM, faster and more expensive than traditional RAM, and added it to the CPU itself. This onboard RAM, which is a type of memory composed of SRAM, is called the *CPU cache*, *primary cache*, or *L1 cache*. This more expensive RAM does not need to be refreshed constantly, making it faster than the DRAM used for regular system memory.

Modern CPUs include both L1 and L2 cache. Memory included on the same microchip as the CPU is Level 1 (L1) or internal or primary cache. This is composed of SRAM, which is very fast. This enables the processor to store code and data temporarily while the CPU is processing information and access it faster than from dynamic RAM used in the computer memory.

Level 2 (L2) cache, also known as external or *secondary cache*, is not located on the same microchip as the CPU. Originally, all L2 cache was on the motherboard. Now, at least some of the L2 cache is included in the CPU package. L2 cache is either 256 K or 512 K. A bus or bridge called the *backside bus* connects this L2 cache to the CPU chip. The bridge between regular memory and the CPU is referred to as the frontside bus. L2 cache is located between the processor and RAM and is normally twice the size of the L1 cache. *Level 3 (L3)* cache is memory on the motherboard between the processor and RAM when there's a built-in L2 cache on the processor.

Banks

You can combine multiple rows of DRAM into a cluster called a *bank*. Each row of DRAM can then be accessed simultaneously. When creating banks, the goal is to match the width of the DRAM to the width of the CPU's external *data bus*, which will generally be 8-bit, 16-bit, 32-bit, or 64-bit. Expressed another way, the number of SIMMs or DIMMs needed to create a bank is the width of the CPU's data bus divided by the width of the SIMM or DIMM. So, for a CPU with a 32-bit data bus, you need 4 SIMMs to create a bank.

Types of ROM

Definition:

ROM is memory that is non-volatile. The original ROM chips could not be altered after the program code was placed on the ROM chip. As time went on, though, users needed the ability to update the information stored on ROM chips. Over the years, various chips have been created that perform the function of ROM, but have the ability to be updated one way or another. These are referred to as programmable ROM.

Example:

The following table describes the ROM types you might encounter.

ROM Type	Description
ROM	A chip that cannot be altered. Technically, this is referred to as a masked ROM chip.
PROM	A blank ROM chip that is burned with a special ROM burner. This chip can only be changed once. After the instructions are burned in, it cannot be updated or changed.
EPROM	Like a PROM except that the data can be erased through a quartz crystal on top of the chip. After removing the chip from the system, a UV light is used to change the binary data back to its original state, all 1s.
EEPROM	A chip that can be reprogrammed using software from the BIOS or chip manufacturer using a process called flashing. Also known as *Flash ROM*. The chip does not need to be removed in order to be reprogrammed.

Memory Packages

Definition:

A *memory package* is a circuit board design that holds the memory chips that are plugged into the memory expansion slots on the motherboard. The memory expansion slots in a computer are collectively known as the *memory bank*. These small, printed circuit boards are either one-sided or two-sided—that is, they contain RAM chips on one or both sides of the board. The circuit board has edge connector pins to connect it to the motherboard. Memory packages might or might not use parity for error-checking. Memory packages come in 8-bit, 16-bit, 32-bit, and 64-bit modules.

Originally, RAM chips were installed individually directly onto the motherboard. This made it difficult to upgrade the amount of RAM in a system or to pinpoint which chip was bad if there was a problem. For this reason, memory packages were introduced. This makes it much easier to upgrade the RAM in a system. If there is a problem with a chip, the memory package module can be easily removed and replaced, eliminating the need to determine exactly which chip is bad.

Example:

The following table describes the standard memory packages you are likely to encounter.

 Additional information about how to visually identify memory can be found at **http://dewassoc.com/performance/memory/how_to_ID_memory.htm**.

Memory Package	Description
SIMM	Individual pins on each side of the module are connected to the same memory chip. Used in 486 systems. Contains a 32-bit path. Must be installed in pairs. Comes in 30- and 72-pin configurations to connect to the memory expansion slot.
DIMM	Pin connections on each side of the module connect to different memory chips. Contains a 64-bit path. Can be installed singly. Has a 168-pin connection to the slot. Used in Pentium systems.
RIMM	Used in Pentium IV systems. Uses different pin connections than DIMMs. Rather than using a single data channel, RIMM uses multiple high-speed channels, enabling each channel to supply dedicated bandwidth to multiple devices simultaneously. It is composed of RDRAM chips. The chips are used in series on parallel channels as compared to DIMM which uses DRAM chips in parallel. These modules have 184-pin connections to the expansion slot.
SODIMM	Small Outline Dual Inline Memory Module. Used in some notebook systems and Apple iMac systems. Measures about 2 inches by 1 inch and has 144 pins. Capacity ranges from 16 to 256 MB per module.

Memory Package	Description
MicroDIMM	Micro Dual Inline Memory Module. Used in small, sub-compact notebooks. Measures about 1.5 inches long and has 144 pins.
Proprietary	Many notebook manufacturers use proprietary formats for their memory modules. So, when you want to upgrade or replace the memory in those systems, you will need to purchase the memory from the notebook manufacturer in most cases.

Parity

Parity is an error correction method that is used on some memory modules for error-checking. The data is sent as eight bits and a ninth bit is included, which is the parity bit.

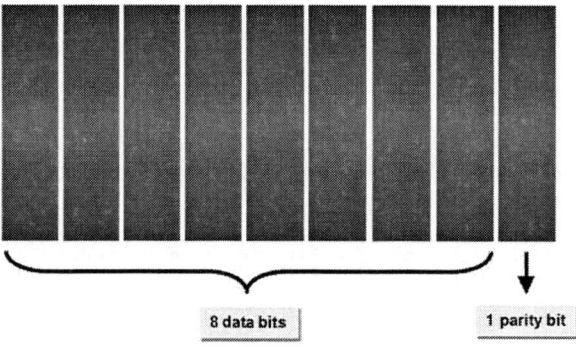

Figure 4-1: *Parity.*

Parity can be odd or even. The parity bit (the ninth bit) is set to 0 or 1, as needed, to provide an even number of 1s for even parity or an odd number of 1s for odd parity. For even parity, 8 bits of data are received and the total number of 1s are added together. If there is an odd number of 1s, the parity bit is set to 1. If the results are even, the parity bit is set to 0. When the data is read, the totals are added again and compared for each bit to the parity bit. If the sum is odd and the parity bit is set to 1, the data is sent to the CPU with the assumption that the data was valid. If the sum is odd and the parity bit was set to 0, the data is not sent to the CPU, because this result indicates there is an error somewhere within the 8 bits of data. If an error is detected, nothing is done to fix it. The system simply tries again after discarding the data.

Parity is rarely used; other system components are relied on to verify that the data contained in memory is accurate when non-parity memory is used. Some chips use fake parity. In this case, the values are always 1s and it is assumed that there are never any memory problems. Other pieces of hardware and/or software take over in verifying that the information contained in the memory is correct.

ECC

Another error-checking method is *Error Correction Code (ECC)*. This method uses several bits for error-checking. A special algorithm is used to detect and then correct any errors it finds. ECC is only used in upper-end systems such as high-end workstations and servers; other desktop systems use non-ECC memory.

How to Add RAM to a System

Procedure Reference: Add Additional RAM to a System

To add RAM to a system:

1. Determine how much RAM is currently installed. You can use the System Properties dialog box to find this or the CMOS settings. From the Start menu, choose My Computer, and then in the System Tasks box on the left side of the window, click View System Information. This is an important step. By knowing how much RAM is currently in the system, you will be able to determine whether the additional RAM you are about to install has been recognized by the system when you are done.

2. Shut down your computer and disconnect the power cord.

3. Discharge any static electricity from yourself or your clothes. While this is always important to do, it is especially important to do when working with memory cards. These components are more delicate and more easily damaged by static charges than other system components.

4. Locate an empty memory expansion socket on the system board or remove a smaller memory module to make room for one containing more memory. If there are no empty slots for memory, you will need to remove one or more existing memory modules and replace them with modules containing more memory. To remove an existing memory module:

    a. Press down on the ejection tabs.

    b. Firmly grasp the memory module and pull it out of the slot.

5. Align the notches in the connector edge of the memory module with the notches in the memory expansion socket, and then firmly press the memory module down into the socket.

6. If the ejection tabs did not lock into the notches on the ends of the memory module, push them up until they lock.

7. Restart the system.

8. Follow any on-screen prompts or perform any steps described in your system's documentation for getting the system to recognize additional memory. This is not required on all systems.

9. Verify that the additional memory was recognized by the system. You can use CMOS or the System Properties dialog box to check this.

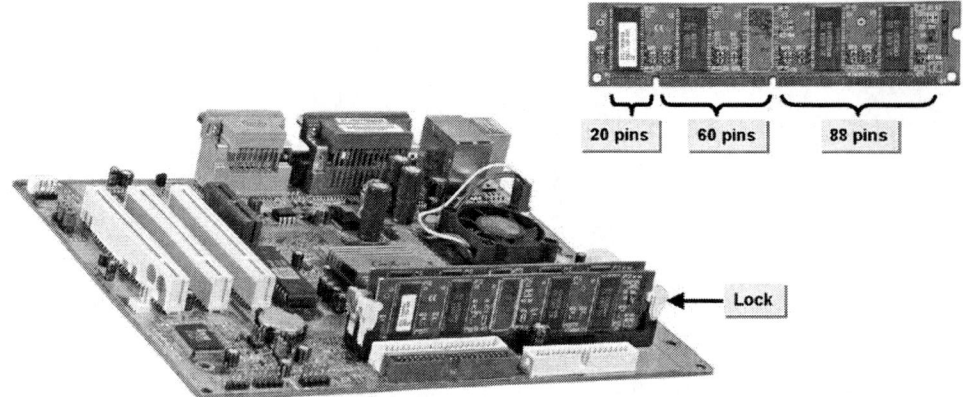

Figure 4-2: *Adding RAM to a system.*

Topic B
Upgrade the CPU

You just added memory to your system. Often, this is all you need in order to make systems respond better. Other times, you will also need to put in a faster processor. In this topic, you will upgrade the CPU.

Have you ever tried to get a new piece of software or a game to run only to find out that your processor is too slow? If so, then you are going to be very interested in this topic. In some cases, it is less expensive to upgrade the CPU than it is to purchase a new system if everything else on your system provides acceptable performance.

CPU

Definition:

The *Central Processing Unit (CPU)* is the integrated circuit that controls all of the system components. The CPU is composed of the control unit, the arithmetic and logic unit, and memory.

 If you would like additional information about processor terminology, you can refer to the glossary of terms at http://processorfinder.intel.com/scripts/help3.asp.

Each processor comes in a variety of speeds. Different CPUs use different connection methods to connect to the motherboard. This includes various sockets, slots, and connection types such as ZIF, LZIF, Single Edge Connector, and others. Different CPUs are packaged differently. This includes the clock frequency, physical size, and voltage. CPUs sold today include onboard cache and an integrated Floating Point Unit, but older CPUs did not include either. Except for the original Pentium and the Pentium Pro, all processors in the Pentium family contain MMX (multimedia extension) capabilities. The voltage varies between different processors. The width of the data bus varies. The amount of addressable RAM varies. Whether multiple processors are supported varies as well as the number processors. Some processors run very hot, so require heat sinks and fans to help cool them.

 The CPU is the brain of the computer. This is where software instructions are performed and math and logic equations are performed. This little component is the most costly of any system components.

The following table describes each of the CPU components.

Component	Description
Control Unit	Performs the fetch, decode, execute, and store functions. Collectively, these functions are referred to as the machine cycle. Speed is written in reference to the number of cycles that can be performed in a given time period. Each machine cycle performs the following steps: • Fetch—Places the address of the next instruction to be executed on the address bus and reads in the word at that instruction register (high speed memory locations within the CPU) location. If an instruction is more than one word long, several fetches will be performed. • Decode—Determines which gates to open between the CPU's functional units and buses, and what the Arithmetic and Logic Unit needs to do. This is determined based on the instruction register contents. • Execute—Passes values between function units and buses, and the operation of the Arithmetic and Logic Unit. • Store—Writes the results of an instruction either to a register location or a memory location.
Arithmetic and Logic Unit (ALU)	Performs integer math and *boolean* operations. The decode logic from the control unit determines which operation should be performed, the *operands* to use, and where the results should be placed in memory.
Memory	Memory locations can be registers, cache, RAM, or ROM.

Example:

Figure 4-3 contains an example of a CPU. Intel, AMD, and Cyrix are the most commonly encountered CPU manufacturers. They each have a series of CPUs that are compatible with each other.

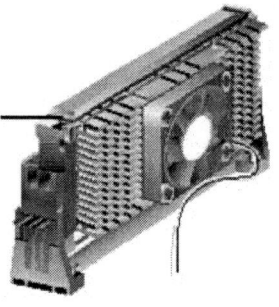

Figure 4-3: *CPUs.*

Non-Example: Math Coprocessors

Math coprocessors are not examples of CPUs. *Math coprocessors*, or floating point units, were designed to be added to a system to help with math calculations. The coprocessor chip must match the CPU. These are 80 x 87 chips that match up with the 80 x 86 CPU, including being the same speed. For example, a 33 MHz 80386 chip must be paired with a 33 MHz 80387 if you're going to add a math coprocessor to the system. Math coprocessors were integrated into the main CPU with the advent of the 80486DX and the Pentium.

CPU Cooling Methods

As processors became more powerful, they also generated more heat, introducing the possibility of damage to or failure of the chip due to overheating. Damage can cause unpredictable processor behavior such as system lockups, sudden reboots, and the like. Failure obviously means that the chip is no longer usable.

 A whining noise from inside the computer could mean the CPU fan is starting to go bad. It's a good idea to periodically clean any dust from the fan by removing it from the chip (if necessary) and using a computer vacuum to remove accumulated dust.

Starting with the 486 processor, *heat sinks* with fans were added to address the problem of overheating processors. These devices are either glued to the CPU using a *thermal compound* or attached with a clamp. (Thermal compounds are manufactured to provide maximum heat transfer from the CPU to the heat sink.) An example of a heat sink is shown in Figure 4-4. To prevent the CPU from overheating, the fan blows heated air away from the heat sink metal elements, allowing cooler air to be pulled across the heat sink's fins and keeping the air around the processor cool. It is imperative that the connection to the CPU is tight.

Figure 4-4: *A heat sink.*

CPUs are also kept cool using a device to circulate a liquid, such as water, around the CPU. The heat from the CPU is absorbed by the cooler liquid, and then the heated liquid is circulated away from the CPU so it can disperse the heat into the air outside the computer. Liquid cooling systems are not as prevalent as heat sinks in most desktop systems or low-end servers.

High-end servers will sometimes have a temperature sensor to detect a rise in temperature. You can often configure your system to notify you when the temperature is too high or to shut down to protect the components if the temperature reaches a certain level.

Factors that Affect CPU Performance

The following table shows factors that affect the performance of a CPU.

Factor	Description
Clock speed	The number of processing cycles that a microprocessor can perform in a given second. Some microprocessors require several cycles to assemble and perform a single instruction, whereas others require fewer cycles.
Millions of Instructions Per Second (MIPS)	The number of instructions that a microprocessor can perform in a given second. A microprocessor can have a slower clock speed than another and a higher MIPS rating if the slower processor uses clock cycles more efficiently.
Amount of RAM that a processor can access	Corresponds directly to the width of the address bus. The formula to calculate addressable memory is 2^n where n equals the address bus width. Most CPUs in use today can address either 4 GB or 64 GB.
Multiprocessing	Using more than one CPU to provide additional processing power.
Cache	Dedicated high-speed memory for storing recently used instructions and data.
Superscalar	Technology that enables the CPU to execute two instructions simultaneously using two different pipelines.
Superpipelining	Ability of the CPU chip to overlap the execution steps (fetch, decode, execute, and write) of four instructions.
Speculative execution	Process of the CPU trying to guess which instruction will be used next, and executing one or more instructions as a result of the guess.
Branch prediction	Process of the CPU trying to anticipate which code will be used next, based on history, and executing that code.
Register renaming	Technology that uses multiple sets of registers in the processor to provide multiple execution paths.
Out-of-order completion	Technology that enables superscalar processors to reassemble the results of instructions that were finished out of order into the correct order, thus assuring correct program execution.
Dual Independent Bus (DIB)	Architecture used in Pentium processors. Uses a bus between the processor and main memory and another bus between the processor and L2 cache. This increases throughput.
Multimedia Extensions (MMX)	A set of additional instructions to support sound, video, and graphics multimedia functions.
Single Instruction Multiple Data (SIMD)	Used in MMX, this processing technique allows a single instruction to work on multiple pieces of data.

Intel Processors

Intel CPUs include 8086, 8088, 80286, 80386sx, 80386DX, 80486sx, 80486DX, Pentium, Pentium MMX, Pentium Pro, Pentium II, Pentium III, Pentium 4, Celeron, Xeon, and Itanium to name a few of the most popular CPUs. AMD CPUs include K5, K6, K7, Duron, Athlon, and the variations on each of those models. Cyrix CPUs include MediaGX and M II, among others.

The following table summarizes some of the specifications for popular Intel processors.

Processor	Clock Speeds	Data Bus	Addressable RAM	Caches	Internal/External Voltage	Multiprocessor Support
Pentium	60, 66, 75, 90, 100, 120, 133, 150, 166, 180, 200 MHz	64-bit	4 GB	Two 8 KB L1	5 V/5 V (not split), or 3.3 V/3.3 V (not split)	Yes, up to two processors.
Pentium Pro	150, 166, 180, 200 MHz	64-bit	64 GB	Two 16 KB, and one 256 KB, 512 KB, or 1 MB L2	3.3 V/3.3 V	Yes, up to four processors.
Pentium with MMX	133, 150, 166, 200, 233, 266, 300 MHz	64-bit	4 GB	Two 16 KB L1	1.8 V to 3.3 V/2.5 V or 3.3 V	Yes, up to two processors.
Pentium II	233, 266, 300, 333, 350, 400, 450 MHz	64-bit	64 GB	Two 15 KB L1, and one 512 KB L2	2.0 V or 2.8 V/3.3 V	Yes, up to two processors.
Celeron	266, 300, 333, 366, 400, 433, 466, 500, 533, 566, 600, 633, 667, 700 MHz	64-bit	64 GB	Two 16 KB L1, and one 128 KB L2 on models 300A and above	1.30 V to 2.1 V/3.3 V	No.

Processor	Clock Speeds	Data Bus	Addressable RAM	Caches	Internal/ External Voltage	Multiprocessor Support
Pentium III	450, 500, 533, 550, 600, 650, 667, 700, 733, 800, 850, 866, 933, 1000 MHz	64-bit	64 GB	Two 16 KB L1, and one 256 or 512 KB L2	1.5 V to 2.05 V (earlier models 2.8 V)/3.3 V	Yes, up to two processors.
Pentium III Xeon	600, 667, 700, 733, 800, 866, 933, 1000 MHz	64-bit	64 GB	Two 16 KB L1, and 256 KB, 512 KB, 1 MB, or 2 MB L2	2.8 V or 5/12 V/3.3 V	Yes, up to eight processors.
Pentium 4	1.32 to 8 GHz	64-bit accelerated	64 GB	8 KB L1 and 512 KB L2	1.525 to 1.75 V	No

CPU Speeds

CPU speed is the speed at which instructions are processed. There are two speeds that affect the CPU speed. One is the core speed or the internal speed at which instructions are processed within the CPU. The other is the bus speed which is the speed at which instructions are transferred to the motherboard. The following table lists the speeds of some of the popular Intel CPUs.

CPU	Core Speed	Bus Speed
Pentium	75-200 Mhz	50-66 MHz
Pentium Pro	150-200 Mhz	60-66 MHz
Pentium with MMX	150-266 Mhz	66 MHz
Pentium II	233-400 Mhz	66-100 MHz
Pentium II Xeon	400-450 Mhz	100 MHz
Celeron	266 Mhz-2 GHz	66-400 MHz
Pentium III	533 Mhz-1.4 GHz	100-133 MHz
Pentium III Xeon	500 Mhz-1 GHz	100-133 MHz

CPU	Core Speed	Bus Speed
Pentium 4	1.32-8 GHz	400-533 MHz
Xeon	1.42-8 GHz	400 MHz

All CPUs are connected to the motherboard in some way. The CPU needs to be able to communicate with most every other component in or connected to the computer through pathways called *buses*.

The buses that have an affect on the CPU speed are shown in the following table.

Bus	Description
Internal	A communication pathway located within the CPU.
External	A communication pathway located outside of the CPU that connects the CPU to other system components.
System, Frontside, or Local	The primary communication pathway between a CPU and other parts of the chipset. Enables data transfer between the CPU, BIOS, and RAM.
Data	A subset of the system bus that carries instructions and data values between the CPU and RAM.
Address	A subset of the system bus that carries the memory locations indicating the source or destination of data or instructions being transferred over the system bus.

While chip makers might advertise that a CPU runs at a certain speed, the truth is that the computer won't necessarily run at that speed 100 percent of the time or maybe at any time. The advertised speed is actually the maximum speed at which the chip can run. In fact, the speed your computer will run at is probably less than the advertised speed. Other components, such as memory, frontside bus, and video cards, have an affect on the actual speed of your computer, depending on what you're doing on the computer at any given time.

Socket and Slot Types

Sockets and slots are the connectors that connect a CPU to the motherboard. There are many varieties of sockets and slots that have been developed over the years.

 Information about which processor in which packaging will fit into which socket or slot is available at **www.sandpile.org**.

Processors come in a variety of packages. The two most general categories of packages include slot-based and socketed. Slot-based processors plug into a system board in much the same way as an expansion board; socketed processors plug into a system board using a grid array of pins. When you replace a processor, you must select a processor that is compatible with the type supported by the sys-

Chapter 4: Upgrading System Components

tem board. Also, you must be careful to line up Pin 1 on the processor with Pin 1 on the socket; otherwise, the processor won't work and might even be damaged. Also, with socketed processors, you must be careful not to bend the pins when removing or inserting the processor; otherwise, you can ruin the processor, which is costly to replace. You can also purchase adapters that allow you to use a socketed processor in a slot-based system board.

The following table describes some of the sockets you might encounter.

Socket Type	Pin Layout	Processor Used For
Socket 0	168 pin inline	5v 486DX
Socket 1	169 pin inline	5v 486DX and 486SX
Socket 2	238 pin inline	5v 486DX, 486SX, 486DX2
Socket 3	237 pin inline	3.3v and 5v 486DX, 486SX, 486DX2, 486DX4
Socket 4	273 pin inline arranged in 21 x 21 PGA grid	5v Pentium 60 and 66
Socket 5	320 pin staggered arranged in 37 x 37 SPGA grid	3.3v early Pentium
Socket 6	235 pin inline arranged in 19 x 19 PGA grid	3.3v 486DX4
Socket 7	321 pin staggered arranged in 37 x 37 SPGA grid	Later Pentium, AMD K6, Cyrix 6x86, IDT
Super 7	321 pin staggered arranged in 37 x 37 SPGA grid	AMD K62 and K63
Socket 8	386 pin staggered ZIF arranged in 24 x 26 SPGA grid	3.3v Pentium Pro
Socket 370	Supports PPGA	Original Celeron
Socket 423	SPGA	Pentium 4
Socket 478	SPGA	Pentium 4
Socket A	Supports PPGA	AMD Athlon, Duron, Palomino, and Morgan

 For detailed information about Intel Desktop CPUs, you can refer to **http://infohq.com/Computer/intel-cpu.shtml**. Be sure to capitalize the word Computer or else this URL won't work.

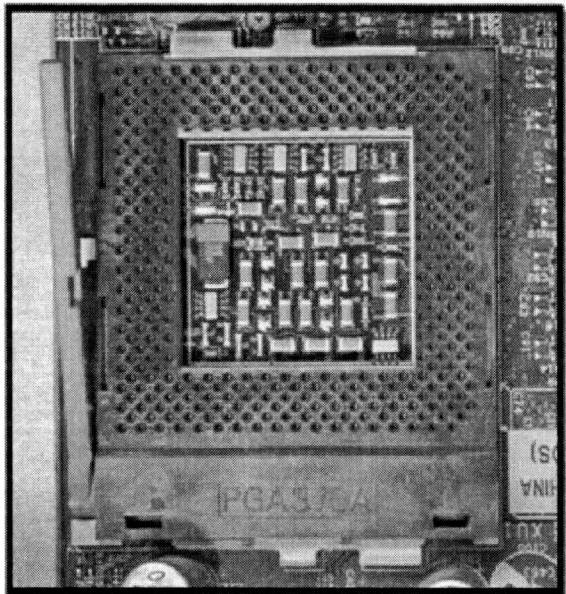

Figure 4-5: *Several types of CPU sockets.*

Some processors use slots to connect the CPU to the motherboard. The following table describes some of the slots you might encounter.

Slot Type	Description
Slot 1	Contains a 242-pin edge connector. Used for Celeron SEPP, Pentium II SECC and SECC2, and Pentium III processors.
Slot 2	Contains a 330-pin edge connector. Used for Pentium II Xeon and Pentium III Xeon processors. Designed for multi-processor systems.
Slot A	Contains a 242-pin edge connector. Used for AMD Athlon processors. Pinouts are incompatible with Slot 1.
Slot M	Used for Itanium processors.

Figure 4-6: *Slot 1 (for SECC packaging).*

CPU Package Types

Definition:

A CPU package is a package that describes the physical packaging or form factor of a CPU. This includes the size and shape of the CPU, along with the number and layout of the pins or contacts.

The CPU is relatively easy to locate because it is the biggest chip on the motherboard. Newer PCs make it even easier to find because it is usually installed in a larger socket, referred to as a Zero Insertion Force or *ZIF socket*. It uses a lever to tighten or loosen the pin connections between the processor chip and the socket, requiring no force to insert or remove a processor chip.

Figure 4-7: *A ZIF socket.*

Original CPUs were sometimes soldered onto the motherboard. Others used standard 169-pin screw machine sockets. You needed to use a special type of tool called a chip extractor to remove the chip. These look like big tweezers with bent over ends that go under the edge of the chip so you can pull it out. It takes around 100 pounds of force to install a chip in this type of socket. It was easy to damage the socket, the pins, or the chips.

As chips developed, they became faster. More features were integrated into the CPU that were previously carried on outside of the CPU.

Example:

The following table describes the package types used for some of the popular Intel CPUs.

 Photo examples of each of these package types can be found through links at **http://support.intel.com/support/processors/procid/ptype.htm**.

Package Type	Description
Flip Chip Pin Grid Array (FC-PGA)	Referred to as a flip chip, because the die (the part that makes up the chip) is exposed on the top of the processor to enable better chip cooling. Power and Ground signals are uncoupled to improve performance. Uses separate capacitors and resistors on the bottom of the processor. Contains 370 pins in a staggered arrangement so that the processor can only be inserted into the socket one way. Used in Pentium III and Celeron processors.
FC-PGA2	Contains 370 pins in Pentium III and Celeron versions. Contains 423 pins in the Pentium 4 version. Different from the FC-PGA in that this version includes an integrated heat sink attached directly to the processor.
OOI or Organic Land Grid Array (OLGA)	Uses a flip chip design. Integrated heat spreader to assist the heat sink. Used in Pentium 4 processors. Contains 423 pins.
Pin Grid Array (PGA)	Pins insert into a socket. Uses nickel-plated copper heat slug on top of the processor to improve thermal conductivity. Used by Intel Xeon processors. Contains 603 pins.
Staggered Pin Grid Array (SPGA)	Staggered arrangement of pins around socket's outer edge. Staggering enables more pins to be placed in the same surface area.

Chapter 4: Upgrading System Components

Package Type	Description
Plastic Pin Grid Array (PPGA)	Contains 370 pins. Used by early Celeron processors.
Single Edge Contact Cartridge (SECC)	Uses gold contacts rather than pins. Plugs into a slot. Package is covered in a metal shell. Package back is a thermal plate used as a heat sink. Package contains substrate circuit board to link processor, L2 cache, and bus termination circuits. Packages containing 242 contacts used in Pentium II Xeon processors. Packages containing 330 contacts used in Pentium III Xeon processors.
SECC2	Uses less casing material than the original SECC. Does not use the thermal plate found on SECC packages. Contains 242 contacts. Used in some versions of Pentium II and Pentium III processors.
Single Edge Processor (SEP)	Similar to SECC, but without a casing. Substrate circuit board visible from the outside. Contains 242 contacts. Used in early Celeron processors.

Other packaging technologies are used in mobile computing. These include Micro-FCPGA and Micro-FCBGA. The first is a variation on the desktop FCPGA. The second uses balls rather than pins (hence the difference in acronyms). The balls can't be bent like pins can.

Instruction Sets

Definition:

An *instruction set* is the collection of commands that is used by a CPU to perform calculations and other computing operations. All instruction sets perform calculations and other computing operations. They vary by:

- Whether they require fixed length instructions or not.
- Whether the instructions are carried out by hardware only or hardware and software.
- How many instructions it takes to execute a function.

Example:

The following table describes the three available instruction sets for PCs.

Instruction Set	Description
Complex Instruction Set Computer (CISC)	A design strategy for computer architectures that depends on hardware to perform complicated instructions. Do not require instructions to be of a fixed length. Allow for more complicated functions to be executed in one instruction. Most Intel processors fall into this category.
Reduced Instruction Set Computer (RISC)	A design strategy for computer architecture that depends on a combination of hardware and software to perform complicated instructions. Require instructions to be of a fixed length. RISC instructions are simpler and fewer than CISC, but more instructions are required to carry out a single function. Macintosh, IBM RS/6000, and Sun Microsystems computers use RISC. IBM, Motorola, and Sun manufacture RISC chips.
Explicitly Parallel Instruction Computing (EPIC)	A design strategy for computer architecture that is meant to simplify and streamline CPU operation by taking advantage of advancements in compiler technology and by combining the best of the CISC and RISC design strategies. EPIC-based processors are 64-bit chips. Intel IA-64 architecture, including Intel Itanium processors, is based on EPIC.

How to Replace the CPU

Procedure Reference: Upgrade the CPU

To upgrade the CPU:

1. Shut down the system and remove the existing CPU.
    a. Shut down the system.
    b. Unplug the power cord.
    c. Ground yourself and dissipate any static electricity you might be carrying.
    d. Pull up the lever on the side of the ZIF-socket CPU. If you have a different style CPU, refer to the system documentation for how to remove it.
    e. Pick the CPU straight up so that you don't bend any pins.

f. Place the old CPU in a safe location in an appropriate container to prevent damage to the CPU should you need or want to reinstall it later.

2. Install the new CPU.

   a. Align the pins on the CPU with the holes in the ZIF socket on the system board.

   b. Press the CPU lever back down to lock the CPU in place.

   c. Connect any power connections to the appropriate power connectors.

3. Reboot and verify that the CPU works. If the system boots, then the CPU was installed correctly. To verify that the CPU is reporting the correct information, you can view the System Properties dialog box and verify that the specifications listed match those of your CPU.

Topic C
Add a CPU

You just replaced the existing CPU with another CPU. Some system boards have the capacity to support more than one CPU. In this topic, you will add a second CPU to the system board.

You've probably heard that two heads are better than one. You might also have heard the CPU referred to as the brains of the computer. Well, if your system board supports it, you can have two CPUs installed at the same time. Your users might ask you to install a second CPU for them if they have multiprocessor-enabled applications.

How to Add a Second CPU

Procedure Reference: Add a Second Processor

To add a second processor:

1. Shut down the system, disconnect the power, and ground yourself.

2. Remove the terminator from the second processor socket.

3. Insert a CPU that is identical to the processor in the first processor socket.

4. Restart the system and verify that both processors are recognized in the System Properties window.

Procedure Reference: Remove a Second Processor

To remove a second processor:

1. Shut down the system, disconnect the power, and ground yourself.

2. Following the directions shown in the system board or processor documentation, locate the second processor, and remove it from the socket. The primary socket must contain a processor. So, if you are removing one of the processors, it cannot be the one in the primary socket. Refer to documentation for the system to determine which socket this is.

3. Following the directions shown in the system board or processor documentation, insert the terminator or other device in the second processor socket, or set the system board settings for a single processor.

4. Reboot the system and verify that it can boot successfully with the single processor. Through Device Manager, you can display information about the processor or processors in the system.

Topic D
Upgrade the System BIOS

You have made several upgrades to your system at this point. One of these upgrades, or one of those you might perform later, might require that your system BIOS be upgraded. In this topic, you will flash the BIOS to upgrade the BIOS firmware.

The BIOS that shipped with your system was probably fine for the components that were originally installed. However, as you add or replace components, as software is installed, and as enhancements are made available by the BIOS manufacturer, you should check to see if you should install a BIOS upgrade for your users. Sometimes the need will be obvious when the system won't boot; other times, you will be researching something about the system and find that an upgrade is available, so you will install it.

Basic Input Output System (BIOS)

Definition:

The *Basic Input Output System (BIOS)* is the set of instruction commands stored on a ROM chip that is used to start the most basic services of a system.

The instruction set can be changed by replacing the BIOS chip with one containing the new software or, if it is an EEPROM, by flashing the chip. Early systems required replacement of the BIOS chip. Almost every system you encounter will be flashable.

Example:

There are several BIOSs within a computer system. The system BIOS is the one that sets the computer's configuration and environment when the system is powered on. Other expansion cards and components can also contain BIOS chips. The firmware contained on these BIOS chips holds the configuration information for the component and often helps improve the speed of the device. Phoenix, AMI, and Award are popular BIOS manufacturers. PC makers license the BIOS from one of these companies.

Methods for Accessing the System BIOS

Each BIOS manufacturer has their own method for users accessing system setup menus. This is usually displayed when the system is booting and for many manufacturers is only displayed from a cold boot. The key or key combination is different between different BIOS manufacturers. You often need to be very quick to catch it and press the appropriate key(s). Also, sometimes the monitor display does not come on until after the message has passed. Some of the methods to access setup are displayed in the following table.

BIOS	Access System Settings Using
Compaq	F10 or F12
ALR	F2 or Ctrl+Alt+Esc
AMD	F1
AMI	Delete
Phoenix	Ctrl+Alt+Esc, Ctrl+Alt+S, or Ctrl+Alt+Insert

These are just a few of the BIOS manufacturers and the keys you need to access that specific BIOS setup program. There are many other BIOSs and methods. Refer to your screen or your documentation for information on how to access yours.

BIOS Settings

Definition:

BIOS settings are the hardware configuration settings that are stored in the CMOS. Every computer has a BIOS. The settings are always stored in CMOS. Exactly what the settings are called, the menus under which they are found, and the settings you can set vary. They vary based on the BIOS manufacturer and the hardware that is installed in the system.

Example:

The CMOS Setup utility usually has a menu across the top of the screen or down the screen. This will usually have a Main or General menu with settings for things like the system date and time, the language used in the CMOS Setup utility, and so forth. Other menus contain settings for:

- CPUs
- On-board devices (enable/disable)
- Parallel ports (uni- and bi-directional settings, enable/disable, ECP and EPP printer ports)
- COM/serial ports (including base I/O addresses, modes, enable/disable, interrupts, and DMA settings)
- Floppy and hard drives (enable/disable, boot order, speed, density, size, and type)
- Memory (speed, parity, and non-parity)
- Boot (whether the POST messages are displayed, which device to boot from, and in what order the boot devices should be searched)
- Security (passwords)
- Infrared ports
- Plug and Play
- Power (APM, ACPI, and Wake On LAN/PME/Modem Ring)
- Virus protection (enable/disable)

- Event log
- Video configuration settings
- Exiting the utility (with choices to save, discard, set defaults, and load defaults)

Firmware

Definition:

Firmware is a set of computer program instructions (software) that is permanently stored in ROM. It is the controller software for a device. It is most often written on an EEPROM so it can be updated with a flash program to fix any errors in the controller software or to improve device performance.

Example:

The system BIOS is the most common use of firmware you will encounter. The BIOS instructions are permanently stored in the firmware embedded on the BIOS chip. Firmware is also used in other components to off-load instructions from the CPU to the device to help speed up processing. Firmware can often be found in video, network, and modem expansion cards, as well as disk controllers and some drives. The software instructions can be changed by replacing the chip on which they are stored with a chip containing the new instructions, or, if it is stored on an EEPROM chip, by flashing the chip.

Non-Example:

Firmware is not hardware and it is not software. It is stored on a piece of hardware (ROM), but it is not the hardware itself. It is software code, but it can only be stored on a ROM, not in any other location.

How to Upgrade the System BIOS

Procedure Reference: Upgrade the System BIOS

To upgrade the system BIOS:

1. Determine the BIOS manufacturer for your system. You can do this by choosing Start→All Programs→Accessories→System Tools→System Information. The BIOS Version/Date and SMBIOS Version fields show information about the currently installed BIOS.

2. Download the BIOS upgrade from the system manufacturer's Web site. You will need to download the exact BIOS for your system. Using the wrong one can make your system unusable.

3. Following the directions found on the Web site, upgrade the system BIOS. In some cases, this will be to write the appropriate files to a boot or startup floppy disk, and in other cases, it might be to apply the upgrade directly from the Web site. Other options might also be available.

4. Through the System Information window, verify that the new system BIOS is recognized.

Topic E
Upgrade the Power Supply

You have now added several components to your system. While the original power supply might meet your power consumption needs if it is a newer system, older systems typically have relatively small power supplies compared to those in systems today. In this topic, you will upgrade the power supply.

Preventing system lockups, random reboots, and quirky behavior can sometimes be achieved by upgrading the power supply in a system. A system that is under-powered might experience any of those problems in addition to others. If you are upgrading components, be sure that your power supply meets the power needs you are placing on the system. This will prevent problems and hopefully prevent trouble calls to fix power problems.

Power Supply

Definition:

The *power supply* is an internal system component that converts AC power from an electrical outlet to DC power needed by system components. While not actually a component of the system board, it is required in order for system components to receive power. The power supply is attached to the computer case. It is also connected to the system board. It is a metal box in the rear of the system. It contains the power cord plug and a fan to cool it because it generates a lot of heat.

Some power supplies have a voltage switch. This enables you to set the voltage to that used in different countries.

There was no standard for power supply form factor. They could be whatever size fit the case and met the needs of the system board. Now, manufacturers have settled on an ATX-based power standard to fit an industry-standard ATX case and meets the electrical needs of an ATX system board.

Example:

An example of a power supply is shown in Figure 4-8.

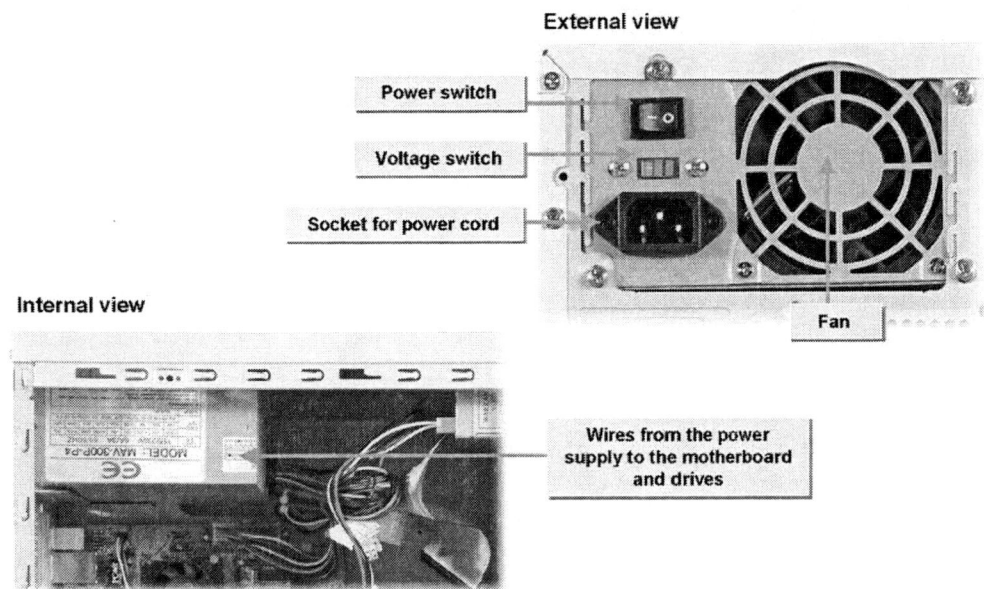

Figure 4-8: *A power supply.*

Watts

Power supply specifications are given in watts. A watt is volts times amps (voltage x amperes). Older systems typically had power supplies under 200 watts, and often even under 100 watts. The power supply sends power to all system components except for components requiring a high current. These components include the fan and disk drives. When you install additional components in a system, you need to make sure you have not exceeded the capacity of the power supply. If you have, you will need to upgrade the power supply.

Internal Power Connections

System components cannot use the 120-volt power coming directly from the electrical outlet. The power supply steps the voltages down to 3.3-, 5-, and 12-volt connections for system components. Wires are color-coded as to their voltages. The following table shows the wire color for each voltage connection.

Color or Component	Voltage
Yellow wire	+12
Blue wire	-12
Red wire	+5
White wire	-5
Motor	+/-12

Color or Component	Voltage
Circuitry	+/-5

System Board Power Supply Connections

The power supply connection to the system board is a keyed or unkeyed connection that enables the power supply to supply power to the internal components of the system. Keyed connectors are designed so that the plug and socket have notches which must line up in order for the plug to fit into the socket. Almost all connections are keyed today so that you can't accidentally plug it in backwards.

The connection also might use a single connector or two connectors. If there are two connectors, they are labeled P8 and P9, as shown in Figure 4-9. Be sure not to switch them when you plug them in or you could damage the system board. The trend has gone to having a single, keyed connector so that it can only be plugged in one way. This virtually eliminates the damage that can be caused to the system board by plugging the power connections in wrong.

A single keyed connector

A pair of connectors

Figure 4-9: *System board power supply connectors.*

Power supplies not only power the components directly connected to the system board through slots, but drives and other internal components as well. The power supply sprouts many connections besides the one to the system board. There are Berg and Molex connections. There is also a connection to the power switch for the system.

The pinouts for the system board ATX-based power connector are shown in the following table.

Pin Numbers	Color	DC Output
1, 2, and 11	Orange	+3.3 V
4, 6, 19, and 20	Red	+5 V
3, 5, 7, 13, 15, 16, and 17	Black	Ground
8	Grey	+5 V
9	Purple	+5 V
10	Yellow	+12 V
12	Blue	-12 V
14	Green	PS-ON
18	White	-5 V

Drive Power Connectors

Definition:

A drive power connector is a connector from the power supply that provides power to the internal drives. There are two types of internal drive power connectors sprouting from the power supply. The Berg connector is a small flat connector. This type of connector is typically used for connecting power to floppy drives, Zip drives, or SuperDisk drives. There are usually only one or two of these connectors. The Molex connector is the standard peripheral connector for powering internal IDE and SCSI drives. There are usually four or more of these connectors.

The peripheral device connector pinout is shown in the following table.

Pin Number	Color	Output
1	Yellow	+12 V DC
2	Black	Ground
3	Black	Ground
4	Red	+5 V DC

Example:

Examples of Berg and Molex connectors are shown in Figure 4-10.

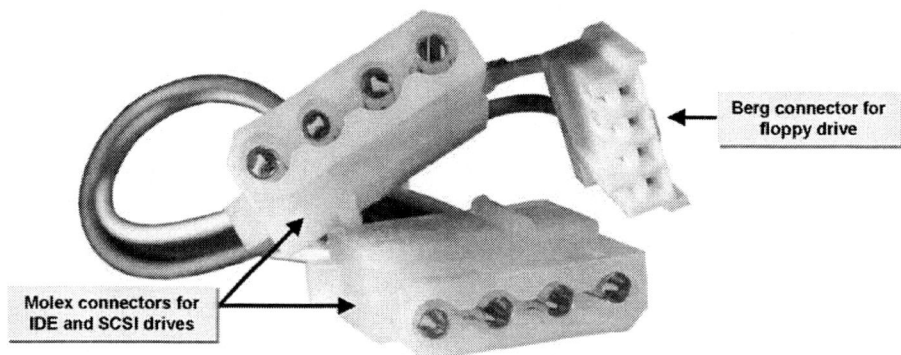

Figure 4-10: *Drive power connectors.*

How to Calculate Your Power Needs

Procedure Reference: Calculate Power Needs

In order to calculate whether your power supply meets your power needs, you will need to add up the maximum power you might use at one time. A range of maximum power consumption for various components has been established. Most components use much less than the maximum. You can check the documentation for the component to determine how much power it actually will use. The following table shows the wattages needed for some of the common components in systems.

Component	Wattage
ISA bus	12.1 watts
PCI bus	56.1 watts
AGP bus	25, 50, or 110 watts
PCI card	5 watts
AGP card	20 to 30 watts
SCSI PCI card	20 to 25 watts
Floppy drive	5 watts
RAM	10 watts per each 128 MB of RAM
7200 RPM hard drive	5 to 15 watts
1 GHz Pentium III CPU	34 watts
1.7 GHz Pentium 4 CPU	65 watts
300 MHz Celeron CPU	18 watts

Component	Wattage
600 MHz AMD Athlon CPU	45 watts
1.4 GHz AMD Athlon CPU	70 watts

To calculate the amount of power needed for your system:

1. Determine the number of watts used by each component. This should include the following components:
   - System board
   - CPU
   - RAM
   - Hard drives
   - CD drives
   - DVD drives
   - Floppy drives
   - Expansion cards
2. Add up all of the power needed by the system components.
3. Look at the label on the power supply to see what the maximum wattage output is.
4. Compare your computation with the power supply output. If you have not exceeded the power available, you won't need to upgrade. If you have, you will need to obtain a suitable power supply and install it.

How to Upgrade the Power Supply

Procedure Reference: Upgrade the Power Supply

To upgrade the power supply:

1. Remove the existing power supply.
   a. Shut down and turn off the system.
   b. Unplug the electrical power cord from the electric outlet and from the power supply.
   c. Remove any components needed to access the power supply and its connection to the system board. Some systems are very cramped inside and components, for instance, drive bay assemblies might cover the power supply to system board connections, part of the power supply, or both.
   d. Unplug all power connections from devices. Be sure to label each connection to make it easier to reconnect them when you are finished installing the new power supply.
   e. Unplug the power supply from the system board.

  f. Unscrew the power supply from the case.

  g. Remove the power supply from the case.

 2. Install the replacement power supply.

  a. Insert the power supply into the case.

  b. Secure the power supply to the case.

  c. Plug all power connections to devices.

  d. Plug the power supply into the system board.

  e. Reinstall any components you removed to access the power supply.

  f. Connect the power cord from the power supply to the electrical outlet.

 3. Test the power supply. To test it, turn on the system, and then try using the components to verify that they are properly powered. This should include all drives, network connections, and any powered devices.

Power Management Standards

The power management standards *Advanced Power Management (APM)* and *ACPI* are standards that were designed to reduce power consumption.

Two other methods of saving power are Hibernation and Suspend modes. Hibernation shuts down the PC saving the state it was in. There is a file created on the hard drive that is the same size as the amount of RAM installed on the system. All of the information in RAM is written to this file. Suspend mode turns off the hard drive and CPU, but it does not shut down the system.

AC Power

While internal system components rely on the power supply, other devices such as printers and external modems require their own direct supply of AC power. In such a case, the device must be plugged directly into a source of AC power such as a wall socket or power strip.

Power Supply Fan

Some power supplies enable you to see the RPMs of the power supply fan. You can then adjust the fan speed to run at only the speed needed to cool your system. This can reduce power consumption and save wear and tear on the fan.

TOPIC F
Upgrade the System Board

You have now installed, removed, or upgraded almost every component in the system. We've been dancing around the last component that we will upgrade. In this topic, you will upgrade the system board.

When it comes time to upgrade the system board, chances are that you also need to upgrade everything else as well, so this is not a very common upgrade that you will be asked to perform. Sometimes, however, you have already spent the money to upgrade everything else, so it makes sense to just upgrade the system board as well.

System Board

Definition:

A *system board* or *motherboard* is a circuit board that is the main circuit board in the computer. It contains the bus, processor, integrated circuits for peripherals, expansion slots, and BIOS chip. System boards come in a variety of shapes and speeds. All system boards are connected to the case and to all components within the system. The form factor varies between system boards. The system board might or might not have a daughter board or riser card, and it might or might not have a *voltage regulator module* (VRM), which is meant to regulate the voltage that's passed to the CPU. The chipset is the collection of all chips used on the motherboard. The functions that a computer supports is determined by the chipset. The chipset usually includes chips for the functions such as the following:

- CPU
- BIOS
- RAM
- Ports, such as parallel, serial, USB, keyboard, and monitor
- Expansion slots
- Drive interfaces

Example: A System Board with a Daughter Board

The system board is usually referred to as the motherboard. This is because other boards can be connected to it. Those boards are referred to as daughter boards or riser cards.

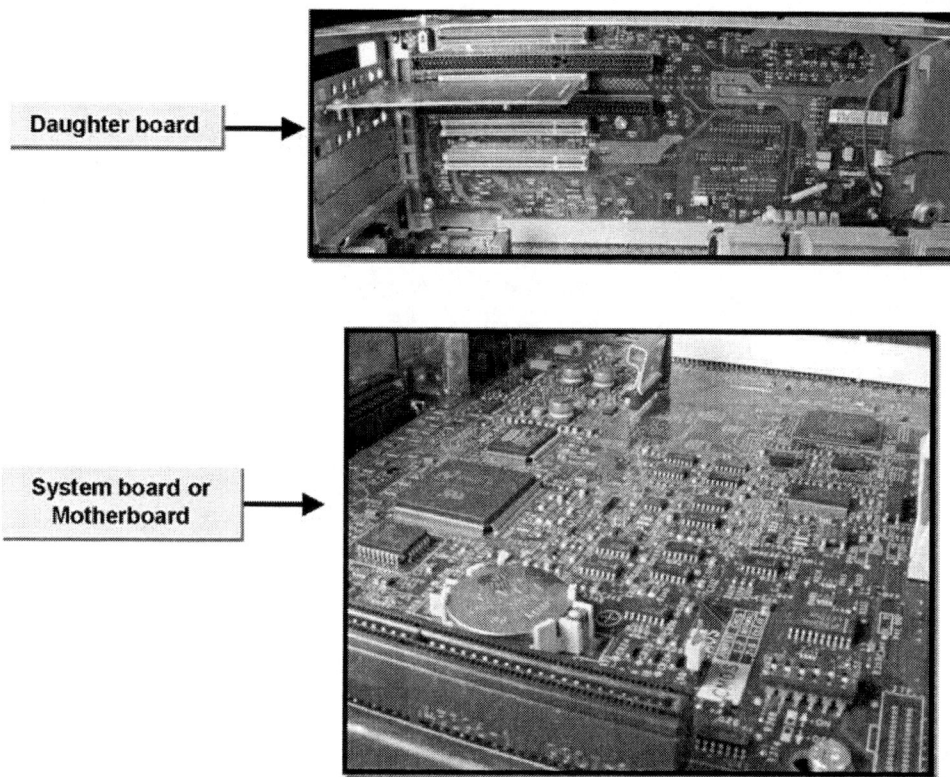

Figure 4-11: *A system board with a daughter board.*

Example: A System Board without a Daughter Board

The system board shown in Figure 4-12 shows a system board without a daughter board.

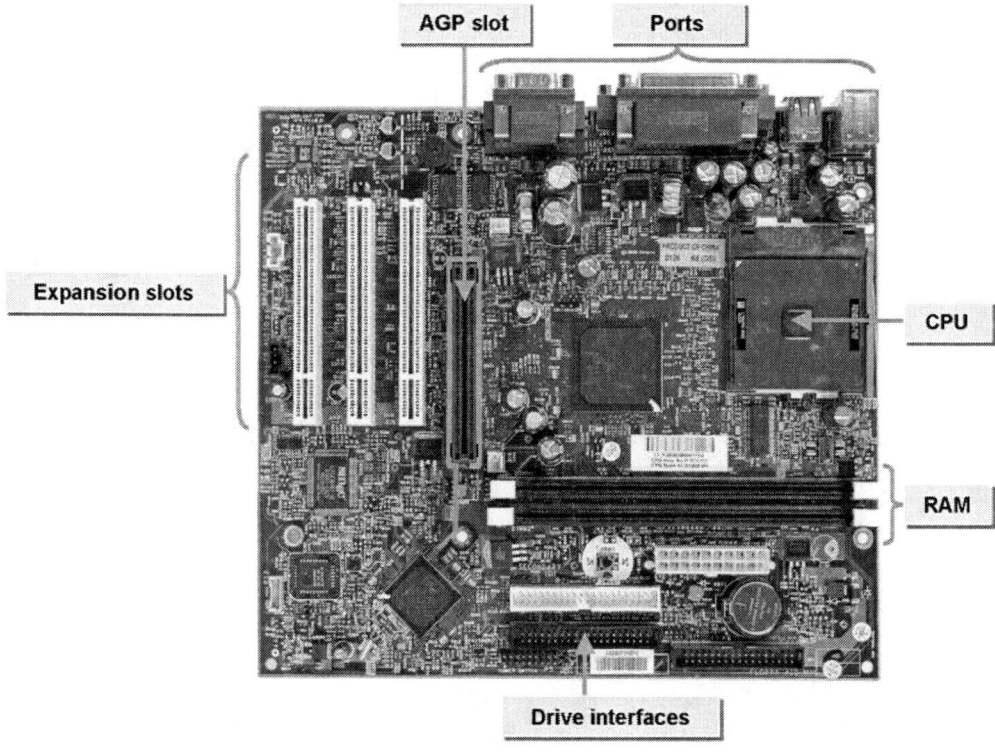

Figure 4-12: *A system board without a daughter board.*

Riser Cards

A riser card is like a daughter board in that it plugs directly into a slot on the motherboard and rises from the motherboard at a 90 degree angle. A riser card contains slots into which you can plug modems, audio cards, or network cards. Riser cards are meant to remove analog I/O processing from the motherboard for modems and audio components to make it easier for motherboard manufacturers to create and gain approval for new motherboard designs.

There are two types of riser cards:

- *Audio/Modem Riser (AMR)*—AMR riser cards plug directly into the motherboard and rise from the motherboard at a right angle. AMR riser cards are used to connect modems, and they support audio cards for higher-quality audio reproduction.
- *Communication and Networking Riser (CNR)*—CNR riser cards plug directly into the motherboard and rise from the motherboard at a 90 degree angle. CNR riser cards were meant to provide support for local area network (LAN) capabilities, modem, and audio cards.

Form Factors

The *form factor* is the size and shape of the motherboard. There are several different form factors that you might encounter, and they are described in the following list:

- Full-size AT—This is usually used in older tower systems. Originally, it was designed from the original XT motherboard. These original full-size systems took up a large amount of desktop space. By orienting tower systems vertically, they can stand on the floor and not take up desktop space, and they can still use the full-size system board. The board is 12 inches by 13.8 inches. A transfer bus of 16-bit or better is required. It uses CMOS to retain configuration settings. It has a 5-pin DIN keyboard connection.

- Baby AT—This is usually used in older desktop systems. In an effort to free up desk space, a smaller computer was needed than what was offered when a full-size AT motherboard was used. The popular AT motherboard was scaled down to create the Baby AT motherboard. It fits into a smaller case than the full-size AT board, but it is otherwise the same as the full-size AT motherboard. It works in any case except for those considered low profile or slimline. This was an extremely popular design. This board is usually 13 inches by 8.5 to 9 inches. It was never developed as a standard, so there are variations on the size of this particular board.

- LPX—Slimline and low-profile cases were being developed about the same time as the Baby AT motherboard was introduced. However, these smaller cases could not use even the Baby AT board. The LPX and Mini-LPX motherboards were developed for these cases. These are your typical desktop cases. A riser card is used to plug expansion cards into the motherboard. This riser card enables the expansion cards to lay sideways (the same orientation as the system board). Thus, the case does not have to be as high as the card. Another difference in this board is that it uses a PS/2-style keyboard connector rather than the 5-pin DIN connector used on the AT boards. Video, parallel, and two serial ports were placed at the rear of the board in standard locations. This board is 9 inches by 11 to 13 inches. A mini-LPX board was also designed which was 8 to 9 inches by 10 to 11 inches.

- ATX—In 1995, Intel introduced the ATX motherboard. It is the standard for new systems. Compared to AT motherboards, the ATX boards provide better I/O support, lower cost, easier use, and better processor support. Some of the features to note about the ATX board are:

    — Power supply with a single, keyed 20-pin connector. Rather than requiring VRMs to reduce voltage down from 5v3, 3v DC is available directly from the power supply.

    — The CPU is closer to the cooling fan on the power supply. Also, the cooling circulation blows air into the case instead of blowing air out of the case.

    — I/O ports are integrated into the board along with PS/2 connectors (instead of 5-pin DIN connectors).

    — You can access the entire motherboard without reaching around drives. This was accomplished by rotating the board 90 degrees.

    — This board cannot be used in Baby AT or LPX cases.

    — The board is 12 inches by 9.6 inches.

> The ATX Specification standard can be found at www.formfactors.org/developer/specs/atx/atx2_1.pdf.

- NLX—Intel's NLX system board replaces the LPX system board. It is a small form factor designed around the Pentium II processor. It supports DIMM technology and AGP technology. It is used in newer slimline design systems. The board is 8 to 9 inches by 10 to 13.6 inches.

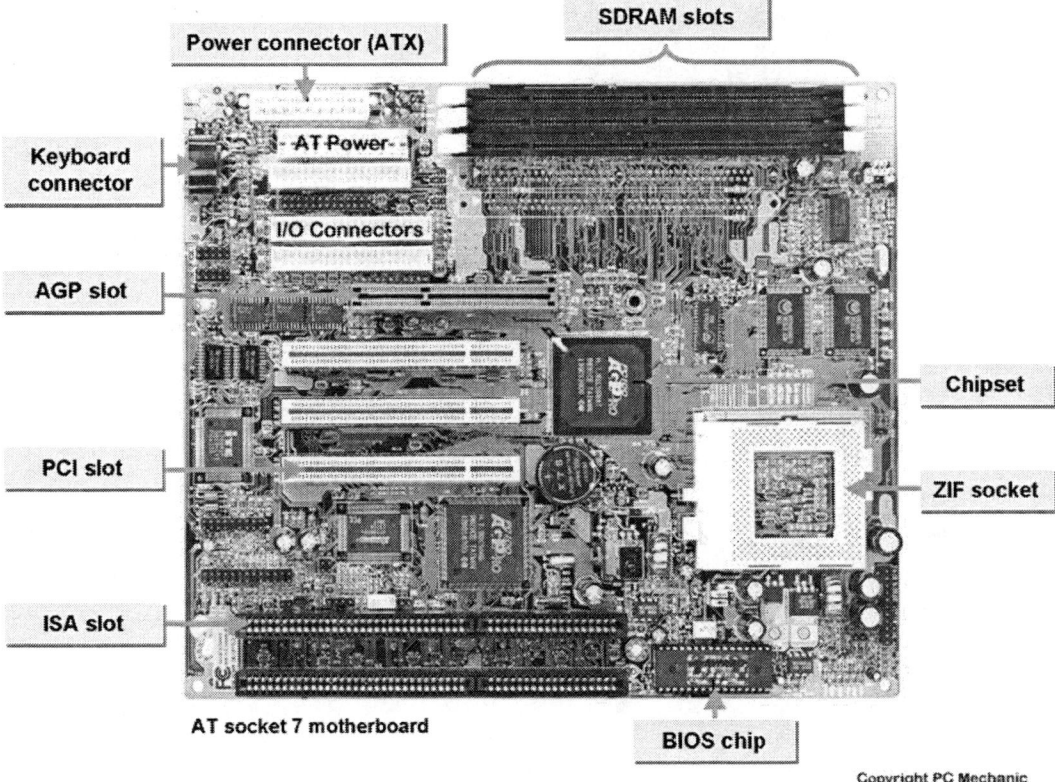

Figure 4-13: *Full-size AT system board.*

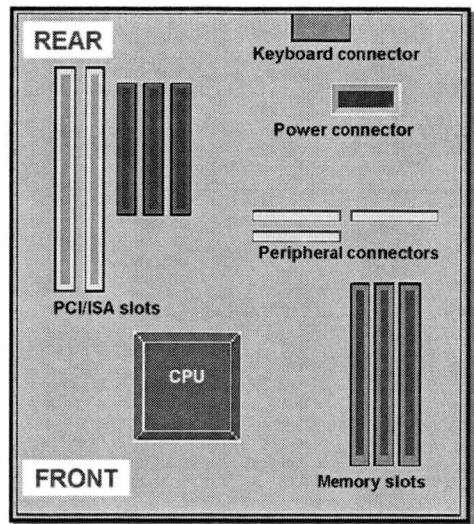

Figure 4-14: *Baby AT system board.*

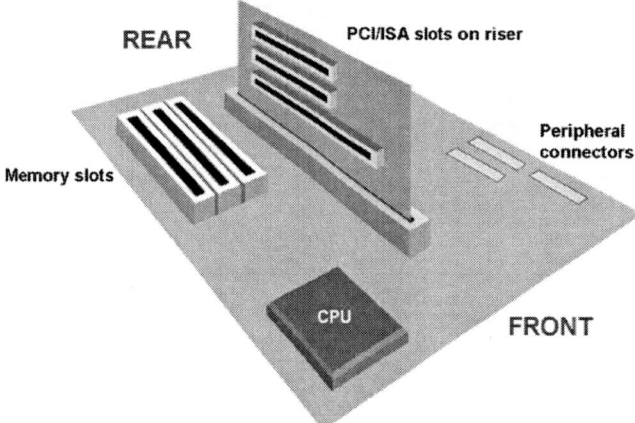

Figure 4-15: *LPX system board.*

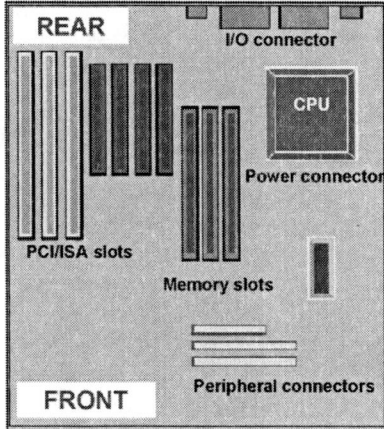

Figure 4-16: *ATX system board.*

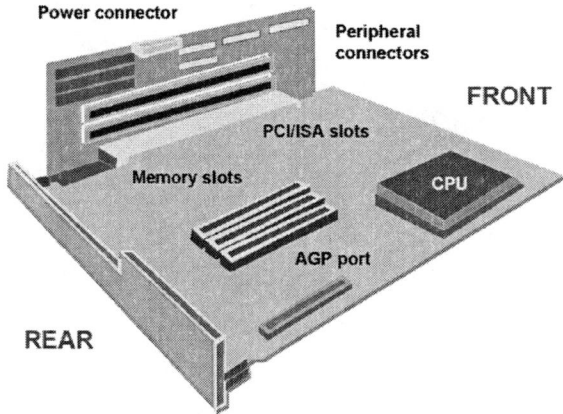

Figure 4-17: *NLX system board.*

Computer Cases

Definition:

The computer case is the enclosure that holds all of the components of your system. Computer cases come in several formats. Some are designed to hold lots of internal components and have lots of room to work around those components. These cases are usually tower cases and take up a good deal of room. Other cases are designed to use a minimum amount of space. The trade-off is often cramped cases with little room for adding additional components.

Since the tower proved to be popular, there are now several versions of the tower model. These include:

- Full tower, which is usually used for servers or when you will be installing many drives and other components.

Chapter 4: Upgrading System Components

- Mid tower, which is a slightly smaller version of the full-size tower.
- Micro tower, which is the size that replaces the original desktop case in most modern systems.

When you are replacing the system board, you need to make sure you get one that fits your case. This is because the holes in the system board need to line up with the connections in the case. The system board is secured to the case using these connections.

Also, when replacing the cover on the case, you must make sure the cover is properly aligned on the case. If the cover isn't properly aligned, it might affect the cooling system and the operating of the internal drives.

Example: Enclosure Styles

Figure 4-18 shows examples of computer cases.

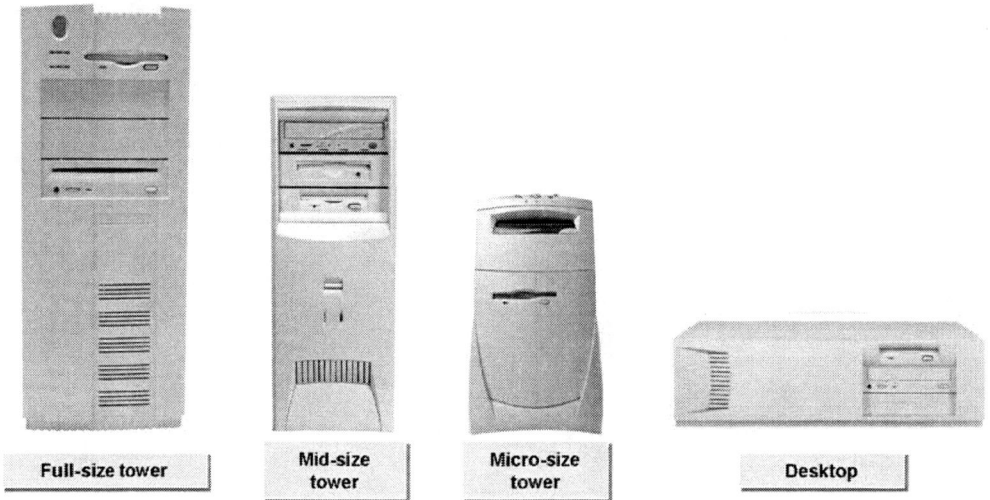

Figure 4-18: *Computer case enclosure styles.*

ATX System Board Components

The following figure shows a generic ATX motherboard. It identifies the basic components of a motherboard. Each of the components is examined in detail throughout this course, but let's examine the purpose of each of these components briefly. The table following Figure 4-19 describes each of the components.

 This example doesn't include infrared or Firewire ports, but yours may.

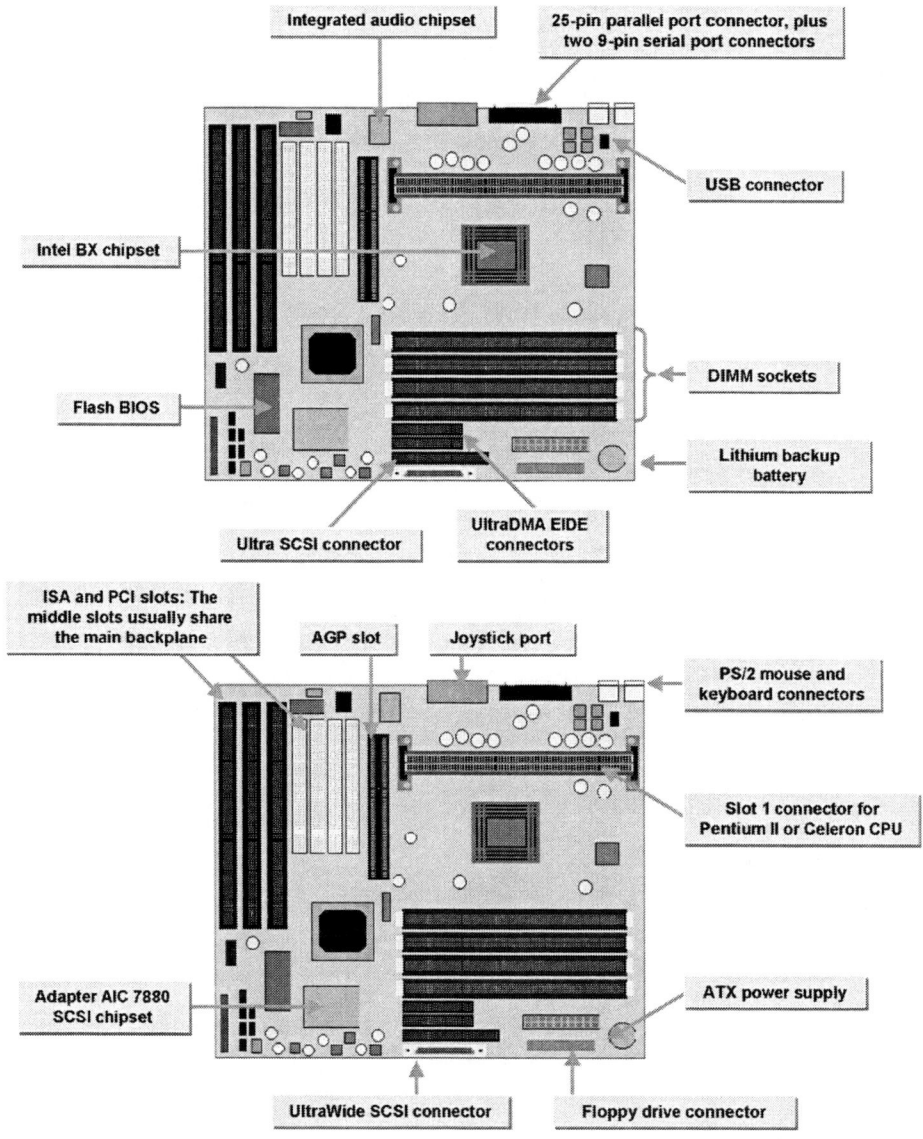

Figure 4-19: *A generic ATX motherboard.*

Component	Description
BIOS	Basic Input Output System; used for configuring system hardware.
Processor slot	Where the CPU is installed.

Chapter 4: Upgrading System Components

Component	Description
Memory slots	Where the system RAM memory is installed.
L2 cache	Where the processor stores frequently used data and instructions.
PCI slots	Slots for 32-bit PCI cards.
ISA slots	Slots for 8-bit and 16-bit ISA cards.
Keyboard connector	PS/2 port.
Mouse connector	PS/2 port.
Serial port	DB9 male connector.
Parallel port	DB25 female connector.
USB port	Peripheral connection designed to be Plug and Play compatible, and to eliminate the need to install expansion cards.
Chipset	Integrated circuit that provides the motherboard's core functionality.
AGP slot	Dedicated video card adapter slot.
Power supply connector	Connects the power supply to the motherboard.
Floppy drive connector	Connects the floppy drive to the system.
IDE connector	Connects fixed and removable IDE drives, such as CD, DVD, and hard drives, to the system.

How to Upgrade the System Board

Procedure Reference: Replace the System Board

Today's system boards are highly integrated and generally not repairable. When you examine a system board, you will find that there are very few components on the board that are actually repairable. For example, if a built-in port fails, you will have to install an expansion card that provides that port's functionality. If an integrated circuit fails, you will have to replace the system board. Even if you are highly skilled in the use of a soldering iron, in most cases, when a system board fails, you will replace it. Other than the battery, there is virtually nothing you can repair.

When you replace a system board, you must ensure that it is properly configured to match the processor that it will host. In essence, you must configure the system board so that the internal and external frequencies of the processor are compatible. You accomplish this by specifying a frequency multiple. Most system boards operate at a specific speed, but some enable you to select the speed via jumpers or through CMOS.

To replace the system board:

If you need to, you can perform these steps in a different order if it makes it easier to physically access components.

1. Remove the original motherboard.
    a. Shut down the system and unplug the power cord.
    b. Disconnect all external devices.
    c. Remove all expansion cards and store them in anti-static bags.
    d. Disconnect cables from the system board, marking each cable as to what it connects to and where it goes.
    e. Unscrew the system board from the case.
    f. Lift the system board out of the case. On some systems, after lifting the system board over the pin(s), you will need to slide it out of the case.

2. Install the replacement motherboard.
    a. Place the new system board into the case and align the mounting holes.
    b. Secure the system board to the case.
    c. Install RAM and processor(s) on the new system board. Some sources recommend installing these components prior to installing the system board. If you do this, be careful not to bend the board or mash any connectors on the bottom side of the system board as you insert the components.
    d. Reinstall cards and cables removed from the old system board.
    e. Test the system.

Other Ports on the System Board

While the following components are not necessarily found on all system boards, you may encounter them on some of the system boards you come across:

- Parallel port
- IEEE 1394/Firewire port
- Infrared port

Topic G
Decide When to Upgrade

Now that you're familiar with all the components in a computer, and you know what it takes to upgrade those components, you'll learn how to make the decision to upgrade. A thorough understanding of upgrade requirements is important to help you make an informed decision.

Upgrading computer hardware can be a costly undertaking. While the price of some hardware components might be lower now than in the past, a company-wide upgrade could mean considerable expense in both the cost of materials and the man-hours needed to actually perform the upgrade. As a result, sometimes companies will need real convincing that a hardware upgrade is absolutely necessary. In this topic, you'll learn how to make the right decision.

Indications You Need to Upgrade

There are many occasions that will indicate when you might need to upgrade system components. Table 4-1 includes some indications that you might need to upgrade your system hardware.

 You might find that upgrading one component will require the upgrade of another component.

Table 4-1: *When You Might Need to Upgrade*

Component	You Might Need to Upgrade When
Memory	You want to upgrade the operating system or install high-end software that requires more RAM; or when users report that system response time is slow and a resultant increase in productivity can be demonstrated to justify the cost.
Processor	You want to upgrade the operating system or install high-end software that requires a faster processor; or when users report that system response time is slow and you can double the speed of the machine, and increased productivity can be demonstrated to justify the cost. (Look for a CPU with a cache, which will be faster than a cache on the motherboard.)
System BIOS (firmware)	You want to install a new hardware component, such as a hard drive or processor, that may not be supported by the current system BIOS; the manufacturer has released a bug fix or security patch; or the newer BIOS supports a necessary feature, such as USB devices, that the current BIOS doesn't support.
Power supply	The power supply isn't adequate for the system components that rely on it.
System boards (motherboards)	You need to install a device or hardware component, such as a processor, that the current motherboard doesn't support, or you need to install a device, such as a network card, but all the motherboard's slots are in use.
Network adapter card	The current network card doesn't support the current or planned network configuration; or if the vendor removes support for a legacy device, because you won't be able to obtain updated drivers or drivers for new operating systems.

Component	You Might Need to Upgrade When
Hard drive	The hard drive is running out of free space when all unnecessary files are deleted, especially important if free space falls below 200 MB.
Video cards	The video card doesn't support the kind of graphics your applications output, or if your video card doesn't support a new monitor.
PCMCIA cards (Type I, II, or III)	The slots on a new notebook don't support your current cards.
Bus	The motherboard is incompatible, or a necessary system component is not supported.

How to Decide to Upgrade

Deciding when to upgrade a system's hardware can be a complex task. But if you make the correct decision, you will have a system that supports all the necessary hardware components, operating systems, and applications that a user needs to be productive.

Guidelines

To make the decision to upgrade:

- Determine if the memory is sufficient for the current operating system, applications, and other system resources, or for the operating system, applications, and other system resources you plan to upgrade to.
- Determine if the processor is adequate for the current operating system, applications, and other system resources, or for the operating system, applications, and other system resources you plan to upgrade to.
- Determine if the system BIOS supports current hardware or hardware you plan to install; if the current system BIOS contains the necessary security configurations; or if there are any bugs in the current system BIOS that are hindering performance.
- Determine if the power supply is adequate for the installed components or for components you're going to install.
- Determine if the motherboard will support a device you need to add.
- Determine if the network card supports the current or planned network configuration.
- Determine if there is sufficient hard disk space to support current or planned operations.
- Determine if the video card supports graphics generated by current applications or those you plan to install, or if the video card adequately supports the current monitor or one you plan to add.
- Determine if the PCMCIA cards are supported by the slots in the current or planned notebook computers.
- Determine if the bus is compatible with the current motherboard and system components or those you plan to install.

Example: New Operating System

You have a Windows 98 system with a Pentium 133 processor, 32 MB of RAM, and a 2 GB hard disk that has 250 MB of hard disk space. You plan to upgrade from Windows 98 to Windows XP, and to determine if the current hardware will support the new operating system, you look at the minimum configuration requirements for Windows XP. You determine that you will need to upgrade the processor, the RAM, and the hard disk to support the new operating system.

Cost/Benefit Analysis

After determining that you need to upgrade system components, you need to determine what the cost of those upgrades will be. After investigating cost, you might find that you can't afford the upgrades, that the cost of performing the upgrades outweighs the potential benefits of the upgrade, or that it is more cost effective to buy an entirely new system.

CHAPTER 4 FOLLOW-UP
Upgrading System Components

In this chapter, you upgraded several system components. In many cases, this is nothing more than installing a new component, or removing an existing component and replacing it with a new one. You upgraded the memory, CPU, system BIOS, power supply, and system board. You also added a second CPU to a multi-processor system.

Essential Terms

- BIOS
- BIOS settings
- computer cases
- CPUs
- CPU cache
- CPU packages
- CPU performance factors
- CPU speed
- firmware
- form factors
- instruction sets
- memory
- memory packages
- motherboards
- multiprocessing
- power connections
- power supplies
- processors
- RAM
- RAM speed
- ROM
- system BIOS
- system boards
- upgrades

Review Questions

1. What is the definition of volitile memory?
2. What type of RAM is used for cache memory? Why?
3. What type of DRAM is used for video cards?
4. Which RAM is slower: 10 ns, 40 ns, or 60 ns?

5. What is the name of memory that is located on the same microchip as the CPU? What kind of memory is it?
6. What is the bus or bridge that connects L2 cache to the CPU chip?
7. What kind of memory is used on SIMMs and DIMMs and needs to be refreshed every few milliseconds?
8. What is EEPROM?
9. What kind of memory package would you expect to find in a Pentium IV system?
10. What kind of memory package has a 168-pin connection to the slot?
11. What is parity and what is its purpose?
12. What is the function of the system BIOS?
13. Where are your system's BIOS settings stored?
14. What is firmware and where is it stored?
15. Older power supplies used two connectors to connect to the motherboard. What were the connectors labeled?
16. What kind of connector is used to power hard drives?
17. What kind of connector is used to connect the power supply to a floppy drive?
18. What is hibernation?
19. What happens when you put the PC in suspend mode?
20. What is the main circuit board of a computer system?
21. What is the function of a riser card?
22. What are two types of riser cards?
23. What is a motherboard form factor?
24. What is the standard motherboard form factor?
25. What form factor typically uses riser cards?
26. What kind of connector does an ATX power supply use?
27. When would you need to upgrade (or "flash") the system BIOS?
28. The Control Unit of a CPU performs several functions which are referred to as the machine cycle. What are the functions?
29. What is the purpose of a math coprocessor?
30. How does a heat sink keep a CPU cool?
31. What is the clock speed of a CPU?
32. What is multiprocessing?
33. What is the amount of RAM that a Pentium III 800 MHz can address?
34. What is the socket type for an AMD Athlon?
35. What is a pin grid array and what type of processor uses it?

Review Projects

Project #1 Introduction to Hyper-threading

Intel has developed Hyper-Threading Technology which enables one physical processor to act like two processors to the operating system. To investigate what hyper-threading is, read the short article, "Hyper-Threading Technology: Maximizing Processor Performance" on Intel's Web site (**http://www.intel.com/labs/features/ht11021.htm#move**). Once you have a general idea of what hyper-threading entails, work through the tutorial titled, "Introduction to Hyper-Threading Technology," located at **http://cedar.intel.com/media/training/hyper_threading_intro/tutorial/index.htm**

If you were preparing a short presentation on the advantages of hyper-threading for a local company, what specific benefits of hyper-threading would you discuss? Why?

Project #2 Investigating Your System BIOS

The system BIOS (basic input/output system) is firmware that controls much of your computer's input and output functions. When you first boot your computer, the BIOS checks communication with devices such as the hard drive, video card, and RAM chips. If no errors are found, you'll hear one beep which means that the POST (power on self test) was good. In this exercise, you'll enter the BIOS setup and explore the different settings available.

Hard boot your PC and watch the screen carefully. At the bottom left of the screen you should see a long string of numbers and the keyboard key or key combination to press to enter the BIOS (your machine may use the term Setup). Press the key or key combination to enter you system's BIOS. Depending on your BIOS setup, there may be headings along the top of the screen or along the side of the screen. Write down each of the headings. Explore the settings under each tab.

While exploring the system BIOS, record the following:

- Can you change the boot order of your PC (for example, set the order so the machine boots from the CD-ROM)? Under what tab is that setting located?
- Does the computer have security settings? If so, what are they?
- What information is available about the processor?
- Does your BIOS tell you the temperature inside the machine?

After you've explored that system BIOS, you should make a copy of the settings. If the BIOS becomes corrupted or if the CMOS chip's battery fails, you'll have all the necessary information to restore your BIOS settings. You'll use PrtSc to print each of the BIOS setup screens. To do this, you must have a print device that uses a parallel port (network, serial, USB, or FireWire connections will not work). Within each of the BIOS setup screens you can press the printscreen key (PrtSc) on the keyboard (this calls the BIOS service). The output of the screen will be sent to the print device. If you make any changes to settings make sure you change back to the original values (unless you're sure you want to make a particular change). Also, when you exit the BIOS you can exit without saving so any changes you make will be lost.

Project #3 How PC Power Supplies Work

When you investigate the individual components in a computer system, it's important to understand how they function so you can make informed purchasing decisions. The power supply is, in essence, the lifeblood of your computer system. To understand how it works (and why you should never work on one), read the tutorial on the How Stuff Works Web site (**http://computer.howstuffworks.com/ power-supply.htm**). After you complete the tutorial, open your computer's case and make a list of all the components. Using the information provided in the tutorial (and use a search engine if you need other, more specific information), determine the minimum wattage your computer's power supply should be based on your research. Log your information in a text file and save it to your Hardware Documentation folder on the C drive.

Reflective Questions

1. What components will you upgrade most often at your job? Why?

2. Will you need to upgrade motherboards at work? How often might you need to perform this task? Why?

CHAPTER 5
Supporting Portable Computing Devices

Chapter Objectives:

In this chapter, you will install, configure, and work with various portable computing devices. You will:

- Set up a notebook using a docking solution.
- Install or remove drives in portable computing devices.
- Install a PC Card into a portable computer.
- Replace a Mini-PCI card.
- Install, add, or remove memory to a portable computing device.
- Connect a PDA to a desktop or portable computer.

Introduction

Up to this point, you have been working on desktop systems; however, not all users are content with being tied to a specific location. In this chapter, you will begin supporting portable computing devices.

In most companies, a hardware technician will need to support more devices than the desktop systems. There are often a variety of portable computing devices you will be asked to support as well. Many of the skills you acquired in supporting desktop systems also apply to portable systems. Being able to support both mobile and non-mobile systems is an important skill you will need to develop to keep your users' systems up and running properly.

TOPIC A
Connect External Peripherals to a Portable Computer

While the skills you have developed up to this point have been practiced on desktop or non-portable computer systems, many of those skills also apply to portable computer devices. In this topic, you will investigate how you can connect external peripherals to a portable computer system.

The first time a user receives a portable computer, they are often very excited about the mobility this gives them. They often quickly realize though that they have made a significant trade-off—they gave up the larger monitor, keyboard, and pointing device they had on their desktop system. For some users, this is not a problem. For others though, the need to have those larger peripherals whenever possible is highly desirable. You will need to be able to connect external peripherals to their portable systems.

Portable Computing Devices

Definition:

A portable computing device is a computer that can easily be moved from one location to another. Some of the features all portable computing devices share include:

- The devices are small and lightweight.
- They have their own internal power source that is typically a rechargeable battery pack, but could be standard consumer batteries.
- They connect to other devices or systems.
- They can function without being connected to other devices or systems while in the portable state.

The following list includes the ways that portable computing devices vary:

- The portable computing device can be a complete system (with all of the functions of a desktop computer) or it can have limited functionality (which acts like a computer peripheral).
- How the batteries are recharged varies. Some systems recharge while the device is plugged in and you are using it through AC power; other devices require that you remove the battery pack and place it in a recharger.
- The length of time the device can run from battery power varies.

- When connected to other systems or devices, its function can vary. It can be a network node, a peripheral, or even an input or output device to the computer.
- It can use the same operating system as desktop systems or it can require its own operating system. Other devices use no operating system, but uses commands written to chips in the device.
- Most devices can be expanded in functionality by adding cards to the device. The cards and types of functionality you can add varies.
- Most devices use some sort of storage medium. This varies from removable drives to flash memory cards. The size, format, and connection type varies for each of these storage devices.
- The power cords are not usually interchangeable between brands or even models of notebook computers.

Example: Notebook Computer

A notebook computer is a small, lightweight portable computing device that runs on battery power. You can connect them to other devices, such as a printer, or they can function without being connected to another device. Notebooks are a complete system. You can also run some notebooks through a DC power adapter that you can plug into a cigarette lighter in a car or into a special outlet on some airplanes. Battery power typically lasts from 45 minutes to 4 hours. After that time, you will need to plug it into an electrical outlet to continue working. The batteries are recharged while it is plugged in. Notebooks use Windows operating systems, and you can expand their functionality by adding cards to them.

The model pictured in Figure 5-1 weighs only 3.5 pounds. Its battery power lasts about 1.5 hours per charge and takes about 8 hours to fully recharge. It includes integrated peripherals and can also use external peripherals and includes standard desktop hardware interfaces. It uses a Windows desktop operating system. It can be connected to a network or used as a standalone system. Functionality can be expanded by adding adapter cards to the system.

Figure 5-1: *A notebook computer as an example of a portable computing device.*

Example: PDA

A Personal Digital Assistant (PDA) can be used as a standalone device or as a peripheral to a notebook or desktop system. An example PDA is shown in Figure 5-2. It is powered by rechargeable batteries. It uses its own operating system, the Palm OS. To recharge it, it is connected to the computer through a standard peripheral port. This connection goes to the USB port and to the electrical outlet. This PDA has a slot to add additional functionality that was not built into the device. This PDA has software installed so the user can view and edit desktop documents. The input for this device is a stylus rather than a keyboard. Input can also be obtained through its connection with the host computer.

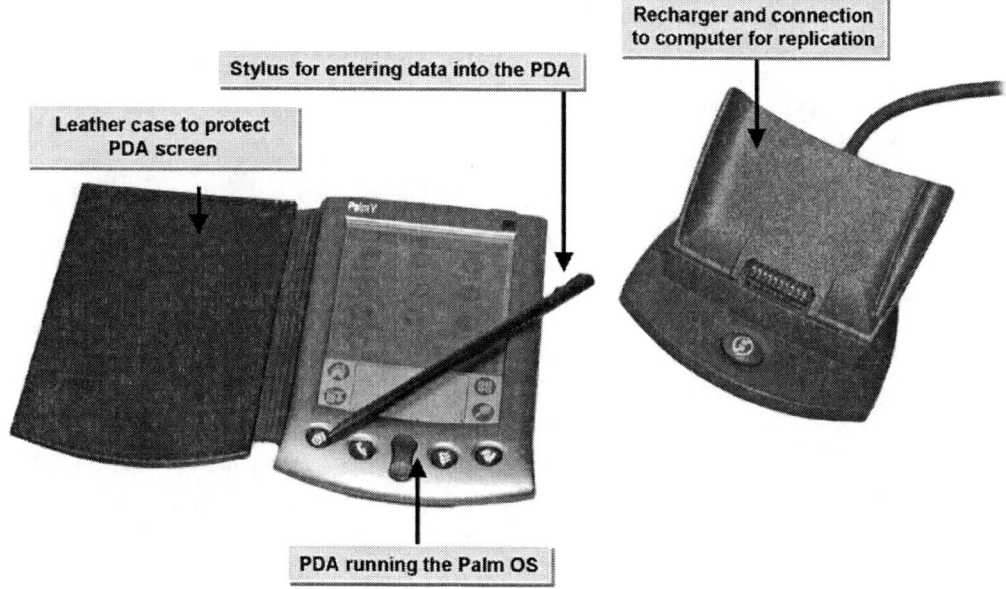

Figure 5-2: *A PDA as an example of a portable computing device.*

Notebook Computers

Definition:

A notebook computer is a portable computer that is small, lightweight, and portable. All notebooks:

- Use a CPU designed especially for use in a portable computer.
- Have hard drives that can be easily removed.
- Have battery packs that can be easily removed.
- Can run on battery or AC power.
- Use memory designed especially for portable computers.
- Use integrated peripherals for the monitor, keyboard, and pointing device.
- Use PC Cards for expansion cards. PC Cards connect to the Card bus.
- Uses SODIMM or proprietary memory.
- The monitor is hinged at the bottom and swings down to form the cover for the laptop. It latches to the body of the computer to secure it for transport.

Notebook computers vary by the following factors:

- Size of the notebook. Some larger ones are referred to as laptops because they fit in your lap. They typically have more features. Some smaller ones are referred to as sub-notebooks and typically have fewer features.
- Display size, quality, and technology.

- Keyboard size, number of keys, and options.
- Pointing device used.
- Power supply type (Lithium Ion or NiMH battery, or a fuel cell).
- Battery type used.
- Length of battery support time.
- How long it takes to recharge the battery.
- Power cord connection.
- Docking solutions.
- Connections for external peripherals.
- The power button can be located inside or outside of the closed case. It is more often located inside so that it isn't accidentally turned on when it is in the user's briefcase or being transported in some other bag.
- Bays or connections for additional drives such as floppy drives, and CD-ROM, CD-RW, or DVD drives.
- Since notebooks are easily stolen, there is usually a security cable slot.

Example: A Notebook Computer

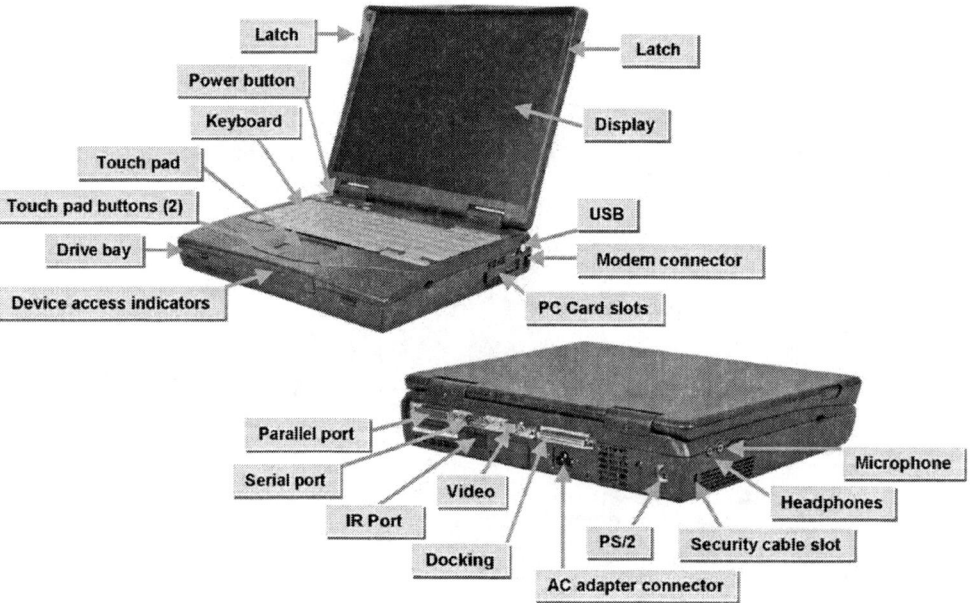

Figure 5-3: *A notebook computer.*

Security Slot and Cable

Most notebooks contain a security slot. A security cable with a plate that fits inside the slot can be secured around a stationary object such as a chair or table. Turning the key rotates the plate so that it cannot be slipped back out of the slot without breaking the computer case. This is shown in Figure 5-4.

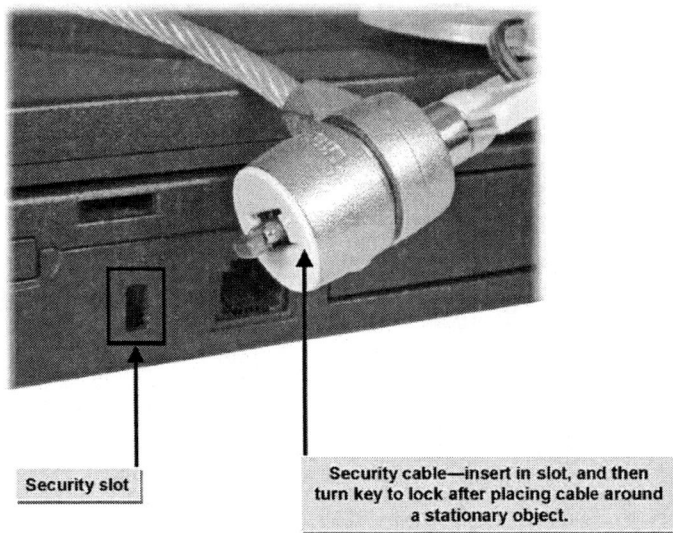

Figure 5-4: *A security slot and cable.*

Integrated Peripherals

Definition:

An integrated peripheral is a peripheral that is built into the computer and contained within the computer's case. In desktop and portable computers, this includes internal drives. In portable computers, this also includes the keyboard, pointing device, and monitor.

Integrated peripherals have a variety of characteristics, some of which are described in the following list.

- The monitor varies by size, resolution, and technology used to create the image. They are LCD displays. LCD displays are used because they are flat, take up less room, and use less power.
- The keyboard varies in the size and number of keys. Some keys that are separate on a desktop keyboard are shared on a notebook keyboard. Keys might be smaller than those on a desktop keyboard and are almost always closer together.
- The pointing device varies in type and location.

Example: Integrated Monitor

Figure 5-5 shows an example of a notebook with an integrated monitor. This notebook uses an active matrix LCD monitor.

Figure 5-5: *An integrated monitor.*

Example: Integrated Keyboard

Figure 5-6 shows an example of a notebook with an integrated keyboard. This keyboard uses the Fn key to access the functions that are shared with standard typewriter keys. These include the number pad keys, brightness and contrast for the integrated monitor, Home, and End, among others.

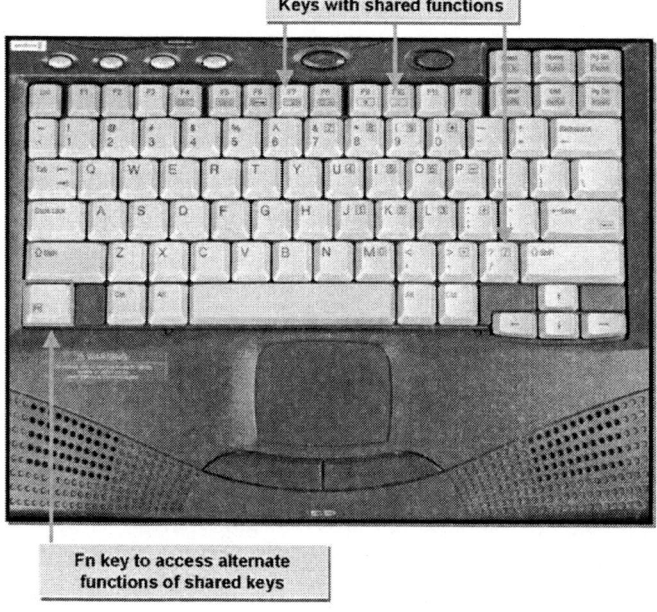

Figure 5-6: *An integrated keyboard.*

Example: Integrated Pointing Device

Figure 5-7 shows an example of a notebook with an integrated pointing device. This notebook computer uses a touch pad pointing device with separate mouse buttons. You can also tap the glide pad device to simulate pressing mouse buttons.

Figure 5-7: *An integrated pointing device.*

Chapter 5: Supporting Portable Computing Devices

Types of LCD Screens

There are two types of LCD screens:

— Active Matrix—This is also known as Thin-Film Transistor or TFT. It uses one transistor for each pixel. It requires more power than a passive matrix monitor, but provides a better quality image with a wider viewing angle and faster screen updates.

— Passive Matrix—Uses two groups of transistors combined with a wire matrix to produce images. Images are lower quality than CRT or active matrix, usually limited to 256 colors. Screen updates are slow as they are drawn line by line.

Commonly Used Pointing Devices

Commonly used pointing devices include

— Trackball—A trackball like those used on a desktop are integrated into the notebook case.

— Trackpoint—Also known as a pointing stick. A small eraser-shaped device in the center of the keyboard that works like a very short joystick.

— Trackpad—Also known as a touch pad or glide pad. An electromagnetically sensitive pad that tracks movement of a finger to move the mouse pointer. Mouse clicks can be simulated by tapping the pad. There are usually buttons for mouse clicks as well. This is less precise than the other integrated pointing options.

Docking Solutions

Definition:

Docking solutions are desktop devices that connect portable computers to standard desktop peripherals without needing to connect and disconnect the peripherals when you switch from being mobile to working at the desk with the external peripherals. All docking solutions:

- Enable you to use full size peripherals such as mouse, keyboard, monitor, and printer which are connected to the docking solution.
- Are proprietary; there are no standards, so you need to purchase the docking solution from the notebook manufacturer that is specific to your model notebook.
- Contain hardware interface ports.

Docking solutions vary in that they might:

- Use the same power cord as is used to plug the notebook in directly to an electrical outlet, or they might use a different power cord.
- Contain slots for desktop expansion cards.
- Contain bays for additional drives.
- Contain additional ports not found on the notebook computer.

Example: A Port Replicator

Figure 5-8 shows a port replicator. This port replicator includes standard desktop ports for full size peripherals, such as a mouse and keyboard, plus a proprietary connector for an external drive. This notebook does not have drive bays for removable media devices such as floppy drives or CD-ROM/DVD drives, so it connects them through a cable as an external device. The connector for the laptop to connect to the port replicator is located on the bottom of the notebook computer.

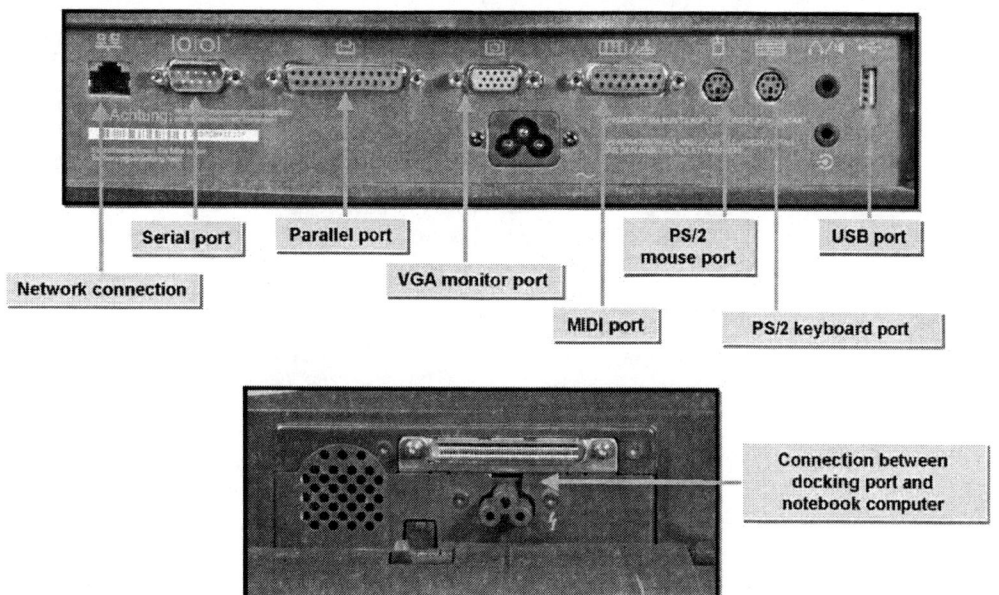

Figure 5-8: *A port replicator.*

Example: A Docking Station

A docking station is also known as a multiport. It is commonly used when the user uses the notebook as a desktop replacement. The notebook is connected to the docking station through a docking port located on the back or bottom of the notebook. Docking stations typically contain duplicates of the standard desktop ports which are also found on the notebook. In addition, there are often slots for desktop PCI or ISA expansion cards, drive bays for additional mass storage devices, and possibly additional ports and connectors. An example of a docking station is shown in Figure 5-9.

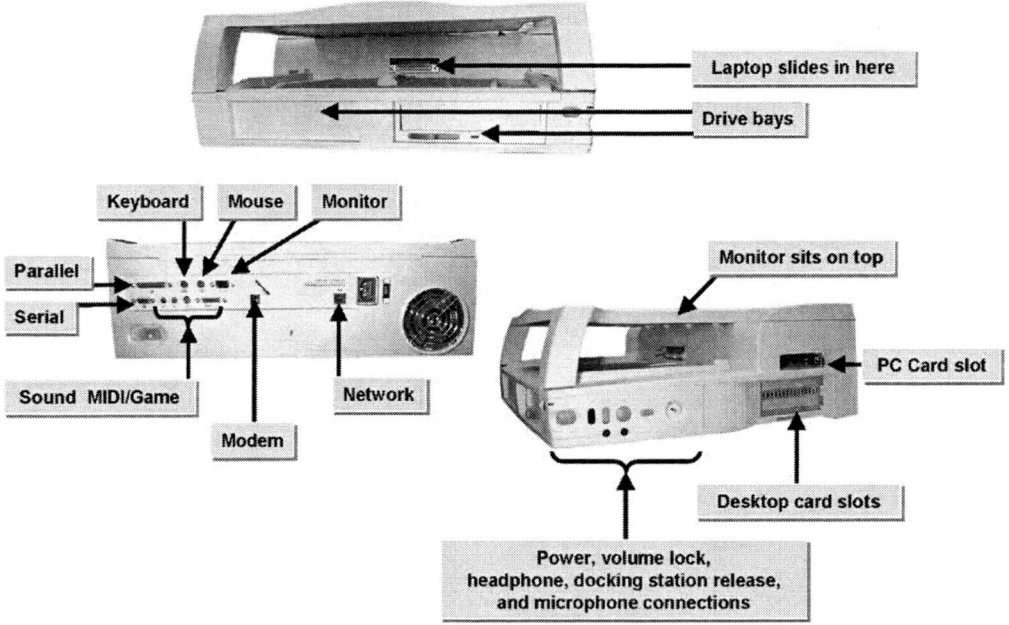

Figure 5-9: *A docking station.*

Non-Example: Direct Connections

Connecting external peripheral devices directly to the ports on the notebook computer is not an example of a docking solution. This is because each time you want to switch between stationary and mobile use, you would need to disconnect or reconnect each of the peripheral devices from the computer. An example of the ports on a notebook computer are shown in Figure 5-10.

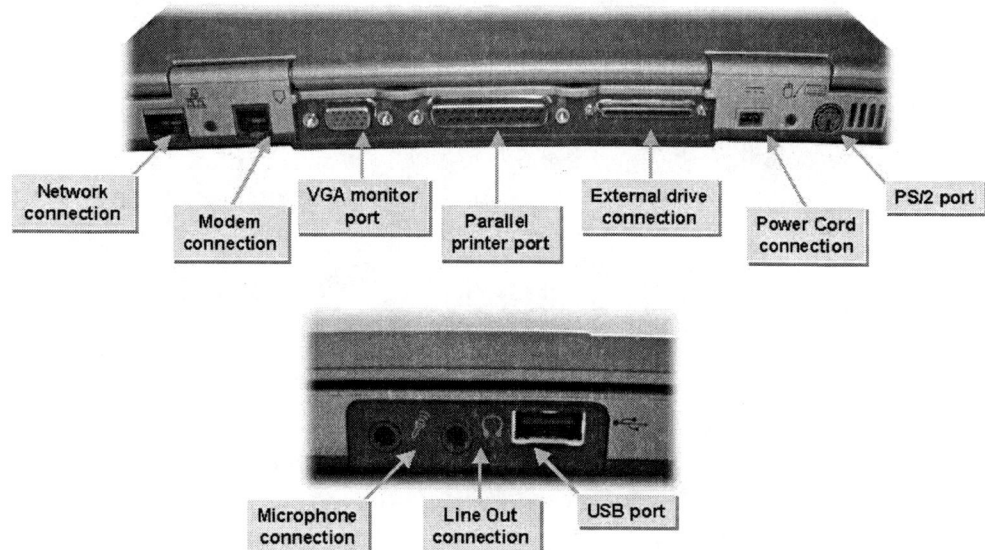

Figure 5-10: *Connecting peripherals directly to a notebook computer.*

Portable Device Power Sources

Power sources for portable devices are either AC (alternating current from an electrical outlet) or DC (direct current from a battery) sources that supply power to the portable device. While the portable device is in its portable state, batteries are used for the power source. When the device is used as a desktop computer or peripheral, the power source can be battery or AC power through a power cord plugged into an electrical outlet.

> A DC power adapter for a portable computer enables you to connect the device to a cigarette lighter outlet.

AC power connectors vary from notebook to notebook. Desktop systems all use the same basic power cord, but often not even multiple notebooks from the same manufacturer use the same power cord on notebook systems. Figure 5-11 shows two different power cord connections. When the notebook is not being used as a portable device, it is usually plugged in using the AC power cord that matches the computer. Through this connection, the battery is also recharged.

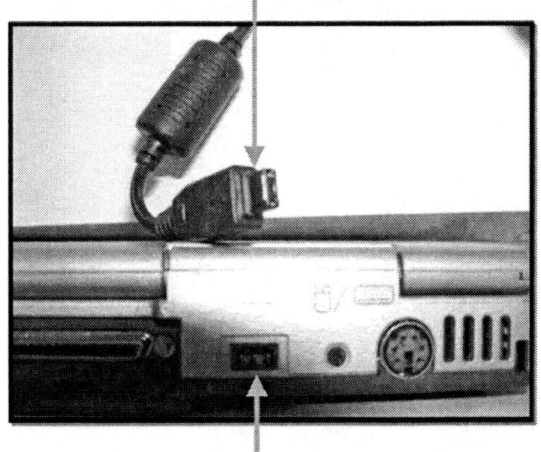
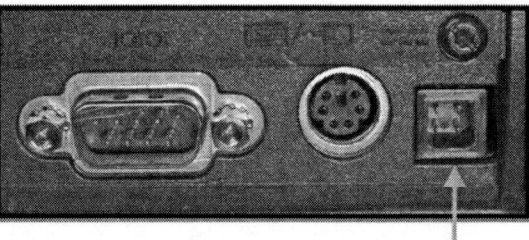

Figure 5-11: *AC power connections.*

Figure 5-12 shows three different batteries from notebook systems. The batteries shown in the figure are all different shapes. They were designed to fit as best as possible around other components in each of the systems they were designed for. Two of them are Li-Ion batteries and one is an Ni-MH battery. The long Li-Ion battery no longer holds a charge. It is about three years old and has been recharged many times. Any battery you use in a portable device must be compatible with the device and the device's operating system. Rechargeable batteries are used in most portable computing devices. Batteries usually last between one and six hours per charge. These are usually packaged in a battery pack.

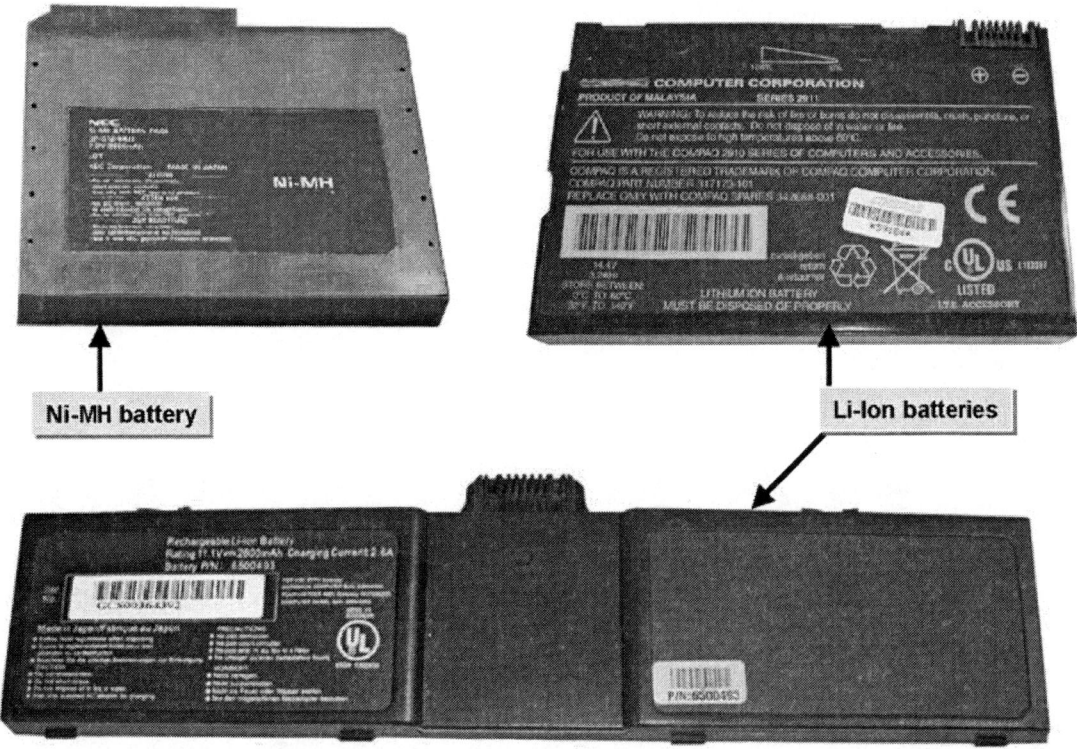

Figure 5-12: *Batteries for portable computer systems.*

Types of Batteries

The batteries in the battery pack might be:

- Nickel Cadmium (*NiCad*).
    - The battery type used in the original portable computers.
    - Heaviest and least expensive.
    - Short life of three to four hours.
    - Recharge can take up to 12 hours.
    - Can be recharged approximately 700 to 1,000 times.
    - Remembers how full it was when last recharged and doesn't go past that point the next time it is charged. This is referred to as the memory effect.
- Nickel Metal-Hydride (*NiMH*).
    - Environmentally friendly because it doesn't contain heavy metals that can be toxic.
    - Uses nickel and metal hydride plates with potassium hydroxide as the electrolyte.
    - Uses a liquid electrolyte which must be contained in protective steel cans to prevent leakage.

- — Doesn't hold charges as well as NiCad when not in use, but provides up to 50 percent more power than NiCad for the same weight.
- — Doesn't suffer from memory effect.
- — More expensive than NiCad.
- — Can be recharged approximately 400 to 500 times.
- *Li-Ion.*
  - — Lithium based. A lightweight metal.
  - — Provides light, long-life battery.
  - — Holds a charge well.
  - — Can't be overcharged.
  - — Holds twice as much power as NiCad.
  - — Weights about half as much as NiCad.
  - — Provides higher power than NiCad.
  - — More expensive than NiCad.
  - — Can be recharged approximately 400 to 500 times.
  - — Uses a liquid electrolyte which must be contained in protective steel cans to prevent leakage.
- *Lithium Polymer.*
  - — Similar to Li-Ion in power.
  - — Uses a jelly-like material as an electrolyte instead of liquid. This enables power cells to be manufactured in various shapes and sizes for custom requirements.
- *Zinc Air.*
  - — Provides more charge per pound than NiCad or NiMH.
  - — Doesn't suffer from the memory effect.
  - — Uses a carbon membrane that absorbs oxygen, a zinc plate, and potassium hydroxide as the electrolyte.

Power a Portable Device

Procedure Reference: Power a Portable Device

To connect a portable device to a power source:

 Using the incorrect power cord can destroy a portable device.

1. If you're going to run the device on battery power, insert the appropriate battery type if the device doesn't already have a rechargeable battery included.
2. If the device has a rechargeable battery and the battery needs to be recharged, plug the device into its cradle or docking station (if there is one) or plug the device directly into an electrical outlet using the supplied power cord (if applicable).

3. If the device needs to be connected directly to an electrical outlet, plug the device into the outlet using the supplied power cord.

How to Dock a Notebook Computer

Procedure Reference: Dock Portable Systems

To connect a portable system to a docking station or port replicator:

1. Connect the external peripherals to the docking station or port replicator.
2. Connect the power supply to the docking station or port replicator.
3. Following the instructions shown in the manual for your system, connect the portable computer to the docking solution you are using.
4. Boot the computer and verify that the portable system can use the external peripherals while docked.
5. Following the instructions shown in the manual for your system, remove the portable computer from the docking solution.
6. Verify that the portable system can use its integrated peripherals while undocked.

Topic B
Install or Remove Portable Computing Device Drives

You have identified what a portable computing device is, including a notebook computer. In this topic, you will be installing and removing drives from those portable computing devices.

Desktop systems usually have lots of drive bays with room for one or more hard drives; one or more CD-ROM, CD-R, CD-RW, DVD, and/or DVD-R drives; one or more floppy drives; and one or more removable cartridge drives. Notebooks try to be as small as possible, and the first thing to go is often space for additional drives besides the hard drive. Knowing how to connect additional drives to portable computers will be important when you are supporting users with notebook systems.

Portable Computer Drives

Definition:

Portable computer drives are storage areas that are specially designed to fit in portable computers. Drives are proprietary to their manufacturer and sometimes even to the computer model. All notebook computers have an internal hard drive. They might or might not include internal bays for other drives such as floppy, CD-ROM, or DVD drives. Some notebooks connect additional drives through a docking station, bay station, or via cable connections. Most notebook hard drives use 2.5-inch platters as compared to the 3.5-inch platters used on desktop hard drives. The height and length of hard drives varies. Notebook hard drives tend to run at slower speeds than desktop hard drives.

Some hard drives are difficult to remove since you need to dismantle the computer. Others have a slide lock to unlock it from the case, and then you can slide the drive out. If the notebook you are working on is difficult to remove the drive from, then you might consider using alternate hard drive solutions such as USB or FireWire hard drives which can be connected externally.

Some notebook computers have room for a hard drive, floppy drive, and an optical drive all to be installed simultaneously. More often though, especially as notebooks have gotten smaller, floppy and optical drives need to be switched out with either one or the other being available at a time.

Example:

Figure 5-13 shows an example of a notebook with the floppy drive being removed so that the CD-ROM drive can be inserted. The computer in this example contains an internal hard drive. It has one additional drive bay in which you can insert either the proprietary floppy drive or CD-ROM drive.

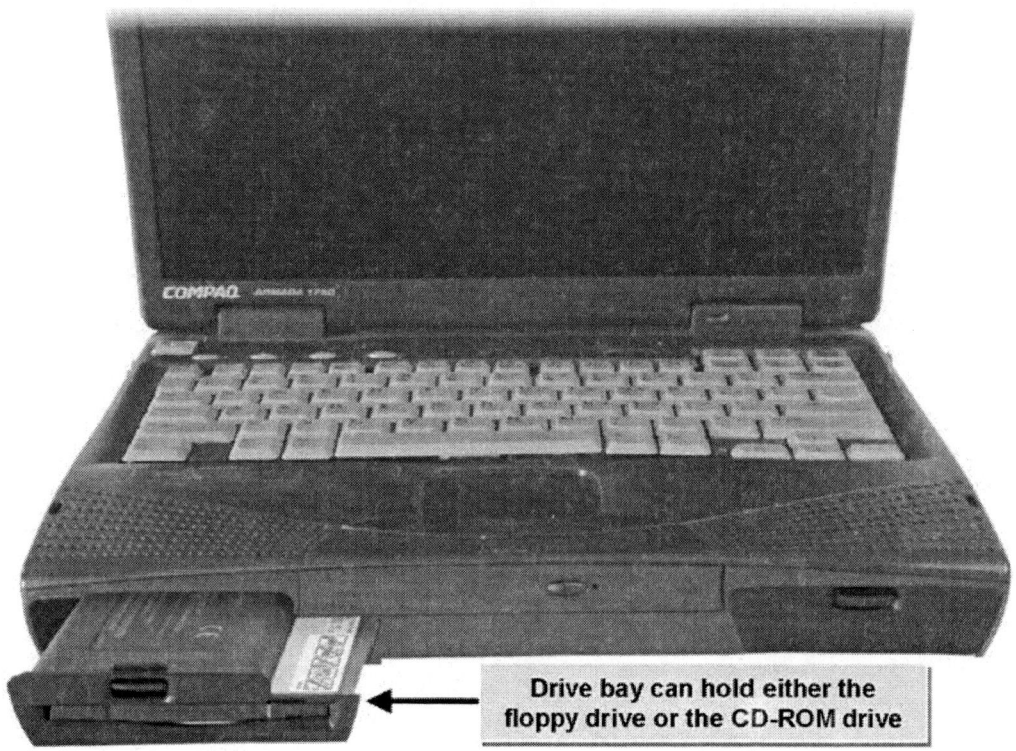

Figure 5-13: *Exchanging drives in a notebook computer.*

How to Install or Remove Drives from Notebooks

Procedure Reference: Exchange Portable Computer Drives

To exchange which drive is installed:

1. In the System Tray, click the Removable Device icon. This will display a list of all of the removable devices which need to be stopped before removing or ejecting the device from the system.

2. Click the description of the device you want to remove. This will begin with the word Stop and be followed by a description of the drive or other device.

3. When the services for the device have been stopped, a Safe To Remove Hardware information box is displayed. Click OK to acknowledge the message.

4. Different systems have various methods of releasing the drive from the bay. Refer to the documentation and any symbols on the system case for information on how to release the drive from the bay. Often it is a slide button that you need to pull down while sliding the drive out of the bay. On other systems, you might need to press a catch or disconnect a cable.

5. Slide the drive out of the bay and place it in a safe storage container where it won't be damaged by ESD factors or other environmental contaminants.

6. You can now slide the other drive into the drive bay. When it has been properly installed, a Removable Device icon will appear in the System Tray again. On some systems, you need to reboot before the replacement drive is available.

7. You can further verify that the drive was correctly installed by accessing the drive through Windows Explorer or some other application.

TOPIC C
Install or Remove PCMCIA Cards

Another component you'll need to install or remove in a notebook computer is a PCMCIA card, which increases a notebooks functionality. In this topic, you'll install a PCMCIA card.

Being able to assist users in installing and removing PC Cards is an important skill for supporting users with portable systems. You will need to be able to recognize the PC Card types so you can advise the user on which types can be installed and how many can be installed at once in a particular system.

PC Cards

Definition:

PC Cards are expansion cards that are used in portable computers to increase functionality of the computer. This is the technology used in portable computers rather than the ISA or PCI expansion cards used in desktop systems. The PC Card standard was developed by the *Personal Computer Memory Card International Association (PCMCIA)*. Some people refer to PC Cards as PCMCIA cards. All PC Cards are credit-card-sized expansion cards. They have a female 68-pin connector that plugs into a 68-pin male connector inside a slot in the side of the computer. They are 54 mm wide by 85.6 mm long.

PC Cards vary in thickness based on the type. PC Card types are shown in the following table.

Type	Thickness	Used Primarily For
I	3.3 mm	Memory.
II	5.0 mm	Memory, modems, network adapters, wireless network adapters, USB, FireWire, and SCSI connectors. Might have pop-out connectors for network cables or phone line connections.
III	10.5 mm	Miniature hard drives.

Most PC Cards use *CardBus*. It enables PC Cards and hosts to use 32-bit bus mastering and to operate at speeds of up to 33 MHz. *Bus mastering* enables the PC Card to communicate directly with other cards without going through the CPU.

Some PC Cards use *Zoomed Video (ZV)*. This is a connection between the PC Card and the computer that enables the card to write video data directly to the video controller, bypassing the system bus.

Some cards use *eXecute In Place (XIP)*. This enables operating system and application code stored on the PC Card to run directly from the PC Card. This eliminates the need to use system RAM to execute the code.

Example: A Type II PC Card

Figure 5-14 shows a Type II card that is 5 mm thick. This is a network adapter that uses the CardBus standard. It is being inserted into a Type II slot in the computer.

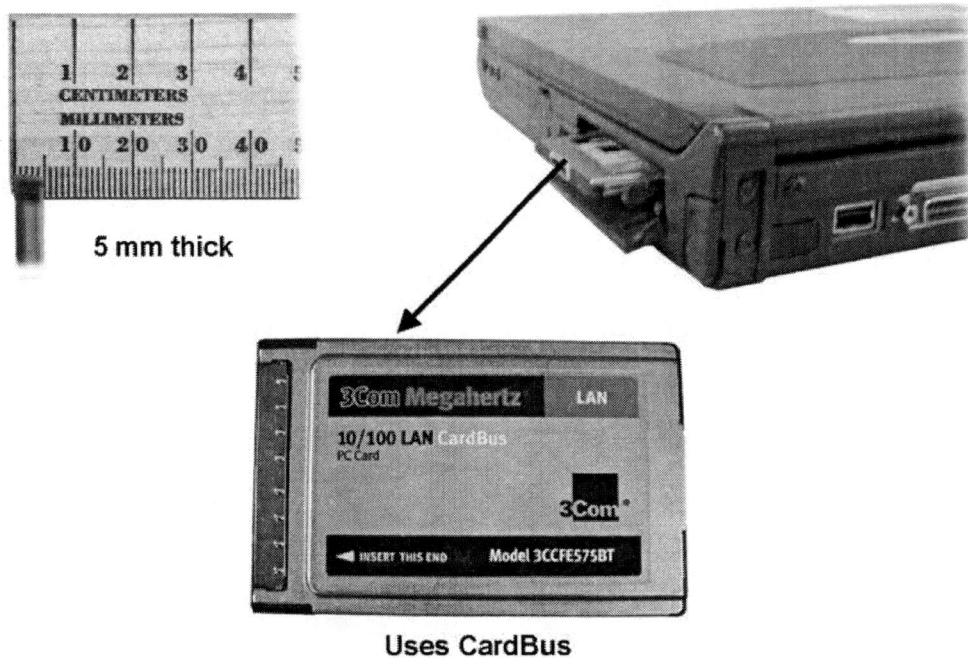

Figure 5-14: *A Type II PC Card.*

Card and Socket Services

All PC Cards use Card and Socket Services. These are layers of software loaded into memory. These two layers of software detect and support a PC Card when it is inserted into the portable computer. They are also responsible for managing the hot-swapping of PC Cards.

- *Socket Services* interacts with the system BIOS. When a PC Card is inserted or removed, socket services communicates that information to the system bus.
- *Card Services* is a software layer above socket services that communicates with the operating system to let it know when a card is inserted or removed. It automatically assigns system resources when the card is inserted.
- *Card Information Structure (CIS)* passes card information to the computer, including features and electrical characteristics, so that the computer can configure the card for use automatically.

PC Card Uses

PC Cards are used in a variety of ways to expand the capabilities of notebook computers. Table 5-1 describes some of the ways PC Cards are used.

Table 5-1: *PC Card Uses*

PC Card Use	Description
Modem	Adds modem capabilities to notebooks that don't have built-in modems. May have a retractable piece in which to plug the phone cord.
Network adapter (NIC)	Adds networking capabilities to notebooks that don't have built-in NICs. Like the modem card, it may have a retractable piece in which to plug a network cable.
Wireless network adapter	Provides wireless networking for notebooks that don't have built-in wireless capability. Often includes a built-in antenna for wireless communication.
SCSI adapter	Allows users to connect SCSI devices, such as a printer or external hard drive, to the notebook if it doesn't have a built-in SCSI adapter.
USB	Allows users to connect USB devices, such as external memory devices or printers, to the notebook if it doesn't have a built-in SCSI adapter.
IEEE 1394/Firewire	Provides a connection for devices such as external hard drives.

How to Install a PC Card

Procedure Reference: Install a PC Card

To install a PC Card:

1. Slide the PC Card into the PC Card slot until it is fully inserted. Make sure the PC Card is right side up. There is usually a label on the top with an arrow and/or the word "Insert" indicating which way to install it. You can bend the pins if you attempt to install it upside down.
2. If prompted, install any required drivers for the PC Card.
3. Verify that the PC Card was recognized by the system. You can look for an icon in the System Tray or you can use Device Manager to verify that the device is working properly. PC Cards must be compatible with the device and the device's operating system.

Procedure Reference: Manage PC Cards

There are times when users will need to exchange cards. This happens often if there is only one PC Card slot in their system or if they need more functionality for their system. To manage PC Cards:

1. Install and use the PC Card for the service you need. This might be a PC Card for network connections, modem connections, SCSI device connections, or other functionalities.

2. If you need to remove the PC Card and insert a different one, in the system tray, click the Removable Device icon and choose the option to stop the device you want to remove. There should be an entry for each removable device in your system. This might include drives as well as PC Cards.

3. Disconnect any devices or cables connected to the card to be removed.

4. Push the PC Card slot release lever once to pop it out.

5. Push the PC Card slot release lever again to release the PC Card from the slot.

6. Slide the card out of the slot.

7. Insert the replacement card into the slot.

Topic D
Install or Remove Mini-PCI Cards

You've installed and removed PC Cards in a notebook system, but there's a newer technology that uses internal cards to provide some of the same capabilities that PC Cards provide. These cards are called Mini-PCI cards, and in this topic, you'll learn how to install and remove them.

While it isn't often that you need to install or remove a Mini-PCI card, there are three likely situations when you might have to: when an existing Mini-PCI card starts to malfunction or stops working altogether; when you need to upgrade an existing Mini-PCI card; or when you want to add a wireless Mini-PCI card to a notebook. And when one of these situations arises, to ensure that the user has the resources necessary to complete his job, you're going to need to know how to identify a Mini-PCI card and install or remove one if necessary.

Mini-PCI Card

Definition:

A Mini-PCI card is an expansion card that is used to increase the functionality of a portable computer. Mini-PCI cards are internal expansion cards, not external like PC Cards, and are installed by the computer manufacturer. Mini-PCI cards are most often used to increase communications abilities by providing network adapters or modems. Mini-PCI are much smaller than other expansion cards, often measuring just a few centimeters in length. There are three types of Mini-PCI cards. They are listed in Table 5-2.

Table 5-2: *Types of Mini-PCI Cards*

Type	Description
I	Can be installed anywhere in the computer chassis, and uses internal cables to connect it to modem (RJ-11) and network (RJ-45) connectors on the computer's chassis. Connected to the motherboard using a mini 100-pin stacking connector with a 4 mm minimum stacking height.
II	Have built-in modem and network connectors, and therefore must be located against the computer's chassis. Connected to the motherboard using a mini 100-pin stacking connector with a 4 mm minimum stacking height.
III	Uses SODIMM connector to slide into a slot onto the motherboard. Uses internal cables to connect it to modem and network connectors on the computer's chassis.

Example: Mini-PCI Card

Figure 5-15 shows a Mini-PCI card. This Mini-PCI card is much smaller than a normal PCI expansion card.

Figure 5-15: *A Mini-PCI card.*

How to Install or Remove a Mini-PCI Card

Procedure Reference: Install a Mini-PCI Card

To install a Mini-PCI card:

1. Shut down the system, close the cover, and unplug the power cord. If necessary, remove the computer from the docking station or disconnect any peripheral devices.
2. Ground yourself and dissipate any static electricity you might be carrying.
3. Turn over the laptop and follow the manufacturer's instructions to locate the Mini-PCI bay cover. If there is no Mini-PCI bay, follow the manufacturer's instruction to access the location where you can install the Mini-PCI card.

4. Remove the screw that secures the Mini-PCI bay cover.

5. Remove the Mini-PCI bay cover.

6. If necessary, connect the card to any cables.

7. Secure the card inside the bay using supplied screws or clamps.

8. Replace the cover on the bay and fasten it with the screw.

9. Plug in the computer or replace it in the docking station. Turn the power on.

10. Verify that the new Mini-PCI card has been recognized. If necessary, install any updated drivers.

Procedure Reference: Remove or Replace a Mini-PCI Card

To remove or replace a Mini-PCI card:

1. Shut down the system, close the cover, and unplug the power cord. If necessary, remove the computer from the docking station or disconnect any peripheral devices.

2. Ground yourself and dissipate any static electricity you might be carrying.

3. Turn over the laptop and follow the manufacturer's instructions to locate the Mini-PCI bay cover. If there is no Mini-PCI bay, follow the manufacturer's instruction to locate the existing Mini-PCI card.

4. Remove the screw that secures the Mini-PCI bay cover.

5. Remove the Mini-PCI bay cover.

6. Remove any screws or clamps holding the Mini-PCI card in place.

7. If necessary, remove any cables connecting the Mini-PCI card to a modem or network connector.

8. If replacing the existing card, connect the new card to the cables.

9. Secure the new card using the screws or clamps you removed from the old card.

10. Replace the cover on the bay and fasten it with the screw.

11. Plug in the computer or replace it in the docking station. Turn the power on.

12. Verify that the new Mini-PCI card has been recognized. If necessary, install any updated drivers.

Topic E
Install or Add Memory to a Portable Computing Device

Just as you were able to install additional memory on a desktop system, you can install additional memory on a portable system. In this topic, you will install memory into a portable computing device.

Users will often require additional memory over what was installed when the system was purchased. Knowing how to determine the kind of memory required for a specific portable system and how to install it will help you install it more quickly and efficiently.

Portable Device Memory Options

Portable devices use memory that was specifically designed for those devices. Since it is not produced in as high quantities as desktop memory, it tends to be much more expensive. Also, there is less standardization. Some notebooks take proprietary memory that must be purchased from the manufacturer of the notebook system. Some notebooks use Small Outline DIMM (SODIMM) modules, which are about half the size of standard desktop DIMMs, or MicroDIMMs, which are even smaller than SODIMMs, so are popular for notebooks. Other portable computing devices and some notebooks use flash memory modules rather than regular RAM. Examples of memory for notebook computers are shown in Figure 5-16.

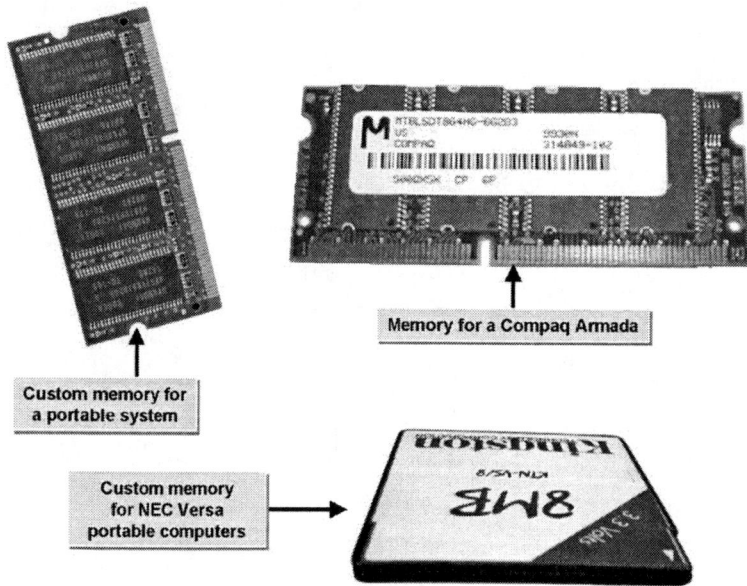

Figure 5-16: *Memory for notebook computers.*

Flash Memory

Definition:

> *Flash memory* is a removable solid-state mass storage device that resides on a small card. All flash memory:

- Uses EEPROM.
- Functions more like a removable disk than typical RAM or ROM.
- Is considered a solid-state device, because there are no moving parts.
- Can be written to and erased in blocks. This makes it fast since it is writing several bits at a time rather than one at a time.
- Is small and lightweight.
- Can be read directly from the device by connecting it to the computer with a cable or other wireless method.
- Can be read using a separate card reader or adapter. The adapters enable the flash memory card to be read through a PC Card slot or through a floppy drive.

Flash memory varies by:

- Type. There are several different flash memory cards. They are not interchangeable or compatible with each other.
- The devices it can be used in. Some types of flash memory can be used in many devices and some can be used in limited devices. See the documentation for your device on which type of flash memory card it uses.
- Some are more fragile than others.
- The size and shape of the memory card.
- Some use a controller built into the memory card and others rely on a controller in the device into which they are inserted.

Example: CompactFlash

Figure 5-17 shows an example of a CompactFlash memory card. CompactFlash memory cards contain a built-in controller.

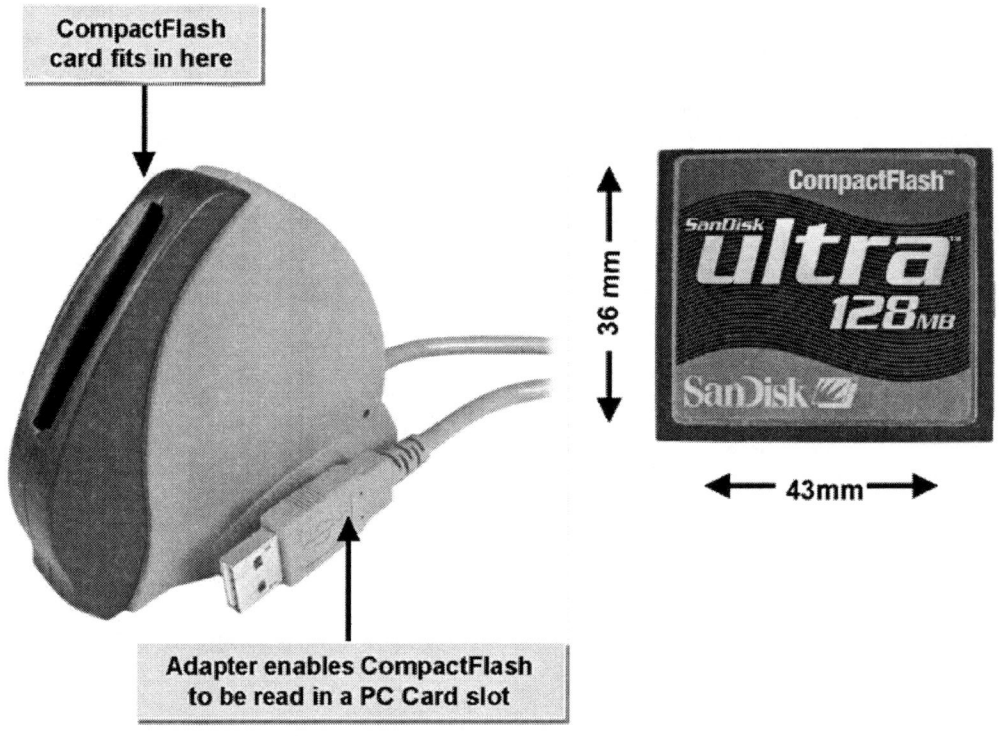

Figure 5-17: *A CompactFlash memory card.*

Example: SmartMedia

SmartMedia is a flash memory card that uses a memory chip and no built-in controller. It uses the controller in the device. Older SmartMedia cards ran at 5 V, but newer cards run at 3.3 V. You can tell the difference by the location of the notch. With the contact side of the card facing up, a notch on the left side indicates a 5 V card and the notch on the right indicates a 3.3 V card. Be sure not to place a 5 V card in a device that is expecting a 3.3 V card.

The SmartMedia card is 45 mm long, 37 mm wide, and 0.76 mm thick. It comes in 2, 4, 8, 16, 32, 64, and 128 MB capacities.

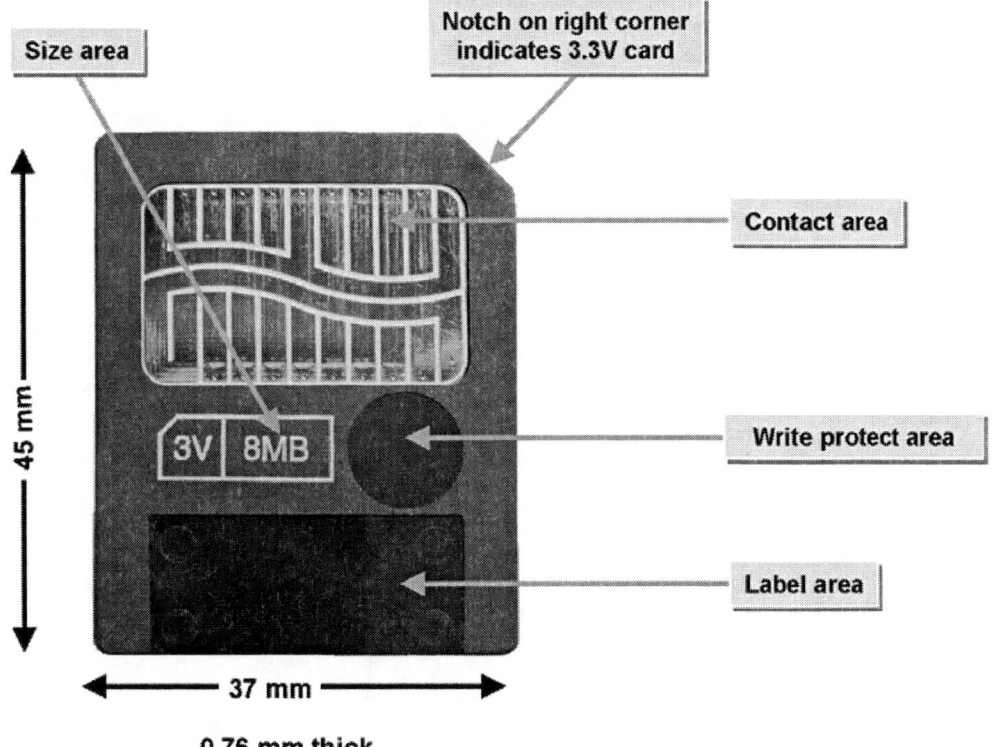

Figure 5-18: *A SmartMedia memory card.*

Types of Flash Memory Cards

The following table compares the features of flash memory cards and how they vary.

Name	Physical Size	Capacity	Description
CompactFlash	43 mm long x 36 mm wide. Type I is 3.3 mm thick and Type II is 5 mm thick.	8 MB to 1 GB	Composed of memory chips and a controller. Has a 50-pin contact. More information can be found at **www.compactflash.org/info/cfinfo.htm**.

Chapter 5: Supporting Portable Computing Devices

Name	Physical Size	Capacity	Description
SmartMedia	45 mm long x 37 mm wide x 0.76 mm thick. Weighs 1.8 grams.	2, 4, 8, 16, 32, 64, or 128 MB	Contains only a memory chip and no controller. Controller is in the device that the card is inserted into. Older cards ran at 5 V and have the notch on the left. Newer cards run at 3.3 V and have the notch on the right.
xD-Picture Card (xD)	20 mm long x 25 mm wide x 1.7 mm thick. Weighs 2 grams.	16 MB to 256 MB with plans for up to 8 GB	Contains only a memory chip and no controller. Controller is in the device that the card is inserted into. Half the size of SmartMedia cards. More information can be found at **www.dpreview.com/ news/0207/ 02073002fujifilmxd.asp**.
Memory Stick (MS)	50 mm long x 21.5 mm wide x 2.8 mm thick. Weighs 4 grams.	4, 8, 16, 32, 64, and 128 MB	Used extensively in Sony products. Memory Stick Pro is one-half the size of a MS card and is 1 GB.
Secure Digital (SD) and MultiMedia Card (MMC)	32 mm long x 24 mm wide x 2.1 mm thick.	4 to 512 MB	Composed of memory chip(s), controller module, and copper balls between chips. SD and MMC are the same physically, but technically they are different. Some systems only can use SD. A new variety, SD-I/O with built-in Bluetooth technology for wireless transfer of data. There are also SD Audio and SD Memory Cards. More information can be found at **http://usa.sdcard.com/ Consumer/page.asp**.

A comparison of the various flash memory cards can be found at **http://usa.sdcard.com/consumer/page.asp?view=&Page=WhatSD/comparison**.

How to Install, Add, or Remove Memory

Procedure Reference: Install Memory in Portable Computing Devices

Different brands and models of portable computing devices use different types of memory. Be sure to check the documentation for your device so that you purchase the correct type of memory to use in your device. To install the memory:

1. In a laptop or notebook portable computer:
    a. Shut down the system and unplug the power cord. You should never install memory while the system is powered on.
    b. Locate the memory cover and remove it. This could be on the bottom, on the side of the system, or under the keyboard. Refer to the documentation for how to access the memory.
    c. If you're going to remove the memory, remove the memory module.
    d. If you're going to add memory, verify that the memory is appropriate for the system. There are many types of memory, often proprietary to a specific system or manufacturer.
    e. Insert the memory module according to the directions in the system or memory documentation.
    f. If no memory slots are available, remove a smaller memory module following the directions in the system or memory documentation, then install the larger memory module.
    g. Replace the cover to the memory slots.
    h. Start the computer and verify that the additional memory was recognized.

2. In an MP3 player, a PDA, or a digital camera:
    a. Turn off the device.
    b. Locate the memory slot. This is often under a cover which needs to be opened to access the slot (in most digital cameras and MP3 players). Other times, it might just connect externally to the device (such as is the case for some PDA devices).
    c. Remove existing memory, if necessary.
    d. Insert the memory according to the directions in the documentation. There is often a picture indicating the orientation of the device in relationship to the slot.
    e. Turn on the device.
    f. Verify that the memory was recognized.

Topic F
Connect PDAs to Computers

The portable computing devices you have worked with so far are all still full-fledged computers. In this topic, you will examine another class of computing devices called Personal Digital Assistants (PDAs).

If you walk through any business district or even the local shopping mall, you usually see at least one person with a cell phone pressed to his ear (or an earphone cord trailing to his pocket). Many of those people also need access to other information that is stored on their computer. In this topic, you will learn how mobile users can take some of that information from their computer with them in their shirt pocket or purse.

PDA

Definition:

A *Personal Digital Assistant (PDA)* is a portable computing device that can be held in one hand. They are also referred to as *palmtops*. All PDAs:

- Use an operating system.
- Have applications.
- Can be used as organizers.
- Can be connected to a computer.
- Can be used as a peripheral to the computer as well as a standalone device.
- Synchronize information between the computer and the PDA.

PDAs vary by:

- Input method. These include:
    - A stylus to write on the screen. You might need to train the PDA to recognize your handwriting, but more often, you need to learn its handwriting characters.
    - An integrated keyboard. This might be a physical keyboard with very tiny keys or a graphical keyboard you type on using the stylus.
    - An add-on keyboard that plugs into the PDA.
- The screen can be color or black and white.
- The operating system the PDA uses. Some of the common operating systems include the following:
    - PalmOS
    - Windows CE
    - EPOC
    - FLEXOS
    - OS/9
    - JavaOS

- The applications installed. It also varies in whether you can add applications and which applications you can add. Applications need to be compatible with the PDA operating system installed on your PDA. Some of the applications include the following:
  - Calculator
  - Document viewers
  - Document editors
  - Games
  - Calendar
  - Address book
  - Expense report tracking
  - To Do list
  - Notepad
- How it connects to a computer. It might connect through the serial port or the USB port. The PDA might need to be connected to a cradle to make the connection or it might connect directly to a cable.
- What other devices besides a computer that it can connect to. Some PDAs can connect to other PDAs, to cell phones, and digital cameras. This might be a hard-wired physical connection or it might be through an IR port.
- Some PDAs enable you to increase the functionality by connecting other devices to it. Others increase functionality through the use of flash memory cards being added to the PDA.
- Some PDAs incorporate mobile communication features to enable you to access email or Web services while on the road from your PDA.
- The battery type varies. Most PDAs use rechargeable batteries that are recharged when you connect the PDA to the computer, but some, especially older PDAs, use standard AA batteries.
- The amount of memory installed. This determines how much information the PDA can hold. On some PDAs, you can add more memory, but others cannot be upgraded.
- Buttons and other physical features including:
  - Power button function and location.
  - Contrast, brightness, and backlight controls.
  - Application buttons. On some PDAs, you can assign specific applications to physical buttons on the PDA to make them easily accessible if you use them often.
- The software on the computer used to synchronize data between the computer and the PDA.

Example: A Palm V PDA

Figure 5-19 shows an example of a PDA. This PDA uses the Palm OS. Features of this example PDA include:

- It has a black and white screen.

- It has 2 MB of memory.
- It includes application buttons across the bottom of the PDA to access applications directly rather than selecting them through the icons on the screen. You can select any application through the icons on the screen from the main menu.
- It uses the Graffiti writing software as the primary input mode. You can also display a keyboard on screen and use the stylus to tap the keys. You can also connect an external keyboard designed specifically for the Palm.
- It connects to the computer through the serial port. You can also purchase an adapter to enable it to be connected to the USB port.
- It contains an Li-Ion battery. You place the Palm in the cradle to recharge its internal battery. The initial charge takes about three hours. Recharge a few minutes each day to maintain full battery power. Under normal use, you can usually go up to a month without recharging.
- It has an IR port. Through it you can connect to other Palm devices or a computer with an IR port.
- The cradle or the IR port are used to synchronize it with the files on your computer. Palm Desktop software is installed on the computer and through it, you can keep a calendar up to date on the computer as well as the PDA. It is also the method for adding new applications and transferring data files between the two devices.
- Accessories are added through the serial connector on the lower edge of the PDA. Accessories include:
  — A portable keyboard.
  — A modem. The modem looks much like the cradle and is the same size as the PDA. The phone line connects to the top edge of the modem.
  — A GSM kit. This works with the modem to enable you to use specific GSM-enabled cell phones to make dial-up connections. GSM stands for Global System for Mobile Communications.

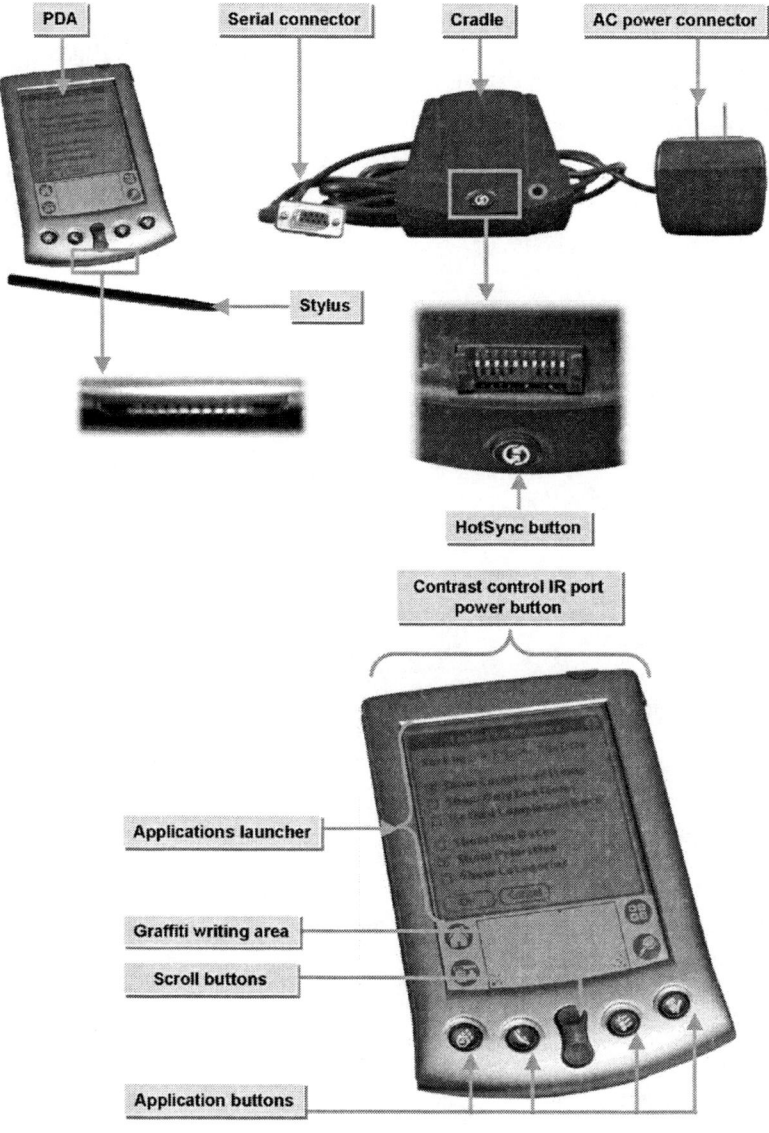

Figure 5-19: *A Palm V PDA.*

Example: Palm m130

Figure 5-20 shows another Palm with different features than our previous example. This PDA has most of the same features as the Palm V. It varies from the previous example in the following ways:

- Cradle uses a USB connection.
- PDA contains 8 MB of memory.
- Has a color display.

- Uses an SD/MMC/SDIO slot to add functionality. This includes additional memory (16 or 32 MB), backs up contents of the PDA to a separate card for safekeeping, eBooks (electronic books on a card), games, reference books and resources, and Bluetooth connection for wireless connection to Bluetooth-enabled devices such as other PDAs, cell phones, and printers.

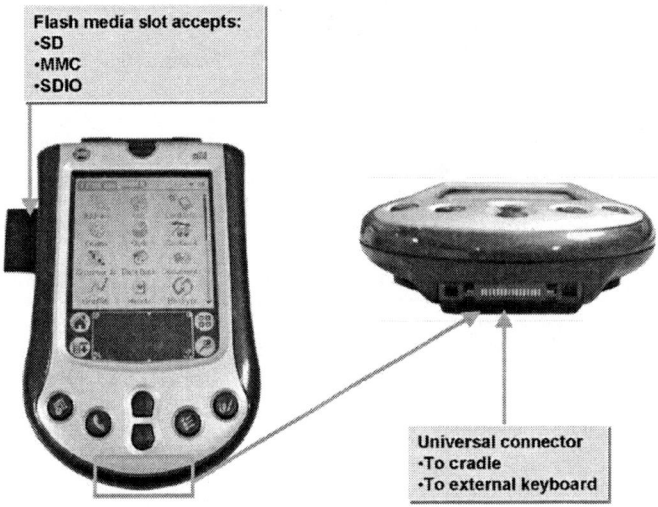

Figure 5-20: *A Palm m130.*

How to Connect a PDA to a Computer

Procedure Reference: Connect a PDA to a Computer

To connect a PDA to a computer:

1. Connect the cable from the cradle or docking station to the appropriate port on the computer. Refer to the PDA documentation and determine which port the PDA should be connected to. Some companies refer to the stand that is used to connect the PDA to the computer and to recharge the PDA as a cradle and others refer to it as a docking station.

2. Connect the PDA to the cradle or docking station as described in the PDA documentation. There is a connector on the device that fits in the PDA to establish the connection.

3. If necessary, install software on the computer to recognize the PDA. In order to synchronize data between the PDA and the computer, software needs to be installed to recognize the PDA and to transfer the data.

Chapter 5 Follow-up
Supporting Portable Computing Devices

In this chapter, you learned how to support a variety of portable computing devices. You connected external peripherals to a portable system. Then you added and/or removed PC Cards and memory to the system. Next, you connected a PDA to a computer.

Essential Terms

- batteries
- Card Services
- docking stations
- drives
- flash memory cards
- integrated peripherals
- memory
- mini-PC cards
- notebook computers
- PC cards
- PCMCIA cards
- PDAs
- peripheral devices
- portable computing devices
- power sources
- Socket Services

Review Questions

1. What are a laptop's expansion cards called and to what kind of bus do they connect?
2. What are the two types of LCD screens?
3. What is the purpose of a docking station?
4. Nickel cadmium (NiCad) batteries have what is referred to as the memory effect. What is the memory effect?
5. Which type of laptop battery cannot be recharged?
6. List the five types of batteries used for laptop computers.
7. How many pins are on a PC card connector?
8. What is a type III PC card used for typically?
9. What is the thickness of a type II PC card?
10. On laptop computers using PC cards, what is the purpose of bus mastering?
11. What is Zoomed Video?
12. What are socket services?
13. What is the function of Card Information Structure (CIS)?
14. What kind of connector is used by Type I and Type II mini-PC cards to connect to the motherboard?
15. What kind of connector does a Type III mini-PC card use?
16. What is flash memory?
17. What is the voltage of a newer SmartMedia flash memory card?
18. How many pins are on a CompactFlash contact?

19. What is the difference between SD and SD-I/O?
20. What is the function of card services?
21. What is the purpose of PC cards?
22. What is another name for a docking station?
23. What is a trackpad?
24. Which LCD screen provides higher quality: Passive Matrix or Active Matrix?
25. What kind of input device does a PDA (Personal Digital Assistant) use?
26. What is the thickness of a Type III PC card?
27. What are Type I PC cards used for typically?
28. Some PC cards use eXecute In Place (XIP). What is XIP?

Review Projects

Project #1 Understanding PC Cards

A PC card is the size of a credit card and the card's inner workings are enclosed in a hard metal case. One end is exposed to reveal the 68-pin connector. This exercise is comprised of two parts. In the first part, you'll examine the inside of a 3Com network PC card. In the second part, you'll discover some of the more recent advances in PC card technology. Open a browser and navigate to Tom's Hardware, **http://www6.tomshardware.com/network/20011210/nic-03.html**. Read the article about 32-bit card-bus technology and examine the image of a PC card that has been opened. To learn more about PC cards and also compact flash, navigate to the PC Guide Web site at **http://www.pcguide.com/ref/hdd/op/formPCCard-c.html**. Note the visual comparison among a quarter, compact flash card, and a PC card.

Project #2 Laptop Security

One of the key strengths of laptops—their size—is also one of their key weaknesses. Companies and individuals must protect both the physical equipment and the data stored on the machine. While it's imporant to secure a laptop physically, many products are not effective deterrents. For example, most laptops allow you to attach a security cable to the machine. This is not a fool-proof method and will deter only the casual opportunist.

To meet increased security needs, companies have devised better methods of securing computers. One company, Absolute Software, offers a software solution to help users and companies monitor and track computers. In the event that a laptop is stolen, the machine can be tracked. CompuTracePlus is name of Absolute Software's product. To learn more about the software, explore their Web site at **http://www.absolute.com/public/products/computraceplus/default.asp**.

Explore the links located under the software's name. Pay particular attention to the FAQs. Since this is a software product, what are its limitations? If someone knew CompuTracePlus was running on a machine, how could they circumvent it? How effective do you think the software would be? There are a number of methods for protecting a laptop physically. Although using a security cable is a popular method, there are also alarms that can be attached to a machine. Computer Security Products a sensor that can be attached to a laptop (or desktop) and if the sensor is removed an alarm will sound. To learn more about this method, read the links provided on the PC Tab Web site (**http://www.computersecurity.com/pctab/**). As you read through the material, do you think a sensoring system would be more or less effective than a software solution?

On the left column of Computer Security Product's Web site are other security options such as cables. Browse the options available. Make a table that lists the most popular methods and record the advantages and disadvantages of each method.

Project #3 How Laptops Work

Although there are many fundamental similarities between laptops and desktops, there are obvious points of difference. There is an immense amount of information available that describes the inner-workings of desktops, including how to build them. There is far less detailed information available about laptops. The How Stuff Works Web site corrects that imbalance by offering an impressive amount of information about laptops.

In this exercise, work through the tutorial on laptops. You'll notice that there are many links at the bottom of the page. Click each link so you work through the entire tutorial. As you do, take advantage of the detailed images the Web site provides. You have the option to print out this tutorial. You should either print out a hard copy of this information or copy and paste it from the Web site for reference. Create a subfolder under your Hardware Documentation folder and name it "laptop reference materials."

Reflective Questions

1. **Do you support more desktop or mobile systems? Why are there more of one than the other in your company?**

2. **What types of portable computing devices are you responsible for supporting?**

CHAPTER 6
Performing Preventative Maintenance

Chapter Objectives:

In this chapter, you will perform preventative maintenance procedures.

You will:

- Maintain hard disks.
- Perform printer maintenance.
- Check UPS batteries.
- Clean peripheral components.
- Clean the inside of the computer.
- Identify how to properly dispose of hazardous materials.

Introduction

You have installed and upgraded all of the system components at this point. Now you'll want to keep them up and running. You can perform preventative maintenance measures to help prevent problems. In this chapter, you will perform some of the most commonly encountered preventative maintenance activities that should be routinely performed.

One of the best ways to prevent calls from users is to perform regularly scheduled preventative maintenance procedures. This is similar to taking your car in for regularly scheduled service work; this prevents you from breaking down on the side of the road as often. If the mechanic notices you have worn belts, she can recommend that you replace them while the car is in the shop. In the same way, by performing periodic PC maintenance, you can help prevent trouble calls from your users.

Topic A
Hard Disk Maintenance

Because hard disks are central to a computer's performance, you need to ensure that they're maintained properly. After first ensuring a computer has a functioning hard disk, you can focus on the rest of the system and its peripherals. In this topic, we'll cover some of the tools you can use to keep hard disks and users productive.

An improperly maintained hard disk can cause a host of problems, including slow performance and system crashes, which lead to lost data and unhappy users. There are a few procedures you can follow to keep your hard disks at an optimum performance level.

Fragmentation

The Windows operating systems do not write a file to disk as a single large block. Instead, they break up the file into smaller pieces. When Windows writes these smaller pieces to the disk, it tries to write them close together so that the disk can retrieve the file quickly whenever a user opens it. As a disk fills up and files are added and removed, it becomes harder for Windows to find enough contiguous space to write all the pieces of a file. As a result, Windows ends up writing the file wherever it can find free space on a disk. The end result is that files can become fragmented, meaning their pieces can be spread out all over the disk. The greater the amount of *fragmentation*, the more work the operating system must perform to retrieve and write files. You can counteract fragmentation by defragmenting a computer's hard disk.

Hard Disk Maintenance Tools

There are a few tools you can use to manage and maintain hard disks in the Windows family of operating systems. Table 6-1 describes some of the tools at your disposal.

Table 6-1: *Hard Disk Maintenance Tools*

Tools	Operating System	Description
Chkdsk.exe	Windows 9x, Windows NT 4.0, Windows 2000, and Windows XP	Command-line tool that enables you to check the hard disk for bad sectors or errors in the file system. Can be used to repair errors. Errors on the disk can cause data loss and intermittent system crashes.
Check Disk	Windows 2000 and Windows XP	Graphical Windows version of the Chkdsk.exe tool that you can use within the operating system. Can be used to repair errors that can slow down the hard disk or cause system crashes and data loss.
Disk Defragmenter	Windows 9x, Windows 2000, and Windows XP	Defragments the hard disk by locating fragmented files and moving the pieces of each file or folder to one location on the volume, so each file then occupies a single, contiguous space on the disk. Seriously fragmented files (more than 5-10 percent fragmentation) can slow down a hard drive.
Scan Disk (Scandisk.exe)	Windows 9x	Performs a thorough check of a hard disk and repairs any errors it encounters.

How to Maintain Hard Disks

Procedure Reference: Check for Hard Disk Errors Using the Command Line in Windows 9x, Windows NT 4.0, Windows 2000, and Windows XP

To check a hard disk for errors in Windows 9x, Windows NT Workstation 4.0, Windows 2000, and Windows XP:

1. Open a Command Prompt window.

2. At the command prompt, enter chkdsk *volume*:, where *volume*: is the volume you want to scan. (When entering a drive, you must use the colon.) Entering just chkdsk will display statistics for the current drive. You may also use any of the switches in Table 6-2.

Table 6-2: *Chkdsk Switches*

Switch	Description
filename	On a FAT volume, specifies the file you want to check for fragmentation.
/f	Specifies that you want to fix errors.
/v	On FAT and FAT32 volumes, will output the file name and path for every file on the disk.

Switch	Description
/r	Used with /f, recovers readable information from bad sectors.
/l:size	On NTFS volumes, lets you set the size of the log file in KB.
/x	Used with /f, this switch forces a volume to dismount before it's checked.
/i	On NTFS volumes, reduces scan time by scaling back the check of index entries.
/c	On NTFS volumes, reduces scan time by scaling back check of folders.

3. If you choose to fix errors using the /f switch, enter the appropriate choice to schedule Chkdsk to run at the next system restart.

4. If necessary, restart the computer.

5. If any errors are found, that information will be displayed. Read the resulting report.

Procedure Reference: Check for Hard Disk Errors in Windows 2000 and Windows XP

To check for hard disk errors in Windows 2000 and Windows XP:

1. Open My Computer or Windows Explorer.

2. Right-click the drive you want to check and choose Properties.

3. Select the Tools tab.

4. In the Error-Checking section, click Check Now.

5. In the Check Disk dialog box, you can choose whether to automatically fix errors and whether to try to recover bad sectors. Click Start.

6. Read the resulting report.

Procedure Reference: Defragment a Hard Disk in Windows 9x

To defragment a drive in Windows 9x:

1. Choose Start→Programs→Accessories→System Tools→Disk Defragmenter.

2. In the Select Drive dialog box, select the drive you want to defragment.

3. In Windows 95, click the Advanced button if you want to change the settings of the defragmentation utility from the default.

In Windows 98, click the Settings button if you want to change the settings of the defragmentation utility from the default.

Click OK to close the Settings dialog box.

4. Click OK.

5. If you want to see the details of the defragmentation process on your hard disk, click Show Details.

Click Hide Details to show only the summary information.

6. Click Yes to close Disk Defragmenter when the defragmentation process is complete.

Procedure Reference: Defragment a Hard Disk in Windows 2000 and Windows XP

To defragment a hard disk in Windows 2000 and Windows XP:

1. Log on as a local administrator.

2. From the Start menu, choose Programs→Accessories→System Tools→Disk Defragmenter.

3. In the top pane of the Disk Defragmenter window, select the disk you want to defragment.

4. If you want to analyze the fragmentation state of the disk before defragmenting, click Analyze.

5. After the analysis, you will see a message box with a recommendation as to whether you should defragment or not. This recommendation is made based on a Disk Defragmenter algorithm, rather than a specific fragmentation level, but it is common practice to defragment disks that are more than five percent fragmented.

Click View Report to see details of the fragmentation state of the disk.

6. To begin the defragmentation, click Defragment in the analysis message box, in the Analysis Report dialog box, or in the Disk Defragmenter window itself. Disk Defragmenter will reanalyze the disk and begin the defragmentation. You can view the progress in the progress bar.

 Defragmentation of a large, highly fragmented, and very full disk can take several hours.

7. When the defragmentation is complete, you can click View Report to see detailed information about the defragmentation.

Procedure Reference: Run ScanDisk in Windows 98

To run ScanDisk in Windows 98:

1. Choose Start→Programs→Accessories→System Tools→ScanDisk.

2. Select the drive you want to check for errors.

3. Choose the type of test you want to perform: Standard will check files and folders for errors, while Thorough performs the same test as Standard and it scans the disk surface for errors.

4. If you want ScanDisk to automatically fix errors it finds, select Automatically Fix Errors.

5. Click Start.

6. Read the resulting report and click Close when you're done.

Topic B
Perform Printer Maintenance

You have given your users printers. They are happily printing away, and you would like to keep your users happy. One way to do that is to have a maintenance schedule and clean your printers regularly. In this topic, you will perform printer maintenance.

Jammed paper, streaky printouts, and low toner are some of the printer service calls you will receive. To avoid these types of calls and keep your printers in good working condition, be proactive in performing regular printer maintenance.

Laser Printers

Definition:

A *laser printer* is a printer that forms images on paper by using a laser beam and an electrophotographic drum. All laser printers:

- Produce high-quality images.
- Output one page at a time.
- Produce images using a combination of electrostatic charges, toner, and laser light.

Components of a laser printer include the following:

- *Toner* cartridge. This is a single, replaceable unit that contains the fine powder used to create images as well as additional components used in image production.
- Laser scanning assembly. This is a unit that contains the laser.
- High-voltage power supply.
- DC power supply.
- Paper transport assembly. This unit contains the rollers and motors that move the paper through the laser printer.
- Transfer *corona* assembly. This is a component that contains the corona wire which is responsible for charging the paper so that it pulls the toner off the drum.
- *Fusing assembly.* This unit, also known as the fuser, applies pressure and heat to the paper to seal the toner particles to the paper.

- Formatter board. This unit processes all of the data received from the computer and coordinates the steps needed to produce the finished page.

Laser printers vary by:

- The hardware interface used to connect the printer to the computer.
- Whether it produces black and white or color output.
- The number of paper trays and the amount of paper each tray can hold.
- How adjustable paper trays are.
- Output locations. Usually this is an output bin on top of the printer, but there might be an additional or alternate straight paper path through a drop-down door on the rear of the printer.
- The printer language used.
- Print resolution or Dots Per Inch (DPI).
- The speed at which they print.
- Whether it uses a single laser or a strip of LEDs.
- Whether consumable components are separate components or built together into a single unit.
- Status lights and their location.
- Paper sizes and weights that can be accommodated by the printer.
- The energy-saving features.
- The toner-saving features.
- The operating systems supported.
- The amount of memory installed, whether the memory is upgradeable, and the type of memory.

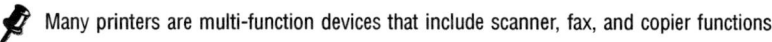
Many printers are multi-function devices that include scanner, fax, and copier functions.

Example: HP LaserJet 6P

Figure 6-1 shows an example of a laser printer. Features of this printer include:

- It can be connected to the computer using:
    - A LocalTalk connection for Macintosh computers or LocalTalk networks.
    - A 1284 B Centronics parallel port.
    - A 1284 C parallel port.
    - An infrared port.
- It has two input trays and two output trays.
- This printer can use either Printer Control Language (PCL) or PostScript commands and can automatically switch between them as needed.
- This printer outputs images at 600 DPI at eight pages per minute.

- It has 2 MB of memory.

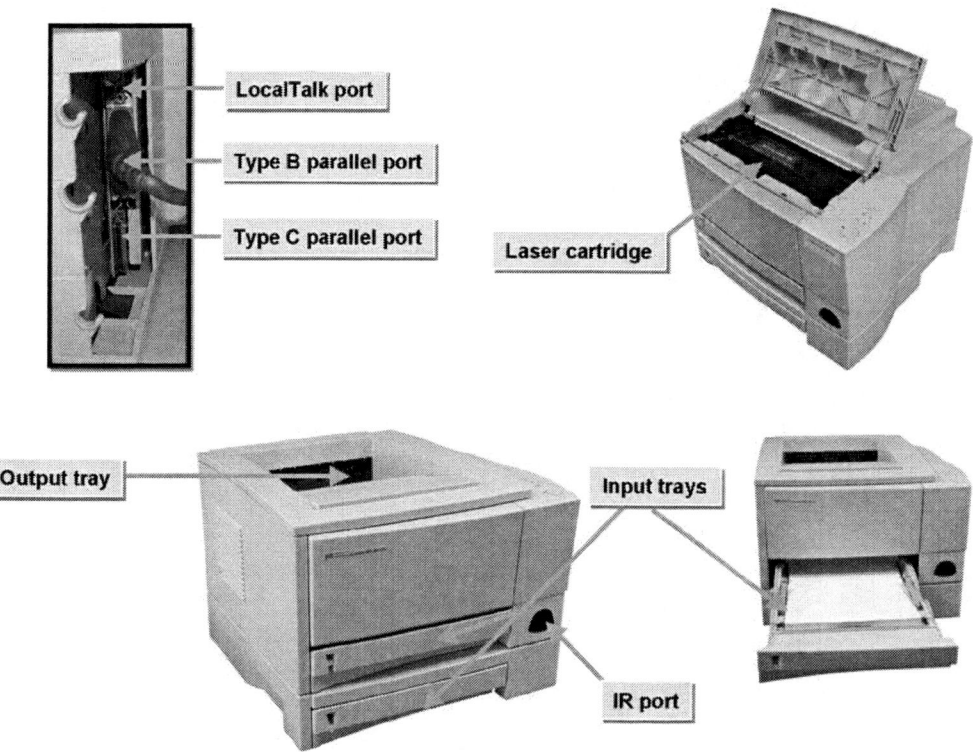

Figure 6-1: *A laser printer.*

Dot-matrix Printers

Definition:

A *dot-matrix printer* is a printer that forms images using a set of pins that strike an inked ribbon. All dot-matrix printers:

- Create letters and images from dots.
- Can print on continuous roll paper.
- Can print multi-part forms that use carbon or No Carbon Required (NCR) paper.
- Have printheads that contain a vertical column of small pins that are controlled by an electromagnet.
- Use ribbons coated with ink to create images.

Dot-matrix printers vary by:

- The number of pins in the printhead.
- The ribbon used in the printer.
- Whether it can produce black-and-white or color output.

- Whether it can print on cut-sheet paper, continuous form paper, or both.
- Whether it can adjust how close the ribbon is to the paper. If it is too close, you might get smear or drag marks. If it is too far away, the output might be too light.
- The speed of printing.
- The paper path.
- The ability to print on cut sheet paper using a cut-sheet feeder.
- The hardware interface used to connect the printer to the computer.
- Size and weight of paper that can be used.
- The tractor feed mechanisms; the number and location of wheels with pins varies. There might also be additional guides that latch over the holes in the paper to guide it through the paper path.
- The menus or buttons to configure settings including default fonts, print quality, and character pitch.
- The number of slots for different fonts (if any).
- The ability to upgrade its memory.

Example: OkiData Microline 390

Figure 6-2 shows an example of a dot-matrix printer. This is a 24-pin printer. It is currently set up to use individual sheets of paper using the cut-sheet feeder rather than the continuous form paper and tractor feed. It has a slot to add more fonts to its memory. Using the buttons on the front of the printer, you can set the default font, print quality, and character pitch.

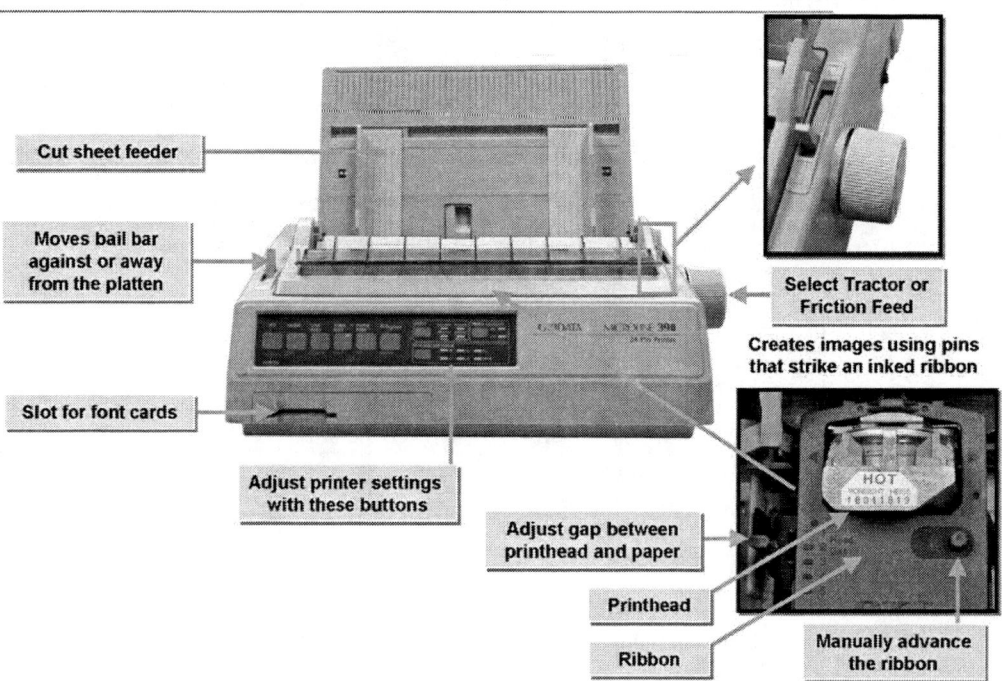

Figure 6-2: *A dot-matrix printer.*

Tractor Feed

Tractor feed uses pairs of wheels with pins evenly spaced around the circumference at a set spacing. Paper with matching holes in the edges fits over the pins. As the wheels turn, the paper is pulled through the printer. Usually just two wheels are used, but there might be additional wheels or pin guides that the paper is latched to in addition. When using the tractor feed mechanism, there is usually a lever or other setting on the printer that needs to be set in order to use the tractor feed. Figure 6-3 shows a printer set up to use tractor feed.

Figure 6-3: *Tractor feed.*

Friction Feed

Friction feed uses two rollers placed one on top of the other. As the rollers turn, the paper is forced through the paper path. This is used to print on individual sheets of paper (cut-sheet paper) and envelopes. Be sure to set the printer lever or other setting to the cut-sheet setting when printing using friction feed. Figure 6-4 shows a printer set up to use friction feed.

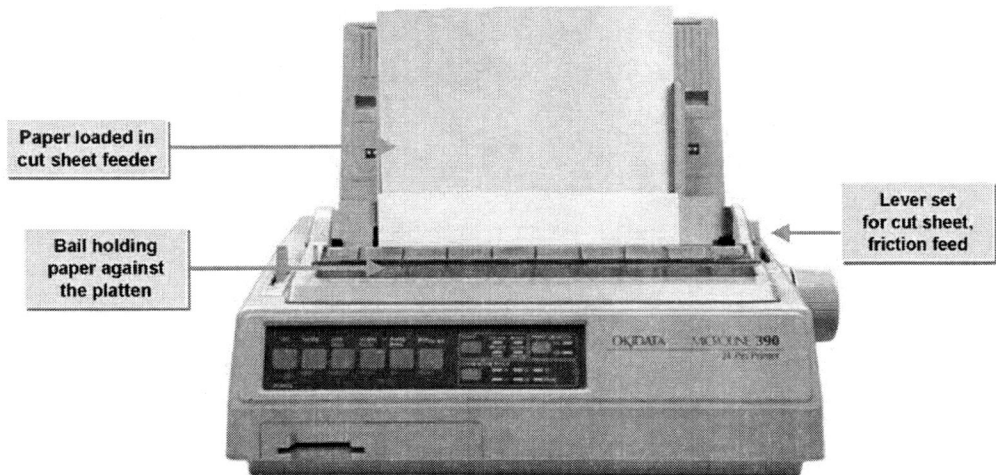

Figure 6-4: *Friction feed.*

Chapter 6: Performing Preventative Maintenance

Inkjet Printers

Definition:

An *inkjet printer* is a printer that forms images by spraying ink on the paper. Inkjet printers are sometimes referred to as *ink dispersion printers*. All inkjet printers:

- Force liquid ink out of nozzles aimed carefully at the paper.
- Use ink cartridges.
- Have a stepper motor to move the printhead across the paper.
- Use rollers to advance the paper.
- Have a cleaning cycle.
- Park the printhead.
- Contain memory buffers.

Inkjet printers vary by:

- The hardware interfaces that can be used to connect the printer to the computer. These might include the following:
    - Parallel
    - USB
    - Serial
    - AppleTalk
    - SCSI
- The media they can print on. This includes the following:
    - Inexpensive copier paper
    - Bright paper made specifically for inkjet printers
    - Photo papers
    - Transparencies
    - Labels
    - Card stock
    - Envelopes
- Whether it produces black and white or color output.
- Whether black is produced using a separate cartridge or by combining the cyan, yellow, and magenta color output.
- Whether there are separate tanks for each color or if they are all in one unit. If the colors are in one unit and one color runs out, the entire cartridge needs to be replaced.
- The size of cartridges and how much ink each cartridge contains.
- The cost of cartridges.
- The speed at which it prints.
- Whether the printhead is part of the printer or part of the print cartridge.

- The paper path. Some printers have a straight-through paper path and others turn the paper over as it passes through the printer.
- The resolution or DPI.
- How the ink is released. It could be by:
  - Piezoelectric used in Epson printers. This is a vibration that releases a droplet of ink from the cartridge.
  - Thermal used in most other printers. This method releases a droplet of ink by heating up the ink.

Example: Epson Stylus Color 500

Figure 6-5 shows an example of an inkjet printer. This printer uses a separate black cartridge, and the color cartridge contains all three colors. The head is parked to the right of the roller. When the printer is turned on, it goes through its cleaning cycle. It has a straight-through paper path in which the paper feeds from the top of the printer and comes out in the output tray the same side up. It uses Piezoelectric technology to release ink onto the paper.

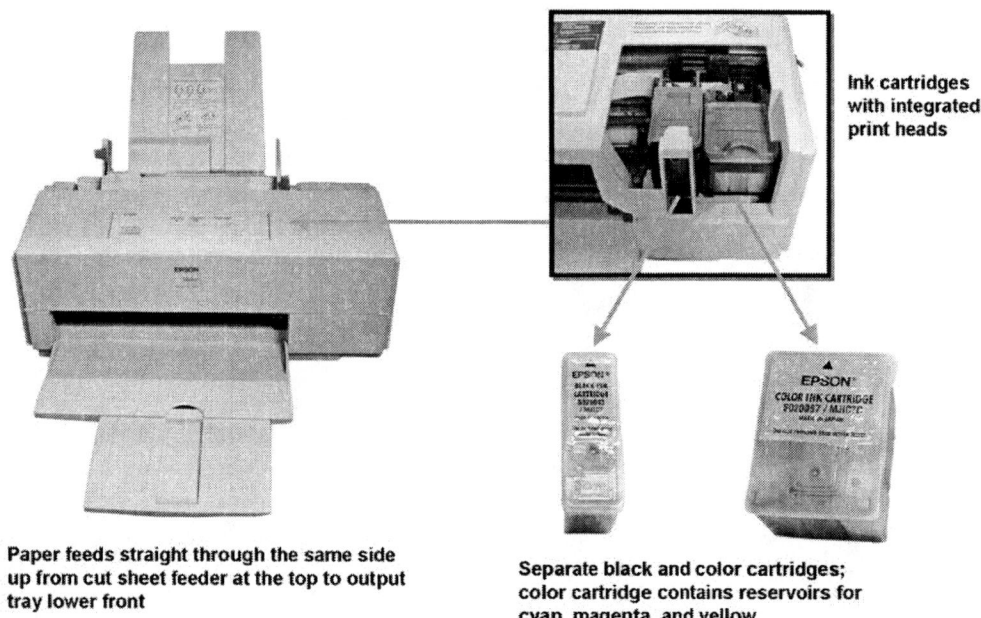

Figure 6-5: *An inkjet printer.*

Solid Ink Printers

Definition:

Solid ink printers are printers that use ink from melted solid-ink sticks. The ink is melted and forced into a printhead, where it's transferred to a drum, which then transfers the image to the paper as it's rolled over it. Solid ink printers can print on standard paper. Some solid ink printers can produce better results than laser printers or inkjet printers because it produces an image with a clearer, finer edge on a wide variety of media, such as paper or transparency.

Example: Xerox Phaser 8200B

The Xerox Phaser 8200B uses melted solid-ink sticks instead of toner. The solid ink sticks are melted during the print process, and the liquid ink is used to create an image on a drum. The paper is then rolled over the drum to transfer the image. The Xerox Phaser 8200 can print on standard paper and on overheads.

Dye Sublimation Printers

Definition:

A dye sublimation printer is a printer that uses a thermal process to transfer dye to paper to create images. Sheets of cyan, magenta, yellow, and black dye are heated, which turns the dye into a gas, which is then transferred to paper where it forms a solid again. Some dye sublimation printers print on photo paper, while others can print a variety of surfaces, including transparencies, which can be used on overhead projectors. Dye sublimation printers are used to print photos because they can create clearer, more realistic photo reproductions and they don't fade as much over time. Dye sublimation printers are often used in scientific research centers because of their ability to create near-perfect, photo-realistic reproductions.

Example: Kodak Professional 8500 Digital Photo Printer

The Kodak Professional 8500 Digital Photo Printer uses dye embedded in a ribbon, which is stored inside a cartridge. When the ribbon is exposed to heat from the thermal head, the dye turns to gas and is absorbed by special photo paper. Once absorbed into the paper, the dye turns to a solid again, reproducing the image that was sent to the printer. The Kodak Professional 8500 Digital Photo Printer is used to print pictures because of it's ability to create near-perfect photo reproductions.

How to Perform Printer Maintenance

Procedure Reference: Maintain Dot-matrix Printers

To maintain a dot-matrix printer:

1. Print a test page to verify that the ribbon prints satisfactorily.

2. If necessary, replace the printer ribbon based on the results of the previous step.

   If the test print shows indications of printhead wear or damage, make arrangements to repair or replace the printhead or printer.

3. Verify that there is enough paper for a day's printing. If necessary, have extra paper available for users to install.

4. Using compressed air or a printer vacuum, remove the dust and paper bits from the inside of the printer. You can also use toothpicks, artist paint brushes, or cotton swabs to assist in removing debris from the printer.

5. Use tweezers to remove any paper caught in the paper feed mechanism. Rolling a manila folder through the paper path also works to remove bits of paper caught in the paper path.

6. Use mild household cleaner to wipe down the exterior of the printer case.

Procedure Reference: Maintain Inkjet Printers

To maintain an inkjet printer:

1. Print a test page to verify that the printer prints satisfactorily.

2. If necessary, replace the ink cartridges based on the results of the previous step. Some printers have separate cartridges for each color and some use one cartridge with separate chambers for each color. The black cartridge is separate on almost all printers, except for some very low-end printers.

   If the test print shows indications of printhead wear or damage, make arrangements to repair or replace the printhead or printer.

3. Verify that there is enough paper for a day's printing. If necessary, have extra paper available for a user to install.

4. Using compressed air or a printer vacuum, remove the dust and paper bits from the inside of the printer. You can also use toothpicks, artist paint brushes, or cotton swabs to assist in removing debris from the printer.

5. Use tweezers to remove any paper caught in the paper feed mechanism.

6. Use mild household cleaner to wipe down the exterior of the printer case.

7. Place an inkjet cleaning sheet in the paper tray. Using the form feed button(s), send the paper through the paper path. This assists you in cleaning the paper path from excess ink and other debris.

Procedure Reference: Maintain a Laser Printer

To maintain a laser printer:

1. Print a test page to verify that the printer prints satisfactorily.

2. If necessary, replace the toner, drum, or other printer components based on the results of the previous step. The components that need replacing will vary depending on the printer. Refer to printer documentation for which component might cause poor print quality as seen on the test printout. Documentation will also show you how to replace the worn component.

3. Verify that there is enough paper for a day's printing. If necessary, have extra paper available for a user to install.

4. Using compressed air or a printer vacuum, remove the dust and paper bits from the inside of the printer. You can also use toothpicks, artist paint brushes, or cotton swabs to assist in removing debris from the printer.

 Only use specially designed laser printer vacuums so you don't reverse the polarity of the electrons on the drum.

 Don't use compressed air if there is a toner spill. This will just spread the toner around, making it harder to clean up and possibly getting it into other parts of the printer.

5. Verify that the fan is working properly and is not clogged. Without the fan, the printer can overheat.

6. Clean the corona wire and check the fuser wand and ozone filter each time you replace the toner.

7. The rollers can be cleaned with alcohol. They get dirty over time and can leave marks on the paper if they are not cleaned.

8. Use tweezers to remove any paper caught in the paper feed mechanism.

9. Use mild household cleaner to wipe down the exterior of the printer case.

10. Place a laser printer cleaning sheet in the paper tray and use the form feed button(s) to send it through the paper path.

Procedure Reference: Maintain a Solid Ink Printer

To maintain a solid ink printer:

1. Print a test page to verify that the printer prints satisfactorily.

2. If necessary, replace the ink sticks based on the results of the previous step. Follow the manufacturer's instructions to replace the solid ink supply.

   If the test print shows indications of printhead wear or damage, make arrangements to repair or replace the printhead or printer.

3. Verify that there is enough paper for a day's printing. If necessary, have extra paper available for a user to install.

4. Using compressed air or a printer vacuum, remove the dust and paper bits from the inside of the printer. You can also use toothpicks, artist paint brushes, or cotton swabs to assist in removing debris from the printer.

5. Use tweezers to remove any paper caught in the paper feed mechanism.

6. Use mild household cleaner to wipe down the exterior of the printer case.

Procedure Reference: Maintain a Dye Sublimation Printer

To maintain a dye sublimation printer:

1. Print a test page to verify that the printer prints satisfactorily.

2. If necessary, replace the dye sheets based on the results of the previous step. Follow the manufacturer's instructions to replace the dye sheets.

3. Verify that there is enough paper for the expected workload. If necessary, have extra paper available for a user to install.

4. Using compressed air or a printer vacuum, remove the dust and paper bits from the inside of the printer.

5. Use mild household cleaner to wipe down the exterior of the printer case.

Printer Safety

While maintaining printers, there are some important safety tips to keep in mind:

- Be careful not to touch some of the internal elements inside inkjet and laser printers. These elements can be very hot and can cause burns.
- Use caution when disposing of used printer supplies; some items are combustible.
- Treat any fire in a printer as an electrical fire; do not try to extinguish it with water or foam.
- Excessive exposure to toner can cause respiratory or skin irritation.
- Plug printers only into appropriately grounded outlets.

Topic C
Use a UPS

So far you have set up PCs and assumed that there will be electrical power available for users to be able to boot without errors and for it to function properly. In some locations, this assumption is frequently challenged by brief (and not so brief) power outages. In this topic, you will learn how you can verify that the Uninterruptible Power Supply (UPS) batteries are up to this challenge.

There is little that is more infuriating than having a flashlight stowed away for power outages, and then when you go to turn it on, you find that the batteries are dead. The same thing can be said of a UPS. However, the consequences of a dead battery in this case can be even more serious—it can cause a loss of data and affect user productivity. So, you need to regularly check that the UPS batteries are still holding a charge and will be there for you when the power goes out.

UPS

Definition:

An *Uninterruptible Power Supply (UPS)* is a battery-operated device that is intended to save computer components from damage due to power problems such as power failures, spikes, and sags. Computer systems require a steady supply of electricity. Interrupts in that power can cause your systems to fail. All UPSs:

- Use battery power to supply power to the devices connected to the UPS.

- Can be configured through the operating system as to what happens when there is a power failure.
- Keep the computer up so you can perform an orderly shutdown.
- Have a method for testing that the UPS works properly.

UPSs vary in that:
- They can be online or standby.
- Some can stay up longer than others.
- Some have more software configuration options.
- Most connect to a hardware interface on the computer such as the USB or serial port. This enables the UPS and the computer to work together in monitoring the available power and shutting down the computer.
- Some are rated on their switching time. This is the time it takes to switch from wall voltage to the battery during a power anomaly.
- They power your equipment from their batteries at all times (an online UPS).
- They power your equipment only when the wall outlet power fails completely (a standby UPS).

Example: Online UPS

An *online UPS* supplies power to your systems from its batteries at all times. An example of an online UPS is shown in Figure 6-6. Power from the normal electrical system is used to constantly charge the batteries. Online UPSs usually supply cleaner battery power than standby UPSs. The batteries usually don't last as long as standby UPS batteries.

Online UPSs generally filter power to reduce or remove power spikes. Since online UPSs supply power from the battery at all times, they can prevent power sags.

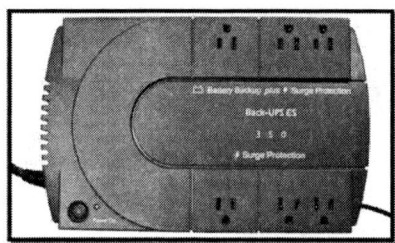 

Figure 6-6: *An online UPS.*

 After a power interruption of more than a few seconds, be sure to turn off the power. This is because a surge of electricity into all system components will occur when the power comes back on.

Example: Standby UPS

A *Standby UPS* (SUPS) uses a battery to supply power when a power problem occurs. At times of normal power operation, power is supplied from the normal electrical system. This method places minimal burden on the batteries and power inverts in the UPS, leading to longer UPS life. These UPSs are rated on their switching time since their batteries are only in use when the regular power is unavailable. These UPSs usually cannot solve sag problems.

Non-Example: Surge Suppressor

A surge suppressor is not a UPS. While it is meant to help protect components from power spikes, it does not protect components from power failures or sags, nor does it provide a steady supply of electricity. It also doesn't provide power to components in the case of a power failure.

Determining UPS Size Needs

To determine the size of UPS you need, you can use one of the following techniques:

- Perform a manual calculation.
    1. Multiply the volts by amps for each device you will connect to the UPS.
    2. Add together the results of each device in step 1.
    3. Purchase this size UPS.
- Use the tool found on most UPS manufacturers' Web sites to determine the size you need. By filling out a form about the equipment you will be plugging into the UPS, the tool will recommend the manufacturer's UPSs that meet your needs.

How to Use a UPS

Procedure Reference: Use and Test a UPS

To use and test a UPS:

1. Plug the UPS into the wall and the computer components to be powered through the UPS into the UPS. You might also need to connect the battery to the terminals within the UPS. Be sure to plug the UPS directly into an electrical outlet and not into a surge suppressor or power strip.

2. Configure what happens when a power failure occurs.

    a. Open Control Panel.

    b. Click Performance And Maintenance.

    c. Click Power Options.

    d. If available, click the UPS tab to display the UPS page. When some UPSs are attached to the computer, the UPS tab is no longer displayed, and is replaced with other tabs such as Alarms and Power Meter.

    e. If your UPS is connected to COM1 or COM2 and the UPS tab is displayed in the Power Options Properties dialog box, in the Details section of the UPS page, click Select and you can select the manufacturer and model.

If the UPS tab is not displayed, you will need to use any other UPS-related tabs or other software that came with the UPS to configure it.

f. If the UPS tab is available, click Configure to configure when you should be notified of power failure and how often. You can also configure what you want the computer to do when it encounters a power failure. You can have it run a specific program when the critical alarm threshold is reached. Next, the computer either performs a shutdown or goes in to hibernation. COM1 and COM2 are the only ports available through the UPS configuration from within Windows XP. If you have a UPS that connects to a USB or some other port, you will need to use the software that came with the UPS.

If the UPS tab is not available, check the documentation that came with your UPS and follow the instructions for configuring what to do when a power failure occurs.

g. Click OK to apply your changes and close the Power Options Properties dialog box.

3. Test the UPS. You can:

- Unplug the UPS from the wall and verify that the components remain powered. If you configured it to run a specific program, shut down the computer, or put it in to hibernation, you can leave it unplugged until this occurs if you want to test that feature as well. When you are done testing, plug the UPS back into the wall.

- Most models have a test button. Press the Test button to verify that the UPS can power the components plugged into the UPS.

TOPIC D
Clean Peripheral Components

You have seen how important it is to be proactive in maintaining printers and UPSs. Keeping users' keyboards, mice, and monitors clean can also help alleviate trouble calls. In this topic, you will identify the materials used to clean these peripherals and perform basic peripheral cleaning procedures.

Users are always getting their peripherals dirty—that's just a fact of life. If you want them to stay clean, leave them in the boxes and they will never get dirty. Your users won't get any work done, but their peripherals will be clean! Finger prints on monitors, crumbs in the keyboards, gunk in the mice are all part of the things you will need to clean up when you perform peripheral component cleaning routines. By routinely cleaning these devices, you can help prevent trouble calls in the future and prevent unhappy users when these components fail.

Cleaning Compounds and Materials

Cleaning materials for computers can be gathered from standard household cleaning supplies in addition to supplies specifically designed for computers and electronics. The following table shows you the cleaning supplies that you can use.

Cleaning Supply	Description
Monitor cleaning wipes	Alcohol-based, lint-free, pre-moistened wipes for cleaning monitor screens. These should only be used on CRT or TV monitors and not on plastic-coated LCD screens.
Keyboard cleaning wipes	Pre-moistened wipes for cleaning keyboards.
Lint-free cloths	If you choose not to use pre-moistened wipes, you can use rubbing alcohol applied to a lint-free cloth to wipe down screens and keyboards. They can also be used to clean other peripherals.
Rubbing alcohol	Used with cotton swabs or lint-free cloths, this is a useful solution for cleaning many peripherals.
Mild household cleaner	Keeping the exterior of peripherals clean helps prevent dirt and debris from getting inside the equipment. (Never spray directly on the equipment. Avoid using ammonia-based cleaners around laser printers; the ammonia may react chemically with the toner.)
Cotton swabs	Tightly wound cotton swabs are useful in getting cleaning solution into tight places. They are also useful when used dry to get dust and debris out from between keys and around buttons or other tight areas.
Window cleaner	Standard household window cleaner can be used if sprayed on a lint-free cloth first. Be sure to use it only on glass screens and not on plastic-based screens.
Toothpicks	Toothpicks come in handy in getting dirt out from around keys, buttons, and other tight spaces. They are also useful for removing the gunk that builds up on the rollers in a mouse. Another use for toothpicks is for when you are trying to retrieve jumpers that have fallen onto the motherboard.
Artist paint brush	A small paint brush can be used to remove dust from between keys on a keyboard. If the brush has long bristles, they can reach under the keys where other cleaning objects would not be able to reach.
Compressed air canister	A canister with a nozzle that can be aimed at components to blow dust out. This is often used when removing dust from the interior of a computer. Be sure to blow the dust away from the power supply and drives. It can also be used to blow dust out of the power supply fan area, on keyboards, and from the ventilation holes on other peripherals.

Cleaning Supply	Description
Computer or electronics vacuum	A computer or electronics vacuum is a non-static vacuum that can be used on the chassis, the power supply, fans, and in printers. Regular vacuum cleaners can create static which will damage computer equipment. It should have a filter and bag fine enough to contain toner particles so that you can use it to clean up toner spills from laser printers or photocopiers. These vacuums can often be used to blow as well as suck, so they can replace the need for compressed air canisters for blowing dust out of machines. Sucking the dust up is usually better, though, since blowing the dust can cause it to get onto or into other components. Sucking it up into a vacuum cleaner bag gets it out of the system without the chance of it getting into something else.
Toner cloth	A special cloth that you stretch that picks up toner particles that are either in the printer or around the printer. Be careful if using it inside the printer so that the cloth doesn't get caught on any components, leaving fibers behind.
Mask	A mask that fits over your mouth and nose should be worn when using a compressed air canister or working around toner spills. This will keep the particles out of your body.
Latex gloves	You should wear latex gloves when cleaning up a toner spill.

How to Clean Peripherals

Procedure Reference: Clean Peripherals

To clean peripherals:

1. Clean the keyboard using compressed air, an artist paint brush or business card, toothpicks, and rubbing alcohol.

2. Clean the mouse by removing the ball and cleaning the rollers with rubbing alcohol, toothpicks, and the mouse interior with compressed air.

3. Clean the monitor by spraying glass cleaner on a lint-free cloth, and then wiping the glass. Clean the vents using a small vacuum.

4. Clean PDAs using a lint-free cloth to wipe the screen and lint-free cloth dampened with rubbing alcohol to wipe down the entire PDA.

5. Clean scanners by spraying glass cleaner on a lint-free cloth, and then wiping the glass. Wipe the exterior with a lint-free cloth dampened with household cleaner.

6. Clean contacts and connections with a lint-free cloth or an artist's paint brush.

Topic E
Clean Internal System Components

It is not enough to clean just peripherals and the outside of computer cases. Lint, dust, hair, and other contaminants are likely to find their way in to users' systems over time. Routine cleaning of internal system components can remove these foreign bodies before they cause real problems for your users. In this topic, you will clean internal system components.

Keeping foreign bodies out of systems is more easily done in a clean office environment than it is in a home with several pets or out on a factory floor, but that doesn't mean the office system won't get junk in it, though. The openings in the case and around the fan seem to draw particulate matter into the system as if they were iron filings being drawn to a magnet. By taking the time to remove this material from a system, you can help prolong the system life and reduce the number of trouble calls you get on systems.

How to Clean Internal System Components

Procedure Reference: Clean the Internal System Components

To clean internal system components:

1. Remove the case and clean with damp lint-free cloth.

2. Clean the system board using a compressed air canister and computer vacuum. Try to hold the case at an angle with the back corner. Blow the air so the dust is blown away from the drives and power supply. If it is extremely dusty, you might want to wear a mask over your mouth and nose since the dust particles will fly up when you spray the compressed air.

3. Clean the CD-ROM drive using a CD-ROM cleaning kit and following the directions it comes with.

4. Clean the floppy drive using a floppy drive cleaning kit and following the directions it comes with.

5. Clean removable media drives using the cleaning kit that is compatible with the drive and following the directions it comes with.

 Iomega Zip and Jaz drives should not be cleaned. This will damage the drives. Imation SuperDrives can be cleaned.

Topic F
Dispose of Computer Equipment

Even if you perform routine maintenance on systems and keep them in good repair, they will eventually come to the end of their useful life. You need to know how to properly dispose of system components, because they contain hazardous materials. In this topic, you will identify how to recycle, reuse, or dispose of old equipment.

You will need to know how to prepare system components for disposal so that your company is in compliance with all laws governing the disposal of hazardous material. You also protect yourself and your co-workers from hazardous materials when you follow the guidelines established for dealing with hazardous materials. You need to identify the hazardous materials contained in the system components you are disposing of, and dispose of them in the appropriate manner.

Material Safety Data Sheets

Material Safety Data Sheets (*MSDS*) are technical bulletins designed to give users and emergency personnel information about the proper procedures of the storage and handling of a hazardous substance. Companies are required by the Occupational Safety & Health Administration (OSHA) to make MSDS information available to employees who might be exposed to hazardous materials.

Manufacturers of a product create the MSDS. They ship it with the first shipment of a product to a new customer. They also need to ship an MSDS any time there is an update to it. MSDSs cover information such as the following:

- Physical data
- Toxicity
- Health effects
- First aid
- Reactivity
- Storage
- Safe-handling and use precautions
- Disposal
- Protective equipment
- Spill/leak procedures

 More information about MSDS can be found at **www.ilpi.com/msds/**.

Hazardous Materials

Definition:

Hazardous materials are any materials that must be handled in a special way in order to prevent injury to people or damage to the environment. All hazardous materials must:

- Be handled to prevent injury to people.

- Be handled properly to prevent environmental damage.
- Be disposed of properly.
- Be handled according to OSHA requirements.
- Have an MSDS available.

Hazardous materials vary in the following ways:

- They might be chemicals or chemical solvents, or cans or other containers that hold chemicals.
- They might be computer components that contain hazardous elements such as the following:
  — Lead
  — Mercury
  — Cadmium
  — Phosphorous
  — Barium
- How exposure to the material should be treated.
- How they are disposed of.
- How they are to be handled and stored.
- Any local, regional, state, or government requirements for handling and disposing of hazardous materials.

Example: Liquid Cleaning Materials

The household cleaning materials you use to clean equipment must be handled to prevent injury to people and to prevent environmental damage. Some contain caustic chemicals and solvents that could cause respiratory distress or skin irritation. Figure 6-7 shows an example of the precautions you need to take when handling glass cleaner.

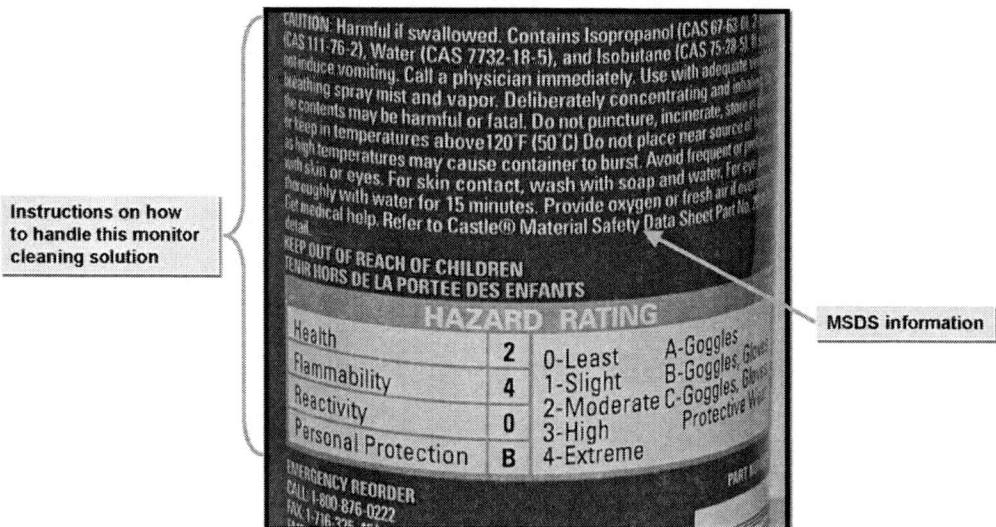

Figure 6-7: *Glass cleaner.*

Example: Laser Printer Toner

Laser printer toner is made of fine particles of iron and plastic approximately 7 to 10 microns in size that can cause problems when exposed to heat. Also, the residual chemicals can do severe damage to the environment. Handling procedures for toner cartridges are usually printed on the cartridge, as well as detailed in documentation that comes with the cartridge. An example of the printed handling instructions is shown in Figure 6-8.

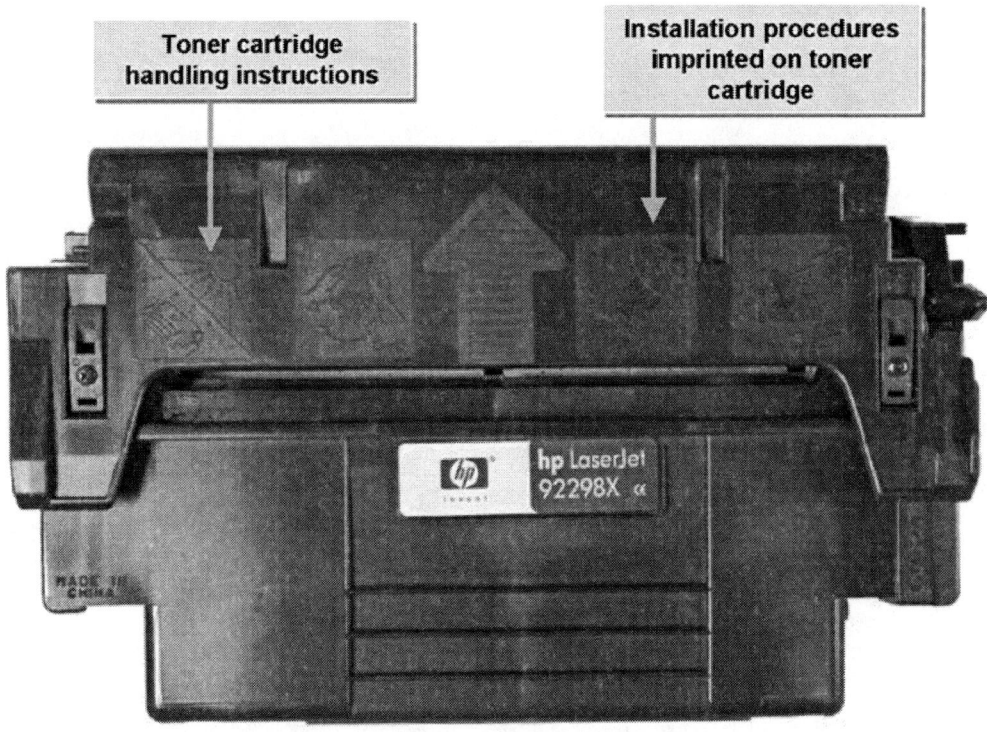

Figure 6-8: *A laser printer toner cartridge.*

Example: Metals

Most computer equipment contains soldered joins, which use lead, as well as other metal such as copper, gold, and silver. The lead is toxic. The other metals can be recycled and reused.

Monitors contain mercury, cadmium, phosphorous, and barium. These are safely enclosed in a vacuum-sealed case when it is in everyday use. If you were to send it to a landfill, though, the glass and plastic housing would be crushed, exposing the dirt to these dangerous elements.

Example: Ozone

Laser printers produce ozone gas, usually when the corona wire produces an electrical discharge during printing. Depending on the levels, ozone can be a mild to severe irritant. Regulatory agencies have established limits regarding the amount of ozone that employees are exposed to. Be sure to replace the ozone filter as recommended by the manufacturer and follow proper procedures to dispose of the used filter.

Example: Batteries

Batteries are used to maintain the data in CMOS chips and to supply power to remote controls, portable devices, and notebook computers. These batteries might contain any one of a number of dangerous chemicals, including:

- Lithium
- Lead
- Nickel metal hydride
- Nickel cadmium

How to Dispose of Hazardous Materials

Procedure Reference: Dispose of Hazardous Materials

To dispose of computer equipment:

1. Determine if any equipment needs to be treated as hazardous materials by referring to the MSDS for the product.

2. When disposing of household cleaners, be sure to read labels and follow instructions for disposing of them and the containers they were stored in. Check whether the container can be recycled.

3. Dispose of batteries according to the type of battery and the recommended method of disposal or recycling. Used batteries should not be tossed in the trash, but disposed of by following proper procedures. Alkaline batteries can usually be disposed of in the regular trash, but check with your municipality to determine if they have a recycling program in place for those batteries. Batteries containing heavy metals must be disposed of by following hazardous materials guidelines.

4. When disposing of toner and toner cartridges, use the following procedures:

   a. Toner spills should be cleaned up using a special printer or electronics vacuum that has a fine filter and bag to contain the material. Using a regular vacuum can melt the toner if it gets on the vacuum motor. Use a dry paper towel, toner spill cloths, or cool water to clean toner from skin or clothing.

   b. Toner cartridges should be refilled or recycled. Empty toner cartridges should not be disposed of in regular trash. Your company should have an established set of guidelines for how to dispose of used toner cartridges.

5. Find a computer recycler who can take your old equipment.

Chapter 6 Follow-up
Performing Preventative Maintenance

In this chapter, you learned about the importance of performing preventative maintenance. You learned how to perform preventative maintenance on printers, UPSs, interior components, exterior components, as well as how to dispose of equipment that has reached the end of its useful life.

Essential Terms

- cleaning supplies
- computer equipment disposal
- fragmentation
- hard disks
- hazardous materials
- internal PC components
- maintenance tools
- MSDS
- peripheral devices
- power problems
- preventative maintenance
- printer maintenance
- printer safety
- printers
- UPSs

Review Questions

1. Why is fragmentation a problem and what can you do to remedy the problem?
2. What is the purpose of chkdsk.exe?
3. What utility performs a check of the hard disk and repairs (or attempts to repair) any errors it finds on a Windows 9x system?
4. If you enter chkdsk /i at a command line, what will be the result?
5. What is the function of a laser printer's transfer corona assembly?
6. What are Material Safety Data Sheets?
7. Laser printers produce ozone gas and, because of this, what should be replaced as needed according to manufacturer recommendations?
8. What should you do to dispose of batteries that contain heavy metals?
9. Who creates a Materials Safety Data Sheet?
10. What should you use to clear dust from the fans of your computer system?
11. Why is it important not to use a regular household vacuum to clean computer equipment?
12. What kind of print device produces near-perfect photo-realistic reproductions?
13. What kind of printer forms images by spraying ink on the paper?
14. What kind of print device uses a tractor feed?
15. What is the function of a laser printer's fusing assembly?
16. What is the unit of measurement for determining print resolution?
17. You've noticed that it's taking longer to start applications and retrieve data. What should you do?
18. Why is it important to check your disk drive for bad sectors and errors?
19. What two operating systems include the graphical version of the chkdsk.exe tool?
20. Why is it important to keep the fans inside your computer system free from excessive dust?
21. What happens if you enter chkdsk at the command prompt on your Windows 2000 machine?
22. What switch do you have to use with the chkdsk command in order to fix errors?
23. You use disk defragmenter to analyze your C drive. When complete, the utility displays its recommendation. On what is the recommendation based?
24. How can you view detailed information about disks you defragmented?

25. Windows 98's Scan Disk allows you to perform two types of tests. What are they?
26. After you set up a UPS, what should you do next?

Review Projects

Project #1 How a Laser Printer Works

As an A+ service technician, you will be responsible for maintaining and troubleshooting print devices. Many businesses use laser printers because they are more efficient and less costly per duty cycle than many other types of print devices. To maintain and troubleshoot a laser printer properly, you must understand the process of how a laser printer works. How Stuff Works provides a good discussion of the laser printing process that will both reinforce and deepen your understanding of laser printers. You can review the information on laser printers at **http://www.howstuffworks.com/laser-printer.htm**. You have the option to print a copy of the tutorial. You should either print a copy or cut and paste the information from the Web site. If you cut and paste the information, create a folder under Hardware Documentation called Printers and save your file to the folder.

Project #2 Computer Disposal and E-cycling

Eventually, every consumer and company that uses computers has to dispose of computer equipment. While you may be able to donate older working equipment, computers and monitors that no longer function must be disposed of properly. As discussed in your readings, computers and peripherals contain hazardous materials and it is vital to follow the correct guidelines for recycling and/or disposing of old equipment.

In this activity you'll learn more about the challenges involved in equipment disposal and recycling. Using PBS's Web site, read the following articles that focus on e-waste, its implications, and e-cycling:

- E-cycling: **http://www.pbs.org/now/science/ecycling.html**
- E-cycling resource map: **http://www.pbs.org/now/science/ecyclemap.html**. This Web site provides a state-by-state listing of recycling centers and contact offices. Make a copy of this list or bookmark the page for future reference.
- CRTs and the recycling process: **http://www.npr.org/programs/morning/features/2002/jul/recycling/index.html**

Project #3 Windows NT Printing - Flow of Control

http://www.microsoft.com/technet/treeview/default.asp?url=/TechNet/prodtechnol/winntas/support/ntprint2.asp

This article focuses on printing in Windows NT 4.0 (and NT 3.x). Even though many companies have migrated to Windows 2000, Windows NT 4.0 still is widely used. Migrating a network to a new operating system can be a daunting task, especially for large enterprises, and such a move takes extensive planning. While some companies have made a full transition from Windows NT to Windows 2000, many will migrate slowly and change out systems as time and budgets allow. As a skilled technician, you're likely to work with Windows NT systems in a mixed environment of Windows NT and Windows 2000. It would not be surprising to see NT 4.0 used as file and print servers. As you'll discover, the NT modular printing subsystem is very flexible and capable of serving a wide range of clients.

This article gives you some insight into the flexibility and capability of the Windows NT printing subsystem. By tracking out the printing "decision-tree," you'll gain a deeper understanding of printer architecture. By following the logic of this article, you'll increase your understanding of the printing process and enhance your troubleshooting skills.

Reflective Questions

1. How often does your company perform periodic maintenance on computer equipment? Would you recommend that the company stay with this policy, perform maintenance more frequently, or less frequently?

2. How does your company handle disposing of old or broken equipment? Would you recommend that the company stay with this policy or change it? Does it meet environmental guidelines?

CHAPTER 7
Troubleshooting Device Problems

Chapter Objectives:

In this chapter, you will troubleshoot and correct device problems.

You will:

- Troubleshoot and correct monitor problems.
- Troubleshoot and correct keyboard and pointing device problems.
- Troubleshoot and correct adapter card problems.
- Troubleshoot and correct hard drive problems.
- Troubleshoot and correct internal removable media device problems.
- Troubleshoot and correct CD or DVD drive problems.
- Troubleshoot and correct printer problems.

Introduction

You installed and configured hardware rather than letting users do it. You performed regularly scheduled preventative maintenance procedures. However, you still get trouble calls from users. No matter how carefully you try to control their systems, there are going to be times components fail or act up. In this chapter, you will learn how to troubleshoot device problems.

Knowing how to quickly and efficiently troubleshoot device problems will lead users to trust you in being able to fix their problems. If you often end up spending hours figuring out that the problem was a loose connection or a dead battery, that will not instill a lot of confidence in your users as to your abilities. While there are times that this will happen, you need to hone your troubleshooting skills so that this is the exception rather than the rule.

TOPIC A
Correct Monitor Problems

You have installed a monitor and performed preventative maintenance on it. The monitor might have installed easily and worked right away or you might have encountered problems. After you installed the monitor, the user might have encountered problems. In this topic, you will correct monitor problems.

A common but critical problem users may experience is a non-functioning peripheral. Since a monitor problem can halt a users work, you must be able to quickly identify the cause and resolve the issue. Experience is the best teacher in many troubleshooting issues. So, let's get you some experience!

The Troubleshooting Process

The troubleshooting process consists of the following phases:

1. The Collect Phase—In this phase, detailed information about the hardware, the software, the operating system in use, the steps that result in the problem, and the perceived problem is gathered. This might be gathered by the hardware technician, by help desk personnel, or through an online trouble reporting form.
2. The Isolate Phase—In this phase, the user is asked a series of questions to isolate the potential causes of the problem. The technician also asks his or her self questions that will help isolate the cause of the problem.
3. The Correct Phase—In this phase, the technician actually performs the steps needed to resolve the problem.

The troubleshooting process is shown in Figure 7-1.

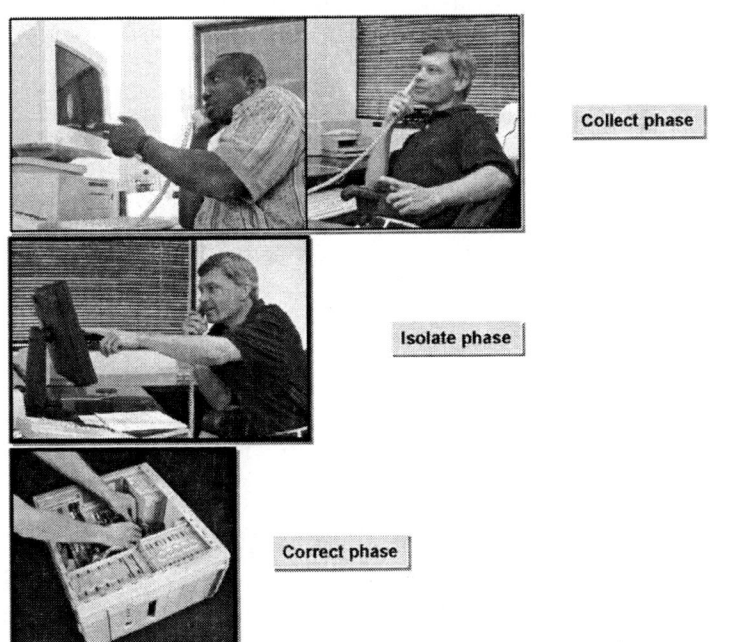

Figure 7-1: *The troubleshooting process.*

Troubleshooting Tips

When you are attempting to resolve a problem, you need to keep some things in mind. The first is to use your common sense. Some solutions are very obvious if you examine the equipment. For example, a cable might be loose or disconnected. Be sure to look for these obvious problems before delving too deeply into troubleshooting mode.

There are three things you will want to try before getting too deep into troubleshooting mode for almost all problems. These are:

- Check the physical connections. This might involve making sure the device is plugged in and connected to the computer, that it is connected to the right port, that an adapter card is fully seated in the slot, and so forth.

- Check the adapter to which the device is connected. If you are having trouble with a device, it might not be a fault in the device. It might be a problem with the adapter or the adapter card to which it is connected. Be sure to troubleshoot the entire interface including the card, port, cable, and device.

- Check Device Manager. An exclamation point (!) or X in red or yellow over a device indicates there is a problem. The Properties sheet of devices has a Device Status box that indicates whether the device is working properly. This box also contains a Troubleshoot button which accesses topics in the Help And Support Center.

- Use the Help And Support Center utility to have Windows guide you through the things you should check when troubleshooting a particular device problem.

Chapter 7: Troubleshooting Device Problems

In the procedure references and activities throughout this course, we have listed many of the possible solutions to a given problem. You might not need to perform all of the steps listed in order to resolve the problem.

On the other hand, in some cases there might be additional causes and solutions that are not listed. You might find these when you access a vendor's Web site. These are often specific to a particular make and model of a device.

Many times when you are troubleshooting a problem, you will find that there is more than one cause for the problem. In this case, you might need to combine several troubleshooting strategies to resolve the problem.

Often you will need to reboot to test whether your attempt to fix the problem has actually resolved the problem. If it did, great! If it didn't, just keep trying to work your way through the rest of the list of possible solutions. If none of the solutions work for your problem, ask a colleague if they can help you. Sometimes that second set of eyes sees the solution that you don't.

How CRTs Produce Images

Most televisions and computer monitors are based on CRT technology. The computer output you see on the monitor screen is the result of a carefully controlled stream of electrons hitting the phosphorous coating on the screen and making parts of it glow. Because the phosphorous glows for only a fraction of a second, the electron stream must return and start it glowing again so the image remains on the screen.

The process for producing an image on a non-interlaced monitor is:

1. Information from main memory is received by the video adapter in digital form. The color information for each visible pixel on the screen, which may be composed of several of the physical phosphorous dots on the screen, is stored in the video memory.
2. The Random Access Memory Digital-Analog Converter (*RAMDAC*) circuit converts the digital information from analog information. A separate digital to analog converter (DAC) is used for red, blue, and green signals.
3. A table containing information about the voltage levels needed to produce a specific color for a pixel is read from the video card.
4. Signals are sent through the monitor cable from the video adapter to electron guns in the monitor. There are three separate guns—one for each color. The guns are in the back of the monitor.
5. The inside of a CRT is a vacuum. The electron guns shoot streams of electrons through this vacuum. Electron stream intensity is specified by the information sent from the video adapter.
6. A magnetic deflection yoke inside the monitor bends the electron streams using electromagnetism. The path is aimed by additional information sent by the video adapter. This information includes what the resolution and refresh rate are.
7. Electron streams are aligned by the shadow mask, aperture grill, or slotted mask that they pass through. The dot pitch is determined by how close the holes in the mask are to each other.
8. The phosphorous coating inside the screen is hit by the electron stream, causing the phosphorous to glow. Each of the three colors uses a different phosphorous substance.

9. The electron stream passes across the screen and is then turned off. The yoke refocuses the electrons on the left of the screen again, this time just below the previous scan line. This is repeated, with the yoke adjusting the angle of the electrons so that all lines on the entire screen are illuminated. One pass over the entire screen is referred to as a frame.

10. Since the phosphorous glows for only a fraction of a second after being hit by the electrons, they need to be hit repeatedly. The usual rate is at least 60 frames per second. So, that means that this entire process is repeated at least 60 times per second.

A graphical representation of how a non-interlaced monitor produces an image is shown in Figure 7-2.

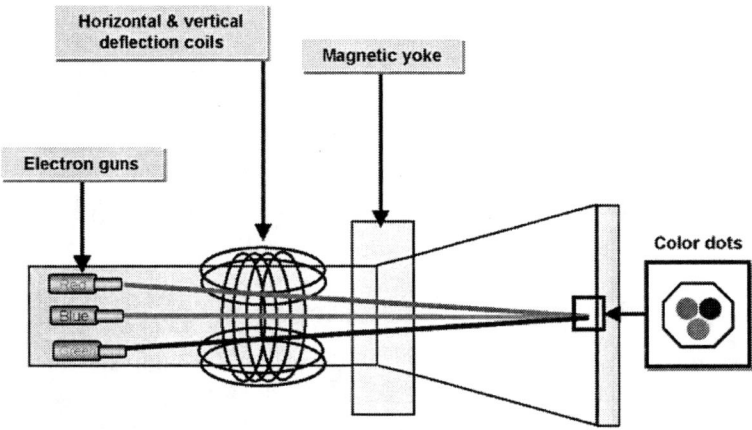

Figure 7-2: *How color CRT monitors work.*

If you have an interlaced display adapter, every other line is scanned during each pass until the entire screen has been covered. This method produces a noticeable flicker as the phosphors lose luminescence before they are hit again.

Aspect Ratio

The aspect ratio is the ratio of width to height of a display. Most software expects a 4:3 ratio, and the display will appear to be distorted if other ratios are used. The aspect ratio is found by reducing the fraction of the number of pixels across the screen over the number of pixels down the screen. For example, a resolution of 640 x 480 has a 4:3 aspect ratio. The following table lists some common resolutions and the aspect ratios.

Resolution	Number of Pixels	Aspect Ratio
320 x 200	64,000	8:5
640 x 480	307,200	4:3
800 x 600	480,000	4:3
1,024 x 768	786,432	4:3
1,280 x 1,024	1,310,720	5:4

Chapter 7: Troubleshooting Device Problems

Resolution	Number of Pixels	Aspect Ratio
1600 x 1200	1,920,000	4:3

Degauss

Monitors aim electrons onto the display screen. These are aimed through a device called a shadow mask. Magnetic forces outside of the monitor, for instance powerful speakers, can magnetize the monitor's shadow mask, pulling it out of alignment. This can result in distorted images and colors.

 Some degaussers are so strong, that when you degauss your monitor, other monitors sitting nearby are also degaussed!

Degaussing a monitor demagnetizes the monitor. Many monitors degauss automatically when they are turned on. Some also include a degauss button so that you can manually degauss the monitor.

Electron Beam Positioning Technologies Used in Monitors

Because the red, green, and blue dots are so small, it is difficult for the electron beam to always hit the center of the right dot. In CRT monitors you will find one of three technologies used to position the electron beams produced by the electron guns at the back of the monitor. These are shadow mask, aperture grill, or slotted mask.

Technology	Description
Shadow mask	One way to keep the beam from hitting the wrong dot is to use a metal sheet with a tiny hole for each trio of adjacent red, green, and blue dots. This grill is a shadow mask; it keeps stray electrons from bleeding over into other colored dots.
Aperture grill	Other monitors use very thin vertical strips of metal to block the stray electrons from hitting the wrong dots on the tube. These strips form an aperture grill. Monitors using the aperture grill may have a brighter display with a sharper image, but wires used to stabilize the strips form very thin horizontal lines on the screen image.
Slotted mask	This is a combination of shadow mask and aperture grill technologies. It uses vertical slots with horizontal masks to produce a stable image that is brighter than shadow mask.

Monitor Safety

Monitors store high-voltage electricity on large capacitors for long periods of time after the monitor is turned off and unplugged. The 20,000 volts are combined with enough current to kill you. The CRT tube can implode and spray you with shards of glass. The 120 V from the wall outlet are present in parts of the monitor, even when it is turned off. For this reason, all the monitor repairs in this course can be done without taking the cover off the monitor or sticking anything inside the cover.

Power Management

Power management is configured in CMOS. It can be configured to specify when power conservation settings are enacted. You can specify which components are automatically powered down and under what conditions.

With the power management enabled in CMOS, you can then use Windows XP Power Schemes to reduce power consumption of specific devices or the computer as a whole. Windows XP comes with several preconfigured power options you can choose from or you can create your own settings. These features must be supported by the hardware in order for XP to implement them. After a specific interval, you can:

- Turn off components such as the monitor or hard drive.
- Go into Standby Mode. This puts devices in a low power state and turns off some devices.
- Go into Hibernate Mode. This saves the contents of RAM to disk, and then turns off the monitor, drives, and, finally, the computer itself.

Common Monitor Problems

There are many problems you might encounter when troubleshooting monitors. The following table lists the most common symptoms of monitor problems and possible problems that cause those symptoms.

Symptom	Possible Problem	Troubleshooting Tool or Technique	Interpretation of Troubleshooting Tool Results
No image displayed on the monitor	Power is not turned on. Power button is turned on, but monitor is plugged into a power strip, surge protector, or UPS that is not turned on. Data cable to the VGA port on the PC is disconnected. Verify that brightness control is adjusted properly. Verify that contrast control is adjusted properly. The monitor is in power saving mode. Press a key or move the mouse to wake up the monitor.	Physically manipulating the monitor.	When you make adjustments to the monitor, determine if they fixed the problem.
Monitor flickers	Monitor cable is not securely connected to the video port or there are bent or broken pins. Incorrect display adapter and monitor device drivers are in use. Display adapter and/or monitor settings are corrupted. Refresh rate is too low. Monitor is non-interleaved. Refresh rate is too low. Monitor is non-interleaved.	Verify that the monitor cable is securely connected to the video port and that there are no bent or broken pins. Through Device Manager, verify that the correct display adapter and monitor device drivers are in use. Through Device Manager, check the Device Status box for the display adapter and monitor. Set the refresh rate higher if supported by the monitor and adapter card. Replace the monitor with an interleaved monitor.	When you make adjustments to the monitor, determine if they fixed the problem.

Symptom	Possible Problem	Troubleshooting Tool or Technique	Interpretation of Troubleshooting Tool Results
No power	Monitor is dark. Power indicator light is not lit.	Check whether the power cord is securely connected on the monitor and to the electrical outlet. Check whether the fuse in the monitor is blown. Check whether the monitor is plugged in to a power strip, surge protector, or UPS that is not turned on. Check whether the monitor is plugged in to an outlet that has tripped its circuit breaker. Check if the monitor power button is stuck. Might be able to unstick it by wiggling it.	When you make adjustments to the monitor, determine if they fixed the problem.
Monitor turns itself off	Power management is enabled.	CMOS utility: Check the ACPI settings in the BIOS. Display Properties, Screen Saver settings.	In CMOS, if the ACPI power settings are enabled, you can use the Display Properties Screen Saver and Monitor Power settings to control when the power is lowered or turned off to the monitor. In Display Properties, on the Screen Saver page, adjust the Wait Time to meet the user's needs. Click the Power button to access the Power Schemes and settings for the Power Options Properties dialog box and set those as appropriate to the user's needs as well.

Symptom	Possible Problem	Troubleshooting Tool or Technique	Interpretation of Troubleshooting Tool Results
Screen is fine until a specific application is started, then the screen goes blank, flickers, or acts bizarrely	Application requires different color quality (also known as color depth) or screen resolution.	Display Properties dialog box.	Adjust settings on the Settings page of the dialog box.
Monitor is on, but rather than displaying an image or being black, it is white	This is usually because the monitor is not connected to the video port on the computer. If it is not due to being disconnected, disconnect it and check for bent or broken pins.	Physically manipulating the monitor.	When you make adjustments to the monitor, determine if they fixed the problem.

How to Troubleshoot Monitor Problems

Procedure Reference: Troubleshoot Monitor Problems

There are many problems that can occur with monitors. Here are some ideas to try for a few of the most common problems you are likely to encounter. You probably will not need to try all of them in order to solve the problem. You might need to reboot after trying some of the fixes to see if they worked or not.

1. If the monitor will not come on and the power light is not lighting up either, verify that the monitor power cord is plugged in. Some steps to take in resolving this problem might include:

    - Plugging in a lamp or other device to the electrical outlet to verify that the outlet is working. If it is not, contact the electrician to fix the outlet and plug the monitor in to another outlet.
    - If the monitor is plugged in to a UPS, power strip, or surge protector, verify that the unit is turned on and has power.
    - Verify that the connections of the power cord and monitor cable are secure on the monitor as well as on the PC and electrical outlet.
    - If there is a fuse on the back of the monitor, remove the fuse and check for a broken wire. Replace the fuse with a good fuse or put the fuse back in if it isn't blown.
    - If the monitor still is not working, replace it with a known good monitor. Unplug the video cable from the monitor port on the computer and unplug the monitor electrical cord from the electrical outlet.

2. If the monitor is flickering and the display is distorted, you might try:

- Verifying that the monitor cable is firmly plugged in to the monitor and to the computer.
- If the monitor has one, press the degauss button. A monitor with a degauss button lets you demagnetize the monitor in an attempt to resolve color blotching problems or distortions. Most monitors automatically degauss when they are turned on.
- Check the monitor cable for any bent pins and straighten if necessary.
- Move the monitor away from florescent lights, speakers, other monitors, or other electronic devices with powerful motors.

3. If the monitor power light is on, but nothing is displayed on the screen, you might check:
   - Determine if the power light is glowing green or orange. If the power light is orange, the monitor is in energy-saving mode or is getting no data from the computer. A green power light indicates that the monitor is on and is receiving data.
   - Verify that the cable is connected to the monitor and to the PC.
   - Adjust the contrast using the buttons on the monitor.
   - Adjust the brightness using the buttons on the monitor.
   - If it is still not working, swap the monitor with a known good monitor.

4. If the monitor comes on, but then goes blank after a few moments, you should check:
   - Determine if the monitor power light is glowing green or orange.
   - If the light is orange, press a key to arouse the system from energy-saving mode. Some monitors only seem to wake up when the Windows key is pressed on the keyboard.
   - Change the Power Management settings in CMOS to disable sleep or doze mode. The exact steps for this vary based on your system BIOS, so the setting might not be called Power Management, and could be under a variety of different options.
   - Change the Power Scheme within Windows.
     1. Right-click the Windows Desktop and choose Properties.
     2. Display the Screen Saver panel and click Power.
     3. Display the Power Schemes drop-down list and choose Always On.
     4. Change all Settings For Always On Power Scheme to Never.

     After you have determined that the monitor is not shutting down due to electrical malfunctions, the user can adjust these settings to meet their needs.

5. If the monitor is making noises, determine whether it is making crackling or whining noise.
   - If it is a crackling noise, clean the monitor and try to vacuum or blow dust out of monitor vents. Remember, **do not open the monitor!** If necessary, send it to a monitor repair facility for more in-depth cleaning.

- If it is a whining noise, try moving the monitor. You might also try changing the refresh rate. If it is still whining, send it out to a monitor repair facility for adjustment and replace it with a quieter monitor.

6. If none of your attempts to correct the problem are successful, it might be because the monitor is dead and needs to be replaced. It is usually less expensive to replace the monitor than to send it out for repairs. To replace the monitor:
   1. Remove the existing monitor.
      a. Shut down the computer.
      b. Turn off the power on the computer and the monitor.
      c. Unplug the monitor from the electrical outlet.
      d. Unplug the monitor data cable from the monitor port.
   2. Install the new monitor.
      a. Connect the data cable from the monitor to the computer's monitor port.
      b. Plug the monitor power cable into an electrical outlet.
      c. Turn on the monitor and computer power.
      d. Start the computer and verify that the new hardware was detected.

TOPIC B
Correct Input Device Problems

You have installed and maintained peripherals so far. What if you get a trouble call about a keyboard or mouse problem? In this topic, you will correct keyboard and mouse problems.

You get a call from a user who says that when they enter their password, an error message is displayed saying that they typed it wrong. The user knows their password and has tried it several times, each time with the same results. The user has a laptop with the numeric keypad integrated with the letters and accessed through a Function button. You immediately know what the problem is and help the user fix the problem, so you have yet another satisfied customer. If you hadn't had this same call from other users, you wouldn't necessarily know what the problem was so quickly. Experience is the best teacher in many troubleshooting issues.

How Keyboards Work

When you press down then release a key, this is what happens:
1. The microprocessor built into the keyboard continuously scans for changes from the key circuits. This comes in as a change in the current for the key. Each key has a scan code for its down state and one for its release state.
2. The scan code for the key being pressed is sent.
3. The scan code is stored in the keyboard buffer.

4. An interrupt is sent to the CPU to alert it to the fact that the keyboard needs attention. IRQ 1 is used to transmit this interrupt for keyboard attention.

5. The scan code is deleted from the keyboard's buffer after it has been transferred. The shift and toggle keys such as Ctrl, Alt, Caps Lock, Scroll Lock, Insert, and so forth also generate scan codes. These are stored in a special area of the keyboard buffer until pressed again and are not deleted when they have been sent. These are not deleted from the buffer until they are pressed a second time to release the state of the key.

6. The keyboard BIOS reads the contents of the special shift and toggle keys along with the scan codes for other keys to determine which state of the key should be sent to the CPU. For example, should it be b or B. Or, if the Ctrl key is being held and the B key is pressed, then it means that the user wants to bold some text or if Alt is being held and the B key is pressed, then the user probably is using the keyboard method to access a menu with B as its key letter.

7. When the key is released, a separate scan code is sent.

Figure 7-3 shows an example of what happens when you press a key on a keyboard.

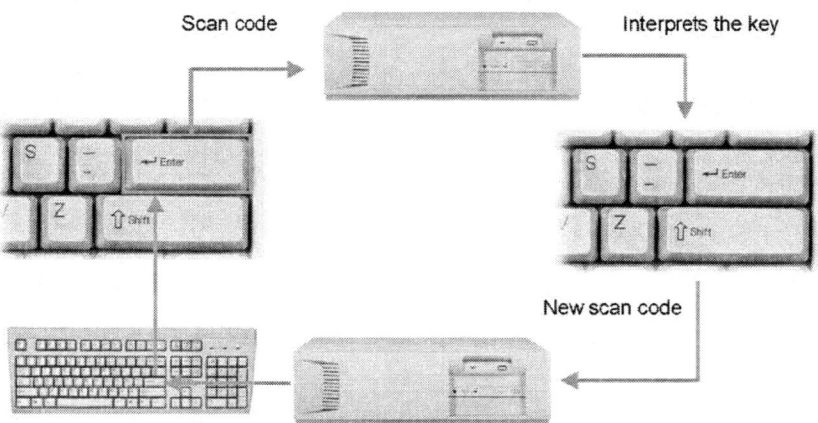

Figure 7-3: *How a keyboard works.*

Keyboard Scan Codes

ASCII (American Standard Code for Information Interchange) and ANSI (American National Standards Institute) have produced well-known number codes for each character in the English language, as well as some special and foreign characters. For example, A is 65, B is 66 and C is 67 in both ASCII and ANSI. Character maps, symbols selection options, and special character codes refer to ASCII numbers. The keyboard scan code for A is 1E, for B is 30, and for C is 2E. Programming language looks at text as a series of ASCII codes, with one number representing each letter.

The keyboard has a special scan code for every key on the keyboard. When a key is pressed, this scan code is sent through the keyboard cable to a keyboard BIOS chip that then sends the proper ASCII code to the computer for processing. When the key is released, another code is sent to the BIOS chip to let it know that the key is up. The Typematic Repeat Rate determines how many times per second the scan code is sent to the BIOS when a key is held down for an extended period of time.

Keyboard Components

The keyboard BIOS is the brains of the keyboard. When the Shift, Ctrl, or Caps Lock keys are pressed, they are treated like any other key by the keyboard. The scan code for the key is sent to the BIOS. BIOS then sends a signal back to the keyboard to light up the LED light for the special key that was pressed.

Keyboards are manufactured using two different techniques:

- The first method uses coiled metal springs to push the key up after the user has depressed it and made the electrical contact that tells the computer which key has been pressed.
- The second method uses rubber or plastic membranes. When a key is pressed, a bump in the rubber membrane is pressed down, and a conductive material on the membrane completes a circuit that lets the keyboard know which key was pressed. The compressed rubber bump then bounces back into its original shape and pushes the key up into its starting position.

Keyboards need a force of about 100 grams to press the key down. Most keyboards require electric current that has a maximum load of 300mA (milliAmps). This power comes to the keyboard through the cable from the main computer power supply.

Common Keyboard Problems

Keyboards are so inexpensive, that there is usually not much troubleshooting that is done on them. Sometimes the problem is with the keyboard port on the computer, so replacing the keyboard will not correct the problem. Here are some of the symptoms and possible problems they indicate.

Symptom	Possible Problem
Keys stick.	Foreign matter under the keys.
User with physical limitations is currently unable to use the standard keyboard.	Accessibility features for the keyboard have not been enabled.
No input is sent when keys are pressed.	Keyboard unplugged. Keyboard plugged into mouse port. Keyboard interface contains bent or broken pins. User attempted to connect the keyboard using a PS/2-to-USB adapter on a keyboard that doesn't support this translation. Keyboard port on the computer is damaged.
Keyboard-related message or beep codes given during computer boot.	Keyboard might be disconnected or plugged into the mouse port. Keyboard might be damaged.

Symptom	Possible Problem
Wrong characters are displayed on the screen when user inputs information.	The language was changed in the Keyboard Properties within Windows. Short or incorrect contacts being made due to beverage spilled into the keyboard or another foreign matter in the keyboard. Keyboard interface on the computer is damaged.
Multimedia buttons not working properly.	Device driver needs updating. File related to the button has been moved, renamed, or modified in some way.

Keyboard Troubleshooting Techniques

Troubleshooting keyboard problems usually involves physically examining the connection, examining the keyboard for foreign materials under the keys, and verifying that the keyboard is connected to the correct port. The following table describes some common problems and how to troubleshoot those problems.

Suspected Problem	Troubleshooting Techniques	Interpretation of Troubleshooting Tool Results
Foreign matter under the keys.	Physically shake the keyboard upside down or use compressed air to blow out debris.	Foreign matter can cause the contact to be made to the wrong key or not be made at all.
Accessibility features for the keyboard have not been enabled.	Control Panel	Enable the Accessibility options such as StickyKeys, FilterKeys and/or ToggleKeys to enable handicapped users to more easily use the keyboard.
Keyboard unplugged. Keyboard plugged into mouse port. Keyboard interface contains bent or broken pins. User attempted to connect the keyboard using a PS/2-to-USB adapter on a keyboard that doesn't support this translation. Keyboard port on the computer is damaged.	Physically check the connections.	Keyboards plugged into the wrong port won't work.

Suspected Problem	Troubleshooting Techniques	Interpretation of Troubleshooting Tool Results
Keyboard might be disconnected or plugged into the mouse port. Keyboard might be damaged.	Physically check the connections.	Keyboards plugged into the wrong port or not plugged in at all won't work.
The language was changed in the Keyboard Properties within Windows. Short or incorrect contacts being made due to beverage spilled into the keyboard or another foreign matter in the keyboard. Keyboard interface on the computer is damaged.	Check the Keyboard Properties settings then physically check the keyboard for foreign matter under the keys.	The wrong characters being displayed can be any number of reasons. These are a couple of the more common reasons.
Device driver needs updating. File related to the button has been moved, renamed, or modified in some way.	Download updated drivers from the manufacturer's Web site. Verify that the file associated with a given button is correctly named, and if any options are needed, that they are correctly formatted.	Be sure that you get the correct driver for your keyboard if you replace the current driver; otherwise, you run the risk of more of the special buttons not working properly.

How Pointing Devices Work

When the user moves the mouse, the computer detects the direction and amount of motion by electrical signals sent through the mouse cord and redraws a pointer that mimics that motion on the screen. The computer knows the position of the pointer relative to other objects drawn on the screen.

 The mouse was invented by Douglas Engelbart of Stanford Research Center in 1963 and pioneered by Xerox in the 1970s. It frees the user from strict keyboard input and makes computers accessible to a much wider audience.

To summarize how a mechanical mouse works:

1. The user moves the mouse over a flat surface.
2. The ball inside the mouse turns in the direction the mouse is moved. This ball is usually a rubber-coated steel ball.

3. The ball rests against two rollers which send X- and Y-axis information to the computer. All mice report their location several times per second. The more reports per second, the smoother the mouse pointer movement on the screen. A third roller holds the ball in place against the other two rollers.

4. The rollers are connected to encoder wheels. These encoders contain metal contacts around the edge. Two bars are connected to the mouse shell which make contact with the metal contacts on the encoder wheels and create an electrical signal. The computer counts the number of signals sent to know how far and how fast you are moving the mouse.

5. The mouse buttons are simple switches. Signals are sent each time the mouse button or buttons are pressed. The computer translates the mouse clicks or presses and the software program interprets them to mean whatever the programmers programmed the mouse signals to mean.

6. When the user clicks one of the buttons on the mouse, the computer determines what icon or graphic the user was pointing at, if anything, and then performs the action that the icon has associated with a mouse click. An icon may have specific actions programmed to run if the mouse moves the pointer into its area, out of its area, or over its area. If a mouse button is pressed while the pointer is in its area, it may have specific actions programmed to run if a mouse button is:

   - Down.
   - Up.
   - Clicked (pressed and released).
   - Double-clicked (clicked two times with a short time span between clicks).
   - Ctrl-clicked (clicked while the Ctrl key on the keyboard is held down).
   - Shift-clicked (clicked while the Shift key on the keyboard is held down).
   - Alt-clicked (clicked while the Alt key on the keyboard is held down).

7. The user can drag an icon by pointing at it, holding the mouse button down, and while holding the button down moving the mouse (press and drag). The icon can be programmed to respond differently if the button used is the left, right, or center (if available or both buttons together) mouse button.

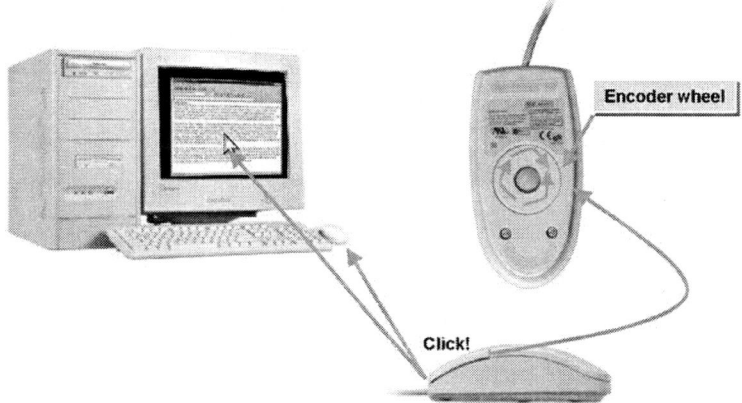

Figure 7-4: *How a mechanical mouse works.*

Optical Mouse

Another type of mouse is an optical mouse. It uses LED signals rather than a ball to track the location. The mouse shines LED on the surface it is being rolled over and scans the light reflected from the surface. An optical mouse is composed of a lens, an optical sensor, and an LED that shines through an opening onto the mousing surface.

Trackball

Another pointing device you will encounter is a trackball. This works the same way as a mouse except that it is upside down with the ball on the top and rolled by the user's hand rather than rolling on a flat mousing surface. It uses the same process as a mechanical mouse with the only difference being the location of the ball.

Common Pointing Device Problems

There are many problems you might encounter when troubleshooting pointing devices. The following table lists some of the most common symptoms of pointing device problems that cause those symptoms.

Symptom	Possible Problem	Troubleshooting Tool or Technique	Interpretation of Troubleshooting Tool Results
Mouse pointer jumps around on the screen.	Mouse ball or rollers are dirty. Mouse has reached the end of its useful life. Mouse is not being rolled over a flat surface. Mouse is being rolled over a dirty mouse pad.	Visually inspect the mouse, the mouse pad, and the area around the mouse. You can use the Device Manager and Help And Support Center utilities to check the pointing device.	This is a common problem and preventative maintenance can reduce this problem, but usually does not eliminate it.

Symptom	Possible Problem	Troubleshooting Tool or Technique	Interpretation of Troubleshooting Tool Results
Cordless mouse is in use and mouse pointer is jumping around or not moving.	Verify that there is no obstruction between the transmitter and the receiver. Press the Reset or Connect buttons on each device to try to re-establish the connection. Replace the batteries in the mouse. Press the Reset or Connect buttons on each device again. Verify that the receiver device is connected to the port. Try a corded mouse connected to the port. If this works, replace the cordless mouse with either a corded mouse or another cordless mouse.	You can use the Device Manager and Help And Support Center utilities to check the pointing device. Check batteries.	If the Windows XP utilities don't show a problem with the mouse, it is probably just a case of worn out batteries.
Mouse works okay sometimes, but other times the mouse doesn't work.	IRQ conflict between the mouse and the modem (or another device).	Device Manager.	Device Manager will list any conflicts it finds between devices. Change the mouse to another IRQ such as IRQ 12.
Mouse is not working.	Mouse is not plugged in. Mouse is plugged in to the keyboard port. Mouse was connected after the computer was started. Some pointing devices require special drivers and possibly additional software to function properly. Pointing device is not on the Windows Hardware Compatibility List (HCL). Driver for the pointing device was corrupted or outdated.	Physically check the pointing device connection. Use Device Manager to verify that the correct driver is installed. Check the pointing device's documentation to see if any additional software is required for it to function properly. Check the Web site of the device manufacturer to see if newer drivers or software should be installed.	Device Manager shows the name of the mice or other pointing device. The Driver page of the properties sheet for the device lists • Driver provider. • Driver date. • Driver version.

Chapter 7: Troubleshooting Device Problems

Symptom	Possible Problem	Troubleshooting Tool or Technique	Interpretation of Troubleshooting Tool Results
USB mouse is not working properly.	A problem with the root hub or USB host controller. Mouse is plugged into an unpowered USB hub and is not getting enough power to operate properly.	You can check the status of the root hub or USB host controller in Device Manager. You can try physically removing some of the devices from the hub to see if the mouse functions then or you can plug it directly into a USB port on the computer.	If the root hub or USB host controller is working properly and plugging the pointing device directly in to the computer makes the device work, then the device is not receiving enough power. Use a powered USB hub or devices requiring more power to another USB port or powered hub.

How Touch Screen Devices Work

Before this process can occur, the hardware needs to be installed and calibrated. After installing the hardware and software for the touch screen device, run the utility that came with it to calibrate it. This sets the dimensions of the screen and the relative distance between points. There will be on screen instructions for where to touch the screen. The following list describes the process a touch screen device uses to retrieve user input and send it to the computer for processing.

1. The touch sensor panel is touched by a user using a finger, a stylus, or other device.
2. A change in the electrical flow through the screen is created by the touch.
3. The system evaluates the change in electrical flow to determine where the touch occurred.
4. The touch screen controller sends the touch sensor data to the computer as input data.
5. The driver for the touch screen device enables the computer to interpret the data that was sent. Usually the data is interpreted as mouse interactions.

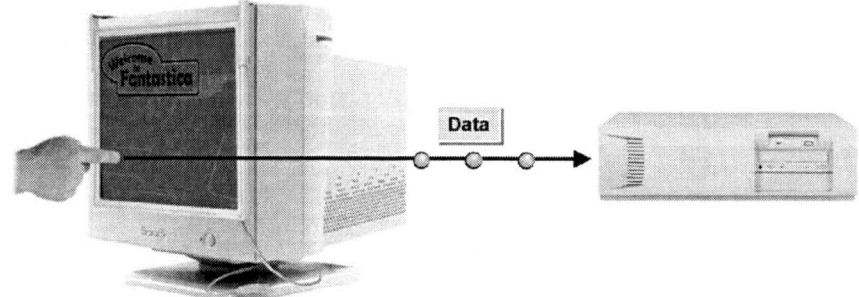

Figure 7-5: *How touch screen devices work.*

Common Touch Screen Device Problems

The following table lists some of the most common symptoms of touch screen device problems and the possible problems that cause those symptoms.

Symptom	Possible Problem	Troubleshooting Tool or Technique
Handheld computer with touch screen interface is having trouble responding to screen input.	Dirty or damaged screen. Calibration settings were lost.	Clean screen. If necessary, replace screen. Run the calibration utility to set screen dimension information. Be sure batteries are charged to retain settings.
Insertion point is not appearing where user touches. It appears well above that location or not on screen at all.	Calibration settings have been lost.	Set the effective area of the screen, then run the calibration utility. You might also need to set the DPI settings to match between the touch screen and what the program is expecting.
User cannot select or activate some areas of the screen.	Calibration utility needs to be re-run. Hardware connections need to be checked.	Run the utilities from the manufacturer to check calibration and other hardware settings. Hardware testing software might also be available from the manufacturer.
Results of touching the screen are not consistent or are inaccurately interpreted.	Calibration settings were lost. Screen surface is dirty or damaged. Connections between touch screen components are loose or damaged. Circuitry within a component of the touch screen system is damaged and needs replacement.	Check the hardware using the manufacturer's calibration and hardware testing utilities. Clean the touch screen surface. Verify that all connections are properly connected.

How to Troubleshoot Input Device Problems

Procedure Reference: Troubleshoot Keyboard and Pointing Device Problems

There are many problems that can occur with keyboards and pointing devices. Here are some ideas to try for a few of the most common problems you are likely to encounter. You probably will not need to try all of them in order to solve the problem. You might need to reboot after trying some of the fixes to see if they worked or not.

1. If the keyboard is not working at all:

- Verify that the keyboard is plugged in to the keyboard port.
- Verify that the keyboard cable is securely connected. Some keyboard cables need to be plugged in to the keyboard as well as to the system's keyboard port.
- If the keyboard still does not work, switch it with a known good keyboard. Pull the connector straight out of the port so as not to bend any of the pins.
- If the keyboard still does not work, verify that CMOS is configured to recognize the keyboard.
- If the keyboard still does not work, test the keyboard port with a multimeter. Pin 4 should have a reading of +5 V and pin 3 is ground. If the port is damaged, you will need to replace the system board.

2. If the keyboard is producing the wrong characters when the user types:
   - Verify that no Function key, Scroll Lock, or other key is enabled or stuck down.
   - Verify that the correct drivers are in use.
   - If that is not the problem, replace with a known good keyboard. Unplug the keyboard and plug in the replacement keyboard.

3. If liquids are spilled on the keyboard:
   - Remind users that all drinks must be covered when used near computer equipment.
   - Unplug the keyboard and turn it upside down over a wastebasket.
   - Move the keyboard around to remove as much liquid as possible.
   - Rinse keyboard in running water if the liquid was sticky (soda pop or sweetened drinks).
   - Set on end to dry for several days.
   - Replace the keyboard with another keyboard so that the user can get back to work until their keyboard is ready to use again.

4. If the mouse pointer is jumping around on the screen:
   - Clean the rollers inside the mouse.
   - Replace the mouse. Unplug the mouse and plug in the new mouse.

5. If a cordless mouse is in use and the mouse pointer is not moving on the screen:
   - Verify that there is no obstruction between the transmitter and the receiver.
   - Press the Reset or Connect buttons on each device to try to re-establish the connection.
   - Replace the batteries in the mouse. Press the Reset or Connect buttons on each device again.
   - Verify that the receiver device is connected to the port.
   - Try a corded mouse connected to the port. If this works, replace the cordless mouse with either a corded mouse or another cordless mouse.

6. If touch screen input is not being read or interpreted correctly:

- Clean the screen.
- Check all connections between all touch screen components.
- Run calibration software.
- Run device testing software.
- Check for damaged components.

 Keyboards and pointing devices are so inexpensive, that unless the device is a special one designed for a specific need, it is more cost effective to simply replace the device.

Topic C
Correct Adapter Card and PC Card Problems

You have seen how to troubleshoot a basic component such as a peripheral. Another component you will need to troubleshoot is adapter cards and PC Cards. In this topic, you will troubleshoot adapter cards and PC Cards.

Your mechanic often knows just what component in your car is acting up based on your description of the way your vehicle is acting. Knowing the common problems associated with adapter cards and PC Cards will enable you to more quickly correct the problems your users encounter. Being able to quickly resolve problems for your users will make them more productive faster.

How Adapter Cards Work

Adapter cards (also known as expansion cards) are inserted into slots on the motherboard. This enables them to communicate with the system's CPU. The process it uses to communicate is outlined in Figure 7-6. The process of communicating between the adapter card and the CPU is:

1. CPU runs processes including the ability to check for requests from peripherals for attention.
2. Peripherals request attention from the CPU by sending an IRQ to the CPU.
3. CPU puts aside whatever it is doing and responds to, or services, the interrupt.
4. Data is transferred and processed.
5. The CPU goes back to doing what it was doing before the interruption occurred.

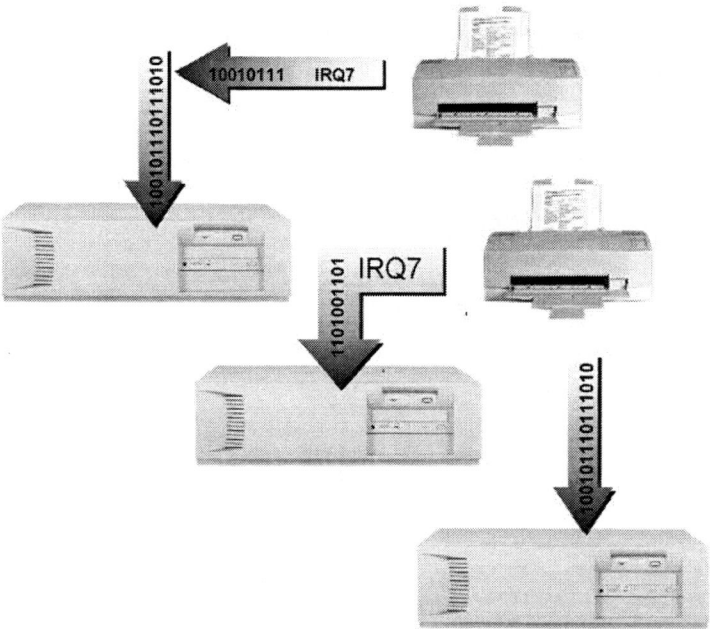

Figure 7-6: *Adapter cards use interrupts to request attention.*

Common Problems with Adapter Cards

The most common problem you will encounter with adapter cards is hardware or system resource conflicts. The following table lists some additional symptoms of adapter card symptoms and possible problems that cause those symptoms.

Symptom	Possible Problem	Troubleshooting Tool or Technique	Interpretation of Troubleshooting Tool Results
Adapter seems to work fine until you replace the system case.	Adapter card is grounded against the case.	Visually inspect card and case for bent or damaged areas.	If the working parts of the adapter card come in contact with the case, it can cause shorts and other faults that affect the working of the adapter card.

Symptom	Possible Problem	Troubleshooting Tool or Technique	Interpretation of Troubleshooting Tool Results
Card works fine in another slot, but when any card is inserted in this particular slot, it doesn't work.	Bus slot damaged.	Multimeter, visual inspection.	Voltages should be within prescribed ranges for the slot and adapter card.
Card tests fine and slot tests fine, but services are unavailable.	Cables not connected, loose, or damaged.	Visually inspect cards and cables.	If a cable needs to connect between a device and an adapter card and it isn't connected properly, then the functions provided through the cable will not be available.
Services provided by the adapter or a device connected to the adapter work intermittently.	Adapter card (or cards) not seated properly. Hardware resource conflict. Adapter card physically damaged. Adapter card electronically damaged.	Reseat adapter card (or cards). Resolves any hardware resource conflicts. Replace any adapter card that is physically damaged. Replace any adapter card that is electronically damaged.	Intermittent problems can be the most tricky to track down and resolve.

Common USB Problems

Generally speaking you should run into few problems with USB ports, hubs and devices. Due to their true Plug and Play nature, things should go smoothly whenever you install a new USB device. However, here are some of the things you need to know, and that you might run into when working with USB.

Problem	Solution
USB support not enabled in the BIOS	USB support must be enabled in the BIOS. Enabling USB support assigns an IRQ to the PCI USB host bus controller. USB may be enabled by default in the BIOS. If it isn't, enter the BIOS during the POST, and locate the area where you enable USB support, and then enable it. You will likely find USB support under the Input/Output Ports menu, under Peripheral Setup, or under Advanced Options. If your BIOS doesn't have USB support, you may need to upgrade it, or, alternatively, install a PCI to USB adapter card in the system.
No USB port on the system	Install a PCI to USB adapter card in the computer.
USB 1.0 system with cable over 5 meters	Make sure that the USB cable doesn't exceed 5 meters. An extension may lead to signal loss, and errors can occur, such as devices not functioning properly or not being detected. The USB 1.0 specification specifically states that extensions are not allowed. Later USB specifications allow for cables with internal repeaters, but signal loss can still occur.
Device cannot be seen	Your operating system may not support USB. Windows 95 provides limited USB support, and requires version B (OSR2) and supplemental USB support files. You're best off with Windows 98 or Windows 2000, which both natively support USB. To check if the USB supplement has been installed in Windows 95, open Add/Remove Programs from Control Panel, and look for USB Supplement to OSR2. If you don't see this item, then the supplement hasn't yet been installed. The supplement file is USBSUPP.EXE, and you can find it on the Windows 95 OEM Service Release 2.1 and 2.5 CDs. You can't download it from Microsoft's Web site. Of course, it's always possible that your USB device simply experienced hardware failure. If everything else is working properly, and you've verified that there are no configuration errors or problems of that sort, suspect the hardware.
USB device displays an unknown device icon in Device Manager	If you see an unknown device in Device Manager, you can check the following. If the USB host controller, but not the Root Hub, is listed as the unknown device, you may have a problem with the USB.INF file. To try to alleviate this problem, remove the USB host controller from Device Manager, and then click Refresh. Windows will then redetect hardware, and should see and install both the USB host controller and the Root Hub. Then, browse to \Windows\Inf, right-click the USB.INF file, and choose Install. Windows should then detect your USB device, and you should be able to find it in Device Manager.

How to Troubleshoot Adapter Card Problems

Procedure Reference: Troubleshoot PC Adapter Card Problems

There are many problems that can occur with PC adapter cards and the peripherals connected to them. Here are some ideas to try for a few of the most common problems you are likely to encounter:

1. If you are having video card problems:
   - Locate the video card and make sure that it is fully seated into the slot, and then see if this fixed the problem.
   - Determine if the video card is in a PCI, ISA, or AGP slot. If it is not in an AGP slot, try moving the card to another slot. There is only one AGP slot on the system board, so if it is in the AGP slot, it cannot be moved to a different slot.
   - Remove the card and press down on all four corners of socketed chips to verify that they are fully seated, and then reinstall the card.
   - If another hardware device has recently been added to the system, check Device Manager and verify that there is not a resource conflict between the device and the video card.

2. If you suspect a resource conflict between devices:
   - Open Device Manager and display the Resources By Connection view.
   - Determine if there is a conflict between any devices. ISA cards cannot use the same IRQ as another card. IRQs have been set aside for PCI cards to share with each other. However, the PCI cards cannot share that IRQ with ISA cards.
   - Change the conflicting resource to an unused setting. This might be the IRQ, DMA, or I/O Address.
   - Verify that both devices now work properly.

3. If you suspect a card was damaged due to electrostatic discharge (be it from improper handling, surges, or a lightning storm):
   - Check whether the card in question is listed in Device Manager.
   - Display Properties for the card and verify whether the Device Status indicates that it is working properly.
   - If the device is not working properly, click Troubleshoot and follow the Troubleshoot Wizard steps.
   - If the problem is not resolved, replace the card and verify that the problem has been resolved.

4. If the speakers connected to your sound card are humming constantly:
   - Verify that it is a humming noise rather than a crackling noise.

- Verify that the speaker is plugged in all the way. If it is only partially plugged in, it will hum.
- Move the speakers apart and away from the system. This will reduce interference.
- If the hum has not stopped, verify that the speaker wires are not tangled with the power cords. This can cause interference as well.
- If the problem persists, try replacing the speakers with higher quality speakers.

5. If the speakers connected to your sound card do not produce any sound:
   - Verify that the speakers are connected to the correct port on the sound card.
   - Verify that the speakers are turned on and the power cord is plugged in.
   - Verify that the speaker sound is turned up. There should be a volume dial on one of the speakers.
   - Verify that the Windows volume control is turned up. The Volume icon in the System Tray can be used to adjust the volume. If there is a Not symbol over the speaker icon, the volume has been muted.
   - Verify that the audio cable from the CD-ROM is connected to the sound card.
   - Use Device Manager to verify that the sound card is working properly.
   - If the problem persists, try replacing the sound card and/or speakers.

6. If you have a problem with a device, and replacing the device doesn't fix the problem, and you have also replaced the cable and power cords, then you should suspect the adapter card is giving you the problem. This applies to any adapter card including SCSI, FireWire, USB, and others. To test if this is the problem:
   - Remove the problem device from the port.
   - Connect a replacement device to the port.
   - If necessary, install drivers for the new device.
   - If it works, then the adapter card is okay.
   - If it doesn't work, then try replacing the cable between the device and the port.
   - If it works, then the adapter card is okay.
   - If it doesn't work, then try disconnecting the cables from the port, unscrewing the adapter card from the case, and pulling it straight out to remove the adapter card. Then insert a replacement card.
   - If it works, then the adapter card replacement solved your problem.

Topic D
Correct Hard Drive Problems

You have installed both IDE and SCSI hard drives at this point. Hopefully everything works wonderfully, but as you know, that is not always the case. In this topic, you will correct hard drive problems.

Being able to recognize hard drive problems is an important part of your job. Sometimes it is not immediately obvious that this is the problem. With some experience you will be able to quickly and efficiently identify the problem and determine if you can fix the problem or if you will need to replace the drive.

How Hard Drives Work

To write to a hard drive:

1. The computer positions the head in a particular track. Read/write heads hover over the platters approximately 2/1,000,000th of an inch above the platter.
2. When the appropriate sector passes by, pulses of electricity are sent through a coil of wire in the head. This creates an electromagnetic field, which aligns magnetic particles on the disk surface.
3. By alternating the flow of the current to the head, ones and zeroes can be encoded magnetically.
4. The data is encoded, or written, in circular tracks as the head floats over the rotating platter. The platters spin at a rate of between 5,200 and 10,000 RPMs.

To read data from a hard drive:

1. The computer positions the head over the appropriate track.
2. When the sector passes by, the magnetic particles on the disk create an electrical current in the head through a phenomenon known as *inductance*. Inductance is a circuit or device in which a change in the current generates an electromotive force.
3. In the head, the alternating patterns of magnetism on the disk translate into alternating flows of electrical current, which can be translated into ones and zeroes.

Figure 7-7: *How hard drives work.*

Common Problems with Hard Drives

There are many problems you might encounter when troubleshooting hard drives. Some problems that appear to be hard drive problems are actually virus infections. These can cause physical hard drive damage as well, but usually just damage the files on the disk and not the disk itself. The following table lists the most common symptoms of hard drive problems and possible problems that cause those symptoms.

Symptom	Possible Problem	Troubleshooting Tool or Technique
Error message at boot Drive Not Ready—System Halted	Drive is damaged. Drive is not configured for Master or Cable Select as appropriate to the system. Data cable is not connected or incorrectly connected to the drive.	Visually inspect the drive and its connections.
POST error codes in the 17xx range	1701: Drive not found. 1702: Hard drive adapter not found. 1703: Hard drive failure. 1704: Hard drive or adapter failure. 1780, 1790: Hard drive 0 failed. 1781, 1791: Hard drive 1 failed. 1782: Hard drive controller failed.	Visually inspect connections. Replace component.
Can't read from or write to the drive	Bad sectors on the drive. IRQ conflicts. Drive failure. Virus attack.	Run Scandisk to try to recover information from bad sectors and to mark those sectors as unusable. Check Device Manager for hardware resource conflicts and for indications of drive failure. Run virus check software and remove any viruses found.
System will not boot	Drive disconnected, damaged, not recognized by the BIOS.	Visual inspection, CMOS setup utility.
Drive is making grinding noises that keep repeating in a regular pattern	Physically damaged drive, most likely due to a head crash.	Remind users and technicians not to move a machine while it is in use since that is the most common cause of head crashes.
Data is frequently being corrupted or utilities are not running properly	System not being shut down properly, drive is in the process of failing, virus.	Educate users on how to properly shut down and run virus protection software.

Troubleshooting SCSI Drive Problems

Keep the following points in mind as you troubleshoot SCSI drive problems:
- The vast majority (up to 95 percent) of problems with SCSI disks are due to incorrect ID settings and improper termination.

- When a SCSI system is booted or reset, SCSI controllers generally need to renew all SCSI device connections before activating the devices, causing a delay during POST.
- SCSI cables should be handled carefully to minimize problems. For instance, rolling SCSI cable onto itself can cause crosstalk and impede the signal. Running long lengths of it next to metal or past power supplies can also cause errors due to signal impedance.
- If you intend for a SCSI disk to be bootable after you install it, you must configure the BIOS to Enabled by using jumper settings or software configuration.
- Verify that all SCSI devices have unique SCSI ID numbers.
- If you are installing an additional SCSI hard drive into a computer where only one connector is available on the SCSI cable and the cable itself is terminated, remove and replace the cable with one that has multiple connectors.

Slow Drives

Some hard drives are just inherently slow. The drive revolves at a slower speed than other drives. In other cases, though, a drive that was quite fast might become slow to retrieve files. This might happen suddenly or it might happen over time, and then one day you just happen to notice it. Some of the possible reasons for slow drives include:

- Drive is too full—Windows needs free drive space to write temp and swap files. It needs at least 100 to 200 MB, but 1 to 2 GB is highly recommended.
- Fragmentation—As you write, then erase files, data can become fragmented. The files are written in contiguous blocks beginning with the first free block found. If there is not enough room before the next file is encountered on the disk, then the rest of the file is written in other areas of the disk. Pointers link all the parts of the file together, but this takes time to reassemble the next time you read the file. Run a disk defragmenter program monthly to clean up defragmentation and put files in contiguous blocks.
- Controller too slow—If you have a fast drive connected to a slower controller, the drive will transfer data at the slower rate.
- The wrong cable is used—IDE drive cables all look about the same. However, if you use a cable for a slower drive, it can result in decreased performance.

Hard Drive Maintenance Tools

Just as you can perform physical maintenance on devices, you can perform software maintenance on some devices as well. Hard drives become fragmented and worn as they are used. The following table lists some of the tools you can use to maintain hard drives.

Utility	Purpose	Syntax
chkdsk	Enables you to check the hard disk for errors. If any errors are reported, you can then use other tools such as ScanDisk to repair those errors.	Enter chkdsk *drive letter*. For example, to check the C drive, enter chkdsk C:.
Disk Defragmenter (Defrag.exe)	Rearranges the files on your computer's hard disk to make them contiguous. Use Disk Defragmenter when a hard disk's performance has slowed down.	Run the Disk Defragmenter by choosing Start→Programs→Accessories→System Tools→Disk Defragmenter, or by choosing Start→Run and entering defrag in the Open text box.
Scandisk (Scandisk.exe)	Scans and repairs problems with your computer's hard disk.	You run the Scandisk utility by choosing Start→Programs→Accessories→System Tools→ScanDisk, or by choosing Start→Run and entering scandisk in the Open text box.

How to Troubleshoot and Correct Hard Drive Problems

Procedure Reference: Troubleshoot Hard Drive Boot Problems

There are many reasons why a hard drive won't boot. Here are some ideas to try for a few of the most common problems you are likely to encounter:

1. Examine the POST codes and other messages displayed at boot time.
   - The numbers in the 17xx range indicate that the hard drive or controller were not found. Check that both devices are connected and functional.
   - The message No Boot Device Available indicates that the BIOS could not find an installed operating system on the hard drive or a bootable floppy disk. Verify that the operating system was installed. If it was, try to boot from floppy disk and access the hard drive, then check the boot partition for errors.
   - The messages No Operating System Found or Ntldr Can't Load are often caused by a non-bootable floppy disk being left in the drive.
   - Configuration or CMOS error indicates that the information reported by CMOS is different than the hard drive found by the POST. Check CMOS settings. If the settings won't stick, check the battery on the system board.

- The message Hard Drive Not Found or Fixed Disk Error indicates that the hard drive was not found during the POST. Check all hard drive and hard drive controller connections. The hard drive or controller might be dead.
- The message Reboot And Select Proper Boot Device Or Insert Boot Media In Selected Boot Device indicates that the BIOS found no bootable device in the system. It could also indicate that a removable media drive does not contain media if no hard disk was found and it found a removable media drive (such as a floppy disk drive, Zip drive, SuperDrive, or the like).

2. Determine why the hard drive won't boot. You might need to do all of the following steps or you might need to perform only a few until you determine what the problem is.
   - Perform a cold boot.
   - Verify that CMOS lists the correct device settings for the hard drive. This includes the correct drive type, whether LBA is enabled, and the CHS (cylinders, heads, and sectors) settings.
   - Listen to the drive or touch the drive to determine if it is spinning during POST. It should be spinning up to full speed during this time. It usually makes noise during this time and you can feel the vibrations of the drive while it is spinning.
   - Use your multimeter to verify that the power connection readings are correct. They should be +12v for Pin 1 and +5v for Pin 4. Pins 2 and 3 should be grounded.
   - Verify that the data cable is correctly oriented. Pin 1 is almost always on the side nearest the power connection. Pin 1 on the cable is on the side with the stripe.
   - Check drive settings. For an IDE drive, verify that it is set to master, slave, or cable select as appropriate to the drive and its location in the drive chain within the system. For a SCSI drive, verify that the termination is correct for its location in the chain and that it has a unique device ID.
   - Look for data recovery options. There are some built-in recovery capabilities in some operating systems. You can also purchase software to assist you in recovering data. In many cases though, you will need to resort to sending the drive out to a company that specializes in recovering data from damaged drives.
   - If none of these fix the problem, replace the drive.

3. Verify that the drive now works.
   - Boot the system.
   - Verify that you can read from and write to the drive you repaired.

Procedure Reference: Troubleshoot why a Newly Installed Hard Drive isn't Recognized

There are many reasons why a newly installed hard drive can't be recognized. Here are some ideas to try for a few of the most common problems you are likely to encounter:

1. Verify that the CMOS settings are correct.
2. Verify that the drive was installed correctly.

3. Try to boot from a bootable floppy disk. When the system comes up, at the DOS prompt, enter the drive letter for the drive in question. If you are unable to access the drive, proceed to the next step in this procedure.

4. Verify that the drive was prepared for use. This includes:
   1. Verifying that the drive has been partitioned.
   2. Verifying that the drive has been formatted.

   If these were not done, partition and format the drive for the user.

5. Even though the FDISK command is not included in Windows XP, if you have this command on a bootable floppy disk, you can boot from it and use it to see the partitions and hard disks recognized by the system. If a hard disk is not listed, verify that it was correctly installed. If no partitions are listed on the selected drive, reboot without the floppy disk and use the Windows XP management utilities to create and format the partition or partitions on the drive.

Procedure Reference: Troubleshoot Hard Drive Data Access Problems

There are many reasons why you cannot access the data on a hard drive. Here are some ideas to try for a few of the most common problems you are likely to encounter:

1. If the system boots and all appears to be working properly until you attempt to access data on one of the drives, and the message Can't Access This Drive is displayed, some reasons might include:
   - There is no drive using the letter the user is entering.
   - If it is a drive that uses removable media, the media might not be in the drive or not fully inserted into the drive.
   - The drive is damaged.

   To diagnose the problem you can:
   - Verify that there really is a drive at the letter being used.
   - Attempt to copy a file from another drive to the drive in question.
   - Attempt to copy a file from the drive in question to another drive.
   - Open My Computer, right-click the drive letter in question, and then display the Hardware pane. Use the Troubleshooting Wizard to attempt to locate the problem.
   - If none of these procedures fixed the problem, back up the data from the drive if possible, and then reformat the drive. Remember, reformatting will destroy any data on the drive.
   - If reformatting does not correct the problem, replace the drive.

2. If the user attempts to access a drive in the system and this causes the system to lock up and you hear a clicking sound, you could try to diagnose the problem by:
   - Running the Windows XP Error-checking option on the Tools pane of the Local Disk Properties dialog box.

- Try using an older version of Scandisk from floppy disk to try to identify and repair the errors it encounters.
- Back up the data if you can get to it.
- In all likelihood, you will need to replace the drive.

Another indication of this same problem is that the user can change to the drive in question, but when attempting to access a file or list the files on the drive, it locks up the system and the drive begins clicking again.

3. If the user reports that some folders have disappeared and folder and file names are scrambled with strange characters in their names, you should troubleshoot it the same as the previous problem. It is most likely a bad hard drive. It could also be caused by a virus.

Procedure Reference: Troubleshoot the Wrong Drive Size Being Reported

There are many reasons why the system might report the wrong hard drive size. Here are some reasons for a few of the most common problems you are likely to encounter:

1. If the system contains an older BIOS that does not recognize large drives, it will report that there is only about a 500 MB drive in the system. To resolve this problem, update the BIOS so that the entire drive can be recognized. If the BIOS cannot be upgraded, a Dynamic Disk Overylay driver can be installed to enable the older BIOS and the large drive to work together.

2. A system running Windows 98 SE might report that the drive is only about 6 GB even though you know the drive is much larger. This is a known problem that can be resolved with a fix from the Microsoft Web site at **http://support.microsoft.com/default.aspx?scid=KB;EN-US;Q263044&**.

3. Users are often misled about the exact size of a drive. When talking in general terms, most people round 1024 bytes to 1000 since it is easier to talk in round numbers. By the time you get up to billions of bytes as you will with the newer drives, those 24 bytes for each 1000 bytes starts to add up to significant amounts.

 For more information about binary multiples as used in denoting drive sizes, see **http://physics.nist.gov/cuu/Units/binary.html**.

TOPIC E
Correct Internal Removable Media Drive Problems

Most of the components you have troubleshot so far have few or no moving parts. Drives for removable media have many movable parts, and this invites problems. In this topic, you will correct removable media drive problems.

Any time there are movable parts, there is the potential for a breakdown. Anywhere there is an opening in a PC, there is the potential for it to become filled with foreign matter. That's two strikes against removable media drives. While they are less frequently used now than they were in the past, you will likely be asked by your users to fix these devices at some point. If they use removable media for storing backups or sensitive data, your users will need you to quickly repair the drive for them.

Removable Cartridge Drive Utility Software

Definition:

Removable cartridge drive utilities are software available with the drive or by download from the manufacturer's Web site that enables you to manage the drive and the drive cartridges. All removable cartridge software programs:

- Enable users to manage files and folders.
- Provide additional management options for files and folders stored on the cartridge.

The software varies based on the manufacturer. Each manufacturer uses software that is specific to their drives and cartridges. Some cartridges cannot be accessed if the software is not installed; other drives are accessible without the need to install additional software.

Example:

The Zip drive from Iomega is an example of a removable cartridge drive. The original parallel port model required that you install either guest software or the full software package. The guest software can be run from a floppy disk in some cases. Figure 7-8 shows an example of the additional options available after the Iomega software was installed to work with the Zip drive.

Figure 7-8: *Additional options available with the Iomega software.*

How Floppy Drives Work

When you insert a cartridge in a removable cartridge drive:

1. The metal door slides open revealing the mylar disk surface. This disk is also referred to as a cookie.
2. Controller motor spins the floppy disk at about 360 RPMs.
3. A worm gear operated by a stepper motor moves the read/write heads (one on each side of the disk) to the desired track.

Figure 7-9: *How floppy drives work.*

How Removable Cartridge Drives Work

When you insert a cartridge in a removable cartridge drive:

1. The metal door slides open revealing the mylar disk surface. This disk is also referred to as a cookie.
2. A hub in the drive engages with the center hole of the disk. The hub enables the disk to spin at roughly 3,000 RPMs. This is faster than a floppy disk spins but not as fast as a hard drive spins.
3. Read/write heads move into the opening on the case. There is one for each side of the disk. The heads lightly touch the disk surface. The heads are smaller than those for floppy drives by a factor of about 10.

 The disk is coated with high energy level particles that enable more bits to be packed into a smaller area. It also uses zoned sectors to increase the capacity of the disk.

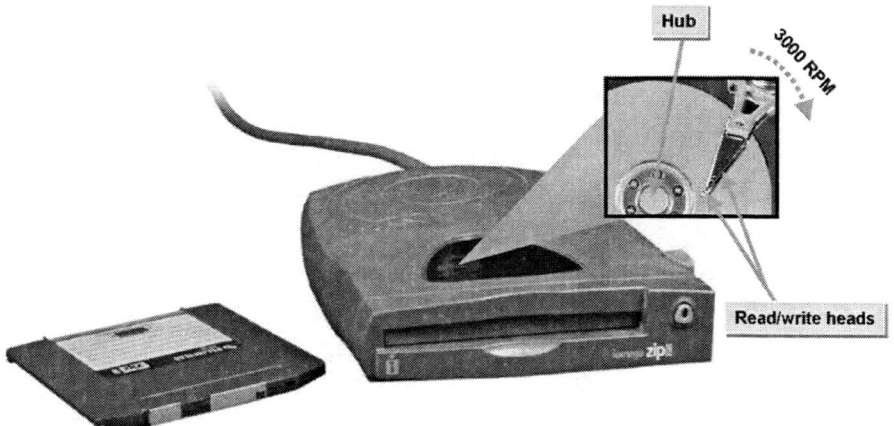

Figure 7-10: *How removable cartridge drives work.*

How Tape Drives Work

Whereas hard drives, floppy drives, and removable cartridge drives are direct access devices, tape drives are sequential access devices. Rather than being able to go to a specific file directly, with a tape, you have to read past every file on the tape until you get to the one you want.

When you insert a tape cartridge in a tape drive and perform a backup of files from your hard drive:

1. The computer reads the FAT table on the hard drive and locates the files that you want to back up.
2. Data is then dumped from RAM to the tape drive controller buffer as memory fills.
3. The controller sends commands to the drive to start spooling the tape.
4. The capstan in the center of the supply reel turns the rollers in the cartridge. The belt around the tape and the rollers provide resistance and keeps the tape taught and tight to the drive heads.
5. Data is sent from the controller to the read/write heads.
6. Tape is composed of parallel tracks. Data is written from the center out towards the edge on each pass. Holes in the end of the tape signal that the direction of the tape needs to be reversed. When it gets to the end, it reverses and moves out one track.

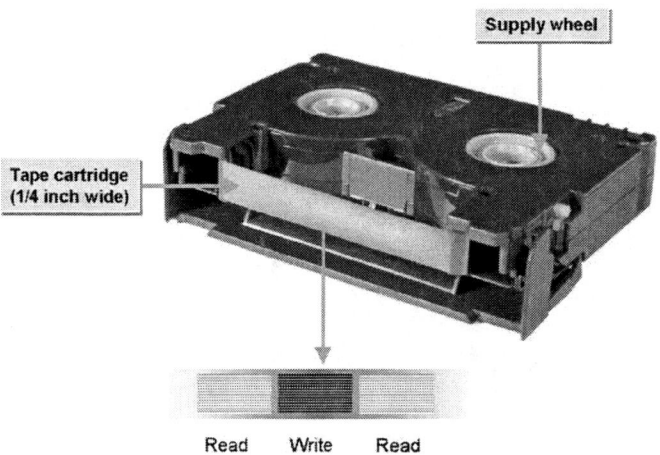

Figure 7-11: *How tape drives work.*

Common Problems with Internal Removable Media Devices

The following concerns might arise when dealing with internal removable media devices:

- If the computer case is not properly aligned with the chassis, the opening for the internal drive might be difficult to access.
- Because there are large openings in the case for these devices, it is common for them to gather large amounts of dust, so be sure to keep them clean.
- Be sure to properly store the media so it is not dirty or damaged. Using dirty or damaged media can damage the drive.

How to Troubleshoot and Correct Internal Removable Media Device Problems

Procedure Reference: Install and Use IomegaWare Utilities

To install and use IomegaWare utilities for Iomega drives:

1. Download the IomegaWare software if you do not have a current version available on CD-ROM.
2. Following the instructions that came with the CD-ROM or the downloaded file, install the software.
3. When you access the Iomega drive through Windows Explorer or other such utilities, you should now see several additional menu options with the Iomega symbol preceding them.

Procedure Reference: Troubleshoot Floppy Drive Problems

There are many problems that can occur with floppy drives. Here are some ideas to try for a few of the most common problems you are likely to encounter:

1. If, when attempting to read data from the floppy disk, the user receives the error message This Disk Is Not Formatted. Do You Want To Format It Now Or Insert Disk Now?, you should:
   - Check that the disk is readable. You can do this by trying to read it on another floppy disk.
   - Try reinserting the floppy disk in the drive.
   - If you received the floppy disk from another user with data on it, determine if it was formatted on another operating system such as Macintosh or Linux. If it was, you will not want to format it as this would erase all of the data on the disk.
   - Verify that the floppy disk functions properly. The shuttle window should open and shut easily. There should be no foreign matter on the mylar disk surface. The mylar disk should spin easily within the plastic case.
   - Check the floppy disk for viruses.
   - Check the floppy disk for bad sectors.
   - Check whether or not other floppy disks can be read in the drive.

2. If the user cannot write to a floppy disk in the drive, you should:
   - Check that the floppy disk is not write-protected. If it is, move the switch to unprotect the floppy disk. Looking at the back side of the floppy disk, the slider on the upper left corner should be down, causing the hole to be blocked in order to write to the floppy disk.
   - Verify that the floppy disk has been properly formatted. A floppy disk formatted using the native format on a Macintosh or Linux system for example cannot be read on a Windows system.
   - Verify that the floppy drive is working properly. Open the system and verify that the floppy drive cable and power connections are properly connected and that the floppy drive mechanisms (you can often see some of them through the holes in the floppy drive case) are functioning properly when you insert a floppy disk in the drive.
   - Clean the floppy drive read/write heads. You can purchase a special cleaning disk with a cleaning solution to insert in the drive. With the cleaning disk in the drive, you attempt to access the drive, causing the disk to spin and thus cleaning the drive.

3. The error message The System Cannot Find The Drive Specified indicates that the operating system cannot locate the floppy disk drive. You should check the CMOS settings to verify that the system knows there is a floppy drive, and then clean the drive, check the alignment of the drive, and check all connections (power and data cables) for the drive.

4. If you attempt to read a floppy disk and receive a message that the disk is not formatted, it was most likely formatted using a different operating system such as Macintosh or Linux. If so, then the original owner of the disk will need to provide the information to you on a medium that Windows can read. This might be over the network, or on a Windows formatted floppy disk (both Macintosh and Linux can read and write to Windows formatted floppy disks).

5. If you can read and write to floppy disks on this system, but they cannot be read on another system, you should suspect that the drive is out of alignment. In a drive that is out of alignment, the read/write head is not properly aligned with the tracks on the disk and covers parts of tracks rather than a single track. While there are tools for adjusting the drive alignment, it is often cheaper to simply replace the drive. More information about the types of misalignment, causes, and methods for repairing the damage can be found at **www.accurite.com/FloppyPrimer.html**.

6. If none of the previous solutions fixed the problem, you might need to replace the floppy drive. To replace the floppy disk drive:

    a. Remove the original floppy disk drive.

    1. Disconnect the power connector from the rear of the disk drive.
    2. Disconnect the controller cable from the rear of the disk drive.
    3. Remove the screws that mount the disk drive in the chassis bay.
    4. Slide the disk drive out of its bay.

    b. Install the replacement floppy disk drive.

    1. Insert the disk drive into its bay.
    2. Mount the disk drive to the chassis using the appropriate screws.
    3. Connect the controller cable to the rear of the disk drive.
    4. Connect the power connector to the rear of the disk drive.
    5. Start the system and verify that the disk drive works properly.

Procedure Reference: Troubleshoot Removable Cartridge Drive Problems

There are many problems that can occur with removable cartridge drives. Here are some ideas to try for a few of the most common problems you are likely to encounter:

1. If no drive letter is displayed in Windows Explorer for a removable cartridge drive, verify that the drivers for the drive have been installed on the system. If that is not the problem, verify that the drive is connected to the proper port with the proper cable. After fixing either of these problems, you should restart the system.

2. If the user cannot write to the removable media:

    - Check that it has not been write protected. This might be a software enabled write protection or a physical write protection on the disk depending on the media you are using.
    - If the disk still cannot be written to, try another disk in the drive.

- If the disk still cannot be written to, verify that the drive is properly connected to the system and that the power supply is plugged in for external models.
- If the disk still cannot be accessed, try moving the drive as far from the monitor, speakers, power supplies or other electronic devices as possible. There might be interference from the devices.

3. If the media was formatted under an operating system other than Windows, you might have problems reading or writing to it. You can sometimes view the properties of the drive to determine the format of the disk.

4. If the disk will not come out of the drive, you can try using a straightened paper clip. Most drives have a hole that you can insert the paper clip wire into then press to manually release and eject the disk from the drive mechanism.

5. The original Zip drive used the Parallel port and the cable that it came with is not always compatible with the default settings on current parallel ports. You might need to change the settings so that the port is not using unidirectional or ECP settings. It should use bidirectional settings. After making the change, restart the computer and now that ECP has been disabled, you should be able to access the drive.

TOPIC F

Correct CD or DVD Drive Problems

In the previous topic, you fixed removable drives. Another closely related drive type is CD and DVD drives. In this topic, you will correct CD and DVD drive problems.

Whether your laser disk drivers are CD-ROM, CD-RW, DVD-ROM, or DVD/R drives, your users are likely to rely on them frequently to perform their job. A problem with these drives can mean that the user will not be able to install or use software if the application requires the disc to be in the drive before using it. You will need to quickly and efficiently correct these problems to get your users back up and running right away.

Common Problems with CD and DVD Drives

CD-ROM, CD-RW, CD-R, DVD-ROM, DVD-R, and DVD-RW drives are often referred to simply as CD and DVD drives. The following list of problems applies to any variation on CD and DVD drives.

- Misaligned case—Prevents drive door from opening and the tray from moving in and out properly.
- Tray out of balance—Inexpensive trays in drives or stickers that don't cover the entire surface of the disc can cause it to wobble because it throws the balance of the drive off. Data can be hard or impossible to read because of the wobble.
- Drive mechanism won't pull disc or tray in—The gears may be stripped, especially if the user pushed on the tray directly rather than using the buttons to manipulate the drive.
- CD drive won't release the CD—Sometimes it is because the software is still accessing the disc. Other times it is because of other reasons. You can use a straightened paper clip to insert in the hole in the front of the drive to release the catch on the drive so that you can remove the disc.

- Disconnected wires—If you can't hear the sounds or music when you attempt to play a CD, then chances are that the wires from the CD drive to the sound card are disconnected. Other possibilities are that the speakers are turned off or down or that the sounds were muted through the Windows settings.
- Driver problems—If the drive is acting strangely and nothing seems to fix it, check the drivers. You might need to uninstall and reinstall the drivers to fix the problem.
- Overheating—If a CD-R or CD-RW drive overheats, there is a good chance that the CD you burn will not be readable. If you have an overheating problem, try fans, or try burning a single CD at a time rather than one right after the other.
- Software—If you want to view DVD movies on a DVD or DVD-R drive, you will need software to play the movie.

How to Troubleshoot and Correct CD or DVD Drive Problems

Procedure Reference: Troubleshoot CD or DVD Drive Problems

There are many problems that can occur with CD-ROM, CD-RW, CD-R, DVD, and DVD-R drives. Here are some ideas to try for a few of the most common problems you are likely to encounter:

1. If the CD/DVD drive door won't open:
   - Verify that there is power to the drive.
   - Press the eject button on the drive.
   - Verify that no applications are attempting to read from the drive.
   - Open My Computer and right-click the drive icon, then choose Eject.
   - If all else fails, use a straightened paper clip to insert in the hole on the drive to manually release the catch.

2. If the CD/DVD drive reads data and program disks, but the user can't hear audio CDs:
   - Verify that you can read a data CD.
   - Verify that speakers are connected properly to the sound card.
   - Verify that the speakers are powered and turned on.
   - Verify that the volume is turned up on the physical speakers.
   - Right-click the Volume icon in the System Tray and choose Open Volume Controls. Verify that Volume Control is not all the way down and that Mute is not checked. You can also adjust the volume through Control Panel.
   - Play a system sound:
     1. Open the Control Panel.
     2. Click Sounds, Search And Audio.
     3. Click Adjust The System Volume.
     4. Display the Sounds panel.

5. Select an event, and then click the Play button next to Sounds to see if the associated sound for the event is played.
- Verify that the correct sound drivers are installed.
  a. In the Control Panel display the Sounds, Speech, And Audio Devices dialog box, and then display the Hardware panel.
  b. Verify that the Devices list includes the proper driver and that Audio Codes is listed.
  c. If not, use the Add/Remove Hardware program to add the appropriate drivers.
- Use the Troubleshooting Wizard for the Sounds, Speak, And Audio Devices.
- Attempt to play the default song in the Windows Media Player.
  1. From the Start menu, choose All Programs→Accessories→Entertainment→ Windows Media Player.
  2. Choose Tools→Options.
  3. Display the File Types panel and verify that all File Types are checked.
  4. Click OK.
  5. Click the Play button to attempt to play the default song.
- Verify that the audio cable inside the system case that connects the CD-ROM drive to the sound card is properly installed and that there are no broken wires.
- Verify that the user can now play the audio CD.

3. If, after upgrading to Windows XP, a user can no longer access their CD/DVD drive:
- Verify that the drive is on the Windows XP hardware compatibility list.
- Verify that the drive is properly installed.
- Verify that Windows Explorer lists a drive letter for the CD/DVD drive.
- Verify that the appropriate driver is installed.
  1. Open My Computer.
  2. Right-click the drive icon and choose Properties.
  3. Display the Hardware panel.
  4. Verify that the appropriate driver is listed.
- Use the Troubleshooting Wizard.
  1. Open My Computer.
  2. Right-click the drive icon and choose Properties.
  3. Display the Hardware panel.
  4. Click the Troubleshoot button and follow the prompts to troubleshoot the problem.

4. To specify a certain drive letter for a drive:
  1. Click Start on the taskbar, right-click My Computer, and then choose Manage.

2. Under Computer Management, click Disk Management.

3. In the list of drives in the right pane, right-click the Removable Device and then click Change Drive Letter And Paths.

4. Click Change, and in the drop-down box, specify a drive letter for the Removable Device, choosing one that is not assigned to the mapped network drives.

5. Click OK twice.

5. If the user inserts a blank CD in the CD-RW drive, and the drive ejects it before the user can write to it:

- Make sure the media is rated for the speed at which you are trying to write.
- Make sure the user is not trying to write more than the disc can hold. A CD can only hold approximately 650 MB of data, so if the user was trying to write 800 MB of data to the CD, then there will be problems.
- Check for software error messages that indicate what the problem might be.

Some less common reasons why the disc is ejected might be:

- The system might be checking the disc and when it doesn't find a table of contents, it is ejecting the disc, thinking it is unusable.
- Debris inside the drive. Dust and other foreign matter can cause a drive to constantly eject the disc.
- Check whether the operating system or the hardware is causing the problem by unplugging the data cable from the drive before inserting the disc. If there is a pause before the disc is ejected or if the drive light blinks steadily, it might be because the media is defective or not high enough quality for the drive to use. Try a different brand of discs.
- If the hardware appears to be fine, the operating system might be causing the problem. Try disabling auto insert for all CD devices.
  1. In Device Manager, display properties for the CD-RW drive.
  2. Display the Settings page.
  3. Under Options, uncheck Auto Insert Notification. Be sure to leave Disconnect checked.
  4. Reboot for the changes to take effect.
- See if the CD-RW drive will write after the system has been off for awhile. Some systems overheat and have trouble writing when the drive gets too hot.

6. DVD drives can read and play CD-ROM and audio CDs as well as read DVD-ROMs. To watch a DVD movie you need to install decoder software. Stand-alone DVD players have a hardware decoder in them. Computer drive based DVD players use software to take the function of the decoder.

Topic G
Correct Printer Problems

You have now learned to troubleshoot and correct many system components. One of the most common components that you will probably receive trouble calls on is printer problems. In this topic, you will troubleshoot and correct printer problems.

You need to be able to resolve printer problems fast. There are few things that make users angrier than not being able to print. Being able to track down where in the printing process the problem is occurring takes practice and experience. Knowing where to look and what to look for helps you resolve these problems quickly.

Common Problems with Printers

Solving printer problems requires imagination and skill, as well as organization and logic. The following is a list of common printer problems.

Problem	Possible Causes	Troubleshooting Tool or Technique
Nothing will print from any application	Physical printer problem Driver	Test button on the printer Control Panel
Printer doesn't print the way the user expects it to	Wrong driver selected in Control Panel Wrong page setup selections made in the application or in Control Panel	Control Panel Application or Control Panel settings
User can't access network printer	User lost network connection or network printer is down	Reattach to the network and check the status of the printer
Printer prints part of a document then garbage for the rest of the document	Printer is low on memory	Check whether additional memory can be installed in the printer

Environmental Effects on Printing

Printers are usually quite robust peripherals and can take quite a beating. However, some of the environments where printers are used are not the ideal situation for printing. Users need their printers where they need them though, so here is a list of some of the factors that might cause printer problems.

- A clean environment prolongs the life and usability of most equipment, including printers. However, printers are often needed on the factory floor, in a pet grooming salon, and other places where dirt, dust, and debris are flying constantly. Keeping the printer in an enclosure can reduce the amount of debris getting into the printer in such a case.

- Relative humidity of 50 to 60 percent is good for computer equipment. High humidity can lead to moisture problems. Low humidity can lead to static problems. An outdoor plant nursery in southern Florida is just as likely to need a printer as an air conditioned office though, so finding ways to deal with the humidity are necessary in such situations. Users need to be aware that they will experience problems in such situations, but with patience, they can print.

Windows Print Process

The Windows XP print process consists of the following stages.

1. A user prints a document in an application.
2. The Graphics Device Interface (GDI) calls the printer driver.
3. The printer driver creates a job in printer language for the target printer. (This is called rendering.) This determines the job's data type. Some data types can be printed directly; others will require additional rendering later in the process.
4. The client side of the print spooler returns control of the computer system to the application.
5. The server side of the print spooler inserts the job into the printing stream.
6. The print router determines whether the job is for a local or remote printer.
   - If the job is for a local printer, the print router routes it to the local print provider.
   - If the job is for a remote printer:
     — The print router routes it to the correct remote print provider for the print server. (For example, a Windows print server and a Novell NetWare print server will have different print providers.)
     — The remote print provider passes the job over the network to the spooler service at the print server, and the process resumes, at the print server, at step 5.
7. The local print provider spools the print job or writes it from memory to disk. By default, print jobs spool to the C:\Windows\System32\Spool\Printers folder. The local print provider also locates a print processor that can render the job's data type.
8. The print processor, WinPrint, completes any rendering needed for the job's data type. WinPrint supports all the general data types. In rare cases, a specialized printer might install a specialized print processor.
9. The separator page processor inserts a separator page, if indicated.
10. The port monitor software for the printer's port handles the physical data communication between the computer and printer.
11. The printer produces the output.

Figure 7-12 graphically represents the Windows print process.

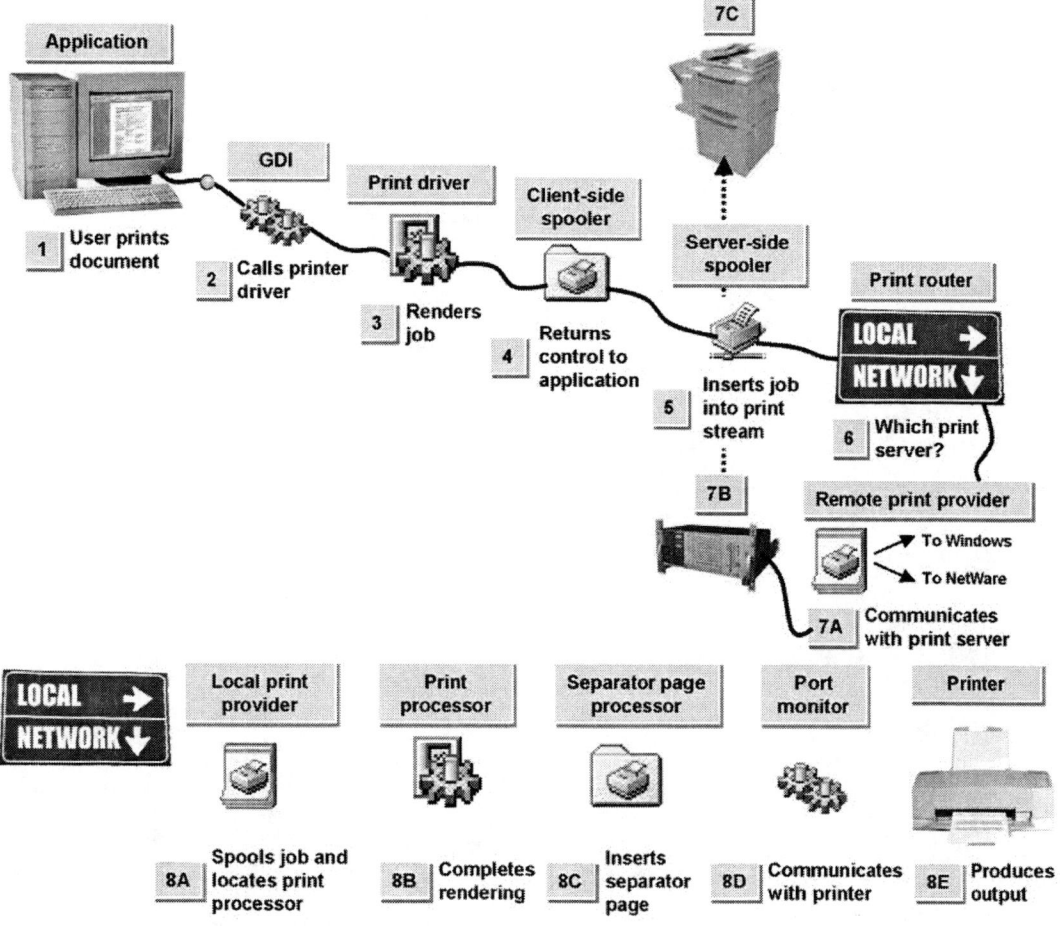

Figure 7-12: *The Windows print process.*

The Laser Printing Process

Laser printers print a page at a time using a combination of electrostatic charges, toner, and laser light. The following steps describe the process the laser printer uses to produce the finished printed page.

1. Cleaning—The Electrostatic Photographic (EP) drum is cleaned with a rubber blade.
2. Erasing—Charges are removed from the EP drum in preparation for the next image.
3. Charging or conditioning—The EP drum is given a negative charge of about -600 volts by the primary corona wire.
4. Writing—A laser beam writes to the EP drum causing portions of the drum to become almost positively charged.
5. Developing—Toner is attracted to the areas of the drum that were hit by the laser light.

6. Transferring—The transfer corona wire charges the paper with a positive charge. The EP drum turns as the paper runs beneath it and loses its toner to the paper.
7. Fusing—The paper runs through the fusing assembly that is heated to 350 degrees F. The fuser's high temperature and pressure fuse or melt the toner into the paper.

A graphical representation of the process is shown in Figure 7-13.

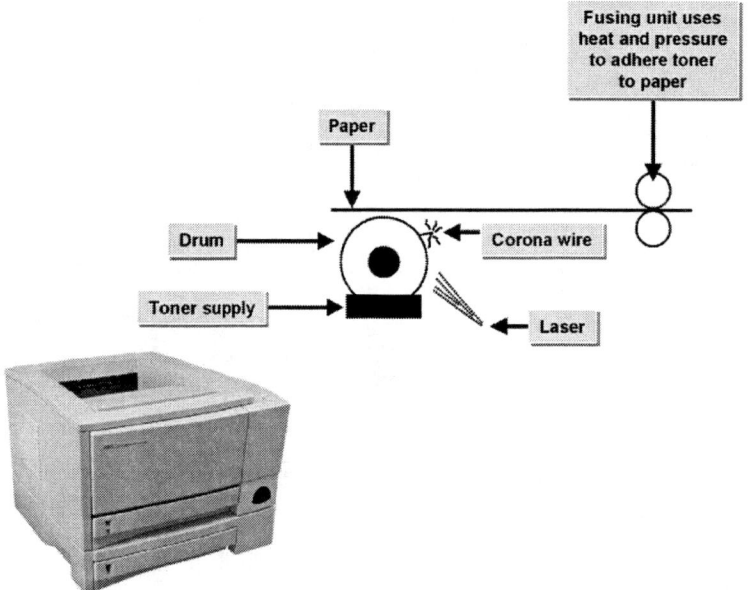

Figure 7-13: *How a laser printer works.*

Common Laser Printer Problems

Laser printers contain chemicals, high voltages, and high-temperature areas that can hurt you. Make sure the printer is off and the parts are cool before you attempt to work on the machine. Some of the exposed wires are very thin and can be damaged easily, so treat the printer gently.

Problem	Cause	Solution
Smeared output, or output rubs off the paper	A fuser problem.	The heat from the fuser melts the toner into the paper. If the fuser roller is uneven or the paper path has a problem, the image will be distorted. If the fuser is not hot enough, or if the paper has too much texture, the toner will not melt into the paper and will rub off.

Problem	Cause	Solution
Low-quality image	Might be caused by any of the laser printer process steps because they all involve creating an image.	Poor-quality paper may not accept a charge from the transfer corona, so the transfer will not take place. Good paper will not be charged enough if the transfer corona is dirty or faulty, or if the power supply that charges the corona has a problem. Along that line, a faulty primary corona or high-voltage power supply will not give the print drum the charge it needs to create a distinct image.
Repeating horizontal lines or white spaces	One of the rollers in the paper path has a problem.	Compare the distance between the repetitions of the lines to the circumferences of the rollers to find which may have the problem. Clean all the rollers before attempting to replace any of them. A good cleaning can fix many problems. A warped or worn fuser roller or a scratched print drum are possibilities.
Repeating vertical lines or white spaces	Problem with the charge wires or the drum.	If debris was caught between the wipe blade and drum, it could scratch a circle around the drum so it would not attract toner. If a portion of either the primary or transfer corona is covered with dust or bits of paper, it will not send out an even charge as the paper goes by, and a vertical defect will appear in the printed image.

How an Inkjet Printer Works

Inkjet technology has been developing since the late 1970s. This has become an inexpensive printing technology. The process used to create inkjet printouts is outlined here. A graphical representation of the process is shown in Figure 7-14.

1. Liquid ink is forced out of carefully aimed nozzles onto the paper.
2. The printhead moves back and forth across the paper, printing one row, several dots wide, of the image at a time. The printhead can produce at least 300 distinct dots per inch (300 dpi). Some printers can print at up to 1200 dpi.
3. The paper advances after every row until the page is covered.
4. The amount of ink shot onto the a page is determined by the driver software that controls where and when each nozzle deposits ink.

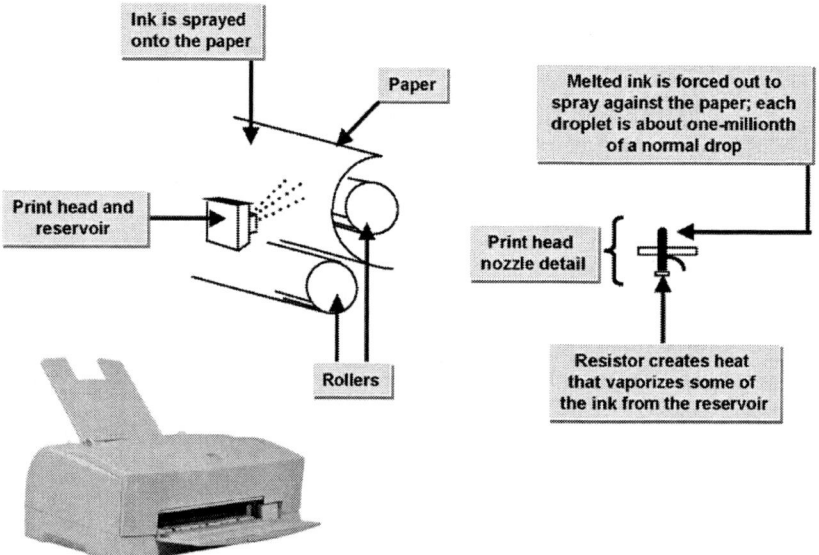

Figure 7-14: *How an inkjet printer works.*

Other Inkjet Technologies

Another inkjet technology used in some printers uses heat rather than forcing ink out. In these printers, ink is heated to create a bubble that bursts and shoots ink onto the paper. The heat is turned off, the element cools, and more ink is sucked into the nozzle when the bubble collapses. Each thermal printhead has about 300 to 600 nozzles that shoot blobs of ink that can create dots about 60 microns in diameter.

Yet another inkjet technology uses piezo-electric technology. This uses a piezo crystal that flexes when current flows through it. When current flows to the crystal, it changes shape just enough to force a drop of ink out of the nozzle and onto the paper.

Common Inkjet Problems

Most problems unique to an inkjet printer can be solved by replacing the print cartridge and using good-quality paper. Except for very high-end models, it may be more cost effective to replace rather than repair the printer.

How a Dot-matrix Printer Works

Dot-matrix printers are still used today, in spite of their slow speed, high noise level, and low quality, because they can print on a continuous roll of paper, as well as multi-part forms that use carbon or no-carbon-required (NCR) paper. The process for creating output using a dot-matrix printer is described here. A graphical representation of the process is shown in Figure 7-15.

1. The dot-matrix printhead has a vertical column of small pins that are controlled by an electromagnet. The pins shoot out of the printhead and strike an ink-coated ribbon.

2. The impact of the pin transfers ink from the ribbon to the printed page. This physical impact is responsible for the printer's ability to print multiple-layer forms.
3. After a set of pins has fired, an electromagnet pulls them back in, the printhead moves a fraction of an inch across the page, and another set of pins is fired.
4. The dots created on the page become the printed text or graphics. Smaller pins create better quality images. Printers come in 9-pin and 24-pin varieties.
5. NLQ printers usually use two or more passes over a line of text to increase the number of dots used per letter. This connects the dots to form sharper and clearer letters.

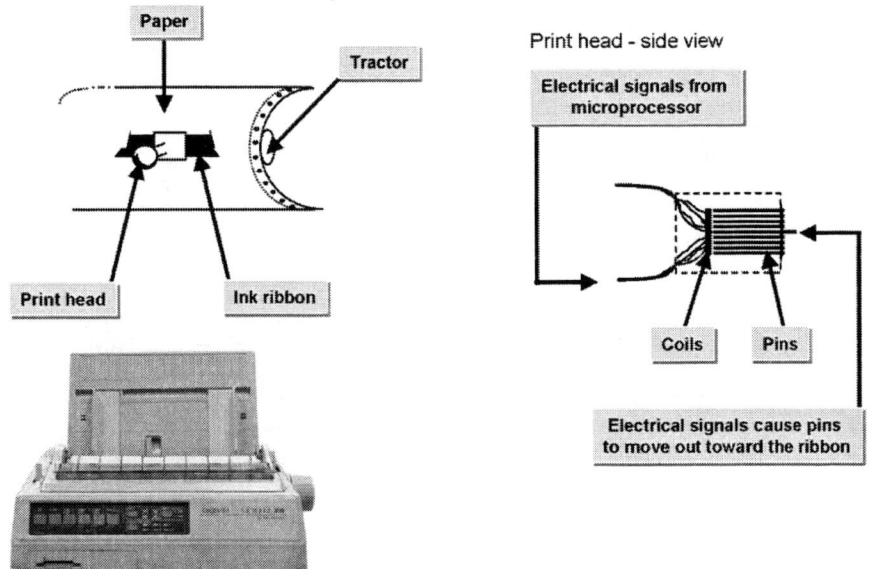

Figure 7-15: *How a dot-matrix printer works.*

Common Dot-matrix Printer Problems

Dot-matrix printers are known to be rugged and dependable. Most repairs are limited to the printhead, which may be hot after a long period of use.

Problem	Cause	Solution
Horizontal lines appear in the print so parts of characters are missing	A pin in the printhead is stuck.	Attempts to repair a printhead can damage it beyond hope. Try cleaning the printhead with a lubricant like WD-40 or alcohol. Remove any visible grime. If this fails, the pin may be bent, rather than just stuck. You can open the printhead and look at the pins, but this is only done as the last resort before buying a new printhead because this step often causes permanent damage to the head. Getting 24 microscopic pins back into line, along with their springs, is a major challenge.
Flecks and smudges on the paper	The ribbon is not aligned correctly, not feeding correctly, or is over-inked.	Reposition the ribbon. If the problem remains, try a different ribbon. The time and effort to repair a ribbon cartridge is rarely cost effective. If the new ribbon does not advance, the problem may be in the gears in the printer that cause the ribbon to move. Make sure they are clean and lubricated.
Poor print quality	The printer adjustment for paper thickness is set to an incorrect value.	Set the thickness to match the paper you are using. Also, use good-quality paper for the best-looking output.

Other Kinds of Printers

Solid-ink printers use wax sticks that are melted. The colored wax is squirted onto a drum that then transfers the ink to the paper one page at a time. Because of the danger from melted wax, these printers are usually kept in isolated areas and shared over the network.

Dye-sublimation printers are special devices widely used in demanding graphic arts and photographic applications. The paper requires four different passes, getting all the yellow on the page first, then cyan, magenta, and finally black. The ink is on large rolls of film. A heating element boils away a tiny dot of the ink that diffuses into a specially manufactured paper's surface where it mixes with other ink to form a colored area. The temperature controls the amount of ink added to the paper, so variations in the temperature setting can control the quantity of each colored ink added to every location on the paper.

Thermo autochrome uses special paper that has cyan, magenta, and yellow layers. A printer uses a specific temperature to activate the colors on one layer at a time. Ultraviolet light fixes the color before the next layer is heated.

Thermal wax is very similar to dye-sublimation but uses plastic films covered with colored wax. A heater melts dots of the wax onto a special thermal paper. This technology is excellent for making transparencies.

How to Troubleshoot and Correct Printer Problems

Procedure Reference: Troubleshoot Printer Problems

There are many problems that can occur with printers. Here are some ideas to try for a few of the most common problems you are likely to encounter:

1. When attempting to print, the job appears in the print queue, but after a few minutes the system notification error message This Document Failed To Print is displayed.
   - Verify that the printer is connected to the parallel port using an IEEE 1284 cable.
   - Verify that LPT1 is configured as a bidirectional or an ECP port.
   - Perform a printer self test and verify that the printer passes this test.
   - If the printer is piggy-backed on another device such as a Zip drive, scanner, or other daisy-chained device to the LPT port, connect the printer directly to LPT1 and attempt to print again.
   - Move the printer and cable to another PC and attempt to print from Notepad or WordPad.
   - Replace the printer cable.
   - Open the print queue from the System Tray. Choose Help, Troubleshooter. Select My Document Doesn't Print At All then click Next. Then work through the troubleshooter trying their suggestions and working your way through the help suggestions until you can resolve the problem.

2. Printer does not successfully print a test page.
   - From the Start menu choose Printers And Faxes.
   - Right-click the printer in question and choose Properties.
   - Click Print Test Page. You should always try to reproduce the problem to verify exactly what the problem is.
   - If the page did not print, click Troubleshoot.
   - Follow the Troubleshooting Wizard to help you resolve the problem.
   - Check the documentation for your printer and print a test page directly from the physical printer using printer controls.
   - If the printer still does not print, refer to the printer documentation for how to resolve this problem on your printer model.

3. To fix a paper jam on a laser printer:
   - Check the printer documentation and follow the directions on how to remove paper from a paper jam for your printer model.
   - Check input and output trays for stuck paper.
   - Check the rest of the paper path for jammed paper or stray bits of paper. A small bit of paper in the wrong location can cause the sensors to believe there is a paper jam.
   - Remove the tray and verify that the plates at the bottom of the tray move freely. Reinsert the tray and try to print again.

- Reset the printer and try printing again.

> ⚠ Be very careful when working inside a laser printer. The fuser assembly can get very hot (180 degrees Celsius).

4. Repeated streaks on the page printed on a laser printer can indicate any number of problems. The spacing of the streaks helps identify which component is causing the problem. Refer to the troubleshooting guide for your printer model to determine the exact cause of the problem.

5. Ink jet printers are prone to problems. These are most often consumer level devices and not designed for the rigors of printing demanded in most business environments. Some of the problems you might encounter, and potential solutions include:
   - *Poor print quality*—If the print quality is poor, perform one or more cleaning cycles. It is often due to clogged nozzles. Clean the printer to make sure there are no lint or other debris dragging across the wet ink. Change to a paper specifically designed for inkjet printers.
   - *No output*—If the printer is not producing any output, but the paper is going through the printer, you should check that the ink cartridges are not empty. You should perform a cleaning cycle on the printers. Some printers require several cleaning cycles if they have not been used for some time before they start producing output. This is usually due to the print head having dried ink clogging the nozzles. Check the documentation or Web site for the printer to see if there are any sequences to perform to get output when there is nothing printing.
   - *Fuzzy output*—If the output is fuzzy, perform several cleaning cycles. If the print head is contained on the ink cartridge, try a fresh ink cartridge. If the print head is separate, you might need to replace the print head.

6. Dot-matrix printers present their own unique problems. The tractor feed, ribbon, and print head are the usual sources of problems. Poor print quality can result from:
   - Dried out or used-up ribbons.
   - The print head being too far from the paper.
   - Worn or damaged print head to name a few of the most common reasons.

   The tractor feed, while providing a good method for guiding the paper through the paper path, can cause problems as well. These might include:
   - Bits of paper getting torn off and stuck in the paper path.
   - Mis-alignment of the holes on the teeth of the tractor feed, causing the paper to feed askew and finally jamming when it gets too far out of alignment.
   - The gears that drive the tractor feed getting worn to name a few of the most common reasons.

7. If you use a piggy-backed parallel port device with the printer plugged in to the device, and you have problems printing to the printer, you should check the documentation for the device on troubleshooting methods. You might find that the best solution is installing a second parallel port in the system or replacing the printer with one that uses USB or some other connection method.

8. USB printers can be plugged in to any USB port on the system. However, USB ports on unpowered devices such as keyboards or unpowered hubs might result in sporadic problems because the port is so far from the power supply within the computer system. The error message The Hub Does Not Have Enough Power Available To Operate The *Device Driver* Name. Would You Like Assistance In Solving This Problem? If You Click No, The Device May Not Function Properly. To resolve this problem, plug the printer into a USB port directly on the system or use a powered hub.

Procedure Reference: Configure the Parallel Port

To configure a parallel port:

1. Access the system BIOS.
2. Enable the parallel port protocol you want to use. This can be EPP, ECP, or SPP.
3. Save the BIOS settings. The system will then restart with the new settings.

CHAPTER 7 FOLLOW-UP
Troubleshooting Device Problems

In this chapter, you learned how to troubleshoot problems for specific devices. This included identifying and resolving problems with peripherals, adapter cards, hard drives, removable media drives, CD/DVD drives, and printers.

Essential Terms

- adapter cards
- CD drives
- drives
- DVD drives
- hard drives
- keyboards
- maintenance tools
- monitors
- mouse
- PC Cards
- peripheral devices
- power management
- printers
- removable cartridge drives
- safety
- SCSI
- touch screens
- troubleshooting
- USB
- Windows print process

Review Questions

1. The troubleshooting process consists of three main phases. What are those phases?
2. If you view an image on the monitor and there is a noticeable flicker, what type of display adapter is used?
3. What is the aspect ratio of a monitor?
4. What does degaussing do to your CRT monitor?
5. What is the function of a shadow mask?
6. What kind of mask combines the technology of a shadow mask and an aperture grill?
7. Where is power management configured?
8. In a CRT, what stores high voltage electricity for extended periods of time?
9. One of the power features in XP is Hibernate mode. What happens when a computer goes into Hibernate mode?
10. If a CRT monitor is making crackling noises, what is the likely problem?
11. What is each key represented by on a keyboard?
12. What does an optical mouse use to track location?
13. To minimize signal loss, a USB cable should not exceed what length?
14. A computer user working on a machine using Windows 95 complains that after a PCI card with a USB port was installed, USB devices will not run. What should you check first?
15. You can't get a USB device to run. When you open Device Manager, only the USB controller and not the USB root hub is listed. What may be the problem?
16. If a hard drive is making grinding noises that repeat in regular patterns, what do you suspect is the problem?
17. The overwhelming majority of problems with SCSI drives are caused by one of two likely problems. What are those two problems?
18. POST codes can help you troubleshoot problems. What does a POST code in the 17xx range indicate?
19. What does the message "No boot device available" indicate?
20. What should you check if you get the message "Hard drive not found" during the POST?
21. You install a new, larger hard drive in an older computer. When you boot the system, the system reports the drive is only 500 MB. What is the problem?
22. Tape devices are sequential access devices. What does this mean?
23. You insert a CD-ROM into the drive tray and push on the tray to close the mechanism. The drive tray won't close. What is the probable reason?
24. If a printer prints only part of a document followed by garbage characters, what do you think is wrong?
25. In Windows XP, what is the default location for spooled print jobs?
26. What are the steps involved in the laser printing process? (List steps in the correct order.)

27. In the laser printing process, when toner is attracted to the areas of the drum that were hit by the laser light, what step in the process is this?
28. You print a memo a few minutes before an important meeting. When you pick the memo up from the laser printer you notice that the ink is smeared. What is the problem?
29. The image quality from your inkjet print device is poor. What would you do first to try to correct the problem?
30. What is the default IRQ for LPT1?

Review Projects

Project #1 Anatomy of a CRT

When supporting computer users you must perform a range of maintenance and troubleshooting tasks to ensure that they can do their work. One of the main output devices your users will utilize is the monitor. Although you are not trained to work on the interior of a monitor, you should understand how a CRT monitor works so you'll be able to determine whether a problem can be fixed by you or a person trained in monitor repair.

Review the tutorial on PC Guide's Web site (**http://www.pctechguide.com/06crtmon.htm**). The first part of the tutorial will reinforce much of the informaton covered in your readings. The second part of the tutorial takes a deeper look into the workings of a monitor.

As you work through the tutorials, make a list of common monitor problems and the solutions. Experiment with basic monitor controls such as degauss, vertical and horizontal settings, and image positioning.

Project #2 Anatomy of Flat Panel Display

As prices continue to decrease for flat panel monitors, more consumers and businesses are making the investment. The benefits to users are many, but perhaps the most compelling reason to use flat panel monitors is because they don't produce the flicker that is visible when using CRT monitors. This decreases user eye strain and general fatigue.

It's important to understand the basic operations of a flat panel monitor for the same reasons as those cited for a CRT. However, an added reason to learn more about both types of monitors is so you'll be able to make well-informed purchasing decisions. In this exercise, review the tutorials about Flat Panel monitors on PC Guide's Web site (**http://desktoppub.about.com/gi/dynamic/offsite.htm?site=http%3A%2F%2Fwww.webopedia.com%2FTERM%2Fl%2Flaser_printer.html**). Bookmark the site for future reference.

Project #3 How Inkjet Printers Work

Inkjet print devices are usually very reliable and they're inexpensive when compared to print devices such as laser printers. Unlike laser printers, inkjet printers are simpler to maintain and there are fewer hazards involved in working on them. The How Stuff Works Web site provides an excellent discussion of inkjet printers and how they work (**http://computer.howstuffworks.com/inkjet-printer.htm**).

If you have an inkjet printer at your disposal, use the tutorial as a guide as you remove the cover of your print device and identify as many parts of the unit as you can. If the interior of your inkjet print device looks different from the one illustrated on the Web site, diagram your inkjet print device and identify its parts by researching the device on the manufacturer's Web site. Keep a copy of your diagram as part of your documentation.

Reflective Questions

1. What specific hardware devices do you have to troubleshoot most often?

2. What steps could you take to reduce the amount of device-specific trouble tickets you receive?

CHAPTER 8
Troubleshooting System Problems

Chapter Objectives:

In this chapter, you will troubleshoot system problems.

You will:

- Troubleshoot and correct network connection problems.
- Troubleshoot and correct modem problems.
- Troubleshoot and correct power problems.
- Troubleshoot and correct boot problems.
- Troubleshoot and correct memory problems.
- Troubleshoot and correct system board problems.
- Troubleshoot and correct problems with portable systems.
- Diagnose system problems.

Introduction

So far you have used your troubleshooting skills to determine the problem with a specific component. However, you won't always know exactly which component is causing the problem. In this chapter, you will troubleshoot system problems that can occur over numerous system components.

Sometimes you need to troubleshoot the entire system to determine what the source of the problem is since some processes occur over a range of system components. This can start with the user entering a request from the keyboard to the system outputting the results in any number of places, and the connections between the user and the resultant output can be many and varied. Being able to follow that communication from the user to the output will help you identify where in the process that the problem is occurring so that you can fix it immediately.

TOPIC A
Correct Network Connection Problems

You have connected your system to the network. This greatly expands what you can do with your system. If you suddenly cannot connect to the network, you need to be able to determine what and where the problem is. In this topic, you will troubleshoot and correct network connection problems.

Why do you, the hardware support tech, care about network connection problems? Isn't this something for the network administrator to support? Well, not always. In many companies, it is the responsibility of the hardware technician to determine if the network card and cable are working properly before the network administrator starts troubleshooting from the network side of things. Or, if the network administrator troubleshoots from her side of things and determines that the problem is at the user's computer, you will be assigned the support call. Therefore, you will need to know how to determine where in the network process the problem is occurring and what the symptoms of those problems are.

Common Problems with Network Connections

Users rely on being able to access files, Web sites, server applications, and networked hardware to do their jobs. When their connection to any of those networked resources is disrupted, they need to have it restored as soon as possible. The following table lists some of the common problems and possible causes.

Problem	Possible Cause
User cannot connect to the network.	TCP/IP settings are incorrect. Ethernet frame type is incorrect. Network settings are incorrectly set.
User had a connection to the network, but during their work session, lost their connection.	Workstation network connection hardware is damaged. Cable became disconnected from workstation. Network hardware or software experienced a problem.

Problem	Possible Cause
User is connected to the network, but cannot access desired resources.	User does not have access rights to the desired resource. Resource is experiencing a technical problem.

Help And Support Center

Windows XP includes a utility labeled the Help And Support Center. It provides access to the help system and to assistance from online sources. It also includes guided troubleshooting wizards to help you locate a problem. Through this utility you can view help, perform diagnostics, use troubleshooters, ask for help from another user, get help from online support groups, and more.

Network Troubleshooting Utilities

The following table is a list of some of the commands and utilities that you might find useful in troubleshooting network problems. These are run from the command prompt.

Command or Utility	Description
ipconfig	Shows the network settings for the computer.
ping	Shows whether the computer can reach a given site.

How to Troubleshoot Network Connection Problems

Procedure Reference: Troubleshoot Network Connections

There are many problems that can occur with network connections. Here are some ideas to try for a few of the most common problems you are likely to encounter:

1. Troubleshoot the network connection settings. You can use network troubleshooting utilities such as the Windows XP commands Ping, Ipconfig, and the properties of the LAN Connection document to verify that the settings are correctly configured for your network. You can get the settings from the network administrator.

   Using ping from another system enables you to verify that the network is up and others can indeed connect. You might try this command at the workstation having the problem, one nearby, and one on another part of the network. This will help you isolate the problem.

   The ipconfig command is used to list the network connection settings for a system. Use the /all option to display all of the information for all network interface cards in the system.

> Other operating systems use different commands rather than ipconfig. For example, Windows 95/98 use winipcfg and Linux uses ifconfig.

2. Troubleshoot the local system network connection hardware and cables.
   - The cable should be firmly connected to the network card and the wall, hub, router, or other connection to the network.
   - Verify that the correct cable is being used. Some cables look alike if you aren't careful. For example, the TV cable and the Ethernet thin cable look similar, but the wire is different and the connectors might be different. It might work sporadically, but it might not work at all. A twisted pair cable comes in various categories. Most networks use Category 5 cable. Category 3 cable looks the same except that the casing says Cat 3 rather than Cat 5.
   - Run the diagnostics test for the network card. This is usually software that comes with the network card and is specific to that network card.
   - If necessary, replace the network cable.
   - If necessary, replace the network card.

3. Verify that the system can connect to the network. You should be able to log in and access resources. For example, if the network connection enables you to access the Internet, you can try to Ping a site such as **www.google.com**.

TOPIC B
Correct Modem Problems

You have added a modem to your system. The modem on either end of the connection or the phone line in between can have configuration or other hardware problems. In this topic, you will troubleshoot and correct modem-related problems.

When the users you are supporting need to work from home or on the road, they expect their modem to be configured and working. All they should need to do is plug in the phone line to their modem and click the connection document to establish a connection to the server they want to access. If everything is working the way it should, this is an accurate picture of the users' world. However, as you know, things don't always work the way they should. To keep your users happy and productive, you will need to be able to figure out why they can't connect over their modem.

Common Problems with Modems

There are many problems you might encounter with modem connections. The problem could be with the settings on your end or the other end, with the hardware on either end, or with the phone company or phone lines in between. The following table lists some of the problems you are likely to encounter and possible causes of those problems.

Problem	Possible Causes
Modem doesn't work.	Modem is not on the HCL for the operating system. Modem is not properly connected and powered on. This might show up as the error message Modem Not Responding also.
Cannot connect to the ISP.	Using the wrong phone number. Entering the user name and/or password incorrectly. Phone line is damaged, is not an analog line (is digital), or phones are down.
ISP server not responding.	ISP server is down. Your modem speed is set too high for the phone line conditions or compatibility between your modem and the ISP modems.
Connection is dropped.	Call waiting was not configured and a call was received through call waiting. Some ISPs disconnect a connection after a certain period of inactivity. The modem cable or phone line got physically disconnected. Modem drivers need to be updated. The ISP made changes and the user needs to make changes to their settings to match.
Error messages when you attempt to make the connection.	No Dialtone. This could be due to the phone line not being connected, there being a phone company problem with the line, or with settings on your modem. Also, EMI and EFI can cause such problems Dial-Up Networking Could Not Negotiate a Compatible Set of Network Protocols. This could be due to modem settings or to incompatibilities between you and the host into which you are attempting to dial.
Busy signal.	If there is always a busy signal no matter when you attempt to connect, make sure that the cables are not tangled, that the user is dialing properly, and that you can manually dial the number through a utility such as HyperTerminal. Also, check that the phone company is not experiencing problems.

How to Troubleshoot and Correct Modem Problems

Procedure Reference: Troubleshoot Modem Problems

There are many problems that can occur with modems. Here are some ideas to try for a few of the most common problems you are likely to encounter:

1. The message No Dialtone is displayed when the user tries to place a call through the modem.
   - Verify that there really is a dial tone by picking up a phone connected to the same phone line and listening for the dial tone. If there is no dial tone, determine whether the problem is with the phone lines in the neighborhood or within your home or office.
   - Verify that the telephone line is connected to the correct port on the modem. This might be marked as line-in, Line, or Telco.
   - Verify that the other end of the telephone line is plugged into the wall phone jack.
   - Unplug any other devices attached to the telephone line such as an answering machine or fax machine.
   - Verify that your telephone receiver is not off the hook.
   - Untangle the phone line, especially from power cords.
   - Add X3 to the modem init string to ignore the message and continue trying to dial into the server.

2. If the error message Modem Not Responding is displayed:
   - If you are using an external modem, verify that it is plugged in, turned on, and properly connected to the system.
   - From Control page, open the Network And Internet Connections page, and then click Phone And Modem Options.
   - Display the Modems page and verify that the correct modem make and model is listed.
   - Select the modem and click Properties.
   - Display the Diagnostics page.
   - Click Query Modem, and then review the results of the query.
   - Click View Log. After reviewing the log file, close Notepad. Close the Modem Properties dialog box.
   - In the Network And Internet Connections window, click Network Diagnostics.
   - Click Scan Your System.
   - Expand Modems and verify that the settings are accurate for the modem to connect to the network.
   - If it is still not working, remove the modem and reinstall it or replace it.

3. If the error message Dial-Up Networking Could Not Negotiate A Compatible Set Of Network Protocols is displayed:

- Verify that the correct driver for your make and model of modem is installed.
- Display the Modem Properties dialog box.
- Display the Advanced page, and then click Change Default Preferences.
- Verify that Port Speed, Data Protocol, Compression, and Flow Control match the settings needed to connect to the network.
- Display the Advanced page.
- Verify that the Hardware Settings for Data Bits, Parity, Stop Bits, and Modulation are the appropriate settings for your network connection.

4. If the remote system always appears to be busy, you can see if any of the following might be the problem:
   - Determine whether the user is trying to dial internationally. Additional setup might be required.
   - Open HyperTerminal and enter the command ATX0. Then enter the phone number. This manually sets the modem and dials the number.
   - Straighten any kinks or tangled phone lines. The line might be getting feedback if the lines are kinked or tangled.

5. If a newly installed modem does not respond, you should:
   - Verify that the phone line is correctly connected to the modem.
   - Verify that external modems are securely connected to the system. The power supply needs to be connected to the modem and plugged in to a power outlet as well.
   - Close any other open applications and attempt dialing again.
   - Verify that the modem settings in Control Panel match the physical modem COM and IRQ settings.
   - Reset the modem through HyperTerminal with the command ATXF.
   - Try dialing again.

6. If the connection acts like it is connected, but the user can't log in:
   - Verify that the user is using the correct login name.
   - Verify that the user is using the correct password.
   - Verify that the settings for the connection are correctly configured.

Topic C
Correct Power Problems

As you have learned, many problems are somewhat obvious as to their source: you can't print, you can't connect to the network, or something similar. Power problems can also be obvious (your system won't turn on) or very mysterious. In this topic, you will examine some of the common power problems you might encounter.

We have seen some problems that get users pretty frustrated so far. One of the most frustrating can be power problems. They can manifest themselves in many ways and sometimes it is not obvious that a power problem is the reason for the problem the user is experiencing. You will need to be able to determine the cause of power problems before you can correct them and get the user back up and running. If power problems are allowed to continue, your company data can be seriously corrupted and users will be less productive, so you need to be able to fix these problems for users.

Common Power Problems

Power problems can result in data loss, erratic behavior, system crashes, and hardware damage. More severe power problems cause more severe computer problems. The following table lists some of the most common power problems and possible causes.

Power Problem	Possible Causes	Can Result In
Line noise	EMI interference. RFI (radio frequency interference) interference. Lightning.	Erratic behavior, data loss.
Power sag	Many electrical systems starting up at once. Switching loads at the electric company utility. Electric company equipment failure. Too small of a power source.	Erratic behavior, data loss, system crashes, hardware damage.
Power undervoltage or brownout (may last several minutes to several days). A variation on this is switching transient or instantaneous undervoltage which lasts only a matter of nanoseconds.	Decreased line voltage. Demand exceeds power company supply. Utility company reduced voltage to conserve energy.	Erratic behavior, data loss, system crashes, hardware damage.

Power Problem	Possible Causes	Can Result In
Frequency variation	Usually occurs when using a small generator of power. As loads increase or decrease, the power frequency varies.	Erratic behavior, data loss, system crashes, hardware damage.
Overvoltage	Suddenly reduced loads. Equipment with heavy power consumption is turned off. Power company switches loads between equipment.	Erratic behavior, data loss, system crashes, hardware damage.
Power failure	Lightning strikes. Electrical Power lines down. Overload of electrical power needs.	Data loss, system crashes, hardware damage.

Electrical Safety

Electricity can cause a lot of damage, so you need to be careful working around it. Contact with electrical energy can cause injuries including:

- Electrocution—It is the result of the body being exposed to a lethal amount of electrical energy. For death to occur, the body must become part of an active electrical circuit with a current capable of overstimulating the nervous system or damaging internal organs.
- Electric shock—This can be painful and cause severe damage to you and the equipment.
- Electrical burns—Contact with a source of electrical energy can cause external as well as internal burns.
- Collateral injuries—These are injuries caused by involuntary muscle movement which can be caused by an electric shock. Electricity flowing through your body can cause your muscles to twitch uncontrollably. These motions can cause you to hurt yourself on objects around you.

Working on a computer can be safe and enjoyable if you protect yourself from electrical hazards by taking the appropriate precautions. These include:

- Perform only work for which you have sufficient training.
- Don't attempt repair work when you are tired; you may make careless mistakes, and your primary diagnostic tool, deductive reasoning, will not be operating at full capacity.
- Don't assume anything without checking it out for yourself.
- Don't wear jewelry or other articles that could accidentally contact circuitry and conduct current.
- Suspend work during electrical storms.
- Don't handle electrical equipment when your hands or feet are wet or when you are standing on a wet surface.
- Perform as many tests as possible with the power off.

- When removing circuit boards, place them on a dissipative ground mat or put them in an anti-static bag.
- Use an anti-static wrist strap when handling static-sensitive components like system boards, sound cards, and memory chips, but remove the strap if you are working on any part of a computer monitor.
- After cleaning the equipment, be very sure it is dry before powering it up.
- Label wires and connectors as you detach them, and make sure you plug them back into the proper sockets in the proper order.
- When you replace the computer's case, make sure all the wires are inside. The case may have sharp edges that can cut through exposed cables.
- Power supplies have a high voltage in them any time the computer is plugged in, even if the computer power is turned off. Disconnect the power cord before you start work on a power supply and leave it off until you are done. Turn off the computer but leave the cord plugged in to maintain a good ground connection if you are not working on the power supply.
- Never stick anything into the power supply fan to get it to rotate. This approach doesn't work, and it's dangerous.
- Do not take the case off a monitor. The risk to your life is not worth any repairs you might make.
- Don't bang on the monitor screen with your tools; an explosion will propel shards of glass in every direction.
- To clean the monitor, turn it off and unplug it; do not wear an anti-static wrist strap. Use isopropyl alcohol rather than a general-purpose cleaner; it doesn't create a safety hazard if dripped inside the case. Use an anti-static cleaner to clean the glass on the monitor; never wash the glass with the power on.

How Surge Protectors Protect Computer Equipment

When electrical current voltage varies too much, it can cause lots of problems for computers and for you the computer user. If there are sags, surges, or noise on the electrical line, it can lead to damage of hardware. Plugging your equipment into a surge surpressor, UPS, or line conditioner can even out the electrical current so that it is more even.

1. Electrical current flows from the outlet to the line conditioner. It can be a surge protector, a UPS, or a separate line conditioner.
2. Electrical current that is within tolerance limits for the current, flows on through and powers the components plugged into the unit.
3. Power surge electrical current extra voltage is diverted to the unit's ground or neutral wire.
4. The unit includes circuitry to work to even out wide fluctuations in the power.
5. If you are using a UPS, it can also deal with undervoltages and sags by providing additional power to the hardware being served.

Figure 8-1 shows a graphical representation of the process used to condition power.

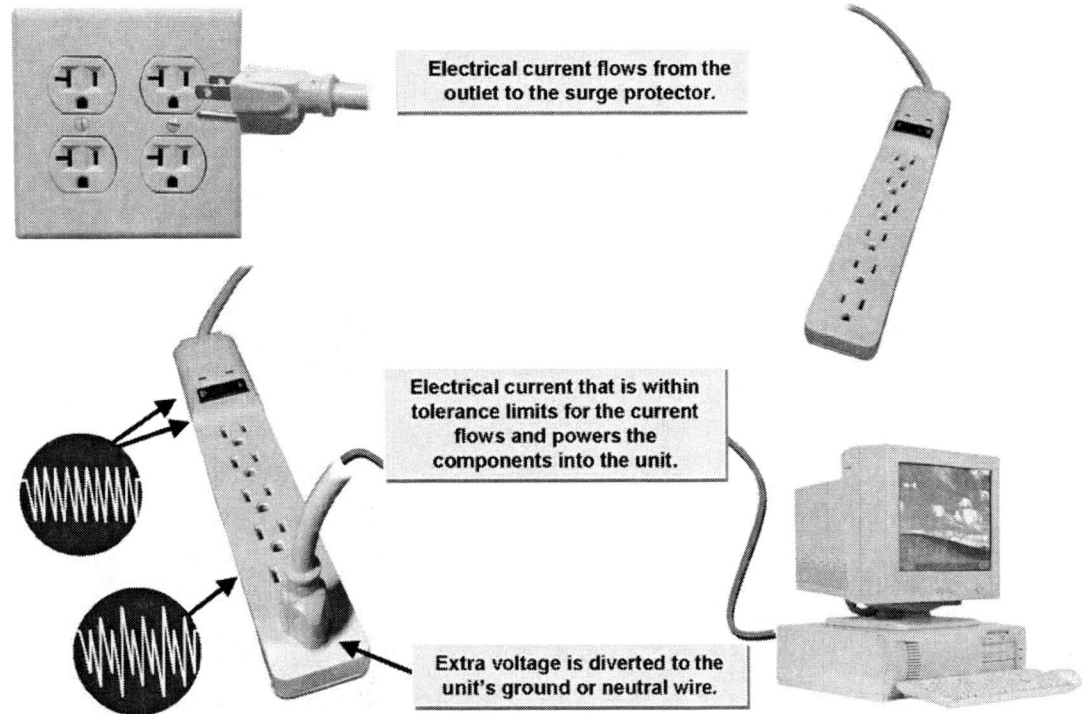

Figure 8-1: *How surge protectors protect computer equipment.*

How to Troubleshoot and Correct Power Problems

Procedure Reference: Troubleshoot Power Problems

There are many problems that can occur related to power. Here are some ideas to try for a few of the most common problems you are likely to encounter:

1. If the system doesn't come on, or abruptly shuts itself down and the fan does not appear to be working:

    - Unplug the system and remove the system cover.
    - Using compressed air, blow out any dust around the fan spindle.
    - Verify that there is no obvious reason that the fan is not spinning.
    - If these suggestions do not fix the problem, replace the power supply. Remember, do not open a power supply as there is a high danger of electrocution.

    This problem should be addressed as soon as possible. Leaving the problem alone would allow heat to build up to dangerous levels, causing serious damage to the system, and possibly fire.

2. If you turn on the power switch and the system does not come on, listen for the fan and check for the power light. Some things to check include:

- Verify that the power cord is securely connected to the power supply and to the electrical outlet on the UPS or surge protector (or the wall, but you should always protect it through a UPS or surge protector).
- Verify that the UPS or surge protector is turned on and plugged in.
- Verify that the UPS or surge protector is working by plugging in a lamp with a known good light bulb and turning on the light.
- If the lamp did not light, check to see whether any reset buttons need to be reset on the UPS or surge surpressor, or check the electric outlet's circuit breaker.
- If none of these fixed the problem, prepare to replace the power supply.
  a. Power off and remove any external power cables from the power supply connections.
  b. Remove the cover, and then disconnect all connections from the internal devices.
  c. If necessary, remove any components needed to have complete access to the power supply. Some systems have such tight space, that you need to remove other components to get to the power supply.
  d. Unscrew the power supply from the back of the system case.
  e. Determine if, and in which direction, the power supply needs to be slid to remove it from the slots holding it in place then remove it from the system.
  f. Slide the replacement power supply into place and screw it to the system case. Modern power supplies have been standardized with the ATX-power supply specification, but older power supplies and those for portable systems vary in size and the location of the screw holes. So, you will want to measure the power supply to ensure that it will fit in the space the old power supply occupied and that you can secure it to the case. Also, verify that the power supply uses the same connection type to the system board as the previous power supply. The replacement power supply should be at least the same wattage as the one you removed. If it was of low wattage, this would be a good time to upgrade the wattage of the power supply.
  g. If you removed any components to remove the power supply, reinstall those components.
  h. Reconnect the power connections to internal and external devices. Be sure to plug the power supply back into the system board. If it uses two connectors or unkeyed connectors, be sure to connect them correctly or you run the risk of damaging the system board.
  i. Verify that all components are working properly.

3. Some power problem indications can be seen in error codes and messages at boot time. These might include:
   - No beeps.
   - Continuously repeating beep pattern.
   - Power On Self Test (POST) errors between 020 and 029.

- Parity error messages.
- No power indicator light.
- No sound from the power supply fan.

4. If an ATX motherboard will not power up, check the voltage of the power being supplied.
    a. Set the multimeter for DC volts over 12V.
    b. Locate an available internal power supply connector. If none are free, you will need to power off the system and unplug it first, then remove one from a floppy drive or CD drive.
    c. Insert the black probe from the multimeter into one of the two center holes on the internal power supply connector.
    d. Insert the red probe from the multimeter into the hole for the red wire.
    e. Verify that the multimeter reading is +5V DC.
    f. Move the red probe into the hole for the yellow wire.
    g. Verify that the multimeter reading is +12V DC.
    h. If either reading is incorrect, test again. If the reading is still incorrect, replace the power supply.
    i. If the reading was correct, check the documentation for the ATX system board on how the logic circuit switch that signals power to be turned on or off is to be connected.
    j. Verify that the system board, processor, memory, and video card are all correctly installed and working.

Topic D
Correct Boot Problems

You just examined power problems which often affect being able to boot. Another closely related category of problems is problems with the boot process. In this topic, you will identify what should happen during the boot process and examine how to correct some of the common problems you might encounter.

Knowing how the boot process is supposed to work will help you identify potential reasons for boot problems. Being able to recognize where in the boot process the problem is occurring helps you resolve the issue more quickly, getting the user back to work sooner.

The Boot Process

When you turn on the computer a whole series of actions are performed. The process is depicted in Figure 8-2. The steps are:

1. The power supply initializes, and then sends a power good signal to the CPU.
2. Reset process signals the CPU to find the BIOS boot jump address.

3. POST is run by the BIOS.
4. POST results in either:
   - A beep code to indicate an error was encountered.
   - The video BIOS is located, loaded, and run.
5. Any other hardware BIOS are located, loaded, and run.
6. BIOS information is displayed on the screen.
7. BIOS runs system tests including a memory test.
8. Devices identified in CMOS are detected, configured, and tested.
9. PnP devices are detected and configured.
10. BIOS checks CMOS to locate the disk drive from which to boot.
11. The system boots from the specified device or displays an error message if none is found.
    - Master Boot Record (MBR) of the hard drive.
    - First sector of floppy disk.

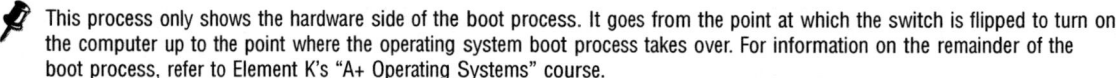
This process only shows the hardware side of the boot process. It goes from the point at which the switch is flipped to turn on the computer up to the point where the operating system boot process takes over. For information on the remainder of the boot process, refer to Element K's "A+ Operating Systems" course.

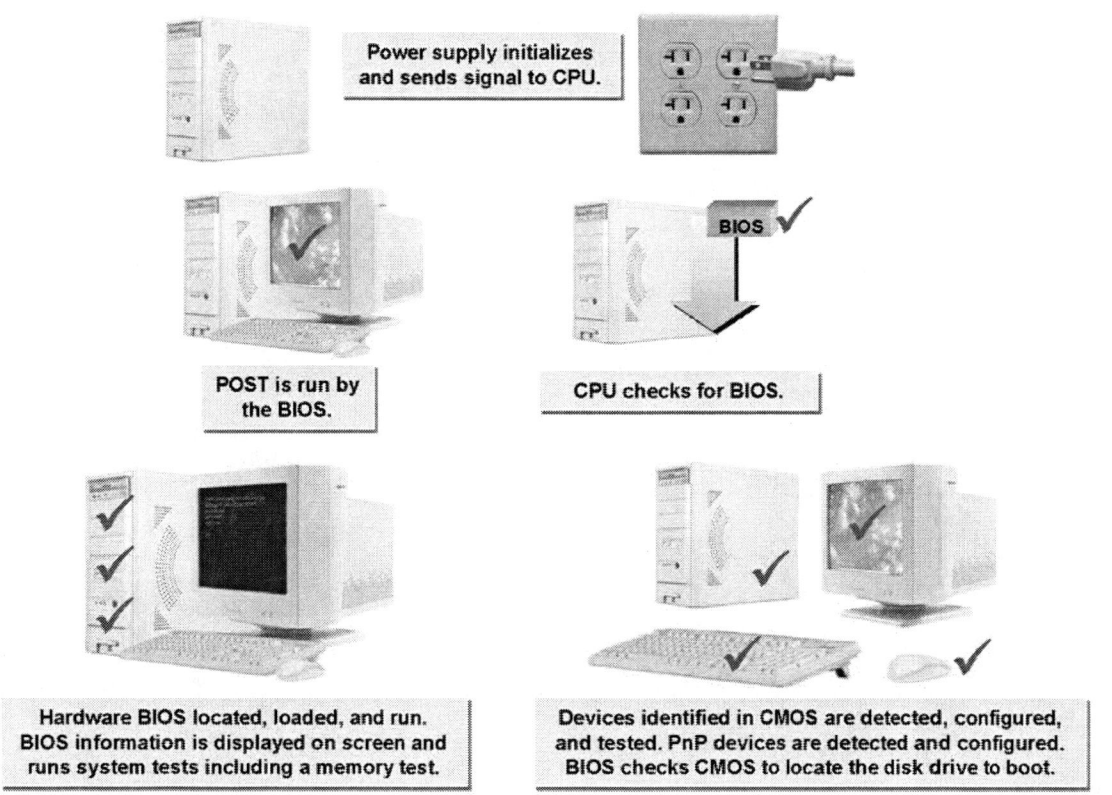

Figure 8-2: *The boot process.*

Common Boot Problems

Boot problems typically show up as either POST beep codes or error messages displayed on the screen. These vary based on the BIOS manufacturer. Refer to the documentation for your system BIOS for information on what the codes or messages indicate and how to resolve them.

Procedure Reference: Troubleshoot Boot Problems

There are many problems that can occur at boot time. Here are some ideas to try for a few of the most common problems you are likely to encounter:

1. If the system is slow to boot, it could be because of any number of things. Some specific boards have known problems related to this. You can best resolve such problems by referring to the support documents provided by the system board manufacturer.

2. Beep codes at boot time are specific to the BIOS manufacturer. Refer to the manufacturer's documentation to determine the meaning of the beep codes.

3. An Operating System Not Found error message is usually the result of the user leaving a non-bootable floppy disk in the floppy drive. If that is not the cause, you should follow the directions for troubleshooting hard disk boot problems.

4. If the power-on password for a system has been lost, you can usually reset it by removing the CMOS battery for a period of time. You will, of course, lose all of the CMOS settings, so hopefully you have them recorded somewhere.

TOPIC E
Correct Memory Problems

You have installed many components and later learned how to troubleshoot and correct problems that might arise with those components. One of the components you installed was memory modules. In this topic, you will troubleshoot and correct problems that might occur with the memory installed in your system.

There are several different symptoms of memory problems. The solutions can be boiled down to just a handful of things you need to try and to check. Being able to pinpoint that it is a memory problem is the hard part. After you do figure out that the problem is being caused by memory problems, you will be able to resolve it relatively quickly.

Symptoms of Memory Problems

Memory problems typically show themselves as errors, erratic behavior of the system, or frequent crashes. The following table lists some of the common symptoms and possible causes of the problems.

Symptom	Possible Causes
Computer crashes or reboots itself periodically.	ESD, over heating, or other power related problems that cause the memory to have problems. Registry writing to bad memory, General Protection Faults (GPFs), and exception errors caused by software and operating system.
Memory errors are displayed on the screen.	Memory address errors at boot time. Memory mismatch errors in which you are prompted to specify how much RAM is installed to clear the message. When using applications that require more memory, or don't properly release memory, you might get error messages displayed.
Computer appears to boot, but the screen remains blank.	Memory is not correct for the system. For instance, the computer is expecting memory that uses error checking and you installed non-parity memory. Memory module is not fully inserted into the slot.

Symptom	Possible Causes
Computer does not boot. POST beep codes are heard.	CPU cannot communicate with hardware due to the hardware being improperly installed or the BIOS not recognizing the hardware. Beep codes are specific to the BIOS manufacturer and the ones for memory can be found in the manufacturers' beep codes list.
Newly installed memory is not recognized.	You exceeded the maximum amount of RAM that can be addressed by the system. Even though the slots can accept SIMS containing more memory, the system can only recognize a certain amount of memory on most systems. The wrong memory type was installed.

How to Troubleshoot Memory Problems

Procedure Reference: Troubleshoot Memory Problems

When strange things begin happening to the data in your computer, one of the first things to check is for a virus. If that is not the problem, the next thing to check is the memory. You should evaluate the following when attempting to correct memory problems:

1. Verify that the correct memory modules were installed in the system. You can check the part numbers against the memory or PC manufacturer's Web site. For example, be sure that you aren't trying to use DDR RAM in an EDO RAM system.

2. Verify that the memory was installed and configured properly. Older systems required that memory be installed in pairs. In all cases, verify that the memory modules are fully seated. Always start with memory in the first bank. Check your documentation for other requirements specific to your system.

3. Try swapping the memory between slots. For example, if you only experience problems when many applications are open, the chance is that one of the memory modules in the higher banks is the problem. If the system won't boot, try one of the other modules in the first bank to see if it then boots. Try putting a known good module in the first slot and removing all of the other memory modules.

4. Check for BIOS upgrades. If there are known problems, then a fix has probably been issued. This usually applies to older systems.

Topic F
Correct System Board Problems

You have used your troubleshooting skills to resolve many problems by now. The last component we will troubleshoot is the system board.

One of your users is experiencing a problem with their system. You have checked the memory and found that to be just fine. You checked the cards, the drives, and the power supply and they all show no problems either. The only thing left to check is whether there is a problem with the system board. When nothing else seems to be fixing the problem, this is the next (and hopefully last) component to check.

Symptoms of System Board Problems

System board problems can be among the most difficult to recognize and diagnose. If you have eliminated all of the components, the software, and the operating system as not being the problem, then you should check that the system board is not the problem. Typically, the computer won't boot or the computer is displaying erratic behavior that can't be resolved otherwise.

When installing components into the system board, be sure not to bend or break any of the pins. This includes the pins on the cards as well as the system board. Also, the system board could be cracked if you pushed down too hard. When you secure the system board to the case, be sure not to overtighten the screws as this could also crack or damage the system board.

ESD damage such as that caused by lightning strikes can fry the system board electronics. Be sure to use proper surge protection to help prevent such problems.

You should check the following as causes of the problem:

- Power connections.
- Power supply.
- CMOS battery is not holding the information.
- CPU. Overheating can be a problem in addition to the CPU being electrically damaged. Use a temperature sensor along with cooling systems to combat this problem.
- Memory.
- Virus check the system including the BIOS.
- Short due to components not being properly seated.
- BIOS being out of date.
- Loose connections.

CPU Cooling Systems

You have seen how a heat sink and fan can help keep a CPU from getting too hot. Sometimes you need even more cooling than what these provide. Two solutions you might implement are liquid cooling and thermal compound cooling.

Liquid cooling solutions are similar to the radiator's function in your car. A special heat sink contains liquid that passes through the heat sink attached to the CPU. Heat is transferred from the CPU to the liquid. The liquid passes outside of the case to be cooled as it moves its way back into the case and through the system again.

Thermal cooling compound comes in a tube and is used between the CPU and the heat sink or liquid cooling system. Compounds from different manufacturers are composed of different metals and the different solutions in which those metals reside. The idea is to provide as much particle contact between the CPU and the heat sink or liquid cooling solution as possible to transfer heat away from the CPU, through the compound, and onto the heat sink or liquid cooling solution.

How to Troubleshoot and Correct System Board Problems

Procedure Reference: Troubleshoot System Board Problems

If a user has a hardware problem and you have exhausted all of the other potential causes for the problem, you might suspect it is the system board. The following are some of the potential issues in troubleshooting system board problems.

1. Some of the common system board problems are due to ESD damage (due to storms, improper handling, power surges or spikes, or shorting out on the system case), bent or broken pins, and crack(s) in the system board itself.

2. The system board is a likely culprit if all other components have been checked and/or replaced with no resolution to the problem. You will want to thoroughly check all of the other components since they are more likely to be the problem, but if they do check out satisfactorily or you replace them with known good equipment with no relief in sight, then this points to a problem with the system board.

TOPIC G
Correct Portable System Problems

Now that you have used your troubleshooting skills to solve problems related to desktop systems, it is time to turn your attention to the portable system problems. Many of the same symptoms can be seen on portable devices. In this topic, you will troubleshoot problems that occur on portable devices.

Users want portable devices so that they aren't tied to one location. These devices are built to take the knocks of life on the road, but are sometimes more prone to problems than their desktop cousins. You need to be able to resolve the issues so users and their equipment can get back on the road as soon as possible.

Common Portable System Problems

Each portable computer system has a unique method for gaining access to the internal components. The way in which you access them should be documented in the technical service manual or on the manufacturer's Web site. You will need to refer to the documentation for information on how to open them up and locate the connectors for the components you are working on.

Some of the common problems you might encounter are:

- Power problems. This could be related to the battery power or to the power supply.
- Damaged integrated components such as the screen, keyboard, or pointing device. These are connected with ribbon cables to the system board. They can be replaced only with the same part number from the manufacturer.
- Memory. This is often located under the keyboard. In order to access the memory, you need to know how to remove the keyboard from the case. Other notebook computers have a cover on the bottom of the computer that you remove to access the memory slot(s).

Some specific problems you might encounter and potential causes are listed in the following table.

Problem	Potential Causes
When the user switches from using the external monitor to using the internal monitor, the internal monitor does not work.	Press the key combination on the internal keyboard for switching between the external and internal monitor as indicated in the portable system documentation.
Portable computer enters hibernation mode while the user is using it.	Some systems go into hibernation mode if they overheat. Overheating is a big problem in some portable systems. Verify that the system has sufficient battery power or that it is plugged in to an electrical power source. Verify that the power saving features are not set with too short of a time setting.
Computer will not run from battery power.	Verify that the computer was fully inserted into the docking solution (or recharging unit) when you are attempting to recharge the battery. If the battery is older than two years, it will probably not hold a charge any longer. Verify that the charger is not feeding back on itself and depleting the power as it is attempting to charge the battery.

Problem	Potential Causes
Memory is added to the portable computer system, and now the system will not boot.	Verify that the memory modules are fully seated in their slots. Verify that the battery is charged or that it is plugged in. Verify that no other components were accidentally disconnected when you added the memory.

How to Troubleshoot and Correct Portable System Problems

Procedure Reference: Troubleshoot Portable System Problems

There are many problems that occur with portable systems. Here are some ideas to try for a few of the most common problems you are likely to encounter:

1. When the user switches from the docked state to the undocked state, sometimes the user needs to press a key combination to indicate to the computer that the integrated peripherals are to be used rather than external peripherals. The exact key combination can be found in the documentation for the system. It usually is a key marked Fn and another key such as a Function key.

2. If the user's computer enters hibernation mode even when they are still typing on it, check for the following:
   - Overheating.
   - That there is sufficient power.
   - That the power saving settings are set to reasonable lengths for the user's work flow.

3. Batteries don't last forever, so if the battery will not hold a charge, verify that the user is properly charging it, that the system is not feeding back on itself and depleting the power, then replace the battery. You will likely need to purchase it from the manufacturer of the portable system as they are uniquely shaped to fit around other portable system components.

4. When you install memory in a portable system, you need to verify that it is fully seated. Also, afterwards you should check that no other components were disconnected and that the system has power before giving it back to the user.

Topic H
Diagnose System Problems

So far, we have pointed you directly to the malfunctioning system component. However, on the job, the user will not always be able to tell you what component is causing a problem. They just know that they can't get their work done. In this topic, you will learn how to diagnose system problems.

Your car breaks down on the side of the road. All you know is that the Check Engine light has come on. This is similar to when your system breaks down. You might get a cryptic error message or you might get nothing. Using the collect, isolate, and correct troubleshooting method, you can systematically determine where the problem is and fix it so that your users can be up and running as soon as possible.

Collect, Isolate, and Correct Troubleshooting Model

Definition:

The Collect, Isolate, and Correct method is a troubleshooting model that divides the troubleshooting process into three large stages, each containing several steps. There are many different troubleshooting models with varying numbers of steps, but this generic process contains all of the steps needed to go from being notified of a problem to being able to resolve it.

What ever troubleshooting method you decide to use, document the troubleshooting process. This will ensure that you are consistent in your approach to solving problems.

You should have a supply of working replacement parts. Test the parts that have been previously deployed to ensure that they work. Having this stockpile of spare parts ensures that you will have them available to use when problems appear rather than having to order the parts and wait for them to come in before you can resolve the problem.

Track any known problems and bugs. You can do this by consulting with other experts and online sources. You can also keep abreast of them by reading periodicals and trade magazines. Another good source of information is local user groups. All of these sources help you stay informed of known problems.

You should maintain accurate log files for all equipment, for network settings, and for the user environments. This will enable you to check for changes that occurred to the equipment, the network, or the user environment when you are attempting to resolve a problem.

Example:

A user calls the help desk to report a problem. In the collect phase the technician gathers information about the user and the problem. In the isolate phase the technician narrows down exactly what the problem is. During the correct phase the technician actually resolves the problem.

Collecting Troubleshooting Information

The Collect phase of the Collect, Isolate, and Correct troubleshooting model helps you determine which general area of the computer you need to troubleshoot. Using the collect phase guidelines, you can determine which category the problem falls into. For example, does it appear to be a problem related to the video system, the print system, the drive system, or other systems.

Guidelines

Guidelines for collecting information about the problem will help you be consistent in your approach to gathering information. Some of the guidelines you should consider using are:

- Gather user reports of the trouble. Gathering information from the user is usually the first that you are made aware of a problem. This usually comes as a call to the support group or person that the user is having a problem. The user often has an idea of what they think might be wrong.
- Looking for obvious problems. For example, verify that the component is plugged in before assuming it is broken.
- Check for any error messages. The message can help you determine which component you need to troubleshoot. For example, it can help narrow the problem down to something in the video system rather than something related to the drive system.
- Find out what the user has been doing right before they started experiencing the problem. See if there were any changes to hardware or software recently.
- Make sure that the user is following proper procedures. You might want to check the order that the user performs certain steps. For example, if they need to log in to a server before accessing data on it, verify that they are indeed logging in.

Example:

A user calls the support center. They say that they are experiencing problems with their printer. The technician should then ask the user to verify that all of the printer power and data cables are properly connected. Next, find out if any error messages were displayed on the user's system or on the printer. Ask the user when the last time that they were able to successfully print to the printer was and what has changed since then. Finally, verify that the user is following all of the steps needed to send a print job to the printer.

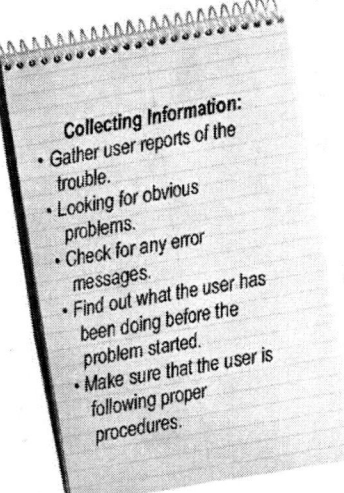

Figure 8-3: *Collecting troubleshooting information.*

Isolating the Problem

The Isolate phase of the Collect, Isolate, and Correct troubleshooting model helps you narrow down which part of the computer you need to troubleshoot. Using the isolate phase guidelines, you determine exactly which component is causing the problem.

Guidelines

Guidelines for isolating the problem will help you be organized in your approach to determining the exact cause of the problem. The Isolate stage is a balancing act between a methodical series of steps and a best guess attempt at solving problems. In some cases, an intuitive reaction will lead you quickly to the source of the trouble. In other cases, you will need to methodically proceed with the troubleshooting process to discover the root of the problem. Some of the guidelines you should consider using are:

- Start with the easiest problems first. Check to see that the power cord is plugged in before you check to see if the internal power supply is burned out. Check for obvious problems before looking for strange or unlikely problems.

- Follow a sequential method in your troubleshooting. Complete one testing or isolating process before beginning another. This helps you eliminate problems one at a time.

- Document each step you take in isolating the problem. This will help you follow a sequential process. Also, you can check that you have tried all of the possible solutions you can think of for a particular problem. Also, if you need to undo a particular fix that you tried, you will know exactly what you did.

- Ask further isolating questions to narrow the range of possibilities for the cause of the problem. The questions are any that will help you eliminate possible problems and get you closer to figuring out exactly which component in a system is causing the problem.

- Make sure that the proper versions of hardware and software are being used. Keeping a detailed record of versions, upgrades, and known problems can help you in troubleshooting a problem down the road.

- Swap parts as necessary to determine the cause of the problem. This will help you to find faulty components faster and hopefully, more easily. However, swapping parts won't necessarily help you find problems arising from the interaction between two or more parts that you are swapping.

- Challenge your own assumptions. Or, better yet, don't make assumptions when you are troubleshooting. If you find yourself saying of course *that* can't be the problem, you might need to challenge your assumption and try changing that anyway. This is especially true when you seem to have exhausted all other possibilities.

 The Isolate stage is often completed nearly simultaneously with the Correct stage.

Example:

For this example, let's say you are responding to a user's call for printing help. The easiest thing to check is that the printer is turned on, is online, is connected, and properly powered. You should ask isolating questions such as whether the user successfully printed previously, whether the correct driver is installed for the printer, whether they can print from any applications or from the command line, and if it is shared printer whether others can print to it. As you try various fixes, be sure to document exactly what you did and only apply one fix at a time. Swap out the printer for another printer and try printing again. If you are still having problems, maybe it isn't the printer with the problem. It might be a resource conflict or a port problem. When you have exhausted all of the potential solutions you can think of, make sure you didn't overlook anything and challenge any assumptions you might have made.

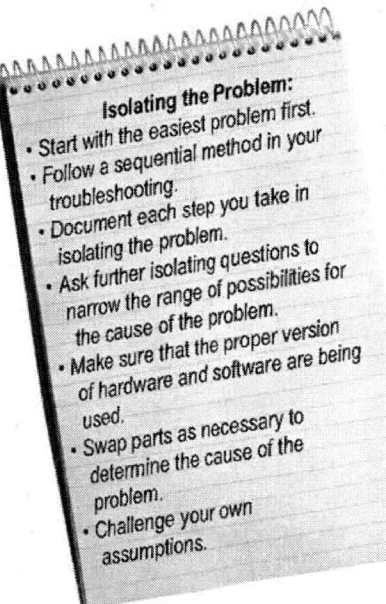

Isolating the Problem:
- Start with the easiest problem first.
- Follow a sequential method in your troubleshooting.
- Document each step you take in isolating the problem.
- Ask further isolating questions to narrow the range of possibilities for the cause of the problem.
- Make sure that the proper version of hardware and software are being used.
- Swap parts as necessary to determine the cause of the problem.
- Challenge your own assumptions.

Figure 8-4: *Isolating the problem.*

Troubleshooting Resources

When you are troubleshooting a problem, you will need to use various resources to aid you. The following table lists some of the common resources you might use and when they are most appropriate for a situation.

Resource	Most Appropriate For
Reference manuals	How to install, configure, and use a particular piece of hardware.
Web support	More up-to-date information than that included in the reference manuals. Also usually includes updated drivers and other support issues and their resolutions.
Phone support	When the information in the reference manuals or Web site does not resolve the issue you are experiencing.

Resource	Most Appropriate For
Forums and newsgroups	Help from peers. Useful for getting input from others who might have experienced the problems you are facing.
Other people	When you are new to a job or new to supporting a particular piece of hardware, if other people are familiar with it, they might have information that will help you in resolving problems.
Magazines	More in-depth articles than what is usually found on Web sites and more up-to-date than what is found in books and manuals.

Correcting the Problem

Procedure Reference: Correct the Problem

The Correct stage involves the steps that actually fix the problem, as well as preventive measures. The prioritized list from the Isolate stage helps you set a plan for solving the problem. Follow your plan. Proceed down your list of potential causes, step by step, from top to bottom. Document your progress and don't skip any steps. The steps involved in the Correct stage of this troubleshooting method might include:

1. Document any attempts you make to solve the problem. Note the conditions before and after you implemented the correction.

2. Take one step at a time. Make only one change; then test to see if the problem has been solved. If so, you've found the problem. Document your solution and take the necessary steps to complete the trouble call. However, if your step didn't fix the problem, undo your changes. Make a change only if you can undo it.

3. Test your final solution for full functionality. Ask the end-users to test as well. Their perception of fully functional may not match yours. It is best to discover further problems immediately than to get another trouble call from the user.

4. Take any steps you can to prevent future problems. For example, if you noted a potentially faulty network cable connector on the user's network connection, even if that did not turn out to be the cause of this trouble ticket, you would be wise to fix it while you are there. This will save you the time of returning later to fix a problem you are already aware of.

5. Document the problem and its solution. You might notice that you have already documented steps in the Isolate stage of this troubleshooting method and documented fixes in the Correct stage. All of this documentation is useful in troubleshooting future similar problems.

6. Develop standards to prevent problems. Having a set list of equipment that you support will enable you to become more familiar with the potential problems and you will be able to resolve the problems more quickly. If you have a wide variety of brands to support, you will need to become familiar with the way each works when they are working correctly and the list of possible problems and the solutions to those problems for each brand.

How to Diagnose System Problems

Procedure Reference: Diagnose System Problems

When you are asked to diagnose a system problem, you should use a troubleshooting model such as the one presented previously. Some of the key points you should remember to implement are:

1. Ask open ended questions of the user requesting assistance.
2. Determine if the problem can be resolved over the phone or if resolution of the problem requires desk-side assistance from a hardware technician.
3. Ask further questions to help isolate reasons for the problem.
4. Follow the troubleshooting model to make sure you respond appropriately to service calls.

CHAPTER 8 FOLLOW-UP
Troubleshooting System Problems

In this chapter, you learned how to troubleshoot problems that occur over the entire system or over several system components. You used your skills to troubleshoot network, dial-up, power, boot, memory, motherboard, and portable system problems. You then pulled your skills together to diagnose a system problem when you didn't know which component was experiencing the problem.

Essential Terms

- BIOS
- boot process
- electrical safety
- memory
- modems
- motherboards
- network connections
- portable computing devices
- power supplies
- surge protectors
- system boards
- troubleshooting
- troubleshooting models
- UPSs

Review Questions

1. What command would you enter at the command prompt to see your IP address and subnet mask on a Windows NT/2000/XP machine?
2. What command would you use to verify connectivity between one machine and another?
3. If a user tries to place a call through the modem and the message "No dial tone" displays on the screen, what should you check first?
4. What kind of power problem can occur when many electrical systems start up at once?
5. Why should you not wear jewelry when working inside a computer?
6. What do POST errors between 020 and 029 indicate?
7. What does POST stand for?
8. You set the power-on password on a system that has since been pulled from the network. You've hired some people and you've taken the system out of storage. When you boot the computer you have to enter the password but you've forgotten it. What can you do?
9. A technician in your department has been performing basic upgrades to systems. After he has worked on your machine the computer boots but the screen remains blank. You suspect a problem with the memory and the technician checks to make sure it is seated properly. The problem is not resolved. What should he check next?
10. While one of your users is using a portable computer it enters hibernation. What do you think is the likely cause?
11. In troubleshooting, why is it important to try to replicate the problem?
12. Where would you go for the most up-to-date information about a particular product?
13. When trying to isolate a system problem, what should you do as you move through each step in the troubleshooting process?
14. What are the three phases of the troubleshooting model?
15. Why should you maintain a stockpile of spare parts?
16. Why should you maintain logs for all equipment, network settings, and user environments?
17. You add new memory to a laptop computer. When you turn on the computer the system will not boot. What should you check first?
18. A user running a laptop computer switches from using an external monitor to using the internal (laptop) monitor. However, the internal monitor does not work. What should you tell the user to do?
19. What is liquid cooling?
20. When would you suspect that the system board has failed?
21. What can happen to the system board if you push down too hard when inserting expansion cards?
22. A user tells you that applications crash when several are open. However, if only one or two applications are running, there are no problems. What do you suspect is the problem?
23. A user boots a computer and receives the error message "Operating System Not Found." What should the user check first?

24. In device manager, what does an "X" represent when it's displayed over the icon of a device?
25. You try to use your modem to connect to the Internet but your ISP's server is not responding. You were able to make a connection the day before. What is the likely problem?
26. What is the command used by Windows 9x to display the computer's IP address?
27. In Windows NT/2000/XP you use the Ipconfig command to display an IP address. What switch would you use to display other statistics such as the physical address of the network card?
28. You add more memory to a user's machine. When you boot the machine to verify the new memory, the computer seems to boot, but the screen remains blank. What do you suspect the problem to be?
29. Why should you document the troubleshooting process you use?

Review Projects

Project #1 Monitoring and Troubleshooting Windows 2000

Microsoft publishes resource kits for their operating systems. Each resource kit offers an immense amount of information about the operating system's architecture and features. This exercise focuses on chapter 14 of the Windows 2000 resource kit. Titled "Troubleshooting Strategies," this article augments your readings to help you develop strong troubleshooting skills. The chapter is located at **http://www.microsoft.com/technet/treeview/default.asp?url=/TechNet/prodtechnol/windows2000serv/reskit/serverop/part4/sopch14.asp**.

The article provides you with insight into the many utilities native to Windows 2000. Included in this article is a guideline to follow when confronted with difficult, hard to identify problems. The main points are worth listing here:

- Analyze symptoms and factors.
- Check to see if the problem is a common issue.
- Isolate the source of the problem.
- Define an action plan.
- Consult technical support resources.

Taking a methodical approach to any system or network problem will help you stay focused and use your time effectively. You should always maintain a log of the issues you've encountered and how you resolved them.

As you can see, the steps outlined by Microsoft are very similar to those discussed in your readings. As you work through this chapter, you'll be introducted to commands and utilties that probably are new to you. Explore the commands and utilities on a Windows 2000 machine.

Project #2 Troubleshooting Windows 98 Startup Problems

The Troubleshooting Windows 98 Startup Problems article is located at **http://support.microsoft.com/default.aspx?scid=KB;en-us;q188867**. This is a Microsoft Knowledge Base article that focuses specifically on Windows 98 startup problems. Microsoft maintains a vast knowledge base comprised of thousands of articles concerning all aspects of its operating systems. As an A+ technician, your most valuable skills will be in knowing not only how to troubleshoot computers, but in knowing where to go and how to search for answers to various problems you encounter.

Beyond reading this article, click each link and explore related articles. Even though you likely have a fully functioning operating system, follow some of the suggestions offered by Microsoft to familiarize yourself with Window 98's startup options.

Project #3 Troubleshooting Iomega Zip Drives

Iomega zip drives are popular storage devices for consumers and business users alike. You can easily attach a zip drive to a desktop or a laptop to gain a significant amount of storage space. Given the popularity of this device, you should be aware of potential problems that can occur and appropriate troubleshooting methods.

Iomega maintains a support page on their Web site that describes a "clicking" problem that can happen with zip drives. The support page is located at **http://www.iomega.com/support/documents/30109.html**. Read through the support page and access the links that are provided. If you have an old zip drive or one that is no longer working, take it apart to better understand the discussion of disk alignment/non-alignment. Copy the support page from Iomega's Web site and add it to your Hardware troubleshooting folder.

Reflective Questions

1. What type of system-wide problem do you see (or expect to see) most often?

2. Which problems do you think will be most difficult to track down the cause for and resolve?

CHAPTER 9
Windows Tools

Chapter Objectives:

In this chapter, you will list Windows and command-line tools.

You will:
- Describe Windows graphical tools.
- Describe command-line tools.

Introduction

When you installed and supported the hardware on various types of personal computers, you employed a set of administrative tools to help you get the job done. When you install and support the software on personal computers, there are even more tools of various types that you'll need to use to accomplish a variety of tasks. So before you learn how to administer and support the operating systems and other software on Windows computers, you should learn about all the tools you have at your disposal and when to use them.

Imagine having to troubleshoot a user's network connection, or having to copy a file from a floppy disk to a hard drive. And picture the situation where you need to install a new network card or a new application. Which tools do you use? Where do you find them? Are they the same tools in Windows NT Workstation 4.0 as they are in Windows XP? You can't do your job, or even learn to do your job, without knowing which tools to use and how to find them. So in this chapter, you'll learn about two sets of tools: graphical tools and command-line tools. Once you know the basics, you can sit down at any Windows computer and instantly find the tools you need.

TOPIC A
Windows Graphical Tools

When you sit down in front of a Windows computer to perform routine maintenance, because Windows has a graphical interface, most times you're going to open a graphical tool. Because the most common Windows tools are graphical, we're going to cover them first in this chapter.

There are a wide variety of graphical tools available in the Windows operating systems, so knowing which one to use and when to use it is important for any Windows support personnel. If you don't know which tools are available, and which tools perform which functions, you'll find you won't get very far as an A+ technician.

Graphical Tools

Definition:

> A graphical tool is a program that is opened within a Windows operating system and is displayed in a colorful window with a mixture of text and icons to represent files and programs on the computer. Graphical tools enable users to manage operating systems using a combination of input from mouse clicks and a keyboard. Output from the computer is displayed in the same window or new windows, which represent the results of the user's input.

Example: My Computer

> As you can see in Figure 9-1, My Computer is an example of a graphical utility. The tool is opened from within the operating system by double-clicking the My Computer icon on the desktop. The tool combines text and icons to represent files and programs on the computer. Users can use a mouse to click the files and programs to open them, or they can use the keyboard to open files and programs by pressing Enter. Results are displayed right in the My Computer window or in new windows that open when a user launches a program.

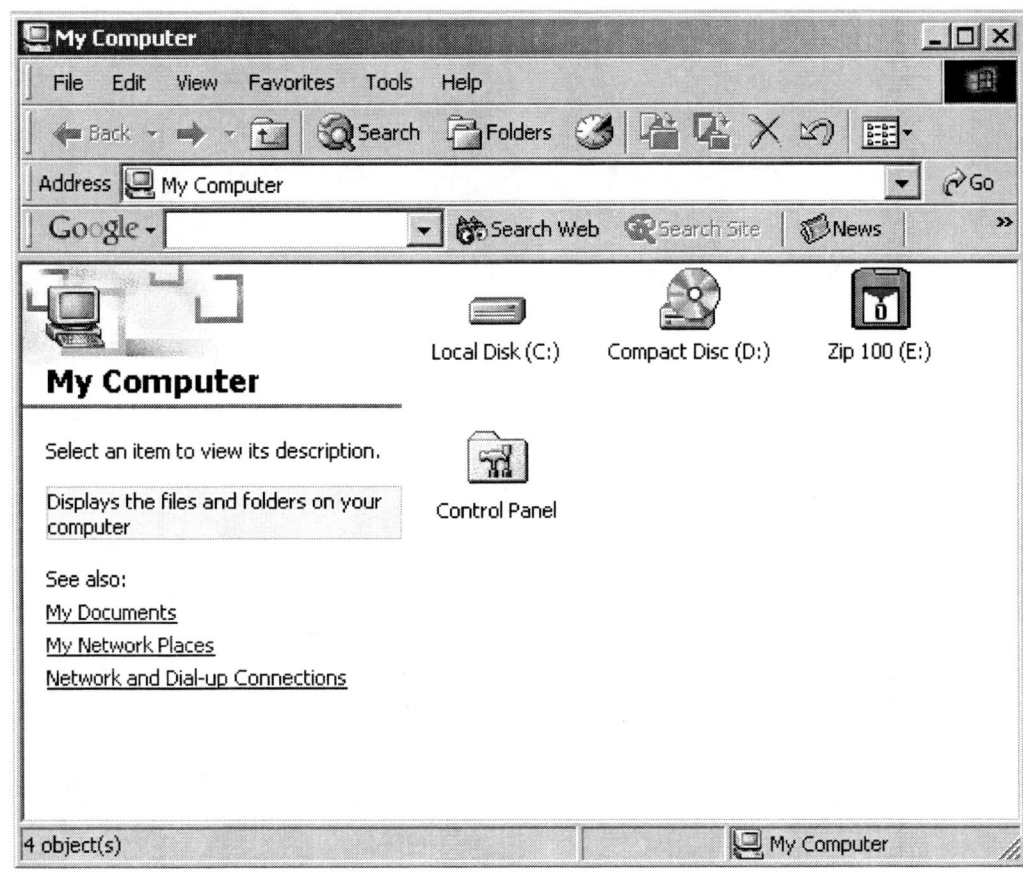

Figure 9-1: *My Computer graphical tool in Windows 2000.*

Taskbar

The taskbar is located at the bottom of a Windows screen, as shown in Figure 9-2. It contains the following items:

- The Start button.
- The Quick Launch toolbar (Windows 98 and Windows 2000), which has icons that let you quickly launch the most often used programs, including Internet Explorer and Outlook Express. You can add other programs to this toolbar by dragging shortcuts onto it.
- Buttons for any open programs.
- The system tray, which includes the clock, and icons for any programs that have been configured to add an icon to the system tray. You can often access the properties of these programs by clicking or right-clicking the icons in the system tray.

Figure 9-2: *The taskbar in Windows XP Professional.*

While the taskbar might appear slightly different in the various versions of the Windows operating systems, it's default location and function is the same.

Start Menu

The Start menu, shown in Figure 9-3, is the main starting point in the Windows operating system. You can access almost any graphical tool you need on the Start menu, including Windows Explorer and Control Panel, by choosing it directly from the Start menu or from one of the sub-menus that open off of it. You can open the Start menu by clicking the Start button on the taskbar, in the lower-left corner of the Windows screen. While the Start menu might have a slightly different appearance from one version of Windows to the next, it still provides a central location for all the important system tools you'll need to manage the operating system.

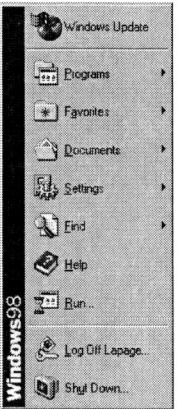

Figure 9-3: *The Windows Start menu in Windows 98.*

The default installations of the different Windows operating systems will arrange the Start menu in slightly different ways. Table 9-1 shows which menus and items you'll see when you open the Start menu in fresh installations of Windows 98, Windows NT 4.0, Windows 2000, and Windows XP. In addition to these items, the Start menu might also contain programs that have been configured to add menu items to it.

Table 9-1: *Start Menu Contents*

Operating System	What's on the Start Menu When You Open It
Windows 98	Windows Update, Programs menu, Favorites menu, Documents menu, Settings menu, Find menu, Help, Run, Log Off *username*, and Shut Down.
Windows NT Workstation 4.0	Programs menu, Documents menu, Settings menu, Find menu, Help, Run, and Shut Down.
Windows 2000 Professional	Windows Update, Programs menu, Documents menu, Settings menu, Search menu, Help, Run, and Shut Down.
Windows XP Professional	Internet Explorer, Outlook Express, MSN Explorer, Windows Media Player, Windows Movie Maker, Tour Windows XP, Files And Settings Transfer Wizard, All Programs menu, My Documents, My Recent Documents menu, My Pictures, My Music, My Computer, My Network Places (if networking properties have been configured), Control Panel, Printers And Faxes, Help And Support, Search, Run, Log Off, and Turn Off Computer. The Start menu might also contain any commonly used programs (added automatically).

Chapter 9: Windows Tools

In Windows 98, Windows 2000, and Windows XP, the Programs menu has an Accessories submenu, which itself contains a System Tools submenu. You can use the System Tools menu to open a variety of tools, which are listed in Table 9-2. System Tools, such as Disk Cleanup, which is used to find and delete unnecessary temporary files or Internet cache files to help recover disk space, are important management tools that you can use to optimize a computer's performance.

Table 9-2: *System Tools on Windows Operating Systems*

Operating System	System Tools Menu Contents
Windows 98	Backup, Disk Cleanup, Disk Defragmenter, Drive Converter, Maintenance Wizard, ScanDisk, Scheduled Tasks, System Information, and Welcome To Windows.
Windows 2000	Backup, Character Map, Disk Cleanup, Disk Defragmenter, Getting Started, Scheduled Tasks, and System Information.
Windows XP	Activate Windows, Backup, Character Map, Disk Cleanup, Disk Defragmenter, Files And Settings Transfer Wizard, Scheduled Tasks, System Information, and System Restore.

Windows Explorer

You use Windows Explorer, shown in Figure 9-4, to manage files and folders on your computer, including the contents of your hard disk, floppy drives, CD-ROM/CD-R/CD-RW drives, DVD/DVD-R drives, and any other storage device attached to your computer. Windows Explorer might look slightly different on the different versions of Windows, but you still use it for the same purpose. You can find Windows Explorer on the Programs menu in Windows 98 and Windows NT 4.0, and you can find it on the Accessories menu off the Start menu in Windows 2000 and Windows XP.

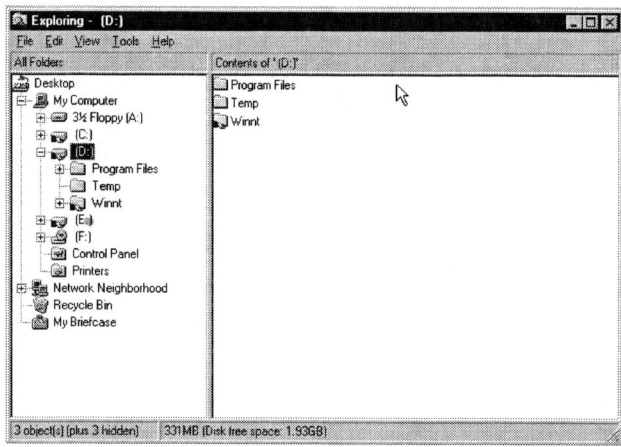

Figure 9-4: *Windows Explorer in Windows NT Workstation 4.0.*

When naming files and folders in Windows Explorer, keep in mind that the maximum depth of a folder structure is dictated by the maximum number of characters in a file path, which is 255. Included in this total is the character representing the C drive and any file extension. The three-letter file extension is used to represent the contents of the file. Some of the more common file name extensions are listed in Table 9-3. In Windows, file extensions are used to associate files with applications, such as text documents with Word or spreadsheets with Excel. If you alter a file name extension, you might find that the file won't run properly or that you can't open it with its associated application, so take care when modifying file names to preserve their extensions.

 Text files can be read using a common text editor, such as Notepad, while binary files (executable programs) can be read only by the computer.

Table 9-3: *Common File Extensions*

File Extension	File Type
bat	Batch file
bin	Binary file
com	Command file
exe	Programs/applications
hlp, chm	Help files
htm, html	HyperText Markup Language (HTML) files
inf	Setup configuration settings
ini	Configuration settings
msi	Windows Installer package
sys	System files
tif, jpg, jpeg, gif, bmp	Image files
txt, rtf	Text files
vbs	VBScript file

My Computer

Like Windows Explorer, My Computer is used to manage files and folders on your computer and on any storage devices attached to your computer. You can also access other Windows tools, such as Control Panel, using My Computer, which you can open by double-clicking the My Computer icon on the desktop in Windows 98, Windows NT 4.0, and Windows 2000. You can open My Computer from the Start menu in Windows XP.

Control Panel

Control Panel contains programs that you use to configure the Windows operating system or the computer's hardware. In Table 9-4, we list the most commonly used Control Panel programs.

You'll sometimes hear the Control Panel programs referred to as applets.

Table 9-4: *Control Panel Programs*

Applet	Use To
Add New Hardware (Windows 9x); Add/Remove Hardware (Windows 2000); Add Hardware (Windows XP)	Install or remove hardware devices from the computer.
Add/Remove Programs (Windows 9x, Windows NT/2000); Add or Remove Programs (Windows XP)	Install or remove application software from the computer.
Display	Configure the wallpaper, screen saver, color scheme, and screen resolution for the computer's monitor.
Mouse	Configure mouse properties such as whether you're using the mouse left-handed or right-handed, the double-click speed, pointer style, and acceleration.
Passwords (only in Windows 9x)	Change the current user's password and to implement user profiles in Windows 9x.
System	Configure hardware profiles, devices (Windows 9x/2000/XP), and performance settings such as virtual memory.

Figure 9-5: *Control Panel in Windows 2000.*

Like other graphical tools, Control Panel may look slightly different from one Windows version to the next, but essentially its function is the same. Control Panel in Windows 2000, shown in Figure 9-5, looks much the same as it does in Windows 98 and Windows NT 4.0. However, Control Panel in Windows XP, shown in Figure 9-6, looks different because similar tools are grouped together in categories, and it is the categories and not the programs that you see when you first open Control Panel in Windows XP.

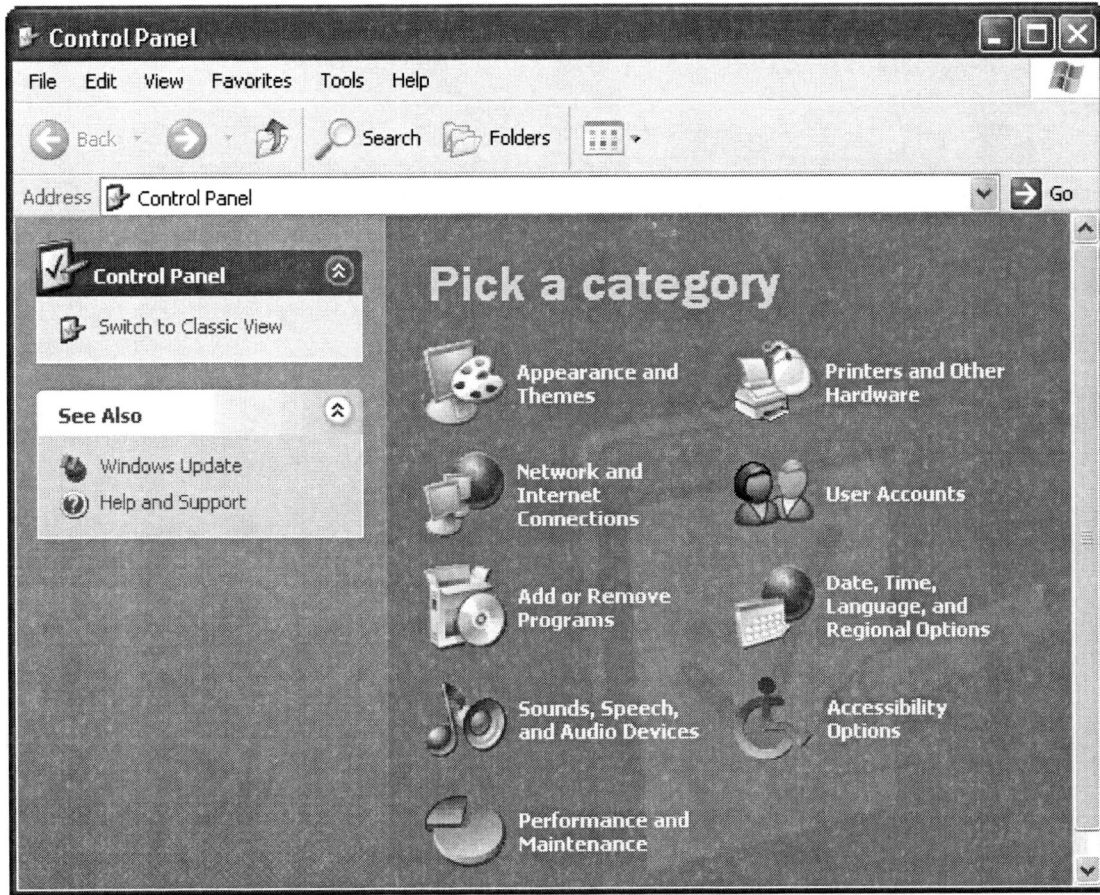

Figure 9-6: *Control Panel in Windows XP.*

You can find Control Panel off the Settings submenu on the Start menu in Windows 98, Windows NT 4.0, and Windows 2000. In Windows XP, Control Panel can be opened directly from the Start menu.

Computer Management in Windows 2000/XP

One central place to find just about every system administration or information tool in Windows 2000 and Windows XP is Computer Management, shown in Figure 9-7. You can open Computer Management by right-clicking My Computer and choosing Manage. You can use Computer Management to perform a wide variety of administrative tasks, including:

- View and manage logs in Event Viewer.

- View system information, such as processor speed and RAM configuration.
- View and configure performance monitors.
- Manage shared folders.
- Manage and configure devices.
- Manage local user and group accounts.
- Configure hard disks and partitions.
- Defragment the hard disk.
- Manage logical drives.
- Configure removable storage devices.
- Configure system services.

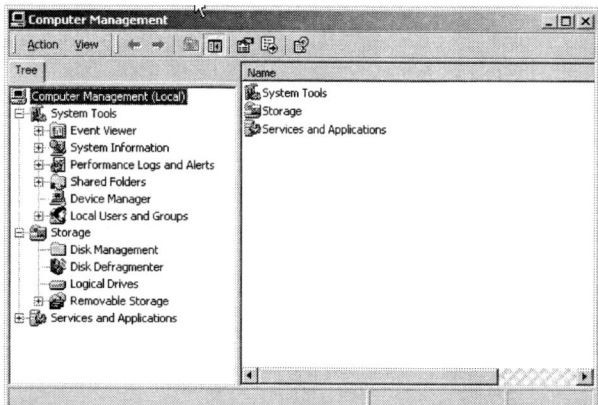

Figure 9-7: *The Computer Management screen.*

Network Neighborhood and My Network Places

Network Neighborhood and My Network Places are similar to My Computer in that they allow you to manage files and folders. The difference is you use Network Neighborhood and My Network Places to manage files and folders on other computers in the network. Of course, you must have the necessary permissions to connect to another computer and manage files and folders on that computer.

You can use Network Neighborhood and My Network Places to perform the following tasks:

- Connect to another computer on the network.
- Transfer files and folders from another computer to your computer.
- Transfer files and folders from your computer to another computer.
- Manage files and folders on another computer in the network.

Figure 9-8: *Network Neighborhood in Windows NT 4.0.*

Network Neighborhood, shown in Figure 9-8, is the tool you use in Windows 98 and Windows NT 4.0. My Network Places, shown in Figure 9-9, is the tool you use in Windows 2000 and Windows XP. You can find the tool in the desktop in Windows 98, Windows NT 4.0, and Windows 2000. You can find the tool in Windows XP in the Network And Internet Connections category in Control Panel. To access any of the computers or shared folders you see in Network Neighborhood and My Network Places, just double-click them. (You might be prompted to enter another user name and password to access the resources in Windows NT 4.0, Windows 2000, or Windows XP.)

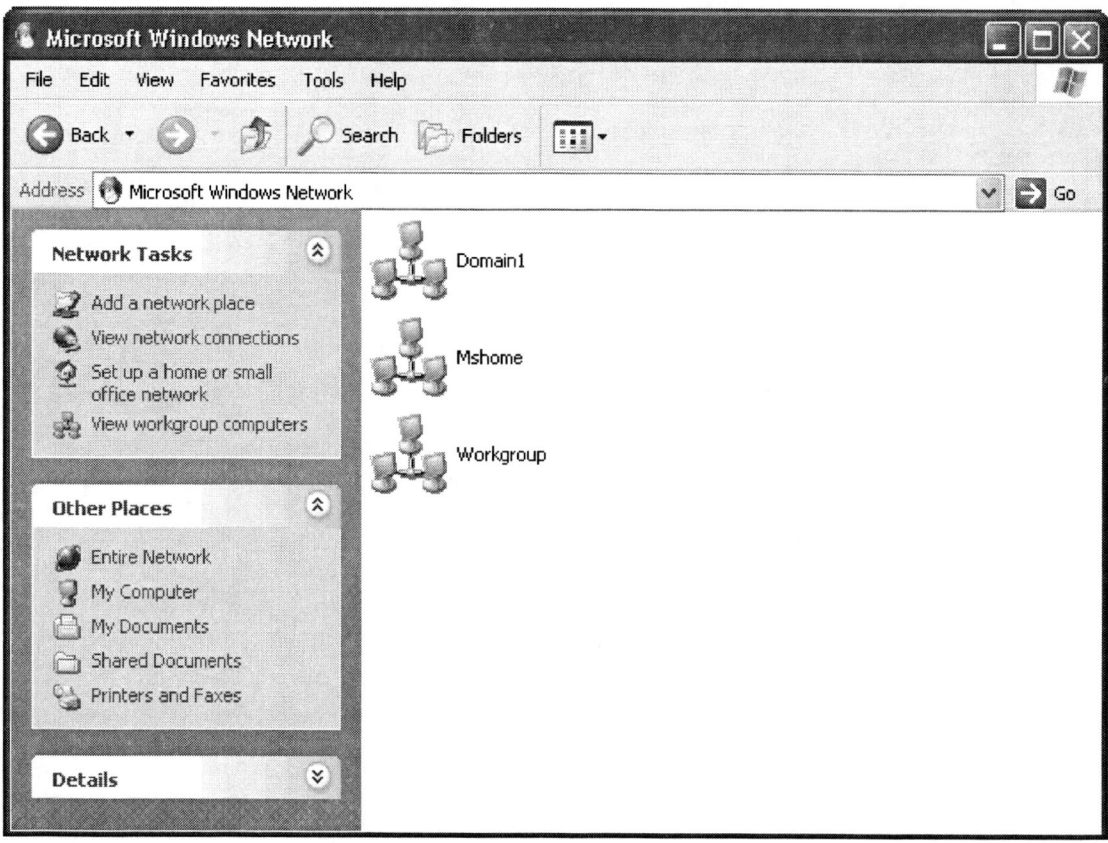

Figure 9-9: *My Network Places in Windows XP.*

Device Manager

In Windows 9x, Windows 2000, and Windows XP, you can determine the hardware devices currently installed in a computer by using the Device Manager. Device Manager is not available in Windows NT. You can use Device Manager to determine the following information:

- The name of a particular hardware component installed in a computer.
- The status of each hardware device.
- The hardware driver installed for each component.
- The hardware resources in use by each component.

You can also use Device Manager to determine the status of your hardware devices. If Device Manager detects a problem, it displays one of the following icons next to the device:

- A red X over a device if it's disabled, as shown in Figure 9-10.
- A yellow circle with an exclamation point if a device's driver is not installed.
- A question mark if a device's configuration conflicts with another device in the computer.

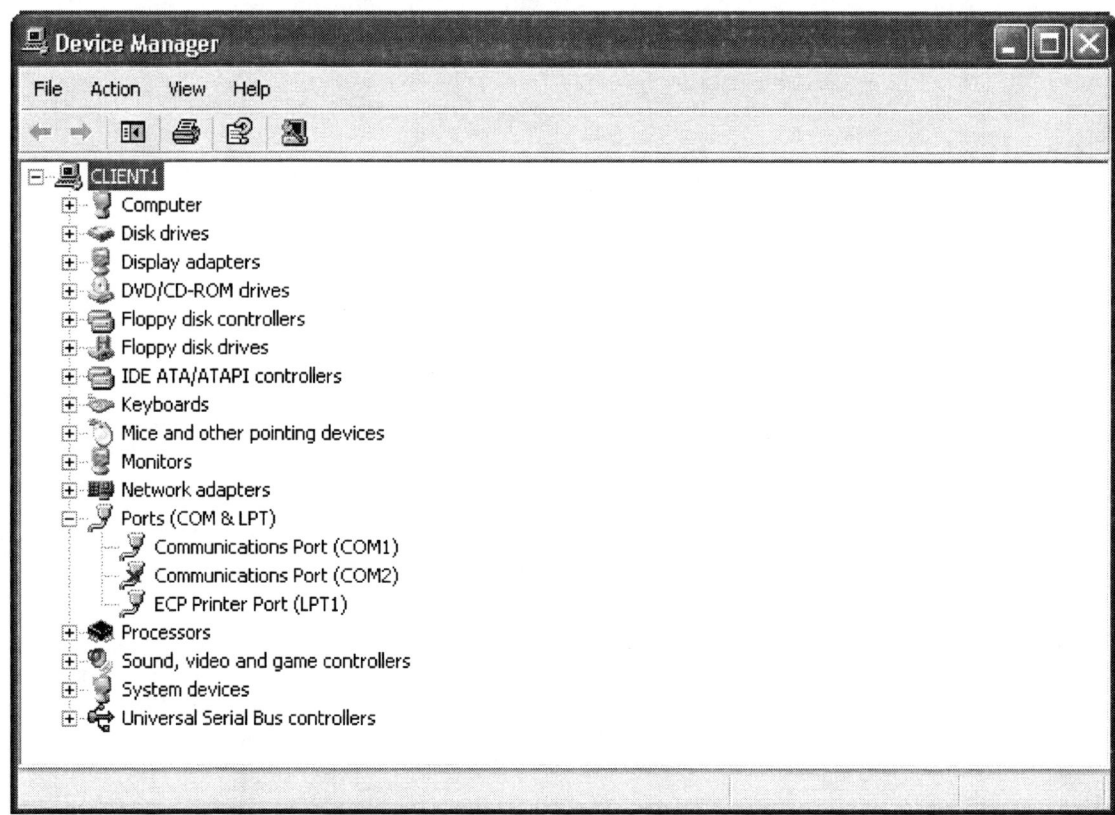

Figure 9-10: *Device Manager in Windows XP.*

Disk Management Tools

In Windows 2000 and Windows XP, you manage hard disks by using the Disk Management utility within the Computer Management console. In Windows NT, you manage hard disks by using the Disk Manager administrative tool. Regardless of which operating system you're using, you access the disk management tool from Administrative Tools.

System Monitoring Tools

Each version of Windows provides a tool that you can use to track the performance of various key components of your system, including the memory, processor, and hard disk. These tools enable you to select different system components, and monitor performance counters that are associated with each component. The counters display component-specific performance statistics; for example, a processor counter can display the percentage of time that the CPU is busy.

The names of the system monitoring tools vary with each version of Windows.

- Windows 98 includes System Monitor, but the tool is not installed by default. Use Add/Remove Programs to install System Monitor. Then, open the Start menu and choose Programs→ Accessories→System Tools→System Monitor.

- Windows NT includes Performance Monitor. Run Performance Monitor from the Administrative Tools group in Control Panel.
- Windows 2000 and Windows XP include System Monitor as part of the Performance management console. Run Performance from the Administrative Tools group in Control Panel.

Account Management Tools

Windows 2000, Windows XP, and Windows NT each include a utility for creating, managing, and deleting user and group accounts. In Windows 2000 and Windows XP, you use Computer Management. In Windows NT, you use User Manager.

TOPIC B
Windows Command-line Tools

Command-line tools are an additional set of tools that you can use to manage Windows computers. You won't use them as often as graphical tools, but they can be just as important in successfully managing the Windows environment.

What happens when your computer won't boot to Windows? Or what do you do when you find a graphical tool too clumsy to use? Fortunately, the command-line tools are available for use within a Windows operating system and outside the operating system in a DOS environment if you can't boot to Windows or if a graphical tool doesn't provide the functionality you need to perform a simple task. In this chapter, you'll learn which command-line tools are available to help you manage your Windows computers.

Command-line Tool

Definition:

A command-line tool is a program that is run by entering appropriate command syntax at a command prompt. The command prompt can be either a command prompt in a DOS environment or in a Command Prompt window in a Windows environment. Command-line tools accept only text input, and they output information in text format or sometimes by opening a window to display information in graphical form. Some command-line tools can only be run in a DOS environment and some can be run in both a DOS and Windows environment. You can also use command-line tools to automate certain administrative functions, such as defragmenting a hard drive, with custom made scripts, such as a batch file or a Visual Basic script.

Example: Format

Format is a program that you run by entering the correct command syntax at a command prompt. You can use Format in a DOS environment or in a Command Prompt window in a Windows environment, which you can see in Figure 9-11. Format accepts text input, and it outputs information in text format.

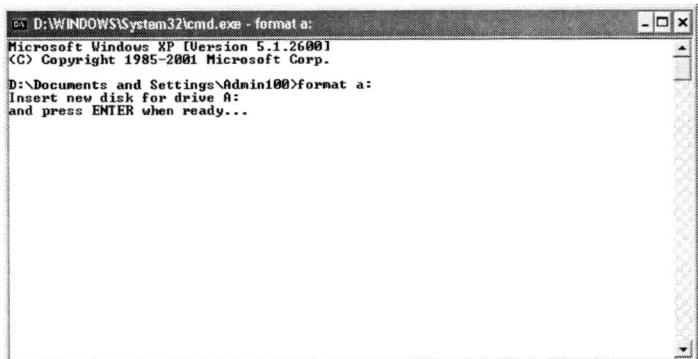

Figure 9-11: *The Format command-line tool in a Windows XP Command Prompt window.*

Popular Command-line Tools

There are a variety of command-line tools you can use to manage your Windows computers. Some popular command-line tools are listed in Table 9-5. Because the syntax may vary slightly in the different operating systems, you should check online help for the exact syntax. To view online help, enter the command followed by a forward slash and a question mark (/?). For a list of all the available commands, type help at the command prompt in Windows NT 4.0, Windows 2000, and Windows XP.

 Not all tools are available in all operating systems.

Table 9-5: *Popular Command-line Tools*

Tool	Used to	Sample Syntax	Supported Operating Systems
Cd	Change to another folder (directory).	cd *drive:path*	Windows 98, Windows NT, Windows 2000, and Windows XP
Cmd	Open the command interpreter.	cmd	Windows NT, Windows 2000, and Windows XP
Command	Open the command interpreter.	command *drive:path*	Windows 98
Copy	Copy files.	copy *source_files destination*	Windows 98, Windows NT, Windows 2000, and Windows XP
Defrag	Defragment hard drives.	defrag *volume*	Windows 98 and Windows XP
Del	Delete files.	del *filename*	Windows 98, Windows NT, Windows 2000, and Windows XP

Chapter 9: Windows Tools

Tool	Used to	Sample Syntax	Supported Operating Systems
Deltree	Delete a directory structure (a directory and all its subdirectories).	deltree *filepath*	DOS and Windows 98
Echo	Display a message or enable/disable echoing.	echo *on	off* or echo *message*	Windows 98, Windows NT, Windows 2000, and Windows XP
Extract	Extract cabinet (.cab) files	extract *cabinet filename*	Windows 98, and Windows 2000 (with download)
Md	Create a folder (directory).	md *foldername*	Windows 98, Windows NT, Windows 2000, and Windows XP
Rd	Delete a folder (directory).	rd *foldername*	Windows 98, Windows NT, Windows 2000, and Windows XP
Rename	Rename a file.	rename *drive:path oldfilename newfilename*	Windows 98, Windows NT, Windows 2000, and Windows XP
Set	Configure environment variables.	set *variable=string*	Windows 98, Windows NT, Windows 2000, and Windows XP
Setver	Configure the version of DOS Windows reports to a program. Used to simulate an older version of DOS if an application won't run in Windows 2000/ XP/NT.)	setver *drive:path filename DOSversion*	Windows 98, Windows NT, Windows 2000, and Windows XP
Type	Display a text file.	type *drive:path filename*	Windows 98, Windows NT, Windows 2000, and Windows XP
Ver	Display operating system version.	ver	Windows 98, Windows NT, Windows 2000, and Windows XP

Tool	Used to	Sample Syntax	Supported Operating Systems
Xcopy	Copy files, folders, and directory trees.	xcopy *source destination*	Windows 98, Windows NT, Windows 2000, and Windows XP

Command-line Troubleshooting Tools

One of the common problems you can encounter is a hard disk that won't boot to Windows or won't boot at all. There are several tools that you can use to troubleshoot problems that are preventing a computer from booting. In Table 9-6, you'll find a list of these tools, a description that includes an explanation of when you might use the tool, and the command's syntax if applicable. You can also use many of these tools within a Command Prompt window; check the operating system Help files for more information.

 Use a DOS boot disk to boot a computer that otherwise won't boot from the hard disk.

Table 9-6: *DOS Boot Troubleshooting Tools*

Tool	Purpose	Syntax
Attrib	Enables you to change the attributes of files. You might use this command if you need to edit a file that has the read-only attribute.	Enter attrib *filename* + or - *attribute*. For example, to remove the read-only attribute from the boot.ini file, you would enter attrib boot.ini -r.
chkdsk	Enables you to check the hard disk for errors. If any errors are reported, you can then use other tools such as ScanDisk to repair those errors.	Enter chkdsk *drive letter*. For example, to check the C drive, enter chkdsk C:.
Dir	Use to view the contents of a directory. For example, you might use the dir command to verify that a file exists in a directory.	Enter dir *path options*. For example, to view a list of the files in the C:\ directory, you would enter dir C:\. If you want to display the list of files in alphabetical order, enter dir C:\ /on. (/on in this syntax stands for "order by name.")
Edit	Use to edit a file. For example, you might use edit to correct problems with the Autoexec.bat or Config.sys files.	Enter edit *filename*. For example, if you need to edit the boot.ini file, enter edit boot.ini.
Fdisk	Use to view, create, or delete partitions, and to mark a primary partition as active.	

Chapter 9: Windows Tools

Tool	Purpose	Syntax
`Format`	Use to format a disk. You can also use it to format a disk and make it bootable.	Enter `format A: /s` to format a floppy disk and make it bootable.
`Mem`	View the memory usage on a computer including the conventional, upper memory, and high memory area segments.	Enter `mem`.
`Msd`	View system information.	Enter `msd` to start the Msd utility.
`Scandisk`	Performs a thorough check of a hard disk and repairs any errors it encounters.	Enter `scandisk` *`drive letter`*.
`Sys.com`	Transfer the Io.sys and Msdos.sys files from a bootable floppy disk to a hard disk so that the computer can boot from the hard disk.	Enter `sys C:`.

CHAPTER 9 FOLLOW-UP

Windows Tools

In this chapter, you learned about Windows graphical and command-line tools that an A+ technician needs to perform his or her job. Knowing which tools to use in a given situation and how to find them is an important skill that every technician who supports Windows computers needs to have in order to perform such basic functions as installing applications and troubleshooting network connections. And now that you know which tools you have at your disposal, you're ready to begin managing and supporting Windows computers.

Essential Terms

- command-line tools
- graphical tools
- troubleshooting tools
- Windows tools

Review Questions

1. What is the purpose of graphical tools?
2. On Windows machines, where is the taskbar located?
3. On Windows 98 and 2000, what is the Quick Launch toolbar?
4. What is the purpose of the Start menu?

5. Which Windows operating systems include a System Tools submenu of the Programs menu?
6. What is Windows Explorer?
7. In Windows NT 4.0 and 98, where can you find Windows Explorer listed?
8. What is the maximum number of characters that can be in a Windows path?
9. What is the function of the three-character file extension in Windows?
10. To what does the file extension .bat refer?
11. Which Windows operating system includes My Computer on the Start menu?
12. What Control Panel applet would you access to change the screen resolution?
13. A user is left-handed and wants you to adjust the mouse which is set up for a right-handed person. Where do you change the properties of the mouse on a Windows 2000 machine?
14. In Windows 98, which Control Panel program do you use to implement user profiles?
15. What is the extension used by a standard text application such as Notepad?
16. Control Panel icons are represented differently in XP than in previous Windows versions. What is the difference?
17. What are two ways to access Computer Management in Windows XP and Windows 2000?
18. What is the purpose of Network Neighborhood in Windows 9x/NT 4.0 and My Network Places in Windows 2000/XP?
19. In Device Manager, what does a yellow circle with an exclamation point mean?
20. In Windows 2000 and XP, what utility do you use to manage hard disks?
21. In Windows NT 4.0, what utility do you use to create, manage, and delete user and group accounts?
22. You need to replace a system file on your Windows 98 machine. The file is located in a .cab file on your Windows 98 CD-ROM. What command will you need to use to extract the files from the .cab?
23. What command enables you to change to another folder at the command line?
24. What output would you receive after entering the command syntax Dir D:\ at the command line?
25. What would the command syntax Attrib +h +r <filename> do?
26. What is the function of the Deltree command?
27. What command would allow you to view information about the memory usage on a computer?
28. What is the purpose of the Set command?
29. What command can you type into the Run box on the Start menu to open a command prompt on a machine running Windows NT 4.0, Windows 2000, or Windows XP?
30. What would you enter at the command prompt to remove a folder named Tasks on the C drive?

Review Projects

Project #1 Windows XP Command-line Tools

Microsoft offers an archive of Web casts that cover many different aspects of their operating systems. In this exercise you'll view the Web cast titled "New Microsoft Windows XP Command-line Tools and Troubleshooting Uitilities." To view the Web cast, go to **http://support.microsoft.com/default.aspx?scid=kb%3Ben-us%3B324617**. Note that under Additonal Resources there is a link if you want to download the PowerPoint slides used in the Web cast. You also can read the transcript of the Web cast.

As you watch and listen to the presentation, make note of some of the commands you find interesting. When you finish watching the Web cast, experiment with some of the commands discussed. As you work with some of the commands, make a list of the ones you find most useful so you'll have a personal command reference. You should also add screen shots to your file so your reference materials are thorough.

Project #2 Batch Files

In your readings you were introduced to common file extensions. The extension .bat is used to create batch files. A batch file is a simple text file. When you add the extension .bat to the file, the file becomes an execuable that you can run at a command prompt. Batch files are particularly useful when you want to automate repetetive tasks.

In this exercise, you'll create a batch file. When you launch the file from the command prompt, it execute the Cd command which will change the directory so you are at the root of the C drive. Then it will execute the md (make directory command) command and create the directory called Documentation. Next, the batch file will exectute the Cd command to take you to the path of the Documentation folder just created. Finally, the batch command will make three subdirectories: video, modems, and monitors.

Open Notepad and enter the following:

@echo on

::This batch file will create two directories on the root of C

cd C:\

md documentation

cd C:\documentation

md video; modems; monitors

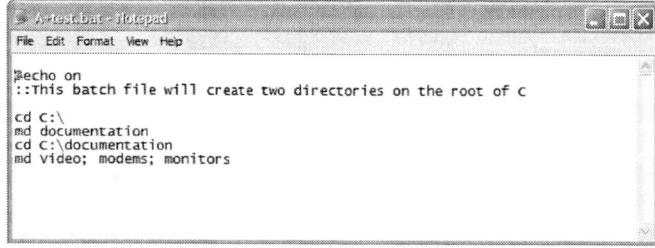

Save the text with an extension of .bat and save it to the proper location. If the file is saved to the wrong location, the system won't be able to find the file to execute it. For example, when you open a command prompt in Windows XP, the path you see will be to your profile. You should see something like C:\Document and Settings\Your name.

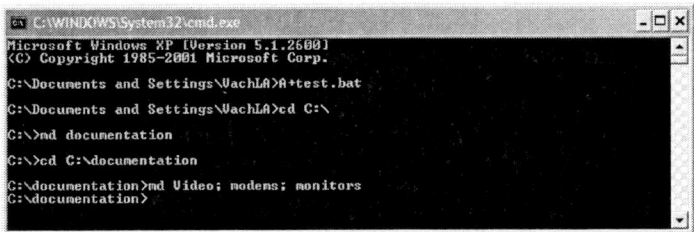

You would have to be sure the batch file was saved in the folder with your name. In the batch file above, the first line means that the commands will be displayed in the command prompt as they execute. If you don't want to see the command output displayed, change echo on to echo off. The double-colon is used to make comments in your batch files. The operating system ignores anything you place after the double colons. If your comments stretch for more than one line, you'd have to place the double colons at the start of each line.

Once you create the file, name it A+test and save it with the .bat extension. Open a command prompt and type the name of the batch file, A+test.bat. The batch file should execute and create a folder named Documentation on the root of your C drive, as well as three sub-folders named Video, Modems, and Monitors.

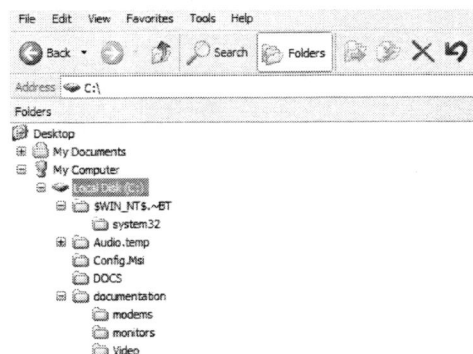

If the batch does not execute, make sure the batch file is located in the right folder, make sure it has an extension of .bat, and make sure the syntax of the batch is correct.

Project #3 Navigating the Control Panel

The Control Panel is a central repository that holds many of the utilities that you'll use to configure your machines. In this exercise, you'll explore the control panels of several operating systems: Windows 98, NT 4.0 workstation or server, Windows 2000 Professional or server, and Windows XP Professional (Note: If all of these operating systems are not available to you, perform this exercise on the operating systems available).

The Control Panel is a graphic interface to the registry. That is, when you make configuration changes at the Control Panel, you are making them to the registry. The advantage of the Control Panel is that you can modify any changes you make easily. If you made all of your configuration changes in the operating system's registry, you'd run the risk of making a mistake and of possibly rendering the system inoperable.

Explore each Control Panel applet and record any Control Panel options unfamiliar to you. Use the operating system's Help feature (in XP, Help and Support Center) to learn more about configuration features you have not used.

Reflective Questions

1. Which Windows tools do you think you'll be using most often?

2. Which command-line tools do you think you'll use most often?

CHAPTER 10
Managing Applications

Chapter Objectives:

In this chapter, you will manage applications.

You will:

- Install a Windows application.
- Configure virtual memory.
- Install a non-Windows application.
- Configure a non-Windows application.
- Remove an application.

Introduction

As an A+-certified Operating Systems technician, you don't just support the operating system; you also support the software applications that run on that operating system. Application support is a very common task for an A+ technician, because your users need applications, such as Microsoft Office or Lotus Notes, to do their jobs. In this chapter, you'll learn how to install, configure, and remove applications.

Without properly installed applications, your users won't be able to get any work done on their computers. If your users can't get any work done, your company won't be productive—which means your company might lose money until the users can access the applications they need to perform their jobs. For these reasons, it's important that you know how to install, configure, and remove applications so that your users can be productive.

TOPIC A
Install a Windows Application

This chapter focuses on managing applications. The first step in managing applications is to install them on computers. Windows applications are the most common type of application you'll encounter in the workplace. So, in this topic, you'll learn how to install a Windows application on your users' computers.

Before your users can work with an application, you must install it so that it's available for the user on the Start menu. Not only must you install the application, but you must also make sure that you install it correctly. Installing the application correctly the first time around will prevent you from having to spend time later troubleshooting or even re-installing the application.

Installation Types

You have three choices for installing an application: Autorun, Executable File (Local), and Executable File (Network). In Table 10-1, we describe the different installation types from which you can choose.

Table 10-1: *Installation Types*

Installation Source	Installation Type	Enables You to Perform an Installation Using
Local	Autorun	The application's installation CD-ROM. If a CD-ROM contains an Autorun file, the Windows computer automatically runs this file whenever you insert the CD-ROM. The Autorun file typically launches a wizard that guides you through installing that application.

Installation Source	Installation Type	Enables You to Perform an Installation Using
Local	Executable file	An executable file such as Setup.exe or Install.exe or an installation package (.msi) file; this file can be stored on local media such as the computer's local hard disk, the application's installation CD-ROM, or a floppy disk. When you double-click the executable file for installing an application, it typically launches a wizard that guides you through installing that application.
Network	Shared folder or CD-ROM	An executable file such as Setup.exe or Install.exe or an installation package (.msi) file stored on a shared network folder or CD-ROM. When you connect to the shared folder and double-click the application's installation executable file, it typically launches a wizard that guides you through installing that application.

 Many companies share their application's installation files on a server so that those applications can be easily installed on computers throughout the network. Installing an application from a shared folder makes the installation easier because you won't have to insert the installation CD-ROM in each computer.

The Background Logon Authentication Process

When you connect to a shared resource, such as a shared folder or printer on a network, Windows verifies that you're authorized to access that share.

1. Your computer provides the user name and password you used to log on to the local computer to the computer containing the shared resource to which you're attempting to connect. (This authentication process takes place in the background. You are prompted to interact with the authentication process only when the credentials you provided on your computer are not valid on the computer to which you're attempting to connect.)

2. The computer with the shared resource checks either its user account database or the domain's account database to verify that your user name and password are valid.

3. If your user name and password are valid, the computer with the shared resource checks the resource's access permissions list to verify that you have sufficient permissions to connect to the shared resource.

    If your user name and password are not valid, you receive an unknown user name or password error message and must enter valid credentials.

4. If you have sufficient permissions, you're permitted to access the shared resource.

If you do not have sufficient permissions to access the resource, you receive an Access Denied error message.

Registry

Definition:

The *Registry* is a configuration database in the Windows 9x, Windows NT, Windows 2000, and Windows XP operating systems that specifies how the computer is configured. This database contains configuration information for:

- Applications that are installed on the computer.
- The computer's hardware.
- Security settings.

In Windows 9x, the Registry consists of two files: system.dat and user.dat; these files are stored in the \Windows folder. In Windows NT, Windows 2000, and Windows XP, the Registry consists of five files stored in the \Winnt\System32\Config folder: Default, SAM, Security, Software, and System, plus a file named Ntuser.dat that's unique for each user who logs on to the computer. This file is stored in the user's profile folder.

If you're using Windows 9x, Windows NT, Windows 2000, or Windows XP, the Registry consists of the HKEY_CLASSES_ROOT, HKEY_CURRENT_USER, HKEY_LOCAL_MACHINE, HKEY_USERS, and HKEY_CURRENT_CONFIG subtrees. Windows 9x contains an additional subtree, HKEY_DYN_DATA. Table 10-2 describes the purpose of each of these subtrees.

Table 10-2: *The Registry Subtrees*

Subtree	Contains
HKEY_CLASSES_ROOT	All the file association information. Windows 9x uses this information to determine which application it should open whenever you double-click a file with a specific extension. For example, Windows 9x automatically opens Notepad whenever you double-click a file with the extension .txt.
HKEY_CURRENT_USER	The user-specific configuration information for the user currently logged on to the computer. For example, information about the user's selected color scheme and wallpaper is stored in this subtree.
HKEY_LOCAL_MACHINE	All the configuration information for the computer's hardware. For example, this subtree contains information about any modems installed in the computer, any defined hardware profiles, and the networking configuration.
HKEY_USERS	User-specific configuration information for all users who have ever logged on at the computer.

Subtree	Contains
HKEY_CURRENT_ CONFIG	Information about the current configuration of the computer's hardware. Because Windows 9x supports Plug and Play, the configuration of the hardware can vary even while the computer is running.
HKEY_DYN_DATA	Information that's stored in RAM on the computer for fast retrieval. For example, Windows 98 stores performance statistics in this subtree. Please note that this subtree is present only in the Windows 9x Registry.

Example:

In Figure 10-1, you find an example of application configuration information in the Windows 2000 Registry.

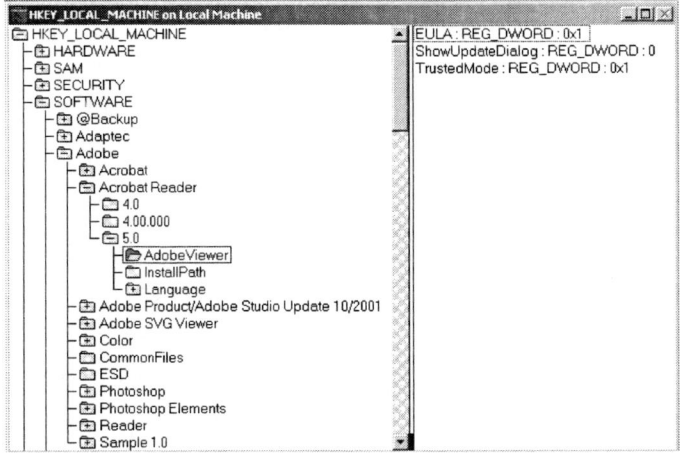

Figure 10-1: *The Registry with application configuration information.*

In Figure 10-2, you see the hardware configuration information as it's stored in the Registry.

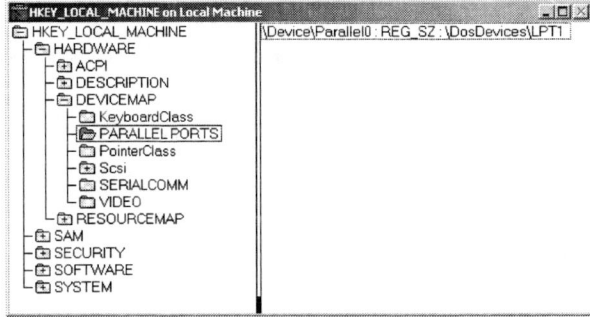

Figure 10-2: *The Registry with hardware configuration information.*

In Figure 10-3, you see the security information stored in the Registry.

Figure 10-3: *The Registry with security configuration information.*

Registry Entries

Definition:

A Registry entry is a configuration specification that defines how the computer's hardware, software, or security settings are configured. A Registry entry must have a *key* and a value. You can optionally create a key to contain other keys and values. A key consists of only a name. A *value* consists of a name, a data type, and the *data* stored in the value. The data types you can assign to values include string, multiple strings, binary, and hexadecimal.

Data Types

In Windows 9x, you can assign the String, Binary, or Dword data types to a value. In Windows NT, Windows 2000, and Windows XP, you can assign the REG_BINARY, REG_SZ, REG_DWORD, REG_MULTI_SZ, or REG_EXPAND_SZ data types to a value. We describe each of these data types in Table 10-3.

Table 10-3: *Registry Value Data Types*

Supported Types of Data	Value Data Type
An alphanumeric string	String (Windows 9x); REG_SZ (Windows NT/2000/XP)
Multiple alphanumeric strings	REG_MULTI_SZ (Windows NT/2000/XP)
An expandable alphanumeric string	REG_EXPAND_SZ (Windows NT/2000/XP)
A binary value	Binary (Windows 9x); REG_BINARY (Windows NT/2000/XP)
A hexadecimal value	Dword (Windows 9x); REG_DWORD (Windows NT/2000/XP)

Binary refers to a number system that consists of only two digits: 0 and 1. A binary value, then, is one that contains only 0s or 1s.

 Hexidecimal refers to a number system that consists of 16 digits: 0 through 9, and A through F. A hexidecimal value is one that contains only these numbers or letters.

Example:

Figure 10-4 shows an example of a Registry key that contains several values.

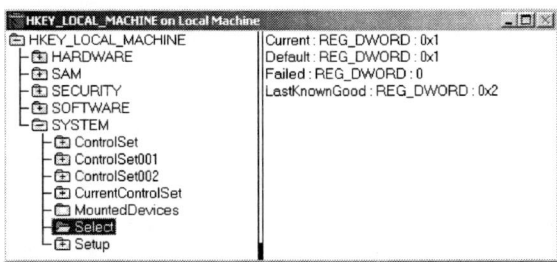

Figure 10-4: *A Registry key containing four values, each with a data type of REG_DWORD.*

Editing the Registry

Procedure Reference: Edit the Registry in Windows 9x

To edit the Registry in Windows 9x:

 You should back up the Registry before making any changes to it.

1. From the Start menu, choose Run.
2. In the Open text box, type `regedit` and click OK.
3. Navigate to the location where you want to make a change to the Registry.
4. If you want to change the data for a Registry value:
   a. Double-click the value.
   b. In the Value Data text box, type the data for this value.
   c. Click OK.

   If you want to rename a key or value:
   a. Right-click the key or value and choose Rename.
   b. Enter a new name.

   If you want to add a new value to the Registry:
   a. Choose Edit→New, and then select the appropriate value type (String, Binary, or DWORD).

b. Enter the name for the value.
c. Double-click the new value.
d. In the Value Data text box, type the data for this value and click OK.

If you want to add a new key to the Registry:
a. Choose Edit→New→Key.
b. Enter a name for the new key.

If you want to remove a key or value from the Registry:
a. Right-click the key or value you want to remove.
b. From the shortcut menu, choose Delete.
c. Click Yes to confirm the deletion.

5. Close Registry Editor.

Procedure Reference: Edit the Registry in Windows NT, Windows 2000, and Windows XP

To edit the Registry in Windows NT, Windows 2000, and Windows XP:

 You should back up the Registry before making any changes to it.

1. Log on as a user with administrator privileges.
2. From the Start menu, choose Run.
3. In the Open text box, type `regedt32` and click OK.
4. Navigate to the location where you want to make a change to the Registry.
5. If you want to change the data for a Registry value:
   a. Double-click the value.
   b. In the text box, type the data for this value.
   c. Click OK.

   If you want to add a new value to the Registry:
   a. Choose Edit→Add Value.
   b. In the Value Name text box, type a name for the value.
   c. From the Data Type drop-down list, select the data type for the value.
   d. Click OK.
   e. Enter the data for the new value and click OK.

   If you want to add a new key to the Registry:
   a. Choose Edit→Add Key.

b. Enter a name for the new key and click OK.

If you want to remove a key or value from the Registry:

a. Select the key or value you want to remove.

b. Choose Edit→Delete.

c. Click Yes to confirm the deletion.

6. Close Registry Editor.

Installation Changes

When you install a new application, you'll find several changes to your computer. These changes include:

- A new menu on the Programs menu with one or more shortcuts for launching the application.
- Optionally, a shortcut on the computer's desktop that you can use to launch the application.
- One or more folders within the \Program Files folder for storing the application's files.
- Modifications to the computer's Registry. These changes include any new file associations for the application (for example, if you install Microsoft Excel, you'll find an association linking .xls files to Excel in HKEY_CLASSES_ROOT).

User Profiles

Definition:

A user profile is a specific grouping of folders, files, and configuration settings created by the operating system to store the user interface configuration for each user who logs on to the computer. In Windows NT, Windows 2000, and Windows XP, the operating system automatically creates a profile for each user who logs on to the computer. In Windows 9x, each user shares the same user profile unless you explicitly set up Windows 9x to maintain separate profiles for each user. A user profile contains:

- All desktop appearance settings such as color scheme, wallpaper, and screen saver.
- The Start menu and taskbar settings.
- The contents of several folders.

A user profile might also contain:

- Shortcuts on the desktop.
- User-specific application configuration settings.
- Any Web sites added to the Favorites menu in Internet Explorer.
- Connections to network printers.
- Connections to shared network folders.
- Internet Explorer configuration settings.

A user profile stores configuration information such as the selected color scheme or the Start menu configuration settings. In Windows 9x, these settings are stored in a file named user.dat. In Windows NT, Windows 2000, and Windows XP, these same settings are stored in a file named ntuser.dat.

Example:

In Figure 10-5, you see the Display Properties that are stored in a user profile.

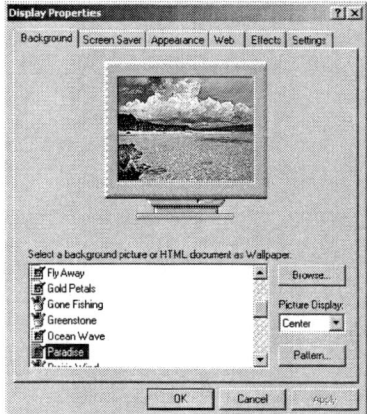

Figure 10-5: *The Display Properties of a user profile.*

In Figure 10-6, you see the Start menu and Taskbar properties that are stored in a user profile.

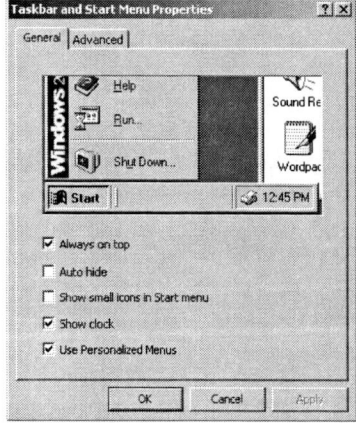

Figure 10-6: *The Start menu and Taskbar properties of a user profile.*

In Figure 10-7, you see the My Documents folder that is part of a user profile.

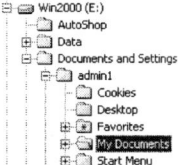

Figure 10-7: *The My Documents folder in a user profile.*

User Profile Folder Locations

A user profile consists of the following folders:

- \My Documents
- \Application Data
- \Cookies
- \Desktop
- \Favorites
- \NetHood
- \Recent
- \SendTo
- \Start Menu

In Windows 9x, all of these folders are stored within the \Windows folder with the exception of the \My Documents folder—it's stored in the root directory of the hard disk. In Windows NT, the user profile folders are stored within the \Winnt\Profiles folder. In Windows 2000 and Windows XP, the user profile folders are stored within the \Documents and Settings folder. In Windows 9x, the user.dat file is stored in the \Windows folder. In Windows NT, the ntuser.dat file is stored in the \Winnt\Profiles*username* folder. In Windows 2000 and Windows XP, the ntuser.dat file is stored in the \Documents and Settings*username* folder.

In Windows 2000 and Windows XP, you'll find two special user profiles within the \Documents and Settings folder: Default User and All Users. Windows 2000 and Windows XP use the Default User profile as a template for creating new users' profiles. So, whatever folders, files, and configuration settings are contained within this profile are automatically copied to a new user's profile whenever that user first logs on to the computer. By default, Windows 2000 and Windows XP automatically hide the Default User profile. You can use the All Users profile in Windows 2000 and Windows XP to store folders, files, and configuration settings you want to be accessible to all users who log on to the computer.

How to Install a Windows Application

Procedure Reference: Install a Windows Application on Windows 2000

To install a Windows application on Windows 2000:

1. Log on as a user with sufficient permissions to install an application.
2. If the application has an installation CD-ROM with an Autorun file:

a. Insert the CD-ROM.

   b. The Autorun file automatically starts the installation wizard. Follow the prompts in the installation wizard to install the application.

3. If the application does not have an Autorun file on its installation CD-ROM or you're installing the application from floppy disk, you can use either of the following methods to install it:
   - Install the application using Control Panel, as follows:
     a. In Control Panel, double-click Add/Remove Programs.
     b. Click Add New Programs.
     c. Perform one of the following tasks, depending on your installation source:

     To install a program from an installation file, click CD Or Floppy (even if the file is on your hard disk or on a shared network folder).

     To download programs from Microsoft's Web site, click Windows Update and follow the instructions on the Web site.

      We're going to cover Windows Update in more detail in Chapter 13.

     d. If you clicked CD Or Floppy, a wizard will run. Click Next.
     e. If the wizard doesn't find an installation file on a CD or floppy disk, enter or browse for the path to the installation file and click Finish.
     f. If you choose to install an application from a network share, you might see a Connect As dialog box prompting you for a valid user name and password for the computer on which the share resides. Enter a valid user name and password and click OK.
     g. An installation wizard might run, depending on the application you're installing. If so, follow the prompts in the software program's installation wizard to install the software.
     h. Close Control Panel.
   - Install the application by accessing its installation files directly:
     a. Double-click the installation file. (This file typically ends in .exe or .msi.)
     b. Follow the prompts in the installation wizard to install the application.

4. Test the application to verify that it works properly.

Procedure Reference: Install a Windows Application on Windows XP

To install a Windows application on Windows XP:

1. Log on as a user with sufficient permissions to install an application.
2. If the application has an installation CD-ROM with an Autorun file:
   a. Insert the CD-ROM.

b. The Autorun file automatically starts the installation wizard. Follow the prompts in the installation wizard to install the application.

3. If the application does not have an Autorun file on its installation CD-ROM or you're installing the application from floppy disk, you can use either of the following methods to install it:

- Install the application using Control Panel, as follows:

  a. In Control Panel, click Add Or Remove Programs.

  b. Click Add New Programs.

  c. Perform one of the following tasks, depending on your installation source:

  To install a program from an installation file, click CD Or Floppy (even if the file is on your hard disk or on a shared network folder).

  To download programs from Microsoft's Web site, click Windows Update and follow the instructions on the Web site.

   We're going to cover Windows Update in more detail in Chapter 13.

  d. If you clicked CD Or Floppy, a wizard will run. Click Next.

  e. If the wizard doesn't find an installation file on a CD or floppy disk, enter or browse for the path to the installation file and click Finish.

  f. If you choose to install an application from a network share, you might see a Connect As dialog box prompting you for a valid user name and password for the computer on which the share resides. Enter a valid user name and password and click OK.

  g. An installation wizard might run, depending on the application you're installing. If so, follow the prompts in the software program's installation wizard to install the software.

  h. Close Control Panel.

- Install the application by accessing its installation files directly:

  a. Double-click the installation file. (This file typically ends in .exe or .msi.)

  b. Follow the prompts in the installation wizard to install the application.

4. Test the application to verify that it works properly.

Procedure Reference: Install a Windows Application on Windows NT

To install a Windows application on Windows NT:

1. Log on as a user with sufficient permissions to install an application.

2. If the application has an installation CD-ROM with an Autorun file:

   a. Insert the CD-ROM.

   b. The Autorun file automatically starts the installation wizard. Follow the prompts in the installation wizard to install the application.

3. If the application does not have an Autorun file on its installation CD-ROM or you're installing the application from floppy disk, you can use either of the following methods to install it:
   - Install the application using Control Panel, as follows:
     a. In Control Panel, double-click Add/Remove Programs.
     b. Click Install.
     c. Click Next to install a program from either a CD or a floppy disk (even if the file is on your hard disk or on a shared network folder).
     d. If the wizard doesn't find an installation file on a CD or floppy disk, enter or browse for the path to the installation file and click Finish.
     e. If you choose to install an application from a network share, you might see a Connect As dialog box prompting you for a valid user name and password for the computer on which the share resides. Enter a valid user name and password and click OK.
     f. An installation wizard might run, depending on the application you're installing. If so, follow the prompts in the software program's installation wizard to install the software.
     g. Close Control Panel.
   - Install the application by accessing its installation files directly:
     a. Double-click the installation file. (This file typically ends in .exe or .msi.)
     b. Follow the prompts in the installation wizard to install the application.
4. Test the application to verify that it works properly.

Procedure Reference: Install a Windows Application on Windows 98

To install a Windows application on Windows 98:

1. If the application has an installation CD-ROM with an Autorun file:
   a. Insert the CD-ROM.
   b. The Autorun file automatically starts the installation wizard. Follow the prompts in the installation wizard to install the application.
2. If the application does not have an Autorun file on its installation CD-ROM or you're installing the application from floppy disk, you can use either of the following methods to install it:
   - Install the application using Control Panel, as follows:
     a. In Control Panel, double-click Add/Remove Programs.
     b. Click Install.
     c. Click Next to install a program from either a CD or a floppy disk (even if the file is on your hard disk or on a shared network folder).
     d. If the wizard doesn't find an installation file on a CD or floppy disk, enter or browse for the path to the installation file and click Finish.

e. If you choose to install an application from a network share, your Windows 98 user account must be defined on the computer on which the share resides (if that computer is running the Windows 2000, Windows XP, or Windows NT operating systems). If the password for this account is different on Windows 98 from the password on the computer with the shared folder, enter the password and click OK.

   f. An installation wizard might run, depending on the application you're installing. If so, follow the prompts in the software program's installation wizard to install the software.

   g. Close Control Panel.

- Install the application by accessing its installation files directly:

   a. Double-click the installation file. (This file typically ends in .exe or .msi.)

   b. Follow the prompts in the installation wizard to install the application.

3. Test the application to verify that it works properly.

Topic B
Configure Virtual Memory

In the previous topic, you learned how to install a Windows application. But, to make many Windows applications run the way they're intended, you'll need to configure virtual memory to meet the requirements of each application. In this topic, you'll learn how to configure a Windows-based computer's virtual memory.

Configuring virtual memory properly enables you to optimize the performance of your users' computers for running applications. You can also configure virtual memory to optimize the performance of the Windows operating system itself. For example, before you optimize a computer's virtual memory, a user who is a data entry clerk would see very slow performance in the company's point-of-sale system and would have to spend her day apologizing to customers. By optimizing this computer's virtual memory, you can make the data entry clerk's application run much faster. Optimizing the performance of your users' applications as well as their operating systems enables your users to be more productive with their computers.

Virtual Memory

Virtual memory enables the computer to use hard disk space as if it is Random Access Memory (RAM). Virtual memory must be assigned to at least one drive and have a minimum size. In Windows 9x, Microsoft recommends that you let the operating system configure the virtual memory settings. In Windows NT, Windows 2000, and Windows XP, you can configure the drive, minimum, and maximum size of virtual memory. You can also configure virtual memory to use multiple hard disks. Virtual memory accesses the hard disk space through a file called the *paging file*; this file is named *pagefile.sys*. The paging file is created by default in the root of the drive on which Windows is installed. You can optionally move the virtual memory file to a different hard drive.

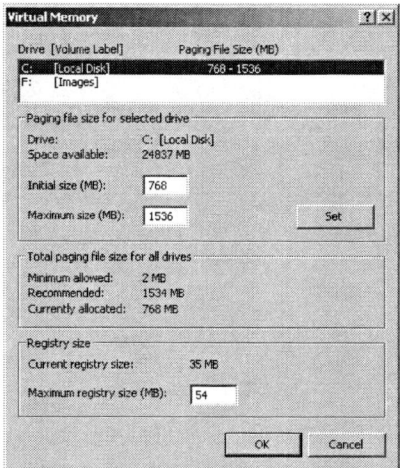

Figure 10-8: *Windows 2000 Virtual Memory settings.*

How to Configure Virtual Memory

Procedure Reference: Configure Virtual Memory in Windows 2000

To configure virtual memory in Windows 2000:

1. Log on as a user with sufficient permissions to configure the computer.
2. Open the System Properties dialog box:
   - In Control Panel, double-click System.
   - On the desktop, right-click the My Computer icon and choose Properties.
3. Select the Advanced tab.
4. Click Performance Options.
5. In the Virtual Memory portion of the Performance Options dialog box, click Change.
6. Modify the Virtual Memory settings:
   - To add a page file, begin by selecting the drive on which you want to place the new page file. Enter both an initial size and a maximum size for the page file and then click Set.
   - To move the page file to a different hard drive, begin by selecting the drive on which you want to place the page file. Enter both an initial size and a maximum size for the page file and then click Set. Next, select the drive from which you want to remove the page file. Set its initial and maximum sizes to 0 and click Set.
   - To change either the initial or maximum size (or both) of the page file, begin by selecting the drive on which they are stored. Enter the value for the Initial Size or Maximum Size and then click Set.
7. Click OK to close all open dialog boxes.

8. If necessary, close Control Panel.

9. Test your change by restarting the computer and verifying that it works.

Procedure Reference: Configure Virtual Memory in Windows XP

To configure virtual memory in Windows XP:

1. Log on as a user with sufficient permissions to configure the computer.

2. Open the System Properties dialog box by using either of the following methods:
   - In the Category view of Control Panel, click the Performance and Maintenance link. In Performance and Maintenance, click the System link.
   - In the Classic view of Control Panel, double-click System.

3. In the System Properties dialog box, select the Advanced tab.

4. Below Performance, click Settings.

5. In the Performance Options dialog box, select the Advanced tab.

6. Below Virtual Memory, click Change.

7. Modify the Virtual Memory settings:
   - To add a page file, begin by selecting the drive on which you want to place the new page file. Enter both an initial size and a maximum size for the page file and then click Set.
   - To move the page file to a different hard drive, begin by selecting the drive on which you want to place the page file. Enter both an initial size and a maximum size for the page file and then click Set. Next, select the drive from which you want to remove the page file. Set its initial and maximum sizes to 0 and click Set.
   - To change either the initial or maximum size (or both) of the page file, begin by selecting the drive on which they are stored. Enter the value for the Initial Size or Maximum Size and then click Set.

8. Click OK to save your changes.

9. Click OK to close all open dialog boxes.

10. If necessary, close Control Panel.

11. Test your change by restarting the computer and verifying that it works.

Procedure Reference: Configure Virtual Memory in Windows NT

To configure virtual memory in Windows NT:

1. Log on as a user with sufficient permissions to configure the computer.

2. Open the System Properties dialog box by using either of the following methods:
   - In Control Panel, double-click System.
   - On the desktop, right-click the My Computer icon and choose Properties.

3. Select the Performance tab.

4. Below Virtual Memory, click Change.

5. Modify the Virtual Memory settings:
   - To add a page file, begin by selecting the drive on which you want to place the new page file. Enter both an initial size and a maximum size for the page file and then click Set.
   - To move the page file to a different hard drive, begin by selecting the drive on which you want to place the page file. Enter both an initial size and a maximum size for the page file and then click Set. Next, select the drive from which you want to remove the page file. Set its initial and maximum sizes to 0 and click Set.
   - To change either the initial or maximum size (or both) of the page file, begin by selecting the drive on which they are stored. Enter the value for the Initial Size or Maximum Size and then click Set.

6. Click OK twice.

7. If necessary, close Control Panel.

8. Test your change by restarting the computer and verifying that it works.

Procedure Reference: Configure Virtual Memory in Windows 98

To configure virtual memory in Windows 98:

1. Open the System Properties dialog box by using either of the following methods:
   - In Control Panel, double-click System.
   - On the desktop, right-click the My Computer icon and choose Properties.

2. Select the Performance tab.

3. Click Virtual Memory.

4. In the Virtual Memory portion of the Performance Options dialog box, click Change.

5. Choose Let Me Specify My Own Virtual Memory Settings.

6. Modify the Virtual Memory settings:
   - To move the page file to a different hard drive, from the Hard Disk drop-down list, select the disk on which you want Windows 98 to place the page file.
   - To limit the size of the page file, specify a maximum size. By default, Windows 98 sets the maximum page file size equal to the amount of free space on the hard drive.
   - To change the initial size of the page file, specify a minimum size.

7. Click OK to save your changes.

8. Click OK to close the System Properties dialog box.

9. If necessary, close Control Panel.

10. Test your change by restarting the computer and verifying that it works.

If a computer is running low on RAM and you want to increase the available memory by using virtual memory, use trial and error to determine the appropriate value. For example, you might try increasing virtual memory by 128 MB if you have enough available disk space on the computer.

Topic C
Install a Non-Windows Application

In Topic 10A, you learned how to install a Windows application. A second type of application you might be expected to install is an application that wasn't written for the Windows operating system. In many cases, the non-Windows applications are custom applications developed for a company by either an in-house programmer or a consultant. These applications were typically designed to run on older computers. In fact, computers have changed faster than companies can update these custom applications. Because such applications are so common, in this topic, you'll learn the steps you should use to install a non-Windows application.

If a company has invested a lot of money in a custom application, they will want to continue using that application even though it wasn't designed to run on a Windows-based operating system. Custom applications typically do just the tasks users need to perform their jobs. In fact, companies typically invest in custom applications when there aren't any available applications to perform these tasks. Having the skills to install a non-Windows application will enable you to install such custom applications properly. By installing the application properly, the company's users will be able to work productively in the non-Windows application.

Non-Windows Applications

Definition:

A non-Windows application is a software program that was written to run in the MS-DOS environment. Non-Windows applications do not have a graphical interface; you navigate the application by using the arrow keys or letters on the computer's keyboard. When you run a non-Windows application on a Windows-based computer, Windows simulates the MS-DOS environment for that application.

Example:

Figure 10-9 shows you an example of a non-Windows application.

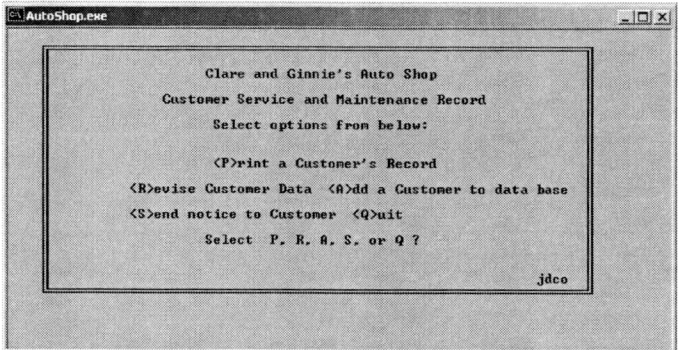

Figure 10-9: *A non-Windows application.*

How to Install a Non-Windows Application

Procedure Reference: Install a Non-Windows Application Without a Setup Program

To install a non-Windows application without a setup program:

1. Create a folder on the computer's hard disk in which to store the non-Windows application.

2. Copy the non-Windows application's files to this folder.

3. Choose where you want to create a shortcut to run the non-Windows application.

    - In Windows 2000 or Windows XP, if you want the shortcut to be available only to a specific user, create the shortcut in either the \Documents And Settings*username*\Start Menu\Programs folder or the \Documents And Settings*username*\Desktop folder. If you want the shortcut to be available to all users, create the shortcut in either the \Documents And Settings\All Users\Start Menu\Programs folder or the \Documents And Settings\All Users\Desktop folder.

    - In Windows NT, if you want the shortcut to be available only to a specific user, create the shortcut in either the \Winnt\Profiles*username*\Start Menu\Programs folder or the \Winnt\Profiles*username*\Desktop folder. If you want the shortcut to be available to all users, create the shortcut in either the \Winnt\Profiles\All Users\Start Menu\Programs folder or the \Winnt\Profiles\All Users\Desktop folder.

    - In Windows 98, if you want the shortcut to be available on the Start menu, create the shortcut in the \Windows\Start Menu folder. If you want the shortcut to be available on the desktop, create it in the \Windows\Desktop folder.

4. To create a shortcut, complete the following steps:

    a. In the appropriate folder or on the desktop, right-click and choose New→Shortcut.

    b. Specify the location of the program's executable file:

       - If you know the exact path to the program's executable file, type it in the Type The Location Of The Item text box.

- If you do not know the exact path to the program's executable file, click Browse and browse the hard disk until you find the executable file. Double-click this file to select it.

c. Click Next.

d. In the Type A Name For This Shortcut text box, type the name you want to appear under the shortcut (on the desktop or Start menu).

e. Click Next.

f. Below Select An Icon For The Shortcut, select the icon you want to use for the shortcut.

g. Click Finish.

5. Test the application to verify that it works properly. If you're installing the application for use by multiple users, test it by logging on as each user.

Procedure Reference: Install a Non-Windows Application With a Setup Program

To install a non-Windows application with a setup program:

1. In Control Panel, use the appropriate utility for installing an application on the computer's operating system.
   - If you're using Windows 2000, double-click Add/Remove Programs and then click Add New Programs. Click CD Or Floppy.
   - If you're using Windows XP, click the Add Or Remove Programs link and then click Add New Programs. Click CD Or Floppy.
   - If you're using Windows NT, double-click Add/Remove Programs and then click Install. Click Next to install from either a CD or a floppy disk.
   - If you're using Windows 98, double-click Add/Remove Programs and then click Install. Click Next to install from either a CD or a floppy disk.

2. If the wizard doesn't find a setup program on a CD or floppy disk, a wizard will run. Enter or browse for the path to the setup program and click Finish.

3. An installation wizard might run, depending on the non-Windows application you're installing. If so, follow the prompts in the software program's installation wizard to install the software.

4. Close Control Panel.

5. If necessary, create a shortcut on the Start menu or the user's desktop to run the non-Windows application.

6. Test the application to verify that it works properly. If you're installing the application for use by multiple users, test it by logging on as each user.

Topic D
Configure a Non-Windows Application

In Topic 10C, you learned how to install a non-Windows application. But, you'll often find that such applications require additional configuration before they will run properly on your users' computers. In this topic, you'll learn the skills you need to configure non-Windows applications.

Non-Windows applications, along with their installation programs, typically aren't very user-friendly. This means that you'll frequently find that you'll have to perform additional configuration tasks in order for the application to meet your users' needs. Knowing the techniques for configuring non-Windows applications will help you get your users working in their non-Windows applications faster. In addition, configuring the non-Windows applications properly the first time will help you avoid having to make repeated visits to your users' computers to change the configuration of the applications.

Operating System Startup Files

DOS and Windows 9x use two startup files: C:\autoexec.bat and C:\config.sys. In DOS, you use these files to configure the operating system, load drivers such as the CD-ROM driver, and configure memory. In Windows 9x, you use these files primarily to configure settings required by non-Windows applications. Both DOS and Windows 9x execute the startup files each time you boot the computer.

Windows NT, Windows 2000, and Windows XP support two startup files: autoexec.nt and config.nt. These files are stored in the \Winnt\System32 folder on the drive on which Windows is installed. These startup files are executed only when you run a non-Windows application within Windows NT, Windows 2000, or Windows XP.

DOS Memory Segments

There are five memory segments in MS-DOS: conventional memory, upper memory, high memory, extended memory, and expanded memory. When you run a non-Windows application in Windows, you might find that you will need to configure some of these five memory segments in order for the application to run. We describe the DOS memory segments in Table 10-4. You configure the DOS memory segments for a non-Windows application by modifying the properties of the shortcut you use to run the application.

Table 10-4: *DOS Memory Segments*

Memory Segment	Size	Description
Conventional Memory	640 KB	Because of the limitations of MS-DOS and the processors for which it was originally designed, DOS could address only the first 640 KB of RAM. For each non-Windows application you run on a computer, Windows must allocate a certain portion of the computer's RAM to simulate conventional memory.

Memory Segment	Size	Description
Upper Memory Area	384 KB	This segment of RAM, the memory between 640 KB and 1 MB, was designed for use by hardware devices. In DOS, you could use memory management techniques to force DOS to use the available memory (called *upper memory blocks* or UMB) within the upper memory area. When you run a non-Windows application on a Windows-based computer, Windows also simulates the upper memory area for that application.
High Memory Area	64 KB	This segment of RAM represents the memory between 1,024 KB and 1,088 KB. In DOS, you could use this memory segment to store a single *terminate-and-stay-resident (TSR)* program, a device driver, or DOS itself. Windows does not simulate this segment of memory when you run a non-Windows application.
Extended Memory (XMS)	All memory above 1,088 KB in the computer	This segment of RAM corresponds to all memory in the computer above 1,088 KB. When you run a non-Windows application, Windows can provide extended memory for the application on an as-needed basis. In Windows, extended memory is automatically available. In DOS, you must load the *himem.sys* driver in the config.sys file to make the extended memory accessible. Himem.sys is a driver that enables DOS to access extended memory.
Expanded Memory (EMS)	Limited to the size of the expanded memory card	Unlike the other DOS memory segments, expanded memory refers to an older specification that enabled you to install an expansion card containing memory in the computer. DOS accessed the memory on this card by using a 64 KB upper memory block. Although you won't encounter computers with expanded memory anymore, you might encounter applications that were written to use it. If so, you can configure Windows to provide the non-Windows application with expanded memory. In DOS, if you want to make expanded memory accessible, you must load the *emm386.exe* driver in the config.sys file. Emm386.exe is a driver that must be loaded before DOS can access expanded memory. You can also use the emm386.exe driver to make the upper memory area accessible for storing TSRs by modifying Config.sys.

Environment Variables

Both MS-DOS and the Windows operating systems support a variety of environment variables that control the behavior of the operating system or an application (or both). Table 10-5 lists some of the common environment variables and how they are used. In Windows 9x, you configure these environment variables by modifying the Windows startup files. In Windows NT, Windows 2000, and Windows XP, you configure environment variables using the System applet within Control Panel.

Table 10-5: *Common Environment Variables*

Environment Variable	Use To
Path	Identify the folders in which you want the operating system to search for executable files.
Temp	Specify the folder in which you want the operating system or application to store temporary files.
Tmp	Define the folder in which you want an application to store temporary files.

 Some applications use the Temp environment variable to identify the folder in which they should store temporary files. Alternatively, other applications use the Tmp environment variable instead.

Files and Buffers

The *files* configuration setting controls how much memory is reserved for the number of files opened by a DOS application. The *buffers* configuration setting specifies how much memory is reserved for transferring temporary information between a non-Windows application's data in RAM and an I/O device such as the monitor. In Windows, you configure the files and buffers configuration settings by modifying the appropriate Windows startup files.

How to Configure a Non-Windows Application

Procedure Reference: Configure DOS Memory Segments in Any Windows Operating System

To configure DOS memory segments in any Windows operating system:

1. Right-click the shortcut for starting the non-Windows application and choose Properties.
2. Select the Memory tab.
3. Use the Conventional Memory, Expanded (EMS) Memory, Extended (XMS) Memory, and MS-DOS Protected Mode (DPMI) Memory text boxes to configure memory to meet the requirements of the non-Windows application. Notice that you can use either a drop-down list to select pre-defined memory settings or type in a specific value in MB in each of the text boxes.
4. Click OK to save your changes.

5. Test the application to verify that it works properly.

Procedure Reference: Configure Environment Variables in Windows 2000

To configure environment variables in Windows 2000:

1. Open the System Properties dialog box by using either of the following methods:
   - In Control Panel, double-click System.
   - On the desktop, right-click the My Computer icon and choose Properties.
2. Select the Advanced tab.
3. Click Environment Variables. You can modify the variables as follows:
   - To edit an existing variable, select the variable and click Edit. Enter the changes and click OK.
   - To delete a variable, select the variable and click Delete.
   - To add a new user variable, click New in the User Variables section. Enter the variable name and value and click OK.
   - To add a new system variable, click New in the System Variables section. Enter the variable name and value and click OK.
4. Click OK twice.
5. If necessary, close Control Panel.
6. Test any non-Windows applications to verify that they work properly.

Procedure Reference: Configure Environment Variables in Windows XP

To configure environment variables in Windows XP:

1. Open the System Properties dialog box by using either of the following methods:
   - In the Category view of Control Panel, click the Performance and Maintenance link. In Performance and Maintenance, click the System link.
   - In the Classic view of Control Panel, double-click System.
2. Select the Advanced tab.
3. Click Environment Variables. You can modify the variables as follows:
   - To edit an existing variable, select the variable and click Edit. Enter the changes and click OK.
   - To delete a variable, select the variable and click Delete.
   - To add a new user variable, click New in the User Variables section. Enter the variable name and value and click OK.
   - To add a new system variable, click New in the System Variables section. Enter the variable name and value and click OK.
4. Click OK twice.

5. If necessary, close Control Panel.

6. Test any non-Windows applications to verify that they work properly.

Procedure Reference: Configure Environment Variables in Windows NT

To configure environment variables in Windows NT:

1. Open the System Properties dialog box by using either of the following methods:
   - In Control Panel, double-click System.
   - On the desktop, right-click the My Computer icon and choose Properties.

2. Select the Environment tab. You can modify the variables as follows:
   - To edit an existing variable, select the variable and click Edit. Enter the changes and click OK.
   - To delete a variable, select the variable and click Delete.
   - To add a new user variable, click New in the User Variables section. Enter the variable name and value and click OK.
   - To add a new system variable, click New in the System Variables section. Enter the variable name and value and click OK.

3. Click OK to save your changes.

4. If necessary, close Control Panel.

5. Test any non-Windows applications to verify that they work properly.

Procedure Reference: Configure Environment Variables in Windows 98

To configure environment variables in Windows 98:

1. From the Start menu, choose Run.

2. In the Open text box, type sysedit and click OK to run the System Configuration Editor.

3. Select the C:\AUTOEXEC.BAT window.

4. Add or edit the statements for configuring the PATH and TEMP variables.
   - To add a PATH variable, type PATH= followed by the folder for which you want Windows 98 to search for executable files.
   - To add a new folder to an existing path statement, type a semi-colon (;) after the current path and then the path to the folder for which you want Windows 98 to search for executable files.
   - To add a TEMP variable, type TEMP= followed by the path to the folder in which you want Windows 98 to store temporary files.
   - To change the folder in which you want Windows 98 to store temporary files, edit the line containing the TEMP= statement in the AUTOEXEC.BAT file.

5. Choose File→Save to save your changes to the AUTOEXEC.BAT file.

6. Close System Configuration Editor.

7. Restart the computer so that Windows 98 will execute the changes you made in the AUTOEXEC.BAT file.

8. Test any non-Windows applications to verify that they work properly.

Procedure Reference: Configure Files and Buffers in Windows 2000, Windows XP, and Windows NT

To configure files and buffers in Windows 2000, Windows XP, and Windows NT:

1. In Notepad, open *X:\%SystemRoot%*\System32\Config.NT. (Replace *X* with the drive letter on which the operating system is installed; replace *%SystemRoot%* with the folder in which the operating system is installed—typically Winnt.)

2. Scroll to the end of the file.

3. If necessary, add the line files= followed by the number of files the non-Windows application needs. If the line files= already exists, edit the value as needed.

4. Add the line buffers= followed by the number of buffers required by the non-Windows application.

5. Save the file.

6. Test any non-Windows applications to verify that they work properly.

Procedure Reference: Configure Files and Buffers in Windows 98

To configure files and buffers in Windows 98:

1. In Notepad, open C:\CONFIG.SYS.

2. Scroll to the end of the file.

3. If necessary, add the line files= followed by the number of files the non-Windows application needs. If the line files= already exists, edit the value as needed.

4. Add the line buffers= followed by the number of buffers required by the non-Windows application.

5. Save the file.

6. Restart the computer so that Windows 98 will execute the changes you made in the CONFIG.SYS file.

7. Test any non-Windows applications to verify that they work properly.

Topic E
Remove an Application

Up to this point in the chapter, we've focused on what you need to do to install, configure, and troubleshoot applications. But what happens if you need to remove an application from a computer? You might run into this problem if you're upgrading users' computers to a new application or if your users no longer need an application on their computers. In this topic, you'll learn how to remove both Windows and non-Windows applications.

It's important that you know how to remove both Windows and non-Windows applications so that you can avoid problems such as unused program files using up the computer's disk space. Removing an application properly enables you to make sure that you've reclaimed the space used by that application on a user's computer. Another situation that might require you to remove an application is during an upgrade of that application. In some cases, you might need to remove the old version of the application before you'll be able to install the new version of that application.

How to Remove an Application

Procedure Reference: Remove an Application in Windows 2000

To remove an application in Windows 2000:

1. In Control Panel, double-click Add/Remove Programs.
2. Select the installed program and click Remove.
3. Follow the prompts to remove the application.
4. Close Add/Remove Programs and Control Panel.
5. Verify that the application was removed successfully.

Procedure Reference: Remove an Application in Windows XP

To remove an application in Windows XP:

1. In Control Panel, click Add Or Remove Programs.
2. Select the installed program and click Change/Remove.
3. Follow the prompts to remove the application.
4. Close Add Or Remove Programs and Control Panel.
5. Verify that the application was removed successfully.

Procedure Reference: Remove an Application in Windows NT

To remove an application in Windows NT:

1. In Control Panel, double-click Add/Remove Programs.
2. Select the installed program and click Add/Remove.
3. Follow the prompts to remove the application.

4. Close Add/Remove Programs and Control Panel.

5. Verify that the application was removed successfully.

Procedure Reference: Remove an Application in Windows 98

To remove an application in Windows 98:

1. In Control Panel, double-click Add/Remove Programs.

2. Select the installed program and click Add/Remove.

3. Follow the prompts to remove the application.

4. Close Add/Remove Programs and Control Panel.

5. Verify that the application was removed successfully.

CHAPTER 10 FOLLOW-UP
Managing Applications

In this chapter, you learned how to install and remove both Windows and non-Windows applications. In addition, you also learned how to configure the properties of non-Windows applications and virtual memory to optimize application performance. With these skills, you can install any application in the Windows 2000, Windows XP, Windows NT, and Windows 9x environments.

Essential Terms

- applications
- DOS
- environment variables
- memory
- non-Windows applications
- RAM
- Registry
- user profiles
- virtual memory
- Windows applications

Review Questions

1. There are three methods for installing an application on a computer. What are they?
2. What is the file extension of an installation package?
3. You have to install an application on 10 computers on the network. What installation would you use?
4. What is the Registry?
5. Where are the Registry files stored on a 9x machine?
6. On Windows NT, 2000, and XP the Registry consists of five files. What are those files?
7. In Windows NT 4.0, 2000 and XP, where are the Registry files stored?

8. In Windows NT 4.0, 2000, and XP, there is a file that's unique to each user that is stored in the user's profile. What is the file?
9. In Windows 9x the Registry consists of what two files?
10. What are the five Registry subtrees?
11. What kind of information is stored in the subtree HKEY_USERS?
12. In what Registry subtree is your wallpaper preference stored?
13. What is the subkey that is present only in the Windows 9x Registry?
14. What Registry subtree contains file association information?
15. What is a Registry entry?
16. A Registry must have a key and a value. What is a key and value?
17. What should you do before you make any changes to the Registry?
18. How do you access the Registry in Windows 9x?
19. What should you enter at the run command to access the Registry on a Windows NT, 2000 or XP machine?
20. How is the user profile created in Windows 2000?
21. In Windows XP, where are the user profile folders stored?
22. You want to install the Support tools on your Windows 2000 system. Where are the tools located?
23. How does virtual memory access the hard drive?
24. In Windows 9x, when would you use the config.sys and autoexec.bat files?
25. Windows NT 4.0, 2000, and XP support two startup files that are executed only when you run a non-Windows application. What are the two files?
26. What are the five memory segments, or levels, in MS-DOS?
27. What was designed to use the upper memory area?
28. What memory segment of RAM represents memory between 1024 KB and 1088 KB?
29. What is the function of the emm386.exe driver?
30. What is the purpose of the files configuration setting?

Review Projects

Project #1 Backing Up the Registry

In Windows 2000 Professional and Windows XP Professional, Microsoft has made it very easy to back up your system's registry. Included in the backup utility is an option to back up only system state data. What consitutes system data depends on the components and configuration of your system, but generally, system data includes the following:

- The Registry
- COM+ Class registration database
- Boot files, including system files

- Certificate services database
- Active Directory
- SYSVOL directory
- Cluster Service
- IIS

In this exercise, you'll back up the system state data on your machine so you have a backup copy of your computer's Registry specifically. If your machine has a CD-R installed, you can back up the system data to a file and then burn the file to CD. Otherwise, save the data to another medium (such as tape or zip drive cartridges). Please note that you must be a member of the administrators group or the backup operators group to use the backup utility.

To review information about system state data, open the Help and Support Center on Windows XP (Start→Help And Support). Read about system state data. Next, you'll perform a backup of your system's state data. Open the backup utility (Start→All Programs→Accessories→System Tools→Backup). Once you open the backup utility, click the Backup Wizard (Advanced) Tab. The Welcome To Backup Wizard will display. Click Next. In the What To Backup box, click the Only Backup The System State Data radio button. Click Next. Browse to a location to save the file and complete the wizard prompts. Once you've backed up the system state data, you're ready to explore your operating system in more depth.

Project #2 Tweaking the Registry

You can modify any setting in your computer by editing the Registry manually. In most cases, you'll edit the Registry automatically by using configuration tools such as those located in your system's Control Panel.

There are circumstances in which you can only enable a specific feature by modifying the Registry directly. Making changes to the Registry is fairly simple. It is important, however, to follow directions precisely because the Registry does not warn you about changes that may damage your operating system setup. For that reason, you should always make a backup of the Registry before you make any changes.

In this exercise, you'll remove My Computer from the desktop and the Start menu. To do this, you'll follow the steps provided by Winguides, located at **http://www.winguides.com/registry/category.php/16/**. Click Remove My Computer From The Desktop And Start Menu. This task is discovery-based, which means you should familiarize yourself with all of the headings in your system's Registry. Make sure you understand exactly what the task requires you to do. If you have never made changes to a Registry before, you should do a dry run first: Print out the winguides page and work through the task without making any actual changes. Once you feel confident navigating the Registry and exploring its properties, make the changes to your Registry. Once complete, close the Registry and reboot your machine. Verify that the My Computer icon has been removed from the desktop (and from the Start menu if the operating system is XP).

Next, reverse your steps. Go back into the Registry and edit it to undo your changes. When complete, reboot the machine and verify that your changes took effect.

Project #3 The Windows 9x Registry

The Registry is a database that holds all of an operating system's configuration information. Most of the modifications you'll make to your systems will not involve editing the Registry. However, if you work in networking environments, you'll find that some changes can only be made in the Registry. For this reason, it is important to tour the Registry and examine its structure.

In this exercise, you'll read a chapter from the Microsoft Windows 98 resource kit. The article will act as your tour guide as you investigate the Registry. Chapter 31 of the Windows 98 Registry resource kit is located at **http://www.microsoft.com/technet/treeview/default.asp?url=/TechNet/prodtechnol/ win98/reskit/part6/wrkc31.asp**. Almost anytime you come across an article about the Registry you'll be warned that making changes to the registry can render your operating system unusable. This warning should be taken seriously. The Registry does not confirm changes that you make, so if you inadvertently change a value, for example, no window will come up asking you to confirm the change.

Up until this point, you've seen that the Windows 98 Registry consists of two files: system.dat and user. dat. This chapter introduces you to a third file, the .pol, or policy file. In a network situation it is possible to generate machine and user-specific policies that enhance the machine's performance and/or limit user customization options. The goal of this activity is to examine the Registry. You'll notice there are several exercises in this chapter and you may want to experiment with as many of these exercises as you can.

Your next task will be to explore a Web site that provides thousands of Registry tweaks. Explore the Web site, http://www.jsiinc.com. If you make any changes to your system's Registry, make sure you have a backup.

Reflective Questions

1. In your work environment, what types of applications will you be expected to install?

2. If you have any non-Windows applications, have you been required to customize their properties in order for the applications to run successfully? If so, what properties have you had to customize?

CHAPTER 11
Installing Network Components

Chapter Objectives:

In this chapter, you will install network components.

You will:

- Update a network card driver.
- Install TCP/IP.
- Troubleshoot IP connectivity.
- Install NetBEUI.
- Install IPX/SPX.
- Install a NetWare client.
- Configure a network connection in Windows 9x.

Introduction

Most companies don't use stand-alone computers. Instead, they network computers together so that users can share resources such as programs, data, and printers. Because the majority of companies have networks, as an A+ technician, you'll be expected to configure networked computers. In this chapter, you'll learn how to configure the network software components that provide basic connectivity from each PC to the network. In addition, you'll learn how to troubleshoot problems with network connectivity.

Without network connectivity, users can't access the shared resources they need to perform their jobs. Installing and configuring network components correctly will ensure that your users will have the access they need.

Topic A
Update a Network Card Driver

There are several network components that must be working properly before you can connect a computer to the network. Before you can configure a network connection, the network card driver must be installed and functioning correctly. In this topic, you'll learn how to update a network card driver in the Windows NT, Windows 2000, and Windows XP operating systems.

Until the network card driver is functioning properly, you can't install or configure any of the other network software components. And until you can configure the necessary network software components, you won't be able to connect the computer to a network—which means that the computer's user won't be able to access the network's resources. Installing the network card driver properly enables you to get that much closer to connecting a computer to the network so that the computer's user can access the network resources he needs to be productive.

Hardware Driver

The Windows operating systems use hardware *drivers* to communicate with the specific hardware in your computer. Depending on the manufacturer of a particular hardware component, the methods by which Windows must communicate with that component can vary. For example, you can install an Ethernet network card made by manufacturers such as 3Com or Intel. Even though both are Ethernet network cards, the methods by which your computer communicates with each network card varies. For this reason, you must install the appropriate hardware driver for the particular network card you're using.

Some hardware drivers are digitally signed to indicate that the drivers have been tested and are of a certain level of quality. With the release of Windows 98, Microsoft began signing drivers that passed Windows Hardware Quality Labs (WHQL) testing. You can use unsigned drivers, but be aware that unsigned drivers have not been tested and certified as compatible with the Windows 98, Windows Me, Windows 2000, or Windows XP operating systems. If a driver hasn't been signed, you will be prompted whether to continue installation when you try to install it on one of your Windows operating systems. While many unsigned drivers are safe and compatible with Windows, you must decide whether you need to use them or whether you can find another driver that has been tested and signed.

Plug and Play

Beginning with Windows 95, and with the exception of Windows NT, Microsoft implemented support for *Plug and Play*. Plug and Play enables the computer's BIOS and the Windows operating system to work together to identify any new hardware you install or attach to a computer. For example, many printers now support Plug and Play. This means that when you attach such a printer to a Windows-based computer, the operating system will automatically detect the new printer and attempt to install the correct printer hardware driver.

How to Use Device Manager

Procedure Reference: Use Device Manager to Identify Hardware Devices

To use Device Manager to identify the hardware devices in a computer:

1. If you're using Windows 2000 or Windows XP, log on as a local administrator.
2. Open Device Manager.
   - In Windows 2000:
     a. Open Control Panel.
     b. Double-click System.
     c. Select the Hardware tab.
     d. Click Device Manager.

    You can also open the System dialog box by right-clicking the My Computer icon on the desktop and choosing Properties.

   - In Windows 9x:
     a. Open Control Panel.
     b. Double-click System.
     c. Select the Device Manager tab.
   - In Windows XP:
     a. On the Start menu, right-click My Computer.
     b. Choose Properties.
     c. Select the Hardware tab.
     d. Click Device Manager.
3. Expand the category of a hardware device (for example, Network Adapters). The name of the hardware device is listed below its category.

Procedure Reference: Use Device Manager to Verify Hardware Device Status

To use Device Manager to verify that a hardware device is working properly:

1. If you're using Windows 2000 or Windows XP, log on as a local administrator.
2. Open Device Manager.

- In Windows 2000:
    a. Open Control Panel.
    b. Double-click System.
    c. Select the Hardware tab.
    d. Click Device Manager.
- In Windows 9x:
    a. Open Control Panel.
    b. Double-click System.
    c. Select the Device Manager tab.

 You can also open the System dialog box by right-clicking the My Computer icon on the desktop and choosing Properties.

- In Windows XP:
    a. On the Start menu, right-click My Computer.
    b. Choose Properties.
    c. Select the Hardware tab.
    d. Click Device Manager.

3. Expand the category of a hardware device (for example, Network Adapters).
4. Right-click the hardware device and choose Properties.
5. Review the Device Status portion of the Properties dialog box. You use this information to determine if the device is working properly.

Procedure Reference: Use Device Manager to Install a Different Device Driver

1. To install a different device driver in Windows 98:
    a. Open Device Manager.
    b. Right-click a device and choose Properties.
    c. In the device's Properties dialog box, select the Driver tab.
    d. Click Update Driver to start the Update Device Driver Wizard. Click Next.
    e. Select Search For A Better Driver Than The One Your Device Is Now Using. Click Next.
    f. Select the locations where you want the wizard to search. You can choose to search the floppy disk drive, the CD-ROM drive, the Microsoft Windows Update site on the Internet, or you can specify a location on the local computer or the network. Click Next.
    g. If the wizard finds another driver, you'll be prompted to use that driver or keep the current driver. Make your selection and click Next.
    h. Complete the wizard to install the selected driver.

2. To install a different device driver in Windows 2000:
   1. Log on as a local administrator.
   2. Open Device Manager.
   3. Right-click a device and choose Properties.
   4. In the device's Properties dialog box, select the Driver tab.
   5. Click Update Driver to start the Update Device Driver Wizard. Click Next.
   6. Select Search For A Suitable Driver For My Device. Click Next.
   7. Select the locations where you want the wizard to search. You can choose to search floppy disk drives, CD-ROM drives, a specific location on the local computer or network, or the Microsoft Windows Update site on the Internet. Click Next.
   8. If the wizard finds another driver, you'll be prompted to use that driver or keep the current driver. Make your selection and click Next.
   9. Complete the wizard to install the selected driver.
3. To install a different device driver in Windows XP:
   1. Log on as a local administrator.
   2. Open Device Manager.
   3. Right-click on a device and choose Update Driver.
   4. Choose Install From A List Or Specific Location. Click Next.
   5. Select Search Removable Media or specify a location to search, or both. Click Next.
   6. If the wizard finds another driver, you'll be prompted to use that driver or keep the current driver. Make your selection and click Next and complete the wizard to install the driver.
   7. If the wizard can't find a driver, the wizard will end. Click Finish.

Procedure Reference: Use Device Manager to Configure Driver Signing Options

1. To configure driver signing options in Windows 2000 and Windows XP:
   a. Right-click My Computer and choose Properties.
   b. Select the Hardware tab.
   c. In the Device Manager section, click Driver Signing.
   d. Configure Windows 2000 to ignore file signatures, prompt you before installing unsigned drivers, or block the installation of unsigned drivers.

How to Update a Network Card Driver

Procedure Reference: Update a Network Card Driver in Windows 2000

To update a network card driver in Windows 2000:

1. Log on as a user with administrative permissions.
2. From the Start menu, choose Settings→Network And Dial-up Connections.

3. Right-click Local Area Connection and choose Properties.
4. In the Local Area Connection Properties dialog box, click Configure.
5. Select the Driver tab.
6. Click Update Driver.
7. On the Welcome To The Upgrade Device Driver Wizard page, click Next.
8. In the Upgrade Device Driver Wizard, verify that Search For A Suitable Driver For My Device is selected and click Next.
9. On the Locate Driver Files page, select the locations you want the Wizard to search for a new driver. You can install the updated driver from any of the following locations:
   - Floppy Disk
   - CD-ROM
   - Local or shared network folder
   - The Microsoft Windows Update Web site

   You might find it necessary to obtain an updated driver for the computer's network card by going directly to the manufacturer's Web site.

10. Click Next to begin the search.
11. If necessary, insert the appropriate disk in either the computer's floppy disk drive or the CD-ROM drive.
12. Click Next to install the updated driver (or to continue with the Wizard if no new driver was found).
13. Click Finish to close the Wizard.
14. Click Close to close the Properties dialog box for your network card.
15. Click OK to close the Local Area Connection Properties dialog box.
16. Verify that the network card and its driver are working properly by right-clicking Local Area Connection and choosing Status. You should see a status of Connected. Click Close to close the Local Area Connection Status dialog box.
17. Close Network And Dial-Up Connections.

Procedure Reference: Update a Network Card Driver in Windows XP

To update a network card driver in Windows XP:

1. Log on as a user with administrative permissions.
2. From the Start menu, choose My Network Places→View Network Connections.
3. Right-click Local Area Connection and choose Properties.
4. In the Local Area Connection Properties dialog box, click Configure.

5. Select the Driver tab.
6. Click Update Driver to start the Hardware Update Wizard.
7. If you want to load the new driver from CD-ROM or floppy disk, complete the following steps:
   a. Choose Install The Software Automatically.
   b. Click Next.
   c. If the Hardware Update Wizard finds an updated driver, click Next to install it.
   d. Click Finish to close the Hardware Update Wizard.

   > The Hardware Update Wizard doesn't include an option to search for a new driver on the Microsoft Windows Update Web site. We cover how you can access the Windows Update Web site to search for not only updated network card drivers but also other Windows updates in Chapter 13.

8. If you want to load the new driver from a local or shared network folder, complete the following steps:
   a. Choose Install From A List Or Specific Location.
   b. Click Next.
   c. Uncheck Search Removable Media.
   d. Check Include This Location In The Search.
   e. Click Browse to select the local or shared network folder from which you want to update the driver.
   f. Select the folder that contains the driver.
   g. Click OK to close the Browse For Folder dialog box.
   h. Click Next to begin searching for a new driver.
   i. If the Hardware Update Wizard finds an updated driver, click Next to install it.
   j. Click Finish to close the Hardware Update Wizard.
9. Click Close to close the Properties dialog box for your network card.
10. Verify that network card and its driver are working properly by right-clicking Local Area Connection and choosing Status. You should see a status of Connected. Click Close to close the Local Area Connection Status dialog box.
11. Close Network Connections.

Procedure Reference: Update a Network Card Driver in Windows NT

To update a network card driver in Windows NT:

1. Log on as a user with administrative permissions.
2. From the Start menu, choose Settings→Control Panel.
3. Double-click Network.

4. Select the Adapters tab.

5. In the list of Network Adapters, select the driver you want to update.

6. Click Update.

7. In the Windows NT Setup dialog box, enter the path to the updated driver files. (You can load the updated driver from floppy disk, CD-ROM, local folder, or shared network folder.)

> You can't update the network card driver from the Microsoft Windows Update Web site using this procedure. You'll learn how to update Windows NT including its network card driver in Chapter 13.

8. Click Continue.

9. Click Close to close the Network dialog box.

10. When prompted, click Yes to restart the computer.

11. Log back on to the computer.

12. Close Control Panel.

13. Verify that network card and its driver are working properly by using Network Neighborhood to browse the network.
    a. On the desktop, double-click Network Neighborhood.
    b. Verify that you see other computers listed in the Network Neighborhood.
    c. Close the window.

TOPIC B
Configure TCP/IP

Now that you've seen how to verify that you have a working network card driver, the next step in configuring network connectivity is to install and configure a network protocol. The primary protocol for both Windows-based networks and the Internet is TCP/IP. In this chapter, you'll learn how to configure TCP/IP in the Windows NT, Windows 2000, and Windows XP operating systems.

Without TCP/IP properly configured on their computers, your users won't be able to communicate with other TCP/IP-based computers on their local network. They also won't be able to access resources on the Internet. Because TCP/IP is so critical, both for connecting to local network resources and the Internet, you can expect frequent requests from your users to install TCP/IP. Knowing how to install TCP/IP properly will help you to get your users up and running quickly, and avoid spending time correcting mistakes.

Network Protocols

A network protocol is responsible for formatting the data packets that are sent between computers on a network. In order for two computers to communicate over a network, they must have a network protocol in common. Windows 9x, Windows NT, and Windows 2000 support the TCP/IP, NWLink IPX/SPX, and NetBEUI network protocols. Windows XP supports the TCP/IP and NWLink IPX/SPX network protocols.

IP Address

Definition:

An IP address is a series of four numbers that you assign to a computer on a TCP/IP network. These four numbers will look something like this: 192.168.200.200. The IP address must consist of four numbers, separated by periods. Each number can be from 0 to 255, with the exception that the first number in the series cannot be 0. In addition, all four numbers cannot be 0 (0.0.0.0) or 255 (255.255.255.255).

Analogy:

An IP address is like a mailing address. A portion of the numbers in the IP address identify the network on which a computer resides, just as a person's mailing address uses a street name to identify the street on which they live. The other portion of the numbers in the IP address uniquely identify the computer on the network, just as the house number uniquely identifies a specific house on a street. So, just as your mailing address consists of both a street name and a house number, so does an IP address consist of numbers to identify the network and numbers to identify the computer on the network.

Example:

In Figure 11-1, you see an example of an IP address with the network and computer portions of the address labeled.

Figure 11-1: *An IP address.*

Subnet Mask

Definition:

A subnet mask is a series of four numbers that the computer uses to determine how many of the four numbers in the IP address are being used to specify the computer's network address. A subnet mask typically looks like this: 255.255.0.0. The first number of the subnet mask must be 255; the remaining three numbers can be any of the following numbers:

- 255
- 252
- 248
- 240
- 224
- 192
- 126
- 0

The four numbers in the subnet mask cannot consist of all 255s (255.255.255.255).

Where you see a number other than zero in the subnet mask, you can determine that the number in the same position in the IP address is part of the computer's network address. For example, if the computer's IP address is 192.168.200.200 and the subnet mask is 255.255.255.0, the numbers in the subnet mask tell you that the first three numbers in the IP address are being used to identify the network on which the computer resides. Likewise, where you see a zero in the subnet mask, this tells you that the number in the same position in the IP address is being used to identify the computer itself.

Example:

In Figure 11-2, you see an example of a subnet mask. The subnet mask is 255.255.255.0, which means that the first three numbers in the computer's IP address are being used to identify the network on which the computer resides.

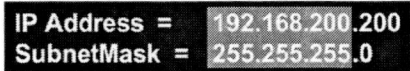

The network address is 192.168.200.

Figure 11-2: *A subnet mask.*

TCP/IP

Definition:

TCP/IP is a non-proprietary, routable network protocol that enables computers to communicate over a network. (A protocol is called routable if it is able to communicate across routers.) The TCP/IP protocol is the foundation for the Internet. In order to communicate on the Internet, a computer must be using the TCP/IP protocol. When you install TCP/IP, you must configure the following properties:

- *IP address*—Four numbers that uniquely identifies the network on which the computer is installed and the computer itself.
- *Subnet mask*—Four numbers used to identify how much of the IP address is being used to identify the network on which the computer is installed.

You might optionally be called upon to configure the following properties for TCP/IP:

- *Default gateway* address. This is the IP address of a router on the network. The computer uses this address to access computers on the other side of the router.
- Preferred and alternate DNS server addresses. Computers use the DNS server address(es) to enable users to access network or Internet resources by name (such as **www.elementk.com**) instead of IP address.
- One or more WINS server addresses. Computers use the WINS server address to access Microsoft Windows network resources by name.

Example:

In Figure 11-3, you find an example of the required and some of the optional TCP/IP configuration properties.

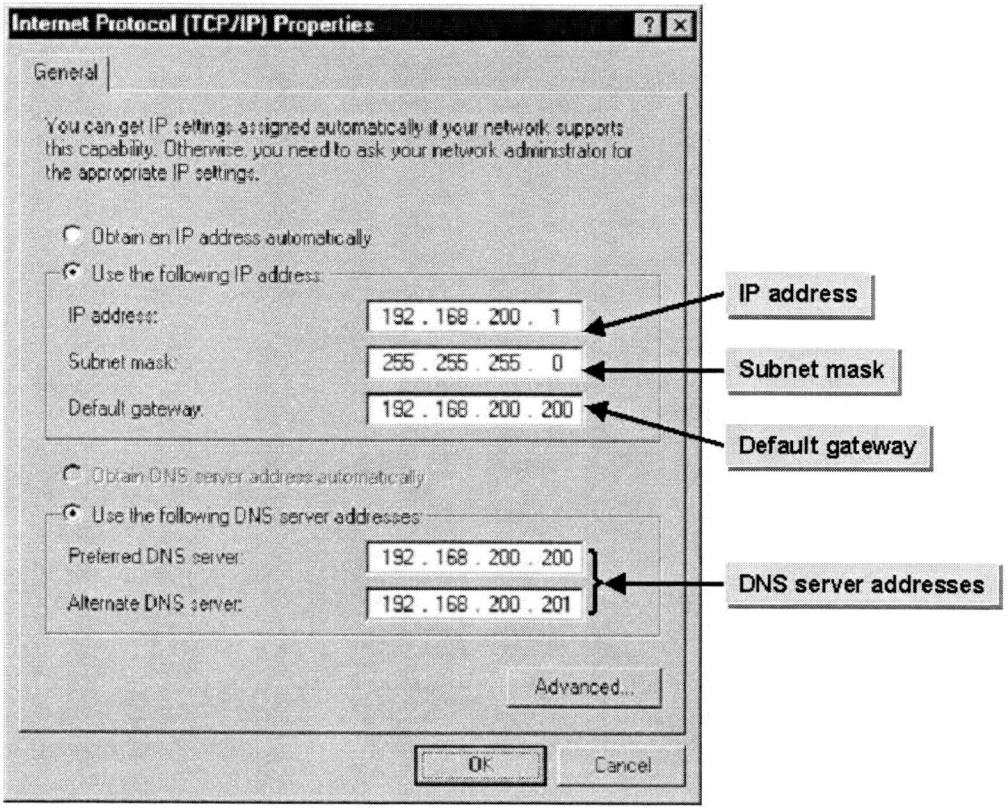

Figure 11-3: *TCP/IP configuration properties.*

Name Servers

On a TCP/IP-based network and even the Internet, you connect to computers by using their names, not their IP addresses. For example, you connect to a computer on your network by using a name such as 2000srv; on the Internet, you connect to computers by using names such as **www.cnn.com**. In order for you to communicate with another computer, however, your computer must know that computer's IP address. There are two ways computers find the IP addresses for specific computer names: *Domain Name System (DNS)* and *Windows Internet Naming System (WINS)* servers. These servers contain databases that consist of computer names and their associated IP addresses.

 You'll sometimes hear computer names referred to as host names.

Automatic TCP/IP Configuration Methods

Windows 98, Windows 2000, and Windows XP support two methods for automatically assigning IP addresses to computers: by using a *Dynamic Host Configuration Protocol (DHCP)* server or by using *Automatic Private IP Addressing*. Windows NT supports automatic IP address assignment only through a DHCP server. Table 11-1 describes each of these configuration methods. Using an automatic TCP/IP configuration method reduces your workload because you won't have to manually assign an IP address and subnet mask to each computer you configure with TCP/IP.

Table 11-1: *Automatic TCP/IP Configuration Methods*

Method	Description
DHCP Server	A server that a network administrator configures with a pool of IP addresses (along with other IP addressing information such as the subnet mask, default gateway, and so on) to assign to clients.
APIPA	A service that automatically configures a computer with an IP address on the 169.254.0.0 network. For example, this service might configure a computer with the IP address of 169.254.217.5.

The TCP/IP Configuration Process

When you configure TCP/IP on a computer, you can configure its properties manually, by assigning a static IP address, subnet mask, and any optional IP addressing parameters such as the default gateway, DNS server address(es), or WINS server address(es). You can also configure the TCP/IP protocol's properties automatically. When you select automatic configuration in Windows 98, Windows 2000, and Windows XP, the computer uses the following process to obtain the necessary IP addressing information for the computer:

1. The computer attempts to communicate with a DHCP server to obtain an IP address. If a DHCP server responds with an offer of IP addressing information, the computer uses the information to automatically configure its IP address, subnet mask, and any other optional properties assigned by the DHCP server.

2. If the computer does not receive a response from a DHCP server, it will use an IP address within the 169.254.0.1 to 169.254.255.254 address range. The computer will also automatically set its subnet mask to 255.255.0.0. The computer does not configure any optional IP addressing parameters such as the default gateway.

If you are configuring the TCP/IP protocol on a Windows NT computer, you can configure its properties manually or automatically. If the Windows NT computer does not find a DHCP server, the computer will not have an IP address and will be unable to communicate on the network. Windows NT does not support APIPA.

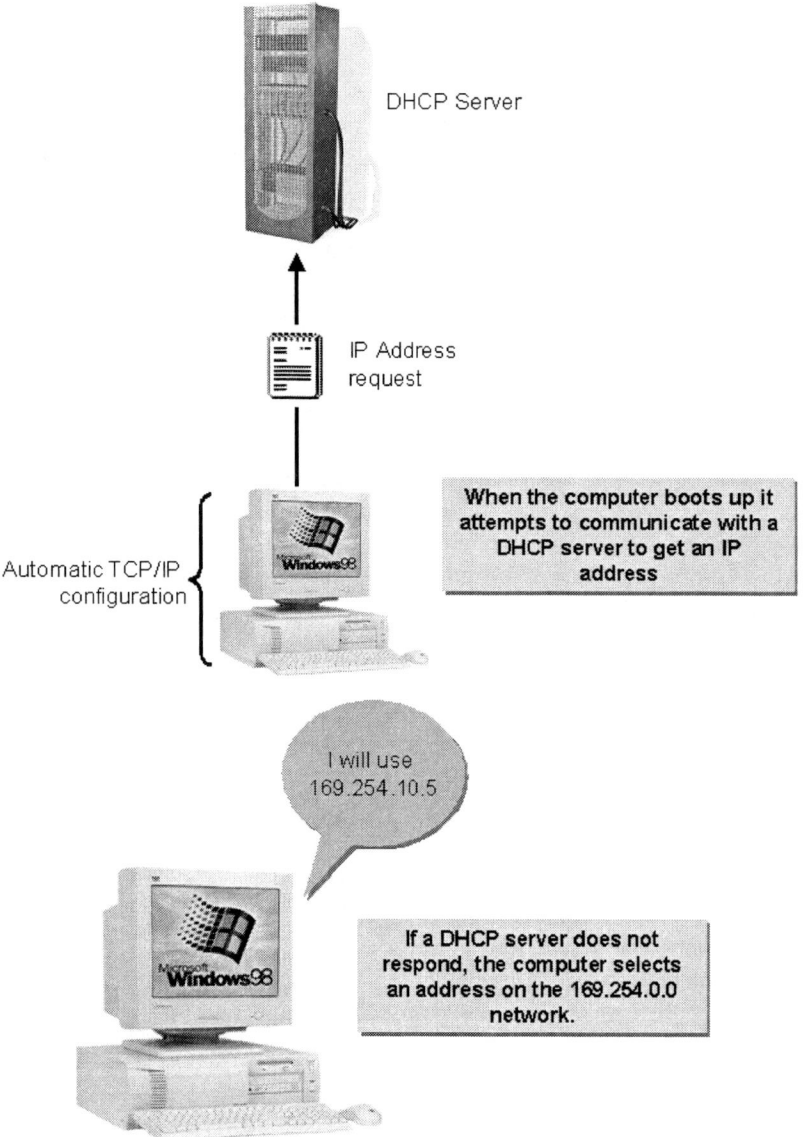

Figure 11-4: *The TCP/IP configuration process.*

The IPConfig Command

You use the `ipconfig` command to verify the configuration of TCP/IP on a computer. In Table 11-2, we list the configuration parameters you can use with the `ipconfig` command along with a description of what each does.

Table 11-2: *IPConfig Command Parameters*

Parameter	Enables You To
`ipconfig`	View the computer's DNS domain name, IP address, subnet mask, and default gateway information.
`ipconfig /all`	View the computer's host name, DNS domain name, network card driver, IP address, subnet mask, default gateway, DNS server(s), and WINS server(s). In addition, you can use this display to determine whether the computer was configured through DHCP or APIPA. If the computer obtained its addressing through DHCP, you also see the IP address of the DHCP server.
`ipconfig /release`	Release the IP addressing information assigned to the computer by the DHCP server or APIPA.
`ipconfig /renew`	Obtain IP addressing information from a DHCP server or APIPA.

The Ping Command

The `ping` command enables you to verify that a computer can communicate across the network using the TCP/IP protocol. The syntax of `ping` is `ping IP address`, where `IP address` is the IP address of another computer on the network. When you use the `ping` command, your computer sends four queries out to the computer associated with the IP address you specified. If your computer can successfully communicate with that computer, you'll see four replies to the `ping` command, as shown in Figure 11-5.

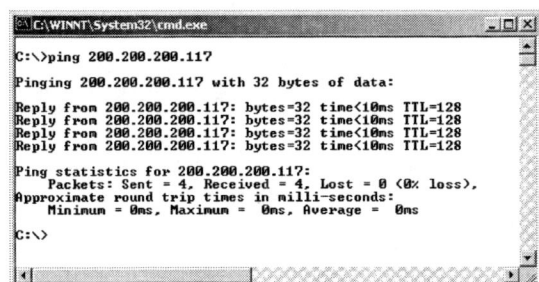

Figure 11-5: *A successful test of TCP/IP connectivity using the ping command.*

Internet Service Provider (ISP)

When you connect a computer or network to the Internet, you typically connect it via a modem to a company that provides Internet access; this company is called an Internet Service Provider (ISP). Most ISPs charge a fee for this connection and, in turn, provide you with a user name, password, email address, and a list of access phone numbers. You connect to the Internet by dialing one of these access phone numbers; the ISP then connects you to the Internet.

 The modem you use to connect to an ISP can be the typical dial-up modem, or it can be a DSL or cable modem for higher-speed connections.

How to Configure TCP/IP

Procedure Reference: Configure TCP/IP in Windows 2000

To configure TCP/IP in Windows 2000:

1. Consult the network administrator to determine if you should manually assign the IP addressing information to the computer or use either DHCP or APIPA. If you're going to manually assign the IP addressing information, obtain the following required information:
   - IP address
   - Subnet mask
   - Default gateway address (if applicable)
   - Preferred and alternate DNS server addresses (if applicable)

2. Log on as a user with administrative permissions.

3. Open Network And Dial-Up Connections. (From the Start menu, choose Settings→ Network And Dial-up Connections.)

4. Right-click Local Area Connection and choose Properties.

5. Select the Internet Protocol (TCP/IP) and click Properties.

6. Configure the TCP/IP properties.
   - If you're configuring the IP address information for the computer manually, select Use The Following IP Address and type in the IP address and subnet mask at a minimum. Optionally, type in a default gateway address, preferred DNS server address, and an alternate DNS server address (if available).
   - If you're configuring the computer to use either DHCP or APIPA, select Obtain An IP Address Automatically and Obtain A DNS Server Address Automatically.

7. Click OK to save your configuration changes.

8. Click OK to close the Local Area Connection Properties dialog box.

9. Close Network And Dial-up Connections.

10. Verify the TCP/IP configuration.

a. From the Start menu, choose Programs→Accessories→Command Prompt.
   b. Enter `ipconfig /all`.
   c. Verify that the TCP/IP addressing parameters are correct.
   d. Close the Command Prompt window.

11. Use `ping` to verify the TCP/IP configuration. (See the following procedure for how to use `ping`.)

Procedure Reference: Configure TCP/IP in Windows XP

To configure TCP/IP in Windows XP:

1. Consult the network administrator to determine if you should manually assign the IP addressing information to the computer or use either DHCP or APIPA. If you're going to manually assign the IP addressing information, obtain the following required information:
    - IP address
    - Subnet mask
    - Default gateway address (if necessary)
    - Preferred and alternate DNS server addresses (if necessary)
2. Log on as a user with administrative permissions.
3. Open Network Connections. (From the Start menu, choose My Network Places→View Network Connections.)
4. Right-click Local Area Connection and choose Properties.
5. Select the Internet Protocol (TCP/IP) and click Properties.
6. Configure the TCP/IP properties.
    - If you're configuring the IP address information for the computer manually, select Use The Following IP Address and type in the IP address and subnet mask at a minimum. Optionally, type in a default gateway address, preferred DNS server address, and an alternate DNS server address (if available).
    - If you're configuring the computer to use either DHCP or APIPA, select Obtain An IP Address Automatically and Obtain A DNS Server Address Automatically.
7. Click OK to save your configuration changes.
8. Click OK to close the Local Area Connection Properties dialog box.
9. Close Network Connections.
10. Verify the TCP/IP configuration.
    a. From the Start menu, choose All Programs→Accessories→Command Prompt.
    b. Enter `ipconfig /all`.
    c. Verify that the TCP/IP addressing parameters are correct.
    d. Close the Command Prompt window.

11. Use ping to test the TCP/IP configuration. (See the procedure below for how to use ping.)

Procedure Reference: Configure TCP/IP in Windows NT

To configure TCP/IP in Windows NT:

 Windows NT does not support Automatic Private IP Addressing (APIPA).

1. Consult the network administrator to determine if you should manually assign the IP addressing information to the computer or use DHCP. If you're going to manually assign the IP addressing information, obtain the following required information.
   - IP address
   - Subnet mask
   - Default gateway address (if necessary)
   - Preferred and alternate DNS server addresses (if necessary)
2. Log on as a user with administrative permissions.
3. Open the Network dialog box. (From the Start menu, choose Settings→Control Panel. Double-click Network.)
4. Select the Protocols tab.
5. In the Network Protocols list, select TCP/IP Protocol.
6. Click Properties.
7. Configure the TCP/IP properties as follows:
   - If you're configuring the IP address information for the computer manually, complete the following steps:
     1. Select Specify An IP Address and type in the IP address, subnet mask, and, optionally, a default gateway address.
     2. If you have DNS server addresses to configure, select the DNS tab.
     3. In the DNS Service Search Order portion of the dialog box, click Add.
     4. In the DNS Server text box, type the IP address of the first DNS server.
     5. Click Add.
     6. Add any additional DNS server addresses.
   - If you're configuring the computer to use DHCP, select Obtain An IP Address From A DHCP Server. (This setting will also automatically configure the computer's DNS server addresses.)
8. Click OK to close the Microsoft TCP/IP Properties dialog box.
9. Click OK to close the Network dialog box.
10. Close Control Panel.

11. Click Yes to restart the computer.
12. When prompted, log back on to the computer.
13. Verify the TCP/IP configuration.
    a. From the Start menu, choose Programs→Accessories→Command Prompt.
    b. Enter `ipconfig /all`.
    c. Verify that the TCP/IP addressing parameters are correct.
    d. Close the Command Prompt window.
14. Use `ping` to test and verify the TCP/IP configuration. (See the procedure below for how to use `ping`.)

Procedure Reference: Test Connectivity Using Ping

To use `ping` to test and verify TCP/IP connectivity:

1. Obtain the IP address of another computer on the network.
2. From the Start menu, choose Programs→Accessories→Command Prompt to open a Command Prompt window.
3. Enter `ping another computer's IP address`. By pinging the IP address of another computer on the network, you verify that the network portion of the computer's IP address and its subnet mask are correct, and that it can communicate with other computers on its network segment.
4. Close the Command Prompt window.

AppleTalk Protocol

Windows NT and Windows 2000 computers natively support the AppleTalk protocol. AppleTalk is the routable network protocol for Macintosh networks. AppleTalk arranges network components into three main subsets:

- Nodes, which are individual devices, such as computers or printers, that have network access. Nodes are addressed by a single 8-bit binary number, represented by the decimal numbers 1 to 254 (the number 255 is reserved for broadcasting). Each node generates its own node number when it comes online, but before using it, the node broadcasts a request to make sure there is no duplicate address.
- Networks, which are the physical segments (network cables).
- Zones, which are workgroups arranged by the administrator to aid in the sharing and access of resources. Members of a zone don't need to be on the same network (physical segment).

Newer Apple computers, including those with the Mac OS X (version 10.2 and higher) operating system, support TCP/IP connectivity, which makes it easier to share files and printers in a Windows network.

Topic C
Troubleshoot TCP/IP Connectivity

As an A+ technician, you'll find that many of the calls you receive for troubleshooting involve problems with network connectivity. The majority of these support calls are due to mistakes in configuring the network connectivity, not a failure in the network hardware itself. Now that you've seen how to install TCP/IP on client computers, you need to learn the steps you can take to troubleshoot problems with the TCP/IP configuration. In this topic, you'll learn how to troubleshoot the TCP/IP configuration on Windows NT-, Windows 2000-, and Windows XP-based computers.

The goal with network connectivity is for your users to be able to be productive by accessing network resources. When your users encounter network connectivity problems, it's important for you to be able to diagnose and resolve these problems as soon as possible. In many cases, you'll be able to resolve these problems by troubleshooting the TCP/IP configuration. Knowing the steps to troubleshooting TCP/IP, along with the tools you can use to help you identify problems, will help you resolve TCP/IP connectivity problems quickly so that your users can get back to work.

The Troubleshooting Process

The troubleshooting process consists of the following phases:

1. The Collect Phase: You should gather information about the computer you're troubleshooting. This information includes:

    - For each computer that is experiencing the problem, obtain detailed information about its hardware, including the manufacturer, processor type and speed, RAM, hard disks, and any peripheral devices such as tape and CD-ROM drives.
    - If all computers on a network are experiencing the problem, document the type of network hardware in use, such as the network cards and cabling. If possible, obtain a diagram with the layout of the network cabling.
    - Document the software in use on the computers affected by the problem. Make sure you record not only the version of Windows, but also any updates installed. If the problem occurs when you run a specific application, record the application's version also.
    - Wherever possible, record the exact steps that result in the problem. Also record any error messages displayed on the screen.
    - Check the System and Application Logs in Windows 2000, Windows NT, or Windows XP for any error messages.
    - Collect the necessary resources to troubleshoot the problem, such as boot disks and diagnostic utilities.

2. The Isolate Phase: Use a series of questions to isolate the potential causes of the problem. Questions to ask include:

    - Is the computer's hardware on the Windows Hardware Compatibility List?
    - Have you installed the latest updates for the version of Windows you're using?

- Is the problem happening to all users or only one user? If the problem is with only a particular computer, you can focus your attention on that computer. In contrast, if the problem is occurring on all computers, focus on the network configuration.

- Is the problem happening when you attempt to access shared resources on one computer or shared resources on multiple computers? If the problem is happening when you attempt to access shared resources on multiple computers, focus on the network configuration of your computer. If the problem is happening when you attempt to access shared resources on only one computer, focus on the computer to which you're trying to connect. Can other users access this computer? If so, it might be a permissions problem. If no other users can access this computer, then suspect a problem with the computer's network configuration.

- Were you ever able to do the task you're attempting to do? If not, the problem is probably that the application or operating system isn't properly configured.

- Have you changed anything or installed any new software or hardware? If so, the problem might be caused by a conflict between your computer and the new software or hardware.

3. The Correct Phase: When you have narrowed down the scope of the problem to a specific area, you can then develop a plan for resolving the problem. When correcting the problem, make sure that you attempt only one change at a time so that you can determine which solution worked.

The TCP/IP Connectivity Process

When you attempt to connect to a computer on a TCP/IP-based network, Windows completes the following steps:

1. Your computer first attempts to find the IP address associated with the name of the computer to which you're attempting to connect.

    - If you're connecting to a computer on the Internet, your computer queries a DNS server to find the computer's IP address.

    - If you're connecting to a computer on the local network and you're using Windows 9x or Windows NT, your computer queries a WINS server to find the computer's IP address.

    - If you're connecting to a computer on the local network and you're using Windows 2000 or Windows XP, your computer queries a DNS server to find the computer's IP address.

    - If you're connecting to a computer on the local network and neither a DNS server nor a WINS server is available (or installed), your computer will broadcast a request to find the computer's IP address. If the computer to which you're attempting to connect responds, your computer can communicate with that computer.

2. Next, your computer determines if you're attempting to connect to a computer on another network. If you are, your computer forwards your communication attempt to the IP address of its default gateway.

3. Your computer establishes a connection with the remote computer. Depending on the computer, your computer might be required to provide your user name and password before you're granted access.

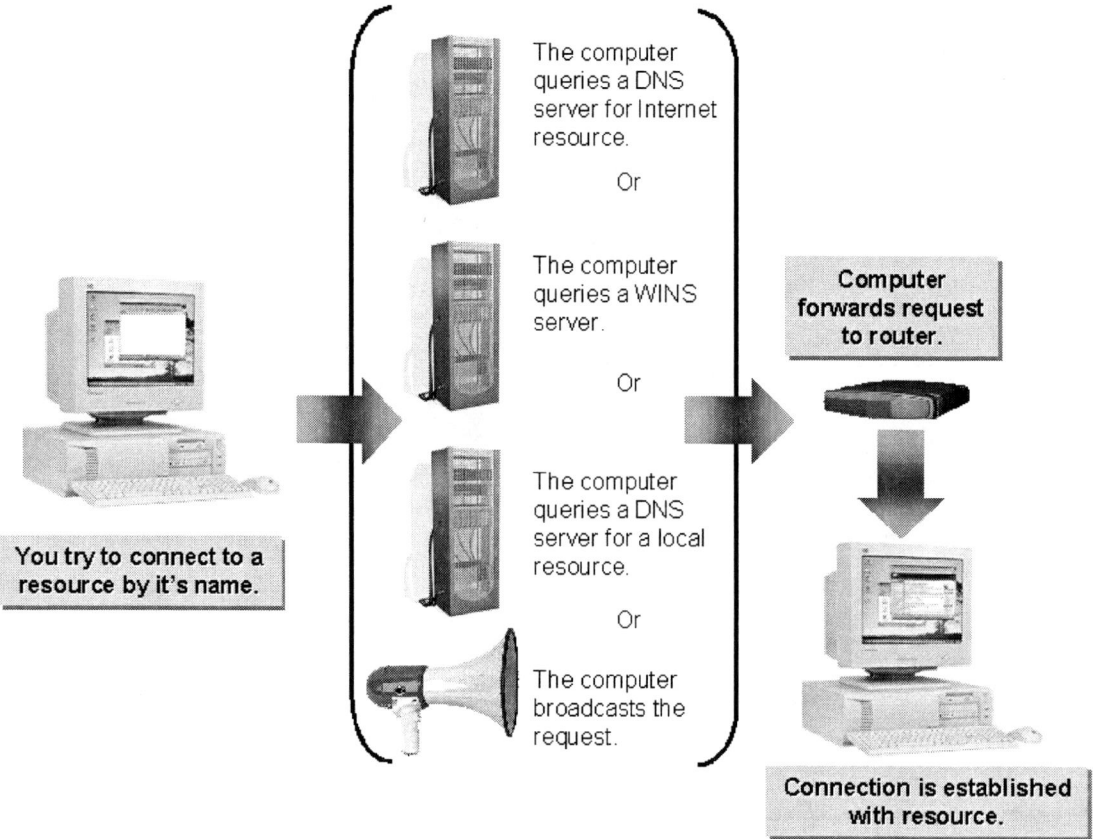

Figure 11-6: *The TCP/IP connectivity process.*

Common Connectivity Problems

There are several common problems you can encounter when troubleshooting TCP/IP. In Table 11-3, you find a list of the common problems and their symptoms.

Table 11-3: *Common TCP/IP Connectivity Problems*

Problem	Symptom
Incorrect subnet mask	Cannot communicate with other hosts. Usually can't communicate with other hosts on the same subnet at all.
Duplicate host address exists on network	Unable to initialize TCP/IP.
Incorrect default gateway address	Cannot communicate with remote networks.

Problem	Symptom
DHCP server unavailable	Cannot obtain an IP address. In Windows 98, Windows 2000, and Windows XP, TCP/IP initializes with an IP address in the APIPA range (169.254.#.#).
Physical connectivity problems	Unable to communicate past the point of the connectivity break.
Incorrect DNS server address; DNS server unavailable	Cannot resolve host names or Internet URLs.
Incorrect WINS server address; WINS server unavailable	Cannot resolve NetBIOS names.

Troubleshooting Tools

Microsoft includes a variety of tools in its Windows operating systems that you can use to troubleshoot TCP/IP. In Table 11-4, you find a description of each of these tools and why you might use them.

Table 11-4: *Troubleshooting Tools*

Tool	Use To
ipconfig	Verify the configuration of TCP/IP and to release or renew DHCP IP address leases.
Local Area Connection Status	Verify that the Local Area Connection is connected to the network and able to send and receive data.
ping	Test communications between two TCP/IP-based hosts.
nslookup	Verify that the computer can connect to a DNS server and successfully find an IP address for a given computer name.
tracert	Determine the route the computer uses to send a packet to its destination. If tracert is unsuccessful, you can use the results generated to determine at what point communications are failing.

How to Troubleshoot TCP/IP Connectivity

Procedure Reference: Troubleshoot TCP/IP Connectivity Problems:

To troubleshoot TCP/IP connectivity problems:

1. Identify the scope of the problem. Is it happening to only one user? If so, you should troubleshoot only that user's computer. On the other hand, is the problem happening on multiple computers? If so, the problem might be the network hardware such as the cabling, hubs, or routers.

2. Ask the user questions and use troubleshooting tools (such as `ping` and `ipconfig`) to isolate the problem. You'll find that most of the TCP/IP connectivity problems fit into one of the following categories:
   - IP addressing problems—Verify that the client has addressing information that matches your network's configuration.
   - Physical network problems—Suspect this if the client's IP configuration otherwise appears correct. Make sure that the computer's network cable is plugged in and check its connection to the wall jack. Verify that the network card is functioning properly. Use `tracert` to verify that you can communicate with other computers across routers.
   - Name resolution problems—See if your client can connect to a target computer by IP address instead of by name. Use `nslookup` to verify that the computer can communicate with the DNS server and obtain the target computer's IP address.

3. Correct the problem.
   - For IP addressing problems, use `ipconfig /release` and `ipconfig /renew` to attempt to lease an IP address on dynamically configured clients. If the clients are manually configured, enter the correct addressing information.
   - For physical network problems, replace or reconnect the network card, cable, jack, or hub.
   - For name resolution problems, correct either the DNS and WINS server addresses in the TCP/IP configuration for manually configured clients. If the DNS or WINS server addresses are incorrect on dynamically configured clients, bring it to the network administrator's attention.

4. Use `ipconfig` and `ping` to verify that you can communicate with other hosts on the network.

5. Document your solution for future reference.

Procedure Reference: Troubleshoot Connectivity Using Ping

To use `ping` to troubleshoot TCP/IP connectivity:

1. Open a Command Prompt window.

2. Enter `ping 127.0.0.1`. Pinging the IP address of 127.0.0.1 (also called the loopback address) generates a response from the IP protocol on your own computer. This verifies that TCP/IP is installed and working, even if the computer doesn't yet have a valid IP address. The loopback address is a standard address that's reserved by the TCP/IP protocol for testing. An equivalent command is `ping localhost`.

3. Enter `ping your IP address`. (Replace "your IP address" with the IP address of the computer.) Pinging the computer's own IP address enables you to verify that the IP address is unique and valid.

4. Enter `ping default gateway address`. (Replace "default gateway address" with the IP address of the default gateway.) By pinging the IP address of the default gateway (or another computer on the computer's network segment if you don't have a default gateway), you verify that the network portion of the computer's IP address and its subnet mask are correct, and that it can communicate with other hosts on its network segment.

5. Enter `ping remote IP address`. (Replace "remote IP address" with the IP address of a host on a different network segment; in other words, a host with a different network address from the computer's own.) Pinging a remote IP address verifies that the computer can communicate across the router (default gateway).

6. Close the Command Prompt window.

Procedure Reference: Troubleshoot Name Resolution Problems Using Ping

To use `ping` to troubleshoot TCP/IP name resolution:

1. Open a Command Prompt window.

2. Enter `ping host name`. (Replace host name with the name of a computer on the network or an Internet URL such as **www.cnn.com**.) If the computer on which you're working attempts to ping a computer (even if that computer doesn't respond), the computer is successfully able to access either a DNS or WINS server to resolve the host name.

3. Close the Command Prompt window.

Procedure Reference: Troubleshoot Name Resolution Problems Using NSLookup

To use `nslookup` to troubleshoot TCP/IP name resolution:

1. Open a Command Prompt window.

2. Enter `nslookup computer name`. For example, if you're testing name resolution for a computer named server1 on your own network, enter `nslookup server1`. If you're testing name resolution for Internet addresses, enter `nslookup www.cnn.com`.

3. Close the Command Prompt window.

Procedure Reference: Troubleshoot Connectivity Using Tracert

To use `tracert` to troubleshoot TCP/IP connectivity:

1. Open a Command Prompt window.

2. Enter `tracert IP address or computer name`.

3. Close the Command Prompt window.

Procedure Reference: Troubleshoot Connectivity Using IPConfig

To use IPConfig to verify your IP addressing information:

1. Open a Command Prompt window.

2. Enter `ipconfig /all`. This command displays not only the computer's IP address, but also information about its DNS server addresses as well as the IP address of the DHCP server from which it leased an address (if applicable).

3. Close the Command Prompt Window.

Procedure Reference: Troubleshoot Automatic TCP/IP Configuration Using IPConfig

To use IPConfig to troubleshoot dynamic IP addressing:

1. Open a Command Prompt window.

2. Enter `ipconfig /release` to release the IP address you leased from the DHCP server.

3. Enter `ipconfig /renew` to attempt to lease a new IP address.

4. Close the Command Prompt window.

Topic D
Install or Remove NetBEUI

As you've seen in this chapter, a network protocol is required for clients to be able to communicate on a network. Just as you might install TCP/IP as a client's network protocol, so might you install NetBEUI. On the other hand, you might encounter a computer on which unnecessary protocols for the user's network environment have been installed. So, in this topic, you'll learn how to install or remove NetBEUI as a network protocol on your users' Windows 2000- and Windows NT-based computers.

There are some situations in which using NetBEUI as the only network protocol might be the best choice for a network. For example, a network administrator might choose to use NetBEUI on a small network that doesn't connect to the Internet. Alternatively, you might encounter situations where you need to install NetBEUI as an additional network protocol in order for your clients to be able to access older, NetBEUI-based resources. Regardless of whether NetBEUI is the only network protocol or an additional protocol, it's important for you to know how to install it properly so that your users will be able to communicate with your network's resources. Conversely, network protocols do use additional resources such as RAM and network bandwidth on a computer. If the network environment doesn't require a particular protocol such as NetBEUI, you should be prepared to remove it from any clients to improve their performance.

The NetBEUI Protocol

The *NetBEUI* protocol is a small, *non-routable*, proprietary Microsoft network protocol. (A non-routable protocol cannot send data across routers.) It is supported by Windows 9x, Windows NT, and Windows 2000, but not Windows XP. When you install NetBEUI, it has no parameters to configure.

 By default, Windows XP does not include support for the NetBEUI protocol. If you're interested in configuring NetBEUI on Windows XP, refer to the Knowledge Base article # Q301041at **http://support.microsoft.com/default.aspx?scid=kb;en-us;Q301041**.

How to Install or Remove NetBEUI

Procedure Reference: Install NetBEUI in Windows 2000

To install NetBEUI in Windows 2000:

1. Log on as a user with administrative permissions.
2. Open Network And Dial-Up Connections.
3. Right-click Local Area Connection and choose Properties.
4. Click Install to install a new network component.
5. In the Select Network Component Type dialog box, select Protocol.
6. Click Add.
7. In the Network Protocol list, select NetBEUI Protocol.
8. Click OK to install the NetBEUI protocol.
9. Click Close to close the Local Area Connection Properties dialog box.
10. Close Network And Dial-Up Connections.
11. Test the NetBEUI protocol by verifying that you can see other NetBEUI-based computers in My Network Places.
    a. On the desktop, double-click My Network Places.
    b. Double-click Computers Near Me.
    c. Verify that you see other computers listed in Computers Near Me.
    d. Close the window.

Procedure Reference: Remove NetBEUI from Windows 2000

To remove NetBEUI from Windows 2000:

1. Log on as a user with administrative permissions.
2. Open Network And Dial-Up Connections.
3. Right-click Local Area Connection and choose Properties.
4. In the list of network components, select NetBEUI Protocol.

5. Click Uninstall to remove the protocol.
6. Click Yes to confirm that you want to remove the protocol.
7. Click Yes to confirm that you want to restart the computer.
8. Log back on to the computer.
9. Verify that the protocol is removed.
    a. Display the properties of the Local Area Connection.
    b. Make sure that the NetBEUI protocol is no longer displayed in the list of installed network components.
    c. Close any open dialog boxes and windows.

Procedure Reference: Install NetBEUI in Windows NT

To install NetBEUI in Windows NT:

1. Log on as a user with administrative permissions.
2. Open the Network dialog box. (From the Start menu, choose Settings→Control Panel. Double-click Network.)
3. Select the Protocols tab.
4. Click Add so that you can install a new protocol.
5. In the Network Protocol list, select NetBEUI Protocol and click OK.
6. In the Windows NT Setup dialog box, enter the path to the Windows NT installation files. (If necessary, insert the Windows NT CD-ROM into the computer's CD-ROM drive.)
7. Click Continue.
8. Click Close to close the Network dialog box.
9. When prompted, click Yes to restart the computer.
10. Log back on to the computer.
11. Test the NetBEUI protocol by verifying that you can see other NetBEUI-based computers in the Network Neighborhood.
    a. On the desktop, double-click Network Neighborhood.
    b. Verify that you see other computers listed in the Network Neighborhood.
    c. Close the window.

Procedure Reference: Remove NetBEUI from Windows NT

To remove NetBEUI from Windows NT:

1. Log on as a user with administrative permissions.
2. Open the Network dialog box.
3. Select the Protocols tab.

4. In the list of protocols, select NetBEUI Protocol.
5. Click Remove.
6. Click Yes to confirm that you want to remove the protocol.
7. Click Close to close the Network dialog box.
8. When prompted, click Yes to restart the computer.
9. Log back on to the computer.
10. Verify that the protocol is removed.
    a. In the Network dialog box, select the Protocols tab.
    b. Verify that you do not see the NetBEUI protocol listed.
    c. Close all open dialog boxes.

TOPIC E
Install or Remove NWLink IPX/SPX

So far in this chapter, you've learned how to install, configure, and troubleshoot the TCP/IP and NetBEUI protocols. But these aren't the only protocols you can use on a network. In this topic, you'll learn how to install the NWLink IPX/SPX protocol in Windows NT, Windows 2000, and Windows XP. And in case you encounter a computer on which the NWlink IPX/SPX protocol isn't needed, you'll also learn how to remove the protocol from these operating systems.

Although TCP/IP is the network protocol most commonly used on today's networks, it's possible that you'll encounter a situation where you'll need to install an alternative or additional protocol such as NWLink IPX/SPX. For example, you might be responsible for configuring clients to connect to older Novell NetWare servers that are running the IPX/SPX protocol. Knowing how to install NWLink IPX/SPX will enable you to configure computers to successfully communicate with IPX/SPX-based resources. You might also encounter computers on which the NWLink IPX/SPX protocol is no longer needed. Knowing how to remove the protocol will enable you to free up both memory and network bandwidth.

The NWLink IPX/SPX Protocol

The *NWLink IPX/SPX* network protocol is Microsoft's implementation of Novell's proprietary transport protocol, Internet Packet Exchange/Sequenced Packet Exchange (IPX/SPX). IPX/SPX was the default network protocol for older versions of Novell NetWare (all versions prior to NetWare 5). NetWare 5 and later versions use TCP/IP as their network protocol instead of IPX/SPX. You'll typically install NWLink IPX/SPX only if your Windows computers need access to an older NetWare server for file and print services or for accessing an application such as a database server.

NWLink IPX/SPX Configuration Settings

Table 11-5 provides you with a guide to the properties you might configure when you install the NWLink IPX/SPX protocol.

Table 11-5: *NWLink IPX/SPX Configuration Settings*

Setting	Description
Frame Type	Determines the format in which the computer sends data and expects to receive data. Computers running different frame types can't communicate. By default, Windows automatically attempts to find the frame type in use on the network and configures the computer to use this frame type. If Windows detects more than one frame type in use on the network, it configures the computer to use the default Ethernet frame type (called 802.2). If you have a mix of servers running different frame types, you might need to set the frame type manually.
External Network Number	Identifies the number assigned to the network. (This number is configured on the NetWare server.) By default, Windows automatically detects the External Network Number.
Internal Network Number	Uniquely identifies the computer; this number is also autodetected by Windows. You configure the Internal Network Number only if you are installing a computer with multiple network cards or running specialized network services on that computer.

How to Install or Remove NWLink IPX/SPX

Procedure Reference: Install NWLink IPX/SPX in Windows 2000

To install NWLink IPX/SPX in Windows 2000:

1. Log on as a user with administrative permissions.
2. Display the properties for the Local Area Connection. (In Network And Dial-up Connections, right-click Local Area Connection and choose Properties.)
3. Click Install to install a new network component.
4. In the Select Network Component Type dialog box, select Protocol.
5. Click Add.
6. In the Network Protocol list, select NWLink IPX/SPX/NetBIOS Compatible Transport Protocol.
7. Click OK to install the protocol.
8. If necessary, configure the frame type.

a. In the list of network components, select the NWLink IPX/SPX/NetBIOS Compatible Transport Protocol.

   b. Click Properties.

   c. From the Frame Type drop-down list, select the appropriate frame type for the network.

   d. Click OK to save your changes.

9. Click Close to close the Local Area Connection Properties dialog box.

10. Close Network And Dial-Up Connections.

11. Test the NWLink IPX/SPX protocol by verifying that you can see other computers in My Network Places.

    a. On the desktop, double-click My Network Places.

    b. Double-click Computers Near Me.

    c. Verify that you see other NWLink IPX/SPX-based computers listed in Computers Near Me.

    d. Close the window.

Procedure Reference: Remove NWLink IPX/SPX from Windows 2000

To remove NWLink IPX/SPX from Windows 2000:

1. Log on as a user with administrative permissions.

2. Display the properties for the Local Area Connection. (In Network And Dial-up Connections, right-click Local Area Connection and choose Properties.)

3. In the list of network components, select NWLink IPX/SPX/NetBIOS Compatible Transport Protocol.

4. Click Uninstall.

5. Click Yes to confirm that you want to remove the protocol.

6. Click Yes to restart the computer.

7. Log back on to the computer.

8. Close Network And Dial-Up Connections.

9. Verify that the protocol is removed.

   a. Display the properties of the Local Area Connection.

   b. Make sure that the NWLink IPX/SPX/NetBIOS Compatible Transport Protocol is no longer displayed in the list of installed network components.

   c. Close any open dialog boxes and windows.

Procedure Reference: Install NWLink IPX/SPX in Windows XP

To install NWLink IPX/SPX in Windows XP:

1. Log on as a user with administrative permissions.
2. Display the properties for the Local Area Connection. (In Network Connections, right-click Local Area Connection and choose Properties.)
3. Click Install to install a new network component.
4. In the Select Network Component Type dialog box, select Protocol.
5. Click Add.
6. In the Network Protocol list, select NWLink IPX/SPX/NetBIOS Compatible Transport Protocol.
7. Click OK to install the protocol.
8. If necessary, configure the frame type.
   a. In the list of network components, select the NWLink IPX/SPX/NetBIOS Compatible Transport Protocol.
   b. Click Properties.
   c. From the Frame Type drop-down list, select the appropriate frame type for the network.
   d. Click OK to save your changes.
9. Click Close to close the Local Area Connection Properties dialog box.
10. Close Network Connections.
11. Test the NWLink IPX/SPX protocol by verifying that you can see other computers in My Network Places.
    a. On the Start menu, click My Network Places.
    b. Click View Workgroup Computers.
    c. Verify that you see other NWLink IPX/SPX-based computers listed.
    d. Close the window.

Procedure Reference: Remove NWLink IPX/SPX from Windows XP

To remove NWLink IPX/SPX from Windows XP:

1. Log on as a user with administrative permissions.
2. Display the properties for the Local Area Connection. (In Network Connections, right-click Local Area Connection and choose Properties.)
3. Select the NWLink IPX/SPX/NetBIOS Compatible Transport Protocol.
4. Click Uninstall to remove the protocol.
5. Click Yes to confirm that you want to remove the protocol.

6. Click Yes to restart the computer.
7. Log back on to the computer.
8. Verify that the protocol is removed.
    a. Display the properties of the Local Area Connection.
    b. Make sure that the NWLink IPX/SPX/NetBIOS Compatible Transport Protocol is no longer displayed in the list of installed network components.
    c. Close any open dialog boxes and windows.

Procedure Reference: Install NWLink IPX/SPX on Windows NT

To install NWLink IPX/SPX on Windows NT:

1. Log on as a user with administrative permissions.
2. Open the Network dialog box.
3. Select the Protocols tab.
4. Click Add so that you can install a new protocol.
5. In the Network Protocol list, select NWLink IPX/SPX Compatible Transport and click OK.
6. In the Windows NT Setup dialog box, enter the path to the Windows NT installation files. (If necessary, insert the Windows NT CD-ROM into the computer's CD-ROM drive.)
7. Click Continue.
8. If necessary, configure the frame type.
    a. In the list of network protocols, select the NWLink IPX/SPX Compatible Transport.
    b. Click Properties.
    c. From the Frame Type drop-down list, select the appropriate frame type for the network.
    d. Click OK to save your changes.
9. Click Close to close the Network dialog box.
10. When prompted, click Yes to restart the computer.
11. Log back on to the computer.
12. Test the NWLink IPX/SPX protocol by verifying that you can browse the Network Neighborhood.
    a. On the desktop, double-click Network Neighborhood.
    b. Verify that you see other NWLink IPX/SPX-based computers listed in the Network Neighborhood.
    c. Close the window.

Procedure Reference: Remove NWLink IPX/SPX from Windows NT

To remove NWLink IPX/SPX from Windows NT:

1. Log on as a user with administrative permissions.
2. Open the Network dialog box.
3. Select the Protocols tab.
4. In the list of protocols, select NWLink IPX/SPX Compatible Transport.
5. Click Remove.
6. Click Yes to confirm that you want to remove the protocol.
7. Click Close to close the Network dialog box.
8. When prompted, click Yes to restart the computer.
9. Log back on to the computer.
10. Verify that the protocol is removed.
    a. In the Network dialog box, select the Protocols tab.
    b. Verify that you do not see the NWLink IPX/SPX Compatible Transport protocol listed.
    c. Close all open dialog boxes.

TOPIC F
Install a NetWare Client

As you saw in Topic 11E, installing the IPX/SPX protocol enables your clients to access applications on servers that are using the IPX/SPX protocol. But what if your clients also need to access shared file and print resources on these servers? If so, you'll need to install the NetWare client to enable your clients to access the servers' file and print resources. In this topic, you'll learn how to install the Windows NT, Windows 2000, and Windows XP clients for connecting to a NetWare server.

By default, all of the Windows operating systems automatically install a client for connecting to shared resources on Windows-based computers. But if you have NetWare servers on your network, without a NetWare client, your users won't be able to connect to the shared file and print resources on the NetWare servers. Installing the NetWare client on your users' computers will provide them with easy access to the resources on a NetWare server.

Network Client

Definition:

A *network client* is a software component that enables a computer to access a shared resource on another computer. The network client redirects requests for accessing shared resources to the appropriate computer on the network. By default, Windows 2000 and Windows XP automatically load the Client for Microsoft Networks if Windows setup detects a network card in the computer during installation. This client enables you to connect to shared resources on other Windows-based computers. (In Windows NT, the equivalent of the Client for Microsoft Networks is the Workstation service.) You can optionally install the Novell NetWare network client, the Client Service For NetWare, if you need to connect to shared resources on a NetWare server.

 On Windows 2000 and Windows XP, there is no configuration needed for the Client for Microsoft Networks. On Windows 9x, you can configure the client to validate a user's logon against the user database on a Windows domain.

Example:

In Figure 11-7, you see an example of how a network client sends a user's request for accessing a shared folder to the appropriate server on the network.

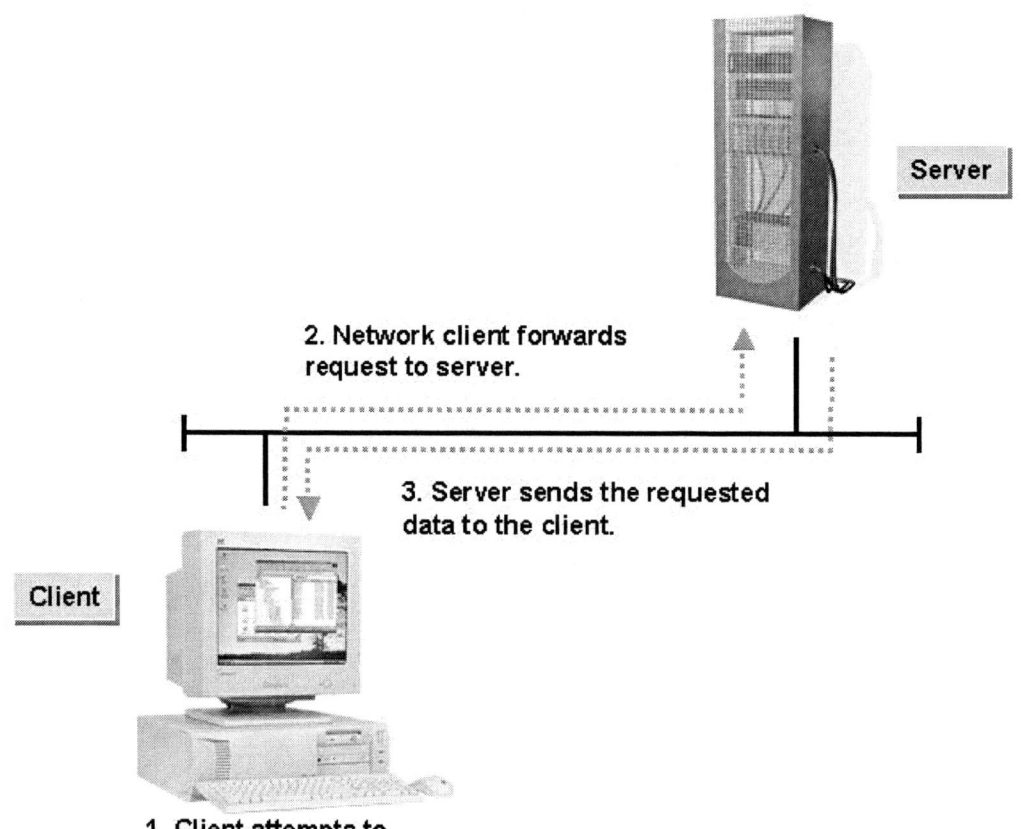

Figure 11-7: *A network client.*

NetWare Client Properties

When you install Client Service For NetWare, you can configure the properties listed in Table 11-6.

Table 11-6: *NetWare Client Properties*

Property	Description
Add Form Feed	This option configures Client Service For NetWare to add a form feed at the end of the user's print jobs to force the paper to feed out of the printer. With most application software, the applications send a form feed to force the paper out of the printer. So, if you enable this option, you'll typically see a blank sheet after each of the user's print jobs.

Property	Description
Default Tree And Context	If you're connecting the computer to NetWare 4.0 or a later version, use this property to specify the name of the NetWare server's directory tree and context.
Notify When Printed	By default, Client Service For NetWare configures the computer so that you're automatically notified when your print jobs are complete.
Preferred Server	If you're connecting the computer to a NetWare 3.12 server or earlier version, use the Preferred Server property to specify the name of the server to which you want to log on.
Print Banner	By default, Client Service For NetWare configures the computer to automatically print a banner page (a page that displays the user's login name for the NetWare server) whenever the user prints to a NetWare printer.
Run Login Script	This property enables you to choose whether you want the computer to run the NetWare server's login script whenever the user logs on to the computer.

How to Install a NetWare Client

Procedure Reference: Install NetWare Client in Windows 2000 and Windows XP

To install NetWare Client in Windows 2000 and Windows XP:

1. Log on as a user with administrative permissions.
2. Open the properties for the Local Area Connection.
3. If necessary, install the NWLink IPX/SPX/NetBIOS Compatible Transport Protocol.
4. Click Install.
5. Verify that Client is selected and click Add.
6. Select Client Service For NetWare and click OK.
7. If you're using Windows 2000, after a moment, in the Select NetWare Logon dialog box, configure the NetWare logon location information for the current user account.
   - If you're logging on to a NetWare 3.12 server or earlier version, verify that Preferred Server is selected. From the Preferred Server drop-down list, select the name of your NetWare server. Click OK.

- If you're logging on to a NetWare 4.0 server or later version, select Default Tree And Context. In the Tree text box, type the name of the NDS tree. In the Context text box, type the context within that tree where the user account exists. Click OK.
- If you don't currently have a NetWare server available to you, verify that <None> is selected in the Preferred Server drop-down list. Click OK.

8. Click Yes to restart the computer.

9. Log back on to the computer.

10. If you're using Windows XP, in the Select NetWare Logon dialog box, configure the NetWare logon location information for the current user account.
    - If you're logging on to a NetWare 3.12 server or earlier version, verify that Preferred Server is selected. From the Preferred Server drop-down list, select the name of your NetWare server. Click OK.
    - If you're logging on to a NetWare 4.0 server or later version, select Default Tree And Context. In the Tree text box, type the name of the NDS tree. In the Context text box, type the context within that tree where the user account exists. Click OK.
    - If you don't currently have a NetWare server available to you, verify that <None> is selected in the Preferred Server drop-down list. Click OK.

11. Configure the Print Options as necessary.
    a. Open Control Panel.
    b. If you're using Windows 2000, double-click CSNW.

       If you're using Windows XP, click the Other Control Panel Options link and then click CSNW.
    c. Below Print Options, uncheck Print Banner if you do not want to include a banner page in each print job.
    d. Uncheck Notify When Printed to prevent Windows from sending notifications when the print jobs are complete.
    e. Check Add Form Feed if you want the Client Service For NetWare to add a form feed at the end of the user's print jobs.
    f. Click OK to save your changes.

12. Close all open windows.

Procedure Reference: Remove NetWare Client in Windows 2000 and Windows XP

To remove NetWare Client from Windows 2000 and Windows XP:

1. Log on as a user with administrative permissions.

2. Open the properties for the Local Area Connection.

3. Select Client Service For NetWare and click Uninstall.

4. Click Yes to confirm that you want to uninstall Client Service For NetWare.

5. Click Yes to restart the computer.
6. Log back on to the computer.
7. Remove the NWLink IPX/SPX protocol if you no longer need it.

Procedure Reference: Install NetWare Client in Windows NT

To install NetWare Client in Windows NT:

1. Log on as a user with administrative permissions.
2. Open the Network dialog box.
3. If necessary, install the NWLink IPX/SPX Compatible Transport protocol.
4. Select the Services tab.
5. Click Add so that you can install a new network service.
6. In the Network Service list, select Client Service For NetWare.
7. Click OK to install the client.
8. In the Windows NT Setup dialog box, enter the path to the Windows NT installation files. (If necessary, insert the Windows NT CD-ROM into the computer's CD-ROM drive.)
9. Click Continue.
10. Click Close to close the Network dialog box.
11. Click Yes to restart the computer.
12. Log back on to the computer.
13. In the Select NetWare Logon dialog box, configure the NetWare logon location information for the current user account as follows:
    - If you're logging on to a NetWare 3.12 server or earlier version, verify that Preferred Server is selected. From the Preferred Server drop-down list, select the name of your NetWare server. Click OK.
    - If you're logging on to a NetWare 4.0 server or later version, select Default Tree And Context. In the Tree text box, type the name of the NDS tree. In the Context text box, type the context within that tree where the user account exists. Click OK.
    - If you don't currently have a NetWare server available to you, verify that <None> is selected in the Preferred Server drop-down list. Click OK.
14. Configure the Print Options as necessary.
    a. Open Control Panel.
    b. Double-click CSNW.
    c. Below Print Options, uncheck Print Banner if you do not want to include a banner page in each print job.
    d. Uncheck Notify When Printed to prevent Windows from sending notifications when the print jobs are complete.

  e. Check Add Form Feed if you want the Client Service For NetWare to add a form feed at the end of the user's print jobs.

  f. Click OK to save your changes.

Procedure Reference: Remove NetWare Client from Windows NT

To remove NetWare Client from Windows NT:

1. Log on as a user with administrative permissions.
2. Open the Network dialog box.
3. Select the Services tab.
4. In the Network Service list, select Client Service For NetWare.
5. Click Remove.
6. Click Yes to confirm that you want to remove Client Service For NetWare.
7. Remove the NWLink IPX/SPX protocol if you no longer need it.
8. Click Close to close the Network dialog box.
9. Click Yes to restart the computer.
10. Log back on to the computer.

TOPIC G
Configure a Network Connection in Windows 9x

Up to this point in the chapter, you've learned the steps for configuring the various network components for connecting Windows NT-, Windows 2000-, and Windows XP-based computers to a network. But what if you're called in to configure a network connection on a Windows 9x-based computer? To make sure you're prepared for such a call, in this topic, you'll learn the steps for configuring a network connection on a Windows 9x-based computer.

Not all companies have the latest and greatest computers for their users. In fact, it's quite common to encounter companies with older computers—and thus older operating systems such as Windows 98. As an A+ technician, you'll need to have the skills necessary for configuring network connections on such computers so that the computers' users can access the network resources they need to perform their jobs.

Primary Network Logon Types

Windows 98 supports four *primary network logon types*: Client For Microsoft Networks, Client For NetWare Networks, Microsoft Family Logon, and Windows Logon. These logon types are described in Table 11-7.

Table 11-7: *Windows 98 Network Logon Types*

Logon Type	Select as Primary Logon Type If You Want to Configure
Client For Microsoft Networks	The computer to log on to a Windows NT or Windows 2000 domain.
Client For NetWare Networks	The computer to log on to a NetWare server.
Microsoft Family Logon	The computer to list all user profiles on the computer. Use this option if you want users to be able to select their account names from a list and you have enabled user profiles.
Windows Logon	The computer to prompt for a user name and password, but not display a list of users on the computer.

 If you do not configure Client For Microsoft Networks with the name of a domain, there is no difference between using Client For Microsoft Networks and Windows Logon as the primary network logon type.

How to Configure a Network Connection in Windows 9x

Procedure Reference: Configure a Network Connection in Windows 9x

To configure a network connection in Windows 9x:

1. If necessary, update the network card driver.
    a. From the Start menu, choose Settings→Control Panel.
    b. Double-click System.
    c. Select the Device Manager tab.
    d. In the list of devices, expand Network Adapters.
    e. Select the network card driver and click Properties.
    f. Select the Driver tab.
    g. Click Update Driver.
    h. In the Update Device Driver Wizard, click Next.
    i. Verify that Search For A Better Driver Than The One Your Device Is Using Now is selected and click Next.
    j. Select the locations you want the wizard to search for a new driver. You can install the updated driver from any of the following locations:
        - Floppy disk
        - CD-ROM
        - The Microsoft Windows Update Web site
        - Local or shared network folder
    k. Click Next to search for an updated driver.

l. If the wizard found an updated driver, click Next.
m. Click Continue.
n. Click Finish to close the Update Device Driver Wizard.
o. Click Close to close the Properties dialog box for the network card.
p. Click Close to close System Properties.
q. Close Control Panel.

2. Configure the TCP/IP protocol.
   a. From the Start menu, choose Settings→Control Panel.
   b. Double-click Network.
   c. In the list of network components, select the TCP/IP→*network card type* component, where "network card type" is the name of the computer's network card.
   d. Click Properties.
   e. On the IP Address tab, configure the IP addressing information.
      - If you're configuring TCP/IP manually, select Specify An IP Address. Type the computer's IP address in the IP Address text box and the subnet mask in the Subnet Mask text box.
      - If you're configuring TCP/IP dynamically, select Obtain An IP Address Automatically.
   f. If you're configuring TCP/IP manually and the computer is on a network with a default gateway, configure the default gateway.
      1. Select the Gateway tab.
      2. In the New Gateway text box, type the IP address of the default gateway.
      3. Click Add.
   g. If you're configuring TCP/IP manually and the computer is on a network with DNS servers, enable and configure DNS.
      1. Select Enable DNS.
      2. In the Host text box, type the computer name.
      3. In the DNS Server Search Order text box, type the DNS server address and click Add.
      4. If another DNS server is available, type the IP address of the server in the DNS Server Search Order text box and click Add.

   (If you're configuring TCP/IP dynamically, you don't have to change anything on the DNS Configuration page. The DHCP server will automatically assign the IP addresses of the DNS servers to the computer.)

   h. If you're configuring TCP/IP manually and the computer is on a network with WINS servers, use the WINS Configuration tab to configure the WINS server information.
      1. Select Enable WINS Resolution.

2. In the WINS Server Search Order text box, type the WINS server address and click Add.

3. If another WINS server is available, type the IP address of the server in the WINS Server Search Order text box and click Add.

(If you're configuring TCP/IP dynamically, you don't have to change anything on the WINS Configuration page. The DHCP server will automatically assign the IP addresses of the WINS servers to the computer.)

    i. Click OK to save your TCP/IP configuration changes.

    j. Click OK to close the Network dialog box.

    k. When prompted, click Yes to restart the computer.

    l. Log back on to the computer.

    m. Close Control Panel.

3. If necessary, install the NetBEUI protocol.

    a. Open the Network dialog box (from the Start menu, choose Settings→Control Panel. Double-click Network).

    b. Click Add.

    c. In the Select Network Component Type dialog box, select Protocol and click Add.

    d. In the Manufacturers list, select Microsoft.

    e. In the Network Protocols list, select NetBEUI.

    f. Click OK to install the protocol.

    g. Click OK to close the Network dialog box.

    h. In the Insert Disk message box, click OK.

    i. In the Copying Files dialog box, enter the path to the Windows 98 installation files (if necessary, insert the Windows 98 CD-ROM into the computer's CD-ROM drive).

    j. When prompted, click Yes to restart the computer.

    k. Log back on to the computer.

    l. Close Control Panel.

4. If necessary, install the IPX/SPX-compatible Protocol.

    a. Open the Network dialog box (from the Start menu, choose Settings→Control Panel. Double-click Network).

    b. Click Add.

    c. In the Select Network Component Type dialog box, select Protocol and click Add.

    d. In the Manufacturers list, select Microsoft.

    e. In the Network Protocols list, select IPX/SPX-compatible Protocol.

    f. Click OK to install the protocol.

    g. Click OK to close the Network dialog box.

h. On the Insert Disk message box, click OK.

i. In the Copying Files dialog box, enter the path to the Windows 98 installation files and click OK (if necessary, insert the Windows 98 CD-ROM into the computer's CD-ROM drive).

j. When prompted, click Yes to restart the computer.

k. Log back on to the computer.

l. Close Control Panel.

5. If necessary, install Client For NetWare Networks.

> If you install Client For NetWare Networks and you do not have the IPX/SPX-Compatible Protocol installed, Windows 9x automatically installs it for you.

a. Open the Network dialog box.

b. In the Manufacturers list, select Microsoft.

c. In the Network Clients list, select Client For NetWare Networks.

d. Click OK to install the client.

e. Click OK to close the Network dialog box.

f. On the Insert Disk message box, click OK.

g. In the Copying Files dialog box, enter the path to the Windows 98 installation files and click OK. (If necessary, insert the Windows 98 CD-ROM into the computer's CD-ROM drive.)

h. When prompted, click Yes to restart the computer.

i. Log back on to the computer.

6. If necessary, configure the Primary Network Logon.

a. Open the Network dialog box.

b. From the Primary Network Logon drop-down list, select the logon type appropriate for the computer.

- Use Client For Microsoft Networks if you want the computer to log on to a Windows NT or Windows 2000 domain.
- Use Client For NetWare Networks if you want the computer to log on to a NetWare server.
- Use Microsoft Family Logon if you want to provide users with a list of available user accounts from which to choose.
- Use Windows Logon if you want to have Windows 98 prompt the user for a user name and password.

c. Click OK to save your changes.

d. When prompted, click Yes to restart the computer.

e. Log back on to the computer.

7. Test the network connection by using a utility such as the IP Configuration utility (Winipcfg) or browsing the Network Neighborhood.

Procedure Reference: Test TCP/IP Connectivity with the IP Configuration Utility (Winipcfg)

To test TCP/IP connectivity with the IP Configuration Utility:

1. From the Start menu, choose Run.
2. In the Open text box, type winipcfg.
3. Click OK to run Winipcfg.
4. Click More Info to display detailed IP addressing information.
5. If necessary, from the drop-down list, select the computer's network card.
6. Review the IP addressing information.
7. If the computer's IP address is assigned dynamically and you're experiencing problems, you can click the Release and Renew buttons to force it to renew its IP address lease.
8. Click OK to close the IP Configuration dialog box.

CHAPTER 11 FOLLOW-UP
Installing Network Components

In this chapter, you learned how to install the components necessary for connecting Windows 2000, Windows 9x, Windows NT, and Windows XP computers to a network. For example, you learned how to make sure a computer is using the latest driver for its network card and how to install any of the supported network protocols. In addition, you learned how to troubleshoot problems with TCP/IP. By mastering all of these skills, you'll be able to quickly and easily set up users' connections to the network.

Essential Terms

- connectivity
- drivers
- IP addresses
- ISPs
- NetBEUI
- NetWare clients
- network cards
- network clients
- network connections
- network protocols
- NWLink IPX/SPX
- Plug and Play
- subnet masks
- TCP/IP
- troubleshooting
- troubleshooting tools

Review Questions

1. What utility do you use to verify the status of hardware devices?

2. What is the default gateway?
3. What must be the first number always be in a subnet mask?
4. What three Windows operating systems support TCP/IP, NWLINK IP X/SPX, and Net Beui network protocols?
5. Which Windows operating system does not support NetBeui?
6. What is the purpose of the subnet mask?
7. What information is stored in the databases of both the DNS and the WINS server?
8. In computer networking, what is a host?
9. Windows 98, 2000, and XP support two methods of assigning IP addresses to computers automatically. What are the two methods?
10. What method of assigning IP addresses to computers automatically does Windows NT 4.0 support?
11. Your computer has an IP address of 192.168.2.200 and a subnet mask of 255.255.255.0. What part of the IP address refers to the network?
12. When booting up your Windows 2000 computer, you machine attempts to communicate with a DHCP server to get an IP address. If the DHCP server does not respond, what address will the machine receive?
13. What command do you use to verify the configuration of TCP/IP on a computer?
14. Your computer receives a private address of 169.254.2.20 and you want to release the IP addressing information so the computer receives its address from a DHCP server that came online. What two commands and parameters should you use?
15. What command do you use to verify that a computer can communicate across the network using the TCP/IP protocol?
16. Windows NT 4.0 and Windows 2000 computers support Macintosh's routable network protocol natively. What is the Macintosh network protocol?
17. When you issue the ping command, how many queries does your computer send out to the computer associated with the IP address you specified?
18. AppleTalk arranges network components into three main subsets. What are the three subsets?
19. What are the three phases of the troubleshooting process?
20. What is the purpose of Nslookup?
21. You test the connectivity of a computer you set up and the computer cannot communicate with other hosts on the same subnet. What is the most likely problem?
22. What is netbeui?
23. On Microsoft systems, what protocol allows you to configure clients to connect to older Novell NetWare servers that are running the IP protocol?
24. What are the four primary network logon types that Windows 98 supports?
25. What does it mean to say that a protocol is routable?
26. What network protocol is used by Apple computers running the Mac OS X (version 10.2 and above)?

27. Before you purchase new hardware for a computer running Windows, what Microsoft database should you consult?
28. What is the function of tracert?
29. What is the loopback address?
30. Why would you ping the loopback address?
31. In order for your Windows clients to access resources on a Novell NetWare server, what network client should you install on the Windows machines?

Review Projects

Project #1 Discovering IBM's Redbooks

IBM offers publications called Redbooks, which are detailed discussions about various technologies, concepts, and architecture. The TCP/IP Tutorial and Technical Overview Redbook is a book-length treatment of TCP/IP. Although the Redbook is long, IBM published it as a PDF so you can move thoughout the doument easily and print only those areas of specific interest to you. Further, the document includes a table of contents so you can quickly identify the material covered in each chapter.

The Redbook is located at **http://www.redbooks.ibm.com/pubs/pdfs/redbooks/gg243376.pdf**. Once the document opens, click the icon that looks like a floppy disk located on the toolbar. Create a subfolder on your hard drive (located under the folder hardware documentation) and name it TCP.

In this activity, read through the first two to three chapters and skim the rest. The beginning of the document provides historical information about the development of TCP/IP and it introduces you to some of the terminology. You'll also find that this document will provide information about some of the material covered later in this course.

As you read through some of the Redbook, there may be terms unfamiliar to you. The Core Technology Glossary should prove to be a helpful reference (**http://www.cren.net/know/glossary/glossary.html**).

Project #2 TCP/IP Troubleshooting

Most networks run the TCP/IP protocols and there will be times when you'll need to troubleshoot various connectivity problems. Your course text introduces you to some of the more important utilities that will help you localize problems. The ipconfig command allows you to verify your TCP/IP configuration and the ping command enables you to verify that the computer can communicate with other computers across the network. You'll revisit the ipconfig and ping commands and you'll be introduced to commands that will help you diagnose a range of TCP/IP problems. The TCP/IP troubleshooting guide from Microsoft's Technet Web site is located at **http://www.microsoft.com/technet/treeview/default.asp?url=/technet/prodtechnol/winxppro/reskit/prcc_tcp_gfhp.asp**. When the page opens, you'll see a short introductory page in the main window. On the left side of the page is a list of topics. Work through each of the topics listed under TCP/IP Troubleshooting. As you work, keep a command prompt open and test as many utilities as you can. To see the full syntax of any of the commands discussed, type the command followed by /? . For example, to see the full syntax of the print command, type ping /? at the command prompt.

Project #3 Introduction to DNS

The domain name system enables you to use friendly names to locate computers and other resources on an IP network. It's easier for people to recall names than it is to recall the quad notation used for IP addresses. For example, when you surf the Web, you know that Microsoft's Web site is **http://www.microsoft.com** and Element K's Web site is **http://www.elementk.com**. Imagine how difficult it would be if you had to recall the IP addresses of both of those sites. It's much easier to remember the "friendly name" than it is to recall the IP address.

In this activity, you'll learn more about DNS and its importance on an IP network. Microsoft provides an excellent overview of the system, its namespace, and concepts. You'll find that DNS is a fairly involved system, but the key to this activity is to familiarize yourself with the name resolution process. Read through the material located at **http://www.microsoft.com/technet/treeview/default.asp?url=/technet/prodtechnol/windows2000serv/reskit/tcpip/part2/tcpch05.asp**. If your computer is on a network that's running a DNS server, ping computers around you by their names to test name resolution. If your computer is not on a network but you're connected to the Internet, open a command prompt and point Yahoo: ping www.yahoo.com. You should receive 4 echo replies back which indicates that the server was found. Take a snapshot of the output using print screen (PrtSc).

Reflective Questions

1. In your work environment, what network protocols will you be using?

2. If you have worked with TCP/IP in a network environment, what types of problems have you encountered? How did you troubleshoot these problems?

CHAPTER 12
Implementing Local Security in Windows 2000/NT/XP

Chapter Objectives:

In this chapter, you will implement local security in Windows 2000/NT/XP.

You will:

- Create or delete local user accounts.
- Modify user account properties.
- Set the workgroup or domain membership.
- Configure file and folder security.
- Encrypt files and folders.

Introduction

As an A+ technician, one of the big concerns you'll be expected to address for your users and clients is how to secure their computers. Security is important for both networked and stand-alone computers. In this chapter, you'll learn the techniques and strategies you can use to secure a Windows 2000-, Windows NT-, or Windows XP-based computer.

If you don't properly secure a computer and its data, you leave it vulnerable to accidental or intentional loss and misuse. It is essential, as an A+ technician, that you implement security to prevent these threats from resulting in costly intrusions, loss of critical data, and lost productivity.

TOPIC A
Create or Delete Local User Accounts

One of the first things a user must do when she sits down at a Windows 2000-, Windows XP-, or Windows NT-based computer is to log on. In these operating systems, any activity the user performs must be in the context of a logged-on user account. Before your users can log on, they must have user accounts. On the other hand, you also need to know how to delete a local user account so that you can protect the computer from unauthorized access. In this topic, you'll learn how to create and delete local user accounts.

Logging on to a computer is like giving a user a key to unlock your company's front door. Without the key, the user won't be able to get to her office to begin working. And without being able to log on to her computer, the user won't be able to do the tasks she needs to perform her job. As an A+ technician, setting up and configuring local user logon accounts will be one of the tasks you'll be expected to perform. Setting up these logon accounts properly for any situation will help your users gain access to their computers so that they can get their work done. Knowing how to delete user accounts enables you to protect the computer from situations such as preventing a user who leaves the company (especially if the user is fired) from logging on to a computer. Such disgruntled users may attempt to damage the computer's data—which can cost your company a lot of time and money due to the loss of productivity.

Local Security

Windows 2000, Windows XP, and Windows NT are secure operating systems, which means that you cannot access a computer running one of these operating systems without logging on as a valid user. A valid user is one that has an account in the Windows 2000, Windows XP, or Windows NT user database on the specific computer to which you're attempting to log on. Such a user account is called "local," because it must be created in the user database on the computer where you log on.

The Built-in User and Group Accounts

Windows 2000 Professional, Windows NT Workstation, and Windows XP Professional include two user and six group accounts that are created automatically when you install the operating system. The *built-in user accounts* are Administrator and Guest. These accounts are described in Table 12-1. Windows XP comes with two additional built-in user accounts; we describe them in Table 12-2. The group accounts are Administrators, Backup Operators, Guests, Power Users, Replicator, and Users. The *built-in groups*, along with their default members, are described in Table 12-3. As you saw with user accounts, Windows XP includes three additional built-in groups. We describe these groups in Table 12-4.

Table 12-1: *Built-in User Accounts*

User Account	Provides
Administrator	Complete administrative access to the computer.
Guest	Limited computer access to persons without a logon user account. By default, the Guest account is disabled when you install the operating system. You enable this account only if you want to permit users to log on as Guest.

Table 12-2: *Windows XP-only Built-in User Accounts*

User Account	Provides
HelpAssistant	Access to the computer during a Remote Assistance session.
Support	Access to Microsoft's Web-based Help and Support services.

Table 12-3: *Built-in Group Accounts*

Group Account	Enables Members To	Default Members
Administrators	Perform all administrative tasks on the computer.	Administrator. In Windows XP, this group also includes an account you create during installation.
Backup Operators	Back up and restore files to which the members do not otherwise have permissions.	None
Guests	Perform any tasks for which the group has permissions.	Guest

Group Account	Enables Members To	Default Members
Power Users	Run pre-Windows 2000 applications, modify some system-wide settings (such as the time), install some programs, and manage some local accounts.	None
Replicator	Participate in domain-based file replication.	None
Users	Run applications and perform other day-to-day computer tasks. Perform any task for which the group has been granted permissions.	All user accounts

Table 12-4: *Windows XP-only Built-in Group Accounts*

Group Account	Enables Members To	Default Members
Network Configuration Operators	Manage network configuration.	None
Remote Desktop Users	Log on to the computer remotely.	None
HelpServicesGroup	Connect to Microsoft's Web-based Help and Support service.	Support user account

How to Create or Delete Local User Accounts

Procedure Reference: Create a Local User Account in Windows 2000

To create a local user account in Windows 2000:

1. Log on as a local computer administrator.
2. From the Start menu, choose Settings→Control Panel.
3. Double-click Administrative Tools.
4. Double-click Computer Management.
5. Below System Tools, expand Local Users And Groups.
6. Select the Users folder.
7. Right-click Users and choose New User.
8. In the User Name text box, type the new user's account name.
9. In the Full Name text box, type the user's full name.

10. In the Password text box, type the user's password.

11. In the Confirm Password text box, re-type the user's password.

12. Select the desired account options. (See Table 12-5.)

13. Click Create to create the new user account.

14. Click Close to close the New User dialog box.

15. Close Computer Management.

16. Close Control Panel.

17. Test the account by logging on as the user.

Table 12-5: *Local Account Options*

Check This Box	Use To
User Must Change Password At Next Logon	Force the user to change the password you assign when you create the account.
User Cannot Change Password	Prevent the user from changing the password you assign to the account.
Password Never Expires	Prevent the user's password from expiring, regardless of any password-expiration policies you establish.
Account Is Disabled	Prevent someone from logging on as this user.

Procedure Reference: Delete a Local User Account in Windows 2000

To delete a local user account in Windows 2000:

1. Log on as a local computer administrator.

2. Open Computer Management. (In Control Panel, double-click Administrative Tools and then double-click Computer Management. Alternatively, you can right-click the My Computer icon and choose Manage.)

3. Below System Tools, expand Local Users And Groups.

4. In the console tree, select Users.

5. In the details pane, right-click the user you want to delete and choose Delete.

6. Click Yes to confirm that you want to delete this user account.

7. Close Computer Management (and Control Panel if necessary).

Procedure Reference: Create a Local User Account in Windows XP

To create a local user account in Windows XP:

1. Log on as a local computer administrator.

2. In Control Panel, select the Performance And Maintenance category.
3. Click Administrative Tools.
4. Double-click Computer Management.
5. Below System Tools, expand Local Users And Groups.
6. Select the Users folder.
7. Right-click the Users folder and choose New User.
8. In the User Name text box, type the new user's account name.
9. In the Full Name text box, type the user's full name.
10. In the Password text box, type the user's password.
11. In the Confirm Password text box, re-type the user's password.
12. Select the desired account options. (See Table Table 12-5.)
13. Click Create to create the new user account.
14. Click Close.
15. Close Computer Management and Control Panel.
16. Test the account by logging on as the user.

Procedure Reference: Delete a Local User Account in Windows XP

To delete a local user account in Windows XP:

1. Log on as a local computer administrator.
2. In Control Panel, select the Performance And Maintenance category.
3. Click Administrative Tools.
4. Double-click Computer Management.
5. Below System Tools, expand Local Users And Groups.
6. Select the Users folder.
7. In the details pane, right-click the user you want to delete and choose Delete.
8. Click Yes to confirm that you want to delete this user.
9. Close Computer Management and Control Panel.

Procedure Reference: Create a Local User Account in Windows NT

To create a local user account in Windows NT:

1. Log on as a local computer administrator.
2. From the Start menu, choose Programs→Administrative Tools→User Manager.

3. Choose User→New User.
4. In the Username text box, type the new user's account name.
5. In the Full Name text box, type the user's full name.
6. In the Password text box, type the user's password.
7. In the Confirm Password text box, re-type the user's password.
8. Select the desired account options. (See Table 12-5.)
9. Click OK to create the new user account.
10. Close User Manager.
11. Test the account by logging on as the user.

Procedure Reference: Delete a Local User Account in Windows NT

To delete a local user account in Windows NT:

1. Log on as a local computer administrator.
2. From the Start menu, choose Programs→Administrative Tools→User Manager.
3. Select the user you want to delete.
4. Choose User→Delete.
5. Click OK to acknowledge the warning message about deleting user accounts.
6. Click Yes to delete the account.
7. Close User Manager.

Procedure Reference: Delete a Local User Profile in Windows 2000

To delete a local user profile in Windows 2000:

1. Log on as a local computer administrator.
2. Open Control Panel and double-click System. (Alternatively, you can right-click the My Computer icon and choose Properties.)
3. Select the User Profiles tab.

   A user profile with a name of Account Unknown indicates that the user account no longer exists on the computer. You can safely delete these profiles.

4. Select a profile with the name of Account Unknown.
5. Click Delete.
6. Click Yes to confirm that you want to delete the profile.
7. Repeat these steps to delete any other profiles with the name of Account Unknown.

8. Click OK to close System Properties.
9. Close Control Panel.
10. In Windows Explorer, verify that you no longer see folders within \Documents and Settings for users whose accounts you have deleted.

Procedure Reference: Delete a Local User Profile in Windows XP

To delete a local user profile in Windows XP:

1. Log on as a local computer administrator.
2. On the Start menu, right-click My Computer and choose Properties.
3. Select the Advanced tab.
4. Below User Profiles, click Settings.

 A user profile with a name of Account Unknown indicates that the user account no longer exists on the computer. You can safely delete these profiles.

5. Select a profile with the name of Account Unknown.
6. Click Delete.
7. Click Yes to confirm that you want to delete the profile.
8. Repeat these steps to delete any other profiles with the name of Account Unknown.
9. Click OK to close the User Profiles dialog box.
10. Click OK to close System Properties.
11. In Windows Explorer, verify that you no longer see folders within \Documents and Settings for users whose accounts you have deleted.

Procedure Reference: Delete a Local User Profile in Windows NT

To delete a local user profile in Windows NT:

1. Log on as a local computer administrator.
2. Open Control Panel and double-click System. (You can also right-click the My Computer icon and choose Properties.)
3. Select the User Profiles tab.

 A user profile with a name of Account Unknown indicates that the user account no longer exists on the computer. You can safely delete these profiles.

4. Select a profile with the name of Account Unknown.
5. Click Delete.
6. Click Yes to confirm that you want to delete the profile.

7. Repeat these steps to delete any other profiles with the name of Account Unknown.
8. Click OK to close System Properties.
9. In Windows Explorer, verify that you no longer see folders within the \Winnt\Profiles folder for users whose accounts you have deleted.

Topic B
Modify User Account Properties

In Topic 12A, you learned how to both create and delete user accounts with the default set of properties. In many cases, these default properties won't fit the needs of your company. In this topic, you'll learn how to modify the properties of local user accounts.

You're bound to run into situations where a user doesn't like his logon name or another user forgets her password after her two-week vacation. You'll also encounter situations such as a user not having the privileges he needs. As an A+ technician, it will be your job to straighten out these problems. The good news is that you can solve these problems by modifying the user accounts.

User Account Properties

After you have created a user account, there are several properties for the user account you can change. Some of the properties you can change include:

- Renaming the account. You might do so if a user leaves your company and a new person takes the user's job. Instead of creating a new account for the new person, you can provide them with access to the computer by renaming the old user's account.
- Changing the user's password. You'll typically be asked to change a user's password when he forgets it.
- Adding the user as a member of a group or removing the user from a group.

How to Modify User Account Properties

Procedure Reference: Rename a User Account in Windows 2000/XP/NT

To rename a user account in Windows 2000, Windows XP, and Windows NT:

1. Log on as a local computer administrator.
2. Open the appropriate user account management tool for the computer's operating system:
   - If you're using Windows 2000 or Windows XP, open Computer Management.
   - If you're using Windows NT, open User Manager.
3. If you're using Windows 2000 or Windows XP, complete the following steps:
   a. Expand Local Users And Groups.
   b. Select the Users folder.

      c. Right-click the user you want to rename and choose Rename.

      d. Type the new name for the user and press Enter.

4. If you're using Windows NT, complete the following steps:

      a. In the list of users, select the user you want to rename.

      b. Choose User→Rename.

      c. In the Change To text box, type the new name for the user.

      d. Click OK.

5. Close the user account management tool.

Procedure Reference: Rename a User's Profile in Windows 2000 or Windows XP

To rename a user's profile in Windows 2000 or Windows XP:

1. Log on as a local computer administrator.
2. Open Windows Explorer.
3. Select the appropriate user profiles folder.
   - If you're using Windows 2000 or Windows XP, select \Documents And Settings.
   - If you're using Windows NT, select \Winnt\Profiles.
4. Right-click the folder you want to rename and choose Rename.
5. Enter a new name for the folder.
6. Close Windows Explorer.

Procedure Reference: Change a User's Password in Windows 2000/XP/NT

To change a user's password in Windows 2000, Windows XP, and Windows NT:

1. Log on as a local computer administrator.
2. Open the appropriate user account management tool for the computer's operating system:
   - If you're using Windows 2000 or Windows XP, open Computer Management.
   - If you're using Windows NT, open User Manager.

   ⚠️ In Windows XP, resetting a user's password will prevent them from accessing any encrypted files. You should reset a user's password only as a last resort.

3. If you're using Windows 2000 or Windows XP, complete the following steps:

      a. Expand Local Users And Groups.

      b. Select the Users folder.

      c. Right-click the user for whom you want to change the password and choose Set Password.

      d. If you're using Windows XP, click Proceed.

e. In the New Password text box, type the new password for the user.

f. In the Confirm Password text box, type the password again.

g. Click OK.

4. If you're using Windows NT, complete the following steps:

   a. In the list of users, double-click the user whose password you want to reset.

   b. In the Password text box, type the new password for the user.

   c. In the Confirm Password text box, type the password again.

   d. Click OK.

5. Close the user account management tool.

Procedure Reference: Modify a User's Group Memberships in Windows 2000/XP/NT

To modify a user's group memberships in Windows 2000, Windows XP, and Windows NT:

1. Log on as a local computer administrator.

2. Open the appropriate user account management tool for the computer's operating system:
   - If you're using Windows 2000 or Windows XP, open Computer Management.
   - If you're using Windows NT, open User Manager.

3. If you're using Windows 2000 and you want to add the user as a member of a group, complete the following steps:

   a. Expand Local Users And Groups.

   b. Select the Users folder.

   c. Double-click the user for whom you want to change group memberships.

   d. Select the Member Of tab.

   e. Click Add.

   f. Select the group or groups to which you want to add the user and click Add.

   g. Click OK to close the Select Groups dialog box.

   h. Click OK to close the user's Properties dialog box.

4. If you're using Windows XP and you want to add the user as a member of a group, complete the following steps:

   a. Expand Local Users And Groups.

   b. Select the Users folder.

   c. Double-click the user for whom you want to change group memberships.

   d. Select the Member Of tab.

   e. Click Add.

   f. If you know the name of the group to which you want to add the user, enter it under Enter The Object Names To Select and click OK.

    g.   If you want to search for the group to which you want to add the user:

          1.   Click Advanced.

          2.   Click Find Now to display a list of groups.

          3.   Select the desired group or groups and click OK.

    h.   Click OK to close the Select Groups dialog box.

    i.   Click OK to close the user's Properties dialog box.

5.   If you're using Windows NT and you want to add the user as a member of a group, complete the following steps:

    a.   Double-click the user.

    b.   Click Groups.

    c.   From the Not Member Of list, select the group to which you want to add the user and click Add.

    d.   Click OK to close the Group Memberships dialog box.

    e.   Click OK to close the user's Properties dialog box.

6.   If you're using Windows 2000 or Windows XP and you want to remove the user from a group, complete the following steps:

    a.   Expand Local Users And Groups.

    b.   Select the Users folder.

    c.   Double-click the user for whom you want to change group memberships.

    d.   Select the Member Of tab.

    e.   Select the group from which you want to remove the user.

    f.   Click Remove.

    g.   Click OK to close the user's Properties dialog box.

7.   If you're using Windows NT and you want to remove the user from a group, complete the following steps:

    a.   Double-click the user.

    b.   Click Groups.

    c.   From the Member Of list, select the group from which you want to remove the user and click Remove.

    d.   Click OK to close the Group Memberships dialog box.

    e.   Click OK to close the user's Properties dialog box.

8.   Close the user account management tool.

Procedure Reference: Modify Other User Account Properties in Windows 2000/XP/NT

To modify other user account properties in Windows 2000, Windows XP, and Windows NT:

1.   Log on as a local computer administrator.

2. Open the appropriate user account management tool for the computer's operating system:
   - If you're using Windows 2000 or Windows XP, open Computer Management.
   - If you're using Windows NT, open User Manager.
3. If you're using Windows 2000 or Windows XP and you want to modify the user's full name, description, or password options, complete the following steps:
   a. Expand Local Users And Groups.
   b. Select the Users folder.
   c. Double-click the user for whom you want to change properties.
   d. On the General page, enter the new full name, description, or desired password options.
   e. Click OK to close the user's Properties dialog box.
4. If you're using Windows NT and you want to modify the user's full name, description, or password options, complete the following steps:
   a. Double-click the user.
   b. Enter the new full name, description, or desired password options.
   c. Click OK to close the user's Properties dialog box.
5. Close the user account management tool.

Topic C
Set Workgroup or Domain Membership

Another security task you might be called to do is to configure the local computer's workgroup or domain membership. As an A+ technician, you'll need the skills for setting and changing a computer's workgroup or domain membership. For example, you might be assigned the task of configuring the workstations on a network to join a new domain that the network administrator has just installed. In this topic, you'll identify the differences between a workgroup and a domain and learn how to configure a computer as a member of each.

Configuring a computer as a member of a domain or a workgroup enables you to make sure that the shared resources on the computer are available to the appropriate users. For example, by configuring the computer's domain or workgroup membership, you make it possible for users to connect to that computer by browsing the appropriate domain or workgroup in either My Network Places (in Windows 2000) or the Network Neighborhood (in Windows NT).

Workgroup

Definition:

A *workgroup* is a Microsoft network model that groups computers together for organizational purposes. The computers that make up a workgroup appear together when you browse the Network Neighborhood in Windows NT or My Network Places in Windows 2000 and Windows XP. In addition, each Windows 2000, Windows XP, and Windows NT computer in the workgroup maintains its own user account database. This means that if a user wants to log on at any computer within the workgroup, you must create the user's account on each computer in the workgroup.

Example:

In Figure 12-1, you see an example of a workgroup. Notice that each computer has its own user account database.

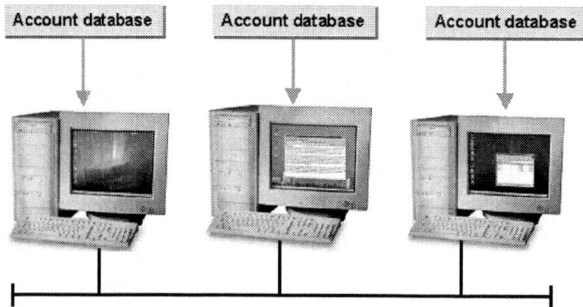

Figure 12-1: *Computers in a workgroup.*

Domain

Definition:

A *domain* is a Microsoft network model that groups computers together for security and to centralize administration. Computers that are members of a domain have access to a shared central user account database, which means that a user can use a single user account to log on at any computer within the domain. Administration is centralized because you need to create the user accounts only in the domain, not on each computer. The shared central user account database is stored on specialized servers called *domain controllers*. Like a workgroup, computers that are members of a domain appear together when you browse the Network Neighborhood in Windows NT or My Network Places in Windows 2000 and Windows XP.

Example:

In Figure 12-1, you see an example of a domain. Notice that each computer has access to the shared domain user account database.

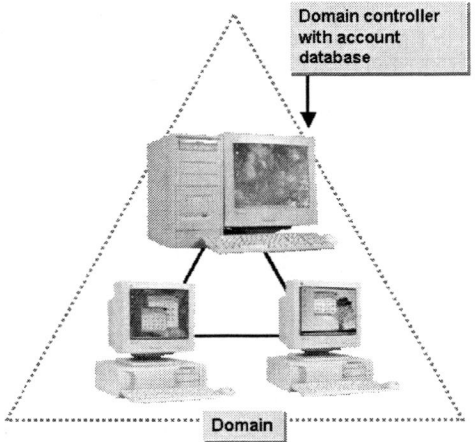

Figure 12-2: *Computers in a domain.*

Domain Policies

When a computer is a member of a domain, it's possible for the administrator of the domain to create policies to restrict the activities that a user can perform on the computer. For example, an administrator can establish a policy that prevents users from changing the color scheme or wallpaper on the computer. In a Windows 2000 or Windows Server 2003 Active Directory domain, this type of policy is called a *group policy object* and is administered as part of the Active Directory. In a Windows NT domain, the equivalent policy is called a *system policy*; the domain administrator implements this system policy by creating a file with the necessary restrictions. As an A+ technician, it's possible that you might encounter a scenario where you are restricted from performing a specific configuration task due to a policy assigned by the domain administrator.

How to Set the Workgroup or Domain Membership

Procedure Reference: Configure Workgroup Membership in Windows 2000

To configure workgroup membership in Windows 2000:

1. Log on as a local computer administrator.
2. Open Control Panel.
3. Double-click System.
4. Select the Network Identification tab.
5. Click Properties.
6. In the Workgroup Name text box, type the name of the workgroup and click OK. The default workgroup name is WORKGROUP.
7. Click OK to close the Network Identification message.

8. Click OK to close the message stating that you must reboot the computer before your change will take effect.
9. Click OK to close the System Properties dialog box.
10. Click Yes to confirm that you want to reboot the computer.
11. Log back on to the computer.
12. Close Control Panel.

Procedure Reference: Configure Domain Membership in Windows 2000

To configure domain membership in Windows 2000:

1. Log on as a local computer administrator.
2. Open Control Panel.
3. Double-click System.
4. Select the Network Identification tab.
5. Click Properties.
6. Below Member Of, select Domain.
7. In the Domain text box, type the name of the domain and click OK.
8. In the Domain Username And Password dialog box, enter the name and password of a domain user account with the authority to add a computer to the domain.
9. Click OK.
10. Click OK to close the Network Identification message.
11. Click OK to close the message stating that you must reboot the computer before your change will take effect.
12. Click OK to close the System Properties dialog box.
13. Click Yes to confirm that you want to reboot the computer.
14. Verify that you can log on to the domain.
    a. When the Welcome To Windows dialog box is displayed, press Ctrl+Alt+Delete.
    b. In the User Name text box, type the domain user account name.
    c. In the Password text box, type the domain user account's password.
    d. From the Log On To drop-down list, select the domain name.
    e. Click OK to log on to the domain.

Procedure Reference: Configure Workgroup Membership in Windows XP

To configure workgroup membership in Windows XP:

1. Log on as a local computer administrator.

2. From the Start menu, right-click My Computer and choose Properties.

3. Select the Computer Name tab.

4. Click Change.

5. In the Workgroup Name text box, type the name of the workgroup and click OK. The default workgroup name is WORKGROUP.

6. Click OK to close the Computer Name Changes message.

7. Click OK to close the message stating that you must reboot the computer before your change will take effect.

8. Click OK to close the System Properties dialog box.

9. Click Yes to confirm that you want to reboot the computer.

10. Log back on to the computer.

Procedure Reference: Configure Domain Membership in Windows XP

To configure domain membership in Windows XP:

1. Log on as a local computer administrator.

2. From the Start menu, right-click My Computer and choose Properties.

3. Select the Computer Name tab.

4. Click Change.

5. Below Member Of, select Domain.

6. In the Domain text box, type the name of the domain and click OK.

7. In the Domain Username And Password dialog box, enter the name and password of a domain user account with the authority to add a computer to the domain.

8. Click OK.

9. Click OK to close the Computer Name Changes message.

10. Click OK to close the message stating that you must reboot the computer before your change will take effect.

11. Click OK to close the System Properties dialog box.

12. Click Yes to confirm that you want to reboot the computer.

13. Verify that you can log on to the domain.

    a. When the Welcome To Windows dialog box is displayed, press Ctrl+Alt+Delete.

    b. In the User Name text box, type the domain user account name.

    c. In the Password text box, type the domain user account's password.

    d. Click Options.

    e. From the Log On To drop-down list, select the domain name.

f. Click OK to log on to the domain.

Procedure Reference: Configure Workgroup Membership in Windows NT

To configure workgroup membership in Windows NT:

1. Log on as a local computer administrator.
2. Open Control Panel.
3. Double-click Network.
4. Click Change.
5. In the Workgroup text box, type the name of the workgroup and click OK. The default workgroup name is WORKGROUP.
6. Click OK to close the Network Configuration message box.
7. Click Close to close the Network dialog box.
8. Click Yes to confirm that you want to reboot the computer.
9. Log back on to the computer.
10. Close Control Panel.

Procedure Reference: Configure Domain Membership in Windows NT

To configure domain membership in Windows NT:

1. Log on as a local computer administrator.
2. Open Control Panel.
3. Double-click Network.
4. Click Change.
5. Below Member Of, select Domain.
6. In the Domain text box, type the name of the domain. If you're joining a Windows NT computer to a Windows 2000 Active Directory domain, type the NetBIOS name for the domain, not the DNS name. For example, if the name of the Active Directory domain is "company.com," type "company" for the domain name.
7. If a computer account hasn't already been created for this computer in the domain, check Create A Computer Account In The Domain. In the User Name and Password text boxes, enter the credentials of a user with the authority to create a computer account in the domain.
8. Click OK.
9. Click OK to close the Network Configuration message box.
10. Click Close to close the Network dialog box.
11. Click Yes to confirm that you want to reboot the computer.

12. Verify that you can log on to the domain as follows:
    a. When the Welcome To Windows dialog box is displayed, press Ctrl+Alt+Delete.
    b. In the User Name text box, type the domain user account name.
    c. In the Password text box, type the domain user account's password.
    d. From the Log On To drop-down list, select the domain name.
    e. Click OK to log on to the domain.

TOPIC D
Configure File and Folder Security

Up to this point in the chapter, you've worked with how to secure a computer through logon accounts. But once the user logs on to the computer, you might not want the user to have access to all files and folders on the computer. In this topic, you'll learn how to secure files and folders.

On almost all of the computers you'll work with, you'll encounter multiple user accounts. You might just see the user's account plus the Administrator; on the other hand, you might encounter multiple users sharing the same computer. In any situation where you have multiple users of the same computers, you can encounter problems with users accessing and modifying each other's files. You need to be sure that each of the users of the computer can access only their own files. You might also need to configure a folder to which all the users of the computer have access so that they can share files with each other. By assigning the file and folder permissions properly, you make sure that the users of the computer can access the files and folders they need without accessing the files and folders they shouldn't.

File Systems

Operating systems use a file system to determine how to store files on a computer's hard disk. There are six different file systems: File Allocation Table (FAT), File Allocation Table 32 (FAT32), NT File System version 4 (NTFS4), NT File System version 5 (NTFS5), High Performance File System (HPFS), and CD File System (CDFS). Each Windows operating system supports some of the available file systems. In Table 12-6, you find a description of each file system along with the versions of Windows that support it.

 You'll sometimes hear the FAT file system referred to as FAT16.

Table 12-6: *File Systems*

File System	Description	Supported By
FAT	The FAT file system is an older file system that's best suited for use with drives that are less than 4 GB in size. Advantages to the FAT file system include: it uses very little overhead on a disk and it's compatible with many different operating systems. If you want to configure a dual-boot computer between Windows 9x and Windows 2000/NT/XP, you must configure the C drive to use the FAT file system.	Windows 9x, Windows NT, Windows 2000, Windows XP
FAT32	The FAT32 file system is an enhanced version of the FAT file system. It scales better to large hard disks (up to 2 TB in size), and uses a smaller cluster size than FAT for more efficient space usage.	Windows 98, Windows 2000, Windows XP
NTFS4	NTFS4 is the native file system Microsoft introduced in the Windows NT operating system. It offers many advantages over the FAT-based file systems including support for very large hard disks, file- and folder-level security, and disk compression.	Windows NT, Windows 2000, Windows XP
NTFS5	NTFS5 is an enhanced version of NTFS that adds support for encryption and disk quotas (for limiting users' disk space).	Windows NT with Service Pack 6, Windows 2000, Windows XP
HPFS	HPFS is a file system created by IBM for the OS/2 operating system. This file system enhanced the FAT file system by adding support for larger hard disks and using a smaller cluster size. Microsoft added support for this file system to the Windows NT operating system.	Windows NT
CDFS	CDFS is a specialized 32-bit file system that enables the Windows operating systems to access the information on a CD-ROM.	Windows 9x, Windows NT, Windows 2000, Windows XP

 Windows ME supports both FAT and FAT32.

NTFS Permissions

With NTFS, you have the ability to set permissions on files and folders to grant or deny users access. If you set permissions at the folder level, those permissions are automatically applied to the files within the folder. In some situations, you might find it necessary to set permissions on an individual file. In this scenario, the permissions you set on an individual file override the permissions set at the folder level. You can either allow or deny a specific permission. In Table 12-7, you see a list of the folder permissions you can set, and in Table 12-8 you find a list of the file permissions.

Table 12-7: *Folder Permissions*

Permission	Permits Users To
Full Control	Perform any action on the folder.
Modify	Change files in the folder, change attributes of the folder, see the contents of the folder and the contents of its files, and run program files in the folder.
Read & Execute	See the contents of the folder and the contents of its files, and run program files in the folder.
List Folder Contents	See the contents of the folder and the contents of its files, and run program files in the folder.
Read	See the contents of the folder and the contents of its files.
Write	Change files in the folder.

Table 12-8: *File Permissions*

Permission	Permits Users To
Full Control	Perform any action on the file.
Modify	Change the file and its attributes; run a program file.
Read & Execute	See the contents of the file; run a program file.
Read	See the contents of the file.
Write	Change the file and its attributes.

The NTFS permissions you assign for a file or folder are cumulative. If you assign NTFS permissions to two groups for a folder, and a user is a member of both groups, the user will receive the permissions you assigned to both groups. For example, let's say that you assigned the Read & Execute permission to the Users group for a folder. You then assigned the Modify permission to the Administrators group for the same folder. If a user is a member of both the Users and Administrators group, the user's permissions for the folder will be Read & Execute and Modify.

Attributes

Regardless of which file system a computer is using, you can set four attributes on its files and folders. These attributes include: Archive, Hidden, Read-Only, and System. In Table 12-9, you find a description of each file attribute and how it's used.

Table 12-9: *File Attributes*

File Attribute	Used To
Archive	Indicate that a file has not been backed up. Windows automatically sets the Archive attribute on any file you create or modify. When you back up a computer, you can choose to back up only the files on which the Archive attribute is set.
Hidden	Hide a file from view in Windows Explorer or My Computer.
Read-Only	Enables users to read the contents of a file or execute it if it's a program file, and prevents users from changing the contents of a file.
System	Indicate that a file is used by the operating system.

 We talk more about the Archive attribute and how you can use it to perform a backup in Chapter 11.

How to Configure File and Folder Security

Procedure Reference: Assign File And Folder Permissions in Windows 2000

To assign file and folder permissions in Windows 2000:

1. Log on as a user with Full Control to the file or folder for which you want to assign permissions.

2. Open Windows Explorer.

3. Right-click the file or folder and choose Properties. The file or folder you select must be on an NTFS partition for you to be able to configure permissions.

4. Select the Security tab.

5. If you want to prevent users from inheriting permissions to the file or folder, uncheck Allow Inheritable Permissions From Parent To Propagate To This Object.
   - If you want to copy the previously inherited permissions to the file or folder, click Copy.
   - If you want to remove the previously inherited permissions from the file or folder, click Remove.

6. Click Add.

7. If the computer is a member of a domain and you want to assign permissions to local users or groups, from the Look In drop-down list, select the local computer.

8. In the Select Users Or Groups dialog box, select the user or group to which you want to grant permissions.

9. Click Add.

10. Click OK.

11. In the Name list, verify that the user or group you just added is selected.

12. Check or uncheck the permissions you want to assign to this user or group for the file or folder.

13. Click OK to save your changes.

14. Close Windows Explorer.

15. Test the permissions you assigned by attempting to access the file or folder as both an authorized user and an unauthorized user.

Procedure Reference: Assign File And Folder Permissions in Windows XP

To assign file and folder permissions in Windows XP:

1. Log on as a user with Full Control to the file or folder for which you want to assign permissions.

2. Open Windows Explorer.

3. Right-click the file or folder and choose Properties. The file or folder you select must be on an NTFS partition for you to be able to configure permissions.

4. Select the Security tab.

5. If you want to prevent users from inheriting permissions to the file or folder, disable inheritance.

    a. Click Advanced.

    b. Uncheck Inherit From Parent The Permission Entries That Apply To Child Objects.

    c. If you want to copy the previously inherited permissions to the file or folder, click Copy.

    If you want to remove the previously inherited permissions from the file or folder, click Remove.

    d. Click OK.

6. Click Add.

7. If the computer is a member of a domain and you want to assign permissions to local users or groups, complete the following steps:

    a. Click Locations.

b. If you're prompted to log on to the domain, click Cancel.
c. In the Location list, select the computer name and click OK.
8. If you know the name of the user or group to which you want to assign permissions, enter it under Enter The Object Names To Select and click OK.
9. If you want to search for the user or group to which you want to assign permissions:
   a. Click Advanced.
   b. Click Find Now to display a list of users, groups, and computers.
   c. Select the desired user or group and click OK.
10. Click OK to close the Select Users Or Groups dialog box.
11. In the Name list, verify that the user or group you just added is selected.
12. Check or uncheck the permissions you want to assign to this user or group for the file or folder.
13. Click OK to save your changes.
14. Close Windows Explorer.
15. Test the permissions you assigned by attempting to access the file or folder as both an authorized user and an unauthorized user.

Procedure Reference: Assign File And Folder Permissions in Windows NT

To assign file and folder permissions in Windows NT:

1. Log on as a user with Full Control to the file or folder for which you want to assign permissions.
2. Open Windows Explorer.
3. Right-click the file or folder and choose Properties. The file or folder you select must be on an NTFS partition for you to be able to configure permissions.
4. Select the Security tab.
5. Click Permissions.
6. Click Add.
7. If the computer is a member of a domain and you want to assign permissions to local users or groups, from the Look In drop-down list, select the local computer.
8. If you want to assign permissions to a group, select the group and click Add.
9. If you want to assign permissions to a user:
   a. Click Show Users.
   b. In the Names list, select the user to which you want to assign permissions.
   c. Click Add.

10. From the Type Of Access drop-down list, select the permissions you want to assign to the user or group.

11. Click OK to close the Add Users And Groups dialog box.

12. If you're assigning permissions to a folder, check the appropriate options:
    - Check Replace Permissions On Subdirectories if you want to also grant the same permissions to the user for the subdirectories within the folder.
    - Check Replace Permissions On Existing Files if you want to grant the permissions to the user for all files within the folder.

13. Click OK.

14. Click OK to close the file or folder Properties dialog box.

15. Close Windows Explorer.

16. Test the permissions you assigned by attempting to access the file or folder as both an authorized user and an unauthorized user.

Procedure Reference: Configure File Attributes in Windows 2000/XP/NT

To configure file attributes in Windows 2000, Windows XP, and Windows NT:

1. Log on as a user with Full Control to the file or folder for which you want to assign permissions.

2. Open Windows Explorer.

3. Right-click the file or folder for which you want to set attributes and choose Properties.

4. On the General page, check or uncheck Read-Only.

5. Check or uncheck Hidden.

6. Click OK to save your changes.

7. Close Windows Explorer.

Topic E
Encrypt Files and Folders

Another technique you can use to further secure Windows 2000 and Windows XP computers is file and folder encryption. As an A+ technician, you might be expected to implement encryption for clients and users that work with sensitive data and thus require high security on their computers. So, in this topic, you'll learn how to implement encryption of both files and folders in Windows 2000 and Windows XP.

It's possible that a user might share a folder with his workgroup and not want those users to have access to some of the files within that folder. In this scenario, using encryption is one way that you can prevent the users from accessing those files. As an A+ technician, by encrypting users' sensitive files and folders, you'll be able to protect the intellectual assets of your company.

Encryption

Windows 2000 and Windows XP use *encryption* to translate data into a coded version for increased security. These operating systems use an encryption rule (also called a key) to determine how to encrypt the data. Windows 2000 and Windows XP use a key that's associated with your user account to encrypt or decrypt a file. Because each user's key is different, you can't open a file that another user has encrypted. Likewise, another user can't open a file that you have encrypted. In an emergency, the domain Administrator user account can decrypt an encrypted file.

 The domain Administrator user can also designate other user accounts as authorized to recover encrypted files.

How to Encrypt Files and Folders

Procedure Reference: Encrypt Files and Folders in Windows 2000 and Windows XP

To encrypt files and folders in Windows 2000 and Windows XP:

1. Log on as a user with Full Control to the file or folder for which you want to enable encryption.
2. Open Windows Explorer.
3. Right-click the folder or file you want to encrypt and choose Properties.
4. On the General page, click Advanced.
5. Check Encrypt Contents To Secure Data and click OK.
6. Click OK to close the Properties dialog box.
7. If you chose to encrypt a folder, in the Confirm Attribute Changes dialog box, make the appropriate selection:
   - If you want to encrypt all files in the folder, as well as its subfolders and their files, select Apply Changes To This Folder, Subfolders, And Files and click OK.
   - If you want to encrypt only the files in the folder and not its subfolders or their files, select Apply Changes To This Folder Only and click OK.
8. If you chose to encrypt a file, in the Encryption Warning dialog box, make the appropriate selection:
   - If you want to encrypt the file and its parent folder, select Encrypt The File And The Parent Folder and click OK.
   - If you want to encrypt only the file, select Encrypt The File Only and click OK.
9. Close Windows Explorer.

Procedure Reference: Decrypt Files and Folders in Windows 2000 and Windows XP

To decrypt files and folders in Windows 2000 and Windows XP:

1. Log on as the user who encrypted the file or folder for which you want to disable encryption.

2. Open Windows Explorer.
3. Right-click the folder or file you want to modify and choose Properties.
4. On the General page, click Advanced.
5. Uncheck Encrypt Contents To Secure Data and click OK.
6. Click OK to close the Properties dialog box.
7. If you chose to decrypt a folder, in the Confirm Attribute Changes dialog box, make the appropriate selection:
   - If you want to remove encryption from all files in the folder, as well as its subfolders and their files, select Apply Changes To This Folder, Subfolders, And Files and click OK.
   - If you want to remove encryption from only the files in the folder and not its subfolders or their files, select Apply Changes To This Folder Only and click OK.
8. If you chose to encrypt a file, in the Encryption Warning dialog box, make the appropriate selection:
   - If you want to encrypt the file and its parent folder, select Encrypt The File And The Parent Folder and click OK.
   - If you want to encrypt only the file, select Encrypt The File Only and click OK.
9. Close Windows Explorer.

CHAPTER 12 FOLLOW-UP
Implementing Local Security in Windows 2000/NT/XP

In this chapter, you learned how to implement local security in Windows 2000, Windows NT, and Windows XP. Knowing how to properly configure these operating systems' security enables you to protect the computers' data. In addition, these skills help you avoid having to spend time recovering data in the event of a data loss.

Essential Terms

- domains
- encryption
- file and folder security
- file attributes
- file encryption
- file systems
- folder encryption
- local security
- local user accounts
- NTFS permissions
- security
- user accounts
- workgroups

Review Questions

1. Windows 2000 Professional, Windows NT 4.0 workstation, and Windows XP Professional include two built-in user accounts. What are they?
2. What account has full privileges to the computer?
3. By default, what user account is disabled when you install Windows NT 4.0, 2000, and XP?
4. Windows XP includes three built-in group accounts that are not available on Windows 2000. What are the three built-in group accounts?
5. What Windows XP built-in user account provides access to Microsoft's Web-based help and support services?
6. What Windows XP built-in group account enables members to log on the computer remotely?
7. In Windows XP, why should you reset a user's password only as a last resort?
8. A user in your workgroup tries to log onto a computer that is being used by someone else. The user cannot log on. Why?
9. What kind of network model uses centralized administration?
10. In a domain network model a user can utilize a single user account to log on at any computer in the domain. Why?
11. What kind of server stores the shared, central account database?
12. What are group policies?
13. What are system policies?
14. What is Windows 2000's native file system?
15. If you were dual booting between Windows 98 and Windows NT 4.0, what file system would you have to use?
16. FAT 32 includes two enhancements to the FAT file system. What are the two enhancements?
17. What file system allows you to set permissions on files?
18. If you set permissions at the file level, what happens to the permissions set at the folder level?
19. What are the five NTFS file permissions?
20. What are the four attributes you can assign to a file?
21. What folder permission allows you to change the attributes of a folder?
22. What is CDFS?
23. A user belongs to two groups, marketing and sales. Both groups have access to the folder, New Items. The user has the NTFS permission full control in the marketing group and the NTFS permission read in the sales group. What is the user's effective permissions for the New Items folder?
24. What is encryption?
25. Who can decrypt encrypted folders?
26. What is a key?

Review Projects

Project #1 Adding the Encrypt Option to File and Folder Shortcuts

In this activity, you'll implement the steps outlined in a Microsoft knowledge base article. The article, "How to Enable the Encryption Command on the Shortcut Menu," shows you how to add the Encrypt command to the shortcut menu on files and folders. To perform this exercise you'll have to edit the Registry on a Windows 2000 or Windows XP machine. You should always back up your system's Registry before editing it.

The steps are detailed below, but you should first read the knowledge base article located at **http://support.microsoft.com/support/kb/articles/Q241/1/21.ASP**.

1. Open your Registry editor and drill down to the following path: HKEY_LOCAL_MACHINE\Software\Microsoft\Windows\CurrentVersion\Explorer\Advanced.

    Under Edit on the menu bar, select NEW and then DWORD value. You'll see the new value listed in the right pane.

2. Notice that the text "new value #1" is in a white box. Press Backspace once to clear the box and type "EncryptionContextMenu" (make sure there are no spaces between words), then change the value data number from 0 to 1.

3. You must reboot your system for the change to take effect.

4. Right-click a folder or file.

    You'll see "Encrypt" added to the shortcut menu.

Project #2 Understanding the NTFS file system

Using the Web site, **http://www.ntfs.com/**, investigate Microsoft's proprietary file system for Windows 2000 and Windows XP. Windows NT 4.0 also supports NTFS (v. 4), but Windows 2000 and XP support more options such as disk quotas, dynamic volumes, and encryption.

Read through the short tutorials. What features of NTFS (NTFS 5.0) are new to you? Document those features that are new to you and use that information to conduct a search.

If you use Google's search engine, you can filter your search for Microsoft-specific information by entering the following URL into your Web browser's address bar: http://google.com/microsoft. What sites did you visit? Bookmark the ones you found most helpful. Modify your search criteria to include Windows NT 4.0 (NTFS 4.0).

Project #3 Encryption and the Cipher command

Encryption

The cipher command displays or modifies the encryption of folder and files on NTFS volumes. Information about the command is available from several sources. You can access detailed information about the command switches by opening a command prompt and typing cipher /?. You can also consult the Help files and Microsoft's Web site. When learning a command, it's easiest to locate it on Microsoft's Web site or in the help files and print a copy of it. To print the syntax for the cipher command from Microsoft's Web site, copy the following address into your Web browser: **http://www.microsoft.com/technet/treeview/default.asp?url=/technet/prodtechnol/windowsserver2003/proddocs/standard/cipher.asp**.

In this exercise, you'll create two folders on either a Windows 2000 or Windows XP machine that uses the NTFS file system. Open Windows Explorer and under the C drive create one folder called Test and a subfolder called Testsub. Open Notepad and create several test files. Save some to the Test folder and some to the Testsub folder. Open the command prompt (enter cmd at the run box) and type cipher /?. This will display the cipher command's syntax.

To experiment with the cipher command, use your printout of the command's syntax. Explore the command and its switches using your two folders, the directory Test and the subdirectory, Testsub. Next, try your hand at writing a short batch file using the cipher command. For example, clear the encyption on the Test folder (if it is encrypted from your experiments). Open Notepad and enter your command or commands. If you want your command output to display at the command prompt, place the following command at the top of the text file: @echo on. If you don't want the command output to display, place the following command at the top of the text file: @echo off. After you finish entering your command(s), save the file with the .bat extension. Open a command prompt, navigate to the location where you saved the batch file (if other than the default location displayed at the command prompt), enter the name of the batch file, and press Enter.

Note: If the batch file does not run, check to make sure the path is correct.

What was the result of running the batch file?

Reflective Questions

1. In your company, or the companies you support, will you be working in a domain or workgroup environment? Why was this environment chosen?

2. Describe a scenario in which you would configure NTFS permissions on a folder.

CHAPTER 13
Managing File and Print Resources in Windows 2000/NT/XP

Chapter Objectives:

In this chapter, you will manage file and print resources in Windows 2000/NT/XP.

You will:
- Share folders.
- Connect to a network printer.
- Capture a printer port.
- Install a local printer.
- Troubleshoot printing.

Introduction

Earlier in this course you learned how to connect Windows-based computers to a network, and you learned how to create user accounts. Well, the point of connecting a computer to a network and creating user accounts is to enable users to access the resources on your network. The most common network resources users want to access are files and printers. For this reason, in this chapter, you'll learn the skills you need to provide users with access to file and print resources in Windows 2000, Windows NT, and Windows XP.

The ability to retrieve, store, and print data is the mainstay of users completing tasks and functioning in their job. As an A+ technician, it is your responsibility to make sure that users have access to the file and print resources they need to be effective.

TOPIC A
Share Folders

Earlier in this course, you learned how to configure permissions for users to access files on the local computer. But in a network environment, your users can access files on other computers as well. In this topic, you'll learn how to share folders so that users can access these folders across the network.

Without a network, if your users want to share files, they'll have to copy them to some form of removable media (such as a floppy disk or CD-ROM) and walk them over to whoever needs access to those files (you'll sometimes hear this process of walking from one computer to the next to transfer files called "sneaker-netting"). Because copying files to removable media and manually moving them from one computer to the next takes time, your users won't be as productive. And because any loss of productivity costs your company money, it's important that you know how to share folders so that your users can take full advantage of the network.

Share Permissions

When you share a folder, you can assign permissions to users or groups to control their access to that shared folder. Windows 2000 and Windows NT support three share permissions: Read, Change, and Full Control. You can configure these same three share permissions in Windows XP as long as the computer is a member of a domain. If the Windows XP computer is a member of a workgroup, you must configure it to use the Classic security model before you can configure shared folders with share permissions. Windows NT supports an additional share permission: No Access. This permission prevents the specified user or group from accessing the shared folder. Table 13-1 contains a description of each of these share permissions.

Table 13-1: *Share Permissions*

Permission	Enables Users To
Read	Connect to the folder, open the folder, open files, and run programs.

Permission	Enables Users To
Change	Connect to the folder, open the folder, open files, run programs, and create, delete, and modify files and subfolders.
Full Control	Perform any action on files and folders within the shared folder.

The Effective Permissions Process

When a user attempts to connect to a shared folder, Windows 2000, Windows XP, and Windows NT must determine the user's effective permissions for that folder before granting (or denying) access. These operating systems use the following steps to determine the user's effective permissions:

1. The operating system examines the share permissions on the folder to see if the user has been granted share permissions directly to the folder or is a member of a group to which share permissions have been granted.
2. If the shared folder is on an NTFS partition, the operating system determines if the user (or a group of which the user is a member) has been granted NTFS permissions for that same folder.
3. If the user has been given both share permissions and NTFS permissions for the same folder, the operating system grants the user the *most restrictive* permissions of the two.

For example, as you see in Figure 13-1, a user named Sarah is attempting to access a shared folder named Reports. You have given the Users group (of which Sarah is a member) the Change share permission for this shared folder. But, you have assigned the Read NTFS permission to Sarah for this same folder. Because the operating system will apply only the most restrictive permission in this scenario, Sarah's effective permissions are Read.

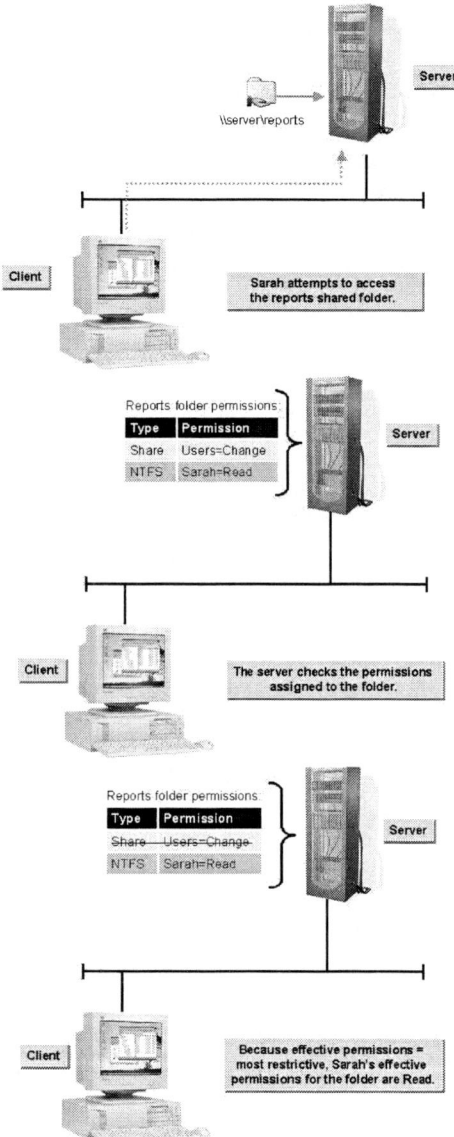

Figure 13-1: *The effective permissions process.*

How to Share Folders

Procedure Reference: Share a Folder

To share a folder in a Windows 2000, Windows NT, or Windows XP computer that is a member of a domain:

1. Log on as a local computer administrator.

2. Open Windows Explorer.

3. Right-click the folder you want to share and choose Sharing.

4. If you're using Windows 2000 or Windows XP, select Share This Folder.

5. If you're using Windows NT, select Shared As.

6. The default share name will match the folder name. If necessary, edit the default share name.

7. If you're using Windows 2000 or Windows NT and you want to limit the number of users who can connect to the share, complete the following steps:

    a. By User Limit, select Allow.

    b. In the Allow text box, type the maximum number of users you want to connect to the share simultaneously.

8. If you're using Windows XP and you want to limit the number of users who can connect to the share, complete the following steps:

    a. Select Allow This Number Of Users.

    b. In the Allow text box, type the maximum number of users you want to connect to the share simultaneously.

    If the computer is a member of a domain, you can assign permissions to either local or domain accounts.

9. Set the desired share permissions.

    a. Click Permissions.

    b. Add the necessary users, groups, or both.

    c. Assign the appropriate share permissions to these accounts.

    d. Click OK to close the Permissions dialog box.

10. Click OK. The appearance of the folder's icon changes to indicate that it is shared.

    Once you have shared the folder, you can share it again under more than one name. On the Sharing tab of the Properties dialog box, click Add New Share to add a second share name. You can set different permissions on each share name.

11. Test access to the share to verify that it is available to users and that you have set the permissions correctly.

Topic B
Connect to a Network Printer

As we mentioned in Topic 13A, implementing a network makes it possible for users to access resources located throughout the network instead of only the resources on their own computers. In fact, one of the big advantages to a network is that it enables users to share expensive resources such as printers. So, in this topic, you'll learn how to connect your users' computers to network printers.

Unfortunately, there's no such thing as a paperless office—yet. Until the paperless office becomes a reality, users will need the ability to print in order to perform their jobs. Connecting users to shared printers enables you to keep your company's hardware costs low because each user won't need his or her own printer. As an A+ technician, you'll be expected to configure users' computers to take advantage of shared printers so that users can print and your company can minimize its printer hardware investment.

Network Printer

Windows 2000, Windows XP, and Windows NT support two types of network printers: a shared printer on a workstation or server, and a printer with a network card that's connected directly to the network. You access a printer with a network card through its IP address. A printer with a network card is also called a *network-attached printer*.

Print Driver

Before the Windows operating systems can print to printers, you must install the printer's driver. This driver provides Windows with the exact commands for printing to the printer. Without this driver, Windows will not be able to print successfully to the printer.

Device Settings

When you connect to a network printer, you'll find that there are several settings you can configure for the printer. These settings vary depending on the printer model. In Table 13-2, we list the most common printer device settings you can expect to encounter.

Table 13-2: *Common Printer Device Settings*

Device Setting	Use To
Form To Tray Assignment	Specify which size paper is stored in each of the printer's paper trays.
Installed Font Cartridge(s)	Configure any font cartridges you have installed in the printer.
Installable Options	Configure any additional options supported by the printer. For example, you might use this option to configure optional paper trays for the printer or to specify any additional RAM installed in the printer.

How to Connect to a Network Printer

Procedure Reference: Connect to a Network Printer in Windows 2000

To connect to a printer that is shared on the network in Windows 2000:

1. Log on with a user account and password that is valid for the print server. For example, if the network printer is shared on a domain controller, log on with a domain user account and password.

2. From the Start menu, choose Settings→Printers to open the Printers dialog box.

3. Double-click the Add Printer icon to start the Add Printer Wizard.

4. Click Next.

5. Select Network Printer.

6. Click Next.

7. On the Locate Your Printer page, make the appropriate selection:
   - If the printer is shared in an Active Directory domain, select Find A Printer In The Directory.
   - If the printer is shared in a workgroup, select Type The Printer Name, Or Click Next To Browse For A Printer. If you know the printer name, type it in the Name text box.
   - If the printer is on the Internet or an intranet, select Connect To A Printer On The Internet Or On Your Intranet. In the URL text box, type the URL for the printer.

8. Click Next.

9. If you already have other printers installed on the computer, you'll be prompted to choose which printer you want as the default printer. Under Do You Want Your Windows-based Programs To Use This Printer As The Default Printer, select one of the following:
   - Yes, if you want all Windows programs to use this printer as their default printer.
   - No, if you want this printer available to Windows programs to use, but it is not their default printer.

10. Click Next and then click Finish.

11. Close the Printers window.

Procedure Reference: Connect to a Network-attached Printer in Windows 2000

To connect to a printer with a network card in Windows 2000:

1. Log on as a local administrator.

2. From the Start menu, choose Settings→Printers to open the Printers window.

3. Double-click the Add Printer icon to start the Add Printer Wizard.

4. Click Next.

5. Select Local Printer.
6. If you want Windows 2000 to use Plug and Play to attempt to detect the printer, check Automatically Detect And Install My Plug And Play Printer.
7. If you want to manually specify the printer manufacturer and type, uncheck Automatically Detect And Install My Plug And Play Printer.
8. Click Next.
9. On the Select The Printer Port page, complete the following steps:
    a. Select Create A New Port.
    b. From the Type drop-down list, select Standard TCP/IP Port.
    c. Click Next. The Add Standard TCP/IP Printer Port Wizard opens.
    d. Click Next.
    e. In the Printer Name Or IP Address text box, type the IP address of the printer.
    f. Click Next.
    g. Click Finish.
10. If you specified that you did not want Windows 2000 to use Plug and Play to attempt to detect your printer, or Plug and Play was unsuccessful, complete the following steps:
    a. Below Manufacturers, select the manufacturer of the printer.
    b. Below Printers, select the printer model.
    c. Click Next.
11. In the Printer Name text box, type a name for your printer.
12. If you already have other printers installed on the computer, you'll be prompted to choose which printer you want as the default printer. Under Do You Want Your Windows-based Programs To Use This Printer As The Default Printer, select one of the following:
    - Yes, if you want all Windows programs to use this printer as their default printer.
    - No, if you want this printer available to Windows programs to use, but it is not their default printer.
13. Click Next.
14. On the Printer Sharing page, select one of the following:
    - If you want to share the printer with other users, select Share As:. In the text box, type a share name for the printer.
    - If you do not want to share the printer with other users, select Do Not Share This Printer.
15. Click Next.
16. Under Would You Like To Print A Test Page, select one of the following:
    - Yes, if you want to print a test page to verify the printer is set up properly.

- No, if you want to skip printing the test page.

17. Click Finish.

18. If you are prompted for the Windows 2000 installation files, insert the disk in the CD-ROM drive and click OK.

19. If you selected Yes to print a test page, click one of the following:
    - Yes, if the test page printed properly at the printer.
    - No, if the test page did not print properly at the printer.

20. Close the Printers window.

Procedure Reference: Connect to a Network Printer in Windows XP

To connect to a printer that is shared on the network in Windows XP:

1. Log on with a user account and password that is valid for the print server. For example, if the network printer is shared on a domain controller, log on with a domain user account and password.

2. From the Start menu, choose Settings→Printers And Faxes to open the Printers dialog box.

3. Click the Add Printer link to start the Add Printer Wizard.

4. Click Next.

5. Select A Network Printer, Or A Printer Attached To Another Computer.

6. Click Next.

7. On the Specify A Printer page, select the appropriate option.
    - If the computer is a member of a workgroup:
        - If you want to search for the printer name, select Browse For A Printer.
        - If you know the printer name, select Connect To This Printer and type the printer name in the Name text box.
        - If the printer is on the Internet or a home or office network, select Connect To A Printer On The Internet Or On A Home Or Office Network. In the URL text box, type the URL for the printer.
    - If the computer is a member of a domain:
        - If you want to search for the printer in the Active Directory, select Find A Printer In The Directory.
        - If you want to search for the printer or know the printer name, select Connect To This Printer (Or To Browse For A Printer).
        - If the printer is on the Internet or a home or office network, select Connect To A Printer On The Internet Or On A Home Or Office Network. In the URL text box, type the URL for the printer.

8. Click Next.

9. If you already have other printers installed on the computer, you'll be prompted to choose which printer you want as the default printer. Under Do You Want To Use This Printer As The Default Printer, select one of the following:
   - Yes, if you want all Windows programs to use this printer as their default printer.
   - No, if you want this printer available to Windows programs to use, but it is not their default printer.
10. Click Next and then click Finish.
11. Close the Printers window.

Procedure Reference: Connect to a Network-attached Printer in Windows XP

To connect to a printer with a network card in Windows XP:

1. Log on as a local administrator.
2. From the Start menu, choose Printers And Faxes to open the Printers And Faxes window.
3. Click the Add A Printer link to start the Add Printer Wizard.
4. Click Next.
5. Select Local Printer Attached To This Computer.
6. If you want Windows 2000 to use Plug and Play to attempt to detect the printer, check Automatically Detect And Install My Plug And Play Printer.
7. If you want to manually specify the printer manufacturer and type, uncheck Automatically Detect And Install My Plug And Play Printer.
8. Click Next.
9. On the Select A Printer Port page, complete the following steps:
   a. Select Create A New Port.
   b. From the Type Of Port drop-down list, select Standard TCP/IP Port.
   c. Click Next. The Add Standard TCP/IP Printer Port Wizard opens.
   d. Click Next.
   e. In the Printer Name Or IP Address text box, type the IP address of the printer.
   f. Click Next.
   g. Click Finish.
10. If you specified that you did not want Windows 2000 to use Plug and Play to attempt to detect your printer, or Plug and Play was unsuccessful, complete the following steps:
    a. Below Manufacturer, select the manufacturer of the printer.
    b. Below Printers, select the printer model.
    c. Click Next.
11. In the Printer Name text box, type a name for your printer.

12. If you already have other printers installed on the computer, you'll be prompted to choose which printer you want as the default printer. Under Do You Want To Use This Printer As The Default Printer, select one of the following:
    - Yes, if you want all Windows programs to use this printer as their default printer.
    - No, if you want this printer available to Windows programs to use, but it is not their default printer.
13. Click Next.
14. On the Printer Sharing page, select one of the following:
    - If you want to share the printer with other users, select Share Name. In the text box, type a share name for the printer.
    - If you do not want to share the printer with other users, select Do Not Share This Printer.
15. Click Next.
16. Under Do You Want To Print A Test Page, select one of the following:
    - Yes, if you want to print a test page to verify the printer is set up properly.
    - No, if you want to skip printing the test page.
17. Click Next.
18. Click Finish.
19. If you are prompted for the Windows XP installation files, insert the disk in the CD-ROM drive and click OK.
20. If you selected Yes to print a test page, click one of the following:
    - Yes, if the test page printed properly at the printer.
    - No, if the test page did not print properly at the printer.
21. Close the Printers And Faxes window.

Procedure Reference: Connect to a Network Printer in Windows NT

To connect to a printer that is shared on the network in Windows NT:

1. Log on with a user account and password that is valid for the print server. For example, if the network printer is shared on a domain controller, log on with a domain user account and password.
2. From the Start menu, choose Settings→Printers to open the Printers dialog box.
3. Double-click the Add Printer icon to start the Add Printer Wizard.
4. Select Network Printer Server.
5. Click Next.
6. In the Connect To Printer dialog box, expand the print server and select the printer.

7. Click OK to close the Connect To Printer dialog box.
8. If the print server doesn't have a suitable Windows NT driver for the printer, you'll see a message box informing you of such. Complete the following steps:
   a. Click OK to close the message box.
   b. In the File Needed dialog box, enter the path to the Windows NT installation files. If necessary, insert the Windows NT installation CD-ROM.
   c. Click OK.
9. If you already have other printers installed on the computer, you'll be prompted to choose which printer you want as the default printer. Under Do You Want Your Windows-based Programs To Use This Printer As The Default Printer, select one of the following:
   - Yes, if you want all Windows programs to use this printer as their default printer.
   - No, if you want this printer available to Windows programs to use, but it is not their default printer.
   - Click Next.
10. Click Finish.
11. Close the Printers window.

TOPIC C
Capture a Printer Port

Topic 13B showed you how you can configure a computer to print to a network printer. Unfortunately, only Windows-based applications recognize network printers and permit you to print to them. If your users are using any non-Windows applications, you'll need to capture a printer port in order to print from these applications. So, in this topic, you'll learn the steps for configuring access to printers so that your users can print within their non-Windows applications.

Most non-Windows applications are custom applications that companies have had developed for them. Such applications typically cost quite a bit of money and perform a specific function for the company that isn't available in commercial, off-the-shelf applications. As an A+ technician, you're bound to encounter a non-Windows application on a computer, and you'll be expected to configure that computer so that the user can print from the custom application. Knowing how to configure printing from non-Windows applications will help you to keep your users working productively in such applications.

Printer Ports

When you connect a printer to a computer, you connect it to a printer port. Windows 2000, Windows XP, and Windows NT support the following printer ports:
- Line Printer 1 (LPT1), Line Printer 2 (LPT2), and Line Printer 3 (LPT3). These ports are also referred to as parallel ports.
- COM1, COM2, COM3, and COM4. These ports are also referred to as serial ports.

Most computers contain a single parallel port (LPT1) and two serial ports (COM1 and COM2).

In addition to the LPT and COM ports, Windows 2000 and Windows XP also support printers connected to USB ports.

 You very rarely see serial ports used for printers because their throughput is significantly slower than that of parallel or USB ports.

Port Capture

MS-DOS applications cannot print directly to the network printers you define in the Printers folder on a Windows computer. Instead, to print from these applications, you must first execute the net use command to capture the print jobs sent to an LPT printer port (such as LPT1 or LPT2) so that those jobs are sent to your network printer. Next, configure the application to print to whichever port you captured. The print jobs you create within the MS-DOS application will thus be "captured" and sent to the network printer.

How to Capture a Printer Port

Procedure Reference: Capture a Printer Port

To capture a printer port:

1. Log on as a local administrator.

2. From the Start menu, choose Programs→Accessories→Command Prompt.

    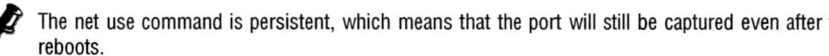 The net use command is persistent, which means that the port will still be captured even after the computer reboots.

3. Enter net use lpt# \\computer_name\shared printer name.

    If the computer has its own local printer on lpt1, use a different port such as lpt2.

4. Enter exit to close the Command Prompt window.

5. In each non-Windows application on the computer, complete the following steps:

    a. Install the printer driver for the shared printer.

    b. Configure the printer driver to use the port you specified in Step 3 (for example, lpt1).

6. Verify that you can print from each application.

Procedure Reference: View Captured Print Jobs

To view captured print jobs:

1. Open a Command Prompt window.

2. Enter `net print \\computer_name\shared printer name` to display a list of the print jobs redirected to the network printer.

3. Close the Command Prompt window.

Procedure Reference: Disconnect a Captured Printer Port

To disconnect a captured printer port:

1. Log on as a local administrator.

2. Open a Command Prompt window.

3. Enter `net use lpt# /delete`.

4. Close the Command Prompt window.

TOPIC D
Install a Local Printer

In Topic 13B, you learned how to connect users' computers to shared network printers. Another printing scenario you might encounter, though, is setting up a locally attached printer. In this topic, you'll learn how to install and configure a local printer in Windows 2000, Windows NT, and Windows XP.

There are valid reasons why a user might need his or her own printer. For example, think about the accounts payable clerk who's responsible for printing checks on a daily basis. Because printing checks requires that the clerk load the printer with expensive pre-printed check forms instead of plain paper, you typically wouldn't want the clerk to print checks on a shared printer. Having the clerk use a shared printer might lead to other users accidentally printing letters or reports on the pre-printed checks. Likewise, you might not want other users to be able to read the check information. In some situations, the checks the clerk prints might contain sensitive information that your company wouldn't want other users to access. As an A+ technician, knowing how to configure a local printer will enable you to respond to users' requests for local printers whether these requests are for convenience or security reasons (or both).

Print Permissions

When you share a printer in Windows 2000, Windows XP, and Windows NT, there are three print permissions you can assign: Print, Manage Printers, and Manage Documents. In Table 13-3, you find a description of each of these print permissions along with who these permissions are assigned to by default when you share a printer.

Table 13-3: *Print Permissions*

Permission	Enables Users To	Assigned By Default To
Print	Print to the shared printer.	Everyone

Permission	Enables Users To	Assigned By Default To
Manage Printers	Print to the printer and fully administer the printer.	Administrators, Power Users
Manage Documents	Manage other users' documents. This permission does not include the ability to print to the printer.	Creator Owner

 Creator Owner is a special group that refers to the creator (and thus, owner) of a print job.

How to Install a Local Printer

Procedure Reference: Install a Local Printer in Windows 2000

To install a printer that is attached to the local computer in Windows 2000:

1. Log on as a local administrator.
2. From the Start menu, choose Settings→Printers to open the Printers window.
3. Double-click the Add Printer icon to start the Add Printer Wizard.
4. Click Next.
5. Select Local Printer.
6. If you want Windows 2000 to use Plug and Play to attempt to detect the printer, check Automatically Detect And Install My Plug And Play Printer.
7. If you want to manually specify the printer manufacturer and type, uncheck Automatically Detect And Install My Plug And Play Printer.
8. Click Next.
9. From the Use The Following Port list, select the port to which your printer is connected.

    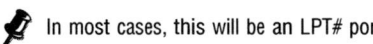 In most cases, this will be an LPT# port.

10. Click Next.
11. If you specified that you did not want Windows 2000 to use Plug and Play to attempt to detect your printer, or Plug and Play was unsuccessful, complete the following steps:
    a. Below Manufacturers, select the manufacturer of the printer.
    b. Below Printers, select the printer model.
    c. Click Next.
12. In the Printer Name text box, type a name for your printer.

13. If you already have other printers installed on the computer, you'll be prompted to choose which printer you want as the default printer. Under Do You Want Your Windows-based Programs To Use This Printer As The Default Printer, select one of the following:
    - Yes, if you want all Windows programs to use this printer as their default printer.
    - No, if you want this printer available to Windows programs to use, but it is not their default printer.
14. Click Next.
15. On the Printer Sharing page, select one of the following:
    - If you want to share the printer with other users, select Share As:. In the text box, type a share name for the printer.
    - If you do not want to share the printer with other users, select Do Not Share This Printer.
16. Click Next.
17. Under Would You Like To Print A Test Page, select one of the following:
    - Yes, if you want to print a test page to verify the printer is set up properly.
    - No, if you want to skip printing the test page.
18. Click Finish.
19. If you are prompted for the Windows 2000 installation files, insert the disk in the CD-ROM drive and click OK.
20. If you selected Yes to print a test page, click one of the following:
    - Yes, if the test page printed properly at the printer.
    - No, if the test page did not print properly at the printer.
21. Close the Printers window.

Procedure Reference: Install a Local Printer in Windows XP

To install a printer that is attached to the local computer in Windows XP:

1. Log on as a local administrator.
2. From the Start menu, choose Printers And Faxes to open the Printers And Faxes window.
3. Click the Add A Printer link to start the Add Printer Wizard.
4. Click Next.
5. Select Local Printer Attached To This Computer.
6. If you want Windows XP to use Plug and Play to attempt to detect the printer, check Automatically Detect And Install My Plug And Play Printer.
7. If you want to manually specify the printer manufacturer and type, uncheck Automatically Detect And Install My Plug And Play Printer.

8. Click Next.
9. From the Use The Following Port drop-down list, select the port to which your printer is connected.

   > In most cases, this will be an LPT# port.

10. Click Next.
11. If you specified that you did not want Windows XP to use Plug and Play to attempt to detect your printer, or Plug and Play was unsuccessful, complete the following steps:
    a. Below Manufacturer, select the manufacturer of the printer.
    b. Below Printers, select the printer model.
    c. Click Next.
12. In the Printer Name text box, type a name for your printer.
13. If you already have other printers installed on the computer, you'll be prompted to choose which printer you want as the default printer. Under Do You Want Your Windows-based Programs To Use This Printer As The Default Printer, select one of the following:
    - Yes, if you want all Windows programs to use this printer as their default printer.
    - No, if you want this printer available to Windows programs to use, but it is not their default printer.
14. Click Next.
15. On the Printer Sharing page, select one of the following:
    - If you want to share the printer with other users, select Share Name. In the text box, type a share name for the printer.
    - If you do not want to share the printer with other users, select Do Not Share This Printer.
16. Click Next.
17. Under Do You Want To Print A Test Page, select one of the following:
    - Yes, if you want to print a test page to verify the printer is set up properly.
    - No, if you want to skip printing the test page.
18. Click Finish.
19. If you are prompted for the Windows XP installation files, insert the disk in the CD-ROM drive and click OK.
20. If you selected Yes to print a test page, click one of the following:
    - Yes, if the test page printed properly at the printer.
    - No, if the test page did not print properly at the printer.
21. Close the Printers And Faxes window.

Procedure Reference: Install a Local Printer in Windows NT

To install a printer that is attached to the local computer in Windows NT:

1. Log on as a local administrator.
2. From the Start menu, choose Settings→Printers to open the Printers window.
3. Double-click the Add Printer icon to start the Add Printer Wizard.
4. Select My Computer.
5. From the Use The Following Port list, select the port to which your printer is connected.

    In most cases, this will be an LPT# port.

6. Click Next.
7. Below Manufacturers, select the manufacturer of the printer.
8. Below Printers, select the printer model.
9. Click Next.
10. In the Printer Name text box, type a name for your printer.
11. On the Printer Sharing page, select one of the following:
    - If you want to share the printer with other users, select Shared. In the Share Name text box, type a share name for the printer.
    - If you do not want to share the printer with other users, select Not Shared.
12. Click Next.
13. If you already have other printers installed on the computer, you'll be prompted to choose which printer you want as the default printer. Under Do You Want Your Windows-based Programs To Use This Printer As The Default Printer, select one of the following:
    - Yes, if you want all Windows programs to use this printer as their default printer.
    - No, if you want this printer available to Windows programs to use, but it is not their default printer.
14. Click Next.
15. Under Would You Like To Print A Test Page select one of the following:
    - Yes (Recommended), if you want to print a test page to verify the printer is set up properly.
    - No, if you want to skip printing the test page.
16. Click Finish.
17. If you are prompted for the Windows NT installation files, insert the disk in the CD-ROM drive and click OK.
18. If you selected Yes to print a test page, click one of the following:

- Yes, if the test page printed properly at the printer.
- No, if the test page did not print properly at the printer.

19. Close the Printers window.

Topic E
Troubleshoot Printing

So far in this chapter you've seen how to configure a Windows 2000, Windows NT, or Windows XP computer to print to both local and networked computers from Windows and non-Windows applications. But what should you do if a user is still unable to print? In this topic, you'll learn about the printing process and then use this process to troubleshoot printing problems.

As an A+ technician, you can expect to be called immediately whenever a user can't print. Users use printers to perform their jobs, and they won't be able to complete their work if they can't print. Some printing problems might be caused by a hardware failure; still others arise from improperly configured software or printers. Knowing the printing process and the steps for troubleshooting printing will enable you to quickly isolate any problems that occur so that you can fix them quickly. Fixing printing problems quickly gets your users back to work performing the necessary tasks for their jobs.

Print Components

There are two major components that comprise printing: the *print driver* and the *print spooler*.

- The print driver is responsible for setting up the print job for the specific printer destination. Windows 2000, Windows XP, and Windows NT include a system service, the Graphics Device Interface (GDI), which provides a standardized communication mechanism between applications and print drivers.
- The print spooler is a collection of dynamic link library files (DLLs) that manages the rest of the printing process. It accepts the print job from the print driver and stores it until the printer can produce it. In Table 13-4, we list the components that make up the print spooler.

Table 13-4: *Print Spooler Components*

Component	What it Does
Client Spooler	Receives the print job from the print driver; returns system control to the operating system.
Server Spooler	Inserts the print job into the printing stream.
Print Router	Determines the correct print provider.
Print Provider	Handles communication between the computer and the print device.
Print Processor	Makes sure a print job is fully ready for printing. Inserts a separator page if specified.

Component	What it Does
Separator Page Processor (part of the Print Processor)	Creates a page or printer code instructions that can be sent to the printer ahead of the print job.

Print Process

The Windows 2000, Windows XP, and Windows NT print processes consist of the following steps:

1. A user prints a document in an application.
2. The GDI calls the printer driver.
3. The printer driver creates a job in printer language for the target printer. (This process is called *rendering*.)
4. The client side of the print spooler returns control of the computer system to the application.
5. The server side of the print spooler inserts the job into the printing stream.
6. The print router determines whether the job is for a local or remote printer.
    - If the job is for a local printer, the print router routes it to the local print provider.
    - If the job is for a remote printer:
        a. The print router routes it to the correct remote print provider for the print server.
        b. The remote print provider passes the job over the network to the spooler service at the print server, and the process resumes, at the print server, at step 5.
7. The local print provider *spools* the print job or writes it from memory to disk. By default, print jobs spool to the \Winnt\System32\Spool\Printers folder in Windows 2000, \Windows\System32\Spool\Printers folder in Windows XP, and \Winnt\System32\Spool\Printers in Windows NT. The local print provider also locates a print processor that can render the job's data type.
8. The print processor completes any rendering needed for the job's data type.
9. The separator page processor inserts a separator page, if indicated.
10. The port monitor software for the printer's port handles the physical data communication between the computer and the printer.
11. The printer produces the output.

Common Print Problems

In Table 13-5, you find a list of common problems you can encounter with printers. For each problem listed in this table, you'll find a step in the following procedure that helps you troubleshoot that problem.

Table 13-5: *Common Print Problems*

For These Symptoms	Suspect Problems With The
Jobs accumulate in the print queue but do not print.	Printer's hardware; Spooler service; print spool stalled.
Print output is garbled.	Incorrect or incompatible print driver; application; incorrect parameter (improperly configured application or hardware).
Print jobs do not reach the print queue.	Application; user permissions; printer share name; network connectivity.

How to Troubleshoot a Printer

Procedure Reference: Troubleshoot a Printer

The troubleshooting steps below are in order of basic to complex. As you gain experience, you may be able to recognize symptoms of a particular problem and immediately go to the step that solves that particular problem. In general, to troubleshoot a printing problem in Windows 2000, Windows XP, or Windows NT:

 While troubleshooting printers, you should consult the manufacturer's documentation and user manuals and any relevant training materials.

1. Check your printer's hardware:
   - Verify that the printer is connected to a working power source.
   - Verify that the printer is online.

     Some printers have an online-offline button.

   - Verify that the printer is not out of paper or the paper is not jammed.
   - Verify that the printer is not low or out of ink or toner.
   - Reset the printer by turning it off for 5 to 10 seconds to purge the printer's memory.

     Full printer memory can cause printing problems.

   - Verify that the printer is properly connected to the computer's printer port.
   - If available, perform a self-test on the printer.

     Many printers come with self-diagnostic programs that can resolve basic hardware issues. Refer to the printer's manual on the specific steps required to perform the diagnostics.

2. Print a test document from Notepad.
   a. Restart your computer.

b. From the Start menu, choose Programs→Accessories→Notepad.

c. Enter some text.

d. Print the page. If the page prints successfully, your printing issue may be specific to one program. You will need to troubleshoot that particular application.

3. If you have a non-USB printer, print from a Command Prompt:

  a. Verify that no printer-sharing devices (such as printer switch boxes) or daisy-chained devices (such as Zip drives) are connected between the computer and the printer.

  b. Open a Command Prompt window. (From the Start menu, choose Programs→ Accessories→Command Prompt.)

  c. At the command prompt, enter one of the following:

   For a standard printer: `copy c:\windows\mouse.txt lpt1`

   For a laser printer: `copy c:\windows\mouse.txt lpt1 /b`

   For a postscript printer: `copy c:\windows\system\testps.txt lpt1`

You can substitute another .txt file for mouse.txt if it doesn't exist on your system. You can also specify a different port if the printer is not connected to the default printer port—LPT1.

On some inkjet and laser printers, you might need to press the Form Feed or Resume button after the printer has received the job.

If the page prints successfully, you can rule out hardware or physical connection problems. The problem might be caused by incorrect spool settings or a stalled Print Server service.

4. If print jobs do not accumulate in the print queue, and you're printing to a shared printer, verify that you have the necessary permissions:

  a. Open the Printers folder.

  b. Right-click the shared printer and choose Properties.

  c. Select the Security tab.

  d. Verify that the user account that's attempting to print has at least the Print permission for the printer. (Keep in mind that permissions can be assigned either to the user account or to a group of which the user is a member.)

  e. If necessary, assign permissions to the user account.

  f. Close the printer's properties and the Printers folder.

5. If print jobs do not accumulate in the print queue, verify that the computer on which the printer is defined has enough available disk space to spool the print jobs.

  • If the printer is defined on a Windows 2000 or Windows NT computer, make sure that the drive containing the \Winnt\System32\Spool\Printers folder has free disk space.

- If the printer is defined on a Windows XP computer, make sure that the drive containing the \Windows\System32\Spool\Printers folder has free disk space.

6. If print jobs are accumulating in the print queue but not printing, and if you're using Windows 2000 or Windows XP, stop and restart the Print Spooler service:
   a. Open Computer Management.
   b. Below Services And Applications, select the Services object.
   c. In the details pane, right-click the Print Spooler service and choose Stop.
   d. Right-click the Print Spooler service and choose Start.
   e. Close Computer Management.

7. If print jobs are accumulating in the print queue but not printing, and if you're using Windows NT, stop and restart the Spooler service:
   a. In Control Panel, double-click Services.
   b. In the Services list, select the Spooler service.
   c. Click Stop.
   d. Click Yes to confirm that you want to stop the service.
   e. Verify that the Spooler service is still selected and click Start.
   f. Close Services and Control Panel.

8. If stopping and restarting the Print Spooler service doesn't resolve the problem, test the spool settings:
   a. If you're using Windows 2000 or Windows NT, from the Start menu, choose Settings→Printers.
   b. If you're using Windows XP, from the Start menu, choose Printers And Faxes.
   c. Right-click the printer and choose Properties.
   d. Select the Advanced tab.
   e. Select Print Directly To The Printer.
   f. Click OK twice.
   g. Print a test page from Notepad. If the page prints successfully, try different combinations of spool settings until you can print from all Windows programs.

9. Confirm the printer's properties are set correctly:
   a. If you're using Windows 2000 or Windows NT, from the Start menu, choose Settings→Printers.
   b. If you're using Windows XP, from the Start menu, choose Printers And Faxes.
   c. Right-click the printer you are troubleshooting and choose Properties.
   d. Verify that the settings correspond to those specified in the printer's manual.

10. Remove and re-install the printer driver. If you are using a printer driver installed from the Windows 2000/XP/NT CD-ROM:

a. If you're using Windows 2000 or Windows NT, from the Start menu, choose Settings→Printers.
b. If you're using Windows XP, from the Start menu, choose Printers And Faxes.
c. Right-click the printer and choose Delete.
d. Click Yes to remove all files associated with the printer.
e. Use the Add Printer Wizard to re-install the printer.
f. Print a test page from Notepad.
g. If the test page is not successful, use the Add Printer Wizard to install the Generic/Text Only printer driver.
h. Print a test page from Notepad.
i. If the second test page is successful, contact your printer's manufacturer for an updated printer driver.

11. Make sure that the user hasn't executed the `net use` command to redirect output from a local printer port to a shared network printer.
    a. In a Command Prompt window, execute the command `net use` to determine what if any local printer ports have been captured.
    b. To disconnect a captured printer port, execute the command `net use lpt# /delete`.

12. Verify the printer port is working properly.
    a. If you're using Windows 2000 or Windows NT, right-click My Computer and choose Properties.
    b. If you're using Windows XP, from the Start menu, right-click My Computer and choose Properties.
    c. If you're using Windows NT, select the Device Manager tab.
    d. If you're using Windows 2000 or Windows XP, select the Hardware tab and then click Device Manager.
    e. Expand Ports (COM & LPT) by clicking the plus sign (+).
    f. Select your printer port.
    g. Click Properties.
    h. Verify the Device Status reads This Device Is Working Properly.
    i. Select the Resources tab.
    j. Verify the Conflicting Devices List reads No Conflicts. If the port is not working correctly, try removing and re-installing the port. If another device is conflicting with the printer port, you need to correct the device conflict.

13. If the port is not working correctly, remove and re-install your printer port:
    a. If you're using Windows 2000 or Windows NT, right-click My Computer and choose Properties.

b. If you're using Windows XP, from the Start menu, right-click My Computer and choose Properties.

c. If you're using Windows NT, select the Device Manager tab.

d. If you're using Windows 2000 or Windows XP, select the Hardware tab and then click Device Manager.

e. Click the Device Manager tab.

f. Expand Ports (COM & LPT) by clicking the plus sign (+).

g. Select your printer port.

h. Click Remove.

i. Click OK.

j. Restart your computer. The printer port should automatically be detected by Windows when it restarts. Follow the prompts to re-install the printer port. If Windows does not automatically detect the printer port, manually add the port using the Add New Hardware wizard.

CHAPTER 13 FOLLOW-UP
Managing File and Print Resources in Windows 2000/NT/XP

In this chapter, you learned how to manage file and print resources in Windows 2000, Windows XP, and Windows NT. Knowing how to manage these resources will enable you to quickly respond to technical support calls. By correctly configuring access to file and print resources, and quickly resolving any problems that arise, you'll be able to keep users working productively on the network.

Essential Terms

- captured printer ports
- effective permissions
- folder sharing
- local printers
- network printers
- print components
- print problems
- print permissions
- printer ports
- printer troubleshooting
- printers
- share permissions
- troubleshooting
- Windows print process

Review Questions

1. Windows 2000 and NT support three share permissions. What are they?

2. Windows NT supports an additional share permission not available in Windows 2000. What share permission is it?

3. If a user has been assigned share permissions and NTFS permissions for the same share, what is the user's effective permission?

4. How does a folder icon change so you know the folder is shared?
5. Windows 2000, XP, and NT support two types of network print devices. What are the two types?
6. Users on your network run non-Windows applications. What must you do so users can print from the applications?
7. What two Windows operating systems support printers connected to USB ports?
8. What command must you execute to print from MS-DOS applications?
9. What is the full command structure you'd use to print to a print device that's shared on the network?
10. What is the full command you enter at the command prompt to delete a captured printer port?
11. What are the three print permissions you can assign when you share a printer in Windows 2000, XP, or NT?
12. In Windows 2000, what two groups can manage printers?
13. You are using Windows NT. Print jobs are accumulating in the print queue but not printing. What should you do?
14. What is the purpose of the separator page processor?
15. What print spool component makes sure a print job is fully ready for printing?
16. What is rendering?
17. In Windows 2000, what is the path to the Printer folder where the print jobs spool?
18. What print spooler component receives the print job from the print driver?
19. What role does the print provider play in the spooler process?
20. What are the two major components that comprise printing?
21. What is the function of the system service, graphics device interface (GDI)?
22. In Windows NT, 2000, and XP, what permission level is given to the everyone group by default?
23. Many users print to the same centrally located network printer. What can you do so users can distinguish among print jobs when they pick up their documents?
24. You attach a new print device to your workstation and download the driver from the manufacturer's Web site. When you print, the output is garbled. What do you suspect is the problem?
25. In Windows NT, 2000, and XP, what print permission does not include the ability to print to the printer?

Review Projects

Project #1 File Sharing and Permissions in Windows XP

The Microsoft Knowledge Base article, "Description of File Sharing and Permissions in Windows XP" introduces you to features specific to Windows XP. Specifically, you'll read about a new user interface that is known as Simple File Sharing. Included in the article is a short video that demonstrates how to enable and disable simple file sharing. Also, the article includes a short troubleshooting section. To access the article, copy the following address into your computer's Web browser: **http://support.microsoft.com/default.aspx?scid=kb%3Ben-us%3B304040**. In this activity, work through the exercises presented in the article. Bookmark the site for future reference.

To better understand file sharing in Windows XP, compare the processes of file sharing and setting permissions with Windows 2000. How, specifically, are they different? Document your discoveries.

Project #2 Accessing Microsoft's Windows 2000 Administrator's Pocket Consultant

The following URL directs you to an article archived on Microsoft's site. The article is a slice of a book excerpt from Microsoft Windows 2000 Administrator's Pocket Consultant. The focus of the article is limited to data sharing and security (permissions). To access the article, enter the following URL into your Web browser: **http://www.microsoft.com/technet/treeview/default.asp?url=/technet/prodtechnol/windows2000serv/deploy/confeat/13w2kada.asp**. Data sharing is what allows remote users to access network resources such as files, folders, printers, and drives. If you're sharing sensitive for a specific user or group, it's important that permissions are set on the resource correctly. Many file and folder access violations occur because permissions are set incorrectly. In situations where security is particularly important, you can enable auditing on resources. This particular article doesn't cover auditing, but it is covered extensively in Windows 2000's help files and Windows XP's Help and Support Center.

In this activity, read through the article and take note of sharing features with which you are unfamiliar (for example, Web sharing)

- What are the advantages of the sharing features?
- From a security standpoint, what do you see as disadvantages of resource sharing, particularly of Web sharing?

    Document your ideas.

On a Windows 2000 machine that uses the NTFS file system, create several folders and share them. Open Notepad and create at least one file for each share. If others don't use the machine, open Computer management and under Local Users and Groups create several users. Experiment with the permissions for files and folders. Assign users different permissions, then log in as each user and access the folders. Document what you did, the "user" who accessed the file, and the result.

Project #3 Investigating Internet Printing

Windows 2000 includes a new printing feature which enables you to print or manage documents from a Web browser. Internet printing (also referred to as IPP which stands for Internet Printing Protocol) demonstrates Microsoft's efforts to incorporate a Web browser into daily operations such as printing. Most users are very familiar with a Web browser and IPP incorporates a new feature into a standard interface. This activity is exploratory in nature. IPP depends on a Microsoft Server (though it is possible to use it from a client running the personal Web server, PWS) running Internet Information Server.

The objective of this activity is to understand the basics of how IPP works. Read through the articles. The articles are short and give you a basic understanding of what IPP is and how it may be implemented:

- "Overview of Internet Printing in Windows 2000" **http://support.microsoft.com/default.aspx?scid=kb%3Ben-us%3B248344**

- "How to Install and Use the Internet Printing Protocol Client" **http://support.microsoft.com/default.aspx?scid=kb;en-us;294439**

What do you see as the advantages of Internet Printing? What specific advantages does it offer over local and standard network printing? If you have access to Windows 2000 Server and IIS (if IIS is running IPP is installed by default), use the articles cited above as well as your operating system's help section to set up and use IPP.

Reflective Questions

1. In your company, or the companies you support, how will you implement file sharing?

2. In your company, or the companies you support, how will you implement printer sharing?

CHAPTER 14
Managing File and Print Resources in Windows 9x

Chapter Objectives:

In this chapter, you will manage file and print resources in Windows 9x.

You will:

- Set workgroup or domain membership.
- Configure the security level.
- Share folders.
- Install a printer.
- Troubleshoot a printer.
- Enable user profiles.

Introduction

In the last chapter, you learned how to manage file and print resources in Windows 2000, Windows XP, and Windows NT computers. Because you might be called upon to perform these same tasks on Windows 9x computers, in this chapter, you'll learn the procedures for managing file and print resources in Windows 9x.

As an A+ technician, you may encounter older yet still viable hardware and operating system technology such as Windows 9x. Your ability to manage file and print resources in these older systems will enable you to support a wider variety of systems and users.

TOPIC A
Set Workgroup or Domain Membership

Because it affects how you configure folder and printer security in Windows 9x, the first task you should complete when managing security is to configure the computer's workgroup or domain membership. In this topic, you'll learn how to configure a Windows 9x computer as a member of either a workgroup or a domain.

Configuring the computer as a member of a domain has an impact on how you go about securing the computer's local resources such as folders and printers. If you don't configure a Windows 9x computer as a member of a domain first before you secure its local resources, you'll have to reconfigure these security settings again if you later add the computer as a member of a domain. To avoid having to redo work, you should always set the computer's workgroup or domain membership first before securing its local resources.

NetBIOS Names

Microsoft designed Windows to be user-friendly. As such, they designed Windows so that you could assign names to computers and then access them by name. In earlier versions of Windows such as Windows 9x and Windows NT, this computer name is called a NetBIOS name. In more recent versions of Windows (such as Windows 2000 and Windows XP), Microsoft replaced the NetBIOS name with a DNS name. A DNS name consists of the computer's name plus the name of the DNS domain. For example, you might have a Windows 2000 server with a DNS name of 2000srv.company.com.

In some situations when you're configuring Windows 9x, you'll find that you will need to enter the NetBIOS-equivalent name for a DNS name. The NetBIOS-equivalent name is the first part of the DNS name without the DNS domain name. Continuing with our example, the NetBIOS-equivalent name for the DNS name of 2000srv.company.com is 2000srv.

How to Set Workgroup or Domain Membership

Procedure Reference: Set Workgroup or Domain Membership

To set your computer's workgroup or domain membership:

1. Choose Start→Settings→Control Panel.

Instead of going through Control Panel, on the Desktop, you can right-click Network Neighborhood and choose Properties to open the Network dialog box.

2. Open Network.
3. Select the Identification tab.
4. In the Workgroup text box, type the name of your workgroup or domain.
5. Click OK.
6. Click Yes to restart the computer.
7. Log back on to the computer.

 Because Windows 9x computers cannot have computer accounts in a Windows domain, they aren't truly members of the domain. When you set their workgroup membership to a domain, they are simply grouped with other domain resources for browsing purposes.

Logging on to a Domain

You can configure Windows 9x to request that a domain controller authenticate a user name and password at log on. The authenticated user would then be able to access shared domain resources from within Windows 9x. However, it is important to remember that Windows 9x itself is not a secure operating system. Even without an authenticated user name and password, a user can access the Windows 9x desktop and use the local operating system and resources.

To configure a Windows 9x computer to request user account authentication by a domain controller:

1. Choose Start→Settings→Control Panel.
2. Open Network.
3. In the The Following Network Components Are Installed list box, select Client For Microsoft Networks.
4. Click Properties.
5. In the Logon Validation box, check Log On To Windows NT Domain.
6. In the Windows NT Domain text box, type the name of your domain.
7. In the Network Logon Options box, select either:
   - Quick Logon to validate your user account and password with the domain controller, but not automatically reconnect any network drives.
   - Logon And Restore Network Connections to validate your user account and password with the domain controller and connect to and verify each network drive mapping.
8. Click OK.
9. Click OK to close the Network dialog box.
10. Click Yes to restart the computer.

11. In the logon dialog box, which automatically displays the domain name, enter your user name and password.
12. Click OK to logon.

Topic B
Configure the Security Level

Because it controls how you share resources, the first task you'll need to complete before sharing files and printers on a Windows 9x computer is to configure its security level. So, in this topic, you'll learn about the different security levels you can implement on a Windows 9x computer and how to configure your chosen security level.

Setting the security level on a Windows 9x computer properly accomplishes two goals: First, it enables you to secure the computer appropriately for its environment. Second, because changing the computer's security level removes all shares on the computer, setting the security level properly in the first place enables you to avoid having to redo the work of establishing shares on the computer.

Security Levels

There are two security levels that can be set on a Windows 9x computer then used to secure shared resources: share-level and user-level. The *share-level security* setting enables you to set a password on each individual shared resource. Anyone connecting to the shared resource who enters the correct password is granted access. The *user-level security* setting enables you to specify which users and groups have access to each individual shared resource. You grant access using the user and group accounts list from the local user accounts database or from a Windows domain. Anyone connecting to the shared resource must have their user name and password validated by the designated user accounts database before they are granted access to the resource.

How to Configure the Security Level

Procedure Reference: Configure the Security Level of a Windows 9x Computer

To configure the security level of a Windows 9x computer:

1. If you plan to implement User-level Access Control, log on to Windows 9x with a user name and password that exists on the computer from which you want to obtain the master list of users. For example, if you plan to obtain the master list from an Active Directory domain, log on as a user within that domain.
2. Choose Start→Settings→Control Panel to open Control Panel.
3. Double-click Network to open the Network applet.
4. Click the Access Control tab to switch to the Access Control page.
5. In the Control Access To Shared Resources Using box, select either of the following:

- Share-level Access Control to apply security where you set a password on each individual shared resource.
- User-level Access Control to apply security where you specify which users and groups have access to each individual shared resource.

6. If you selected User-level Access Control, in the Obtain List Of Users And Groups From text box, type in the name of the computer or network domain where the master list of users is stored.

   If you configure Windows 9x to obtain its list of users from an Active Directory domain, type in the NetBIOS name of the domain instead of the DNS domain name. For example, if the DNS domain name for the domain is "company.com," type "company" in the Obtain List Of Users And Groups From text box.

7. Click OK to close the Network applet.
8. Close the Control Panel window.
9. Click Yes to restart your computer.

 You will be prompted to restart your computer each time you change the security level on your computer. Once the computer restarts, the new security level is applied to your computer. Any resources that were shared with the previous security level will need to be reshared.

TOPIC C
Share Folders

Earlier in this course, you saw how to share folders in the Windows 2000, Windows NT, and Windows XP networked environments. Now, we want to show you how to perform those same tasks with Windows 9x-based computers. In this topic, you'll learn the steps for implementing shared folders in Windows 9x.

Just as you saw with the Windows 2000, Windows NT, and Windows XP operating systems, Windows 9x users also want to be able to share files without using a sneaker net. Providing your Windows 9x users with access to shared folders will help you avoid the loss of productivity that comes with manually copying files between non-networked computers.

Share Permissions in Windows 9x

Definition:

A *Windows 9x share permission* is a collection of defined rights that allow access to a shared resource. A Windows 9x share permission specifies the functions a user can perform using the shared resource. A Windows 9x share permission may include preassigned rights by the operating system or may be customized by the user.

Example: Windows 9x Share Permissions

Windows 9x includes three share permissions:

- The Read-Only access permission allows the user to view the contents of the shared resource, but not save changes. Its rights are preassigned by Windows 9x.
- The Full access permission allows the user to fully control the shared resource and its functionality. Its rights are preassigned by Windows 9x.
- The Custom access permission allows the user setting the permission to decide which rights to allow. This share permission is available only with user-level security.

How to Share Folders

Procedure Reference: Share a Folder Using Share-level Security

To share a folder on a Windows 9x computer where the security level is set to share-level:

1. If necessary, enable file sharing.
    a. Open the Network dialog box (right-click Network Neighborhood and choose Properties).
    b. Click File And Print Sharing.
    c. Check I Want To Be Able To Give Others Access To My Files.
    d. Click OK.
    e. Click OK to close the Network dialog box.
    f. If prompted, click Yes to restart the computer.
    g. Log back on to Windows 98.
2. Locate the folder you want to share using Windows Explorer, My Computer, or another local browsing tool.
3. Right-click the folder.
4. From the shortcut menu, choose Sharing.
5. On the Sharing page, select Shared As:
6. In the Share Name text box, type a maximum of 12 characters as the name for your share. This is the name other users will see when they browse for and access the share.
7. In the Comments text box, type any comments you want to display about the share. Comments are optional.
8. In Access Type, select one of the following:
    - Read-Only to allow other users to view, but not make changes to the contents of the folder.
    - Full to allow users to view and make changes to the contents of the folder.
    - Depends On Password to set users' abilities to read-only or full depending on the password they enter when accessing the share.

9. In Passwords, enter one of the following:
   - If you selected the Read-Only access type, in the Read-Only Password text box, type your desired password.
   - If you selected the Full access type, in the Full Access Password text box, type your desired password.
   - If you selected the Depends On Password access type, in the Read-Only Password text box, type your desired password for read-only access and in the Full Access Password text box, type your desired password for full access.
10. Click OK.
11. In the Password Confirmation dialog box, re-enter the passwords you typed in the appropriate text boxes.
12. Click OK.
13. Verify that users can access the shared folder.

Procedure Reference: Share a Folder Using User-level Security

To share a folder on a Windows 9x computer where the security level is set to user-level:

1. If necessary, enable file sharing.
   a. Open the Network dialog box (right-click Network Neighborhood and choose Properties).
   b. Click File And Print Sharing.
   c. Check I Want To Be Able To Give Others Access To My Files.
   d. Click OK.
   e. Click OK to close the Network dialog box.
   f. If prompted, click Yes to restart the computer.
   g. Log back on to Windows 98.
2. Locate the folder you want to share using Windows Explorer, My Computer, or another local browsing tool.
3. Right-click the folder.
4. From the shortcut menu, choose Sharing.
5. On the Sharing page, select Shared As:
6. In the Share Name text box, type a maximum of 12 characters as the name for your share. This is the name other users will see when they browse for and access the share.
7. In the Comments text box, type any comments you want to display about the share. Comments are optional.
8. Click Add.
9. From the Name list box, select the users or groups you want to grant similar access to.

> You can hold down the Ctrl key to select multiple users and groups.

10. For the users or groups selected, click one of the following:
    - Read-Only to allow other users to view, but not make changes to, the contents of the folder.
    - Full Access to allow users to view and make changes to the contents of the folder.
    - Custom to select the individual rights assigned to the selected users or groups.
11. Repeat steps 8 and 9 for each set of users and groups you want to grant similar access to.
12. Click OK.
13. If you granted custom access to any users or groups, check the desired rights:
    - Read Files
    - Write to Files
    - Create Files and Folders
    - Delete Files
    - Change File Attributes
    - List Files
    - Change Access Control

    Then click OK.
14. Click OK to close the folder's Properties dialog box.
15. Verify that users can access the shared folder.

Topic D
Install a Printer

Earlier in this course, you saw how to install both a local printer and a network printer on Windows 2000, Windows NT, and Windows XP computers. If you encounter a company with older computers, you'll need to know how to perform these same tasks in Windows 9x. In this topic, you'll learn how to install both types of printers on Windows 9x computers.

No matter what operating system they're using, users need to print in order to perform their jobs. As an A+ technician, it will be your job to configure users' Windows 9x computers to print to either a local printer, network printer, or both. Knowing how to configure printing in Windows 9x will enable you to get users up and printing and working productively on their computers.

How to Install a Printer

Procedure Reference: Install a Local Printer

To install a printer that is attached to the local computer:

1. From the Start menu, choose Settings→Printers to open the Printers dialog box.
2. Double-click the Add Printer icon to start the Add Printer Wizard.
3. Click Next.
4. Select Local Printer.
5. Click Next.
6. From the Manufacturers list box, select the manufacturer of your printer.
7. From the Printers list box, select the model of your printer.
8. Click Next.
9. From the Available Ports list box, select the port your printer is connected on.

    In most cases, this will be an LPT# port.

10. Click Next.
11. In the Printer Name text box, type a name for your printer.
12. Under Do You Want Your Windows-based Programs To Use This Printer As The Default Printer, select one of the following:

    You'll be prompted as to whether you want to make this printer the default printer only if you have other printers defined in the Printers folder. If this is the first printer in the Printers folder, Windows 9x automatically makes the printer the default printer.

    - Yes, if you want all Windows programs to use this printer as their default printer.
    - No, if you want this printer available to Windows programs to use, but it is not their default printer.

13. Click Next.
14. Under Would You Like To Print A Test Page select one of the following:
    - Yes (Recommended), if you want to print a test page to verify the printer is set up properly.
    - No, if you want to skip printing the test page.
15. Click Finish.
16. If you are prompted for the Windows 9x setup disk, insert the disk in the CD-ROM drive and click OK.
17. If you selected Yes (Recommended) to print a test page, click one of the following:

- Yes, if the test page printed properly at the printer.
- No, if the test page did not print properly at the printer.

18. Close the Printers window.

Procedure Reference: Install a Network Printer

To install a printer that is shared on the network:

1. Log on to Windows 9x with a user account and password that is valid for the print server. For example, if the network printer is shared on a domain controller, log on to Windows 9x with a domain user account and password.
2. From the Start menu, choose Settings→Printers to open the Printers dialog box.
3. Double-click the Add Printer icon to start the Add Printer Wizard.
4. Click Next.
5. Select Network Printer.
6. Click Next.
7. In the Network Path Or Queue Name text box, type or browse to find the name of the printer.
8. Under Do You Print From MS-DOS-based Programs select one of the following:
   - Yes, if you will be printing from programs that run under MS-DOS.
   - No, if you will be printing from only Windows-based programs.
9. Click Next.
10. If the drivers for your version of Windows 9x are not installed on the print server, you are prompted to select the manufacturer and type of printer:
    a. From the Manufacturers list box, select the manufacturer of your printer.
    b. From the Printers list box, select the model of your printer.
    c. Click Next.
11. In the Printer Name text box, type a name for your printer.
12. If you have installed other printers on this computer, you'll be prompted to choose which printer you want as the default printer. Under Do You Want Your Windows-based Programs To Use This Printer As The Default Printer, select one of the following:
    - Yes, if you want all Windows programs to use this printer as their default printer.
    - No, if you want this printer available to Windows programs to use, but it is not their default printer.
13. Click Finish.
14. If you are prompted for the Windows 9x setup disk, insert the disk in the CD-ROM drive and click OK.

15. Close the Printers window.

Topic E
Troubleshoot a Printer in Windows 9x

In Topic 14D, you learned how to install both network and local printers in the Windows 9x environment. Unfortunately, printing problems are bound to crop up. For this reason, in this topic, you'll learn how to troubleshoot printing in Windows 9x.

As we've said, nothing generates technical support phone calls faster than users who are unable to print. Your job as an A+ technician is to be able to respond to these calls quickly to diagnose and repair the printing problem. Knowing how to troubleshoot printing will enable you to get your users back printing and working productively on their Windows 9x computers.

How to Troubleshoot a Printer in Windows 9x

Procedure Reference: Troubleshoot a Printer in Windows 9x

The troubleshooting steps below are in order of basic to complex. As you gain experience, you may be able to recognize symptoms of a particular problem and immediately go to the step that solves that particular problem. In general, to troubleshoot a printing problem in Windows 9x:

 While troubleshooting printers, you should consult the manufacturer's documentation and user manuals and any relevant training materials.

1. Check your printer's hardware:
   - Verify that the printer is connected to a working power source.
   - Verify that the printer is online (some printers have an online-offline button).
   - Verify that the printer is not out of paper or the paper is not jammed.
   - Verify that the printer is not low or out of ink or toner.
   - Reset the printer by turning it off for 5 to 10 seconds to purge the printer's memory (full printer memory can cause printing problems).
   - Verify that the printer is properly connected to the computer's printer port.
   - If available, perform a self-test on the printer (many printers come with self-diagnostic programs that can resolve basic hardware issues. Refer to the printer's manual on the specific steps required to perform the diagnostics).

2. Print a test document from Notepad.
   a. Restart your computer to clear all programs out of memory.
   b. From the Start menu, choose Programs→Accessories→Notepad.
   c. Enter some text.

d. Print the page.

If the page prints successfully, your printing issue may be specific to one program. You will need to troubleshoot that particular application.

3. If you have a non-USB printer, print from a Command Prompt:
   a. Verify that no printer-sharing devices (such as printer switch boxes) or daisy-chained devices (such as Zip drives) are connected between the computer and the printer.
   b. Restart your computer in SafeMode Command Prompt Only.
   c. At the command prompt, enter one of the following:

   For a standard printer: `copy c:\windows\mouse.txt lpt1`

   For a laser printer: `copy c:\windows\mouse.txt lpt1 /b`

   For a postscript printer: `copy c:\windows\system\testps.txt lpt1`

   You can substitute another .txt file for mouse.txt if it doesn't exist on your system. You can also specify a different port if the printer is not connected to the default printer port—LPT1.

   On some inkjet and laser printers, you might need to press the Form Feed or Resume button after the printer has received the job. If the page prints successfully, you can rule out hardware or physical connection problems. The problem might be caused by incorrect spool or bi-directional printer settings. Go to Step 4.

   If the page does not print successfully, check the printer's properties. Go to Step 6.

4. Test the spool settings:
   a. From the Start menu, choose Settings→Printers.
   b. Right-click the printer and choose Properties.
   c. Click the Details tab.
   d. Click Spool Settings.
   e. Select Print Directly To The Printer (if the local printer is being shared, Print Directly To The Printer will be grayed out. Stop sharing the printer to enable the choice).
   f. Click OK twice.
   g. Print a test page from Notepad.

   If the page prints successfully, try different combinations of spool settings until you can print from all Windows programs.

5. If your printer cable does not conform to the 1284 IEEE specification bi-directional printing will not work in Windows 9x. Disable bi-directional support.
   a. From the Start menu, choose Settings→Printers.
   b. Right-click the printer and choose Properties.
   c. Click the Details tab.

d. Click Spool Settings.

e. Select Disable Bi-Directional Support For This Printer.

f. Click OK twice.

g. Print a test page from Notepad.

If the page prints successfully, replace the printer cable with one that conforms with the 1284 IEEE specification.

6. Confirm the printer's properties are set correctly:

   a. From the Start menu, choose Settings→Printers.

   b. Right-click the printer you are troubleshooting and choose Properties.

   c. Verify that the settings correspond with those specified in the printer's manual.

7. Remove and re-install the printer driver. If you are using a printer driver installed from the Windows 9x CD-ROM:

   a. From the Start menu, choose Settings→Printers.

   b. Right-click the printer and choose Delete.

   c. Click Yes to remove all files associated with the printer.

   d. Use the Add Printer Wizard to re-install the printer.

   e. Print a test page from Notepad.

   f. If the test page is not successful, use the Add Printer Wizard to install the Generic/Text Only printer driver.

   g. Print a test page from Notepad.

   h. If the second test page is successful, contact your printer's manufacturer for an updated printer driver.

8. Verify the printer port is working properly.

   a. Right-click My Computer and choose Properties.

   b. Click the Device Manager tab.

   c. Expand Ports (COM & LPT) by clicking the plus sign (+).

   d. Select your printer port.

   e. Click Properties.

   f. Verify the Device Status reads This Device Is Working Properly.

   g. Select the Resources tab.

   h. Verify the Conflicting Devices List reads No Conflicts. If the port is not working correctly, try removing and re-installing the port. If another device is conflicting with the printer port, you need to correct the device conflict.

9. If the port is not working correctly, remove and re-install your printer port:

   a. Right-click My Computer and choose Properties.

  b. Click the Device Manager tab.

  c. Expand Ports (COM & LPT) by clicking the plus sign (+).

  d. Select your printer port.

  e. Click Remove.

  f. Click OK.

  g. Restart your computer.

The printer port should automatically be detected by Windows when it restarts. Follow the prompts to re-install the printer port. If Windows does not automatically detect the printer port, manually add the port using the Add New Hardware wizard.

Print Troubleshooter

Windows 9x has a Print Troubleshooter within the Help system that can guide you in diagnosing common problems and solutions.

To run the Print Troubleshooter in Windows 95:

  a. From the Start menu, choose Help.

  b. On the Contents page, double-click Troubleshooting.

  c. Double-click the If You Have Trouble Printing topic.

  d. Respond to the prompts.

To run the Print Troubleshooter in Windows 98:

  a. From the Start menu, choose Help.

  b. On the Contents page, select Troubleshooting.

  c. Select Windows 98 Troubleshooters.

  d. Select Print.

  e. Respond to the prompts.

 The Windows 95 Resource Kit includes a more detailed Print Troubleshooter tool called Epts.exe.

TOPIC F
Enable User Profiles

Earlier in this course, you learned about user profiles in the Windows 2000, Windows NT, and Windows XP environments. Windows 9x also supports user profiles. In this topic, you'll learn how to enable user profiles in Windows 9x.

Enabling user profiles in Windows 9x makes it possible for each user of the computer to have his or her own desktop and Start menu. If you don't enable user profiles, users of the same Windows 9x computer won't be able to have unique desktops and Start menus. If your users aren't very sophisticated, sharing a desktop can lead to a lot of support phone calls with questions such as: "Why did my icons move around on the desktop?" and "How come the wallpaper has changed?" and "Where did my files go?" Configuring Windows 9x so that each user maintains their own profile will help you avoid spending a lot of time answering such questions and reconfiguring computers.

Windows 9x User Profile Folders

On Windows 9x computers where user profiles have been enabled, in the \Windows\Profiles directory, the operating system creates a folder for each user who logs on. This folder is named with the user's logon name. Be aware that the Desktop, Favorites, My Documents, Start Menu, and Temporary Internet folders are only available if they have been enabled in the Personalized Item Settings in the Users option of Control Panel. The NetHood folder is only available if it has been enabled by a system policy. This folder can contain the subfolders listed in the following table.

Folder	Stores
Application Data	Information specifying the installed application settings for this user. This might include items such as an Outlook address book (User.wab) file and list of recently opened Microsoft Office documents.
Cookies	Cookie files for Microsoft Internet Explorer.
Desktop	Contents of the Active Desktop.
Favorites	Channels for Microsoft Internet Explorer.
History	History list for Microsoft Internet Explorer.
My Documents	Contents of the My Documents folder on the user's desktop. Unlike the other folders, this folder is stored in C:\. All users of the computer share the same My Documents folder.
NetHood	Shortcuts available in Network Neighborhood.
Recent	Contents of the Start→Documents menu.
Start Menu	Contents of the Start menu, including the Programs menu.
Temporary Internet Files	Contents of the \Temporary Internet Files directory.

Windows 9x Users

Because Windows 9x is not a secure operating system, you can enter any user name and password when you log on to a Windows 9x-based computer. If you have configured Windows 9x to maintain separate profiles for each user, Windows 9x will then create a series of folders in which to store the profile for the new user name you specified.

How to Enable User Profiles

Procedure Reference: Enable User Profiles

To enable user profiles on a Windows 9x computer:

1. From the Start menu, choose Settings→Control Panel.
2. Double-click Passwords.
3. Select the User Profiles tab.
4. Select Users Can Customize Their Preferences And Desktop Settings.
5. In the User Profile Settings box, check any of the following options:
   - Include Desktop Icons And Network Neighborhood Contents In User Settings if you want the current desktop icons and contents of Network Neighborhood to be copied to any new user profiles.
   - Include Start Menu And Program Groups In User Settings if you want the current Start menu items and program groups to be copied to any new user profiles.

    At the time you enable user profiles, the configuration of the computer becomes the default for all subsequent user profiles.

6. Click OK.
7. Click Yes to restart the computer.

Logging On as a New User

When a new user logs on to a computer where user profiles are enabled, the system prompts them to decide whether or not they want the computer to retain their individual settings. If they click Yes, a new user profile is created for their user name. If they click No, they log on with the default user profile.

CHAPTER 14 FOLLOW-UP
Managing File and Print Resources in Windows 9x

In this chapter, you learned how to manage file and print resources in Windows 9x. Many companies have computers with older operating systems such as Windows 9x. Knowing how to configure file and print resources in Windows 9x expands your marketability because you are able to configure and support a wider variety of computers beyond just the latest technology.

Essential Terms

- domains
- folder sharing
- local printers
- network printers
- printer troubleshooting
- printers

- security
- security levels
- share permissions
- troubleshooting
- user profiles
- workgroups

Review Questions

1. What is a NetBIOS name?
2. In Windows 2000 and Windows XP, what name replaced the NetBIOS name?
3. A DNS name is comprised of what two elements?
4. What are the two security levels that can be set on a Windows 9x computer to secure resources?
5. On a Windows 9x machine, what security setting enables you to set a password on each individual shared resource?
6. What do user-level security settings enable you to do?
7. To configure security levels on a Windows 9x machine, what Control Panel applet do you access?
8. What are the three share permissions available on a Windows 9x computer?
9. Which share permission is available only with user-level security on a Windows 9x machine?
10. Which two Windows 9x share permissions are pre-assigned by the operating system?
11. When troubleshooting a printer problem, you should work in the order of basic to complex. What should you first check when there is a printer problem?
12. To what specification must your print cable conform in order to use bi-directional printing in Windows 9x?
13. Where is the print troubleshooter located in Windows 9x?
14. You want to configure a Windows 9x computer so each user who logs on has a unique desktop and Start menu. What must you configure on the machine?
15. Where do you enable personalized item settings on a Windows 9x machine?
16. What do you have to enable to make the NetHood folder available?
17. What must you do before a new security level you configured is applied to your computer?
18. In Windows 9x, which share permission allows the user to view the contents of a shared folder, but not save the changes?
19. To share a folder on a Windows 9x computer where the share level is set to user-level, what is the maximum number of characters you can use for the share name?
20. When sharing a folder, you use the name list box to select the users or groups you want to grant access. What key do you hold down to select multiple users and groups?
21. Where do you look to verify that the printer port is working correctly?
22. Windows 9x computers cannot truly be members of a domain. Why?
23. What is the first task you should complete when managing security in Windows 9x?
24. What part of a DNS name is the NetBIOS equivalent?
25. What is the effect of changing the security level on a Windows 9x computer?

Review Projects

Project #1 Printing Device Manager Contents

This activity applies to Windows 9x and Windows Millennium.

Device Manager enables you to view your installed hardware and quickly determine if there are problems with any of the devices on your computer. As part of your documentation, you should have a copy of Device Manager's contents.

In this activity, you'll print the contents of Device Manager to a file. By default, when you print the contents of Device Manager to a file, the information is unreadable. This is because Windows uses printer-specific language instead of plain text. The following knowledge base article, "How to Print Device Manager Contents to a Text File," outlines the steps to perform so you can print the Device Manager's contents to a file.

Perform the steps outlined in the knowledge base article. Save the Device Manager contents file to your hardware documentation folder.

Project #2 Using WINS

WINS, which stands for Windows Internet Name Service, is a name resolution method. WINS, like DNS, is a database, but unlike DNS, WINS maps NetBIOS names to IP addresses. For example, at a computer command line you could ping another computer either by its IP address or by its NetBIOS (computer name) name when WINS is enabled.

The "Implementing the WINS Service" article, written by Brien M. Posey, introduces you to WINS and guides you through a basic setup. The primary reason for using WINS is to help reduce broadcast traffic on your network. This article actually precedes Windows 2000's launch; however, the information is still very relevant. Unless you are working in pure Windows 2000 networks, you'll likely find WINS in use. Clients such as 9x, Windows Millenium, and Windows NT 4.0 use WINS.

The article is located at **http://www.microsoft.com/technet/treeview/default.asp?url=/technet/prodtechnol/winntas/tips/techrep/wins.asp**. If you're familiar with WINS, you may be interested in a more exhaustive treatment of the subject. The white paper, "MS Windows 4.0 - WINS Architecture and Capacity Planning," provides you with some history about NetBIOS and NetBIOS networks, LMHOSTS and their limitations, the WINS database, and replication. Although this white paper was written a while ago, it still offers one of the better treatments of the topic available.

If possible, install WINS, and review its menus and options. Configure WINS to work on a small network (2 computers is sufficient).

Project #3 Active Directory Overview

Active Directory is Microsoft's implementation of a directory service in Windows 2000. It provides a central location for all resources so you can manage the network efficiently. There are many advantages to deploying Active Directory on a network:

- Central administration to all users, groups, and computers.
- Group policy implementation.
- Security features such as a more robust authentication protocol.

- Scalability, which means that Active directory can grow in scope to meet the changing needs of your network and of your users.

This list barely scratches the surface of possibilities offered by Active Directory. Microsoft offers a good overview of Active Directory. Although the article provides only an overview, it tells you not only what Active Directory is, but also how it works.

In this activity, read the article, "Active Directory Overview," located at **http://www.microsoft.com/windows2000/server/evaluation/features/dirlist.asp#heading1**. After you've completed the article, you'll review what you've read by creating a fictional company and diagramming your company's Active Directory structure. Following are some questions to get you started:

- What is the full name of your company (for example, widgets.com)?
- How many domain controllers are on the network? What are the conrollers named?
- What kind of operating systems are used?
- How many employees are in your company?
- How many departments are there? Would you make an organizational unit for each department?

This activity is meant to help you review concepts and gain a understanding of the "big picture." Experiment with ideas and use your imagination.

Reflective Questions

1. **In your organization, or the organizations you support, how will you implement shared file resources?**

2. **In your organization, or the organizations you support, how will you implement printer sharing?**

CHAPTER 15
Managing Disk Resources in Windows 2000/NT/XP

Chapter Objectives:

In this chapter, you will manage disk resources in Windows 2000/NT/XP.

You will:

- Create or delete a partition.
- Convert a partition to NTFS.
- Compress files and folders.
- Defragment a hard disk.

Introduction

So far in this course, you've managed applications, implemented network connectivity, and configured file and print resources in the Windows 2000, Windows NT, Windows XP, and Windows 9x operating systems. You might think of these tasks as basic configuration tasks—the tasks you must perform to get users up and working. Now, it's time to turn your attention to managing the computer's disk resources. In this chapter, you'll learn how to manage disk resources in Windows 2000, Windows NT, and Windows XP.

The hard drive is a computer's key storage resource. At best, if it isn't configured properly, disk performance and data security will be compromised. At worst, users will be unable to access the data and applications they need. As an A+ technician, you will be responsible for managing critical disk resources.

Topic A
Create or Delete a Partition

An important part of managing partitions is knowing how to create or delete a partition. As an A+ technician, you need the skills to create the appropriate disk configuration for each user. To do so, you'll need to be able to create or delete partitions whenever necessary. So, in this topic, you'll learn the steps for creating and deleting partitions in the Windows 2000, Windows NT, and Windows XP environments.

There are a lot of reasons why you might need to create or delete the partitions on a hard disk. For example, you might encounter a situation in which you're asked to configure a user's old computer for a new user's use. In this scenario, you won't want the new user to have access to the old user's data, so the best solution is to delete the computer's existing partitions and create the partitions the new user will need. Another scenario in which you might be called upon to create a partition is if you encounter a hard disk with unused free space. Creating a partition in this free space will enable the user to take advantage of otherwise unusable disk space.

Partitions

Definition:

A *partition* is an area of a hard disk that is treated logically as a single unit of storage. A partition can use some or all of the available disk space on a hard disk. In order for a partition to be accessible, you must format it and assign a drive letter to it. A partition can be either primary or extended. A *primary partition* can be used to boot the computer; an *extended partition* cannot. You must mark a primary partition as active in order for it to be used to boot the computer. In the disk management utilities, Windows 2000 and Windows XP indicate which partition is active by displaying (System) for that partition. In the disk management utility for Windows NT, the active partition is indicated with an asterisk (*). The MS-DOS, Windows 9x, Windows NT, Windows 2000, and Windows XP operating systems all use partitions to access disk space.

When you format a disk, you assign a file system to it. Windows 2000 and Windows XP support the following file systems:

- FAT
- FAT32
- NTFS

Windows NT supports the following file systems:

- FAT
- HPFS
- NTFS

Example:

In Figure 15-1, you see the disk information for a drive with three primary partitions. Notice that each partition is assigned its own drive letter.

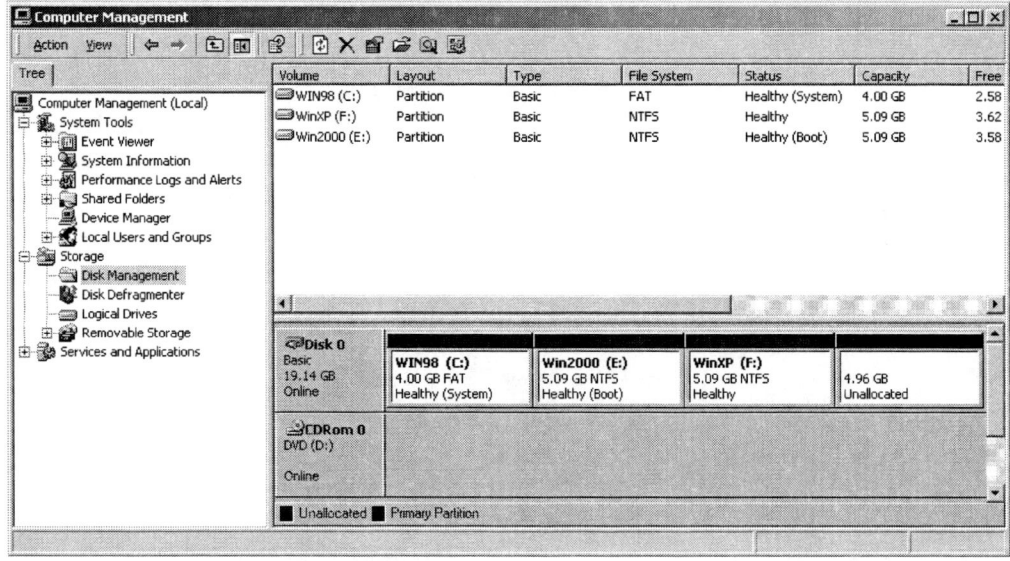

Figure 15-1: *A hard disk with three partitions.*

Other Names for Partitions

You'll find that you often hear different names used for partitions. Although the names differ, they all refer to some or all of the disk space on a particular hard disk. These synonymous names include:

- Disk
- Drive
- Volume

Basic Disks

Definition:

A *basic disk* is a physical hard disk that is divided logically into partitions. Windows NT, Windows 2000, and Windows XP support basic disks. You can create a maximum of four partitions on a basic disk. If you create four partitions, you can either create all four as primary partitions or one extended partition and three primary partitions (you can have a maximum of one extended partition on a hard disk).

 Windows 9x and MS-DOS do not support basic disks. Instead, you can configure a maximum of one primary and one extended partition on these operating systems.

Example:

In Figure 15-2, you see a computer with two basic disks. Each basic disk contains a single primary partition.

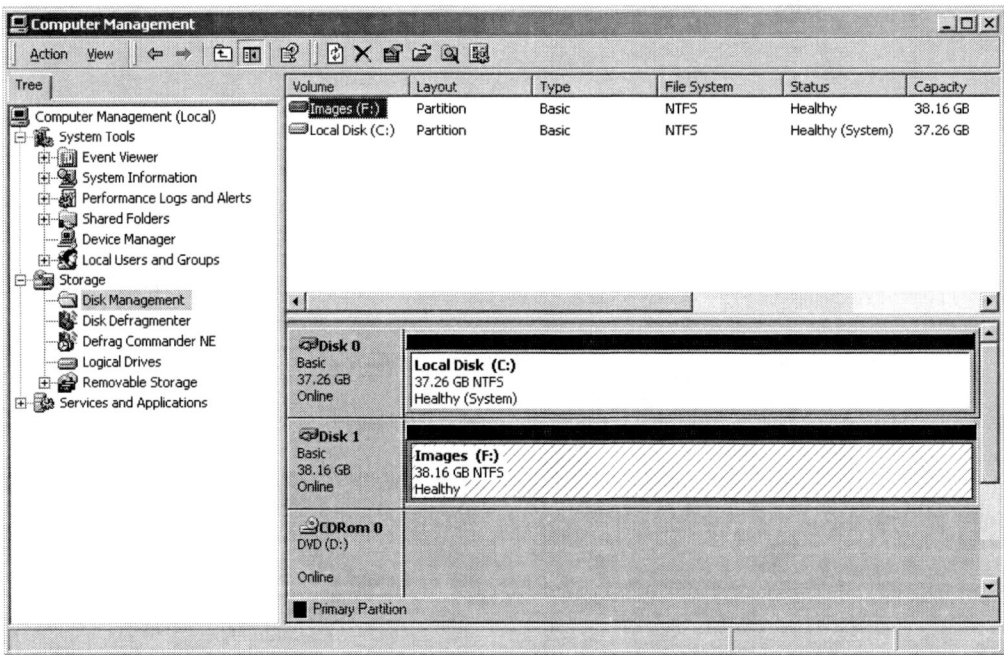

Figure 15-2: *A computer with two basic disks, each containing a single partition.*

Dynamic Disks

Definition:

A *dynamic disk* is a physical hard disk that is divided logically into volumes. Only Windows 2000 and Windows XP support dynamic disks. You create a dynamic disk by converting an existing basic disk to a dynamic disk. Once converted, you cannot convert a dynamic disk back to a basic disk. There is no limit to the number of volumes you can create and format on a physical hard disk. The types of volumes you can create include:

- A simple volume, which is an area of a single dynamic disk that you format and to which you assign a drive letter. (A basic volume is essentially the same as a partition.) If you format the basic volume to use the NTFS file system, you can increase the volume's size by extending it to unformatted free space on the same disk.
- A striped volume, which is multiple areas of space from two or more dynamic disks that you treat as a single logical volume. Windows 2000 and Windows XP write to all disks in the volume simultaneously for improved disk performance.
- A spanned volume, which is multiple areas of space from two or more dynamic disks that you treat as a single logical volume. Windows 2000 and Windows XP write to each disk in sequence. You typically use a spanned volume when you want to increase the amount of disk space in an existing volume.

Windows Server 2003 also supports dynamic disks.

See Appendix C for more information on how to convert a basic disk to a dynamic disk.

Example:

In Figure 15-3, you see a computer with two basic disks and a dynamic disk. The dynamic disk contains two simple volumes.

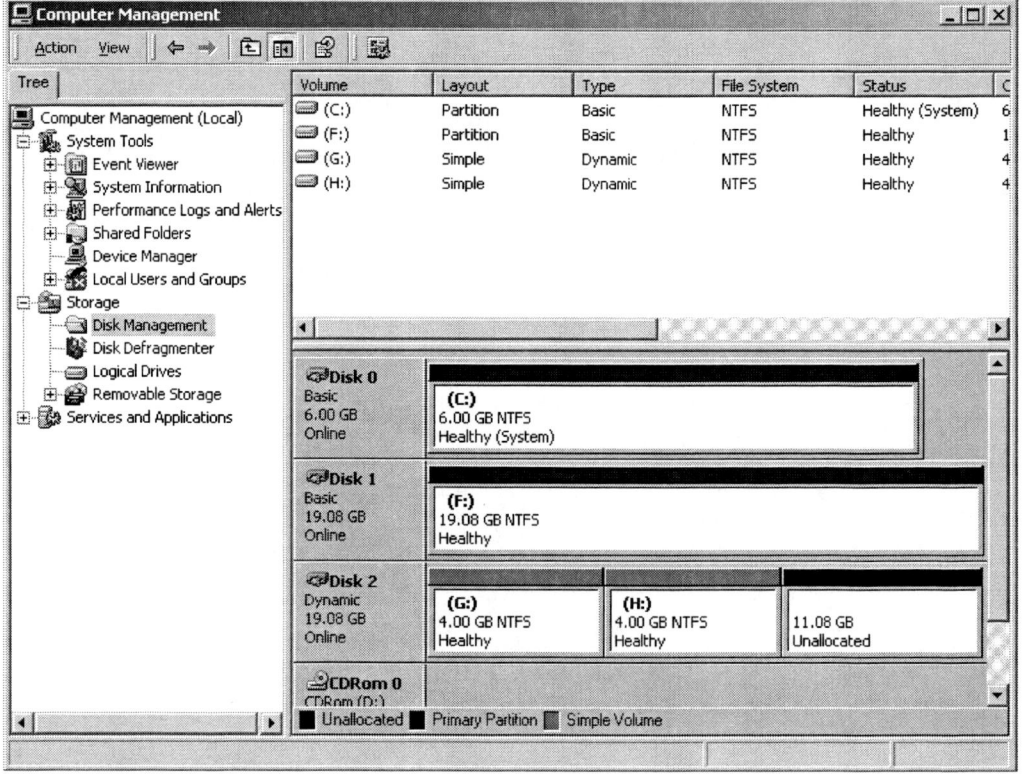

Figure 15-3: *A computer with a dynamic disk containing two simple volumes.*

How to Create or Delete a Partition

Procedure Reference: Create a Primary Partition in Windows 2000 and Windows XP

To create a primary partition in Windows 2000 and Windows XP:

1. Log on as a local administrator.

2. Open Computer Management (right-click My Computer and choose Manage).

3. In the console pane, select the Disk Management folder.

4. If you're using Windows 2000, right-click the available free space in the disk on which you want to create a new partition and choose Create Partition. The Create Partition Wizard starts.

5. If you're using Windows XP, right-click the available free space in the disk on which you want to create a new partition and choose New Partition. The New Partition Wizard starts.

6. Click Next.

7. On the Select Partition Type page, select Primary Partition.

8. Click Next.

9. If you're using Windows 2000, in the Amount Of Disk Space To Use text box, type the size of the partition you want to create.

10. If you're using Windows XP, in the Partition Size In MB text box, type the size of the partition you want to create.

11. Click Next.

12. On the Assign Drive Letter Or Path page, select one of the following:
    - If you want to assign a permanent drive letter to the new partition, choose a drive letter from the drop-down list.
    - If you want to mount the partition into an empty NTFS folder, enter the path to the folder or click Browse to select a folder.
    - If you do not want to assign a drive letter or mount path, select Do Not Assign A Drive Letter Or Drive Path.

13. Click Next.

14. Select whether or not to format this partition. If you choose to format the partition, you can select from the following options:
    - The file system to use (FAT, FAT32, or NTFS).
    - The allocation unit size. This is the size of the smallest available file-storage unit on the disk, and determines the size of the file clusters.
    - The volume label, a name that's assigned to the partition.
    - Check Perform A Quick Format if you want to perform a quick format instead of a full format.
    - Check Enable File And Folder Compression to enable compression on the entire partition.

15. Click Next.

16. Click Finish.

17. Close Computer Management.

18. Verify that the new partition is accessible by using a utility such as Windows Explorer or My Computer.

Procedure Reference: Create a Primary Partition in Windows NT

To create a primary partition in Windows NT:

1. Log on as a local administrator.

2. From the Start menu, choose Programs→Administrative Tools→Disk Administrator.

3. If this is the first time you have run Disk Administrator, click OK in the message box stating that your system configuration will be updated.

4. Right-click the available free space in the disk on which you want to create a new partition and choose Create.

5. In the Confirm message box stating that this partition will not be accessible if you boot the computer under MS-DOS, click Yes.

6. In the Create Partition Of Size text box, type the size of the partition you want to create.

7. Click OK to create the partition.

> Until you commit the changes in Disk Administrator, Windows NT does not actually create or delete partitions on the drive.

8. Choose Partition→Commit Changes Now.

9. Click Yes to confirm that you want to commit your changes.

10. Click OK to close the Disk Administrator message box.

11. Format the partition by completing the following steps:
    a. Right-click the new partition and choose Format.
    b. From the File System drop-down list, select the file system (FAT or NTFS).
    c. From the Allocation Unit drop-down list, select the allocation unit size.
    d. Optionally, in the Volume Label text box, assign a name to the partition.
    e. Check Quick Format to perform a quick format.
    f. Check Enable Compression to enable compression on the new partition.
    g. Click Start.
    h. Click OK to confirm that you want to format the new partition.
    i. Click OK to close the Format Complete message box.
    j. Click Close to close the Format dialog box.

12. Close Disk Administrator.

13. Verify that the new partition is accessible by using a utility such as Windows Explorer or My Computer.

Procedure Reference: Create an Extended Partition in Windows 2000 and Windows XP

To create an extended partition in Windows 2000 and Windows XP:

1. Log on as a local administrator.

2. Open Computer Management (right-click My Computer and choose Manage).

3. In the console pane, select the Disk Management folder.

4. If you're using Windows 2000, right-click the available free space in the disk on which you want to create a new partition and choose Create Partition. The Create Partition Wizard starts.

5. If you're using Windows XP, right-click the available free space in the disk on which you want to create a new partition and choose New Partition. The New Partition Wizard starts.

6. Click Next.

7. On the Select Partition Type page, select Extended Partition.

8. Click Next.

9. In the Amount Of Disk Space To Use text box, type the size of the partition you want to create.

10. Click Next.

11. Click Finish.

12. Create at least one logical drive within the extended partition:
    a. If you're using Windows 2000, right-click an extended partition with free space and choose Create Logical Drive. The Create Partition Wizard starts.
    b. If you're using Windows XP, right-click an extended partition with free space and choose New Logical Drive. The New Partition Wizard starts.
    c. Click Next.
    d. On the Select Partition Type page, click Next.
    e. In the Amount Of Disk Space To Use text box, type the size of the logical drive you want to create.
    f. Click Next.
    g. On the Assign Drive Letter Or Path page, select one of the following:
       - If you want to assign a permanent drive letter to the new logical drive, choose a drive letter from the drop-down list.
       - If you want to mount the logical drive into an empty folder, enter the path to the folder or click Browse to select a folder.
       - If you do not want to assign a drive letter or mount path, select Do Not Assign A Drive Letter Or Drive Path.
    h. Click Next.
    i. Select whether or not to format the logical drive. If you choose to format the logical drive, you can select from the following options:
       - The file system to use (FAT, FAT32, or NTFS).
       - The allocation unit size. This is the size of the smallest available file-storage unit on the disk, and determines the size of the file clusters.
       - The volume label, a name that's assigned to the partition.
       - Check Perform A Quick Format if you want to perform a quick format instead of a full format.
       - Check Enable File And Folder Compression to enable compression on the entire partition.

j. Click Next.

k. Click Finish.

13. Close Computer Management.

14. Verify that the new partition is accessible by using a utility such as Windows Explorer or My Computer.

Procedure Reference: Create an Extended Partition in Windows NT

To create an extended partition in Windows NT:

1. Log on as a local administrator.

2. From the Start menu, choose Programs→Administrative Tools→Disk Administrator.

3. If this is the first time you have run Disk Administrator, click OK in the message box stating that your system configuration will be updated.

4. Right-click the available free space in the disk on which you want to create a new partition and choose Create Extended.

5. In the Create Partition Of Size text box, type the size of the partition you want to create.

6. Click OK to create the partition.

> Until you commit the changes in Disk Administrator, Windows NT does not actually create or delete partitions on the drive.

7. Choose Partition→Commit Changes Now.

8. Click Yes to confirm that you want to commit your changes.

9. Click OK to close the Disk Administrator message box.

10. Create at least one logical drive within the extended partition by completing the following steps:

    a. Right-click the free space in the extended partition and choose Create.

    b. In the Create Logical Drive Of Size text box, type the size of the logical drive you want to create.

    c. Click OK to create the logical drive.

11. Choose Partition→Commit Changes Now.

12. Click Yes to confirm that you want to commit your changes.

13. Click OK to close the Disk Administrator message box.

14. Format the partition by completing the following steps:

    a. Right-click the new logical drive and choose Format.

    b. From the File System drop-down list, select the file system (FAT or NTFS).

    c. From the Allocation Unit drop-down list, select the allocation unit size.

d. Optionally, in the Volume Label text box, assign a name to the logical drive.

e. Check Quick Format to perform a quick format.

f. Check Enable Compression to enable compression on the new logical drive.

g. Click Start.

h. Click OK to confirm that you want to format the new logical drive.

i. Click OK to close the Format Complete message box.

j. Click Close to close the Format dialog box.

15. Close Disk Administrator.

16. Verify that the new partition is accessible by using a utility such as Windows Explorer or My Computer.

Procedure Reference: Delete a Primary Partition in Windows 2000 and Windows XP

To delete a primary partition in Windows 2000 and Windows XP:

1. Log on as a local administrator.

2. Open Computer Management (right-click My Computer and choose Manage).

3. In the console pane, select the Disk Management folder.

4. Right-click the partition you want to delete and choose Delete Partition.

5. Click Yes to confirm that you want to delete the primary partition.

6. Close Computer Management.

7. Verify that the partition is no longer accessible by using a utility such as Windows Explorer or My Computer.

Procedure Reference: Delete a Primary Partition in Windows NT

To delete a primary partition in Windows NT:

1. Log on as a local administrator.

2. From the Start menu, choose Programs→Administrative Tools→Disk Administrator.

3. Right-click the partition you want to delete and choose Delete.

4. Click Yes to confirm that you want to delete the primary partition.

5. Choose Partition→Commit Changes Now.

6. Click Yes to confirm that you want to commit your changes.

7. Click OK to close the Disk Administrator message box.

8. Close Computer Management.

9. Verify that the partition is no longer accessible by using a utility such as Windows Explorer or My Computer.

Procedure Reference: Delete an Extended Partition in Windows 2000 and Windows XP

To delete an extended partition in Windows 2000 and Windows XP:

1. Log on as a local administrator.
2. Open Computer Management (right-click My Computer and choose Manage).
3. In the console pane, select the Disk Management folder.
4. Delete any logical drives within the extended partition first:
   a. Right-click a logical drive and choose Delete Logical Drive.
   b. Click Yes to confirm that you want to delete the logical drive.
   c. Repeat these steps for each logical drive within the extended partition.
5. Right-click the extended partition you want to delete and choose Delete Partition.
6. Click Yes to confirm that you want to delete the extended partition.
7. Close Computer Management.
8. Verify that the partition is no longer accessible by using a utility such as Windows Explorer or My Computer.

Procedure Reference: Delete an Extended Partition in Windows NT

To delete an extended partition in Windows NT:

1. Log on as a local administrator.
2. Open Disk Administrator.
3. Delete any logical drives within the extended partition first:
   a. Right-click a logical drive and choose Delete.
   b. Click Yes to confirm that you want to delete the logical drive.
   c. Repeat these steps for each logical drive within the extended partition.
   d. Choose Partition→Commit Changes Now.
   e. Click Yes to confirm that you want to commit your changes.
   f. Click OK to close the Disk Administrator message box.
4. Right-click the extended partition you want to delete and choose Delete.
5. Choose Partition→Commit Changes Now.
6. Click Yes to confirm that you want to commit your changes.
7. Click OK to close the Disk Administrator message box.
8. Close Computer Management.
9. Verify that the partition is no longer accessible by using a utility such as Windows Explorer or My Computer.

Topic B
Convert a FAT Partition to NTFS

In Topic 15A, you learned how to create a partition and format it with the FAT or FAT32 file systems. Now, for extra security, the network administrator has asked that you change all FAT partitions to use the NTFS file system instead. As you know, re-formatting the partition to use the NTFS file system will destroy the data that's currently stored on it. So in this topic, you'll learn exactly the steps you need to convert a FAT or FAT32 partition to use the NTFS file system without destroying the data that's currently stored on the partition.

To appreciate the ease of converting a partition to NTFS, let's take a look at a scenario: Imagine you're working the Help Desk when the CEO of the company calls in and tells you he's concerned about the security of his computer. "No problem," you say. "I can easily help you to lock down your computer." But when you arrive at his desk, you find that his computer's partitions are using the FAT file system. The CEO is breathing down your neck because he doesn't want you to lose any of his sensitive and valuable data. In this situation, knowing how to convert a FAT-based partition to NTFS will really make you a hero. You'll be able to quickly convert the CEO's partitions to the NTFS file system, which means he'll be able to take advantage of NTFS's advanced security features such as encryption and file- and folder-level security. And, you'll be able to make this change without any risk of losing the CEO's data!

File System Conversion

In Windows 2000, Windows XP, and Windows NT, if you decide that you want to take advantage of the enhanced capabilities of the NTFS file system, you can convert a FAT partition to the NTFS file system without the risk of losing any data on the partition. This conversion is a one-way process. In other words, once you have converted a FAT partition to NTFS, you can't later convert the NTFS partition back to the FAT file system.

How to Convert a FAT Partition to NTFS

Procedure Reference: Convert a FAT Partition to NTFS in Windows 2000/XP/NT

To convert a FAT partition to NTFS in Windows 2000, Windows XP, and Windows NT:

1. Log on as a local administrator.
2. Determine the drive letter or mount path and the volume label of the partition you want to convert (use Computer Management in Windows 2000 and Windows XP, or Disk Administrator in Windows NT).
3. Open a Command Prompt window.
4. Enter `convert drive /fs:ntfs`. You can use the drive letter, mount path, or volume label for the *drive* variable. If you use the drive letter in Windows 2000 or Windows XP, you'll need to enter the volume label of the drive to confirm the conversion.
5. If prompted, enter the volume label for the drive.
6. If you're converting the boot partition or an active partition, you'll be prompted to restart the computer to complete the conversion.

Topic C
Compress Files and Folders

Up to this point in the chapter, we've talked about the strategies you can use to create, manage, and delete partitions on your users' computers. But what happens if your users run out of disk space? In this topic, you'll learn how you can optimize the available disk space on users' computers by implementing compression.

As an A+ technician, it's likely that you'll encounter a situation where a user is running out of disk space and upgrading to a larger hard disk (or adding a second hard disk) isn't an option that's available to you. In this scenario, your best solution to keep the user's computer functioning productively is to implement file and folder compression. Using compression will enable you to conserve precious disk space so that the user can continue to work on the computer.

Compression

In Windows 2000, Windows NT, and Windows XP, you can use compression on NTFS partitions to reduce the amount of space required to store files on the hard disk. Compression reduces the amount of disk space used by files by changing the way the characters in a file are written to disk. For example, when you compress a file, the operating system removes any blank or null characters from the file. When you open the file, the operating system adds these characters back in.

How to Compress Files and Folders

Procedure Reference: Compress a File or Folder

To compress a file or folder:

1. Log on as a user with full control over the file or folder you want to compress.
2. Open Windows Explorer.
3. Right-click the file or folder you want to compress and choose Properties.
4. On the General page, make a note of the amount of disk space in use by the file or folder by recording the value you see next to Size On Disk.
5. If you're using Windows 2000 or Windows XP, complete the following steps:
    a. On the General page, click Advanced.
    b. Check Compress Contents To Save Disk Space.
    c. Click OK.
6. If you're using Windows NT, on the General page, click Compress.
7. Click OK to close the Properties dialog box for the file or folder.
8. If you're using Windows 2000 or Windows XP and you selected a folder to compress, select one of the following:
    - If you want to compress the folder and its files only (and not any subfolders), select Apply Changes To This Folder Only and click OK.

- If you want to compress the folder and its files, along with any subfolders and their files, select Apply Changes To This Folder, Subfolders And Files and click OK.

9. If you're using Windows NT and you selected a folder to compress, check Also Compress Subfolders if you want to compress the subfolders and click OK.

10. Right-click the file or folder to display its properties. Verify that the disk space used is reduced.

    If you want, you can configure Windows Explorer to display compressed files and folders in a different color. For more information, see the Configuring Windows Explorer procedure below.

11. Close Windows Explorer.

Procedure Reference: Compress a Drive

To compress a drive:

1. Log on as a user with at least the Modify NTFS permission for the file or folder you want to compress.

2. Open Windows Explorer.

3. Right-click the drive you want to compress and choose Properties.

4. If you're using Windows 2000 or Windows XP, check Compress Drive To Save Disk Space.

5. If you're using Windows NT, check Compress *drive letter*.

6. Click OK to close the Properties dialog box for the drive.

7. If you're using Windows 2000 or Windows XP, select one of the following:
   - If you want to compress the drive only, select Apply Changes To *drive letter* Only.
   - If you want to compress the drive, its subfolders, and files, select Apply Changes To *drive letter*, Subfolders And Files and click OK.

8. If you're using Windows NT, check Also Compress Subfolders if you want to compress the subfolders and click OK.

9. Close Windows Explorer.

Procedure Reference: Configure Windows Explorer to Display Compressed Files

To configure Windows Explorer to display compressed files in an alternate color:

1. In Windows Explorer, choose Tools→Folder Options.

2. Select the View tab.

3. Below Files And Folders, check Display Compressed Files And Folders With Alternate Color.

4. Click OK.

Topic D
Defragment a Hard Disk in Windows 2000/XP

Part of managing disk resources in Windows 2000 and Windows XP is to keep the disks performing optimally. You can accomplish this task by defragmenting the hard disk on a consistent basis. In this topic, you'll learn the steps for defragmenting a hard disk in Windows 2000 and Windows XP.

Defragmenting your disks improves the performance and life expectancy of your disks by allowing for more efficient storage of files. More efficient storage of files means less physical wear and tear on the heads of the disks themselves, quicker operating system and application startup times, faster application performance, and more rapid retrieval of files.

Fragmentation

The Windows operating systems do not write a file to disk as a single large block. Instead, they break up the file into smaller pieces. When Windows writes these smaller pieces to the disk, it tries to write them close together so that the disk can retrieve the file quickly whenever a user opens it. As a disk fills up and files are added and removed, it becomes harder for Windows to find enough contiguous space to write all the pieces of a file. As a result, Windows ends up writing the file wherever it can find free space on a disk. The end result is that files can become fragmented, meaning their pieces can be spread out all over the disk. The greater the amount of *fragmentation*, the more work the operating system must perform to retrieve and write files. You can counteract fragmentation by defragmenting a computer's hard disk.

How to Defragment a Hard Disk in Windows 2000/XP

Procedure Reference: Defragment a Hard Disk in Windows 2000 and Windows XP

To defragment a hard disk in Windows 2000 and Windows XP:

1. Log on as a local administrator.
2. From the Start menu, choose Programs→Accessories→System Tools→Disk Defragmenter.
3. In the top pane of the Disk Defragmenter window, select the disk you want to defragment.
4. If you want to analyze the fragmentation state of the disk before defragmenting, click Analyze.
5. After the analysis, you will see a message box with a recommendation as to whether you should defragment or not. This recommendation is made based on a Disk Defragmenter algorithm, rather than a specific fragmentation level, but it is common practice to defragment disks that are more than five percent fragmented.

    Click View Report to see details of the fragmentation state of the disk.
6. To begin the defragmentation, click Defragment in the analysis message box, in the Analysis Report dialog box, or in the Disk Defragmenter window itself. Disk Defragmenter will re-analyze the disk and begin the defragmentation. You can view the progress in the progress bar.

> Defragmentation of a large, highly fragmented, and very full disk can take several hours.

7. When the defragmentation is complete, you can click View Report to see detailed information about the defragmentation.

Chapter 15 Follow-up
Managing Disk Resources in Windows 2000/NT/XP

In this chapter, you learned how to create, manage, and delete partitions in the Windows 2000, Windows NT, and Windows XP environments. By properly configuring the partitions in your computers, your users will be able to access the hard disk resources they need to do their jobs.

Essential Terms

- basic disks
- compression
- defragmentation
- disk partitions
- dynamic disks
- FAT partitions
- file compression
- file systems
- folder compression
- fragmentation
- hard disks
- NTFS partitions
- partitions

Review Questions

1. What is a disk partition?
2. On your Windows 2000 computer you have one physical disk that is comprised of three primary partitions. How can you tell which partition is the boot partition?
3. In Windows NT 4.0, you open the disk management utility and you notice the disk has several partitions. How can you tell which partition is the active partition?
4. What file systems do Windows XP and Windows 2000 support?
5. What file system is supported by Windows 98, Windows 2000, and Windows XP, but not Windows NT 4.0?
6. How many partitions can you create on a basic disk?
7. What Windows operating systems do not support basic disks?
8. How many extended partitions can you create on one hard disk?
9. What is a dynamic disk?
10. What kind of volume uses multiple areas of space from two or more dynamic disks that are treated as a single logical volume?
11. When would you create a spanned volume?

12. You want to convert a FAT32 partition to NTFS on a Windows 2000 machine. What is the full command statement you must enter at the command line?
13. What is the function of compression?
14. Why is it important to defragment hard disks on a regular basis?
15. After you defragment a disk where can you find detailed information about the defragmentation?
16. You create a logical drive within an extended partition on your Windows XP machine. You choose to format the volume FAT32 and you notice the allocation unit size. What is an allocation unit size?
17. You want to install MS-DOS, Windows 98, and Windows 2000 on one computer in a multi-boot configuration. What file system will you have to use?
18. Windows XP supports basic disks. How many primary partitions can you have on a Windows XP machine?
19. What determines the size of the file clusters?
20. Which Microsoft operating systems support dynamic disks?
21. What is the minimum number of disks necessary to create a striped volume?
22. What file system would you use on Windows 2000 if you want to use compression?
23. You install a new disk in a computer and then you create a partition. What is the next step you'd perform before installing an operating system?
24. What are the file systems supported by Windows NT 4.0?
25. You convert a basic disk to a dynamic disk on a Windows XP machine. You want to convert the disk back to basic. How do you do that?
26. What permission level must you have to enable compression on a folder on your system's hard drive?
27. Several files on your hard drive are compressed. You move some compressed files from one folder to another folder on the same partition. What will the compression status be of the files you moved?
28. What would happen if you copied compressed files from a folder to another uncompressed folder on the same partition?
29. You've spent the weekend working on some large files. You notice over the next several days that it's taking longer to open and close files. What should you do?
30. You move an uncompressed file to a compressed folder on the same partition. What will the compression state of the file be once it's moved?

Review Projects

Project #1 Windows XP's Disk Management

Windows XP Professional improves upon the disk management options and utilities available in Windows 2000 and Windows NT 4.0. Microsoft's Technet article, "New in Disk Management," outlines the improvements. The URL for the Web page is **http://www.microsoft.com/technet/treeview/default.asp?url=/technet/prodtechnol/winxppro/reskit/prkb_cnc_ruga.asp**. Read through the article to acquaint yourself with the new features. Using a computer running Windows XP Professional, you'll experiment with the disk management utility, diskpart.exe. This utility allows you to manage the system's disks from a command line rather than from the GUI-based disk management utility snap-in.

The diskpart.exe utility is a complex command. Open Windows XP's Help and Support Center and search for diskpart. Once you click the link for the utility you'll see that the command syntax runs for several pages. The great advantage diskpart has over the GUI disk management tool is that you can write scripts (and batch files) to automate disk tasks. In this activity you need to make sure the hard disk has some free space because you'll create a new partition using the diskpart utility. At the command prompt, activate the diskpart environment by entering diskpart at the command line. Press Enter. You'll see the following prompt that indicates you're in the diskpart environment:

diskpart >

Next, you have to select the disk (Microsoft calls this setting the focus on the disk). If you are unsure what the first disk number is on your system, open the GUI-based disk management tool. Notice the number of your hard disk (probably 0). Return to the command prompt and set the focus to disk 0 (or whatever disk number is appropriate). If your hard disk is disk 0, enter the following:

SELECT disk 0

Disk 0 is selected and will now be the focus of your action. Next, use the CREATE command to create a primary partition. Then set the size of the partition. In this example, the partition size will be 2GB

CREATE partition primary size 2048

Diskpart will create the primary partition which you can verify by opening disk management to view your changes. Using the documentation in the Help and Support Center, try other disk operations. Once you are comfortable performing a few minor operations, delete your test partition(s) and create a batch file that performs one or two simple operations automatically.

Project #2 Disk Defragmentation

This tutorial dispels many myths about disk defragmentation. Read through the article to ensure you are familiar with the reasons why disk defragmentation is so important. Access the article at **http://216.239.51.100/search?q=cache:yajM6iW-N2AJ:www.raxco.be/pages/info/PD2000/Version%25206/Defrag%2520Tutorial.pdf+an imation+of+how+disk+defragmentation+works&hl=en&ie=UTF-8**. After reading through the tutorial, navigate to diskeeper's Web site. Diskeeper is a well-known disk defragmentation utility and its lite version is what is used on Windows 2000 natively. In this exercise, read the information about diskeeper on its Web site and download an evaluation copy of diskeeper (listed under new downloads on the home page).

After you download the utility, install it. When installation completes, open the defragment utility on a Windows 2000 machine. Defragment your drive (or a partition on the drive) using Windows 2000's native utility. View the report when the defragmentation completes.

Next, open the full version of diskeeper you just installed. Defragment the same drive (or partition) to observe if the full version performs a more comprehensive scan of your system and thus a more thorough defragmentation. Did the full version do a more thorough job? View the report.

Once you have compared the lite and the full versions' performance, view the menus of both utilities. What does the full version offer you that the lite version does not offer you?

Project #3 Disk Concepts and Troubleshooting

One of your greatest challenges as an A+ technician will be troubleshooting a wide range of hardware and software problems. For Windows operating systems, one of the best sources for troubleshooting information is Microsoft. The company maintains extensive databases of information to help you identify most problems.

In this activity, you'll focus on disk concepts and disk troubleshooting. There are many possible causes of disk problems and ways of recovering from them. The support articles archived on Microsoft's site will help you identify a variety of disk problems and guide you as to how you may resolve them.

The "disk concepts and troubleshooting" page is located at **http://www.microsoft.com/windows2000/techinfo/reskit/en-us/default.asp?url=/windows2000/techinfo/reskit/en-us/prork/prcb_dis_mhrr.asp**. In the left column you'll see the Troubleshooting Disk Problems heading highlighted. In this activity, work through the heading's sub-sections. The sub-sections are as follows:

- Viruses
- Damaged MBRs and Boot Sectors
- Checking for Disk corruption
- Other Disk Problems

You'll be introduced to some tools that will be new to you. Where appropriate, experiment with some of the utilities discussed in the support pages. Make note of those which are more complex, but may be of use later. Bookmark this page as a resource for disk troubleshooting.

Reflective Questions

1. **In your organization, or the organizations you support, what disk management tasks are you expected to perform? Why?**

2. **In your organization, or the organizations you support, what is the configuration of the hard disk partitions on your Windows 2000 computers? Why?**

CHAPTER 16
Managing Disk Resources in Windows 9x

Chapter Objectives:

In this chapter, you will manage disk resources in Windows 9x.

You will:

- Create or delete a partition.
- Compress a hard disk.
- Convert a FAT partition to FAT32.
- Defragment a hard disk.

Introduction

Earlier in this course you learned how to manage the disk resources in the Windows 2000, Windows NT, and Windows XP environments. Because many companies have quite an investment in Windows 9x-based computers, odds are that as an A+ technician you'll also be called on to perform the same management tasks on Windows 9x computers. In this chapter, you'll learn how to create, manage, and delete partitions in the Windows 9x environment.

Hard drives and their associated partitions are critical resources in any computer, and a 9x-based system is no exception. Without properly configured disk resources, your users won't be able to access the files they need. Since you may encounter these older but still viable systems, your ability to manage disk resources is critical.

TOPIC A
Create or Delete a Partition

Just as in Windows 2000, Windows NT, and Windows XP, creating and deleting partitions is an important part of managing partitions in the Windows 9x environment. If your company or clients have Windows 9x computers, as an A+ technician, you'll be expected to know how to configure such computers' hard disks. For this reason, you'll learn the steps to create and delete partitions in this topic.

One of the most common reasons why you'll be asked to create a partition on a computer is when a new hard disk has been installed. A computer (and thus the computer's user) won't be able to use the new hard disk unless it has at least one partition. To enable a user to take advantage of the new hard disk, you'll need to know how to create partitions on that disk. On the other hand, you might encounter a situation where a user no longer needs a hard disk and you want to move that hard disk to a different computer. Because that hard disk might have sensitive data stored on it, you should always delete the disk's partitions before moving the disk to a new computer. Knowing how to delete the old partitions will enable you to protect against the new user accessing the old user's data.

Large Disk Support

Windows 95 OSR2 and Windows 98 provide support for EIDE hard disks larger than 2 gigabytes (GB) when using the FAT32 file system. With the *FAT32 file system*:

- Hard disk space is used 10 to 15 percent more efficiently than FAT or FAT16 drives due to the smaller cluster size used.

- Your hard disks can be from 512 megabytes up to 2 terabytes in size. However, some system BIOS will not accept more than a 7.8 GB bootable partition.

Windows ME also provides support for FAT32.

On a dual-boot system, FAT32 partitions can be accessed only by the Windows 95 OSR2, Windows 98, Windows ME, Windows 2000, and Windows XP operating systems.

MS-DOS Mode

In Windows 9x, you can simulate the MS-DOS environment by starting the operating system in MS-DOS mode. You typically use MS-DOS mode when troubleshooting an application that won't run in Windows 9x. In addition, you use MS-DOS mode to run the programs that enable you to create, format, and delete partitions. In Figure 16-1, you see the option for restarting in MS-DOS mode on the Shut Down Windows menu.

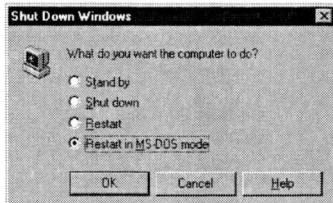

Figure 16-1: *Restarting a Windows 9x computer in MS-DOS mode.*

How to Create or Delete a Partition

Procedure Reference: Create Partitions on a Windows 9x Computer

To create a partition on a Windows 9x computer using Fdisk.exe:

1. Restart the computer in MS-DOS mode.
    a. Choose Start→Shut Down.
    b. In the Shut Down Windows dialog box, select Restart In MS-DOS Mode.
    c. Click OK.
2. At the C:\Windows prompt, type `fdisk` and press Enter.
3. If you have a Windows 98 computer with a hard disk larger than 512 MB, type one of the following and press Enter:
    - Y to enable large disk support and use 32-bit FAT as the file system on your computer. Do not choose this option if you plan to configure the computer to dual-boot between Windows 9x and Windows 2000, Windows NT, or Windows XP.
    - N to bypass enabling large disk support and use 16-bit FAT as the file system on your computer.
4. If the computer is configured to dual-boot with Windows 2000, Windows NT, or Windows XP, and your computer has an NTFS partition, you will be asked if you want to treat NTFS partitions as large. Type N and press Enter.
5. Type 1 and press Enter to create a DOS partition or logical DOS drive.
6. Type one of the following and press Enter:
    - 1 to create a primary DOS partition.
    - 2 to create an extended DOS partition.

> Fdisk allows you to create one primary and one extended partition per hard disk. You must create the primary partition before you can create the extended partition.

7. If you are creating a primary DOS partition, type one of the following and press Enter:
   - Y to specify that you want Fdisk to create a primary partition from the maximum space available and mark the partition active.
   - N to specify you want to manually enter a size for your primary partition and manually mark it active.

8. If you are creating a primary DOS partition and you entered N to specify you want to manually enter a size for your primary partition and manually mark it active, type the size for your primary partition in percentage or megabytes and press Enter. You might see that Fdisk adjusts the size you enter.

9. If you are creating a primary DOS partition and you manually entered a size for your primary partition, set the primary partition as active:
   1. Type 2 and press Enter.
   2. Use the arrow keys to highlight the partition you want to be marked active.
   3. Press Enter.

10. If you are creating an extended DOS partition, type the size for your extended partition in percentage or megabytes and press Enter.

11. Press Esc to return to the Fdisk main menu.

12. If you are creating an extended DOS partition, press Enter to confirm that you want to create a logical drive within your computer's extended partition.

13. If you are creating an extended DOS partition, the logical drive information is displayed. Press Esc to return to the Fdisk main menu. You might see that Fdisk adjusted the size you entered for the partition.

14. Press Esc to exit out of Fdisk.

15. Press Esc to exit from the message prompting you to shut down Windows.

16. Press Ctrl+Alt+Delete to restart your computer.

17. If the computer is configured to dual-boot, from the boot menu, choose Microsoft Windows.

18. Format the newly created partition so that it is usable within Windows 9x:
    - Using the `format` command line utility:
      a. At the C:\Windows prompt, type `format drive_letter:`.

         > The drive letter is the letter assigned to the partition by Fdisk.

      b. Press Enter.

- c. Type Y and press Enter to confirm you want to format your drive.
- d. When the format is complete, either type a label for your drive and press Enter, or press Enter to leave the label blank.
- Using Windows Explorer:
    - a. Open Windows Explorer.
    - b. Right-click the new partition's drive letter and choose Format.
    - c. Click Start.
    - d. Click OK to confirm that you want to format the partition.
    - e. Click OK again to confirm formatting the partition.
    - f. Click Close to close the Format Results dialog box.
    - g. Click OK to close the message box prompting you to run ScanDisk.
    - h. Close Windows Help.
    - i. Close the Format dialog box.
    - j. Close Windows Explorer.
19. In Windows Explorer, verify that you can access the new drive.

Procedure Reference: Delete Partitions on a Windows 9x Computer

To delete a partition on a Windows 9x computer using Fdisk.exe:

1. Restart the computer in MS-DOS mode.
    - a. Choose Start→Shut Down.
    - b. In the Shut Down Windows dialog box, select Restart In MS-DOS Mode.
    - c. Click OK.
2. At the C:\Windows prompt, type `fdisk` and press Enter.
3. If you have a Windows 98 computer with a hard disk larger than 512 MB, type one of the following and press Enter:
    - Y to enable large disk support and use 32-bit FAT as the file system on your computer.
    - N to bypass enabling large disk support and use 16-bit FAT as the file system on your computer.
4. If the computer is configured to dual boot with Windows 2000, Windows NT, or Windows XP, and your computer has an NTFS partition, you will be asked if you want to treat NTFS partitions as large. Type N and press Enter.
5. Type 3 and press Enter to delete a DOS partition or logical DOS drive.
6. Type one of the following and press Enter:
    - 1 to delete a primary DOS partition.
    - 2 to delete an extended DOS partition.

- 3 to delete a logical drive within an extended DOS partition.
- 4 to delete a non-DOS partition, such as NTFS partitions created by Windows 2000.

When you are deleting partitions, you must delete any existing partitions in the following order:

A. Any logical drives within the extended MS-DOS partition.
B. The extended partition.
C. The primary MS-DOS partition.

7. Type the number of the partition or the letter of the logical drive you want to delete and press Enter.
8. If prompted, enter the volume label and press Enter.
9. Type Y and press Enter to verify you want to delete the entered partition or drive.
10. Press Esc to return to the Fdisk main menu.
11. Press Esc to exit out of Fdisk.
12. Press Esc to exit from the message prompting you to shut down Windows.
13. Press Ctrl+Alt+Delete to restart your computer.

 If you deleted your primary partition, you will need an MS-DOS boot disk to restart the computer.

TOPIC B
Compress a Hard Disk

An important part of managing a Windows 9x-based computer's hard disk resources is optimizing its disk space usage. If disk space on a computer is tight, you'll want to take any steps you can to maximize the available disk space. Compressing the hard disk is one technique you can use to increase available disk space, and that's what you'll learn in this topic.

Although hard disks these days are becoming bigger and bigger while their prices are steadily dropping, as an A+ technician, you're bound to encounter a situation where a company or client just can't afford to upgrade a computer's hard disk. Or, you might encounter a computer with BIOS that doesn't support the large hard disks available today. In either case, if such a computer is running out of available disk space, your best solution is to compress the hard disk. Compressing the hard disk will enable you to increase the available disk space on the computer without your having to upgrade the computer's hard disk or add a second disk to the computer.

How to Compress a Hard Disk

Procedure Reference: Compress a Drive

To compress a drive in Windows 9x:

Do not compress the C drive if you dual-boot the computer between Windows 98 and Windows 2000, Windows XP, or Windows NT.

1. If necessary, install DriveSpace 3.
   a. In Control Panel, double-click Add/Remove Programs.
   b. Select the Windows Setup tab.
   c. In the Components list, select System Tools and click Details.
   d. Check Disk Compression Tools and click OK.
   e. In the Add/Remove Programs Properties dialog box, click OK.
   f. When prompted, insert the Windows 98 installation CD-ROM into the CD-ROM drive.
   g. Click OK.
   h. Close Control Panel.
2. Choose Start→Programs→Accessories→System Tools→DriveSpace.
3. In the DriveSpace dialog box, select the drive you want to compress.
4. Choose Drive→Compress.
5. If desired, click Options to change the drive letter of the host drive by selecting a letter from the drop-down list box and change the default free space available on the host drive. Click OK.
6. Click Start.
7. Click Yes if you want to update or create a Windows 98 startup disk. Otherwise, click No.
8. If you're compressing a drive on a dual-boot computer, click OK to close the message stating that a Windows 98 compressed drive isn't accessible by Windows NT, Windows 2000, and Windows XP.
9. If you want to back up your files before compressing the disk, click Back Up Files.
10. Click Compress Now to compress the disk.
11. Click Close to close the Compress A Drive dialog box.
12. If you see a message stating that the hard drive is full, click Cancel.
13. Close DriveSpace.
14. Click Yes to restart the computer.

You cannot compress drives that are formatted to FAT32.

Procedure Reference: Uncompress a Drive

To uncompress a compressed drive in Windows 9x:

1. Choose Start→Programs→Accessories→System Tools→DriveSpace.
2. In the DriveSpace dialog box, select the drive you want to uncompress.
3. Choose Drive→Uncompress.
4. Click Start.
5. Click Uncompress Now.
6. If you are uncompressing the last compressed drive, click Yes to remove the compression driver from memory.
7. Click Close to close the Uncompress A Drive dialog box.
8. Close DriveSpace.
9. Click Yes to restart the computer.

TOPIC C
Convert a FAT Partition to FAT32

In Topic 16A, you learned the steps for creating and formatting a FAT partition. However, for large hard disks on Windows 98-based computers, Microsoft recommends that you use the FAT32 file system instead. That's why you'll learn the steps for converting a FAT partition to the FAT32 file system in this topic.

As you know, hard disks just keep getting bigger and bigger in size. Using the FAT32 file system for a partition instead of the FAT file system improves the performance of the hard disk. Because the slowest hardware component in any computer is its hard disk, anything you can do to optimize the performance of the hard disk will improve the overall performance of the computer itself. And converting a FAT partition to FAT32 instead of deleting the partition and creating a new one means that you won't have to worry about losing the user's data. By converting from FAT to FAT32, you can easily switch a computer's hard disk to the optimized FAT32 file system without any loss of data.

The Conversion Process

When you convert a partition from FAT to FAT32, the conversion process:

1. Boots the computer into MS-DOS.
2. Runs ScanDisk to check the integrity of your disk and correct problems it detects.
3. Runs the converter to:
    a. Check your drives.
    b. Remove uninstall, multi-boot, and extended attribute files.
    c. Convert directories.

      d. Create space for the 32-bit file allocation table.
      e. Convert the file allocation table to 32 bits.
      f. Remove any unused clusters.
      g. Update the partition type.
      h. Update the master boot record.
      i. Update the copy of the file allocation table.
      j. Move the root directory to the beginning of the drive.
4. Boots back into Windows.
5. Runs the Disk Defragmenter.

Cluster Size

All operating systems read from and write to hard disks in chunks of bytes rather than byte by byte. These chunks are called *clusters*. Windows automatically selects the cluster size based on the size of the partition and the file system with which it's formatted. In Table 16-1 and Table 16-2, you see the cluster sizes for different partition sizes and the FAT and FAT32 file systems.

The cluster size determines the smallest unit of disk space the Windows operating system can use when writing to disk. For example, if you save a 1 KB file to a FAT partition that is 1,024 MB in size, Windows uses a 32 KB cluster to store that file; Windows cannot use the remaining 31 KB within that cluster. As you can see, the cluster size can affect the amount of available disk space dramatically. On the other hand, if you save that same 1 KB file to a 1,024 MB FAT32 partition, you see that Windows would use only a 4 KB cluster to store that same file. By using a smaller cluster size, the FAT32 partition is more efficient with using disk space.

Table 16-1: *FAT Cluster Sizes*

Partition Size	Cluster Size
0 – 15 MB	512 bytes
16 – 127 MB	2 KB
128 – 255 MB	4 KB
256 – 511 MB	8 KB
512 – 1,023 MB	16 KB
1,024 – 2,047 MB	32 KB
2,048 – 4,096 MB	64 KB (This cluster size is supported only on FAT partitions in Windows 2000, Windows NT, or Windows XP.)

Table 16-2: *FAT32 Cluster Sizes*

Partition Size	Cluster Size
0.256 – 8.01 GB	4 KB
8.02 – 16.02 GB	8 KB
16.03 – 32.04 GB	16 KB
> 32.04 GB	32 KB

How to Convert a FAT Partition to FAT32

Procedure Reference: Convert a FAT Partition to FAT32

To convert an existing FAT partition on a Windows 98 or Windows 95 OSR-2 computer to FAT32:

1. Choose Start→Programs→Accessories→System Tools→Drive Converter (FAT32). This menu shortcut runs the Drive Converter utility, cvt1.exe.

    If you would like information on the Drive Converter (FAT32) utility and limitations of the FAT32 file system, click Details.

2. Click Next.

3. In the Drives list box, select the FAT16 drive you want to convert.

4. Click Next.

5. Click OK to verify you understand the warning regarding OS limitations with FAT32 while dual-booting a computer.

   Drive Converter scans your computer for anti-virus programs and disk utilities that will not work with FAT32.

6. If Drive Converter finds any incompatible programs or utilities, select them and choose Details.

7. Click Next.

8. If you have backup hardware installed on your computer and you want to back up your files before converting your drive to FAT32, click Create Backup.

9. Click Next.

10. Click Next to restart your computer in MS-DOS mode and begin the conversion.

     Depending on the size of the drive, the conversion could take several hours.

     The Drive Converter (FAT32) file, Cvt1.exe, is installed in the Windows folder by default.

Topic D
Defragment a Hard Disk

Part of managing disk resources in Windows 9x is to keep the disks performing optimally. This can be accomplished by defragmenting the hard disk on a consistent basis. In this topic, you'll learn the steps for defragmenting a hard disk in Windows 9x.

Defragmenting your disks improves their performance and life expectancy by allowing for more efficient storage of files. More efficient storage of files means less physical wear and tear on the heads of the disks themselves, quicker operating system and application startup times, faster application performance, and more rapid retrieval of files.

How to Defragment a Hard Disk

Procedure Reference: Defragment a Hard Disk

To defragment a drive in Windows 9x:

1. Choose Start→Programs→Accessories→System Tools→Disk Defragmenter.

2. In the Select Drive dialog box, select the drive you want to defragment.

3. In Windows 95, click the Advanced button if you want to change the settings of the defragmentation utility from the default.

   In Windows 98, click the Settings button if you want to change the settings of the defragmentation utility from the default.

   Click OK to close the Settings dialog box.

4. Click OK.

5. If you want to see the details of the defragmentation process on your hard disk, click Show Details.

   Click Hide Details to show only the summary information.

6. Click Yes to close Disk Defragmenter when the defragmentation process is complete.

Chapter 16 Follow-up
Managing Disk Resources in Windows 9x

In this chapter, you learned how to create, manage, and delete partitions in the Windows 9x environment. By properly configuring the partitions in your Windows 9x computers, your users will be able to access the hard disk resources they need to do their jobs.

Essential Terms

- compression
- defragmentation
- disk compression
- disk partitions
- FAT partitions
- FAT32 partitions
- fragmentation
- hard disks
- partitions

Review Questions

1. What Windows operating systems support the FAT32 file system?
2. How can you simulate an MS-DOS environment in Windows 9x?
3. When would you start a computer in MS-DOS mode?
4. To create a partition on a Windows 9x machine, what utility do you use?
5. How many partitions can you create on a Windows 9x machine using Fdisk?
6. When deleting partitions in Fdisk, you must delete existing partitions in a specific order. What is the order?
7. How can you increase available space on your hard disk in a Windows 9x machine?
8. What file system should you use for large disks on a Windows 98 machine?
9. What is the slowest hardware component in a computer?
10. The hard disk on your Windows 98 computer is formatted with the FAT file system. What can you do to optimize disk performance on the machine?
11. Operating systems read and write to hard disks in chunks of bytes. What are the chunks called?
12. How does Windows select the cluster size of a disk?
13. What does the cluster size determine?
14. The FAT32 file system uses disk space more efficiently than the FAT file system. Why?
15. What is the cluster size of a FAT partition of 512-1023?
16. What is the cluster size of a FAT32 partition larger than 32GB?
17. What is the utility used to convert a Windows 98 disk partition from FAT to FAT32?
18. Some of your users have complained that their Windows 98 machines have slowed considerably. It takes longer for the operating system to load and longer for applications to start. What should you do to optimize the disk?
19. In order to use a new hard disk, how many partitions must it have?
20. Why is it important to delete partitions on a user's hard drive before re-using the drive in another user's computer?
21. What file systems does Windows ME support?
22. Which file system cannot be compressed?
23. A Windows 98 compressed drive is not accessible in what two operating systems?
24. What is the cluster size of a FAT partition larger than 2048 MB?
25. Which Windows operating systems support a 64 KB cluster size on a FAT partition?

Review Projects

Project #1 Partitioning Utilities

In Windows 2000 and Windows XP, the primary utility you'll use for disk management will be the GUI-based disk management snap-in. However, you should be aware of disk partitioning utilities that allow you to bypass some of the disk management limitations of the operating systems. There are several third-party vendors who provide disk parititoning utilities and one of the better known is Powerquest. This vendor manufacturers Partition Magic which is software that allows you to make changes to your disk partition schema on the fly.

Powerquest maintains a catalog of white papers on their site which you can access at **http://powerquest.com/whitepapers/index.cfm**. In this activity, read the first three white papers listed under the Manage heading. The .pdfs are fairly short, but they reinforce the partition information presented in your readings.

Next, Powerquest allows you to download an evaluation copy of Partition Magic. You can experience how the product works, but since it's an evaluation copy, you cannot implement any changes to your disk schema. Download an evaluation copy of partition magic at **http://powerquest.com/downloads/eval-soho.cfm** and install it. Review Powerquest's documentation and experiment with the product. Given what you know about disks and disk partitioning, what specific operations would Partition Magic allow you to perform that the operating system won't allow you to perform?

Project #2 Working with Fdisk.exe

Before Microsoft designed graphical user interfaces (GUIs) to make it easy to work with disks, you had to use the command-line utility, Fdisk.exe. As an A+ technician, you may work on older machines and you need to know how to make changes to disk configurations on those machines. The following Web site focuses on using Fdisk. Even if you're familiar with the command, you may not be familiar with all of the command's switches. The Web site is located at **http://www.computerhope.com/fdiskhlp.htm#02**.

In this activity, work through the entire tutorial, which is a full simulation of Fdisk operations. Copy the commands page into a word processor application and save the file as Fdisk commands. Save the file to a sub-folder you create under Hardware documentation. Name the sub-folder disk management.

Project #3 Disk Types and Features

Each operating system has a native file system. For example, Windows 98 uses FAT 32, Windows NT 4.0 uses NTFS 4.0, and Windows 2000/XP use NTFS 5.0. In this activity you'll read three support articles from Microsoft. The first not only reinforces information in your readings, but it introduces you to HPFS, an older file system that is supported by Windows NT 4.0. The article also rehearses the advantages and disadvantages of the FAT and FAT32 file system. The second and third articles focus on using the FAT32 file system with Windows XP and Windows 2000, respectively. Each article describes the limitations of using the FAT32 file system.

As you read through each article, take notes on any information that is new to you so you can incorporate it into your reference materials. Also, follow the hyperlinks in the articles and read those. Bookmark the support articles you find most useful. First read "Overview of FAT, HPFS, and NTFS File Systems," which is located at **http://support.microsoft.com/default.aspx?scid=kb;en-us;Q100108**. Next, read the Microsoft support article, "Limitations of the FAT32 File System in Windows XP," which is located at **http://support.microsoft.com/default.aspx?scid=kb;en-us;Q314463**. Finally, read "Limitations of the FAT32 File System in Windows 2000," which is located at **http://support.microsoft.com/default.aspx?scid=kb;EN-US;184006**.

Reflective Questions

1. **In your organization, or the organizations you support, what disk management tasks are you expected to perform? Why?**

2. **In your organization or the organizations you support, what is the configuration of the hard disk partitions on your Windows 9x computers? Why?**

CHAPTER 17
Connecting to Internet and Intranet Resources

Chapter Objectives:

In this chapter, you will connect to Internet and intranet resources.

You will:

- Create a dial-up connection.
- Create a VPN connection.
- Configure a Web browser.
- Configure an email client.
- Troubleshoot Internet and intranet connections.

Introduction

Earlier in this course you worked through a number of tasks you'll be expected to perform to connect Windows-based computers to a network. In this chapter, you'll learn about the additional steps you'll need to take to connect computers to the Internet and how to connect remote computers to your corporate intranet. You'll also learn how to configure the software your users will most commonly use when accessing the Internet or intranet: a Web browser and an email client.

The ability for users to access information on the Internet and share information on company intranets is vital to organizations. It is your responsibility, as an A+ technician, to maintain and support these crucial connections so that users have the access they need.

Topic A
Create a Dial-up Connection

Earlier in this course, you configured all of the network components necessary for your users to make local connections to your company's network, including installing a LAN driver, installing and configuring network protocols, and optionally installing a network client. But in today's environment, more and more users telecommute—which means they'll need to be able to access your company's intranet via a remote connection. Likewise, these same users might also need access to the Internet. In order to accommodate remote users, in this topic, you'll learn how to create dial-up connections that your users can use to access your company's intranet and the Internet.

As you know, providing users with reliable access to network resources enables them to perform the tasks they need to accomplish their jobs. This situation is no different when users connect to your network from a remote location: Users still need to be able to access network resources (including the Internet) reliably. By mastering the skills necessary to configure remote users with dial-up connections, you'll be able to keep your company's users working productively regardless of where they are. In addition, properly configuring users' dial-up connections will help minimize the amount of time you must spend troubleshooting their connections.

Outbound Connection

Definition:

An outbound connection, also referred to as a remote connection or remote-access connection, is a network connection that connects clients on one physical network to resources on a remote network. Outbound connections use:

- LAN or WAN media to carry the data from the client to the remote network.
- Remote access protocols, to transmit packets on a variety of WAN media types.
- A server running remote-access software (RAS) on the remote network to act as a gateway between the client and the remote network's resources.
- Remote client adapter hardware.
- Authentication methods to establish secure communications between the client and the RAS server.

The WAN media can be Public Switched Telephone Network (PSTN), Digital Subscriber Line (DSL), Integrated Services Digital Network (ISDN), or X.25 (a technology that breaks transmissions up into packets and transmits them over a worldwide telecommunications network). Client hardware can be a specialized modem, adapter, or packet assembler/disassembler (PAD). The data within the communication might be encrypted. Table 17-1 gives a brief description of each of these media types and the typical client adapter hardware you need for the connection.

Table 17-1: *WAN Media Types*

WAN Media Type	Description	Typical Client Adapter Hardware
qPSTN	Standard analog telephone lines. Also referred to as Plain Old Telephone Service (POTS).	Modem
DSL	High-speed (broadband) network access from telephone service providers that piggybacks over analog phone lines.	DSL modem
Cable	Broadband network access that piggybacks on existing cable TV infrastructure.	Cable modem
ISDN	A network of leased digital phone lines.	ISDN adapter
X.25	A worldwide packet-switching telecommunications network.	Packet Assembler/ Disassembler (PAD)
Satellite	Network transmissions are bounced off satellites orbiting above the Earth.	Satellite dish and decoder
Wireless	Devices can communicate without physical connection through the use of wireless transmissions that use cellular telephone networks.	Wireless network adapter and antenna

 Individual clients rarely connect directly to ISDN and X.25 networks. The connectivity is usually provided by a dedicated server that the client connects to through other means.

Example: Example: Dial-up Connection

A dial-up connection is an example of an outbound connection. In a dial-up connection, a user at the remote client uses a modem attached to their computer to dial in across phone lines to a modem connected to remote access server on the remote network. The client communicates with the server using the most common Windows dial-up RAS protocol Point-to-Point Protocol (PPP).

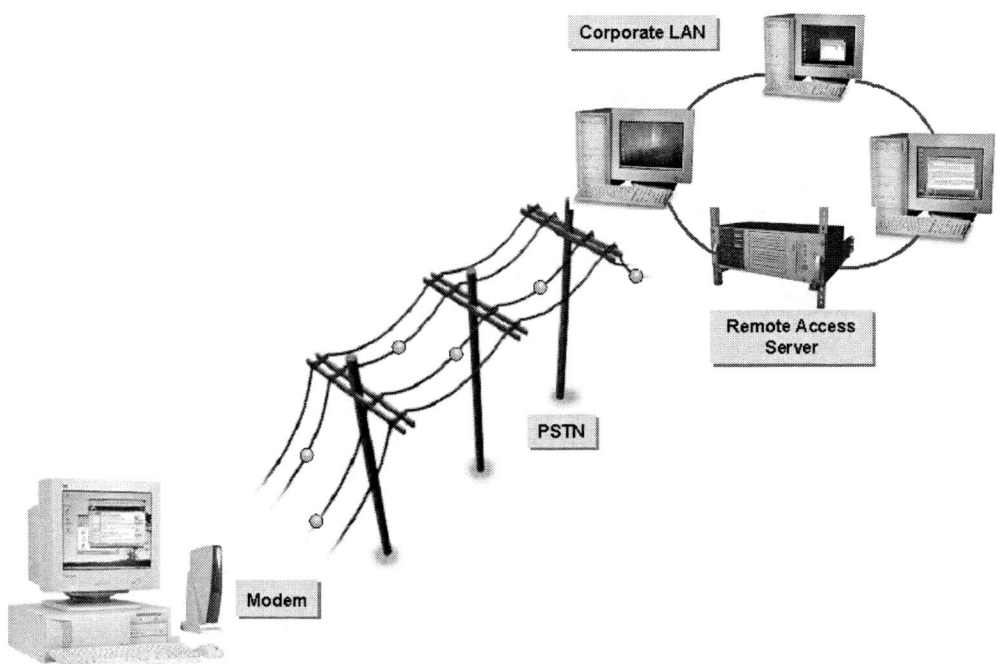

Figure 17-1: *A dial-up connection.*

Example: Example: Virtual Private Network Connection

A Virtual Private Network (VPN) connection is an example of an outbound connection. In a VPN connection, a user dials up to their Internet service provider. The client then establishes a connection with the company's Internet gateway server. The client uses the Internet gateway at that company's LAN to connect to through the Internet to their own company's VPN server. The client communicates with the VPN server using Point-to-Point Tunneling Protocol (PPTP), a Microsoft proprietary VPN protocol.

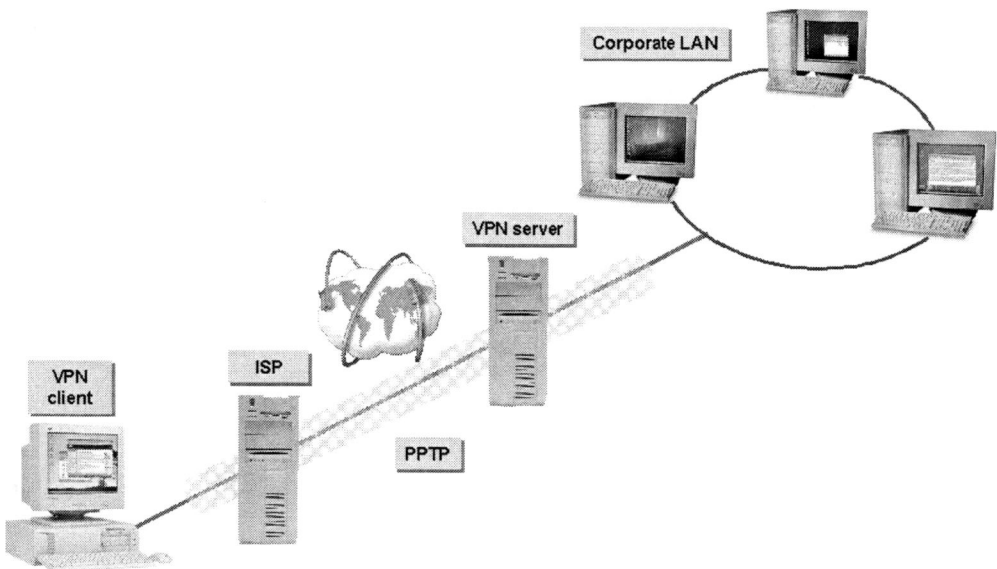

Figure 17-2: *A Virtual Private Network connection.*

Non-Example: Non-example: Cable Modems

Cable modems, another popular method for broadband connectivity from homes to the Internet, operate through the coaxial cable television network, not the phone system. These connections generally appear to the user as local area connections and use LAN protocols to communicate with the remote network.

Dial-Up Connection

Definition:

A dial-up connection is an outbound connection that uses WAN transmission media such as modems and phone lines to connect a client on one physical network to a Remote Access Server (RAS) on a remote network. The client communicates over the connection using a remote access protocol designed for communication over phone lines.

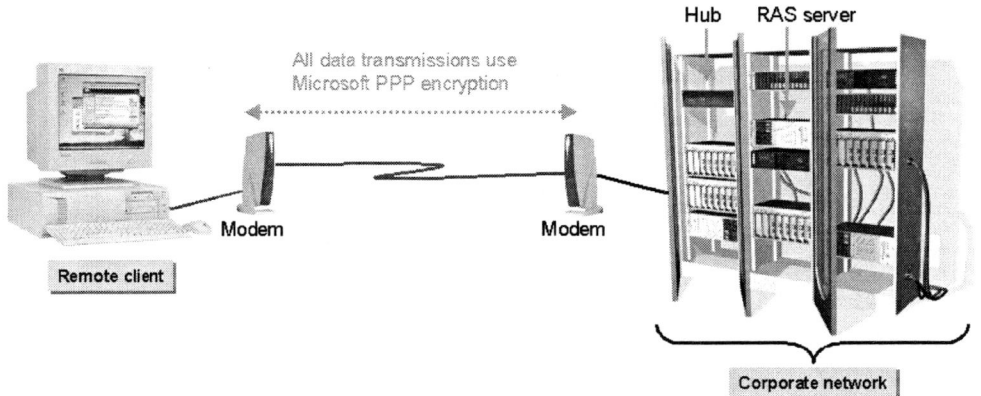

Figure 17-3: *A detailed dial-up connection.*

In Windows, the remote access protocol can be Point-to-Point Protocol (PPP) or Serial Line Internet Protocol (SLIP). PPP is the default remote access protocol in Windows that can transmit packets created with various different LAN protocols such as TCP/IP and NWLink. SLIP is another remote access protocol that can only transmit packets created with TCP/IP and must transmit over serial lines.

A dial-up connection always uses an authentication method to secure the communications from the client to the RAS server as it moves across phone lines. When using PPP, the authentication method can be Microsoft Challenge Handshake Authentication Protocol version 2 (MS-CHAP v2), MS-CHAP, CHAP, Password Authentication Protocol (PAP)/Clear Text, Shiva PAP (SPAP), or Smart Card Authentication. The authentication method chosen might also encrypt the data for additional security. Table 17-2 gives a brief description of each PPP authentication method. To connect to a SLIP server, the user must enter user credentials in a separate terminal window. SLIP does not support data encryption.

Table 17-2: *RAS PPP Authentication Methods*

Authentication Method	Description
MS-CHAP v2	A Microsoft encrypted-password authentication protocol. Supports mutual client-server authentication and data encryption.
MS-CHAP	The original version of MS-CHAP. It does not support mutual authentication.
CHAP	An encrypted-password protocol that supports connection to some third-party PPP servers. It does not support data encryption.
PAP/Clear Text	Sends clear-text passwords. PAP/Clear text should only be used to connect to servers that don't support password encryption.
SPAP	A proprietary version of PAP used to connect to RAS servers manufactured by the Shiva Corporation.

Authentication Method	Description
Smart Card Authentication	Uses authentication information encoded on a smart card. The user must insert the smart card into a reader device connected to the client in order to establish the remote connection. Smart Card and other external authentication methods are supported by the Extensible Authentication Protocol (EAP).

Data Encryption for Dial-up Connections

The authentication method you choose ensures that your client can establish secure communications with the target server. Data encryption ensures that the content of your communication remains secure as it travels over the phone lines. If you use MS-CHAP or EAP authentication, you can also use data encryption on the connection. Outbound PPP connections use proprietary Microsoft Point-to-Point Encryption (MPPE) to encrypt data.

Example:

A remote client uses a dial-up connection to establish communication through their modem and public phone lines to their company's RAS server. The client sends the information to the server using PPP. The PPP communication is secured using MS-CHAP v2. As the data travels to the RAS server over the phone lines it is encrypted using Microsoft Point-to-Point Encryption. The client validates the identity of the server. The server validates the identity of the client and sends data back using PPP as well.

How to Create a Dial-up Connection

Procedure Reference: Create a Dial-up Connection in Windows 2000

To create a dial-up connection on a Windows 2000 computer:

1. Log on as a local administrator.
2. If necessary, install a modem.
   a. Open Control Panel.
   b. Double-click Phone And Modem Options.
   c. In the Location Information dialog box, enter your area code or city code.
   d. If necessary, enter the number you dial to access an outside line.
   e. Select tone or pulse dialing.
   f. Click OK.
   g. Select the Modems tab.
   h. Click Add to add a new modem.
   i. If you have a Plug and Play modem, click Next to have Windows 2000 detect your modem.

If you have a non-Plug and Play modem, check Don't Detect My Modem, I Will Select It From A List.

Click Next.

j. If you are installing a non-Plug and Play modem, below Manufacturers, select the name of your modem's manufacturer. Below Models, select the model of your modem.

If your modem is not in the list, you will need an installation disk from the manufacturer. Insert it in your floppy disk drive and click Have Disk. Select your modem and click OK.

Click Next.

k. In the Select The Port To Use With This Modem list box, select the port your modem will communicate through.

l. Click Next.

m. Click Finish.

n. Click OK to close the Phone And Modems dialog box.

o. Close Control Panel.

3. Create a new connection object.

   a. Choose Start→Settings→Network and Dial-Up Connections→Make New Connection.

   b. Click Next.

   c. Select Dial-Up To Private Network.

   d. Click Next.

   e. If you have more than one communications device installed on your computer, check the device(s) you want the connection to use.

   f. Click Next.

   g. Check Use Dialing Rules.

   h. Enter the area code for the remote access server.

   i. Enter the telephone number for the remote access server.

   j. Select your country or region code.

   k. Click Next.

   l. Select Create This Connection For All Users or Only For Myself.

   m. Click Next.

   n. Enter a name for your connection.

   o. Click Finish.

4. If necessary, make changes to the default configuration information for the connection.

   a. Choose Start→Settings→Network and Dial-Up Connections.

b. Right-click your connection object and choose Properties.

c. On the General page, you can change the following configuration information:
- The modem or device the connection uses.
- Click the Configure button to make configuration changes to the modem hardware.
- Enable or disable all devices using the same phone number.
- Enable or disable using dialing rules.
- Area code.
- Telephone number.
- Country code.
- Enabling or disabling the display of an icon on the taskbar when you're using this connection.

d. On the Options page, you can change the following configuration information:
- Enable or disable dialing options.
- Enable or disable redialing option.
- Configuring multiple devices assigned to the connection.
- Configuring X.25 logon configuration settings.

e. On the Security page, you can change the following configuration information:
- Validation type for passwords.
- Data encryption and logon security.
- Interactive logon and scripting.

f. On the Networking page, you can change the following configuration information:
- Type of dial-up server and its settings.
- The networking components used by the connection and their properties.

g. On the Sharing page, you can specify whether or not the connection will be shared. Along with whether or not you want on-demand dialing for the connection.

h. Click OK.

Procedure Reference: Create a Dial-up Connection to a Private Server in Windows XP

To create a dial-up connection to a private server in Windows XP:

1. Log on as a local administrator.
2. If necessary, install a modem.
   a. Open Control Panel.
   b. Click Printers And Other Hardware.
   c. Click Phone And Modem Options.
   d. Select the Modems tab.

e. Click Add to add a new modem.

f. If you have a Plug and Play modem, click Next to have Windows XP detect your modem.

If you have a non-Plug and Play modem, check Don't Detect My Modem, I Will Select It From A List.

Click Next.

g. If you are installing a non-Plug and Play modem, below Manufacturer, select the name of your modem's manufacturer. Below Models, select the model of your modem.

If your modem is not in the list, you will need an installation disk from the manufacturer. Insert it in your floppy disk drive and click Have Disk. Select your modem and click OK.

Click Next.

h. Select the port your modem will communicate through.

i. Click Next.

j. Click Finish.

k. Click OK to close the Phone and Modem Options dialog box.

3. Create a new connection object.

a. In Control Panel, click Network And Internet Connections.

b. Click Network Connections.

c. Click Create A New Connection.

d. Click Next.

e. On the Network Connection Type page, select Connect To The Network At My Workplace.

f. Click Next.

g. Verify that Dial-Up Connection is selected and click Next.

h. In the Company Name text box, type a name for the connection.

i. Click Next.

j. In the Phone Number text box, type the phone number for the server to which the computer will connect.

k. Click Next.

l. Select Create This Connection For Anyone's Use or My Use Only.

m. Click Next.

n. If you want to create a shortcut to this connection on the desktop, check Add A Shortcut To This Connection To My Desktop.

o. Click Finish.

4. In the Connect dialog box for the new dial-up connection, complete the following tasks:
   a. In the User Name text box, type the user name you must use to connect to the remote server.
   b. In the Password text box, type this user account's password.
   c. If you want to save the user account information with the connection, check Save This User Name And Password For The Following Users and select one of the following:
      - Me Only, if you want to save the user account information for only your user.
      - Anyone Who Uses This Computer, if you want all users of the computer to use the same user account information when connecting to the remote server.
   d. Click Dial to connect to the server, or click Cancel to close the Connect dialog box.
5. If necessary, make changes to the default configuration information for the connection.
   a. In Control Panel, click Network And Internet Connections.
   b. Click Network Connections.
   c. Right-click your connection object and choose Properties.
   d. On the General page, you can change the following configuration information:
      - The modem or device the connection uses.
      - Click the Configure button to make configuration changes to the modem hardware.
      - Enable or disable all devices using the same phone number.
      - Enable or disable using dialing rules.
      - Area code.
      - Telephone number.
      - Alternate phone numbers.
      - Enabling or disabling the display of an icon on the taskbar when you're using this connection.
   e. On the Options page, you can change the following configuration information:
      - Enable or disable dialing options.
      - Enable or disable redialing option.
      - Configuring X.25 logon configuration settings.
   f. On the Security page, you can change the following configuration information:
      - Validation type for passwords.
      - Data encryption and logon security.
      - Interactive logon and scripting.
   g. On the Networking page, you can change the following configuration information:
      - Type of dial-up server and its settings.

- The networking components used by the connection and their properties.

h. On the Advanced page, you can specify the following configuration information:
- Whether or not you want to implement an Internet Connection Firewall.
- Whether or not the connection will be shared, along with whether or not you want on-demand dialing for the connection.

i. Click OK to close the dial-up connection's Properties dialog box.

6. Test the connection.

Procedure Reference: Create a Dial-up Connection in Windows NT

To create a dial-up connection on a Windows NT computer:

1. Log on as a local administrator.
2. If necessary, install a modem.
   a. Open Control Panel.
   b. Double-click Modems.
   c. If you want to have Windows NT attempt to detect your modem for you, click Next.
   d. If you want to manually add your modem, select Don't Detect My Modem; I Will Select It From A List and click Next.
   e. If you are manually adding your modem, or if Windows NT did not correctly locate your modem, below Manufacturers, select the name of your modem's manufacturer. Below Models, select the model of your modem.

   If your modem is not in the list, you will need an installation disk from the manufacturer. Insert it in the floppy disk drive or CD-ROM drive and click Have Disk. Select your modem and click OK.

   f. Click Next.
   g. In the On Which Ports Do You Want To Install It list, select the ports your modem will communicate through.
   h. Click Next.
   i. Click Finish.
   j. Click Close to close the Modems Properties dialog box.
   k. Close Control Panel.
3. From the Start menu, choose Programs→Accessories→Dial-Up Networking.
4. If necessary, click Install to install the Dial-Up Networking components.
   a. If prompted, insert the Windows NT installation CD-ROM or enter a path to the Windows NT installation files.
   b. In the Add RAS Device dialog box, select your modem and click OK.
   c. Click Continue.
   d. When prompted, click Restart to restart your computer.

e. Log back on as a local administrator.

f. From the Start menu, choose Programs→Accessories→Dial-Up Networking.

5. In the What Area (Or City) Code Are You In Now text box, type your area code and click Close.

6. Click OK to begin adding a phonebook entry to the phonebook.

    a. In the Name The New Phonebook Entry text box, type a name for the new connection.

    b. If you are familiar with creating phonebook entries, select I Know All About Phonebook Entries And Would Rather Edit The Properties Directly, or click Next to use the New Phonebook Entry Wizard.

    c. In the Server dialog box, click Next.

    d. Check Use Telephony Dialing Properties.

    e. In the Phone Number text box, type the area code and telephone number of the server you will call. If you have multiple numbers for the same server, click Alternates to add the additional numbers.

    f. Click Next.

    g. Click Finish.

7. If necessary, make changes to the default configuration information for the phonebook entry.

    a. Open Dial-Up Networking.

    b. Select an entry from the Phonebook Entry To Dial drop-down list.

    c. Click More.

    d. Click Edit Entry And Modem Properties.

    e. On the Basic page, you can change the following configuration information:
        - Entry name
        - Comment
        - Country code
        - Area code
        - Phone numbers
        - Whether to use Telephony dialing properties
        - Which modem(s) to use for the entry

    f. On the Server page, you can change the following configuration information:
        - Dial-up server type
        - Network protocols
        - Compression
        - PPP LCP extensions

g. On the Script page, you can change login script information.

h. On the Security page, you can change authentication and encryption settings.

i. On the X.25 page, you can change X.25 network logon options.

j. Click OK to save your changes.

Procedure Reference: Create a Dial-up Connection in Windows 98

To create a dial-up connection on a Windows 98 computer:

1. Install the Dial-Up Networking Windows Setup component.

    a. Choose Start→Settings→Control Panel.

    b. Double-click Add/Remove Programs.

    c. Select the Windows Setup tab.

    d. Select (don't uncheck!) Communications.

    e. Click Details.

    f. Check Dial-Up Networking.

    g. Click OK.

    h. Click OK.

    i. If prompted, enter the path to the Windows 9x setup files and click OK.

    j. Reboot the computer when prompted.

    > If you have a modem already installed on the computer that you want to use for the dial-up connection, you can skip step #1.

2. If you don't have a modem already installed, install a modem.

    a. Open Control Panel.

    b. Double-click Modems.

    c. If a modem is already installed on the computer, click Add to add a new modem.

    d. If you have a plug and play modem, click Next to have Windows 9x detect your modem.

    If you have a non-plug and play modem, check Don't Detect My Modem, I Will Select It From A List.

    Click Next.

    e. If you are installing a non-plug and play modem, in the Manufacturers list box, select the name of your modem's manufacturer. In the Models list box, select the model of your modem.

    If your modem is not in the list, you will need an installation disk from the manufacturer. Insert it in your floppy disk drive and click Have Disk. Select your modem and click OK.

Click Next.

f. In the Select The Port To Use With This Modem list box, select the port your modem will communicate through.

g. Click Next.

h. Click Finish.

3. If you just installed a modem, configure telephony dialing properties.

   a. After you install the first modem on your computer, the Location dialog box opens. Select your country.

   b. Enter your area code or city code.

   c. If necessary, enter the number you dial to access an outside line.

   d. Select tone or pulse dialing.

   e. Click OK.

4. Create a new connection object.

   a. Open My Computer.

   b. Double-click Dial-Up Networking.

   c. Double-click Make New Connection.

   d. Enter a name for your connection.

   e. If you have more than one modem installed on your computer, select the modem you want the connection to use.

   f. Click Next.

   g. Enter the area code for the remote access server.

   h. Enter the telephone number for the remote access server.

   i. Select your country or region code.

   j. Click Next.

   k. Click Finish.

5. If necessary, make changes to the default configuration information for the connection.

   a. In the Dial-Up Networking folder, right-click your connection and choose Properties.

   b. On the General page, you can change the following configuration information:
      - Area code.
      - Telephone number.
      - Country code.
      - Enable or disable Use Area Code and Dialing Properties.
      - The modem the connection uses.
      - Click the Configure button to make configuration changes to the modem hardware.

c. On the Server Types page, you can change the following configuration information:
   - Type of dial-up server.
   - Enabling or disabling logging on to the network.
   - Enabling or disabling software compression.
   - Enabling or disabling password encryption.
   - Enabling or disabling data encryption.
   - Enabling or disabling recording a log file for the connection.
   - Selecting the protocols that will be used by the connection.
   - Click the TCP/IP Settings button to make changes to the TCP/IP protocol for the connection.

d. On the Scripting page, you can specify a script assigned to the connection for manual logon.

e. On the Multilink page, you can specify two or more devices to increase the bandwidth of your dial-up connection.

TOPIC B
Create a VPN Connection

In Topic 17A, you learned how to connect a remote computer to your corporate intranet by defining a dial-up connection. Another and even faster technique you can use to connect users to your intranet is to create a VPN connection. In this topic, you'll learn the steps for creating a VPN connection.

In many cases, users who telecommute will have faster connections to the Internet than a dial-up connection. For example, the typical speed of a DSL connection is up to 1.5 Mbps, whereas the fastest speed of a modem is only 56 Kbps. Because so many users have such fast connections to the Internet, they'll see significantly faster performance if they can connect to your company's intranet via the Internet instead of a dial-up modem. By configuring VPN connections, you'll enable your users to take advantage of their fast Internet connections—which means they'll be able to work more productively when telecommuting.

Virtual Private Network Connection

Definition:

A Virtual Private Network (VPN) connection is an outbound connection that uses existing local or outbound connection objects to connect a client on one physical network, through a private connection over a public network, to a VPN server on a remote network.

The client communicates over the connection using a VPN protocol designed for secure communication over public networks such as the Internet.

In Windows, the VPN protocol can be Point-to-Point Tunneling Protocol (PPTP) or Layer Two Tunneling Protocol (L2TP). PPTP is a Microsoft proprietary VPN protocol for connecting to Microsoft Routing and Remote Access Service (RRAS) servers running PPP. L2TP is an Internet standard VPN protocol for connecting a variety of VPN servers, including RRAS servers running L2TP.

A VPN connection always uses data encryption to keep the connection secure. PPP uses MPPE for data encryption. L2TP requires IP Security (IPSec), an industry-standard set of specification for creating end-to-end security on IP networks.

Example: Example: VPN Connection

A corporate sales representative attaches her laptop to a LAN network port at a client's office to connect to the Internet. Her computer then uses the Internet to connect to a private VPN server at her home office. The communication across the Internet is transmitted using PPTP and is encrypted using MPPE.

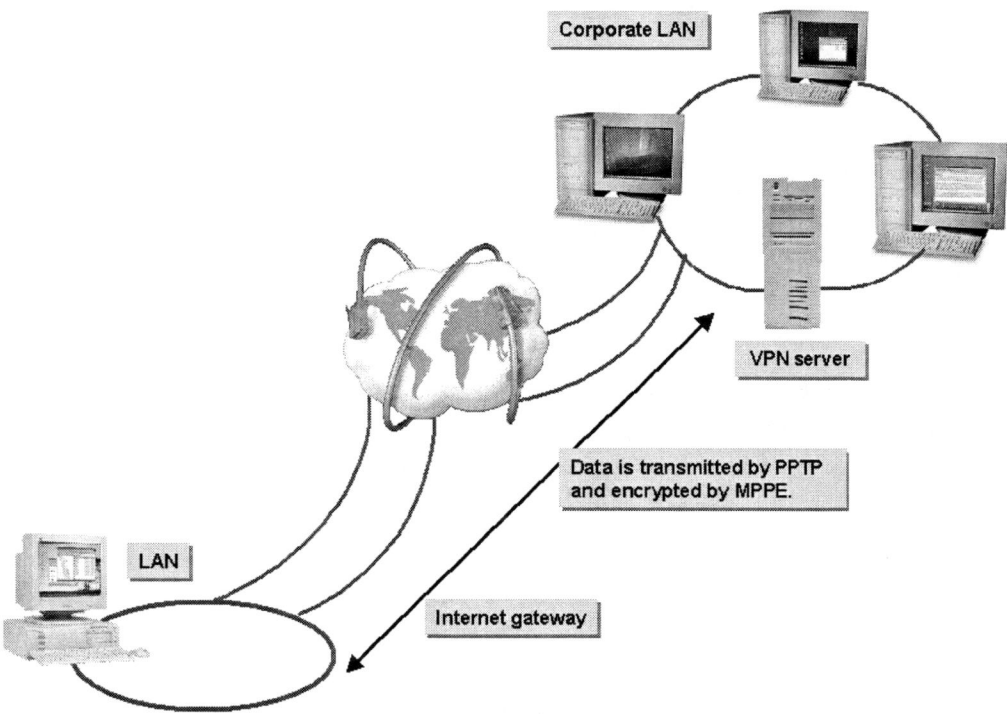

Figure 17-4: *A detailed VPN connection.*

How to Create a VPN Connection

Procedure Reference: Create a VPN Connection in Windows 2000

To create a VPN connection on a Windows 2000 computer:

1. Log on as a local administrator.

2. Create a new connection object.

   a. Choose Start→Settings→Network and Dial-Up Connections→Make New Connection.
   b. Click Next.
   c. Select Connect To A Private Network Through The Internet.
   d. Click Next.
   e. Select one of the following:
      - Do Not Dial This Initial Connection.
      - Automatically Dial This Initial Connection and then select an existing dial-up connection from the drop-down list.
   f. Click Next.
   g. Enter the host name or IP Address for the remote access server.
   h. Click Next.
   i. Select Create This Connection For All Users or Only For Myself.
   j. Click Next.
   k. Enter a name for your connection.
   l. Click Finish.

3. If necessary, make changes to the default configuration information for the connection (in Network Connections, right-click the connection and choose Properties).

4. Click Dial to test the connection.

Procedure Reference: Create a VPN Connection in Windows XP

To create a VPN connection in Windows XP:

1. Log on as a local administrator.
2. If necessary, create a connection to the Internet.
3. Create a new connection object.

   a. In Control Panel, click Network And Internet Connections.
   b. Click Network Connections.
   c. Click Create A New Connection.
   d. Click Next.
   e. On the Network Connection Type page, select Connect To The Network At My Workplace.
   f. Click Next.
   g. Select Virtual Private Network Connection and click Next.
   h. In the Company Name text box, type a name for the connection.
   i. Click Next.

j. On the Public Network page, select one of the following:
- Do Not Dial The Initial Connection, if you do not need to dial in to the Internet before you connect to the VPN server.
- Automatically Dial This Initial Connection, if you need to dial in to the Internet before you connect to the VPN server. From the drop-down list, select the dial-up connection you want to use.

k. Click Next.

l. In the Host Name Or IP Address text box, type the host name or IP address for the server to which the computer will connect.

> If you specify the host name, your computer must be able to resolve the host name to its IP address in DNS.

m. Click Next.

n. Select Create This Connection For Anyone's Use or My Use Only.

o. Click Next.

p. If you want to create a shortcut to this connection on the desktop, check Add A Shortcut To This Connection To My Desktop.

q. Click Finish.

4. In the Connect dialog box for the new dial-up connection, complete the following tasks:

a. In the User Name text box, type the user name you must use to connect to the remote server.

b. In the Password text box, type this user account's password.

c. If you want to save the user account information with the connection, check Save This User Name And Password For The Following Users and select one of the following:
- Me Only, if you want to save the user account information for only your user.
- Anyone Who Uses This Computer, if you want all users of the computer to use the same user account information when connecting to the remote server.

d. Click Connect to connect to the server, or click Cancel to close the Connect dialog box.

5. If necessary, make changes to the default configuration information for the connection (in Network Connections, right-click the connection and choose Properties).

6. Click Dial to test the connection.

Procedure Reference: Create a VPN Connection in Windows NT

To create a VPN connection on a Windows NT computer:

1. Log on as a local administrator.

2. If necessary, create a connection to the Internet.

3. Install the Point-To-Point Tunneling Protocol.
    a. Open Control Panel.
    b. Double-click Network.
    c. Select the Protocols tab and click Add.
    d. Select Point-To-Point Tunneling Protocol and click OK.
    e. If prompted, insert the Windows NT installation CD-ROM and click OK.
    f. In the PPTP Configuration dialog box, enter the number of concurrent VPN connections you need to create and click OK.
    g. Click OK to start Remote Access Setup.
    h. In the Remote Access Setup dialog box, click Add.
    i. Select a VPN connection from the list of RAS capable devices and click OK.
    j. Repeat steps h and i for each VPN connection object.
    k. Click Continue.
    l. Click Close to close the Network Properties dialog box.
    m. When prompted, click Yes to restart the computer.
4. Create a new connection object.
    a. Open Dial-Up Networking.
    b. Click New.
    c. Type a name for the new connection and click Next.
    d. Click Next.
    e. On the Modem Or Adapter page, select a VPN entry and click Next.
    f. On the Phone Number page, uncheck Use Telephony Dialing Properties.
    g. In the Phone Number text box, type the host name or IP address of your VPN server and click Next.
    h. Click Finish to save the new connection.
5. Click Dial to test the connection.

Procedure Reference: Create a VPN Connection in Windows 9x

To create a VPN connection on a Windows 9x computer:

1. Install the Dial-Up Networking Windows Setup component.
2. Install the Virtual Private Networking Windows Setup component.
    a. Choose Start→Settings→Control Panel.
    b. Double-click Add/Remove Programs.
    c. Select the Windows Setup tab.
    d. Select (don't uncheck!) Communications.
    e. Click Details.

    f. Check Virtual Private Networking.
    g. Click OK.
    h. Click OK.
    i. If prompted, enter the path to the Windows 9x setup files and click OK.
    j. Reboot the computer when prompted.
3. Create a new VPN connection object.
    a. Open My Computer.
    b. Double-click Dial-Up Networking.
    c. Double-click Make New Connection.
    d. Enter a name for your connection.
    e. From the Select A Device drop-down list, select the Microsoft VPN Adapter.
    f. Click Next.
    g. Enter the host name or IP Address for the remote access server.
    h. Click Next.
    i. Click Finish.
4. Click Dial to test the connection.

Topic C
Configure a Web Browser

So far in this chapter, you've seen only the steps for connecting a user to the Internet and your corporate intranet. But once you've established these connections, your next task is to configure the software they'll use to access both Internet and intranet resources—their Web browser. In this topic, you'll learn about the options you can configure in a Web browser to tailor it to your company's requirements.

Some companies want all users to access the Internet through a standard home page that requires them to agree to the company's Internet access policy before continuing on to surfing the Internet. Other companies will want you to minimize the amount of disk space that can be eaten up on users' computers with temporary Internet files and cookies. As an A+ technician, it's your job to configure users' Web browsers properly so that users have access to the resources they need while conforming to the company's rules and standards for Internet and intranet access.

Web Browser

Definition:

A Web browser is a software application used to locate and display Web pages. A Web browser can be a text-only browser or a graphical browser, which means it can display graphics and text. In addition, a Web browser may be able to present multimedia elements of sound and video. To present some formats of sound and video, an additional piece of software (called a plug-in) is needed. Web browsers use Internet protocols to establish communication between the client and the Web server. Web browsers contain a field in which you can enter the address of the Web page you wish to display. In addition, your Web browser may contain graphical buttons that you can use for navigation purposes and a menu structure to provide additional functionality.

Example:

Internet Explorer is an example of a graphical Web browser that you can use to locate and display Web pages.

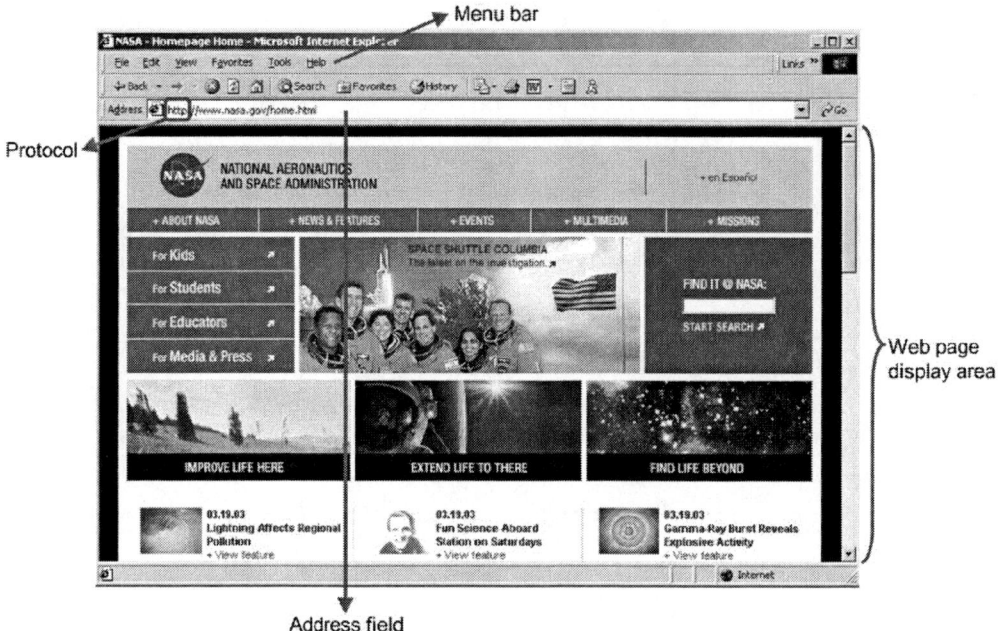

Figure 17-5: *Internet Explorer is a graphical Web browser.*

Web Protocols

Definition:

A Web protocol is a communication protocol that formats data for transmission from a Web client to a Web server. A Web protocol defines how messages are formatted and transmitted, and what actions Web servers and browsers should take in response to various commands. The protocol may or may not provide security for its communications.

Example: Web Protocols

Table 17-3 describes the protocols commonly used with Internet Explorer and Netscape Navigator to communicate between Web clients and Web servers.

Table 17-3: *Web Protocols*

Web Protocol	Description
Hypertext Transfer Protocol (HTTP)	With HTTP, communication is in one direction—only downloading Web page files written in the HyperText Markup Language (HTML) from the Web server to the client browser for viewing. HTTP is the most common protocol used to make Web requests.
File Transfer Protocol (FTP)	A protocol used to upload files to or download files from an FTP file server. With FTP communication is in two directions—allowing both the client to download files from the server or upload files from the server. Most FTP servers require users to log on.
Telnet	Telnet is a terminal emulation protocol that enables a user at one site to simulate a session on a remote host. It does this by translating keystrokes from the user's terminal to instructions recognized by the remote host, then carrying the output back to the user's terminal and displaying it in a format native to the remote host. This service is transparent (it gives users the impression that their terminals are directly attached to the remote host).
Secure Socket Layer (SSL)	A security protocol that uses certificates for authentication and encryption to protect Web communication. SSL is widely deployed on Web sites and the Internet because it's a server-driven process. The client simply has to support SSL; it doesn't need a registered certificate. This means that any of 60 million Internet users can connect to a Web site through a secure connection, as long as their clients can support SSL. Web sites that begin with **https://** are sites that require SSL.

 HyperText Markup Language (HTML) is the authoring language used to create documents on the Web. HTML defines the structure and layout of a Web document as it should present itself in a Web browser.

How to Configure a Web Browser

Procedure Reference: Set up an Internet Connection in Windows 2000

To set up an Internet Connection on a Windows 2000 computer for Internet or intranet access:

1. Choose Start→Programs→Accessories→Communications→Internet Connection Wizard.
2. Select one of the following connection types:
    - I want to sign up for a new Internet account (My telephone line is connected to my modem.)

- I want to transfer my existing Internet account to this computer. (My telephone line is connected to my modem.)
- I want to set up my Internet connection manually, or I want to connect through a local area network (LAN).

> Most businesses will use the last choice—they will either manually set up the connection or connect to the Internet through their LANs. The steps in this procedure document this scenario.

3. Click Next.
4. Select one of the following connection options:
   - I connect through a phone line and a modem.
   - I connect through a local area network (LAN).
5. Click Next.
6. If you selected to connect through a phone line and modem:
   a. Enter the telephone number to connect to the Internet Service Provider.
   b. Use the Advanced button to change the connection type from PPP to SLIP or C-SLIP; change the logon procedure from none to manual logon or use a script; or change the IP address of the computer or the DNS server from automatic to manual. Click OK.
   c. Click Next.
   d. Enter the User Name and Password that will be authenticated by the ISP.
   e. Enter a name for your connection.
   f. Click Next.
7. If you selected to connect through a local area network (LAN):
   a. If you use a proxy server, check the appropriate check box to either automatically discover proxy server settings or manually enter the settings.
   b. Click Next.
   c. If you chose to manually enter the settings, enter your proxy and port information for each service your ISP supports.
   d. Click Next.
   e. If you chose to manually enter the settings, enter any Internet addresses you do not want to use a proxy server and click Next.
8. Select Yes if you want to set up an Internet mail account. Select No if you want to skip the step because you have an existing mail account or you don't want to use mail.
9. Click Next.
10. If desired, uncheck the To Connect To The Internet Immediately check box, so that Windows 9x won't attempt to connect to the Internet immediately.

11. Click Finish.
12. Test the connection.

Procedure Reference: Set Up an Internet Connection in Windows XP

To create an Internet connection in Windows XP:

1. Log on as a local administrator.
2. If necessary, install a modem.
3. Create a new connection object.
    a. In Control Panel, click Network And Internet Connections.
    b. Click Network Connections.
    c. Click Create A New Connection and click Next.
    d. On the Network Connection Type page, select Connect To The Internet and click Next.
    e. Below How Do You Want To Connect To The Internet, select one of the following:
        - Choose From A List Of Internet Service Providers (ISPs), if you want to select from a list of pre-configured connections to ISPs.
        - Set Up My Connection Manually, if you want to manually define your connection to the ISP.
        - Use The CD I Got From An ISP, if you want to use an ISP's installation CD to set up the connection.
    f. Click Next.
    g. If you choose to set up the connection manually, complete the following steps:
        1. On the Internet Connection page, select one of the following:

            Connect Using A Dial-Up Modem.

            Connect Using A Broadband Connection That Requires A User Name And Password, if you have a cable or DSL modem.

            Connect Using A Broadband Connection That Is Always On, if you have a cable modem or DSL connection, or a LAN connection that is always on.
        2. Click Next.
        3. In the ISP Name text box, type the name of your ISP and click Next.
        4. If you selected to connect to the ISP via a dial-up connection, in the Phone Number text box, type the phone number and click Next.
        5. Select Create This Connection For Anyone's Use or My Use Only.
        6. Click Next.
        7. On the Internet Account Information page, complete the following information:

            The user name you selected with the ISP.

The user account's password.

Confirm the user account's password.

You can also select any or all of the following:

Whether you want to use this same user account and password whenever anyone uses this computer to connect to the Internet.

Whether you want this connection to be the default Internet connection.

Whether you want to turn on the Internet Connection Firewall for this connection.

8. Click Next.

9. If you want to create a shortcut to this connection on the desktop, check Add A Shortcut To This Connection To My Desktop.

10. Click Finish.

4. If necessary, make changes to the default configuration information for the connection (in Network Connections, right-click the connection and choose Properties).

5. Test the connection.

Procedure Reference: Set up an Internet Connection in Windows NT

To set up an Internet Connection on a Windows NT computer for Internet or intranet access:

1. Log on as a local administrator.

2. If necessary, install a modem.

3. Open Dial-Up Networking.

4. Click New.

5. In the Name text box, type a name for the connection and click Next.

6. In the Server dialog box, check I Am Calling The Internet and click Next.

7. In the modem or adapter list, select the modem you will use to dial your ISP and click Next.

8. Check Use Telephony Dialing Properties.

9. Type the area code and telephone number of your ISP and click Next.

10. Click Finish.

Procedure Reference: Set up an Internet Connection in Windows 9x

To set up an Internet Connection on a Windows 9x computer for Internet or intranet access:

1. Choose Start→Programs→Accessories→Internet Tools→Internet Connection Wizard.

2. Select one of the following connection types:

- I want to sign up for a new Internet account (My telephone line is connected to my modem.)
- I want to transfer my existing Internet account to this computer. (My telephone line is connected to my modem.)
- I want to set up my Internet connection manually, or I want to connect through a local area network (LAN).

> Most businesses will use the last choice—they will either manually set up the connection or connect to the Internet through their LANs. The steps in this procedure document this scenario.

3. Click Next.
4. Select one of the following connection options:
   - I connect through a phone line and a modem.
   - I connect through a local area network (LAN).
5. Click Next.
6. If you selected to connect through a phone line and modem:
   a. Enter the telephone to connect to the Internet Service Provider.
   b. Use the Advanced button to change the connection type from PPP to SLIP; change the logon procedure from none to manual logon or use a script; or change the IP address of the computer or the DNS server from automatic to manual. Click OK.
   c. Click Next.
   d. Enter the User Name and Password that will be authenticated by the ISP.
   e. Enter a name for your connection.
   f. Click Next.
7. If you selected to connect through a local area network (LAN):
   a. If you use a proxy server, check the appropriate check box to either automatically discover proxy server settings or manually enter the settings.
   b. Click Next.
   c. If you chose to manually enter the settings, enter your proxy and port information for each service your ISP supports.
   d. Click Next.
   e. If you chose to manually enter the settings, enter any Internet addresses you do not want to use a proxy server and click Next.
8. If desired, uncheck the To Connect To The Internet Immediately check box, so that Windows 9x won't attempt to connect to the Internet immediately.
9. Click Finish.

Procedure Reference: Configure the Internet Explorer Web Browser

To configure Internet Explorer on a Windows 2000, Windows XP, Windows NT, or Windows 9x computer:

1. If you're using Windows 2000, Windows NT, or Windows 9x, right-click Internet Explorer on the desktop and choose Properties.

    If you're using Windows XP, on the Start menu, right-click Internet Explorer on the desktop and choose Internet Properties.

     You can also right-click Internet Explorer in the Start→Programs menu and choose Properties.

2. Configure the desired General properties. On the General page you can configure:
    - Your home page.
    - Settings for handling temporary Internet files and refreshing stored pages.
    - Settings for your history list.
    - Colors used in Internet Explorer.
    - Fonts used on Web pages that have no specified text font.
    - The languages displayed on Web sites offering content in several languages.
    - Accessibility options.

3. Configure the desired Security properties. On the Security page, you can configure:
    - The placement of Web sites in local intranet, trusted sites, and restricted sites zones.
    - The security level for each zone. By default, scripts and ActiveX controls are handled differently for each security level. To customize support for scripts and ActiveX controls, select the security level you want to configure and click Customize to open the Security Settings dialog box, where you can also configure how Internet Explorer handles cookies, downloads, Java, and user authentication.

4. Configure the desired Content properties. On the Content page, you can:
    - Enable content ratings to control the Internet content that can be viewed on the computer.
    - Enable certificates that can be used for identification purposes.
    - Enable the AutoComplete feature which lists possible matches for what you are typing from items you've entered previously.
    - On Windows 98, enable the Wallet feature to store personal information for ease of Internet shopping.
    - Configure a personal profile.

5. Configure the desired Connections properties. On the Connections page, you can configure:
    - Select a dial-up or VPN connection to automatically connect when Internet Explorer runs.

- On Windows 98, you can enable the system to perform a security check before dialing a connection.
- Your LAN settings, where you can enable the use of scripts for LAN configuration and a proxy server for your Internet connection. To use a proxy server, check Use A Proxy Server, and then enter the server's IP address and the port to which you want to connect.

You can also start the Internet Connection Wizard by clicking the Setup button.

6. Configure the Programs properties. On the Programs page, you can configure the default programs Internet Explorer will use for:
   - An HTML editor.
   - An email program.
   - A newsgroup server.
   - An Internet meeting program.
   - A calendar program.
   - A contact list.

   You can reset the Internet Explorer programs to their defaults by clicking the Reset Web Settings button.

7. Configure the Advanced properties. On the Advanced page, you can configure the functionality of Internet Explorer by checking (enabling) and unchecking (disabling) features.

8. Click OK.

Procedure Reference: Install the Netscape Navigator 7.01 Web Browser

To install Netscape Navigator 7.01 on a Windows 2000, Windows XP, Windows NT, or Windows 9x computer:

1. Run the NSSetup.exe file.

    The NSSetup.exe file is available for download from the Netscape site at http://channels.netscape.com/ns/borwsers/download.asp or by ordering the CD-ROM.

2. Click Next to begin the Wizard.
3. Click Accept to accept the license agreement.
4. Select the type of setup you prefer.

   The choices available are:
   - Recommended: Installs the most common options. Quickest to download; recommended for most users.
   - Full: Installs a range of options, including Java and several media players.
   - Custom: Recommended for advanced users.

⚠ The remaining steps assume the setup type selected was Recommended.

5. If prompted, click Yes to create a *root_drive:*\Program Files\Netscape\Netscape folder.

6. Select or clear the additional components you want to install.

   Additional components include: SunJava2 and Winamp.

7. Click Next.

8. Enable or disable Quick Launch which keeps portions of the Netscape in memory at all times for quicker launch times.

9. Click Next.

10. Enable or disable Additional Options.

    The additional options available are: Make Netscape.com my home page and, if you are downloading Netscape from the Web site, Save installer files locally.

11. Click Next.

12. Click Install.

13. If you have an existing Netscape or AOL Instant Messenger screen name, enter it along with your password and follow the prompts to log on to the Netscape network.

    If not, click Cancel.

14. Click Finished.

Procedure Reference: Configure the Netscape Navigator 7.01 Browser

To configure Netscape Navigator 7.01 on a Windows 2000, Windows XP, Windows NT, or Windows 9x computer:

1. Run Netscape Navigator.

2. Choose Edit→Preferences.

3. In the Category list box, select Navigator.

4. On the Navigator page, set your general navigator options.

   The options available from the Navigator page are:
   - The page to display when Navigator starts up. The choices are Blank page, Home page, or Last page visited.
   - Enable or disable Netscape as your default browser.
   - Enter the address of a Web page for your home page.
   - Select the buttons you want to see in the toolbars.

5. In the Category list box, select History.

6. On the History page, set your history options.

   The options available from the History page are:
   - The number of days in your History list.
   - The location of your History bar in the Netscape Navigator window.
   - The number of pages in your session history list.

7. Select Languages.
8. On the Languages page, add or remove the languages you would like to view Web pages in.
9. Select Helper Applications.
10. On the Helper Applications page, set your file type association settings.

    The options available on the Helper Applications page are:
    - Adding file type associations.
    - Enabling or disabling the Plug-in Finder Service.
    - Reset your file-opening preferences to the default.

11. Select Smart Browsing.
12. On the Smart Browsing page, set your smart browsing options.

    The options available on the Smart Browsing page are:
    - Enabling or disabling Internet keywords, which enables quick access to services such as stock quotes and Internet searching from the Location bar.
    - Enabling or disabling the Location bar autocomplete feature.

13. Select the Internet Search page.
14. On the Internet Search page, set your Internet search options.

    The options available on the Internet Search page are:
    - Setting your default Internet search engine.
    - Enabling or disabling the auto-open feature of the Search bar.
    - Setting your sidebar search tab preference as a basic or advanced search.

15. Select Tabbed Browsing.
16. Set your Tabbed Browsing options.

    The options available on the Tabbed Browsing page are:
    - Set your tab display options.
    - Set tab versus window settings.

17. Select Downloads.

18. Set your Downloads options.

    The options on the Downloads page specify what behavior Netscape Navigator should display when downloading files.

19. Select Privacy & Security. You can use the pages under Privacy & Security to configure how Navigator handles cookies, manage stored passwords, and configure SSL.

20. Select Advanced. You can use these pages to configure script support and configure proxy servers for your Internet connection.

TOPIC D
Configure an Email Client

In Topic 17C, you learned how to configure users' Web browsers to access Internet and intranet resources. Now, you need to configure users with an email client so that they can send and receive email messages. In this topic, you'll learn the exact steps for configuring users' email clients.

In today's business world, email is considered an essential part of doing business. Without email, many companies just can't compete. Imagine if your company used "snail" mail to deliver its marketing materials to customers (which could take several days) while your competitors deliver the same information via email (which takes only a few seconds). Obviously, the company that uses email will have a competitive edge because it will be able to reach its customers faster. For this reason, your job as an A+ technician is to be prepared to configure users' email clients so that they can access their email. Further, nothing will generate a technical support call quicker than a user who's unable to send or receive email! You need to be prepared to handle such calls so that you can get the user back up and running as quickly as possible.

Email Protocol

Definition:

An email protocol is a communications protocol that enables the transmission of electronic messages over communications networks. The message that is sent can be text entered directly in an email software package or can be electronic files stored on a disk. An email protocol can be used to retrieve email from a server or to send email.

Example: Example: Email Protocols

Table 17-4 describes the protocols commonly used with email software packages.

Table 17-4: *Email Protocols*

Email Protocol	Description
Post Office Protocol (POP) and POP2	Communications protocols used to retrieve email from a mail server. Each must be used in conjunction with the SMTP protocol that can send email to a mail server.

Email Protocol	Description
POP3	A newer version of POP that can be used with or without SMTP.
Internet Message Access Protocol (IMAP)	A communications protocol used to retrieve messages from an email server.
IMAP4	A newer version of IMAP that, like POP, can be used with or without SMTP. It has additional features that allow you to search through your email by keyword and then retrieve just the emails that meet your search criteria.
Simple Mail Transfer Protocol (SMTP)	A communications protocol used to send email to a mail server. It must be used with a communications protocol such as a POP or IMAP protocol to retrieve messages from the mail server.

Email Clients

Definition:

An email client is a software application that runs on a client computer and enables the user to send, receive, and organize email messages.

Example: Email Client

Email clients are used to send, receive, and organize email.

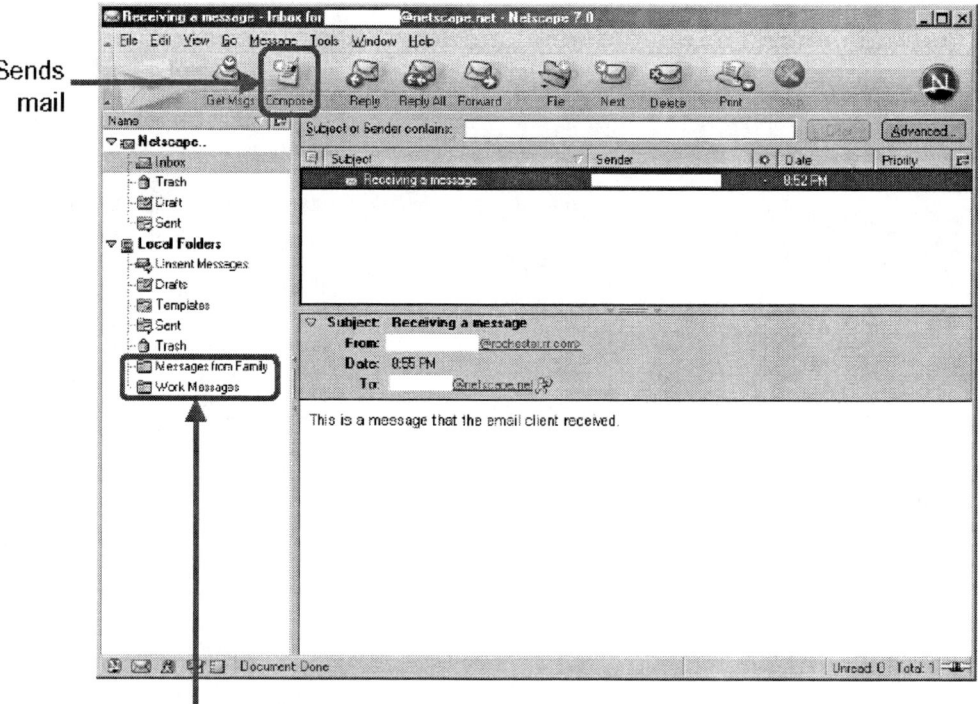

Figure 17-6: *An email client.*

Common Email Client Packages

Common email client packages include:

- Microsoft Outlook—Part of Microsoft Office.
- Microsoft Outlook Express—Free with Windows products.
- Netscape Mail—Free with Netscape Navigator.
- Microsoft Hotmail—Free from MSN.
- Lotus Notes—Must be purchased.
- Qualcomm Eudora—Free for download.
- Novell Groupwise—Must be purchased.

How to Configure an Email Client

Procedure Reference: Configure Outlook Express

To configure Outlook Express to send and receive email:

1. Obtain the necessary email account information.
   - Full name.

- Email address.
- Incoming mail server type: POP3, IMAP, or HTTP.
- Incoming mail server name (required for POP3 and IMAP accounts, but not for HTTP).
- Outgoing mail server name (required for POP3 and IMAP accounts, but not for HTTP).

2. In Windows 2000 and Windows 9x, choose Start→Programs→Outlook Express.

   In Windows XP, choose Start→All Programs→Outlook Express.

   In Windows NT, download and install the latest version of Internet Explorer from Microsoft's Web site at **www.microsoft.com/ie** (Outlook Express will be automatically installed as part of the installation of Internet Explorer). When the installation is complete, choose Start→Programs→Outlook Express.

 If there is an Outlook Express shortcut on your desktop or system tool bar, you can use it to access Outlook Express.

3. In the Display Name text box, type your full name and click Next.

4. In the E-Mail Address text box, type your email address. Click Next.

5. From the My Incoming Mail Server Is A _____ Server drop-down list, select the type of email server (POP3, IMAP, or HTTP).

6. In the Incoming Mail (POP3, IMAP Or HTTP) Server text box, type the fully qualified domain name for this server (for example, pop3.earthlink.net).

7. In the Outgoing Mail (SMTP) Server text box, type the fully qualified domain name for this server.

8. Click Next.

9. On the Internet Mail Logon page, in the Account Name text box, type your user account.

10. In the Password text box, type your user account's password.

11. If you want Outlook Express to save your password, leave Remember Password checked.

    If you want Outlook Express to prompt you for your password before retrieving your email, uncheck Remember Password.

12. Click Next.

13. Click Finish.

14. Test to see that you can send and receive email.

Procedure Reference: Add a New Account to Outlook Express

To add a new email account to Outlook Express:

1. Obtain the necessary email account information.
   - Full name.
   - Email address.
   - Incoming mail server type: POP3, IMAP, or HTTP.
   - Incoming mail server name (required for POP3 and IMAP accounts, but not for HTTP).
   - Outgoing mail server name (required for POP3 and IMAP accounts, but not for HTTP).
2. Open Outlook Express.
3. Choose Tools→Accounts.
4. Select the Mail tab.
5. Click Add and choose Mail.
6. Enter a display name for the person who will be using the account.
7. Click Next.
8. Select one of the following:
   - I Already Have An E-mail Address That I'd Like To Use. Then enter the email address in the text box.
   - I'd Like To Sign Up For A New Account From. Then select an Internet mail provider from the drop-down list box.

    Most companies will have their own mail servers and will provide users with a mail account on that server. The remainder of the steps in this procedure assume a company-provided mail server.

9. Click Next.
10. From the My Incoming Mail Server Is A _____ Server drop-down list box, select the type of mail server Outlook Express will be connecting to.
11. In the Incoming Mail (POP3, IMAP, or HTTP) Server: text box, enter the name of your incoming mail server.
12. In the Outgoing Mail (SMTP) Server: text box, enter the name of your outgoing mail server.
13. Click Next.
14. In the Account Name text box, enter your mail account name.
15. In the Password text box, enter the password for your mail account.

16. To have Outlook Express automatically remember your password, check Remember Password. To enter your password each time you start Outlook Express, uncheck Remember Password.

17. If your mail server requires Secure Password Authentication, check Log On Using Secure Password Authentication (SPA).

18. Click Next.

19. Click Finish.

Topic E
Troubleshoot Internet and Intranet Connections

As you've seen in this chapter, most companies consider Internet and intranet access a critical part of their business. Without such access, many companies are unable to compete against their competitors. As an A+ technician, you'll need to be prepared to quickly identify and resolve any problems with Internet and intranet connections, and that's just what you'll learn in this topic.

Nothing will make you a hero faster than repairing a user's Internet connection. Likewise, nothing will make you more unpopular than if you're unable to resolve a user's Internet or intranet access problem. Many companies rely on the research they can perform on the Internet to make critical business decisions. Without such access, a company will be unable to get the information it needs. As an A+ technician, your job is to make sure that companies are able to access the information superhighway without hitting any potholes or experiencing a breakdown altogether. Knowing how to diagnose and repair Internet/intranet connection problems quickly will enable your users to get back to working productively on their computers.

Common Internet/Intranet Problems

Table 17-5 describes common Internet/intranet connection problems.

Table 17-5: *Common Internet/Intranet Connection Problems*

Symptoms	Possible Causes
Can't establish a dial-up connection	The problem could be with the client hardware (check the modem.log file), the client RAS protocol (check the ppp.log file), or with the dial-up connection settings (verify the phone number, server type, and protocol settings). The RAS server could also be down.
Can't establish a VPN connection	A VPN connection problem could be caused by the same things as a dial-up connection or network connection problem. In addition, you need to verify with the network administrator that the VPN server is up and that the user has permissions to access the network through the VPN server.

Symptoms	Possible Causes
Can't send email	The SMTP server is not configured correctly, the SMTP server is down, or you have a problem communicating with the DNS server.
Page Cannot Be Displayed message in browser	Whenever your browser cannot display a Web page, either the browser can't reach the page or the browser's configuration is set so that it is preventing the Web page from being displayed. On the client end, the cause could be with the Web page address, the connection, or proxy server settings. Check simple things first—verify the Web address is typed correctly in the Address bar. If it is, you'll want to check your connection to your DNS server and that your proxy server settings are correct in your browser.
Not Authorized to View Web Page	The Web page you are attempting to access is private. Contact the Web master of the site or your network administrator to obtain a user name and password for the site.
Browser crashes	If you get an error message when you try to open a Web page, your browser crashes, or your browser won't display a full page, the cause could be that your browser cache or History list contains a bad file, you need updated software to display graphics, an old cookie is causing a problem, or the TCP/IP protocol is corrupt.

How to Troubleshoot Internet/Intranet Connection Problems

Procedure Reference: Troubleshoot Internet/Intranet Connection Problems

An Internet/intranet connectivity problem could range from problems with the actual physical connection to a problem with the application that is trying to use the Internet/intranet connection. To troubleshoot Intranet/intranet connectivity problems:

1. Define the symptoms. Ask questions such as:
   - When did the problem arise?
   - Was there a change in the system at that time? For example, were other applications or operating system patches installed?
   - Does the problem exist within one application that uses Internet access or all applications?

   If it exists in one application, but not others, you can rule out problems with the physical connection and the software for the connection object.

   If it exists in all applications, the problem most likely exists with the physical connection or the software for the connection object.

2. Close all programs, except the one you are trying to connect with. This eliminates the variable of other programs affecting your connectivity and assists in isolating the problem to a particular component or piece of software.

3. Test physical connectivity.
   - Verify modems are properly installed and connected to the computer and turned on.
   - If you have a VPN connection utilizing a network card and cable, verify the network card is functioning and the cable is connected.
   - Try pinging another computer to test the physical link.
   - If you have multilinked devices in your connection object, test the physical connectivity of each device.
4. If the problem is physical, once you narrow the problem to a specific physical component:
   - Review any log files.
   - Check all physical components for hardware failure.
   - Look for patches on the manufacturer's Web site.
   - Re-install the device's driver.
5. If the problem is not physical, based on the symptoms, isolate the problem to either the application you are attempting to access the Internet with (Internet Explorer or Outlook Express), or the connection object (the dial-up or VPN connection software).

   Review any log files of the software components to gather symptoms.
6. Test your connection to your DNS server.
   a. At a command prompt, enter ipconfig /all or use winipcfg to obtain your DNS server address.
   b. At a command prompt, ping the DNS server's IP address. If you receive a response, the problem is not with the DNS server.
7. Verify your proxy server settings.
   a. Choose Start→Settings→Control Panel.
   b. Open Internet Options.
   c. Select the Connections tab.
   d. Verify the Access The Internet Using A Proxy Service check box is checked and the proxy server address and port are entered as given to you by your Internet Service Provider or company's network administrator.
   e. Click OK.
   f. If you are using a dial-up connection, in the Dial-Up Settings list box, select your connection object and click Settings. In the Settings dialog box, select Use A Proxy Server and enter the proxy server address and port as given to you by your Internet Service Provider or company's network administrator.
   g. If you are connected to a LAN that provides Internet access check LAN Settings.
8. If you can't send email:
   a. Verify the email client's SMTP server is set correctly.
   b. Ping the SMTP server to verify it is running.

      c. Check your DNS connection.

9. If your Web browser is crashing, complete the following steps. After each step, stop to see if the problem is resolved. If not, go on to the next step.

    a. Clear your History and delete your temporary files.

        1. Choose Start→Settings→Control Panel.

        2. Open Internet Options.

        3. On the General page, click Delete Files and click OK.

        4. Click Clear History and click Yes.

    b. Enable IE to launch browser windows in a separate process.

        1. In the Internet Options dialog box, select the Advanced page.

        2. Under Browsing, check Launch Browser Windows In A Separate Process.

    c. Install the latest version of DirectX.

    d. Verify TCP/IP is working by pinging your loopback address 127.0.0.1.

    e. If TCP/IP is not working, uninstall and re-install TCP/IP.

    f. Check your cookies:

        1. In Windows Explorer, display the *root_drive*\Windows\Cookies folder.

        2. Select all files in the Cookies folder except index.dat.

        3. Move all the files to a new folder.

        4. Open your browser.

        5. Move each cookie one at a time back into the Windows\Cookie folder. After each move, open your browser to see if it crashes. Continue until you've found the cookie that is causing the crash.

10. On a computer that has Internet connectivity, search Microsoft Knowledge-base articles for known issues and their resolutions based on your defined symptoms.

    a. Go to **www.microsoft.com/technet/default.asp**.

    b. Click Advanced Search.

    c. Uncheck all items except Knowledge Base.

    d. In the Search For text box, enter a word or few words that describe your symptoms.

    e. Click Submit Query.

    f. Review the articles returned for pertinence.

11. Make one suggested change at a time. If the change does not solve the problem, reverse the change before you attempt another suggested change.

CHAPTER 17 FOLLOW-UP
Connecting to Internet and Intranet Resources

In this chapter you learned how to configure software to connect users' networked PCs to the Internet or an intranet. By properly configuring a Web browser, your users will be able to more effectively use information available to them internally via an intranet server and globally via the Internet. When you configure email access for your users, communication becomes quicker and more effective.

Essential Terms

- dial-up connections
- email clients
- email protocols
- Internet connections
- intranet connections
- network connections
- outbound connections
- troubleshooting
- VPN connections
- VPNs
- Web browsers
- Web protocols

Review Questions

1. What is an outbound connection?
2. What kind of client hardware is necessary for X.25 WAN media?
3. In a dial-up connection, the client communicates with the server using the most common Windows dial-up RAS protocol. What is the protocol?
4. What is the Microsoft proprietary protocol used between a client and a VPN server?
5. What is the definition of a dial-up connection?
6. What is SLIP?
7. Over what kinds of lines does SLIP transmit?
8. What remote access protocol does not support encryption: SLIP or PPP?
9. What does MS-CHAP v2 offer that MS-CHAP does not offer?
10. When should PAP/Clear text be used as an authentication method?
11. What is SPAP?
12. What protocol supports smart card authentication?
13. What is a Web browser?
14. Why would you need to install a plug-in for a Web browser?
15. What is the definition of a Web protocol?
16. What is the most common protocol used to make Web requests?
17. What Web protocol do you use to upload files to a server?
18. What is Telnet?
19. What is the security protocol that uses certificates for authentication and encryption to protect Web communication?

20. What must the Web address begin with to indicate sites that require SSL?
21. What is the HyperText Markup Language (HTML)?
22. What is the Post Office Protocol (POP) and POP 2?
23. What communication protocol is used to send email to a server?
24. What is an email client?
25. What is PSTN?
26. What does a client typically need for a satellite connection?
27. What does a client need for wireless communication?
28. What is ISDN?

Review Projects

Project #1 Windows 98: Remote Networking and Mobile Computing

The chapter excerpt from the Windows 98 resource kit titled, "Remote Networking and Mobile Computing," details how to set up and use dial-up networking and virtual private networking. The article also covers Windows 98 mobile computing tools such as the briefcase (forerunner of Windows 2000's offline files) and direct cable connection. The article is located at **http://www.microsoft.com/technet/treeview/default.asp?url=/technet/prodtechnol/win98/reskit/part3/wrkc19.asp**.

The objective of this activity is to familiarize youself with Windows 98's mobile computing options. Not only does the article describe many remote access features, it also provides diagrams and step-by-step setup information.

Using two computers, set up dial-up networking on a Windows 98 computer. Use print screen to document your configuration windows and name the file"Windows 98 dial-up networking." Make a subfolder under your Hardware documentation folder on drive C. Name the folder "Windows 98, configurations." Set up share level security on the Windows 98 dial-up server, and test your connection.

Project #2 Internet Options Overview

Internet Options enables you to set preferences for your Web browser. For a detailed discussion of the options available, got to **C:\Program Files\Microsoft Baseline Security Analyzer\Help\readme.html**. This Web site covers IE 5, but if you're running a later release of Internet Explorer, the preferences will be very similar. If you are running a later version, though, compare the options on your property sheets to those on the Web site. What improvements have been made to the later version?

In this activity, you'll explore the six tabs of the Internet Options control panel: General, Security, Content, Connections, Programs, and Advanced. Click each of the links to read about the settings available to you on each tab.

Experiment with the settings on your own machine. In the left column are links to other Internet-related options and utilities. Explore the options and utilities available. Bookmark this page.

Project #3 Security: Microsoft Baseline Security Analyzer

As companies grow more dependent on remote access and Web-based services, their vulnerability to external attackers increases exponentially. A large company often has the resources to install firewalls and monitoring equipment to strengthen their defenses against outside agents. However, home users and some small companies may not be aware of basic operations they should perform on systems to bolster their defenses. The Microsoft Baseline Security Analyzer is a utility provided by Microsoft that enables you to scan for missing security updates. Often, the first line of defense in security matters is to keep systems up-to-date with the latest patches and service packs. In this activity, download the Baseline Security Analyzer at **http://www.microsoft.com/technet/treeview/default.asp?url=/technet/security/tools/tools/mbsahome.asp**. Also, at the bottom of the page are links to the Analyzer's documentation and to a Web cast that explains it.

Install the analyzer on a computer running either Windows 2000, Windows XP Professional, or Windows Server 2003. After you install the Baseline Analyzer, you'll be prompted to pick a computer to scan as well as options to include in the scan. By default, all options are selected. If, however, you are not running IIS or SQL Server on your computer, deselect those options.

Click Start Scan to allow the Analyzer to scan your system. When the analyzer completes it will display a security report. Review the report. Determine if your system has any vulnerabilities and if it does, take the appropriate steps to correct them.

Reflective Questions

1. In your organization, or the organizations you support, what types of intranet or Internet resources do your users access?

2. In your organization, or the organizations you support, what is the effect on communication using email?

CHAPTER 18
Implementing Virus Protection

Chapter Objectives:

In this chapter, you will implement virus protection.

You will:

- Install virus protection software.
- Configure virus protection software.
- Create a clean boot disk.
- Manually update virus definitions.
- Remove a virus.

Introduction

Unfortunately, one of the skills you'll need as an A+ technician is how to handle viruses. For this reason, it's important that you learn how to both protect computers from viruses as well as to repair a computer in the event it becomes infected, and that's what we'll do in this chapter.

Viruses create costly corruption of data and user downtime. As an A+ technician you will be expected to prevent virus infections and to repair infected computers quickly.

Topic A
Install Virus Protection Software

Your first task in implementing virus protection is to know the types of viruses you can run into and how to install software to protect a computer from these viruses. Because viruses are so prevalent, you need the skills to handle them. In this topic, you'll learn about the types of viruses that can potentially infect a computer. You'll then learn how to install virus protection software so that you can prevent a computer from becoming infected.

Knowing how to install virus protection software enables you to respond to your users' requests to protect their computers from viruses. If you don't know how to install virus protection software, you won't be able to respond to these requests—which can lead to unhappy users or clients (or both!). In addition, knowing how to install virus protection software enables you to protect your users' computers and data from viruses. By installing virus software, you can be proactive by protecting computers against viruses instead of having to be reactive by repairing computers after they've been infected.

Malicious Code Attacks

Definition:

> A *malicious code attack* is a software-based attack in which an attacker inserts malicious code into a user's system to disrupt or disable the operating system or an application. A malicious code attack might:
>
> - Make the operating system or application take action to disrupt or disable other systems on the same network or on a remote network.
>
> - Use an unsuspecting user to spread the code by making the executable file that launches the malicious code appear as if it is from a trusted or safe source.
>
> - Exploit the data stored in the user's own system to spread the code to other remote systems.

Example: Example: Virus

> A *virus* is a piece of malicious code that spreads from one computer to another by attaching itself to other files. The code in the virus might corrupt or erase files (including executable files), the boot sector, or partition information on a user's computer, when an unsuspecting user opens or executes the file to which the virus is attached.

An example of a destructive virus is the Melissa virus, which spread throughout the world attached to Microsoft Word documents that were sent as email attachments.

 In DOS environments, a Terminate and Stay Resident (TSR) virus will attach itself to a computer's memory once it has been loaded by way of an infected executable file.

Example: Example: Worm

A *worm* is a piece of malicious code that spreads from one computer to another on its own, not by attaching itself to another file. The code in a worm might corrupt or erase files on a user's computer, compromise the security of the system, or use up the computer's resources to the point where the system shuts down.

 An example of a destructive worm is the W32.Klez.A@mm worm. The worm spreads through email and network shares.

 A worm that sits dormant on a user's computer until it is triggered by a specific event, such as a specific date, can also be referred to as a logical bomb.

Example: Example: Trojan Horse

A *Trojan Horse* is a piece of malicious code that masquerades as a harmless file. When a user executes it (thinking that it is a harmless application), it can destroy and corrupt data on the user's hard drive, take over your computer and control it remotely, or use your computer to perform attacks that disrupt Web sites.

 An example of a Trojan Horse is the Love Bug which users receive in an email attachment and open, thinking it is a non-threatening letter from someone they know.

Non-Example: Hoaxes

A *hoax* is used to trick users into believing there is a malicious code threat to their systems. Hoaxes typically contain warnings, the purpose of which is to frighten or mislead users and entice them to spread the hoax further by warning others. Hoaxes typically arrive in the form of an email and do little more than clog mail servers and take up network bandwidth when spread by uneducated users.

 An example of a hoax is the Virtual Card for You which is an email warning users to not open any virtual cards sent to them with the subject of Virtual Card for You or it will freeze your computer so that you must reboot the computer and the virus destroys sector zero permanently destroying the hard disk. The email encourages users to pass the word on.

Before passing on any warnings, check out the validity of the warning at one of the following Web sites:

- The United States government Web site at **hoaxbusters.ciac.org**.
- Symantec's Web site at **www.symantec.com/avcenter/hoax.html**.
- McAfee's Web site at **vil.mcafee.com/hoax.asp**.

Virus Protection Software

Definition:

Virus protection software is a software package that is designed to detect and remove viruses. Virus protection software consists of two components: the software engine and the virus definition files. Virus definition files are updated continuously to include protection against newly discovered threats and must be downloaded to the software engine to be effective in protecting against the latest malicious code threats. In some instances, the virus protection software may be able to repair damage done by a malicious piece of code.

Example:

Symantec Norton AntiVirus and McAfee VirusScan are two popular virus protection software packages. Each program has an engine which runs on your computer and definition files that are downloaded from the manufacturers' Web sites.

System Requirements

To install Symantec Norton AntiVirus 2003 or McAfee VirusScan Professional 7.0, your system must meet the minimum requirements for virus protection application. Table 18-1 lists the system requirements for Symantec Norton AntiVirus 2003. Table 18-2 lists the system requirements for McAfee VirusScan Professional 7.0.

Table 18-1: *System Requirements for Symantec Norton AntiVirus 2003*

Operating System	Requirements
Windows XP Home Edition/ Professional	<ul><li>Intel Pentium (or compatible) 300 MHz or higher processor.</li><li>128 MB of RAM.</li><li>70 MB of hard disk space.</li><li>Internet Explorer 5.0 or later (5.5 recommended).</li><li>CD-ROM or DVD-ROM drive.</li><li>A user account with administrative rights.</li></ul>
Windows 2000 Professional	<ul><li>Intel Pentium (or compatible) 133 MHz or higher processor.</li><li>64 MB of RAM.</li><li>70 MB of hard disk space.</li><li>Internet Explorer 5.0 or later (5.5 recommended).</li><li>CD-ROM or DVD-ROM drive.</li><li>A user account with administrative rights.</li></ul>

Operating System	Requirements
Windows 98	• Intel Pentium (or compatible) 133 MHz or higher processor. • 32 MB of RAM. • 70 MB of hard disk space. • Internet Explorer 5.0 or later (5.5 recommended). • CD-ROM or DVD-ROM drive.

Table 18-2: *System Requirements for McAfee VirusScan Professional Version 7.0*

Operating System	Requirements
Windows 98, Windows 2000 Professional, Windows XP Home Edition/Professional	• Intel Pentium (or compatible) 100 MHz or higher processor. • 32 MB of RAM. • 65 MB of hard disk space. • Internet Explorer 4.01 or later, with Service Pack 2 or higher (5.1 or later recommended). • CD-ROM drive. • On Windows 2000 Professional, Windows XP Home Edition/Professional, a user account with administrative rights.

How to Install Virus Protection Software

Procedure Reference: Install Symantec Norton AntiVirus 2003

To install Symantec Norton AntiVirus 2000 in Windows XP, Windows 2000, Windows NT, or Windows 98:

 If you have a 2000 to 2002 version of Norton AntiVirus, the 2003 version will automatically remove the older version. If you have a version prior to version 2000, you must uninstall it before you install version 2003.

1. On Windows 2000, Windows NT, or Windows XP systems, log on to the system using a user account with administrative rights.

2. Start the installation program.
   - Insert the Norton AntiVirus CD into the CD-ROM drive and, in the Norton AntiVirus 2003 window, click Install Norton AntiVirus 2003.

       If you are using the Norton AntiVirus CD and the Norton AntiVirus 2003 window does not open when you insert the CD into the CD-ROM drive, browse the CD and double-click Cdplay.exe.

   - Access the Norton AntiVirus installation files and double-click Setup.exe.

3. If Setup updates any system files, you are prompted to restart your computer. Click OK.

 On Windows 98, Norton AntiVirus scans your computer's memory for viruses before installing. If a virus is found, you will be prompted to use your Emergency Repair Disk to remove the virus before continuing with the installation.

4. In the Norton AntiVirus 2003 Setup wizard, click Next.

5. Click I Accept The License Agreement.

6. Click Next.

7. If you are upgrading from Norton AntiVirus version 2000 to 2002, click Yes to keep your option settings or click No to reset the option settings to the program defaults. Click Next.

8. If desired, use the Browse button to specify a different destination folder for the program.

9. Click Next.

10. Click Next to begin the installation.

11. Read the text of the Readme Information and click Next.

12. Click Finish.

13. If prompted to restart the computer, click Yes.

 To uninstall Norton AntiVirus, use the Add/Remove Programs applet in Control Panel.

14. Log back on to Windows 98.

15. Register your copy of Norton AntiVirus 2003 by filling in the prompts of the Norton AntiVirus Information Wizard.

16. Your displayed subscription service expiration date is one year from your installation date. Click Next.

17. Enable or disable the desired post-installation tasks you wish to complete by checking and unchecking the task boxes.

18. Click Next.

19. Click Finish.

20. If you enabled LiveUpdates, follow the prompts in the wizard to connect to the LiveUpdate site and install any new updates. Click Finish.

21. If you are running Windows 98 and you enabled Rescue Disks, select a destination drive and click Create. If you are using floppy disks, replace the disks when prompted.

22. Click OK and Close to close the Rescue Disk program.

23. If you enabled VirusScan, the scan starts.

24. In the Scan: Summary dialog box, click Details to see specific information on the scan, or Finished to close the scan window.

25. The Norton AntiVirus System Status dialog box opens. Identify any items that need your immediate attention (they are marked in red).

26. To process any items that need your attention, click the link and follow the prompts.

27. When finished, close the Norton AntiVirus window.

Procedure Reference: Install McAfee Security VirusScan Professional 7.0

To install McAfee Security Virus Scan 7.0 in Windows XP, Windows 2000, Windows NT, or Windows 98:

1. On Windows 2000, Windows NT, or Windows XP systems, log on to the system using a user account with administrative rights.

2. Start the installation program by either:
   - Inserting the McAfee VirusScan CD into the CD-ROM drive and, in the Installation Wizard window, clicking Install VirusScan Professional.

     If you are using the McAfee VirusScan CD and the Installation Wizard window does not open when you insert the CD into the CD-ROM drive, browse the CD and double-click setup.exe.

   - Accessing the McAfee VirusScan installation files and double-clicking Setup.exe.

3. In the McAfee Consumer Products Installation dialog box, click Install VirusScan Professional.

4. In the McAfee VirusScan Professional Edition dialog box, click Next.

5. In the McAfee End User License Agreement dialog box, select your country from the drop-down list box. Read the license agreement.

6. Click Accept.

7. Select the Setup Type: Typical Installation or Custom Installation. Choose Custom Installation if you want to specify the installation features you want to install or change the default installation path. (See Step 9.)

8. Click Next.

9. If you chose Custom Installation:
   a. Click Change to modify the destination directory for the McAfee VirusScan files.
   b. Enable or disable Safe & Sound.
   c. Click Next.
   d. Click Change to modify the destination directory for the McAfee Firewall files.
   e. Enable or disable installing McAfee Firewall.
   f. Click Next.

g. Enable or Disable Create Emergency Disk, Run Default Scan After Installation, and Scan Boot Record.

h. Click Next.

10. Click Install.

11. Enable or disable checking for an available McAfee VirusScan Professional update after the installation is complete.

12. Click Next.

13. Enable or Disable Starting McAfee VirusScan Professional Edition immediately.

14. Click Next.

15. Register the software.

    a. On the Product Registration page, click Next.

    b. Complete the required user information (email address, name, address, and so on). Click Next.

    c. Choose any additional options you want to specify.

    - Check I Want To Receive Product Announcements if you want to receive emails from McAfee about new enhancements to the VirusScan software.

    - Check I Want To Receive Special Offers if you want to receive emails from McAfee about any new products they release.

    - Use the drop-down list to specify where you bought McAfee VirusScan.

    d. Click Finish. The McAfee Instant Updater sends your registration information via the Internet. It also checks for any new updates.

    e. If new updates were found, click Update.

    f. If necessary, click Yes to confirm installing the updates.

    g. Click Finish.

    h. Click Yes to restart your computer.

TOPIC B
Configure Virus Protection Software

You have a lot of choices to make after you install virus protection software. For example, do you want the software to scan the computer periodically for viruses? Do you want it to scan all incoming email messages? In this topic, you'll learn the options you can configure in virus protection software that enable you to increase a computer's defenses against viruses.

In some situations, the default configuration of virus protection software won't meet your users' or clients' needs. For example, you might have a client whose work is so critical that he wants his virus protection software to scan for viruses on a daily basis but the default setting is to scan only weekly. As an A+ technician, you must be prepared to configure your users' virus protection software so that it's tailored to their needs.

Common Virus Protection Software Configuration Properties

Many virus protection software packages allow you to set configuration parameters to customize the performance of the product to meet your needs. This customization includes specifying:

- Automatic and manual scans.
- Specific file types to include or exclude in a scan.
- Email scans.
- Automatically and manually obtaining virus definition updates.

Norton AntiVirus configuration options are listed in Table 18-3, Table 18-4, and Table 18-5. The McAfee VirusScan configuration options are listed in Table 18-6, Table 18-7, and Table 18-8.

Table 18-3: *Norton AntiVirus System Options*

Option	Description
Auto-Protect	Checks your computer's programs for viruses as you run them and monitors your computer for activity that is typical of a virus. You can: • Enable or disable auto-protect. • Enable or disable automatic start-up of auto-protect when Windows starts. • Enable or disable an icon in the system tray for auto-protect. • Select how Norton AntiVirus deals with found viruses. You can have Norton AntiVirus automatically repair the infected file, try to repair then quarantine if unsuccessful, deny access to the infected file, or prompt you for a decision each time a virus is found. • Select which types of files to scan for viruses. You choose between a comprehensive file scan or customize the types scanned by file extension or specific file name.
Script Blocking	Monitors Visual Basic and JavaScript scripts for virus-like activities to identify viruses without the need for specific virus definitions. You can: • Enable or disable ScriptBlocking. • Select how Norton AntiVirus deals with found malicious scripts. You can have Norton AntiVirus prompt you for a decision each time a malicious script is found or stop all suspicious activities without prompting you.

Option	Description
Manual Scan	Specifies what items to scan in addition to files when you request a manual scan—memory, boot records, and master boot records. You can: • Select how Norton AntiVirus deals with found viruses. You can have Norton AntiVirus automatically repair the infected file, try to repair then quarantine if unsuccessful, deny access to the infected file, or prompt you for a decision each time a virus is found. • Select which types of files to scan for viruses. You choose between a comprehensive file scan or customize the types scanned by file extension or specific file name. You can also enable or disable the scanning of compressed files.
Bloodhound	Uses scanning technology to identify new and unknown viruses based on the file's structure, its behavior, programming logic, computer instructions, and any data included in the file. You can: • Enable or disable the bloodhound feature. • Select the level of protection—highest, default, or lowest.
Exclusions	Specifies the files or folders to be excluded from scans. You can exclude the individual items selected from virus detection, low level format of the hard disk, write to hard disk boot records, or write to floppy disk boot records.

Table 18-4: *Norton AntiVirus 2003 Internet Options*

Option	Description
Email	Checks your email for viruses and worms. You can: • Enable or disable scanning of incoming email. • Enable or disable scanning of outgoing email. • Select how Norton AntiVirus deals with found viruses or worms. You can have Norton AntiVirus automatically repair the infected file, prompt you for a decision each time a virus is found, try to repair then quarantine if unsuccessful, try to repair then silently quarantine if unsuccessful, or try to repair then quietly delete if unsuccessful. • Enable or disable worm blocking. • Enable or disable alert when scanning email attachments.
Advanced Email	Specifies the default behavior when scanning email. You can: • Enable or disable protection against timeouts. • Enable or disable an icon in the system tray for auto-protect. • Enable or disable progress indicator when sending email.

Option	Description
Instant Messenger	Specifies which instant messenger programs will be protected by Norton AntiVirus 2003. You can: • Select AOL Instant Messenger, MSN Instant Messenger, and Yahoo Messenger to protect. • Select how Norton AntiVirus deals with found viruses. You can have Norton AntiVirus automatically repair the infected file, prompt you for a decision each time a virus is found, or try to repair then quarantine if unsuccessful. • Enable notification of received infected files for MSN.
LiveUpdate	Specify how updates will be applied to the system. You can: • Enable or disable automatic LiveUpdate. • Enable or disable virus protection updates by applying updates without interrupting the user or notification when updates are available. • Enable or disable notification of available program updates.

Table 18-5: *Norton AntiVirus 2003 Other Options*

Option	Description
Inoculation	Available on Windows 98 systems only, monitors changes to system files. You can: • Enable or disable inoculate boot record. • Select how Norton AntiVirus deals with a change in an inoculated boot record. You can have Norton AntiVirus prompt you for a decision each time a virus is found, or just notify you about the change.
Miscellaneous	Specify miscellaneous settings for Norton AntiVirus protection. You can: • Enable or disable creating a backup file in quarantine before attempting to repair a file. • Enable or disable the Office plug-in to scan and protect Microsoft Office documents. • Enable or disable an alert when virus protection is out-of-date. • Enable or disable a system file scan at Windows startup. • Enable or disable password protection to make changes to the configuration of Norton AntiVirus 2003.

Table 18-6: *McAfee VirusScan System Scan Options*

Option	Description
Detection	Used to specify the types of events that cause scanning to occur and the types of files you want to scan. The Advanced button can be used to enable heuristics scanning, which uses scanning technology to identify new and unknown viruses based on the file's structure, its behavior, programming logic, computer instructions, and any data included in the file.
Action	Used to specify how the VShield program will handle viruses that it detects in a file on either a local or network drive.
Report	Used to specify if VirusScan activity will be logged and what types of information will be included in the log. You can use the Browse button to select a new location for the log file.
Exclusion	Used to specify what drives, folders, subfolders, and individual files to exclude from the virus scans.

Table 18-7: *McAfee VirusScan Email Scan Options*

Option	Description
Detection	Enables or disables scanning your email attachments. Specifies the types of attachments to scan. The Advanced button can be used to enable heuristics scanning.
Action	Used to specify how the VShield program will handle viruses that it detects in an email attachment.
Alert	Used to specify warnings that happen if a virus is found in an email.
Report	Used to specify if VirusScan activity will be logged and what types of information will be included in the log. You can use the Browse button to select a new location for the log file.

Table 18-8: *McAfee VirusScan HAWK Options*

Option	Description
Email	Enables or disables HAWK for your email and specifies the settings HAWK will use.
Script Stopper	Enables or disables the Script Stopper feature of HAWK and allows you to add a list of trusted scripts to circumvent the Script Stopper feature.

How to Configure Virus Protection Software

Procedure Reference: Configure Norton AntiVirus 2003

To make changes to the default configuration settings of Norton AntiVirus 2003 in Windows XP, Windows 2000, or Windows 98:

1. From the Start menu, choose Programs→Norton AntiVirus→Norton AntiVirus 2003.
2. Click Options.
3. Make any desired changes to the System options. The System options are listed in Table 18-3.
4. Make any desired changes to the Internet options. The Internet options are listed in Table 18-4.
5. Make any desired changes to the Other options. The Other options are listed in Table 18-5.
6. Click OK.

Procedure Reference: Configure McAfee VirusScan Version 7.0

To make changes to the default configuration settings of McAfee VirusScan version 7.0 in Windows XP, Windows 2000, or Windows 98:

1. From the Start menu, choose Programs→McAfee→VirusScan Professional Edition.
2. Under Tasks, click Configure Automatic Protection Settings.
3. Enable or disable the following protection settings:
   - System Scanning
   - Microsoft Outlook E-Mail Scanning
   - HAWK for E-Mail
   - HAWK for Script Stopper

   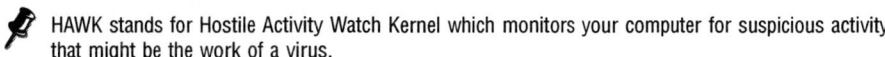
   HAWK stands for Hostile Activity Watch Kernel which monitors your computer for suspicious activity that might be the work of a virus.

4. Click Advanced.
5. Click System Scan.
6. Make any desired changes to the System Scan settings. The System Scan options are shown in Table 18-6. You can set various detection, action, reporting, and exclusion settings for system scans.
7. Click E-Mail Scan.
8. Make any desired changes to the E-mail Scan settings. The E-mail Scan options are shown in Table 18-7.

9. Click HAWK.

10. Make any desired changes to the HAWK settings. The HAWK options are shown in Table 18-8.

11. Click OK.

12. Close the VirusScan Professional Edition dialog box.

TOPIC C
Create a Clean Boot Disk

As you saw in Topic 18A, one of the types of malicious code you can encounter is a virus that affects your boot sector. Depending on the virus protection software you install, you will need a clean (non-infected) boot disk to be able to remove such a virus. In this topic, you'll learn the steps you must take to create a clean boot disk.

Some boot sector viruses can be removed only by first booting the computer with a clean boot disk. You can create this disk only on a computer that isn't already infected with a virus. For this reason, it's essential that you create a clean boot disk before the computer becomes infected. Without a clean boot disk, you might not be able to remove a boot sector virus from a computer, and the user's data and program files can be destroyed.

Boot Disk

Definition:

A boot disk is a diskette that you can use to boot a computer when the operating system installed on the hard disk will not boot. A boot disk contains a minimal set of system files required to boot the computer to a base operating system such as MS-DOS or a Windows product. A boot disk allows you access to the base operating system to make repairs.

A boot disk may be created using your operating system or your virus protection software. A boot disk must be created before there is a problem on the computer. A boot disk created by your virus protection software may contain additional files used to scan your computer for malicious code.

Example: AntiVirus Software Boot Disks

Virus Protection Boot Disks	Contains
Norton Rescue Disk Set	The Norton AntiVirus Rescue Disk set contains backup copies of partition information, CMOS information, master boot record information, and system startup files needed to boot your computer into Windows 98. In addition, it contains a virus scanner and virus definition files. It might contain Norton Utilities if it is installed on your computer.

Virus Protection Boot Disks	Contains
Norton Emergency Disk Set	In addition to containing the system file needed to boot your particular operating system (Windows XP, Windows 2000, Windows 98, or Windows NT), the Norton AntiVirus Emergency Disk set contains a scanning utility that scans your computer and removes viruses.
McAfee Emergency Disk Set	In addition to containing the system files needed to boot your particular operating system, the McAfee Emergency Disk set includes BOOTSCAN.EXE, a specialized, small-footprint command-line scanner that can scan your hard disk boot sectors and master boot record allowing you to boot into a virus-free environment to make repairs.

How to Create a Clean Boot Disk

Procedure Reference: Create a Norton AntiVirus Rescue Disk Set in Windows 98

If you are running Windows 98, you can create a rescue disk set. To create a rescue disk set after you have initially installed the product and run the Norton AntiVirus Information wizard:

1. Open Norton AntiVirus.
2. In the Norton AntiVirus windows, click the Rescue icon at the top of the window.
3. Select drive A.
4. Click Create.
5. If necessary, click Yes to disable virus scanning.
6. Label the disks as prompted and click OK.
7. Insert the disks as prompted.
8. Close Norton AntiVirus.
9. Test your rescue disk set:
    a. Close all open programs.
    b. Insert the rescue disk labeled Basic Rescue Boot Floppy Disk into the A drive.
    c. Shut down and power off your computer.
    d. Turn on your computer.
    e. The computer should restart using the rescue boot floppy and display the Rescue Disk screen. Press Esc to exit to MS-DOS.
    f. Remove your Basic Rescue Boot Floppy Disk from the A drive.
    g. Restart your computer.

Procedure Reference: Updating a Norton AntiVirus 2003 Rescue Disk Set in Windows 98

You can update your existing Rescue Disk set instead of creating a new set:

1. Open Norton AntiVirus.
2. In the Norton AntiVirus window, click the Rescue icon at the top of the window.
3. Select drive A.
4. Click Update.
5. Insert the rescue disk labeled Basic Rescue Boot Floppy Disk into the A drive.
6. Click OK.
7. Insert the disks as prompted.
8. Close Norton AntiVirus.

Procedure Reference: Creating a Norton AntiVirus Emergency Disk Set

To create a Norton AntiVirus Emergency Disk set in Windows XP, Windows 2000, Windows NT, or Windows 98:

1. Insert the Norton AntiVirus CD in the CD-ROM drive.
2. Click Browse CD.
3. Double-click the Support folder.
4. Double-click the Edisk folder.
5. Double-click the Ned.exe file.
6. In the Welcome window, click OK.
7. Label the disk as instructed and insert it in drive A.
8. Click Yes.
9. Repeat labeling, inserting the disk in drive A and clicking OK for all prompted disks.
10. Remove the final disk from the A drive.
11. Click OK.
12. Close all open windows.
13. Remove the Norton AntiVirus CD-ROM from the CD-ROM drive.
14. Test the emergency disk set:
    a. Insert the first disk in the set into the A drive.
    b. Shut down and power off Windows.
    c. Turn on the computer.
    d. In the Norton AntiVirus window, press Enter to scan the C drive.

    e.   When prompted, insert the second disk in the set and press Enter.

    f.   When prompted, insert the third disk and press Enter.

    g.   If you don't want to wait for the scan to complete, turn off the computer, remove the emergency disk, and turn the computer back on.

    h.   When the scan is complete, reinsert the first emergency disk and press any key to continue.

    i.   Turn off the computer, remove the emergency disk, and turn the computer back on.

Procedure Reference: Creating a McAfee VirusScan version 7.0 Emergency Disk

To create a McAfee VirusScan emergency disk in Windows XP, Windows 2000, Windows NT, or Windows 98:

1. Open McAfee VirusScan Professional.

2. Under Tasks, click Other Tasks.

3. Click McAfee Emergency Disk.

4. In the Emergency Disk Wizard, click Next.

5. If your computer contains one or more FAT32 or NTFS partitions, McAfee VirusScan automatically formats the disk to use the NAI-OS file system. Click Next.

    If your computer contains only a FAT partition, select a format for your disk and click Next.
    - Format using the installed operating system.
    - Create an NAI-OS emergency disk.

6. Insert a blank high-density disk in drive A.

7. Click Next.

8. If you chose to format your disk, complete the following steps:

    a. Click OK to verify you understand you must check Copy System Files in the Format Dialog box.

    b. If you chose to format your disk, check Copy System Files in the Format dialog box and click Start.

    c. Click Close twice.

9. Click Finish.

10. Remove the disk, label it, and write-protect it.

11. Close the VirusScan Professional window.

12. Test the emergency disk.

    a. Close all open programs.

    b. Insert the emergency disk into the A drive.

c. Shut down and power off the computer.

d. Turn on the computer.

e. Enter Y to confirm that you performed a cold boot of the computer.

f. Press any key to continue.

g. After a few minutes, virus scanning begins, which means that the emergency disk works properly. When the scanning completes, remove the emergency disk and restart the computer.

If you don't want to wait for the virus scanning to complete, turn off the computer, remove the emergency disk, and then restart the computer.

TOPIC D
Manually Update Virus Definitions

A computer's virus protection software is only as good as its most recent list of viruses. As an A+ technician, if you're called out to work on a computer that you suspect might be infected with a virus, one of the first steps you should take is to make sure that the computer's virus definitions are current. In this topic, you'll learn how to manually update the virus definitions within a computer's virus protection software.

Because hackers are releasing new viruses every day, it's possible for the virus definitions in your users' virus protection software to become out of date. If a computer's virus protection software doesn't have a particular virus' definition, it's possible for that computer to become infected with the new virus. You can avoid leaving your users' computers vulnerable to new viruses by manually updating their virus definitions whenever you hear about new viruses. If you don't act proactively by manually updating a computer's virus definitions, your users' computers won't be protected from new viruses, which leaves them vulnerable to losing their data and applications. Failing to remove a virus may mean the loss of valuable data and productivity by the users, which might mean your job.

How to Manually Update Virus Definitions

Procedure Reference: Manually Update Virus Definitions in Norton AntiVirus 2003

To manually update Norton AntiVirus definition files in Windows XP, Windows 2000, Windows NT, and Windows 98:

1. Open Norton AntiVirus 2003.

2. In the Norton AntiVirus window, click the LiveUpdate icon at the top of the window.

3. Click Next to scan for updates.

4. Click Next to download and install updates.

5. Click Finish.

6. Click OK to reboot the computer.

Procedure Reference: Manually Update Virus Definitions in McAfee AntiVirus Professional

To manually update McAfee AntiVirus definition files in Windows XP, Windows 2000, Windows NT, and Windows 98:

1. Open McAfee VirusScan Professional Edition.
2. Under Tasks, click Check For A VirusScan Update.
3. If updates are found, check the items you want to download and click Update.
4. If prompted, click OK to verify you understand a reboot of your system is necessary.
5. Click Finish.
6. If prompted, click Yes to restart your computer.

   If you installed updates, an automatic scan begins.
7. Close the McAfee Instant Updater dialog box.

TOPIC E
Remove a Virus

So far in this chapter, you've seen the techniques you can use to help avoid a virus infection on a computer. But despite your best efforts to avoid viruses on the computers you support, you're bound to encounter a virus sooner or later. As an A+ technician, it's essential that you know how to remove a virus. For this reason, this topic discusses the techniques you can use to remove a virus from an infected computer.

You can expect to hear immediately when any of your users' computers become infected with a virus. As an A+ technician, your job will often depend on your ability to either talk a user through removing the virus or removing it yourself. It's important for you to master the skills necessary to remove a virus so that you are seen as both able to quickly respond to your users' requests and successful in removing the virus.

Virus Removal Options

If your virus protection software package discovers a piece of malicious code, you will typically have three choices in dealing with the code—attempt to repair the infected file, quarantine the infected file, or delete the infected file. When you quarantine an infected file, the software package will isolate the file so that it cannot be opened or executed. Each software package will have its own way of stating these options, but in general you will be allowed to choose from these three functions.

With a known piece of malicious code, you will want to try to repair or delete the infected file. With a piece of malicious code that you suspect is not yet known, you will want to quarantine it and then submit it to your virus protection software manufacturer for analysis. Both Symantec and McAfee have procedures posted on their security Web sites for submitting malicious code.

How to Remove a Virus

Procedure Reference: Remove a Virus Using Norton AntiVirus 2003

If the virus is found during a scan, the affected files may be automatically repaired or deleted. In some cases, you will need to take action to remove a virus using Norton AntiVirus 2003:

1. You may be prompted to fix the file using the Repair wizard.
   a. Uncheck any files you don't want Norton AntiVirus to fix.
   b. Click Fix.

   Any files that Norton AntiVirus can't fix or delete are added to the Quarantine window.

   c. In the Quarantine window, uncheck any files you don't want to quarantine.
   d. Click Quarantine.

   Any files that Norton AntiVirus can't quarantine are added to the Delete pane.

   e. Uncheck any files you do not want to delete.

   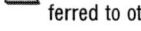 Any infected files that you do not delete remain on your computer and can cause damage or be transferred to other computers.

   f. Click Delete.
   g. Review the details of the summary pane and click Finished.

2. You may be issued an alert that a virus was found and repaired by the Auto-Protect feature.
   - In Windows 98, click Finish to close the alert.
   - In Windows 2000 or Windows XP, click OK to close the alert.

   If you have set your options so that the Auto-Protect feature prompts you to decide what to do with the file, you need to select one of the following:
   - Repair the infected file.
   - Quarantine the infected file.
   - Delete the infected file.
   - Do not open the file, but leave the problem alone.
   - Ignore the problem and do not scan this file in the future.
   - Ignore the problem and continue with the infected file.

   The recommended choice will be selected in the alert dialog box.

3. You may be issued an alert that a virus was found in a script. You must select one of the presented options to remove the threat. The recommended option is to stop running the script.

4. You may be issued an alert that a worm was found in an outgoing email attachment. You must select one of the presented options to remove the worm. The recommended action is to quarantine the file.

5. On Windows 98 systems, you may be alerted to a change in your system files. You must select one of the following options to respond to the inoculation alert:
   - Update the saved copy of your master boot record—select this option if you know there has been a legitimate change to the system files such as applying an operating system patch or repartitioning the hard disk.
   - Restore your master boot record—select this option if you are sure there has not been a legitimate change to the system files.

6. You may be prompted that Norton AntiVirus can't repair a file.
   - If an .exe, .doc, .dot., or .xls file is infected, use the Repair Wizard to fix the problem.
   - If the master boot record, boot record, or a system file is infected, replace the file using the Rescue Disks or your operating system installation disk.

7. If the computer won't boot normally, use the Rescue Disk set to repair or replace infected files.
   a. Insert the basic rescue boot floppy disk in drive A and restart your computer.
   b. Use the arrow keys to select one of the following programs:
      - Norton AntiVirus to scan your computer for viruses and repair any infected files.
      - Rescue Recovery to check and restore boot and partition information.
   c. Press Enter to run the selected program.
   d. Respond to the prompts for inserting and removing disks from the rescue disk set.
   e. When the rescue recovery is complete, remove the rescue disk from the A drive.
   f. Restart your computer.

8. After any alert, you should manually run LiveUpdate to obtain the latest definition files.

9. After you have the most up-to-date virus definition files installed, you should scan your system.

Procedure Reference: Remove a Virus Using McAfee VirusScan Professional

If the virus is found during a scan, the affected files may be automatically repaired or deleted. In some cases, you will need to take action to remove a virus using McAfee VirusScan Professional:

1. You may be prompted to fix the file by selecting one of the following options:
   - *Continue:* This option directs VirusScan to continue with the present scan and not take any other action on the infected file. If you have reporting enabled, the incident will be recorded in the log file.

- *Stop:* This option directs VirusScan to stop the present scan immediately. To continue the scan, you need to click Scan For Viruses Now.
- *Clean Infection or Clean File:* One of these options will be presented depending on the type of problem found. These options direct VirusScan to attempt to remove the virus code from the infected file. If you have reporting enabled, the incident and its resolution will be recorded in the log file. Review the log file to verify the virus.
- *Delete:* This option directs VirusScan to first attempt to remove the virus code from the file and then to delete the infected file if it cannot repair the file.
- *Quarantine:* This option directs VirusScan to move the infected file to the default quarantine folder and continue with the scan.
- *Info:* This option directs VirusScan to run Internet Explorer and go to the AVERT Web site at **www.webimmune.net** where you can research the suspected file or virus.

2. If an infected file is quarantined:
   a. Open McAfee VirusScan Professional.
   b. Click the down arrow for Advanced Tasks.
   c. Click Manage Quarantined Files.

   You will need to manage the file by selecting one of the following options:
   - *Add:* This option allows you to browse for and quarantine a file that VirusScan did not automatically quarantine.
   - *Clean:* This option directs VirusScan to attempt to remove the virus code from the infected file. If the virus cannot be removed, VirusScan notifies you.
   - *Restore:* This option directs VirusScan to restore a file to its original location. It does not clean the file—you should click Clean and verify the virus is removed before restoring a file.
   - *Delete:* This option directs VirusScan to delete the infected file.

     ⚠ Make sure you have a backup copy of the file before you delete.

   - *Submit quarantined files to AVERT via WebImmune:* If you suspect the file is infected with a new, unknown virus, this option directs VirusScan to submit the file to McAfee's investigative labs via the **www.webimmune.net** site.

3. If the computer won't boot normally, use the Emergency Disk to perform an emergency scan that examines your hard disk boot sectors, your Master Boot Record, your system directories, program files, and other common sources of infection on your hard disk.
   a. Insert the Emergency Disk in drive A and restart your computer.
   b. Press Enter to select Next.
   c. Press N to use the DAT files from the Emergency Disk or press L to select another location.

d. Press F to begin the scan.

e. When the rescue recovery is complete, remove the rescue disk from the A drive.

f. Restart your computer.

a. Insert the NAI-OS Emergency Disk in drive A and turn off the power to your computer.

b. Restart your computer.

c. Press Y to indicate that you cycled the power off.

d. When the rescue recovery is complete, remove the rescue disk from the A drive.

e. Restart your computer.

> The Emergency Disk does not scan for macro viruses, script viruses, or Trojan Horse programs.

4. After any alert, you should manually run McAfee's Instant Updater to obtain the latest definition files.

5. After you have the most up-to-date virus definition files installed, you should scan your system.

CHAPTER 18 FOLLOW-UP
Implementing Virus Protection

In this chapter, you learned how to implement virus protection. With properly installed and configured virus protection software, you can both prevent viruses from causing problems on your computer systems and repair computers should they become infected.

Essential Terms

- boot disks
- hoaxes
- malicious code attacks
- Trojan Horses
- virus definitions
- virus protection
- virus removal
- viruses
- worms

Review Questions

1. What is a malicious code attack?
2. What is malicious code that spreads from one computer to another by attaching itself to files?
3. In DOS environments, what kind of virus will attach itself to a computer's memory once it has been loaded by an infected executable file?
4. What kind of virus consists of malicious code that spreads from one computer to another on its own?

5. What kind of worm sits dormant on a computer until it is triggered by a specific event, such as a date?
6. What is a Trojan Horse?
7. What is the purpose of a hoax?
8. How do most hoaxes arrive to users?
9. What should you use to detect and remove viruses?
10. What are the two components of virus software?
11. What must you have to remove a boot sector virus?
12. What is contained in a boot disk?
13. To what does a boot disk give you access?
14. What is the advantage of creating a boot disk using virus protection software?
15. If you suspect a computer has been infected with a virus, what should be your first step?
16. If your virus protection software discovers malicious code, what three choices do you have when dealing with the code?
17. What happens when you quarantine an infected file?
18. What is an example of a Trojan Horse?
19. What do hoaxes contain typically?
20. What is the purpose of a hoax?
21. On Windows 98, what does Norton AntiVirus do to protect your system before installing?
22. How can you keep virus definitions up-to-date when using Norton AntiVirus?
23. What should you do immediately after installing an anti-virus program?
24. What is the function of the auto-protect feature included on many anti-virus packages?
25. What is the function of Script blocking?
26. Norton AntiVirus includes an option called bloodhound. What does bloodhound do to identify viruses?

Review Projects

Project #1 Understanding Computer Viruses

Viruses are a common and omnipresent threat to users who access Web sites, download executables, send and receive email, or even share data on a floppy disk. There are many viruses and more are written every day. Although users should run anti-virus programs and update the definitions frequently, you should be aware of many of the tell-tale signs that a virus may be present on a user's machine. The How Stuff Works Web site discusses viruses in detail. The tutorial is located at **http://www.howstuffworks.com/virus.htm**. In this activity, read through each of the tutorial's topic ideas (the hyperlinks listed). Was there virus information that was new to you? If so, what was it?

Understanding that viruses exist and that they can cause irreparble damage to your user's files isn't always enough. There are some simple steps you can perform to help prevent virus infections on systems. Tend Micro has published a "Safe Computing Guide" on their Web site (**http://www.trendmicro.com/en/security/general/guide/overview.htm**). Read through the guide and implement the steps outlined by Trend Micro. Cut and paste the Safe Computing Guide into a word processor application and save the file to a subfolder named Virus Information on your hard drive.

Project #2 Symantec's Security Response

Symantec's Security Response Web site is dedicated to helping you stay abreast of the latest virus-related threats. The site maintains a "threat list" which categorizes viruses by risk. The URL for the Web site is **http://securityresponse.symantec.com/avcenter/vinfodb.html**. In this activity, click any of the threats listed. Review the information that displays. Since this information is geared to helping you assess specific threats, bookmark this site for future reference. Notice that information about the virus threat is divided into four broad categories:

- Threat assessment: This includes the type of threat, the language used to write it, and the types of files it infects.
- Technical details: This includes the actions that take place when the virus threat is activated.
- Recommendations: This includes best practices so your actions don't inadvertently trigger another breakout of the virus.
- Removal instructions: This includes specific instructions on how to remove a virus from a computer.

Project #3 Tracking Hoaxes

As discussed in your readings, rumors about viruses circulate around the Internet. It's likely you've received various warnings about threats that have turned out to be nothing more than pranks. Unfortunately, a well-played prank may arrive in a user's email with instructions that the user should execute immediately. A frightened and well-meaning user may follow instructions to do something destructive such as format a partition or unhide and delete system files. Hoaxes can only work if the person who receives it acts on the information provided. To combat this, you can check the Snopes database to see if something you or a user received is valid or not. The Snopes Web site is located at **http://snopes.com/**. Click Computer, then click the link for viruses. Scan through the database to view threats that have been identified as actual viruses and those that have been identified as pranks. Do you recognize any of those listed as pranks? Bookmark this site for future reference.

Reflective Questions

1. In your organization, or the organizations you support, what steps have you taken to protect against viruses?

2. In your organization, or the organizations you support, what additional steps do you need to take to protect against viruses?

CHAPTER 19
Preparing for Disaster Recovery

Chapter Objectives:

In this chapter, you will prepare for disaster recovery.

You will:

- Create a boot disk.
- Create an emergency repair disk.
- Install the Recovery Console.
- Back up data.
- Back up system state data.
- Back up the Registry.
- Prepare for an Automated System Recovery.

Introduction

Throughout this course, you've built, step-by-step, completely configured computers. You've configured users' applications, implemented network connectivity, secured the computers, shared folders and printers, managed the computers' hard disks, configured Internet and intranet connectivity, and even installed and configured virus protection software. At this point, your computers are ready for users to begin working productively on them. But what would happen if your computer crashed? Do you have what you need to recover from the problem? To make sure you're prepared for just such an emergency, in this chapter you'll learn how to prepare for disaster recovery so that you can repair a computer as quickly as possible.

It is inevitable that users' computers will crash. It is your responsibility as an A+ technician to prepare for disaster recovery and minimize the down time and cost to your company.

TOPIC A
Create a Boot Disk

The first task you should perform in preparing for disaster recovery is to create a boot disk for each user's computer. Creating a boot disk is a quick and easy task, but one that will pay off tenfold in the event you encounter a computer that won't boot. In this topic, you'll learn the steps for creating a boot disk for each operating system you might encounter, including DOS, Windows 9x, Windows 2000, Windows NT, and Windows XP.

If you're unable to boot a computer, you won't be able to perform any other diagnostics or access any of the operating system's tools for troubleshooting the computer. Having a boot disk handy will enable you to at least boot the computer so that you can begin to troubleshoot and fix the problem that prevented it from booting. By booting the computer successfully, you'll be able to begin the work of repairing the computer.

DOS Boot Files

In order to boot a computer using the MS-DOS operating system, your computer must have the necessary files for booting MS-DOS. In Table 19-1, you see a list of the files used to boot a computer with the MS-DOS operating system. These files must be located wherever the computer is booting from, whether it be the computer's hard disk or a floppy boot disk.

Table 19-1: *MS-DOS Boot Files*

File	Used To
Io.sys	Provide MS-DOS and any programs you run access to the computer's hardware. Io.sys includes drivers for hardware devices such as the keyboard, printer ports, serial ports, floppy drives, and hard drives.
Msdos.sys	Manage input and output to and from the computer's disks.

File	Used To
Command.com	Provide the command prompt interface (C:\>). It also provides you with access to certain DOS commands such as dir, copy, and cd. These commands are called internal DOS commands because they are built into the Command.com file. You'll also hear Command.com referred to as the DOS shell or the command interpreter.
Config.sys	Load device drivers, configure the operating system environment, and optimize memory management. For example, you might use the Config.sys file to load the driver for a computer's CD-ROM drive.
Autoexec.bat	Set the initial configuration of MS-DOS and to run any programs you want to run each time the computer boots.

DOS Boot Process

When you turn on an MS-DOS-based computer, it performs the following steps to boot the computer:

1. The computer performs a power-on self test (POST) to test RAM, disk drives, peripheral devices (such as printers), and other hardware components to verify that they are working.
2. Next, the computer looks for the instructions for loading an operating system. These instructions are called the *Master Boot Record (MBR)*; the computer looks for them on a floppy disk, CD-ROM, or the first hard disk in the computer. (The order in which it looks for boot disks depends on how you configure the computer; by default, computers check for the MBR on the floppy disk drive first, then the CD-ROM drive, followed by the first hard disk.) When the computer finds the MBR, it loads it into RAM.
3. The MBR locates the *boot sector* on the boot disk. The boot sector contains the information that enables the computer to locate the Io.sys file.
4. The computer loads the Io.sys file into RAM.
5. The Io.sys file runs a special routine (called Sysinit) that loads the Msdos.sys file into RAM.
6. The Msdos.sys file then processes the commands in the Config.sys file.
7. The Command.com file is loaded into RAM.
8. The Command.com file calls and processes the commands in the Autoexec.bat file.
9. You now see a system command prompt (typically C:\>).

Windows 9x Boot Files

In order to boot a computer using the Windows 9x operating systems, your computer must have the necessary files for booting Windows 9x. Because Windows 9x is actually integrated with MS-DOS, you'll find that it uses many of the same DOS boot files plus several Windows files to boot the computer. In Table 1–2, you see a list of the files used to boot a computer with Windows 9x. These files are located on the hard disk that's used to boot the computer.

Table 19-2: *Windows 9x Boot Files*

File	Used To
Io.sys	Provide MS-DOS and any programs you run to access the computer's hardware. Io.sys includes drivers for hardware devices such as the keyboard, printer ports, serial ports, floppy drives, and hard drives.
Msdos.sys	Manage input and output to and from the computer's disks.
Config.sys	Load device drivers. The Config.sys file is replaced by the Registry in the Windows 9x environment.
Autoexec.bat	Set the initial configuration of Windows 9x to run programs you want to run each time the computer boots. The Autoexec.bat file is replaced by the Registry and the Startup group in Windows 9x.
Win.ini	Configure specific parameters in the Windows environment. In Windows 9x, this file is typically used to set environment parameters for applications written to run on Windows 3.1; these applications are called 16-bit applications. (Newer applications written for the Windows 9x environment, also called 32-bit applications, use the Registry instead of the Win.ini file.)
Win.com	Load Windows 9x.
System.ini	Configure specific parameters used by DOS and the Windows 9x operating system. For example, you can configure the cache size using System.ini by adding the minfilecache and maxfilecache parameters to [vcache] (maxfilecache shouldn't be more than 25% of total memory). Like the Win.ini file, the System.ini file is used primarily by older Windows applications.
Registry	Identify and load the necessary device drivers for the computer's hardware, software, and the operating system itself.
Virtual Device Driver	Initialize the computer's hardware.

Windows 9x Boot Process

When you turn on a Windows 9x-based computer, it performs the following steps to boot the computer:

1. The computer performs a power-on self test (POST) to test its hardware.

2. The computer locates the Master Boot Record (MBR) and loads it into RAM.
3. The MBR locates the boot sector on the boot disk. The boot sector contains the information that enables the computer to locate the Io.sys file.
4. The computer loads the Io.sys file into RAM.
5. The Io.sys file runs a special routine (called Sysinit) that loads the Msdos.sys file into RAM.
6. The Io.sys file loads the System.dat Registry file into RAM but does not process it at this time.
7. If you have configured multiple hardware profiles, Io.sys prompts the user to select a hardware profile.
8. Io.sys processes the Config.sys and Autoexec.bat files (if they exist).
9. When these tasks are complete, Io.sys executes Win.com.
10. Win.com loads the drivers specified within the Registry.
11. Win.com processes the System.ini and Win.ini files.
12. Win.com loads the necessary virtual device drivers, the basic Windows 9x operating system (called the kernel), and the graphical display interface (GDI).
13. The Windows kernel loads the Explorer user interface, including the Desktop, Start menu, and taskbar.
14. The Windows kernel processes any programs in the Startup folder and restores any network connections.
15. The Windows operating system is now ready for the user to use.

Windows 2000/NT/XP Boot Files

When you attempt to boot a computer using Windows 2000, Windows NT, or Windows XP, your computer must have the necessary files for booting Windows. In Table 19-3, you see a list of the files used to boot a computer with Windows 2000, Windows NT, or Windows XP. The boot files are located on the disk you want the computer to boot from.

Table 19-3: *The Windows 2000/NT/XP Boot Files*

File	Used To
Ntldr	Load the Windows 2000, Windows NT, or Windows XP operating system.
Boot.ini	Point the computer to the disk location where the Windows 2000, Windows NT, or Windows XP files are stored. In a dual-boot environment, the contents of the Boot.ini file are used to build the boot menu so that you can choose which operating system you want to load.
Bootsect.dos	Load any non-Windows 2000, Windows NT, or Windows XP operating system you choose from the menu. For example, if you have configured a computer to dual-boot between Windows 98 and Windows 2000, the boot.ini file loads the bootsect.dos file when you choose Windows 98 from the boot menu.

File	Used To
Ntdetect.com	Examine the hardware, build a hardware list, and pass the list to Ntldr. Ntldr adds this information to the computer's Registry.
Ntbootdd.sys	Initialize SCSI hard disks on which the BIOS is disabled.
Ntoskrnl.exe	Load the basic Windows 2000, Windows NT, or Windows XP operating system kernel.
Hal.dll	Isolate the computer's hardware and its device drivers from the Windows 2000, Windows NT, or Windows XP operating system. Isolating the hardware from the operating system enables Microsoft to use the same basic operating system for different types of hardware (such as different processors).
System	Store the system configuration settings that control how devices and services are loaded during the boot process. System is one of the files that makes up the Windows 2000, Windows NT, and Windows XP Registries.

Windows 2000/NT/XP Boot Process

The Windows 2000, Windows NT, and Windows XP operating systems all use the same boot process. This boot process consists of two main phases: the *boot sequence* and the *load phases*. The Windows 2000/NT/XP boot sequence consists of the following steps:

1. The computer runs its power-on self test (POST) to check the hardware.
2. The computer locates the boot device and loads the Master Boot Record into RAM.
3. The MBR finds the active partition on the boot device and loads the boot sector into RAM.
4. The boot sector loads and initializes the Ntldr file, which takes over control of the rest of the boot process.
5. Ntldr configures the computer's processor to address all of the computer's memory; this mode is called the 32-bit flat memory mode.
6. Ntldr starts the file system that corresponds to the formatting of the disk that Windows 2000, Windows NT, or Windows XP will load from. This could be the FAT file system, or Microsoft's NTFS file system.
7. Ntldr reads the Boot.ini file to locate the Windows 2000/NT/XP operating system, and to build the boot menu on dual-boot computers.
8. Ntldr loads Windows 2000, Windows NT, or Windows XP, or, in a dual-boot environment, whatever operating system the user selects from the boot menu.
9. If the operating system selected is Windows 2000, Windows NT, or Windows XP, Ntldr runs Ntdectect.com to build the hardware list. Ntldr loads Ntoskrnl.exe and the Windows 2000/NT/XP load phases start.

If the operating system selected is anything other than Windows 2000, Windows NT, or Windows XP, Ntldr passes control of the computer to Bootsect.dos.

There are four load phases in the second stage of the Windows 2000/NT/XP boot sequence. These phases include:

1. Kernel Load Phase: The kernel load phase begins when Ntldr loads Ntoskrnl.exe at the end of the boot sequence. You can identify this phase by the Starting Windows progress bar that shows up across the bottom of the screen.

2. Kernel Initialization Phase: In this phase, Ntoskrnl.exe is initialized and takes control of the computer. In Windows 2000 and Windows XP, the computer switches to graphical mode, and you can see a window with an animated Starting Up progress bar. In Windows NT, you can identify this phase when the computer screen turns blue.

3. Service Startup: Ntoskrnl.exe continues by loading the Session Manager (Smss.exe) program. In Windows 2000 and Windows XP, you'll see a window with Please Wait in the title bar during this phase. In Windows NT, you'll see the logon dialog box. During this time, Session Manager loads the high-order services—those necessary for a user to log on.

4. Logon Phase: A Windows 2000/NT/XP boot isn't considered complete until a user logs on successfully. During the logon phase, you can initiate logon. However, Windows 2000/NT/XP will continue to load lower-level services in the background. For this reason, the computer's response time will seem slow to users during the logon phase.

Windows 2000/NT/XP Partition Terminology

In Windows 2000, Windows NT, and Windows XP, Microsoft uses two distinct terms for the computer's partitions. The *system partition* is the partition that contains the files necessary for booting the operating system. In almost all cases, the system partition is the C drive on a computer. The system partition contains the following files:

- Boot.ini
- Bootsect.dos
- Ntldr
- Ntdetect.com

Microsoft refers to the partition that contains all the Windows 2000, Windows NT, or Windows 2000 operating system files as the *boot partition*. The boot partition contains the \Windows folder in the case of Windows 2000 or Windows XP, and the \Winnt folder in Windows NT.

If you have configured the computer with only a single C partition, in this scenario, the system and boot partitions are the same. In contrast, if you have configured the computer with a C partition and a D partition, and installed the operating system into the D partition, the C partition is then the system partition, and the D partition is the boot partition.

The Boot.ini File

Windows 2000, Windows NT, and Windows XP use the Boot.ini file to locate the boot partition (the partition containing the \Windows or \Winnt folder). The Boot.ini file consists of two sections, [Boot Loader] and [Operating Systems], as shown in Figure 19-1. The [Boot Loader] section identifies which operating system you want the computer to default to if no selection is made from the boot menu during the boot process. The timeout parameter specifies how long (in seconds) the computer will display the boot menu before booting the default operating system.

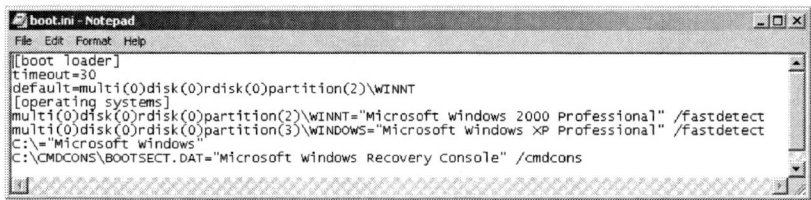

Figure 19-1: *The Boot.ini file.*

The [Operating Systems] section lists the paths to each operating system's files (these are the files stored on the boot partition). Microsoft uses the Advanced RISC Computing (ARC) naming syntax to identify the path to the boot partition. The syntax for ARC path naming is:

- scsi | multi(x)disk(y)rdisk(z)partition(a)\path

In Table 19-4, you find a description of each of the elements that make up the ARC naming syntax.

Table 19-4: *ARC Naming Syntax*

Element	Description
scsi	multi	Indicates the type of hard disk controller in the computer. Uses scsi for SCSI disks with the BIOS disabled; uses multi for all other disks.
(x)	The ordinal number of the disk controller adapter. Ordinal numbering starts with 0. So, if your computer has only one IDE disk controller, the ARC naming syntax would be multi(0).
disk(y)	The SCSI ID of the target disk. If the ARC path starts with multi, (y) is always 0.
rdisk(z)	The disk device's logical unit number. If the ARC path starts with scsi, (z) is always 0. If the ARC path starts with multi, (z) is the ordinal number of the disk on the adapter (usually 0 or 1).
partition(a)	The cardinal number of the Windows 2000/NT/XP boot partition. (Cardinal numbering starts with 1.)
\path	The name of the folder in which the Windows 2000/NT/XP files are stored (typically either \Windows or \Winnt).

How to Create a Boot Disk

Procedure Reference: Create an MS-DOS Boot Disk in Windows 98

You can create a floppy disk to boot a computer using the MS-DOS operating system. To create an MS-DOS boot disk:

1. Start Windows 98.

2. Open Windows Explorer.

3. Format the boot disk using the following steps:
   a. Insert a floppy disk into the floppy disk drive.
   b. In Windows Explorer, right-click 3 1/2 Floppy (A:) and choose Format.
   c. Below Other Options, check Copy System Files.
   d. Click Start.
   e. When the format is complete, click Close to close the Format Results dialog box.
   f. Click Close to close the Format – 3 1/2 Floppy (A:) dialog box.

4. Configure Windows Explorer to display file extensions and hidden files for the C:\Windows\Command folder.
   a. Select the C:\Windows\Command folder.
   b. Choose View→Folder Options.
   c. Select the View tab.
   d. Below Hidden Files, select Show All Files.
   e. Uncheck Hide File Extensions For Known File Types.
   f. Click OK.

5. If you want to use the boot disk to perform such tasks as creating or deleting partitions, correcting boot problems, changing file attributes, or formatting partitions, copy the following program files from C:\Windows\Command to the boot disk.
   - Attrib.exe
   - Edit.com
   - Edit.hlp
   - Fdisk.exe
   - Format.com
   - Scandisk.exe
   - Scandisk.ini
   - Sys.com

   To copy the files, complete the following steps:
   a. In Windows Explorer, select the C:\Windows\Command folder.
   b. Select the first file you want to copy.

    c. Hold down the Control key and select all other files you want to copy.

    d. Right-click the selected files and choose Send To→3 1/2 Floppy (A).

6. Close Windows Explorer.

7. Test the boot disk to verify that it works.

    a. Restart the computer with the floppy disk in the disk drive to verify that you can boot successfully.

    b. If necessary, run the computer's System Setup utility to configure it to boot from floppy first.

    c. The computer boots successfully if you see an MS-DOS prompt displayed.

8. Remove the MS-DOS boot disk, label it, and store it in a safe location. You might also want to write-protect the disk.

Procedure Reference: Create a Startup Disk for Windows 98

You can create a startup disk in Windows 98 that enables you to boot the computer to DOS with support for the computer's CD-ROM. You might create such a disk if you want to re-install Windows 98 on a computer, or if you want to perform diagnostic tests. To create a startup disk for Windows 98:

1. From the Start menu, choose Settings→Control Panel.

2. Double-click Add/Remove Programs.

3. Select the Startup Disk tab.

4. Click Create Disk.

5. When prompted, insert the Windows 98 installation CD-ROM and click OK.

> You do not have to format the floppy disk before creating the startup disk. Windows 98 automatically formats the disk for you.

6. Insert a floppy disk into the floppy disk drive.

7. Click OK.

> It will take several minutes for Windows 98 to create the startup disk.

8. Click OK to close the Add/Remove Programs Properties dialog box.

9. Close Control Panel.

10. Test the startup disk to verify that it works.

    a. Restart the computer with the floppy disk in the disk drive to verify that you can boot successfully.

    b. If necessary, run the computer's System Setup utility to configure it to boot from floppy first.

c. From the Startup menu, choose from one of the following options:
- Start Computer With CD-ROM Support.
- Start Computer Without CD-ROM Support.
- View The Help File.

Alternatively, you can press the following key combinations:
- F5, to start in Safe Mode.
- Shift+F5, to start in Command Prompt mode.
- Shift+F8, to start Windows 98 in Step-By-Step Confirmation Mode.

11. Remove the startup disk, label it, and store it in a safe location. You might also want to write-protect the disk.

Procedure Reference: Create a Boot Disk for Windows 2000/XP/NT

To create a boot disk for Windows 2000, Windows XP, and Windows NT:

1. Log on as a user with permissions to the system partition.
2. Open Windows Explorer.

   You must format the disk in the appropriate operating system for the disk to be bootable.

3. Format the boot disk using the following steps:
    a. Insert a floppy disk into the floppy disk drive.
    b. In Windows Explorer, right-click 3 1/2 Floppy (A:) and choose Format.
    c. Optionally, check Quick Format to reduce the amount of time required to format the disk.
    d. Click Start.
    e. Click OK to confirm that you want to format the disk.
    f. When the format is complete, click OK.
    g. Click Close to close the Format A:\ dialog box.
4. If necessary, if you're using Windows 2000 or Windows XP, configure Windows Explorer to display system and hidden files on the C drive using the following steps:
    a. Select the C drive.
    b. In Windows Explorer, choose Tools→Folder Options.
    c. Select the View tab.
    d. Below Hidden Files And Folders, select Show Hidden Files And Folders.
    e. Uncheck Hide File Extensions For Known File Types.
    f. Uncheck Hide Protected Operating System Files (Recommended).
    g. Click OK.

5. If necessary, if you're using Windows NT, configure Windows Explorer to display system and hidden files on the C drive using the following steps:
   a. Select the C drive.
   b. In Windows Explorer, choose View→Options.
   c. Below Hidden Files, choose Show All Files.
   d. Uncheck Hide File Extensions For Known File Types.
   e. Click OK.
6. Copy the following files to the boot disk:
   - Boot.ini.
   - Bootsect.dos (if it exists). This file will be present only if you dual-boot the computer between Windows 9x and Windows 2000, Windows XP, or Windows NT.
   - Ntbootdd.sys (if it exists). This file will be present only if the computer contains BIOS-disabled SCSI disk drives.
   - Ntdetect.com.
   - Ntldr.

   To copy the files, complete the following steps:
   a. Select the boot.ini file.
   b. Hold down the Control key and select each additional file.
   c. Right-click the selected files and choose Send To→3 1/2 Floppy (A:).
7. Close Windows Explorer.
8. Test the boot disk to verify that it works.
   a. Restart the computer with the floppy disk in the disk drive to verify that you can boot successfully.
   b. If necessary, run the computer's System Setup utility to configure it to boot from floppy first.
   c. If the computer has multiple operating systems, verify that you can start each operating system from the boot disk.
9. Remove the boot disk, label it, and store it in a safe location. You might also want to write-protect the disk.

Procedure Reference: Create an MS-DOS Boot Disk in Windows XP

To create an MS-DOS boot disk in Windows XP:

1. Start Windows XP.
2. Log on as a user.
3. Open Windows Explorer.
4. Format the boot disk using the following steps:

a. Insert a floppy disk into the floppy disk drive.

   b. In Windows Explorer, right-click 3 1/2 Floppy (A:) and choose Format.

   c. Check Create An MS-DOS Startup Disk.

   d. Click Start.

   e. Click OK to confirm that you want to erase all data on the disk.

   f. When the format is complete, click OK.

   g. Click Close to close the Format 3 1/2 Floppy (A:) dialog box.

5. Close Windows Explorer.

6. Test the boot disk to verify that it works.

   a. Restart the computer with the floppy disk in the disk drive to verify that you can boot successfully.

   b. If necessary, run the computer's System Setup utility to configure it to boot from floppy first.

   c. The computer boots successfully if you see an MS-DOS prompt displayed.

7. Remove the MS-DOS boot disk, label it, and store it in a safe location. You might also want to write-protect the disk.

TOPIC B
Create an Emergency Repair Disk

In Windows 2000 and Windows NT, one of the techniques you can use to repair a computer in the event of a crash is to perform an emergency repair. But in order to perform an emergency repair, you'll need a copy of the computer's critical configuration files on a special disk called the emergency repair disk. In this topic, you'll learn how to create an emergency repair disk for both Windows 2000 and Windows NT computers.

Without an emergency repair disk, you won't be able to perform an emergency repair to attempt to correct a computer's problem. Having an emergency repair disk enables you to be prepared for just such an emergency. Further, performing an emergency repair is one of the quickest methods to get a crashed computer back up and running. By having an emergency repair disk at the ready, you'll be able to quickly repair most problems so that your users can get back to work.

Emergency Repair Disk

In Windows 2000 and Windows NT, you can create a disk that contains information about the current configuration of the operating system. You can use this disk, called an *emergency repair disk (ERD)*, to repair your computer if it will not boot up. In addition, you can use the ERD to repair damaged or lost operating system files. When you create an ERD, Windows stores the ERD's information in the \Windows\Repair or \Winnt\Repair folder. In the event you can't find your ERD, the computer can use the information in this folder to repair the computer (provided the hard disk is accessible).

The Emergency Repair Process

After you have created an emergency repair disk, you can use it to repair the computer in the event you encounter a problem. The procedures you use for repairing the computer are as follows:

1. Boot the computer from the Windows 2000 or Windows NT installation CD-ROM. If the computer doesn't support booting from the CD-ROM or the CD-ROM itself is not bootable, you can create installation boot floppies using another computer. (See the Creating Installation Boot Disks procedure.)
2. When prompted to repair the computer, press R.
3. From the Repair Options menu, press R to use the emergency repair process.
4. Choose Fast Repair to perform all repair options, or choose Manual Repair to select the repair options you want to perform.
5. Follow the prompts to repair the computer from the ERD or from the Repair folder on the hard disk.
6. Complete the process and restart the computer.

Creating Installation Boot Disks

Procedure Reference: Create Installation Boot Disks for Windows 2000

To create the installation boot disks for Windows 2000:

1. Obtain three blank floppy disks.
2. Use Windows Explorer to access the \Bootdisk folder on the Windows 2000 installation CD-ROM.
3. Double-click the appropriate program to create the disks.
   - If you're using a Windows 2000, Windows NT, or Windows XP computer to create the disks, double-click makebt32.exe.
   - If you're using Windows 9x, double-click makeboot.exe to create the disks.
4. Label and insert each floppy disk as prompted.
5. Remove the Windows 2000 installation CD-ROM.
6. Close Windows Explorer.

Procedure Reference: Create Installation Boot Disks for Windows NT

To create the installation boot disks for Windows NT:

1. Obtain three blank floppy disks.
2. Insert the Windows NT installation CD-ROM.
3. Run the appropriate program to create the disks.
   - If you're using a Windows 2000, Windows NT, or Windows XP computer to create the disks, from the Start menu, choose Run. In the Open text box, type winnt32 /ox and click OK.

- If you're using Windows 9x to create the disks, from the Start menu, choose Run. In the Open text box, type winnt /ox and click OK.

4. Label and insert each floppy disk as prompted.
5. Remove the Windows NT installation CD-ROM.
6. Close Windows Explorer.

How to Create an Emergency Repair Disk

Procedure Reference: Create an Emergency Repair Disk in Windows 2000

To create an emergency repair disk in Windows 2000:

1. Log on as a local administrator.
2. From the Start menu, choose Programs→Accessories→System Tools→Backup.
3. Insert a blank floppy disk into the floppy disk drive.
4. Click Emergency Repair Disk.
5. Check Also Back Up The Registry To The Repair Directory to store a backup copy of the emergency repair disk information on the computer's hard disk.
6. Click OK to create the disk.
7. Click OK to close the Emergency Repair Diskette message box.
8. Close Backup.
9. Remove the floppy disk, label it, and store it in a safe place.

> The only way to test an ERD is to perform an emergency repair. You'll learn how to perform an emergency repair in Chapter 12.

Procedure Reference: Create an Emergency Repair Disk in Windows NT

To create an emergency repair disk in Windows NT:

1. Log on as a local administrator.
2. From the Start menu, choose Run.
3. Insert a blank floppy disk into the floppy disk drive.
4. In the Open text box, type one of the following:
   - rdisk, if you want to create an emergency repair disk that does not contain the user accounts database.
   - rdisk /s, if you want to create an emergency repair disk that does contain the user accounts database.
5. Click OK.

6. If you typed `rdisk /s` to create the emergency repair disk along with a copy of the user accounts database, complete the following steps:
   a. Click Update Repair Info to store a backup copy of the emergency repair disk information on the computer's hard disk.
   b. Click Yes to confirm that you want to update the repair information.
   c. Click Yes to create the emergency repair disk.
   d. Click OK to confirm that the disk will be reformatted.
   e. Click OK to close the Repair Disk Utility message box.
   f. Click Exit to close the Repair Disk Utility.

    Windows NT automatically backs up the emergency repair disk information to the computer's hard disk when you run `rdisk /s`.

7. If you typed `rdisk` to create the emergency repair disk, complete the following steps:
   a. Click Yes to create the emergency repair disk.
   b. Click OK to confirm that the disk will be reformatted.
   c. Click OK to close the Repair Disk Utility message box.

8. Remove the floppy disk, label it, and store it in a safe place.

    The only way to test an ERD is to perform an emergency repair. You'll learn how to perform an emergency repair in Chapter 12.

TOPIC C
Install the Recovery Console

In Topic 19B, you learned how to create an emergency repair disk so that you can perform an emergency repair on Windows 2000 and Windows NT computers. In Windows XP, the equivalent tool to an emergency repair is the Recovery Console. In this topic, you'll learn how to install the Recovery Console on Windows XP computers so that it's accessible on the computer's startup menu.

The Recovery Console is like a spare tire for Windows XP and Windows 2000. If you have a flat, a spare tire will get you back up and on the road again, but only if you have a spare tire. Likewise, the Recovery Console can get your user's computer up and running again, but only if you can load the Recovery Console software. Installing the Recovery Console on a user's computer is like double-checking that you have a good spare tire in your car's trunk. By installing the Recovery Console, you can be sure that it's always available to you whenever you need it.

Recovery Console

Windows XP and Windows 2000 include a utility that you can use to perform emergency repairs on the computer; it's called the *Recovery Console*. The Recovery Console is a command-line utility that you can use to perform administrative tasks for repairing the computer. For example, you might use the Recovery Console to repair the computer's Master Boot Record. You can start the Recovery Console by booting the computer from the Windows 2000 or Windows XP installation disks, by using the Winnt32 /cmdcons command, or by adding it to the computer's boot menu.

How to Install the Recovery Console

Procedure Reference: Install the Recovery Console

To install the Recovery Console:

1. Log on as a local computer administrator.

2. Execute the `winnt32.exe /cmdcons` command from the appropriate installation CD-ROM.

   - If you're installing the Recovery Console on a Windows 2000 computer, execute this command from the Windows 2000 installation CD-ROM.

   - If you're installing the Recovery Console on a Windows XP computer, execute this command from the Windows XP installation CD-ROM.

   - If you're installing the Recovery Console on a computer configured to dual-boot both Windows 2000 and Windows XP, you MUST execute this command from the Windows XP installation CD-ROM.

   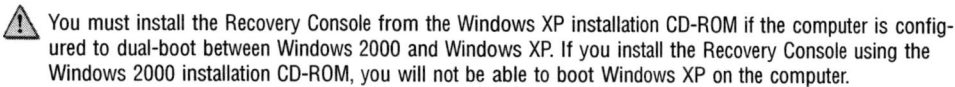
   You must install the Recovery Console from the Windows XP installation CD-ROM if the computer is configured to dual-boot between Windows 2000 and Windows XP. If you install the Recovery Console using the Windows 2000 installation CD-ROM, you will not be able to boot Windows XP on the computer.

3. Click Yes to confirm that you want to install the Recovery Console.

4. If your computer is connected to the Internet, Windows Setup will automatically connect to the Internet and download updated Windows XP or Windows 2000 installation files from the Microsoft Web site.

5. If you want to cancel the automatic updates, complete the following steps:

   a. Press Esc if you do not want to connect to the Internet.

   b. Click Yes to confirm the cancellation.

   c. Select Skip This Step And Continue Installing Windows and click Next.

6. When the Recovery Console installation is complete, click OK.

7. Test the Recovery Console installation by using the following steps:

   a. Shut down and restart the computer.

   b. From the boot menu, select Microsoft Windows Recovery Console.

   c. When prompted, enter the number of the Windows XP Professional installation you want to log on to (if the computer is a single-boot system, this will be installation number 1. If you have Windows 2000 or Windows NT on the computer, you can use the Recovery Console to repair those installations as well).

d. Enter the Administrator password to log on to Windows XP or Windows 2000.

e. To end the Recovery Console session and restart the computer, type exit and press Enter.

Topic D
Back Up Data

Up to this point in the chapter, you've seen the tools you can use to prepare for disaster recovery: creating a boot disk and an emergency repair disk, and installing the Recovery Console. You'll use these tools primarily to recover from problems with a computer's operating system files or configuration. Now it's time to turn your attention to avoiding losing the data stored on a computer. In this topic, you'll learn how to back up data so that you can later restore it.

As an A+ technician, there are several situations in which you'll need a current backup of a user's data. For example, you will need a current backup of a user's data if you're moving that user to a new computer. By having a current backup, you'll be able to quickly transfer the user's data files to her new computer. Other situations you might encounter include a user who accidentally deletes some files (or even an entire folder) that he needs, or the user's hard disk could become damaged. In either scenario, you'll need to be prepared to restore the data so that your user can gain access to the files he needs to perform his job.

The Archive File Attribute

The Windows operating systems automatically assign the Archive file attribute to every file you create or modify on the computer. In Figure 19-2, you see a file with the Archive attribute enabled. You can use this attribute to assist you in performing selective backups of the data on a computer. For example, on one night you might back up all files on the computer's hard disk and remove the Archive attribute from those files. Later, you can back up only those files with the Archive attribute (which means you'll be backing up only the new files the user has created or any existing files modified). Backing up only the files that have changed enables you to reduce the amount of time required to back up the computer.

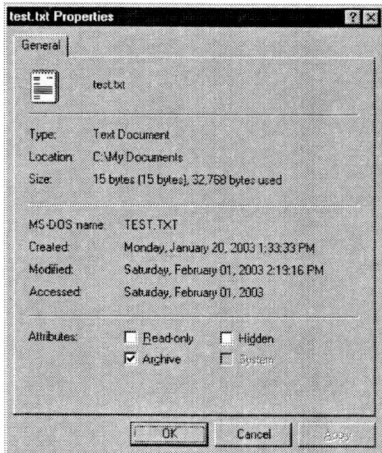

Figure 19-2: *A file with the Archive attribute enabled.*

Backup Types

Windows 2000, Windows NT, Windows XP, and Windows 9x support four backup types: full, copy, incremental, and differential. In Table 19-5, you see a description of each backup type and how it interacts with the Archive attribute. You will typically use one or more of these backup types, as follows:

- Perform a full backup on a nightly basis. Use this strategy if the computer does not contain so much data that the backup cannot complete within the necessary time frame.

- Perform a full backup on a weekly basis. Perform either an incremental or a differential backup on a nightly basis. This strategy enables you to reduce the amount of time required to back up the data on a nightly basis.

Table 19-5: *Backup Types*

Backup Type	Description
Copy	Backs up some or all files on the computer. Does not clear the Archive attribute from the files it backs up.
Full	Backs up some or all files on the computer. Clears the Archive attribute from all files. You'll sometimes hear a full backup referred to as a *normal* backup.
Incremental	Backs up all files since the last full or incremental backup. Clears the Archive attribute from all files.
Differential	Backs up all files since the last full backup. Does not clear the Archive attribute.
Daily	Backs up the files created or modified on the day the backup is performed. Does not clear the Archive attribute.

Backup Media

With the exception of Windows NT, the Windows operating systems support a variety of media to which you can back up. This media includes tape, floppy disks, shared folders on other computers, CD-ROM disks, and Zip disks. Windows NT supports backing up only to tape.

Batch/Script Files

Definition:

Batch and script files are files that contain commands for performing specific tasks on the computer. You can create a batch file or a script file by using any text editor such as Notepad. You must save a batch file with either the .bat or .cmd extensions. You execute a batch file simply by double-clicking it in Windows Explorer or by typing its name in a Command Prompt window.

You create a script file by using the Visual Basic Scripting (VBScript) or JScript languages. You must save a script file with the .wsf extension. Before you execute a script file, you must first run the Windows Script Host (wscript.exe). After you have run the Windows Script Host, you can run the script file by double-clicking it in Windows Explorer.

Example:

In Figure 19-3, you see an example of a batch file. In Figure 19-4, you see an example of a script file.

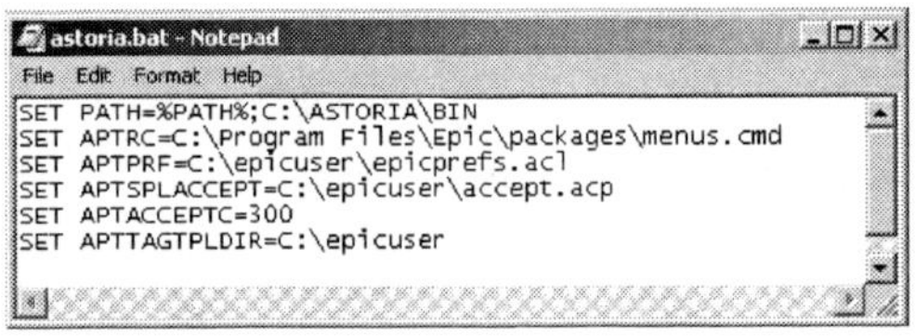

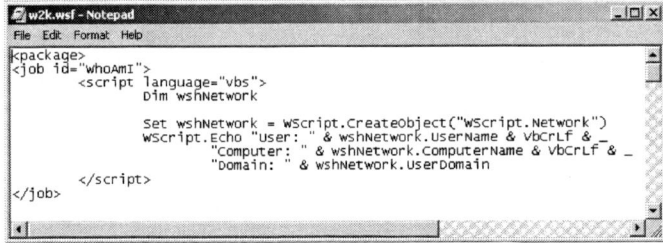

Figure 19-3: *A batch file.*

Figure 19-4: *A script file.*

How to Back Up Data

Procedure Reference: Back Up Data in Windows 2000

To back up data in Windows 2000:

1. Log on as a user who's either a member of the Backup Operators or Administrators groups, owner of a file, or a user who has at least the Read NTFS permissions to back up file data.
2. If you plan to back up to floppy disk, insert a floppy disk into the floppy disk drive.
3. If you plan to back up to tape, insert a tape into the tape drive.
4. From the Start menu, choose Programs→Accessories→System Tools→Backup.
5. Click Backup Wizard.
6. Click Next.
7. On the What To Back Up page, select one of the following:
   - Back Up Everything On My Computer, to back up all files and folders on the computer.
   - Back Up Selected Files, Drives, Or Network Data, to back up only the files you select.
   - Only Back Up The System State Data, to back up just the System State data.
8. Click Next.
9. If you chose to back up only selected files, complete the following steps:
   a. Below What To Back Up, expand the source location of the files and check the check box for each item that you want to back up.
   b. If you want to back up only selected files within a location, below Name, check the specific files you want to back up.
   c. Click Next.
10. On the Where To Store The Backup page:
    a. From the Backup Media Type drop-down list, select the type of backup you want to create (if you do not have a local tape backup device, your only choice will be File).
    b. In the Backup Media Or File Name, type a path and file name for the backup file. The default file name is Backup.bkf.
    c. Click Next.
11. To create the backup using the default settings, click Finish. Otherwise, click Advanced.
12. If you click Advanced, select the type of backup you want to perform.
    - Normal
    - Copy
    - Incremental

- Differential
- Daily

13. Check Backup Migrated Remote Storage Data if you want to back up files that have been migrated to removable media.
14. Click Next.
15. Check Verify Data After Backup to have Backup check that you got a valid backup of the data.
16. Click Next.
17. Below If The Archive Media Already Contains Backups, select one of the following:
    - Append This Backup To The Media
    - Replace The Data On The Media With This Backup
18. Click Next.
19. On the Backup Label page, enter a backup label and a media label.
20. Click Next.
21. On the When To Back Up page, verify that Now is selected and click Next.

See the following procedure for scheduling backups.

22. Click Finish to begin the backup.
23. Review the Backup Progress dialog box to verify that the backup completed successfully.
24. Click Close to close the Backup Progress dialog box.
25. Close Backup.

Procedure Reference: Schedule a Backup in Windows 2000

To schedule a backup in Windows 2000:

1. Use Backup to create a backup job.
2. On the last page of the wizard, click Advanced.
3. Select any advanced options on the Type Of Backup, How To Back Up, Media Options, and Backup Label pages.
4. On the When To Back Up Page, select Later.
5. In the Set Account Information dialog box, complete the following:
   a. In the Run As text box, type the user name of a user with the permissions and rights necessary to back up the files.
   b. In the Password text box, type the password for this user.
   c. In the Confirm Password text box, re-type the password for this user.

d. Click OK.

6. In the Job Name text box, type a name for the job.

7. Click Set Schedule.

8. Select your scheduling options. You can schedule a task to run Once, Daily, Weekly, Monthly, At System Startup, At Logon, or When Idle. For Daily, Weekly, or Monthly schedules, you can configure specific times and days.

9. If you chose a Daily, Weekly, or Monthly schedule, click Advanced, configure the properties, and then click OK. You can configure start and end dates for the task, and configure the task to run more than once at the scheduled time.

10. If you want to run this task on more than one schedule (for example, weekly and also monthly), check Show Multiple Schedules and click New to create additional schedules.

11. To configure how this task will respond to system conditions such as a low battery, select the Settings tab and configure the settings. See the Windows Backup Help system for specific information.

12. When you have finished creating and configuring all schedules, click OK.

13. On the When To Back Up page, click Next.

14. Click Finish.

Procedure Reference: Back Up Data in Windows XP

To back up data in Windows XP:

1. Log on as a user who's either a member of the Backup Operators or Administrators groups, owner of a file, or a user who has at least the Read NTFS permissions to back up file data.

2. If you plan to back up to floppy disk, insert a floppy disk into the floppy disk drive.

3. If you plan to back up to tape, insert a tape into the tape drive.

4. From the Start menu, choose All Programs→Accessories→System Tools→Backup.

5. Click Next.

6. On the What Do You Want To Do page, select one of the following:
   - Back Up Files And Settings.
   - Restore Files And Settings.

7. Click Next.

8. On the What To Back Up page, select one of the following:
   - My Documents And Settings, to back up the current user's My Documents folder, Favorites list, desktop settings, and Internet cookie files.
   - Everyone's Documents And Settings, to back up this same information for all users of the computer.

- All Information On This Computer, to back up everything on the computer.
- Let Me Choose What To Back Up, to back up only the files you select.

9. Click Next.

10. If you chose the Let Me Choose What To Back Up option, complete the following steps:
    a. Below Items To Back Up, expand the source location of the files and check the check box for each item that you want to back up.
    b. If you want to back up only selected files within a location, below Name, check the specific files you want to back up.
    c. Click Next.

11. On the Backup Type, Destination, and Name page:
    a. From the Select The Backup Type drop-down list, select the type of backup you want to create (if you do not have a local tape backup device, your only choice will be File).
    b. From the Choose A Place To Save Your Backup drop-down list, select the location where you want to store your backup (if you do not have a local tape backup device, your default choice will be 3 1/2 Floppy).
    c. In the Type A Name For This Backup text box, type a name for the backup. The default file name is Backup.
    d. Click Next.

12. To create the backup using the default settings, click Finish. Otherwise, click Advanced.

13. If you click Advanced, select the type of backup you want to perform.
    - Normal
    - Copy
    - Incremental
    - Differential
    - Daily

14. Click Next.

15. On the How To Back Up page, check any of the following options:
    - Check Verify Data After Backup to have Backup check that you got a valid backup of the data.
    - Check Use Hardware Compression, If Available, if you're backing up to tape and your tape drive supports compression.
    - Check Disable Volume Shadow Copy, if you want to disable support for backing up files even when they're being written to.

16. Click Next.

17. Below Backup Options, select one of the following:

- Append This Backup To The Existing Backups.
- Replace The Existing Backups.

18. Click Next.

19. On the When To Back Up page, verify that Now is selected and click Next.

    See the following procedure for scheduling backups.

20. Click Finish to begin the backup.

    Windows Backup closes automatically when you click Finish.

21. Review the Backup Progress dialog box to verify that the backup completed successfully.

22. Click Close to close the Backup Progress dialog box.

Procedure Reference: Schedule a Backup in Windows XP

To schedule a backup in Windows XP:

1. Use Backup to create a backup job.

2. On the last page of the wizard, click Advanced.

3. Select any advanced options on the Type Of Backup, How To Back Up, and Backup Options pages.

4. On the When To Back Up Page, select Later.

5. In the Job Name text box, type a name for the job.

6. Click Set Schedule.

7. Select your scheduling options. You can schedule a task to run Once, Daily, Weekly, Monthly, At System Startup, At Logon, or When Idle. For Daily, Weekly, or Monthly schedules, you can configure specific times and days.

8. If you chose a Daily, Weekly, or Monthly schedule, click Advanced, configure the properties, and then click OK. You can configure start and end dates for the task, and configure the task to run more than once at the scheduled time.

9. If you want to run this task on more than one schedule (for example, weekly and also monthly), check Show Multiple Schedules and click New to create additional schedules.

10. To configure how this task will respond to system conditions such as a low battery, select the Settings tab and configure the settings. See the Windows Backup Help system for specific information.

11. When you have finished creating and configuring all schedules, click OK.

12. On the When To Back Up page, click Next.

13. In the Set Account Information dialog box, complete the following:

    a. In the Run As text box, type the user name of a user with the permissions and rights necessary to back up the files.

    b. In the Password text box, type the password for this user.

    c. In the Confirm Password text box, re-type the password for this user.

    d. Click OK.

14. Click Finish.

Procedure Reference: Back Up Data in Windows NT

To back up data in Windows NT:

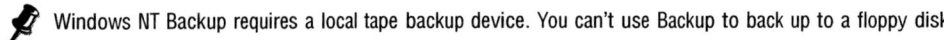 Windows NT Backup requires a local tape backup device. You can't use Backup to back up to a floppy disk.

1. Log on as a user who's either a member of the Backup Operators or Administrators groups, owner of a file, or a user who has at least the Read NTFS permissions to back up file data.

2. Insert a tape into the tape drive.

3. From the Start menu, choose Programs→Administrative Tools→Backup.

4. If you want to back up all data on the computer, in the Drives list, check all drives.

5. If you want to back up only selected files or folders, complete the following steps:

    a. In the Drives list, double-click the drive containing the files you want to back up.

    b. If you want to back up an entire folder, in the left pane, check the folder.

    c. If you want to back up only selected files, in the left pane, select the folder containing the files. In the right pane, check each file you want to back up.

6. On the toolbar, click Backup.

7. Configure any necessary backup options.

- Check Verify After Backup if you want Windows NT Backup to verify the accuracy of the backup.
- Check Restrict Access To Owner Or Administrator if you want to restrict restoring the files in the backup to either the owner of the files or the Administrator.

8. In the Description text box, type a description for the backup.

9. From the Backup Type drop-down list, select the type of backup you want to perform. Windows NT supports the following backup types:

- Normal
- Copy
- Differential
- Incremental
- Daily

10. Below Log Information, select how much information you want to store in the backup log file.

11. Click OK to begin the backup.

12. When the backup is complete, click OK to close the Verify Status dialog box.

13. Close Windows NT Backup.

Procedure Reference: Schedule a Backup in Windows NT

To schedule a backup in Windows NT:

1. Verify that the Task Scheduler service is started and configured to start automatically whenever Windows NT boots.
    a. From the Start menu, choose Settings→Control Panel.
    b. Double-click Services.
    c. In the list of Services, select Task Scheduler.
    d. If necessary, click Start.
    e. If the Startup column displays Manual, click Startup. Below Startup Type, select Automatic and click OK.
    f. Click Close to close Services.
    g. Close Control Panel.

2. Create a batch file that contains the commands to perform the backup.
    a. From the Start menu, choose Programs→Accessories→Notepad.
    b. Enter the command `ntbackup backup path options`. Replace *path* with the path you want to back up (see Table 19-6 for a list of the options you can use with this command). For example, to back up the entire C drive and verify the backup when it's complete, you should enter `ntbackup backup C: /v`.
    c. Choose File→Save As.
    d. In the Save As dialog box, select a drive and folder in which to store the batch file.
    e. From the Save As Type drop-down list, select All Files.
    f. In the File Name text box, type a name for the batch file and use the .cmd extension. (For example, backup.cmd).
    g. Click Save.
    h. Close Notepad.

Table 19-6: *NTBackup Options*

Option	Use to
/a	Append the backup to the existing backups on the tape.

Option	Use to
/b	Back up the Registry. Note: You must also choose another file on the same partition for Windows NT Backup to be able to back up the Registry.
/d "text"	Assign a descriptive name to the backup set.
/e	Log errors that occur during the backup to a file named Backup.log. This file is stored in the \%systemroot% folder.
/l filename	Assign a different file name to the log file.
/r	Restrict access to the tape to members of Administrators or Backup Operators, and the user that created the backup.
/v	Verify that the files were backed up successfully.
/hc:on or /hc:off	Turn hardware compression on or off.

3. Open a Command Prompt window (from the Start menu, choose Programs→Command Prompt).

4. Enter at \\computer_name id time options "command" to schedule the backup batch file to run automatically.

   - Replace \\computer_name with the name of the computer you want to back up.
   - Replace id with the number you want to assign to this scheduled job. You can later use this number to delete or view information about the job.
   - Replace time with the time at which you want the backup job to run. Enter the time as hour: minutes using the 24-hour notation. For example, to schedule a backup at 11:00 p.m., use 23:00 as the time.
   - For a list of available options, see Table 19-7.
   - Replace "command" with the path and name of the batch file. For example, if you stored the backup.cmd batch file in C:\Winnt, the command would be "C:\Winnt\backup.cmd".

Table 19-7: *At Command Options*

Option	Use to
/interactive	Permit the job to interact with the desktop of the user who is logged on at the computer.

Option	Use to
/every:date[,...n]	Configure at to perform the job on specific days of the week or month. Identify days by using the abbreviations M, T, W, Th, F, S, or Su. Identify days of the month by using the number date (1 to 31).
/next:date[,...n]	Configure when the at command will next run the job.

5. Review the schedule for the backup job by entering at at the Command Prompt. If necessary, delete the job using the at *id* /delete command and execute a different at command to correct any mistakes.
6. Close the Command Prompt window.

Procedure Reference: Back Up Data in Windows 98

To back up data in Windows 98:

1. If necessary, install Windows 98 Backup (Msbackup.exe).
    a. In Control Panel, double-click Add/Remove Programs.
    b. Select the Windows Setup tab.
    c. In the Components list, select (don't check or uncheck) System Tools.
    d. Click Details.
    e. Check Backup and click OK.
    f. Click OK to close the Add/Remove Programs Properties dialog box.
    g. When prompted, insert the Windows 98 installation CD-ROM and click OK.
    h. Click Yes to restart the computer.
    i. If necessary, log back on to Windows 98.
    j. Close Control Panel.
2. If you plan to back up to floppy disk, insert a floppy disk into the floppy disk drive.
3. If you plan to back up to tape, insert a tape into the tape drive.
4. From the Start menu, choose Programs→Accessories→System Tools→Backup.
5. If you don't have an attached tape drive, click No in the Microsoft Backup error message box.
6. In the Microsoft Backup dialog box, select Create A New Backup Job.
7. Click OK.
8. In the Backup Wizard, select one of the following:

- Back Up My Computer, to back up everything on the computer.
- Back Up Selected Files, Folders, And Drives, to select the files or folders you want to back up.

9. Click Next.
10. If you chose to back up only selected files, complete the following steps:
    a. Below What To Back Up, expand the source location of the files and check the check box for each item that you want to back up.
    b. If you want to back up only selected files within a location, below Name, check the specific files you want to back up.
    c. Click Next.
11. On the What To Back Up page, select one of the following:
    - All Selected Files, to back up all files in the folder.
    - New And Changed Files, to back up only the files with the Archive attribute.
12. Click Next.
13. On the Where To Back Up page, complete the following:
    a. From the Where To Back Up drop-down list, select the type of backup you want to create (if you do not have a local tape backup device, your only choice will be File).
    b. In the other text box, type a path and file name for the backup file. The default path and file name is C:\MyBackup.qic. If you want to store the backup on a floppy disk, use the A drive instead.
    c. Click Next.
14. On the How To Back Up page, select any or all of these options:
    - Check Compare Original And Backup Files, to verify that your backup was successful.
    - Check Compress The Backup Data, to save space in your backup media (either tape or disk).
15. Click Next.
16. In the Type A Name For This Backup Job text box, type a name for the backup job. You can later re-use this job to perform the same backup.
17. Click Start.
18. Review the Backup Progress dialog box to verify that the backup completed successfully.
19. Click OK to close the Backup Progress dialog box.
20. Close Backup.

You can't schedule a backup in Windows 98.

User Data Files

In some situations, you might find it necessary to back up only the files that a user has created on a computer, and not the program files on that computer. In this situation, you can typically get most of the user's data by backing up the contents of the user's My Documents folder. When looking at other folders on the computer, you can typically identify the data files by their file extensions. In Table 19-8, we list some of the common user data file extensions and the programs used to create them.

Table 19-8: *Common Data File Extensions*

File Extension	Created In
.doc	Microsoft Word
.xls	Microsoft Excel
.ppt	Microsoft PowerPoint
.mdb	Microsoft Access
.txt	Microsoft Word or Notepad

TOPIC E
Back Up System State Data

In Topic 19D, you learned how to back up user data files so that you can be prepared in the event a user accidentally deletes files or the hard disk corrupts some of the user's data files. But if a Windows 2000 or Windows XP computer crashes altogether, another type of backup you'll need is a backup of the computer's system state data. In this topic, you'll learn how to back up a computer's system state data so that it's available to you in the event of a complete computer failure.

If you must recover a computer that's failed altogether, you'll need to not only be able to restore the user's data, but also all of the operating system's configuration information as well. So how do you prepare for such a disaster? You could perform a complete backup of each user's computer on a daily basis, but such backups take a long time to complete and require a lot of room on backup media (such as tapes). By backing up only the system state data, you can create a much smaller backup with the essential information you need to get the computer back up and running. In addition, you'll find it much quicker to restore only the system state data as compared to having to select individual files from a complete backup of the user's computer. So, as you can see, backing up system state data provides you with a quick and easy way to grab a copy of the Windows 2000 or Windows XP configuration information so that you can be prepared in the event disaster strikes.

System State Data

Windows 2000 and Windows XP refer to the critical system components that contain the operating system's configuration information as *system state data*. The system state data includes the following components:

- The Windows 2000 or Windows XP boot files.
- All files installed during the installation of Windows 2000 or Windows XP that have the .sys, .dll, .ttf, .fon, .ocx, and .exe extension.
- The Registry.
- COM+ object registrations, which is a database of program components that are shared between applications.

How to Back Up System State Data

Procedure Reference: Back Up System State Data in Windows 2000

To back up System State Data in Windows 2000:

1. Log on as a user who's either a member of the Backup Operators or Administrators groups, owner of a file, or a user who has at least the Read NTFS permissions to back up file data.

    Backing up the System State Data requires approximately 400 MB of space. You must back it up to a tape, a folder on the local computer, or a shared folder on a server.

2. If you plan to back up to tape, insert a tape into the tape drive.
3. If you plan to back up to a folder, verify that you have enough available disk space. Create the folder.
4. From the Start menu, choose Programs→Accessories→System Tools→Backup.
5. Click Backup Wizard.
6. Click Next.
7. On the What To Back Up page, select Only Back Up The System State Data.
8. Click Next.
9. On the Where To Store The Backup page:
   a. From the Backup Media Type drop-down list, select the type of backup you want to create (if you do not have a local tape backup device, your only choice will be File).
   b. In the Backup Media Or File Name, type the path and name for the backup file. The default file name and path is A:\Backup.bkf.
   c. Click Next.
10. To create the backup using the default settings, click Finish (click Advanced if you want to specify any other backup options).
11. Review the Backup Progress dialog box to verify that the backup completed successfully.
12. Click Close to close the Backup Progress dialog box.
13. Close Backup.

Procedure Reference: Back Up System State Data in Windows XP

To back up System State Data in Windows XP:

1. Log on as a user who's either a member of the Backup Operators or Administrators groups, owner of a file, or a user who has at least the Read NTFS permissions to back up file data.

    Backing up the System State Data requires approximately 400 MB of space. You must back it up to a tape, a folder on the local computer, or a shared folder on a server.

2. If you plan to back up to tape, insert a tape into the tape drive.

3. If you plan to back up to a folder, verify that you have enough available disk space. Create the folder.

4. From the Start menu, choose All Programs→Accessories→System Tools→Backup.

5. Click Next.

6. Verify that Back Up Files And Settings is selected and click Next.

7. On the What To Back Up page, select Let Me Choose What To Back Up.

8. Click Next.

9. Below Items To Back Up, expand My Computer and check System State.

10. Click Next.

11. On the Backup Type, Destination, and Name page, complete the following tasks:

    a. From the Select The Backup Type drop-down list, select the type of backup you want to create (if you do not have a local tape backup device, your only choice will be File).

    b. Next to Choose A Place To Save Your Backup, click Browse to browse for the folder in which you will store the backup. If you're backing up to file, you must store the System State Data backup on a hard disk because you will need approximately 400 MB of storage space.

    c. In the Type A Name For This Backup text box, type a name for the backup file.

    d. Click Next.

12. To create the backup using the default settings, click Finish (click Advanced if you want to specify any other backup options).

13. Review the Backup Progress dialog box to verify that the backup completed successfully.

14. Click Close to close the Backup Progress dialog box.

Windows 98 and System State Data

Windows 98 automatically uses the Windows Registry Checker (scanreg.exe) to make backup copies of the Registry, account information, protocol bindings, software program settings, and user preferences on a daily basis. If the Registry becomes corrupt, you can use the scanreg program in MS-DOS mode to restore the previous day's backup of this information.

TOPIC F
Back Up the Registry

In Topic 19E, you learned how to perform a backup of a computer's system state data, which does include a backup of the computer's Registry. In some cases, though, you might want to back up a computer's Registry but not all of its system state data. Further, neither Windows 9x nor Windows NT include an option for backing up a computer's system state data. Instead, you'll have to manually back up these computers' Registries in order to be prepared for a disaster. In this topic, you'll learn the exact steps for backing up a computer's Registry.

There are a number of situations in which you'll need to manually back up a computer's Registry. For example, you should always perform a backup of the Registry before making any changes to it. That way, you can restore this backup if you make a mistake during the editing process. In another example, you might want to back up a Windows 9x or Windows NT computer's Registry so that you can have its configuration information at the ready in the event of a system failure.

How to Back Up the Registry

Procedure Reference: Back Up a Registry Key with Registry Editor

To back up a Registry key with Registry Editor in Windows 2000, Windows XP, Windows NT, or Windows 98:

 You also back up the Registry when you create an emergency repair disk for these operating systems or back up the system state data.

1. Log on as a local administrator.
2. From the Start menu, choose Run.
3. In the Open text box, type `regedit` and click OK. Using the 16-bit version of Registry Editor (regedit.exe) makes it easier for you to back up the entire Registry.
4. In the left pane, select My Computer.
5. In Windows 2000, Windows NT, and Windows 98, choose Registry→Export Registry File.
6. In Windows XP, choose File→Export.
7. From the Save In drop-down list, select the folder in which you want to store the backup.
8. In the File Name text box, type a name for the backup file.

9. Below Export Range, verify that All is selected.

10. Click Save.

11. Close Registry Editor.

12. In Windows Explorer, verify that the backup file was created successfully.

Procedure Reference: Back Up the Registry with Windows NT Backup

To back up the entire Registry with Windows NT Backup:

The Registry is backed up automatically in Windows 98 and Windows XP when you perform a system state data backup.

1. Log on as a user who's either a member of the Backup Operators or Administrators groups, owner of a file, or a user who has at least the Read NTFS permissions to back up file data.

2. Insert a tape into the tape drive.

3. In Backup, select at least one file on the partition on which the operating system is installed. For example, if Windows NT is on the D drive, create a job to back up a single file on that drive.

4. Click Backup.

5. In the Options dialog box, check Back Up Windows Registry.

6. Configure any necessary backup options.
   - Check Verify After Backup if you want Windows NT Backup to verify the accuracy of the backup.
   - Check Restrict Access To Owner Or Administrator if you want to restrict restoring the files in the backup to either the owner of the files or the Administrator.

7. In the Description text box, type a description for the backup.

8. From the Backup Type drop-down list, select the type of backup you want to perform. Windows NT supports the following backup types:
   - Normal
   - Copy
   - Differential
   - Incremental
   - Daily

9. Below Log Information, select how much information you want to store in the backup log file.

10. Click OK to begin the backup.

11. When the backup is complete, click OK to close the Verify Status dialog box.

12. Close Windows NT Backup.

Procedure Reference: Back Up the Registry with Windows 98 Backup

To back up the Registry with Windows 98 Backup:

1. Create and save a backup job to back up at least one file on the partition on which the operating system is installed. For example, if Windows 98 is on the C drive, create a job to back up a single file on that drive.
2. In Backup, open the backup job.
3. Below How To Back Up, click Options.
4. Select the Advanced tab.
5. Check Back Up Windows Registry and click OK.
6. Choose Job→Save to save the changes to your backup job.
7. If you want to run the backup now, click Start.
8. Close Backup.

Topic G
Prepare for an Automated System Recovery

Up to this point in the chapter, you've been working with the various tools for preparing for disaster and creating a variety of backups that you can use to recover a computer if disaster strikes. But, despite your best efforts to protect your users' computers, you're bound to encounter a situation where your only choice is to completely re-install the computer—a true disaster! The good news is that Windows XP includes a tool called Automated System Recovery that makes it much easier for you to recover in the event of just such a failure, and that's what you'll learn about in this topic.

Take a moment to think about what you would do if you were faced with a computer that has crashed and you're unable to do anything with it. You're unable to boot the computer using a boot disk, so you can't restore any user or system state data. What would you do? Your first instinct might be to re-install Windows XP and then begin the process of restoring your backups. But wait—there's a better way! If you've prepared the computer for an Automated System Recovery, you'll be able to save yourself a lot of work and time because you'll be able to rebuild the computer to its configuration before the crash.

Automated System Recovery Process

Automated System Recovery (ASR) is a process that uses backup data and the Windows XP Professional installation source files to rebuild a failed computer system. To perform ASR, you will need:

- The Windows XP Professional installation CD-ROM.
- An ASR floppy disk, which contains files with the information Windows Setup needs to run ASR recovery.

- An ASR backup set, created with Windows Backup, that contains a complete copy of the Windows XP Professional system files and all configuration information.

You should be aware that an ASR backup set does not include any data from the computer. If you want to return the failed computer to its original state, you will also need to restore a backup of the user data.

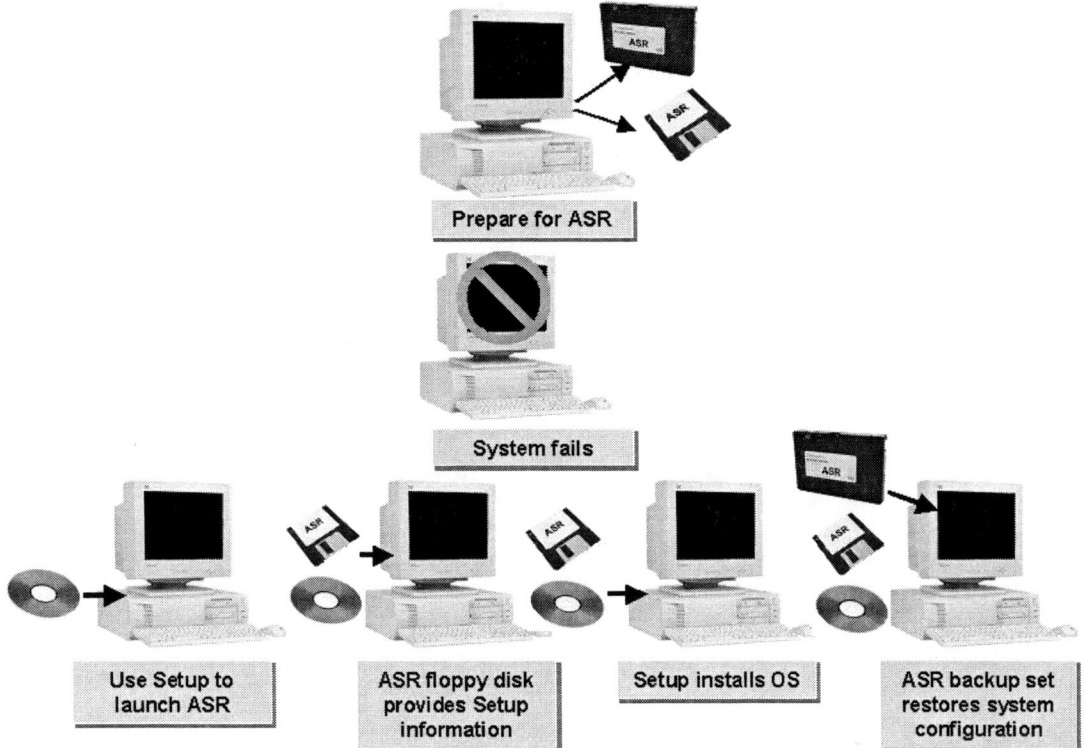

Figure 19-5: *The ASR process.*

The ASR process consists of the following phases:

1. You use Windows Backup to create an ASR backup set and ASR floppy disk.
   - The ASR backup set must be stored on local backup media, not on a network drive.
   - The ASR backup set cannot be stored on the same hard disk as the Windows XP Professional installation, as this disk can be re-initialized during the ASR process.
2. A system suffers a complete and catastrophic failure. For example, the hard disk completely fails.
3. You select a computer to use to restore the system.
4. You run Windows Setup from the Windows XP installation CD-ROM, and initiate ASR.
5. You provide the ASR floppy disk.
6. The computer passes the information in the ASR floppy disk to Windows Setup.
7. Windows Setup installs the operating system as specified on the ASR floppy disk.
8. You provide the ASR backup set.

9. ASR configures the computer according to the information in the backup set.

How to Prepare for an Automated System Recovery

Procedure Reference: Prepare for an ASR

To prepare for an ASR:

1. Log on as a local administrator.
2. Format a floppy disk, and verify that you have enough space on your backup media to hold the complete Windows XP Professional backup (between 1 and 2 GB of data).
3. Run Windows Backup.
4. On the Welcome page, click Advanced Mode.
5. Click Automated System Recovery Wizard.
6. Click Next.
7. Select a backup location and enter a name for the backup file. Click Next.
8. Click Finish. Backup creates the backup set.
9. When prompted, insert the formatted floppy disk and click OK.
10. Click OK to close the message box when the floppy disk creation is complete.
11. Click Close to close the Backup Progress dialog box.
12. Close Backup.
13. Remove the floppy disk and backup media and store them in a safe location.

Procedure Reference: Prepare for an ASR with a Complete Backup

To create an ASR backup set in addition to a complete system backup:

1. Log on as a local administrator.
2. Format a floppy disk, and verify that you have enough space on your backup media to hold the complete Windows XP Professional backup (between 1 and 2 GB of data).
3. Run Windows Backup in Wizard mode.
4. Click Next.
5. On the Backup Or Restore page, verify that Back Up Files And Settings is selected and click Next.
6. Select All Information On This Computer and click Next. You will need enough storage space on your backup media to back up the complete contents of your computer (including all data and application files).
7. Follow the prompts in the wizard to create the ASR floppy disk, ASR backup set, and a backup set with your computer's information.

8. Close Backup.
9. Remove the floppy disk and backup media and store them in a safe location.

CHAPTER 19 FOLLOW-UP
Preparing for Disaster Recovery

In this chapter, you learned tasks such as creating boot disks and emergency repair disks, backing up, and preparing for an Automated System Recovery. By mastering these skills, you can be prepared for any disaster that might head your way. And by being prepared, you can get a computer up and running much quicker, which reduces the computer's downtime.

Essential Terms

- ASR
- backup media
- backup types
- boot disks
- boot files
- boot sector
- disaster recovery
- ERDs
- file attributes
- installation boot disks
- partitions
- Recovery Console
- Registry
- system partitions
- system recovery
- system state data
- user data

Review Questions

1. What is the first task you should perform when preparing for disaster recovery?
2. What are the MS-DOS boot files?
3. What is the function of Msdos.sys?
4. What is the purpose of config.sys?
5. What kind of MS-DOS commands are built into the Command.com file?
6. What is the function of Command.com?
7. When you turn on a computer, the system performs a power-on self test (POST). What is the purpose of the POST rountine?
8. What is the Master Boot Record (MBR)?
9. What is contained in the boot sector?
10. How is the Msdos.sys file loaded into memory?
11. Which MS-DOS boot file processes the commands in the Config.sys file?
12. Which MS-DOS boot file calls and processes the commands in the Autoexec.bat file?
13. In Windows 9x, what replaces the Autoexec.bat file in the boot process?

14. What file is present on Windows 9x that is used to set environment parameters for applications written to run on Windows 3.1?
15. What is the function of Windows 9x's Win.com?
16. In Windows NT/2000 and XP, which boot file loads the operating system?
17. What Windows NT/2000/XP boot file is used to build the boot menu in a dual boot configuration?
18. What boot file must be present to load a non-Windows NT/2000/XP operating system from the boot menu?
19. What boot file examines the computer's hardware, builds a hardware list, and passes the list to Ntldr?
20. Which Windows NT/2000/XP boot file loads the basic operating system kernel?
21. Windows NT, 2000, and XP use the same boot process. What are the two phases of the boot process?
22. What are the four load phases in the second stage of the Windows NT/2000/XP boot sequence?
23. What initiates the kernel load phase?
24. When is a NT/2000/XP boot considered complete?
25. What files are stored in the system partition of a computer running Windows NT/2000/XP?
26. What four files are located on the system partition on a Windows NT/2000/XP computer?
27. What files are stored on the boot partition of a Windows NT/2000/XP machine?
28. What is the function of the Advanced RISC Computing (ARC) naming syntax?
29. What is the syntax for ARC path naming?
30. In Windows NT 4.0 and Windows 2000, what kind of disk contains information about the current configuration of the operating system?
31. What emergency repair utility is avaiable on Windows 2000 and Windows XP?
32. What are the four backup types supported by Windows NT/2000/XP and Windows 9x?
33. Windows 2000 and XP include the option to back up system state data. What components are included in a system state backup?
34. Windows XP includes a tool to rebuild a failed computer system. What tool is it?
35. To perform an Automated System Recovery of Windows XP, what will you need?

Review Projects

Project #1 Automated System Recovery Process

Windows XP Professional includes the Automatic System Recovery Process (ASR), which enables you to recover the operating system in the event of a catastrophe. Your readings introduced you to ASR and detailed how you should prepare for an ASR. The InfiniSource Web site reinforces the material covered in your readings and augments it with images of the setup and restore procedures. To view the descriptions and images on InfiniSource's site, go to **http://www.windows-help.net/WindowsXP/howto-18.html**. Bookmark this site and use it as a supplement to the ASR procedures outlined in your text.

Project #2 Windows XP System Restore

Microsoft XP's system restore feature enables administrators to restore the operating system to a previous state in the event of a disaster. Archived on Microsoft's site is a white paper that describes how ASD monitors the system and creates restore points so the system can revert to a time prior to a system failure.

There are two parts to this activity. In the first part, read the white paper located at **http://msdn.microsoft.com/library/default.asp?url=/library/en-us/dnwxp/html/windowsxpsystemrestore.asp**. Your objective is to gain a general understanding of how the operating system is able to protect itself in the event of a catastrophe. Included in this white paper is a section on interoperability. At this point, you've been introduced to several recovery features and this section will help you better understand how the different recovery options work together to maintain a stable computing environment.

In the second part, investigate the features of Last Known Good and Driver Rollback. Using XP's Help and Support Center located off the Start menu, search for the documentation for each utility and read it. Test both utilities. For Last Known Good you simply reboot the computer and when you see "Please select the operating system to start," press F8. Use the arrow keys to highlight Last Known Good Configuration and press Enter. To test driver rollback, download a driver for a component on your machine such as the sound card. Note: Make sure the sound card driver is compatible with your sound card since this exercise is designed to step you through the process of using driver rollback only. Install the driver by following the prompts. Reboot the computer if you are prompted. Once you log back on to the computer, open Device Manager and locate your sound card. Right-click the sound card and choose Properties. Click the Driver Rollback option and follow the operating system's prompts.

Project #3 Creating Boot Disks

A mainstay of any A+ technician's toolkit is a boot disk. Ideally, you should have a boot disk for every operating system on which you are qualified to work. As pointed out in your readings, you should be well-prepared in the event a system crashes. You may be able to start a system using a boot disk so you can then isolate and repair the point of failure.

The Microsoft article, "How to Create a Bootable for an NTFS or FAT Partition," focuses on Window NT and Windows 2000. Specifically, the article addresses how to create a Windows boot disk to access a drive with a faulty boot sequence. The troubleshooting section located toward the end of the article is particularly valuable. Microsoft documents three common errors that may occur when you try to use the boot disk. You should be aware of the solutions they present.

The objective of this activity is to create the boot disks as outlined in the support article. Either copy the article into a word processing program and save it to disk or print a copy for reference.

At the bottom of the article, there are links that direct you to support articles about making boot disks for other operating systems. Read through each article. Document any information that supplements your course readings. The Microsoft article offered some extra details that you will find valuable when working with Windows NT and Windows 2000. There is another option for locating and creating boot disks. The bootdisk.com Web site offers boot disks that you may download. To evaluate what the Web site offers, navigate to **http://www.bootdisk.com**. You should download and test any boot disk before using it on another person's computer.

Reflective Questions

1. Which techniques presented in this chapter do you currently use in your work environment? Why?

2. What types of disasters have you encountered with computers?

CHAPTER 20
Recovering from Disaster

Chapter Objectives:

In this chapter, you will recover from disaster.

You will:

- Troubleshoot an application.
- Troubleshoot hard disks.
- Restore user data.
- Restore the Registry.
- Restore system state data.
- Recover boot sector files.
- Perform an automated system recovery.

Introduction

In the last chapter, you saw all the steps you should take to prepare for disaster. In this chapter, you'll learn what to do if disaster strikes. You'll begin by troubleshooting applications and a computer that won't boot, move on to how you restore any type of backup, and then master the steps for performing an Automated System Recovery.

As an A+ technician, you can know everything possible about preparing for disaster recovery, but the true test is to actually repair the computer after the disaster strikes. You will be expected to get the computer back up and running as quickly as possible.

TOPIC A
Troubleshoot an Application

Earlier in the course, you learned how to install and configure both Windows and non-Windows applications. Most of the time, installing and configuring an application is all you need to do to get your users up and running. But no application always runs perfectly, and there will be instances in which you'll need to fix a problem. In this topic, you'll learn the skills necessary to troubleshoot an application that isn't working correctly.

An application that doesn't work properly is probably one of the most common problems users face. All too often, system lockups, lost data, and unexplained crashes have their origins in an application that is experiencing problems. Being able to diagnose and fix the problem enables you to respond quickly when an application fails, which means you'll be able to get your users back up and running as soon as possible.

Common Problems

There are many problems you can encounter when troubleshooting applications. Table 20-1 lists the symptoms of problems you can expect to encounter.

Table 20-1: *Common Application Problems*

Symptom	Suspected Problem
Application won't install	You're trying to install an application that needs to overwrite a file that is currently in use on the computer.
Application won't start or load	The application was installed incorrectly, a version conflict between the application and other applications on the computer exists, or your computer is experiencing memory access errors.
Event log is full	The application or system logs have filled up because of too many error messages.

Symptom	Suspected Problem
General Protection Fault	An application is accessing RAM that another application is using or the application is attempting to access a memory address that doesn't exist.
Illegal operation	An application is attempting to perform an action that Windows does not permit. Windows forces the application to close.
Invalid working directory	The application can't find the directory for storing its temporary files (typically \Temp). This can happen if you delete the folder that an application needs for storing its temporary files.
System lock up (Windows 98), Blue screen (Windows 2000/NT/XP)	The computer has too many instructions to process at once given its available RAM and processor resources.
Windows Protection Error	Windows did not load a virtual device driver properly. This error typically occurs at startup or shutdown.

Troubleshooting Tools

The Windows operating systems contain tools and techniques you can use to assist you in troubleshooting problems with applications. In Table 20-2, you see a list of these tools, an analysis of the information they give you, and the operating systems in which they're included.

Table 20-2: *Troubleshooting Tools*

Suspected Problem	Tool/Technique	Analysis	Supported Operating Systems
Open files are keeping you from installing an application.	Close all open applications.	An open application can prevent you from installing an application. Close all applications before starting the installation.	Windows 2000, Windows XP, Windows NT, and Windows 98

Chapter 20: Recovering from Disaster

Suspected Problem	Tool/Technique	Analysis	Supported Operating Systems
Application was installed incorrectly or a version conflict between this application and other applications on the computer exists.	Add/Remove Programs	You can use Add/Remove Programs to install or remove applications. Depending on the application, you might also be able to use Add/Remove Programs to repair the installation of the application.	Windows 2000, Windows XP, Windows NT, and Windows 98
The computer is experiencing memory access errors.	Close Program dialog box	Enables you to view a list of applications currently running on your computer. You can also close any applications that aren't responding.	Windows 98
Windows did not load a device driver properly.	Device Manager	Enables you to view the status of the computer's hardware devices.	Windows 2000, Windows XP, Windows NT, and Windows 98
An application is attempting to access RAM that another application is using or an address that doesn't exist in RAM; an application is attempting to perform an action that Windows does not permit.	Dr. Watson	Provides you with detailed information when an application hangs or ends abnormally. You can run Dr. Watson by choosing Start→Run and entering `drwatson` in the Open text box. Dr. Watson runs in the background and displays information only if you experience a problem with an application.	Windows 2000, Windows XP, Windows NT, and Windows 98

Suspected Problem	Tool/Technique	Analysis	Supported Operating Systems
An application won't install, start, or load.	Event Viewer	Enables you to determine if an application has reported any errors in the Application or System logs.	Windows 2000, Windows XP, and Windows NT
An application won't start or load; Windows did not load a device driver properly.	Expand.exe	Manually extract files from the Windows installation CD-ROM; use these files to replace corrupted system files on the hard disk (you must use Expand.exe because the files are stored in a compressed format on the Windows CD-ROM).	Windows 2000, Windows XP, Windows NT, and Windows 98
An application won't install, start, or load.	Registry Editor	Enables you to view and modify your computer's Registry.	Windows 2000, Windows XP, Windows NT, and Windows 98
An application won't start or load.	Setver	Configure the version of DOS Windows reports to a program (use Setver to simulate an older version of DOS if an application won't run in Windows 2000/XP/NT).	Windows 2000, Windows XP, Windows NT, and Windows 98
An application won't start or load.	System Configuration Utility (MSConfig)	Edit your computer's configuration files.	Windows 98
System lock up or blue screen.	System Properties (in Control Panel)	Use to determine the version of the operating system and which Service Packs are installed.	Windows 2000, Windows XP, and Windows NT (you can use System Properties in Windows 98 to determine the version of Windows installed, but not any patches).

Chapter 20: Recovering from Disaster

Suspected Problem	Tool/Technique	Analysis	Supported Operating Systems
The computer is experiencing memory access errors.	Task Manager	Enables you to list the applications currently running on the computer. You can also use Task Manager to close an application that isn't responding.	Windows 2000, Windows XP, and Windows NT

Application Compatibility

If you are using Windows XP, and you are experiencing problems running an application that was written for an earlier version of Windows, you can run the Application Compatibility Wizard to configure customized operating system settings and display settings for a particular application. You can run the Application Compatibility Wizard from the Accessories group on the All Programs menu.

Web Sites for Troubleshooting Information

Microsoft has several very good Web sites that you can use to research the error messages you encounter on a Windows computer. The Microsoft Help and Support Web site, as shown in Figure 20-1, provides you with access to the Knowledge Base, software downloads, and more. Most importantly, you can use the Knowledge Base to research specific error messages you see. In many cases, Microsoft will provide the solution for this error as well. You can access the Help and Support Web site by going to **support.microsoft.com**.

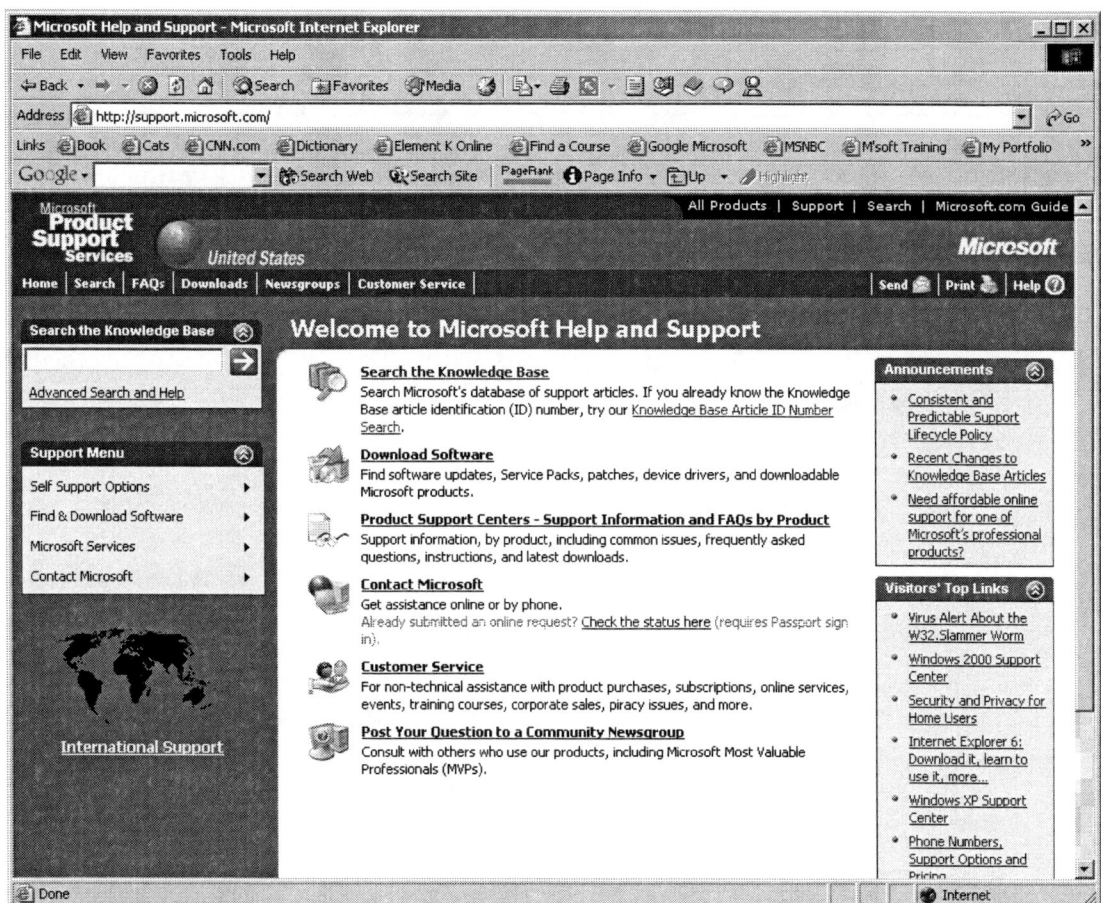

Figure 20-1: *The Microsoft Help and Support Web site.*

Another good Web site to use when troubleshooting is Microsoft Technet. You can access Microsoft Technet by going to **www.microsoft.com/technet**. This Web site also has information you can use to research error messages. In addition, it has the product manuals and Resource Kits (additional documentation) for each Windows operating system.

Finally, you should make sure that you bookmark the Microsoft Web sites for each Windows operating system. In Table 20-3, you see each Windows operating system and the URL for its associated Microsoft Web site.

Table 20-3: *Windows Web Sites*

Windows Version	Web Site
Windows 98	**www.microsoft.com/windows98**
Windows NT	**www.microsoft.com/ntworkstation**
Windows 2000	**www.microsoft.com/windows2000**

Chapter 20: Recovering from Disaster

Windows Version	Web Site
Windows XP	www.microsoft.com/windowsxp

How to Troubleshoot an Application

Procedure Reference: Troubleshoot an Application

To troubleshoot an application:

 While troubleshooting applications, you should consult the manufacturer's documentation and user manuals and any relevant training materials.

1. Collect information about the problem.
   - Try running Dr. Watson and then the application to see if Dr. Watson displays any information about the error.
   - If the problem is occurring on a Windows 2000, Windows NT, or Windows XP computer, check the Application and System logs in Event Viewer to see if the application reported any errors (see the Using Event Viewer to Research Errors procedure below).
   - Use System Properties to determine which version of Windows and Service Packs are installed.
   - Use Device Manager to see if any hardware devices are reporting errors.
2. Isolate the problem.
   - Ask the user if the application ever worked. If it did, find out if anything has been changed on the computer. If it didn't, suspect a configuration problem.
   - Ask the user if she's experiencing problems with all applications or only one application. If it's only one application that's experiencing problems, suspect a problem with that application. If all applications are having problems, suspect a problem with the operating system.
   - Research the problem by using the Knowledge Base on Microsoft's Help and Support Web site or the application manufacturer's Web site.
3. Correct the problem using the following steps.
   a. If you've found a solution in the Knowledge Base or the application manufacturer's Web site, implement the solution. In some cases, Microsoft recommends that you fix a problem by editing the computer's Registry using Registry Editor. Or, you might need to download and install a patch from Microsoft or the application manufacturer's Web site. Proceed to Step 4.
   b. Install the latest Service Pack for Windows 2000, Windows NT, or Windows XP. If you're using Windows 98, connect to the Windows Update Web site and install all recommended patches. Proceed to Step 4.

c. Uninstall the application. Restart the computer. Resintall the application. Go to Step 4.

4. Test the application to verify that you've resolved the problem. If you're still experiencing the problem, return to Step 3.

5. Document the problem and its solution for future reference.

Procedure Reference: Use Windows Event Viewer to Research Errors

To use Windows Event Viewer to review the System and Application error logs in Windows 2000, Windows NT, and Windows XP:

1. Open Event Viewer.
   - If you're using Windows 2000 and Windows XP, open Computer Management. In the console tree, select Event Viewer.
   - If you're using Windows NT, from the Start menu, choose Programs→Administrative Tools→Event Viewer.

2. Open the appropriate log.
   - In Windows 2000 and Windows XP, expand Event Viewer and then select Application or System to display its contents.
   - In Windows NT, choose Log→Application or Log→System.

3. If necessary, filter the events in the Application log.
   a. If you're using Windows 2000 or Windows XP, choose View→Filter.
   b. If you're using Windows NT, choose View→Filter Events.
   c. In the Filter dialog box, select the information on which you want to filter the log. You can filter the messages in the log by any of the following information:
      - Event Source
      - Category
      - User name
      - Computer name
      - Event type (Information, Warning, Error, Success Audit, or Failure Audit)
      - Date
   d. Click OK.

4. Record the details of the error message.

5. Close all open windows.

Procedure Reference: Clear a Log File

If the Application or System logs become full, complete the following steps to clear the log file:

1. Open Event Viewer.

2. Select the log that's full.
3. Back up the log file.
   a. In Windows 2000 and Windows XP, choose Action→Save Log File As.

   In Windows NT, choose Log→Save As.
   b. In the File Name text box, type a name for the log file and click Save.
4. Clear the log file.
   a. In Windows 2000 and Windows XP, choose Action→Clear All Events.

   In Windows NT, choose Log→Clear All Events.
   b. When you're prompted to save the log file, click No.
5. Close all open windows.

TOPIC B
Troubleshoot Hard Disks

Throughout this course, we've been working under the assumption that everything's okay with your users' computers and their hard disks. But what should you do if you suspect a problem with a hard disk? In this topic, you'll learn the common problems you can encounter with hard disks and the troubleshooting tools you can use to diagnose these problems.

A computer without a functioning hard disk is essentially dead in the water. The computer's user won't be able to work on the computer, and thus can't complete her work. Because the hard disk is so critical to the computer, as an A+ technician, many of your technical support cases will involve troubleshooting computer hard disks. It's important that you know how to respond to these calls to quickly repair the hard disk problems so that you can get the computer back up and running and the user back to being productive on her computer.

Common Error Messages

During the boot/startup process, and at other times during normal operation, you're going to encounter a variety of error messages. Table 20-4 lists common boot error messages, Table 20-5 lists common startup error messages, and Table 20-6 lists some other common errors and messages you might see on your Windows computers.

Table 20-4: *Common Boot Error Messages*

Error Message Indicates	Suspect a Problem With the
Invalid boot disk	Hard disk, or the CD-ROM or floppy disk being used to boot the computer.
Inaccessible boot device	Hard disk or hard disk controller.

Error Message Indicates	Suspect a Problem With the
Missing NTLDR	Hard disk, floppy disk, or CD-ROM being used to boot computer. Also, check to see if there's a non-bootable floppy in the floppy drive on a Windows NT/2000/XP computer.
Bad or missing command interpreter	Hard disk or Command.com file.

Table 20-5: *Common Startup Error Messages*

Error Message Indicates	Suspect a Problem With the
Error in Config.sys line *xx*	Config.sys file at the specified line.
Himem.sys not loaded; Missing or corrupt Himem.sys	Config.sys file, or the Himem.sys file itself (missing or corrupt).
Device/Service has failed to start; Option will not function	Device drivers or resource conflicts.

Table 20-6: *Other Common Errors and Messages*

Error Message Indicates	Suspect a Problem With the
A device referenced in System.ini/Win.ini/Registry is not found	Virtual device driver (missing or damaged).
Failure to start GUI	Msdos.sys file or a missing or damaged virtual device driver.

Windows 2000/NT/XP Boot Troubleshooting Tools

Windows 2000, Windows NT, and Windows XP also include tools that you can use to troubleshoot problems with booting the computer. Table 20-7 lists these tools and a description of each.

Table 20-7: *Windows 2000/NT/XP Boot Troubleshooting Tools*

Tool	Purpose
Boot disk	You can use a Windows 2000, Windows NT, or Windows XP boot disk in the event the computer is unable to boot from the hard disk. Once you've booted the computer successfully, you can recopy any missing files to the hard disk from the boot disk.

Tool	Purpose
Emergency Repair	You can perform an emergency repair in Windows NT and Windows 2000 to correct problems with booting the computer, missing or corrupt system files, and Registry problems.
Notepad	If you change the partitioning on your hard disk, you might find that the computer can no longer boot due to the boot.ini file incorrectly pointing to the Windows boot partition. Use Notepad to edit the boot.ini file so that it points to the correct partition.
Recovery Console	You can use the Recovery Console in Windows 2000 and Windows XP to repair problems with the system and boot partitions and copy missing files.
WinMSD	Used to access diagnostic tools and system information, including OS version, system resources, devices, and services.
Recovery CD-ROM	Used to recover the operating system if it will no longer start, often used to boot and copy operating system files from a special partition on the hard drive. Shipped with most Windows computers.
imagineLAN ConfigSafe	Used to take a "snapshot" of the system and restore the system from the snapshot after a critical failure.

Automatic Skip Driver (ASD)

Windows 9x provides another tool for correcting boot problems that result from a failed device driver. Automatic Skip Driver (ASD.EXE) can identify and disable malfunctioning drivers. Run the Automatic Skip Driver Agent from the Tools menu in Microsoft Information.

How to Troubleshoot Hard Disks

Procedure Reference: Troubleshoot a Hard Disk in Windows 2000/XP/NT

To troubleshoot a hard disk in Windows 2000, Windows XP, and Windows NT:

 While troubleshooting hard disks, you should consult the manufacturer's documentation and user manuals and any relevant training materials.

1. If you suspect that a device driver you just installed is preventing the computer from booting, boot the computer with the Last Known Good boot option. Use these steps:

    a. Restart the computer. If necessary, turn the computer off and back on.

b. If you're using Windows 2000 or Windows NT, select the appropriate operating system from the boot menu and press the Spacebar. From the options menu, select Last Known Good.

c. If you're using Windows XP (or if you're using a computer configured to dual boot between Windows XP and Windows 2000 or Windows NT), press F8 after the computer completes the POST. From the Advanced Options Menu, choose Last Known Good Configuration.

d. Start the operating system and log on. Windows automatically restores the last known good Registry information, so the problem should now be resolved.

2. Determine if it is a hardware or software failure.

Use a Windows 2000, Windows XP, or Windows NT boot disk to attempt to boot the computer.

- If Windows 2000, Windows XP, or Windows NT loads successfully, the failure is most likely due to one of the following:
    - An error in the ARC paths in the Boot.ini file.
    - A problem with the Windows 2000, Windows XP, or Windows NT system partition.
- If the operating system fails to load, the failure is most likely due to one of the following:
    - A hardware problem.
    - An error in the ARC paths in the Boot.ini file.
    - A problem with the Windows 2000, Windows XP, or Windows NT system partition.

3. If you suspect the hard disk problem is a hardware failure, complete the following tasks:

a. Verify that the IDE or SCSI hard disk is on the Windows Hardware Compatibility List (HCL). You can check the HCL by going to **http://www.microsoft.com/hwdq/hcl/**.

b. If the computer has an IDE drive:
- Check for bad cables and connectors.
- Verify that the driver for the disk controller is not corrupt or missing.
- Verify that the jumpers are configured correctly.
- Verify the hard disk's BIOS settings: Boot into the computer's CMOS setup utility and verify that the number of heads, cylinders, and sectors per track are set correctly.

c. If the computer has a SCSI drive:
- Check for bad cables.
- Check for incorrect termination.
- Verify the SCSI identifier for the hard disk is correct.

- Disable sync negotiation in the SCSI BIOS.

d. Try installing the hard disk in a computer that you know is not experiencing any problems:

- If the good computer can't access the disk, the hard disk has failed. Replace the disk.
- If the good computer can access the disk, troubleshoot other hardware in the original computer such as the hard disk controller and power supply.

4. Use an MS-DOS boot disk with the Fdisk utility to verify the partitions on the hard disk. Make sure that the appropriate primary partition is marked active.

5. If you suspect that some of the computer's boot files are missing or corrupt, or that the boot.ini file points to the wrong partition, complete the following tasks:

   a. Use the appropriate Windows 2000, Windows XP, or Windows NT boot disk to boot the computer.
   b. Log on as a local administrator.
   c. Correct the problem by replacing the corrupted file with a good copy from the boot floppy disk or by modifying the incorrect entries in the Boot.ini file.
   d. Restart the computer. It should boot normally.

6. If you suspect a problem with the Boot.ini file, edit the ARC paths in the Boot.ini file. To edit the Boot.ini file:

   Windows numbers all primary partitions on the disk first, and then any extended partitions.

   a. Use Disk Management in Windows 2000 and Windows XP or Disk Administrator in Windows NT to determine the partitions on the computer's hard disk. Identify the disk number and the partition number on which Windows 2000, Windows XP, or Windows NT is installed.
   b. Open Windows Explorer.
   c. If necessary, if you're using Windows 2000 or Windows XP, configure Windows Explorer to display system and hidden files.
      1. Select the C drive.
      2. In Windows Explorer, choose Tools→Folder Options.
      3. Select the View tab.
      4. Below Hidden Files And Folders, select Show Hidden Files And Folders.
      5. Uncheck Hide File Extensions For Known File Types.
      6. Uncheck Hide Protected Operating System Files (Recommended).
      7. Click OK.

   If necessary, if you're using Windows NT, configure Windows Explorer to display system and hidden files.
      1. Select the C drive.

2. In Windows Explorer, choose View→Options.
3. Below Hidden Files, choose Show All Files.
4. Uncheck Hide File Extensions For Known File Types.
5. Click OK.
   d. Remove the Read-Only attribute from the Boot.ini file.
   e. Double-click C:\Boot.ini to open it in Notepad.
   f. Change the ARC naming paths to accurately reflect the computer's partitions.
   g. Save your changes.
   h. Restart the computer to verify that the change resolved the problem.
   i. Copy the revised Boot.ini file to the boot disk.
7. If you suspect a problem with the system partition and the computer can boot to Windows, complete the following steps:
   a. Use Disk Management (Windows 2000/XP) or Disk Administrator (Windows NT) to verify that the C partition is marked active.
   b. Re-write the master boot record and boot sector information by using an Emergency Repair (in Windows 2000 and Windows NT) or the Recovery Console (in Windows XP).
8. If the computer attempts to boot but hangs, use the Safe Mode boot options:
   a. Restart the computer (turn the power off and on if necessary).
   b. After the POST phase of the boot sequence, and during the display of the boot menu (if you have one), press F8.
   c. Select the desired Safe Mode boot option from the menu. Use Table 20-8 as a guide.
   d. Log on as a local administrator.
   e. Click Yes in the Safe Mode message box.
   f. Use the appropriate troubleshooting steps to correct the problem. For example, re-install or update a corrupt device driver, copy or delete files, modify a system setting, or uninstall a service or application.
   g. Reboot to normal mode.

Table 20-8: *Safe Mode Boot Options*

Option	Description	Use When
Safe Mode	Starts the computer with a minimal set of drivers and services, including the mouse, keyboard, VGA display, and hard disk.	The problem might be with the networking components.

Option	Description	Use When
Safe Mode with Networking	Starts the computer with the Safe Mode drivers and services, along with the networking drivers and services.	You need to access the network to repair the problem.
Safe Mode with Command Prompt	Starts the computer with the Safe Mode drivers and services, and a command prompt interface.	A problem is preventing Windows from displaying the graphical desktop.

9. Check the event logs for errors.
   a. Log on as a local administrator.
   b. If you're using Windows 2000 or Windows XP, right-click My Computer and choose Manage. Below System Tools, expand Event Viewer.
   c. If you're using Windows NT, from the Start menu, choose Programs→Administrative Tools→Event Viewer.
   d. Review the Application, Security, and System logs for any Warning and Error messages. Look for the most recent messages (these are the messages at the beginning of the log).
   e. Look for any Information events just before the Warning or Error messages; these events might give you a clue as to what was changed on the system prior to the Warning or Error.
   f. After you identify the first event that triggered the problem, review the event's description (along with any related events) to determine the problem's cause.
   g. Research specific error messages by using Microsoft's Knowledge Base at **support.microsoft.com**.
   h. If possible, fix the problem.

10. If the computer is able to boot but the user is experiencing intermittent problems with the disk, or disk access is slow, complete the following steps:
    a. Check the System log in Event Viewer to determine if any disk errors have been recorded by Windows. Such errors could indicate that the disk is failing.
    b. If you're using Windows 2000 or Windows XP, update the driver for the hard disk.
       1. In Device Manager, expand Disk Drives.
       2. Right-click the hard disk and choose Properties.
       3. Select the Driver tab.
       4. Click Update Driver.

c. If you're using Windows 2000 or Windows XP, use Disk Cleanup to remove unnecessary files from the hard disk.

1. In Windows Explorer, right-click the disk and choose Properties.
2. Click Disk Cleanup.
3. On the Disk Cleanup page, check the check boxes for any categories of files that you want to clean up. Disk Cleanup displays the number of KB in the category; if you want to see the actual files you will be deleting, click View Files.
4. To compress old files, check Compress Old Files and click Options to set the length of the expiration window.
5. Click OK to perform the disk cleanup.
6. Click Yes to confirm.

d. Defragment the hard disk.

11. If you're using Windows XP and all else fails, perform an Automated System Recovery (see Topic 20G).

Procedure Reference: Troubleshoot a Hard Disk in Windows 98

To troubleshoot a hard disk in Windows 98:

1. If necessary, create an MS-DOS boot disk on another Windows 98 computer. Include the following files on this boot disk:
   - Attrib.exe
   - Edit.com
   - Edit.hlp
   - Fdisk.exe
   - Format.com
   - Scandisk.exe
   - Scandisk.ini
   - Sys.com

2. Attempt to boot the computer with the MS-DOS boot disk.

3. If the computer will not boot at all, complete the following steps:
   a. If the computer boots from the floppy disk, the problem is with the boot files for Windows 98.
   b. If the computer still won't boot, the problem is with the hardware.

4. If you suspect the hard disk problem is a hardware failure:

   For IDE drives:
   - Check for bad cables and connectors.
   - Verify the driver for the disk controller is not corrupt or missing.

- Verify the jumpers are connected correctly.
- Verify the hard disk's BIOS settings.

  Boot into the system BIOS, verify the # of heads, cylinders, and sectors per track are set correctly.

For SCSI drives:
- Check for bad cables.
- Check for incorrect termination.
- Verify the SCSI identifier for the hard disk is correct.
- Disable sync negotiation in the SCSI BIOS.

5. If the computer boots from an MS-DOS boot disk, run Fdisk and complete the following steps:
   a. Verify that a primary partition exists on the C drive.
   b. Verify that the primary partition is marked active (bootable).
   c. Test to see if the computer can boot now.

   ⚠ If you create a new partition, any data that was previously stored on the hard disk will be erased.

6. If Fdisk doesn't find any partitions on the hard disk, complete the following steps:
   a. Create a primary partition.
   b. Mark the primary partition active.
   c. Exit Fdisk and restart the computer.
   d. At the A: prompt, enter `format c: /s` to format the C drive and make it bootable.
   e. Test to see if the computer can boot now.

7. If Fdisk finds a primary partition that is marked active, complete the following steps:
   a. At the A: prompt, enter `fdisk /mbr` to repair the master boot record on the C drive.
   b. At the A: prompt, enter `sys c:` to re-copy the system files to the C drive.
   c. Test to see if the computer can boot now.

8. If the computer attempts to boot but hangs, use the boot options:
   a. Restart the computer (turn the power off and on if necessary).
   b. After the POST phase of the boot sequence, when you see a flashing cursor at the top of the screen, press and hold F8 (if you have configured the computer to dual-boot, you can press F8 when you see the boot menu).
   c. Select the desired boot option from the menu. Use Table 20-9 as a guide.
   d. Log on as a local administrator.

e. Click Yes in the Safe Mode message box.

f. Use the appropriate troubleshooting steps to correct the problem. For example, re-install or update a corrupt device driver, copy or delete files, modify a system setting, or uninstall a service or application.

g. Reboot to normal mode.

Table 20-9: *Windows 98 Boot Options*

Option	Description	Use When
Command Prompt Only	Does not load the Windows 98 graphical interface.	You want to access the computer's hard disk in order to copy new files to the disk or delete files.
Logged (\Bootlog.txt)	Starts Windows 98 normally, but stores a record of whether Windows 9x components loaded successfully in the Bootlog.txt file.	You want to determine if a device driver isn't loading successfully.
Safe Mode	Starts the computer with a minimal set of drivers and services, including the mouse, keyboard, VGA display, and hard disk.	The problem might be with the networking components.
Safe Mode with Networking Support	Starts the computer with the Safe Mode drivers and services, along with the networking drivers and services.	You need to access the network to repair the problem.
Safe Mode Command Prompt Only	Starts the computer with the Safe Mode drivers and services, and a command prompt interface.	A problem is preventing Windows from displaying the graphical desktop.
Step-by-Step Confirmation	Loads drivers in Config.sys, Autoexec.bat, and Windows 98 one line at a time, enabling you to select which drivers should load.	You suspect that a faulty driver is preventing Windows 98 from booting.

9. If the above steps don't resolve the problem, suspect a problem with the computer's hardware. Things to check include:

   - Replacing the hard disk with a hard disk that you know to be good. If the computer boots successfully from this new hard disk, replace the failed hard disk with a new hard disk.

- If the computer does not boot successfully from a hard disk that you know to be good, try replacing the drive cable and plugging in a different power cable.
- If the computer still does not boot successfully, try installing the hard disk you suspect has failed into a computer that you know boots successfully. If the new computer boots from the hard disk, the problem is with the old computer's hardware. If the new computer does not boot successfully from the hard disk, replace it.

10. If the computer hangs during the startup of Windows 98, complete the following steps:
    a. Check the computer's CMOS settings for a virus protection feature. Some computers have a BIOS setting that prevents applications from modifying the boot sector of the startup disk. Windows 9x must modify the boot sector during Setup or the first time it runs. Disable the virus protection feature by using the computer's CMOS setup.
    b. Use an MS-DOS boot disk to boot the computer. Disable any real-mode drivers in the autoexec.bat and config.sys files. If this resolves the problem, make sure that the devices with real-mode drivers aren't using the same system resources as other devices. Try to obtain new Windows 9x drivers for these devices.
    c. If the problem occurs after you installed device drivers intended for an older version of Windows (such as Windows 3.1), use Sysedit to remove the entries in the System.ini that were added by the device driver's installation software. If the device is displayed in Device Manager, delete it. Restart Windows 98 and use the Add New Hardware Wizard to re-install the device using Windows 98-compatible drivers.

11. If you see the message *Bad or missing <filename>* during startup, complete the following tasks:
    a. Use Sysedit to check the syntax of the entry in the startup file (for example, config.sys).
    b. Verify that the file Windows 98 is attempting to load is stored in the right folder.
    c. Verify that the file is the correct version.
    d. If you suspect that the file might be corrupted, try replacing the file with a known good version from another computer or from a backup set.

12. If you receive a message stating that the Registry is missing or corrupt and you are unable to access Windows 98, complete these steps:
    a. Restart Windows 98.
    b. During the boot process, press and hold the Ctrl key until the Microsoft Windows 98 Startup menu is displayed.
    c. Select Command Prompt only.
    d. At the MS-DOS command prompt, enter `scanreg /restore`.
    e. Select the backup set you want to restore and click Restore.

13. If you receive a message stating that the Registry is missing or corrupt and you are able to access Windows 98, complete these steps:
    a. Restart Windows 98 using the Restart In MS-DOS Mode option.

      b.   At the MS-DOS command prompt, enter `scanreg /restore`.

      c.   Select the backup set you want to restore and click Restore.

14. If you have a particular device that isn't functioning correctly, perform the following steps:

    a. Run Device Manager and display the device's Properties dialog box (from the Start menu, choose Settings→Control Panel. Double-click System. Select the Device Manager tab).

    b. In the Properties dialog box for the device, select the Resources tab.

    c. Look at the Conflicting Device List. Verify that there aren't any resource conflicts.

    d. If you see a resource conflict, try changing the settings as needed. You can also run the Hardware Troubleshooter in Windows Help to obtain assistance in troubleshooting resource conflicts.

    e. If you are unable to resolve the conflicts, remove the device in Device Manager and re-install it by using the Add New Hardware Wizard.

15. If the computer boots to a command prompt instead of Windows 9x, complete the following steps:

    a. Verify the operating system is installed on the computer by entering `ver`.

    b. Make sure that the Msdos.sys file is present in the C:\ folder. If necessary, use `dir C:\ /ah` to display hidden files.

    c. Verify that the Msdos.sys file has not been corrupted:

        1. From the Start menu, choose Programs→Accessories→System Tools→System Information.

        2. Choose Tools→System File Checker.

        3. Select Scan For Altered Files and click Start. If the System File Checker detects an altered system file, it will prompt you to restore the original file from the Windows 98 installation CD-ROM.

    d. Verify that a virtual device driver (VxD) is not the cause of the problem. (If a VxD is preventing Windows 98 from booting, you'll see an error message stating which VxD is causing the problem.) If a VxD is the problem, re-install Windows 98 and choose the Verify or Safe Recovery option to restore the faulty VxD.

16. If the computer boots into Windows 98 but reports disk errors, try the following:

    - Run ScanDisk to examine your disk for invalid file names, file dates, and times, bad sectors, and invalid compression structures, as well as lost, invalid, and cross-linked clusters.

    - If you are running Windows 98, run the Maintenance Wizard to check your hard disk for problems.

Run ScanDisk in Windows 9x

To run ScanDisk from an MS-DOS prompt:

1. Boot to MS-DOS.

2. Enter `scandisk drive:`, where `drive` is the drive letter of the partition you're troubleshooting.

   📌 *A version of scandisk is in the \Windows folder.*

3. Press Enter.
4. If prompted to perform a surface scan, use the arrow keys to select either Yes to perform the scan or No to skip the scan.
5. Use the arrow keys to select Exit.

To run ScanDisk from Windows 9x:

1. Choose Start→Programs→Accessories→System Tools→ScanDisk.
2. In the drives list box, select the drive(s) you want to check for errors.

   📌 *You can use the Shift or Ctrl keys to select multiple disks in the drives list box.*

3. In the Type Of Test box, select Standard or Thorough.
4. If you select Thorough, click the Options button to select the following:
   - Change the area of the disk to scan from System And Data Areas to either System Area Only or Data Area Only.
   - Disable write-testing by checking the Do Not Perform Write Testing check box.
   - Disable repairing bad sectors in hidden and system files by checking the Do Not Repair Bad Sectors In Hidden And System Files check box.

   Click OK to close the Surface Scan Options dialog box.
5. Click the Advanced button to change the following default options:
   - Change Display Summary from Always to either Never or Only if Errors Found.
   - Change Log File from Replace Log to either Append To Log or No Log.
   - Change Cross-linked Files from Make Copies to either Delete or Ignore.
   - Change Lost File Fragments from Convert To Files to Free.
   - Change Check Files For Invalid File Names to also include Invalid Dates and Times and/or Duplicate Names, or to disable Invalid File Names.
   - Disable Check Host Drive First.
   - Enable Report MS-DOS Mode Name Length Errors.

   Click OK to close the ScanDisk options dialog box.
6. If you want Window 9x to automatically fix errors that it finds, check the Automatically Fix Errors check box.
7. Click Start.
8. Click Close to close the ScanDisk Results dialog box.
9. Click Close to close the ScanDisk dialog box.

Run the Maintenance Wizard in Windows 9x

To run the Maintenance Wizard on a Windows 98 computer:

1. Choose Start→Programs→Accessories→System Tools→Maintenance Wizard.
2. Select either Express or Custom. Express completes the following tasks:
   - Defragments your hard disk to speed up your most frequently used programs.
   - Checks your hard disk for errors.
   - Deletes unnecessary files from the hard disk.

   Custom allows you to select your own maintenance tasks.
3. Select one of the following times to run maintenance tasks:
   - Nights—Midnight to 3:00 A.M.
   - Days—Noon to 3:00 P.M.
   - Evenings—8:00 P.M. to 11:00 P.M.
   - Custom—Use current settings (this option is available only if you select Custom in Step 2).

   The computer must be on to run maintenance tasks.

   Click Next.
4. If you selected Custom, select either Yes, Defragment My Disk Regularly or No, Do Not Defragment My Disk.

   If you selected Yes, Defragment My Disk Regularly, use the Reschedule button to alter the default schedule for the defragmentation task. Use the Settings button to change the default drive to defragment.

   Click Next.
5. If you selected Custom, select either Yes, Scan My Hard Disk For Errors Regularly or No, Do Not Scan My Hard Disk For Errors.

   If you selected Yes, Scan My Hard Disk For Errors Regularly, use the Reschedule button to alter the default schedule for the disk scan task. Use the Settings button to change the default drive to scan and scan options.

   Click Next.
6. If you selected Custom, select either Yes, Delete Unnecessary Files Regularly or No, Do Not Delete Unnecessary Files.

   If you selected Yes, Delete Unnecessary Files Regularly, use the Reschedule button to alter the default schedule for the file removal task. Use the Settings button to change the default types of files to remove. Check the check boxes of the file types you want Windows 98 to delete.

   Click Next.

7. If you want to run the maintenance tasks immediately, check the When I Click Finish, Perform Each Scheduled Task For The First Time check box.

8. Click Finish.

Topic C
Restore Data

In Chapter 11, you learned how to back up data so that it's available to you to restore on a user's computer. You'll need this backup in the event the computer crashes or the computer's user accidentally deletes files that he needs. In this topic, you'll learn how to go about restoring your backup of the data.

Nothing will panic a user more than the thought that he's lost some (or even all) of his data. In fact, most users consider the loss of their data the worst possible thing that can happen to them on a computer. As an A+ technician, your job requires that you know how to restore data in just such an emergency.

How to Restore Data

Procedure Reference: Restore Data in Windows 2000

To restore data in Windows 2000:

1. Log on as a user who's either a member of the Backup Operators or Administrators groups, owner of a file, or a user who has at least the Write NTFS permissions to restore file data.

2. Load your backup media.

3. Run Backup.

4. Click Restore Wizard.

5. Click Next.

6. Below What To Restore, expand the backup media (File or Tape).

7. Check the backup set stored on the backup media that you want to restore.

8. Click Next.

9. If you want to configure advanced options such as the destination for the restored files, what you want Backup to do if the files already exist on the computer's hard disk, and whether you want to restore security permissions, click Advanced.

10. Click Finish to restore the backup.

11. Click OK to confirm that you have inserted the backup media.

12. Click Close to close the Restore Progress dialog box.

13. Close Backup.

14. Verify that the files, folders, or both were restored successfully.

Procedure Reference: Restore Data in Windows XP

To restore data in Windows XP:

1. Log on as a user who's either a member of the Backup Operators or Administrators groups, owner of a file, or a user who has at least the Write NTFS permissions to restore file data.
2. Load your backup media.
3. Run Backup.
4. Click Next.
5. Select Restore Files And Settings and click Next.
6. Below Items To Restore, expand the backup media (File or Tape).
7. Expand the backup set you want to restore.
8. Check the files and folders you want to restore from the backup set.
9. Click Next.
10. If you want to configure advanced options such as the destination for the restored files, what you want Backup to do if the files already exist on the computer's hard disk, and whether you want to restore security permissions, click Advanced.
11. Click Finish to restore the backup.
12. Click Close to close the Restore Progress dialog box.
13. Close Backup.
14. Verify that the files, folders, or both were restored successfully.

Procedure Reference: Restore Data in Windows NT

To restore data in Windows NT:

1. Log on as a user who's either a member of the Backup Operators or Administrators groups, owner of a file, or a user who has at least the Write NTFS permissions to restore file data.
2. Load your backup media.
3. Run Backup.
4. Click Restore Wizard.
5. Click Next.
6. Below What To Restore, expand the backup media (File or Tape).
7. Check the backup set stored on the backup media that you want to restore.
8. Click Next.

9. If you want to configure advanced options such as the destination for the restored files, what you want Backup to do if the files already exist on the computer's hard disk, and whether you want to restore security permissions, click Advanced.

10. Click Finish to restore the backup.

11. Click OK to confirm that you have inserted the backup media.

12. Click Close to close the Restore Progress dialog box.

13. Close Backup.

14. Verify that the files, folders, or both were restored successfully.

Procedure Reference: Restore Data in Windows 98

To restore data in Windows 98:

1. Load your backup media.

2. Run Backup (Msbackup.exe) from the System Tools menu.

3. Select Restore Backed Up Files and click OK.

4. From the Restore From drop-down list, select your backup media.

5. If necessary, in the text box, type the path and name of the backup file.

6. Click Next.

7. In the Select Backup Sets dialog box, check the backup set(s) you want to restore and click OK.

8. Below What To Restore, check the files and folders you want to restore.

9. Click Next.

10. From the Where To Restore drop-down list, select where you want to restore the files and click Next.

11. On the How To Restore page, select one of the following:
    - Do Not Replace The File On My Computer (Recommended), if you don't want to restore the backup over the files currently on your computer's hard disk.
    - Replace The File On My Computer Only If The File Is Older, to have Backup restore the files over the copies on your computer only if the files on your computer are older than the ones within the backup set.
    - Always Replace The File On My Computer, if you want to have the files in the backup set replace the files on your computer (regardless of the date stamp on the files).

12. Click Start to begin the restore.

13. Click OK to confirm that you have inserted the backup media.

14. Click OK to close the Operation Completed message box.

15. Click OK to close the Restore Progress dialog box.
16. Close Backup.
17. Verify that the files, folders, or both were restored successfully.

TOPIC D
Restore the Registry

In Topic 20C, you learned how to restore a user's data in the event of a computer crash or accidental deletion of files. But restoring user data files doesn't restore the operating system's configuration information. If you need to restore the operating system's configuration, one technique you can use is to restore a backup of the Registry—and that's what you'll learn how to do in this topic.

Without the Registry, or if the Registry becomes corrupt, a user's computer won't have the information it needs to properly load the operating system. Losing the Registry is like losing the detailed driving directions you got from the American Automobile Association for a month-long cross country trip. Without these directions, you won't know which roads to take. Without the Registry, a computer won't know what device drivers and services to load, nor will it know how the user's applications are configured. Because the Registry is so critical to the Windows operating systems, it's essential that you as an A+ technician know the steps to restore it so that you can get the computer back up and running.

How to Restore the Registry

Procedure Reference: Restore the Registry from a Registry Editor Backup

To restore the Registry from a Registry Editor backup:

1. If you can't start Windows in normal mode, boot to Safe Mode.
2. If you're using Windows 2000, Windows XP, or Windows NT, log on as a local administrator.
3. Verify that you have a backup of the Registry that was created with Registry Editor (regedit.exe).
4. Run Regedit.exe (from the Start menu, choose Run. In the Open text box, type regedit.exe and click OK).
5. In the left pane, select My Computer.
6. Choose Registry→Import Registry File.
7. From the Look In drop-down list, select the drive on which you stored the Registry backup.

   You might see an error message stating that not all Registry keys were imported. Registry Editor can't overwrite the portions of the Registry that are currently in use.

8. Select the backup file and click Open. Registry Editor will import the Registry backup.

9. Click OK to close the Successful Import message.
10. Close Registry Editor.
11. Restart the computer.
12. When the computer has restarted, log back on and verify that the problem has been corrected.

Procedure Reference: Restore the Registry from a Windows NT Backup

To restore the Registry from a Windows NT Backup:

1. Insert the media with your Registry backup.
2. Open Backup.
3. Click Close to close the Microsoft Backup dialog box.
4. Select the Restore tab.
5. Click Yes to have Backup refresh the information it displays in the Restore window.
6. In the Select Backup Sets dialog box, check the backup set containing the Registry backup and click OK.
7. Below What To Restore, select at least one file to restore.
8. Click Options.
9. Select the Advanced tab.
10. Check Restore Windows Registry and click OK.
11. Click Start to begin the restore.
12. Click OK to confirm that you have inserted the backup media.
13. Click Yes to confirm that you want to restore the Windows Registry.
14. In the Microsoft Backup message box, select one of the following:
    - Click Yes if you want to restore the hardware and system settings configuration in the Registry. You don't have to restore these settings if they haven't changed since the last Registry backup.
    - Click No if you do not want to restore the hardware and system settings configuration in the Registry.
15. Click OK to close the Operation Completed message box.
16. If any errors are reported, click Report to view the log file. Close the log file when you're done reviewing it.
17. Click OK to close the Restore Progress dialog box.
18. Click Yes to restart the computer.

Procedure Reference: Restore the Registry from a Windows 98 Backup

To restore the Registry from a Windows 98 backup:

1. Insert the media with your Registry backup.
2. Open Backup.
3. Click Close to close the Microsoft Backup dialog box.
4. Select the Restore tab.
5. Click Yes to have Backup refresh the information it displays in the Restore window.
6. In the Select Backup Sets dialog box, check the backup set containing the Registry backup and click OK.
7. Below What To Restore, select at least one file to restore.
8. Click Options.
9. Select the Advanced tab.
10. Check Restore Windows Registry and click OK.
11. Click Start to begin the restore.
12. Click OK to confirm that you have inserted the backup media.
13. Click Yes to confirm that you want to restore the Windows Registry.
14. In the Microsoft Backup message box, select one of the following:
    - Click Yes if you want to restore the hardware and system settings configuration in the Registry. You don't have to restore these settings if they haven't changed since the last Registry backup.
    - Click No if you do not want to restore the hardware and system settings configuration in the Registry.
15. Click OK to close the Operation Completed message box.
16. If any errors are reported, click Report to view the log file. Close the log file when you're done reviewing it.
17. Click OK to close the Restore Progress dialog box.
18. Click Yes to restart the computer.

System Restore

If you are using Windows XP, you can use System Restore to restore a variety of system settings, including the Registry. The System Restore feature creates restore points, which are snapshots of the system configuration at a given moment in time. The system automatically creates restore points in response to significant system events, such as program installation. You can also create restore points manually.

TOPIC E
Restore System State Data

In Topic 20D, you learned how to restore a computer's Registry in case disaster strikes. In Windows 2000 and Windows XP, however, you have another choice for restoring the Registry (along with other critical operating system information): restoring a system state data backup. In this topic, you'll master the steps for doing just that.

A computer's system state data provides the "how to" instructions for configuring the operating system when the computer boots. Without this information, the computer potentially won't have what it needs to load the necessary drivers and services for the computer to function. In fact, it's possible that the computer won't even boot if the system state data is lost. Enter you, the A+ technician, to the rescue: By mastering the skills in this topic, you'll know just what to do to restore the system state data quickly so that the computer functions normally.

How to Restore System State Data

Procedure Reference: Restore System State Data in Windows 2000

To restore System State data in Windows 2000:

1. If you can't start Windows 2000 in normal mode, boot to Safe Mode.
2. Log on as a local administrator.
3. Load your backup media.
4. Run Backup.
5. Click Restore Wizard.
6. Click Next.
7. If you don't see the backup set containing the System State Data backup, click Import File. In the Catalog Backup File text box, type the path and file name for the backup file and click OK.
8. Below What To Restore, complete the following steps:
   a. Expand the backup media (File or Tape).
   b. Expand the backup set you want to restore.
   c. Check System State.
9. Click Next.
10. Click Finish to restore the backup.
11. Click OK to confirm that you have inserted the backup media.
12. Click Close to close the Restore Progress dialog box.
13. Click Yes to restart the computer (you might need to close some processes manually).
14. When the computer reboots, log on and verify that the problem has been corrected.

Procedure Reference: Restore System State Data in Windows XP

To restore System State Data in Windows XP:

1. Log on as a local administrator.
2. If you can't start Windows XP in normal mode, boot to Safe Mode.
3. Load your backup media.
4. Run Backup.
5. Click Next.
6. Select Restore Files And Settings and click Next.
7. If you don't see the backup set containing the System State Data backup, click Import File. In the Catalog Backup File text box, type the path and file name for the backup file and click OK.
8. Below What To Restore, complete the following steps:
   a. Expand the backup media (File or Tape).
   b. Expand the backup set you want to restore.
   c. Check System State.
9. Click Next.
10. Click Finish to restore the backup.
11. Click Close to close the Restore Progress dialog box.
12. Click Yes to restart the computer. (You might need to close some processes manually.)
13. When the computer reboots, log on and verify that the problem has been corrected.

TOPIC F
Recover Boot Sector Files

In Topic 20E, you learned how to recover a computer's System State Data, part of which includes the computer's boot sector files. If you have a computer that won't boot and you know it's due to one or more missing boot files, or the computer has one of the older operating systems such as Windows NT or Windows 9x, you can use other techniques to repair the computer. In this topic, you'll learn how to recover corrupt or missing boot files in all of the Windows operating systems.

It's not uncommon for a user to accidentally delete some of the files his computer needs to boot the operating system. Or, in another scenario, a virus can corrupt a computer's boot files. In a third example, installing and partitioning a new hard disk might make Windows 2000, Windows NT, or Windows XP unable to find the operating system files to complete loading the operating system. In all of these cases, your best and quickest method for repairing these computers is to recover their boot sector files.

How to Recover Boot Sector Files

Procedure Reference: Use Recovery Console to Repair Windows XP

To use Recovery Console to Repair Windows XP:

1. Boot to the Recovery Console.
   - If you have installed the Recovery Console as a boot option, restart the computer and select Recovery Console from the boot menu.
   - If you haven't installed the Recovery Console as a boot option, boot the computer from the Windows XP Professional CD-ROM. On the Welcome To Setup screen, press R to boot to the Recovery Console.
2. When prompted, enter the number of the Windows XP Professional installation to which you want to log on.
3. Enter the Administrator user's password to log on.
4. Use the appropriate Recovery Console commands to correct the system problem. Refer to Table 20-10 for examples.
5. Enter `exit` to end your Recovery Console session and restart the computer.
6. Verify that Windows XP works correctly by logging on.

Table 20-10: *Recovery Console Examples*

Situation	How to Fix
You need to re-create the boot sector or the master boot record.	Use the `fixboot` or `fixmbr` commands.
A boot file is missing or corrupt and you don't have a boot disk.	Replace the missing file by using the `expand` command to extract a compressed copy of the file from the installation CD-ROM, or the `copy` command to copy the file from another location.
A system file or a device driver file is missing or corrupt.	Replace the file from the installation media for Windows XP Professional or for the device.
There is a problem with a Safe Mode driver or service.	Use the `disable` command to disable the service or driver, and then replace the files.
The pagefile is corrupt.	Use the `delete` command to delete the pagefile.sys file.

Procedure Reference: Perform an Emergency Repair in Windows 2000

To perform an emergency repair in Windows 2000:

Do not attempt an emergency repair on a computer configured to dual boot between Windows 2000 or Windows NT and Windows XP. Doing so will replace the system files installed by Windows XP with the older Windows 2000 or Windows NT system files—which will prevent Windows XP from loading.

1. Boot the computer from the Windows 2000 Professional installation CD-ROM.

   If you don't have a bootable CD-ROM drive, use the `makeboot.exe` (if you're using a 16-bit operating system) or `makeboot32.exe` (if you're using a 32-bit operating system) command to create the three setup boot floppies. Boot the computer from the first floppy disk.

2. When prompted, press R to repair a Windows 2000 installation.

3. Press M to select a manual repair.

4. Select the repair tasks you want to perform:
   - Inspect Startup Environment
   - Verify Windows 2000 System Files
   - Inspect Boot Sector

   By default, all three repair tasks are selected. Press the Spacebar to deselect a task.

5. Select Continue.

6. Press Enter to indicate that you have an Emergency Repair Disk (ERD).

7. Insert the ERD and press Enter. Setup begins the emergency repair process.

8. Remove the ERD when you see the countdown bar for the system to restart.

9. Boot to Windows 2000 and verify that you can log on.

10. Re-apply any Service Packs or hotfixes for Windows 2000 (when you run an emergency repair, it will replace any updated Windows 2000 files with the original versions from the installation CD-ROM. This means that if you've updated Windows 2000 with a Service Pack, the emergency repair process will replace those files with the original files. You should always re-apply any Service Packs or hotfixes after performing an emergency repair).

Procedure Reference: Performing an Emergency Repair in Windows NT

To perform an emergency repair in Windows NT:

1. Insert the Windows NT installation CD-ROM into the computer's CD-ROM drive.

2. Insert the Windows NT Setup boot disk.

3. If the computer is currently running, restart the computer. Otherwise, turn on the computer.

4. When prompted, press R for Repair.

5. Select the desired repair options by using the check boxes. The four options are described in Table 20-11.

Table 20-11: *Windows NT Repair Options*

Option	Description
Inspect Registry Files	You are able to select the Registry trees you want to repair. The Setup program will replace the selected trees with the backup copies contained on your emergency repair disk (this means that all changes made to the Registry since you last updated the emergency repair disk will be lost).
Inspect Startup Environment	If you have Windows NT 4.0 installed on your computer and it does not appear in the list of bootable systems, select this option.
Verify Windows NT System Files	This option verifies the existence and integrity of all Windows NT system files. The repair process has the ability to replace the missing or corrupt files after verification from the user, or to automatically replace all missing or corrupt files.
Inspect Boot Sector	When you cannot boot to any operating system installed on your computer, use this option to replace the boot sector on your disk.

6. When prompted, insert the emergency repair disk.
7. Verify, replace, or reinstall files as necessary.
8. Remove the ERD when the repair is complete.
9. Boot to Windows NT and verify that you can log on.
10. Re-apply any Service Packs or hotfixes for Windows NT.

Topic G
Perform an Automated System Recovery

In Chapter 11, you learned the steps for creating an Automated System Recovery (ASR) backup set for a Windows XP-based computer. In this chapter, you've learned the steps you can take to attempt to recover the computer without performing an ASR. But if all else fails and you're unable to recover the computer, it's time for you to perform an ASR. In this topic, you'll learn the procedures for recovering a computer with ASR.

If you're unable to recover a Windows XP computer by restoring user and system state data, you have two choices to get the computer up and running: You can completely re-install the computer's operating system and then attempt to restore whatever user and system state data backups you have, or you can perform an Automated System Recovery (ASR). Although an ASR is essentially a process for re-installing the operating system, it does offer you one distinct advantage: ASR will attempt to salvage whatever it can of the operating system's configuration.

How to Perform an Automated System Recovery

Procedure Reference: Perform an ASR

To perform an ASR:

1. Run the Windows Setup program by booting from the Windows XP Professional installation CD-ROM, or by running the `winnt32.exe` command manually.

2. When the Press [F2] To Run Automated System Recovery (ASR) message is displayed in the status bar, press F2. This message disappears quickly.

3. When prompted, insert the ASR boot floppy disk and press any key (you can also start the ASR with this disk already in the floppy disk drive).

4. If prompted, press C to confirm that your disk partitions will be deleted and re-created. This is necessary on dynamic disks to prepare them for operating system installation (you can't install Windows XP Professional on a dynamic disk). ASR will convert the disks back to dynamic later on.

5. When prompted, after the disk is scanned and configured, Windows Setup runs, and the Automated System Recovery Wizard runs, insert the ASR backup media.

6. Complete the Automated System Recovery Wizard; ASR will automatically restore the ASR backup set.

 To support unattended system recovery, the screens in the Automated System Recovery Wizard will automatically advance after a time-out.

7. If you are prompted for an installation directory (for example, if ASR is restoring to a clean hard disk), provide the path (typically, C:\Windows). When the installation and restoration are complete, the computer will restart.

8. Log on and verify the computer works properly.

CHAPTER 20 FOLLOW-UP
Recovering from Disaster

In this chapter, you learned how to perform the tasks necessary to recover after a disaster. Specifically, you learned how to troubleshoot problems with applications and computers' hard disks. You also learned how to restore backups of data, the Registry, and System State data, and how to perform an emergency repair. Finally, you learned how to recover a failed Windows XP computer by performing an Automated System Recovery. As an A+ technician, you'll need these skills so that you can respond to troubleshooting support calls and get your clients' computers back up and running after a failure.

Essential Terms

- applications
- ASR
- boot sector
- disaster recovery
- hard disks
- Registry
- restoring data
- system state data
- troubleshooting
- troubleshooting tools

Review Questions

1. What kind of problem exists when an application accesses RAM that another application is using?
2. When does an illegal operation occur?
3. Why would you receive an application error message indicating there's an invalid working directory?
4. What error would you expect to occur if Windows did not load a virtual device driver properly?
5. You're having trouble starting an application. What utility is available in Windows NT/2000/XP that enables you to see if an application has reported any errors?
6. What utility would you use to investigate an application's memory access errors?
7. What utility enables you to access the Registry on a Windows 2000 machine?
8. A user informs you that there are intermittent problems while using a specific application. What utility should you use to capture information about the application?
9. What do you suspect is the problem when an error message indicates a device referenced in System.ini/win.ini/registry is not found?
10. In Windows 2000 and XP, what utility would you use to repair problems with the system and boot partitions?
11. What troubleshooting tool is used to take a "snapshot" of the system and restore the system from the snapshot after a critical failure?
12. You install a new device driver for a component and then restart the system. The system stops loading and displays a STOP message before the logon box displays. What troubleshooting option should you use so the system boots correctly?

13. A computer user using Windows NT 4.0 made some changes to the disk partition layout and now the computer cannot load the operating system. You suspect a problem with the ARC path in the boot.ini file. How does Windows number partitions?

14. You access the boot.ini file on the system partition of your Windows 2000 machine. You make a change to the ARC path but the change is not saved to the file. What's wrong?

15. In Windows NT and Windows 2000 what would you use to rewrite the master boot record and boot sector information?

16. What are the safe mode boot options?

17. In Windows 2000 and XP what utility would you use to remove unnecessary files from the hard disk?

18. After a Windows 98 computer POSTs, what key should you press to enter safe mode?

19. On a Windows 98 machine what boot option would you use when you want to determine if a device driver isn't loading successfully?

20. When would you use the Step-by-Step confirmation boot option in Windows 98?

21. If your computer boots into Windows 98 but reports disk errors, what should you try first?

22. What tasks does the Maintenance Wizard perform in Windows 98?

23. In recovery console, what commands would you use to re-create the boot or the master boot record?

24. You want to make the three setup boot floppies for a Windows 2000 computer. What command creates the three disks?

25. What are the four repair options available on a Windows NT system?

26. To perform an automated system recovery on a Windows XP machine, what key do you press when the ASR message is displayed in the status bar during boot up?

Review Projects

Project #1 Data Recovery Software

Disasters strike and the effects can be costly. Recovering from a disaster requires that you have a plan and the resources to help you get a system back up and in working order. However, what happens if you find yourself unprepared for a particular disaster? For example, if a curious user stumbled upon disk management and accidently reformatted a partition containing sensitive data, what would you do? If there is a recent backup, you can restore the data, but what happens if the restore process stops because the backup is corrupt? Can this happen? Yes.

Although you always should back up data and perform test restores to verify the backup's integrity, recovery software may prove invaluable in emergency situations. This exercise focuses on the recovery software, GetDataBack, which is available from Runtime Software. Their Web address is **http://www.runtime.org**. GetDataBack is recovery software that can help you retrieve data lost because of corruption or accident.

Download an evaluation copy of the data recovery software for either the FAT or NTFS file system. You will need two computers to perform the following activity. Install the software. Read the documentation. Runtime's documentation for their products is exhaustive. Runtime provides evaluation software for examination. To see how well the software works, create a small partition on your hard drive, format it, and populate it with unimportant files. Use GetDataBack to simulate the retrieval of the lost data. Because you are using an evaluation copy and not a fully licensed one, you will not be able to recover the lost data. You will, however, be able to perform all the steps in the recovery process and see the data that would be recovered by the full version.

Project #2 Recovery Console Overview

Microsoft includes an impressive range of troubleshooting utilities in both Windows 2000 and Windows XP. In many situations, safe mode and other startup options can be used to troubleshoot various problems. However, if a system won't boot, you can't access the safe mode advanced options. If you have administrator rights, you can use the recovery console to perform repair operations as well as a variety of administrative tasks.

The documentation on recovery console is located at **http://www.microsoft.com/technet/treeview/ default.asp?url=/technet/prodtechnol/winxppro/proddocs/recovery_console_overview.asp**. This takes you to the recovery console main page. In this activity, you'll install recovery console on your Windows 2000 or Windows XP machine. Although you can start the recovery console using the CD-ROM, in this activity you should install recovery console as a startup option. It will display as a boot option when it's installed. Once recovery console is installed, access the console (you'll need the administrator name and password). Recovery console is very similar to working at a command prompt. There is no GUI to help you navigate configuration screens. Experiment with the console by using some of the commands (do not make changes that may disable or corrupt your system). Based on the commands, what kinds of operations do you think recovery console would be best suited for? (There's a list on commands on the Web page and also in the operating system help files.) If there are commands unfamiliar to you, look them up either on Microsoft's Web site or in the help documentation.

Project #3 Windows XP's Support Tools

Windows XP Professional ships with Support Tools. To access the folder, insert the Windows XP Professional CD-ROM into the drive. Double-click SupTools.msi to launch the Support Tools wizard. After you accept the license agreement, you'll be prompted to perform either a typical or a complete installation. Choose complete and accept the default path for installation. Once the installation completes, you'll notice that Windows support tools is listed under Programs off the Start manu (Start→ Programs→Windows Support Tools). Open the release notes to view information about the tools. Next, open the Support Tools Help which is listed off the Windows Support Tools folder. This will open an alphabetical listing of the tools. Click a link to learn about a tool and its syntax. Return to the Windows Support Tools folder located off the Start menu and click the Command Prompt option. The command prompt will open at the Support Tools folder. For any support tool, enter the name of the tool followed by /?. This will display the command's syntax. Each support tool performs a specific function. Depending on your setup, some of the tools will not apply. However, using XP's Help and Support Center, examine several of the support tools and experiment with some of them at the command line.

- What tools did you use?
- What actions did they enable you to perform?

Document your results and save them to a sub-folder under your Hardware documentation directory

Reflective Questions

1. What types of disasters have you encountered with regards to computers? How did you respond?

2. What is your experience with restoring data from backup?

CHAPTER 21
Installing Client Operating Systems

Chapter Objectives:

In this chapter, you will install client operating systems.

You will:

- Install a Windows client operating system.
- Upgrade from an older Windows operating system to a newer Windows operating system.
- Troubleshoot operating system installations.
- Add or remove operating system components.

Introduction

Throughout this course, you've been learning how to configure and troubleshoot all of the Windows operating systems. You've learned how to connect these operating systems to a network, how to secure their resources, manage and share file and print resources, and manage their hard disks. Now, it's time to use this knowledge you've gained in how to configure these operating systems by learning how to install them from scratch or upgrade them. So, in this chapter, you'll learn how to install the Windows 98, Windows 2000, and Windows XP operating systems. You'll also learn how to upgrade Windows 98 to Windows 2000 or Windows XP, and how to upgrade Windows 2000 to Windows XP.

Without a properly installed operating system, your users' computers will not function. Although most new computers come straight from the manufacturer with an operating system loaded, you will encounter situations in which the operating system will need to be re-installed or upgraded on existing systems.

TOPIC A
Install a Windows Client Operating System

So far in this course, you've learned the steps you must take to configure the various components of each Windows operating system. For example, you learned how to manage Windows 98, Windows 2000, and Windows XP computers' file and print resources. Now it's time for you to learn the steps for installing each operating system from scratch, and that's what you'll learn in this topic.

Knowing how to perform a Windows 98, Windows 2000, or Windows XP installation from scratch is an important part of an A+ technician's toolkit. You need to know how to install a computer from scratch in case you're redeploying a computer from one user to another. You also need to know how to re-install a Windows client operating system when all of your other troubleshooting techniques fail. Although re-installing a Windows client operating system should be your last option for recovering a failed computer, it's an invaluable option nonetheless.

Windows Operating Systems Features

Each new release of the Windows operating systems brings you new and enhanced features. In Table 21-1, you see a list of the features available in Windows 98. Windows 2000 supports all of the features in Windows 98 and adds new features. In Table 21-2, you'll find a list of the features of Windows 2000. Likewise, Windows XP supports all of the features in Windows 2000—but adds new features. You'll find the features of Windows XP in Table 21-3.

Table 21-1: *Features of Windows 98*

Feature	Enables You To
Active Desktop	Display Web pages on your desktop.
Easier Internet Access	Connect to the Internet by typing a URL in any window in Windows 98 or even the taskbar and save Web pages for offline use.

Feature	Enables You To
Multiple Monitor Support	Increase the size of your desktop by configuring the computer to display on two monitors.
Outlook Express	Send and receive POP3, IMAP, and HTTP email.
Quick Launch Toolbar	Run applications by clicking their icons in the taskbar.
Task Scheduler	Automate tasks on your computer.
Tighter Integration with Internet Features	Open items on the computer by clicking a link instead of double-clicking it; navigate through folders using the Forward and Back buttons; and use a Web page as the background for a window.
Troubleshooters	Quickly diagnose problems.
USB Support	Easily install (or remove) devices from USB ports.

Table 21-2: *Features of Windows 2000*

Feature	Description
Active Directory	A directory service that provides access to all objects and resources in a Windows 2000 domain environment.
Backup	Backup supports a wide variety of storage media, such as tape drives, external hard disks, Zip drives, recordable CD-ROMs, and logical drives.
Disk Quotas	Provides a method for managing storage space by enabling you to limit users' disk space.
Encrypting File System (EFS)	Enables you to encrypt files on an NTFS partition.
Microsoft Management Console	Microsoft's new standard interface for all system administration tools. It's the framework that supports specialized tools, called snap-ins, each of which is designed to provide specific management capabilities.
Plug and Play support	Provides support for automatic and dynamic reconfiguration of installed hardware, removable devices, a New Hardware Wizard, and an enhanced Device Manager.

Feature	Description
Power management functionality	These features include system power management, device power management, processor power management, battery management, thermal management, and application-level power management.
Task Scheduler	A graphical utility that makes it easy for you to automate tasks such as backing up the computer.

 Windows NT does not support disk quotas, file encryption, backing up to media other than tapes, and Plug and Play. In addition, Windows NT does not include the Microsoft Management Console or Task Scheduler utilities.

Table 21-3: *Features of Windows XP*

Feature	Description
Adaptive Start menu	The Start menu automatically adapts to the way you work. The programs you use most frequently are listed first on the Start menu.
Consolidated taskbar	If you open multiple files within the same application (such as Microsoft Word), Windows XP consolidates all open windows for that application on the taskbar.
Dramatically reduced reboot requirements	In Windows 2000, many changes you make to the computer's configuration require you to reboot the computer. In Windows XP, many of these same scenarios no longer require you to reboot the computer.
New visual design	The user interface is redesigned in Windows XP to make it easier to perform tasks. For example, common management tasks are grouped together in Control Panel. In addition, Microsoft added new visual cues to help you navigate more easily.
User State Migration Tool	A utility that enables you to easily migrate a user's data, application settings, and operating system settings from an old computer to a new Windows XP computer.
Windows Installer service	A service that helps you track, upgrade, and remove software programs correctly from the computer.

Installation Requirements

Each Windows operating system has different hardware requirements. In Table 21-4, we list the hardware requirements for installing Windows 98. In Table 21-5, you'll find the minimum hardware requirements for Windows 2000 Professional; in Table 21-6, you see the hardware requirements for Windows XP Professional. Keep in mind that these tables list the minimum requirements for installing the respective operating system. For optimal performance, your computer should exceed these hardware requirements. You should also check the Windows Hardware Compatibility List on Microsoft's Web site at **http://www.microsoft.com/hwdq/hcl/**.

Table 21-4: *Windows 98 Hardware Requirements*

Hardware	Minimum Requirement
Processor	486DX 66 MHz
RAM	16 MB
Hard disk	At least 225 MB of free space
Video adapter	VGA
Installation source	CD-ROM or DVD-ROM (without one of these drives, you must install Windows 98 using floppy disks)
Pointing device	Mouse

Table 21-5: *Windows 2000 Professional Hardware Requirements*

Hardware	Minimum Requirement
Processor	Pentium 133 MHz
RAM	32 MB (64 MB recommended)
Hard disk	2 GB with 1 GB free space
Video adapter	VGA
Installation source	12X CD-ROM
Pointing device	Mouse

Table 21-6: *Windows XP Professional Hardware Requirements*

Hardware	Minimum Requirement
Processor	Pentium 233 MHz
RAM	64 MB
Available disk space	1.5 GB
Video adapter	Super VGA

Hardware	Minimum Requirement
Installation source	CD-ROM or DVD-ROM
Pointing device	Mouse

In addition to the hardware requirements listed in Table 21-4, Table 21-5, and Table 21-6, you might find that you need the following hardware regardless of which Windows operating system you're installing:

- A sound card and speakers (or headphones).
- A modem for accessing the Internet or faxing purposes.

In many cases, you'll find that choosing an operating system for a computer is dictated by the computer's hardware. If you support users that have older hardware, using the Windows 98 operating system will typically be the best choice because of its low hardware requirements. On the other hand, if you have users with newer (and faster hardware), using either Windows 2000 or Windows XP will offer them better performance on those systems, with the added benefit of increased security.

Multiple Boot Computer

In certain environments, you might find it necessary to configure a computer with more than one operating system. This type of computer is called multiple boot because it enables you to boot the computer to more than one operating system. If you plan to configure a multiple boot computer with the Windows 98 and Windows 2000, Windows NT, or Windows XP operating systems, you must:

- Configure the C drive to use the FAT file system.
- Install Windows 98 first, and then install Windows 2000, Windows NT, or Windows XP.

If you plan to configure a multiple boot computer with the Windows 2000 and Windows NT or Windows XP operating systems, you must install the older operating system(s) first. Install the most recent operating system last. For example, if you plan to install the Windows 2000 and Windows XP operating systems on a computer, you must install Windows 2000 first, and then install Windows XP.

Windows Setup Programs

If you install a version of Windows by inserting the installation CD-ROM or by booting from a bootable CD-ROM, you'll find that the installation starts automatically for you. But what if you're connecting to installation files on a network share to perform a network installation or if you're performing an upgrade? In this scenario, you'll need to know which file to double-click to start the installation. In Table 21-7, you see the appropriate setup file to use based on the operating system you're currently using and the operating system you want to install.

Table 21-7: *Windows Setup Programs*

Operating System You're Currently Using	Operating System You're Installing	Installation File
MS-DOS	Windows 98	Setup.exe
MS-DOS	Windows 2000 or Windows XP	Winnt.exe
Windows 95	Windows 98	Setup.exe
Windows 98, Windows 2000, Windows NT, or Windows XP	Windows 2000 or Windows XP	Winnt32.exe

Windows Upgrade Paths

As technology changes and newer operating systems are released, at some point you'll probably find yourself as part of the process of deploying a new operating system. Whether you perform an upgrade or a fresh installation depends in part on whether your current operating system supports an upgrade. Table 21-8 described the upgrade paths for the Windows operating systems. If an upgrade path isn't supported, then an upgrade is not possible; the newer operating system will have to be installed over the older operating system, with the older operating system and its settings being deleted in the process.

Table 21-8: *Windows Upgrade Paths*

Current Operating System	Can be Upgraded To
Windows 95	Windows 98, Windows 2000 Professional
Windows 98	Windows 2000 Professional, Windows XP Professional
Windows NT Workstation 4.0	Windows 2000 Professional, Windows XP Professional
Windows 2000 Professional	Windows XP Professional
Windows XP Professional	None at this time

Windows Update

After you have installed an operating system on a computer, you can obtain the latest updates for that operating system by connecting to Microsoft's Windows Update Web site. This Web site is located at **windowsupdate.microsoft.com**. You can also connect to the Windows Update Web site by choosing Windows Update from the Start menu in Windows 98, Windows 2000, and Windows XP.

How to Install a Windows Client Operating System

Procedure Reference: Install Windows 98

To install Windows 98 as the only operating system on the computer:

> This procedure assumes that you do not currently have an operating system on the computer.

1. Verify that the computer's hardware meets the requirements for Windows 98.
2. If necessary, create a Windows 98 Startup disk.
   - If you have access to a Windows 98 computer, use these steps to create a Startup Disk:
     a. In Control Panel, double-click Add/Remove Programs.
     b. Select the Startup Disk tab.
     c. Click Create Disk.
     d. When prompted, insert the Windows 98 installation CD-ROM and click OK.
     e. Insert a floppy disk into the floppy disk drive.
     f. Click OK.
     g. Close Add/Remove Programs and Control Panel.
   - If you do not have access to a Windows 98 computer, but you do have access to a computer, use these steps to create a Startup Disk:
     a. On a working computer, insert the Windows 98 CD-ROM.
     b. If you see a Welcome To Windows 98 dialog box, click Exit to close it.
     c. Open Windows Explorer.
     d. Access the \Tools\Mtsutil\Fat32ebd folder.
     e. Double-click Fat32ebd.exe to create the Startup disk.
     f. When prompted, press Y and Enter to continue.
     g. When you see the message "Done," close the MS-DOS Prompt window.
     h. Write protect and label the floppy disk.
3. Insert the Windows 98 Startup disk into the computer on which you want to install Windows 98.
4. Turn on the computer. If necessary, configure the computer to attempt to boot from floppy disk first.

> You won't need to access the CD-ROM at this point in the installation.

5. When prompted, choose Start Computer Without CD-ROM Support and press Enter.
6. Use Fdisk to partition the computer's hard disk.
   a. If the computer has any existing partitions you no longer need, delete the partitions.
   b. If you want to use the FAT32 file system, enable large disk support.
   c. Create at least one primary partition and mark it active.
   d. When prompted, restart the computer (press Ctrl+Alt+Delete).

7. When prompted, choose Start Computer With CD-ROM Support and press Enter.
8. Format the computer's partitions.
    a. At the A: prompt, enter `format c: /s`.
    b. Format any additional logical drives you created by entering `format drive letter:`. For example, `format d:`.
9. Insert the Windows 98 installation CD-ROM into the computer's CD-ROM drive.
10. At the A: prompt, enter `x:\setup`, where x is the letter assigned to the computer's CD-ROM drive.
11. Press Enter to continue. ScanDisk runs to verify that the disk has no errors.
12. In ScanDisk, press X to exit.
13. The Windows 98 Setup Wizard starts. Complete the following tasks:
    a. On the License Agreement page, select I Accept The Agreement and click Next.
    b. Enter the Windows 98 product key and click Next.
    c. On the Select Directory page, choose one of the following:
        - Select C:\WINDOWS to install Windows 98 in the default folder.
        - Select Other Directory if you want to choose a different folder in which to install Windows 98.
    d. Click Next.
    e. If you chose Other Directory, enter the path to the folder in which you want to install Windows 98, and then click Next.
    f. On the Setup Options page, select one of the following options:
        - Typical
        - Portable
        - Compact
        - Custom
    g. Click Next.
    h. On the User Information page, enter the user's name and the company name. Click Next.
    i. On the Windows Components page, select one of the following:
        - Install The Most Common Components (Recommended).
        - Show Me The List Of Components So I Can Choose.
    j. Click Next.
    k. If you selected Show Me The List Of Components So I Can Choose, check the Windows components you want to install on the computer and then click Next.
    l. Select your country or region and click Next.
    m. Click Next to create a Windows 98 Startup disk.

n. When prompted, insert a blank floppy disk and click OK.

o. When the Startup disk creation is complete, remove the floppy disk and label it. Click OK.

p. Click Next. Setup will now copy the Windows 98 files to your hard disk.

> 📌 The file copy process will take several minutes.

q. When the file copy is complete, click Restart Now.

> 📌 Setup will automatically restart the computer after 15 seconds.

14. After the computer restarts, Setup will attempt to detect the hardware. When hardware detection is complete, click Restart Now to restart the computer again.

15. Click OK to close the Network message box reminding you to define a workgroup name.

16. If Setup detected a network card in the computer, on the Identification page, complete the following tasks:
    a. In the Computer Name text box, type a name for the computer.
    b. In the Workgroup Name text box, type the name of the workgroup to which you want the computer to belong.
    c. Optionally, in the Computer Description text box, type a description for the computer.
    d. Click Close.

17. In the Date/Time Properties dialog box, configure the appropriate date, time, and time zone for your location. Click Close.

18. When the installation is complete, click Restart Now.

> 📌 By default, Windows 98 assumes you want to use the name you typed on the User Information page as your user name.

19. In the User Name text box, type the user name you want to use for the computer.

20. In the Password text box, type the password you want to assign to this user.

21. Click OK.

22. In the Confirm New Password text box, re-type the password and click OK.

23. Configure the computer to connect to the Internet.

24. If necessary, install any hardware drivers that were not automatically installed during setup. For example, make sure that the drivers for devices such as sound cards, modems, and display adapters were installed correctly.
    a. Use Device Manager to view the status of these devices and to look for any devices for which Setup did not install the drivers.

b. If you need new drivers, connect to the manufacturer's Web site to download the drivers for Windows 98.

c. Use Add New Hardware in Control Panel to install the drivers that weren't installed or to install drivers for non-Plug and Play devices. To open Add New Hardware, double-click it. After Windows searches for the hardware and reports that it can't find it, select No, I Want To Select The Hardware From A List. Then select the type of hardware device and click Next. Then click Have Disk if you have the drivers on floppy disk, in a folder on the hard disk, or in a location on the network. Browse to the correct drivers and complete the wizard.

25. Update Windows 98.

    a. From the Start menu, choose Windows Update.

    b. Click Yes to install and run the Windows Update Control Package.

    c. If necessary, click Yes again.

    d. Click Scan For Updates.

    e. Click Review And Install Updates.

    f. Click Yes to continue.

    g. Follow the prompts to install the updates you want. You'll find that some of the updates are "exclusive," which means they can't be installed with other updates. If you choose to install an exclusive update, be sure to go back to the Windows Update Web site to check for other updates.

26. If necessary, restart the computer after the updates are installed.

27. If you have enough available disk space, copy the Windows 98 installation files to a folder on the hard disk.

Procedure Reference: Install Windows 2000 Professional

To install Windows 2000 Professional as the only operating system on the computer:

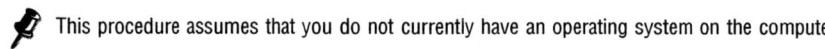
This procedure assumes that you do not currently have an operating system on the computer.

1. Verify that the computer's hardware meets the requirements for Windows.

2. Start the installation.

   - If the computer does not have a bootable CD-ROM drive, boot the computer from the first Setup disk. Use the following steps to create and use the Setup disks if you don't have them:

     a. Verify that you have three blank floppy disks.

     b. At a working computer, insert the Windows 2000 CD-ROM.

     c. If you're using Windows 9x or MS-DOS, run \bootdisk\makeboot.exe from the Windows 2000 CD-ROM to create the Setup disks.

     d. If you're using Windows 2000, Windows XP, or Windows NT, run \bootdisk\makebt32.exe from the Windows 2000 CD-ROM to create the Setup disks.

  e. Insert each disk when prompted.

  f. Label the disks.

  g. Insert the first Windows Setup disk and start the computer. When prompted, insert each additional disk as required.

- If the computer has a bootable CD-ROM drive, insert the Windows 2000 CD-ROM and start the computer. If prompted, press a key to boot from CD.
- If the installation files are on a network share, complete the following steps:

  a. Connect the computer to the network.

  b. Access the network share containing the installation files.

  c. Double-click the appropriate Setup program file (use winnt.exe if you're using MS-DOS to access the network share; use winnt32.exe if you're using Windows 98 to connect to the network share).

3. On the Welcome To Setup page, press Enter to install Windows 2000.

4. Press F8 to agree to the Microsoft Windows 2000 Professional license.

5. Partition and format the computer's hard disk.

  a. If the computer has any existing partitions you no longer need, highlight the partition and press D to delete each partition. Press L to confirm that you want to delete the partition.

  b. To create a partition, highlight Unpartitioned Space and press C. In the text box, type the size for the partition and press Enter.

  c. Highlight the partition in which you want to install Windows 2000 and press Enter.

  d. Select from the following choices to format the new partition:

    - Format The Partition Using The NTFS File System.
    - Format The Partition Using The FAT File System.

  e. Press Enter.

When the format is complete, Setup checks the partitions and then copies some of the Windows 2000 files to the hard disk.

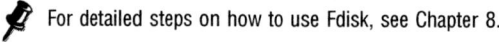 For detailed steps on how to use Fdisk, see Chapter 8.

6. Press Enter to restart the computer. Do not boot from the CD-ROM.

7. On the Welcome page, click Next.

Setup now detects and installs the devices in the computer.

8. When the hardware detection is complete, on the Regional Settings page, configure the locale and keyboard layout if necessary (the default settings are English (United States) for the locale and US for the keyboard layout).

9. Click Next.

10. On the Personalize Your Software page, complete the following:
    - In the Name text box, type the user of the computer's name.
    - In the Organization text box, type the company name.
    - Click Next.
11. On the Your Product Key page, enter your product key and click Next.
12. On the Computer Name And Administrator Password page, complete the following:
    - In the Computer Name text box, type a name for the computer.
    - In the Administrator password text box, type the password you want to assign to the Administrator's user account.
    - In the Confirm Password text box, re-type the password.
    - Click Next.
13. If Setup detected a modem in the computer, on the Modem Dialing Information page, complete the following:
    - From the What Country/Region Are You In Now drop-down list, select the appropriate country or region.
    - In the What Area Code (Or City Code) Are You In Now text box, type the area code.
    - In the If You Dial A Number To Get An Outside Line text box, type a value if applicable.
    - Select either Tone Dialing or Pulse Dialing.
    - Click Next.
14. On the Date And Time Settings page, configure the date, time, time zone, and whether your location adjusts for Daylight Savings Time. Click Next.
15. On the Networking Settings page, select one of the following:
    - If you want to install the network components with TCP/IP as the only protocol and you want the IP address to be assigned dynamically, select Typical Settings.
    - If you want to configure TCP/IP manually, or you want to install additional protocols, select Custom Settings.
16. Click Next.
17. If you select Custom Settings, use the Networking Components page to customize the network connection.
    - Click Install to add additional network components such as protocols.
    - Highlight Internet Protocol (TCP/IP) and click Properties to manually configure the IP addressing information.
    - Click Next when you're finished.
18. On the Workgroup Or Computer Domain, complete the following steps:

a. If you want the computer to be a member of a workgroup, select No, This Computer Is Not On A Network. In the Workgroup Or Computer Domain text box, type the name of the workgroup.

b. If you want the computer to be a member of a domain, select Yes, Make This Computer A Member Of The Following Domain. In the Workgroup Or Computer Domain text box, type the NetBIOS name of the domain (for example, if the Active Directory domain name is company.com, type company for the NetBIOS domain name).

c. Click Next.

d. If you're joining the computer to a domain, in the Join Computer To *Domain* dialog box, type the user name and password of a user with administrative rights for the domain. Click OK.

Setup now completes copying the Windows 2000 files to the hard disk. This process may take 15 to 20 minutes.

19. Click Finish. The computer automatically restarts.

20. If you configured the computer as a member of a workgroup and not a domain, Windows automatically starts the Network Identification Wizard. Use the following steps to complete the wizard:

   a. On the Welcome page, click Next.

   b. On the Users Of This Computer page, select one of the following options:

   - Users Must Enter A User Name And Password To Use This Computer, if you want each user to have to log on to the computer whenever it boots.

   - Windows Always Assumes The Following User Has Logged On To This Computer, if you want Windows 2000 to automatically log on as a specific user whenever the computer boots. In the appropriate text boxes, enter a user name and password, and confirm the password.

   c. Click Next.

   d. Click Finish.

21. If you configured Windows 2000 to require each user to log on, log on as Administrator with the password you defined for the account during installation.

22. Configure the computer to connect to the Internet.

23. If necessary, install any hardware drivers that were not automatically installed during setup. For example, make sure that the drivers for devices such as sound cards, modems, and display adapters were installed correctly.

   a. Use Device Manager to view the status of these devices and to look for any devices for which Setup did not install the drivers.

   b. If you need new drivers, connect to the manufacturer's Web site to download the drivers for Windows 2000.

   c. Use Add/Remove Hardware in Control Panel to install the drivers that weren't installed or to install drivers for non-Plug and Play devices. To open Add New Hardware, double-click it. Select Add/Troubleshoot Device. After Windows searches for Plug and Play hardware, in the list of devices, select the type of hardware device you want to add and click Next. Select No, I Want To Select The Hardware From A List. Select the type of hardware you want to install. Then click Have Disk if you have the drivers on floppy disk, in a folder on the hard disk, or in a location on the network. Browse to the correct drivers and complete the wizard.

24. Update Windows 2000.
    a. From the Start menu, choose Windows Update.
    b. Click Yes to install and run the Windows Update Control Package.
    c. If necessary, click Yes again.
    d. Click Scan For Updates.
    e. Click Review And Install Updates.
    f. Click Yes to continue.
    g. Follow the prompts to install the updates you want. You'll find that some of the updates are "exclusive," which means they can't be installed with other updates. If you choose to install an exclusive update, be sure to go back to the Windows Update Web site to check for other updates.

25. If necessary, restart the computer after the updates are installed.

26. If you have enough available disk space, copy the Windows 2000 installation files to a folder on the hard disk.

27. If necessary, use Computer Management to create any additional user accounts needed on the computer.

Procedure Reference: Install Windows XP Professional

To install Windows XP Professional as the only operating system on the computer:

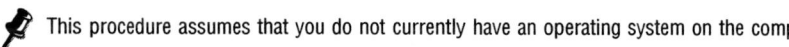
This procedure assumes that you do not currently have an operating system on the computer.

1. Verify that the computer's hardware meets the requirements for Windows XP.
2. Start the installation.
   - If the computer does not have a bootable CD-ROM drive, boot the computer from the first Setup disk. Use the following steps to create and use the Setup disks if you don't have them:
     a. Verify that you have three blank floppy disks.
     b. At a working computer, insert the Windows XP CD-ROM.
     c. If you're using Windows 9x or MS-DOS, run \bootdisk\makeboot.exe from the Windows XP CD-ROM to create the Setup disks.
     d. If you're using Windows 2000, Windows XP, or Windows NT, run \bootdisk\makebt32.exe from the Windows XP CD-ROM to create the Setup disks.

      e.   Insert each disk when prompted.

      f.   Label the disks.

      g.   Insert the first Windows Setup disk and start the computer. When prompted, insert each additional disk as required.

- If the computer has a bootable CD-ROM drive, insert the Windows XP CD-ROM and start the computer. If prompted, press a key to boot from CD.
- If the installation files are on a network share, complete the following steps:

      a.   Connect the computer to the network.

      b.   Access the network share containing the installation files.

      c.   Double-click the appropriate Setup program file (use winnt.exe if you're using MS-DOS to access the network share; use winnt32.exe if you're using Windows 98 to connect to the network share).

3. On the Welcome To Setup page, press Enter to install Windows XP.
4. Press F8 to agree to the Microsoft Windows 2000 Professional license.
5. Partition and format the computer's hard disk.

      a.   If the computer has any existing partitions you no longer need, highlight the partition and press D to delete each partition. Press L to confirm that you want to delete the partition.

      b.   To create a partition, highlight Unpartitioned Space and press C. In the text box, type the size for the partition and press Enter.

      c.   Highlight the partition in which you want to install Windows XP and press Enter.

      d.   Select from the following choices to format the new partition:

          - Format The Partition Using The NTFS File System (Quick)
          - Format The Partition Using The FAT File System (Quick)
          - Format The Partition Using The NTFS File System
          - Format The Partition Using The FAT File System

      e.   Press Enter.

When the format is complete, Setup checks the partitions and then copies some of the Windows XP files to the hard disk.

6. Press Enter to restart the computer. Do not boot from the CD-ROM.

Setup now detects and installs the devices in the computer.

7. When the hardware detection is complete, on the Regional Settings page, configure the locale and keyboard layout if necessary (the default settings are English (United States) for the locale and US for the keyboard layout).
8. Click Next.
9. On the Personalize Your Software page, complete the following:

- In the Name text box, type the user of the computer's name.
- In the Organization text box, type the company name.
- Click Next.

10. Enter the Product Key and click Next.

11. On the Computer Name And Administrator Password page, complete the following:
    - In the Computer Name text box, type a name for the computer.
    - In the Administrator password text box, type the password you want to assign to the Administrator's user account.
    - In the Confirm Password text box, re-type the password.
    - Click Next.

12. If Setup detected a modem in the computer, on the Modem Dialing Information page, complete the following:
    - From the What Country/Region Are You In Now drop-down list, select the appropriate country or region.
    - In the What Area Code (Or City Code) Are You In Now text box, type the area code.
    - In the If You Dial A Number To Get An Outside Line text box, type a value if applicable.
    - Select either Tone Dialing or Pulse Dialing.
    - Click Next.

13. On the Date And Time Settings page, configure the date, time, time zone, and whether your location adjusts for Daylight Savings Time. Click Next.

14. On the Networking Settings page, select one of the following:
    - If you want to install the network components with TCP/IP as the only protocol and you want the IP address to be assigned dynamically, select Typical Settings.
    - If you want to configure TCP/IP manually, or you want to install additional protocols, select Custom Settings.

15. Click Next.

16. If you select Custom Settings, use the Networking Components page to customize the network connection.
    - Click Install to add additional network components such as protocols.
    - Highlight Internet Protocol (TCP/IP) and click Properties to manually configure the IP addressing information.
    - Click Next when you're finished.

17. On the Workgroup Or Computer Domain, complete the following steps:

a. If you want the computer to be a member of a workgroup, select No, This Computer Is Not On A Network, Or Is On A Network Without A Domain. In the Make This Computer A Member Of The Following Workgroup text box, type the name of the workgroup.

b. If you want the computer to be a member of a domain, select Yes, Make This Computer A Member Of The Following Domain. In the text box, type the NetBIOS name of the domain (for example, if the Active Directory domain name is company.com, type company for the NetBIOS domain name).

c. Click Next.

d. If you're joining the computer to a domain, in the Join Computer To *Domain* dialog box, type the user name and password of a user with administrative rights for the domain. Click OK.

Setup now completes copying the Windows XP files to the hard disk. This process may take 25 to 30 minutes. The computer automatically restarts when the copy process completes.

18. In the Welcome To Microsoft Windows page, click Next.

19. Select one of the following options to configure how the computer connects to the Internet:
    - Yes, This Computer Will Connect Through A Local Area Network Or Home Network.
    - No, This Computer Will Connect Directly To The Internet.

20. Click Next.

21. On the Ready To Register With Microsoft page, select whether you want to register the computer with Microsoft at this time. If you select Yes, click Next and complete the steps to register the computer.

22. Click Next.

23. If you configured the computer as a member of a workgroup and not a domain, on the Who Will Use This Computer page, type the names of the users who will use the computer and click Next. Windows XP will automatically create user accounts for these users.

24. Click Finish.

> For more information on how to configure an Internet connection in Windows XP, see Chapter 8.

25. Configure the computer to connect to the Internet.

26. If necessary, install any hardware drivers that were not automatically installed during setup. For example, make sure that the drivers for devices such as sound cards, modems, and display adapters were installed correctly.

    a. Use Device Manager to view the status of these devices and to look for any devices for which Setup did not install the drivers.

b. If you need new drivers, connect to the manufacturer's Web site to download the drivers for Windows XP.

c. Use the Add Hardware Wizard to install the drivers that weren't installed or to install drivers for non-Plug and Play devices. Select Yes, I Have Already Connected The Hardware. Select Add A New Hardware Device. Select Install The Hardware That I Manually Select From A List. Select the type of hardware you want to install. Then click Have Disk if you have the drivers on floppy disk, in a folder on the hard disk, or in a location on the network. Browse to the correct drivers and complete the wizard.

27. Update Windows XP.

    a. From the Start menu, choose All Programs→Windows Update.
    b. Click Yes to install and run the Windows Update Control Package.
    c. If necessary, click Yes again.
    d. Click Scan For Updates.
    e. Click Review And Install Updates.
    f. Click Yes to continue.
    g. Follow the prompts to install the updates you want. You'll find that some of the updates are "exclusive," which means they can't be installed with other updates. If you choose to install an exclusive update, be sure to go back to the Windows Update Web site to check for other updates.

28. If necessary, restart the computer after the updates are installed.

29. If you have enough available disk space, copy the Windows XP installation files to a folder on the hard disk.

30. If necessary, use Computer Management to create any additional user accounts needed on the computer.

Procedure Reference: Install Windows 98 and Windows 2000/XP on a Single Computer

To install both Windows 98 and Windows 2000 or Windows XP on a single computer:

 You must install Windows 98 first.

1. Install Windows 98 first. Make sure the installation meets the following requirements:
   - The C drive must be formatted to be no larger than 2 GB and must use the FAT file system.
   - If you want to create an NTFS partition, you must leave free space on the hard disk when you install Windows 98.

2. Install Windows 2000 or Windows XP. Make sure that you complete the following during installation:

   a. In Windows 98, insert the Windows 2000 Professional or Windows XP Professional CD-ROM.

b. If you're installing Windows 2000, when you're prompted to upgrade Windows 98, click No.

📌 Microsoft strongly recommends that you install each operating system in its own partition.

c. Click Advanced Options. Check I Want To Choose The Installation Partition During Setup so that you can create a new partition on which to store Windows 2000 during installation.

d. Follow the prompts to complete the Windows 2000 or Windows XP installation (refer to the procedures for installing these operating systems for more information).

3. In Windows 2000 or Windows XP, select the default operating system.

a. Open Control Panel.

b. Double-click System.

c. Select the Advanced tab.

d. Click Startup And Recovery.

e. From the Default Operating System drop-down list, select the operating system you want to load by default on the computer.

f. Click OK twice.

g. Close Control Panel.

4. Verify that you can start each operating system from the boot menu.

Procedure Reference: Install Windows 2000 and Windows XP on a Single Computer

To install Windows 2000 and Windows XP on a single computer:

 You must install Windows 2000 first.

1. Install Windows 2000. If you want to install Windows XP into a separate partition, make sure that you leave free space on the hard disk.

2. Install Windows XP Professional. Make sure that you complete the following during installation:

a. In Windows 2000, insert the Windows XP Professional CD-ROM.

b. When you're prompted to upgrade Windows 2000, click No.

📌 Microsoft strongly recommends that you install each operating system in its own partition.

c. Click Advanced Options. Check I Want To Choose The Installation Partition During Setup so that you can create a new partition on which to store Windows 2000 during installation.

d. Follow the prompts to complete the Windows XP installation (refer to the procedures in Topic A for more information).

3. In Windows 2000 or Windows XP, select the default operating system.
    a. Open Control Panel.
    b. Double-click System.
    c. Select the Advanced tab.
    d. Click Startup And Recovery.
    e. From the Default Operating System drop-down list, select the operating system you want to load by default on the computer.
    f. Click OK twice.
    g. Close Control Panel.
4. Verify that you can start each operating system from the boot menu.

Installation Types

During the installation of the Windows 98 and Windows Me operating systems, you'll get to choose which type of installation you want to perform. Generally, there are four types to choose from, all of which are described in Table 21-9.

Table 21-9: *Installation Types*

Installation Type	Description
Typical	This is the default option and is recommended for most users. A Typical installation provides the least customization. It was designed for the least user intervention; thus, it performs most installation steps automatically. The most common Windows 9x components are installed.
Portable	This installation option is recommended for portable or mobile computers. In addition to many of the default options installed with a Typical installation, it installs the Windows 9x features that are designed specifically for mobile computing, such as the Briefcase.
Compact	This installation option installs the minimum files required to run Windows 9x. It is recommended for users who have minimal disk space available on their hard drives, but who cannot run a network-shared copy of Windows 9x.
Custom	This installation option provides the greatest customization, enabling the user to select from every available option provided by the Setup program.

Topic B
Upgrade a Windows Client Operating System

In Topic 21A, you learned how to install a Windows client operating system from scratch on a computer. A user has used this computer to install her applications and has stored quite a bit of data on it. Now, you've been asked to upgrade this computer to a later version of Windows. In this topic, you'll learn the steps for upgrading from an earlier version of Windows to a newer version.

Upgrading a computer's operating system to a newer one enables the computer's user to take advantage of the new features and capabilities added to the newer version. And as you've seen, performing such an upgrade offers you, the A+ technician, the benefit of saving a lot of time. You won't have to completely install the new operating system from scratch along with all of the user's applications. You also won't have to spend time restoring the user's data into the new operating system.

How to Upgrade a Windows Client Operating System

Procedure Reference: Upgrade from Windows 98 to Windows 2000

To upgrade from Windows 98 to Windows 2000:

1. Verify that the computer meets the hardware requirements for Windows 2000 (use Table 21-5 or go to **www.microsoft.com/windows2000/professional/evaluation/sysreqs/default.asp**).
2. Back up the user data files.
3. In Windows 98, insert the Windows 2000 Professional CD-ROM.
4. When prompted, click Yes to upgrade Windows 98.
5. On the Welcome page, select Upgrade To Windows 2000 (Recommended) and click Next.
6. Select I Accept This Agreement and click Next.
7. If necessary, enter the Windows 2000 product key and click Next.
8. On the Preparing To Upgrade To Windows 2000 page, click Click Here to connect to the Windows Compatibility Web site to check your computer's hardware. When you're done, close Internet Explorer.
9. Click Next.
10. On the Provide Upgrade Packs page, select one of the following:
    - Yes, I Have Upgrade Packs. Click Add to add to the Upgrade Pack List.
    - No, I Don't Have Any Upgrade Packs.
11. Click Next.

12. On the Upgrading To The Windows 2000 NTFS File System page, select Yes, Upgrade My Drive if you want to upgrade the hard disk to NTFS. Otherwise, select No, Do Not Upgrade My Drive. Click Next.

13. Review the Upgrade Report. Click Save As if you want to save it. You can also click Print if you want to print the report.

14. Click Next.

15. Click Next to begin the upgrade.

16. When prompted, restart the computer. Do not boot from the Windows 2000 CD. Setup copies some of the Windows 2000 files to the hard disk.

17. Press Enter to restart the computer. Do not boot from the CD-ROM.

18. If you chose to upgrade the disk to NTFS, Setup converts the disk at this point. When the conversion is complete, your computer restarts.

    Setup now detects and installs the devices in the computer. It also automatically installs networking components and adds the computer as either a member of a workgroup or a domain (based on the configuration of Windows 98). Setup now completes copying the Windows 2000 files to the hard disk. This whole automated process may take 20 to 30 minutes.

19. Click Restart Now.

20. In the Password Creation dialog box, type a temporary password to assign to each user account created during the upgrade (at a minimum, you should see one user account plus the Administrator account).

21. Click OK.

22. Log on as Administrator with the password you just defined.

    For more information on how to configure an Internet connection in Windows 2000, see Chapter 8.

23. If necessary, configure the computer to connect to the Internet.

24. If necessary, install any hardware drivers that were not automatically installed during setup. For example, make sure that the drivers for devices such as sound cards, modems, and display adapters were installed correctly.

    a. Use Device Manager to view the status of these devices and to look for any devices for which Setup did not install the drivers.

    b. If you need new drivers, connect to the manufacturer's Web site to download the drivers for Windows 2000.

    c. Use Add New Hardware in Control Panel to install the drivers. When prompted, do not have Windows 2000 search for the device. Instead, select the driver from the files you downloaded.

25. Update Windows 2000.

      a. From the Start menu, choose Windows Update.

      b. Click Yes to install and run the Windows Update Control Package.

      c. If necessary, click Yes again.

      d. Click Scan For Updates.

      e. Click Review And Install Updates.

      f. Click Yes to continue.

      g. Follow the prompts to install the updates you want. You'll find that some of the updates are "exclusive," which means they can't be installed with other updates. If you choose to install an exclusive update, be sure to go back to the Windows Update Web site to check for other updates.

26. If necessary, restart the computer after the updates are installed.

27. If you have enough available disk space, copy the Windows 2000 installation files to a folder on the hard disk.

28. If necessary, use Computer Management to create any additional user accounts needed on the computer.

Procedure Reference: Upgrade from Windows 2000 to Windows XP

To upgrade from Windows 2000 to Windows XP:

1. Verify that the computer meets the hardware requirements for Windows XP (use Table 21-6 or go to **www.microsoft.com/windowsxp/pro/evaluation/sysreqs.asp**).

2. Back up the user data files.

3. In Windows 2000, insert the Windows XP Professional CD-ROM.

4. Click Install Windows XP.

5. From the Installation Type drop-down list, select Upgrade (Recommended) and click Next.

6. Select I Accept This Agreement and click Next.

7. Enter the Product Key and click Next.

8. On the Get Updated Setup Files page, select one of the following:

    - Yes, Download The Updated Setup Files (Recommended).
    - No, Skip This Step And Continue Installing Windows.

9. Click Next.

    If you selected to download updated setup files, Setup will connect to Microsoft's Web site and download updates for installing Windows XP. Your computer will automatically restart after downloading the updates. Do not boot from the CD.

10. After copying files, Setup will restart the computer again. Do not boot from the CD.

11. When the installation is complete, the computer will restart again.

12. On the Welcome To Microsoft Windows page, click Next.

13. On the Ready To Register With Microsoft page, select whether you want to register the computer with Microsoft at this time. If you select Yes, Click Next and complete the steps to register the computer.

14. Click Next.

15. On the Let's Get On The Internet page, select one of the following:
    - Get Online With MSN.
    - Do Not Set Up An Internet Connection At This Time.

    Click Next.

16. If you selected Get Online With MSN, complete the steps to create an account.

17. Click Finish.

18. Log on to Windows XP.

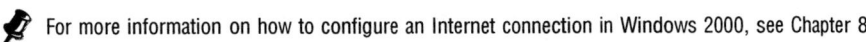 For more information on how to configure an Internet connection in Windows 2000, see Chapter 8.

19. If necessary, configure the computer to connect to the Internet.

20. If necessary, install any hardware drivers that were not automatically installed during setup. For example, make sure that the drivers for devices such as sound cards, modems, and display adapters were installed correctly.
    a. Use Device Manager to view the status of these devices and to look for any devices for which Setup did not install the drivers.
    b. If you need new drivers, connect to the manufacturer's Web site to download the drivers for Windows XP.
    c. Use Add New Hardware in Control Panel to install the drivers. When prompted, do not have Windows XP search for the device. Instead, select the driver from the files you downloaded.

21. Update Windows XP.
    a. From the Start menu, choose All Programs→Windows Update.
    b. Click Yes to install and run the Windows Update Control Package.
    c. If necessary, click Yes again.
    d. Click Scan For Updates.
    e. Click Review And Install Updates.
    f. Click Yes to continue.
    g. Follow the prompts to install the updates you want. You'll find that some of the updates are "exclusive," which means they can't be installed with other updates. If you choose to install an exclusive update, be sure to go back to the Windows Update Web site to check for other updates.

22. If necessary, restart the computer after the updates are installed.
23. If you have enough available disk space, copy the Windows XP installation files to a folder on the hard disk.

Replacing an Operating System

If you want to completely replace the operating system on a computer, you'll need to complete the following steps:

1. Back up all data on the computer that you want to retain after changing the operating system.
2. Install the new operating system. During the installation, delete all partitions on the hard disk, and then create a new partition for the operating system.
3. Restore the backed up files to the computer.

TOPIC C
Troubleshoot Operating System Installations

So far in this chapter you've learned how to install operating systems from scratch. Unfortunately, sometimes an installation will fail. As an A+ technician, you'll be expected to troubleshoot problems with installing an operating system so that you're able to successfully install the operating system. So, in this chapter, you'll learn the common problems that can occur during installation and how to go about troubleshooting them.

In some cases, you'll wish that you could just walk away when you encounter a problem during an installation. Unfortunately, that's not how it works in the real world. As an A+ technician, it's your job not only to attempt to install a computer's operating system, but also to install it successfully. Mastering the skills for troubleshooting installations will enable you to quickly and successfully handle any problem that might crop up during an operating system installation.

Common Problems

Regardless of which Windows operating system you're installing, you'll find that the problems you can encounter are very similar. In Table 21-10, you see a list of common installation problems you can encounter, along with potential solutions for those problems.

Table 21-10: *Common Installation Problems*

Problem	Potential Solution
Media errors	Try using a different CD-ROM or a different set of shared installation files on the network.
Unsupported CD-ROM drive	Try replacing your CD-ROM drive with one that's supported, or install using another method such as connecting to a network share.

Problem	Potential Solution
Insufficient disk space	Try using Setup to create a partition out of free space on your disk that's large enough. You can also try deleting files or folders, moving files or folders to another partition, compressing an NTFS partition, or creating a larger NTFS partition.
Failure of Windows to install or start	Check that all of the hardware on your computer is detected and is compatible with Windows 2000.
Failure of a dependency service to start (in Windows 2000 or Windows XP only)	Use the Back button in the Setup wizard to return to the Network Settings page. Verify that you have installed the correct network card driver and protocol. You'll also need to check the configuration settings for your adapter. Make sure that the computer name is unique on the network.

How to Troubleshoot an Operating System Installation

Procedure Reference: How to Troubleshoot an Operating System Installation

To troubleshoot an operating system installation:

1. If you're installing a Windows operating system on a computer with no existing operating system, and the installation is failing, verify that the computer's hardware is compatible with the version of Windows you're attempting to install. If necessary, upgrade the hardware.

2. If you're upgrading to a new version of Windows and you're receiving errors when Setup tries to write to the hard disk, disable any anti-virus software on the computer. Also, make sure that the computer's CMOS setup is not configured to perform any boot sector virus detection.

    For more information on how to troubleshoot hard disks in Windows 2000, Windows XP, and Windows NT, see Chapter 6. To learn how to troubleshoot hard disks in Windows 9x, see Chapter 5.

3. If you're experiencing hard disk errors, troubleshoot the hard disks. If necessary, replace the hard disks.

4. If the Setup program for the version of Windows you're installing does not recognize the computer's CD-ROM drive and the computer has an existing operating system (or is configured to boot with network support from a floppy disk), install Windows by connecting to a network share with the installation files.

5. If the Setup program for the version of Windows you're installing does not recognize the computer's CD-ROM drive and the computer does not have an existing operating system, install Windows by using the Setup boot disks.

Topic D
Add or Remove Operating System Components

Up to this point in the chapter, you've learned how to install operating systems using the typical installation option. In some cases, though, the Windows components Setup installs when you perform a typical installation won't meet the needs of a particular user. For this reason, in this topic, you'll learn how to add or remove operating system components on a computer.

Tailoring an operating system to meet a particular user's needs is just like custom building a house. One homeowner might like blue walls and grey carpeting, while another homeowner might prefer off-white walls and beige carpeting. Just as you can tailor a house to the homeowner's tastes, so can you tailor the Windows environment to a user's tastes or needs. For example, you might encounter a situation where the owner of a company requires that you remove all games from users' computers. To do so, you'll need to know how to remove an operating system component.

Operating System Components

Each Windows operating system comes with a variety of components. These include Accessories (such as the Calculator and Notepad), Communications, Games, and so on. Depending on how you install Windows, you might find that your installation does not include a component that you need. You can install that component by using Control Panel.

How to Add or Remove Operating System Components

Procedure Reference: Add or Remove Operating System Components

To add or remove operating system components:

1. Log on as a local administrator.
2. If you're using Windows XP, in Control Panel, click Add Or Remove Programs.

   If you're using Windows 2000, Windows NT, or Windows 98, in Control Panel, double-click Add/Remove Programs.
3. If you're using Windows 2000 or Windows XP, click Add/Remove Windows Components.

   In Windows NT, click Windows Setup.

   In Windows 98, select the Windows Setup tab.
4. To install a component, check its check box in the Components list.

   To uninstall a component, uncheck its check box.
5. To install or remove a component within a category, select the component category (such as Accessories) and click Details.

   Check or uncheck the component's check box, and then click OK.
6. Click Next.

7. If prompted, insert the Windows installation CD-ROM and click OK.

8. If necessary, click Finish.

9. Close all open windows.

10. Verify that the component was installed or removed.

CHAPTER 21 FOLLOW-UP
Installing Client Operating Systems

In this chapter, you learned how to install the Windows 98, Windows 2000, and Windows XP Professional computers. You also learned how to upgrade to the Windows 2000 or Windows XP operating system, how to add or remove any of the operating system components, and how to troubleshoot the problems you can encounter during installation. These skills will prepare you to quickly respond to clients' requests for installing or upgrading their computers' operating systems.

Essential Terms

- client operating systems
- multiple boot computers
- operating system components
- operating system installation
- operating systems
- troubleshooting
- updates
- upgrades
- Windows operating systems
- Windows upgrades
- Windows Update

Review Questions

1. Windows 98 features the Active Desktop. What does Active Desktop enable you to do?
2. What does the Quick Launch toolbar in Windows 98 enable you to do?
3. Windows 2000 supports Active Directory. What does Active Directory provide?
4. Why would you enable disk quotas on a Windows 2000 machine?
5. What is the Microsoft Management Console (MMC) that's available on Windows 2000 and XP Professional?
6. What is the Adaptive Start menu in Windows XP?
7. What is the utility in Windows XP that enables you to migrate a user's data, application settings, and operating system settings from an old machine to a new one that's running XP?
8. What is the minimum processor requirement for Windows 98?
9. What is the minimum amount of free hard disk space needed to install Windows 98 on a computer?
10. If you install Windows 98 and Windows 2000 in a dual boot configuration, which operating system do you install first?

11. When installing Windows 2000 or Windows XP from MS-DOS, what is the file that launches the installation?
12. You are using a Windows 95 operating system and you want to upgrade it. What operating systems could you consider upgrading to directly?
13. When installing Windows 98 or Windows ME, you have the choice of four different installation types. What are the four types?
14. Which Windows 98 installation type is the default?
15. What installation type provides features for mobile computers specifically?
16. While trying to upgrade to a new version of Windows you receive error messages when Setup tries to write to disk. What should you do first to correct the situation?
17. You're trying to install a Windows operating system on a computer that has no operating system present. The installation is failing. What should you check?
18. You're trying to install Windows 2000 on a customer's hard disk. You change the boot sequence in the BIOS so the computer can boot from the CD-ROM. You insert the CD-ROM, but the computer won't boot from it. What should you do?
19. If you open multiple files within the same application, such as Microsoft Excel, what does Windows XP do to simplify the look of the taskbar?
20. What service in Windows XP helps you track, upgrade, and remove software programs fully and correctly?
21. What is the minimum processor required for installing Windows XP Professional?
22. Which operating system can you install from a DVD-ROM drive?
23. What is the minimum memory required to install Windows 2000?
24. You want to install several operating systems on your computer. In what order would you install the following operating systems? Windows NT 4.0, MS-DOS, Windows XP, Windows 95.
25. If users have older hardware on their computers, which Windows operating system would be the better choice to install? Windows XP, Windows NT 4.0, Windows 98, or Windows 2000.

Review Projects

Project #1 Windows XP Home Edition Comparison Guide

There are two versions of Windows XP: Home and Professional. As its name implies, the Home edition is targeted to home users who use the operating system in ways different from most businesses. However, you'll likely encounter situations in which people will want to know the advantages of Windows XP Home over earlier operating systems such as Windows 9x and Windows Millennium. Microsoft developed a comparison chart to help you compare the features of the operating systems so you can help people make informed purchasing decisions. Go to **http://www.microsoft.com/windowsxp/home/evaluation/whyupgrade/featurecomp.asp**. After reviewing the chart, what do you consider some of the major selling strengths of Windows XP Home? Create a sub-folder under Hardware documentation on your C drive. Name the folder "operating system information." Copy the chart from the Web site and paste it into your word processing program (first select the chart, use Ctrl+C to copy the chart to the clipboard, and use Ctrl+V to paste the chart from the clipboard into the word processing program). In addition to reviewing the comparison guide, watch some of the short videos Microsoft created to compare Windows 98 and Windows XP. Titled "The Windows XP/Windows 98 Matchup," these short videos provide a quick overview of some of the main differences between the two systems. The Matchup is located at **http://www.microsoft.com/windowsxp/pro/evaluation/whyupgrade/wxpvswin98.asp**. As you watch the videos, create a comparison chart you can use to compare the features of Windows 98 and Windows XP.

Project #2 Windows XP Professional

Windows XP Professional is Microsoft's latest client operating system release as well as its most feature-rich and robust OS to date. Even the GUI interface has been re-designed to ensure that users can find what they want quickly. However, every change to an operating system means you've got to spend time learning the new interfaces. To acquaint yourself with the operating system, Microsoft hosts an XP help center on its Web site. You'll find extensive documentation, tutorials, how-tos, and FAQs. The help center is located at **http://www.microsoft.com/technet/treeview/default.asp?url=/technet/prodtechnol/winxppro/default.asp**.

This activity is exploratory. Windows XP promises to be a popular operating system because it offers features that appeal to much wider audiences than previous Windows versions. Under the title bar, "The Inside Scoop on Windows XP," is a link titled, "Browse the Documentation." Click it. The link re-directs you to a section that outlines XP's new features. Explore the links in the left column. Bookmark any Web pages you want to include in your documentation. When you're done, return to the original page (URL noted above) and review the Answers To Top Customer Questions and the How-to Articles sections.

Project #3 Windows XP Newsgroups

Despite your best efforts, there will be times when the solution to a system problem eludes you. In such cases, you can present the problem to a Microsoft newsgroup. The newsgroups are comprised of other IT professionals like yourself. While newsgroup members will help you with various troubleshooting issues, you'll have the opportunity to hone your skills by helping others in the group. For a list of Windows XP newsgroups, enter the following address in your browser: **http://www.microsoft.com/technet/newsgroups/default.asp?url=/technet/newsgroups/NodePages/winxp.asp**. In this activity, explore the newsgroups. Click a link and you'll have immediate access to the message board. If you have specific questions about XP, first browse the board to make sure the question has not been asked recently. If it hasn't, post it. In most cases you'll receive answers within 24 hours.

Reflective Questions

1. Have you ever installed an operating system? If so, which one? What was your experience with the installation?

2. What is your experience with upgrading computer operating systems? Did you encounter any problems? If so, how did you resolve them?

CHAPTER 22
Automating Client Operating System Installations

Chapter Objectives:

In this chapter, you will automate client operating system installations.

You will:

- Perform an unattended installation.
- Create a computer image.
- Install a computer image.

Introduction

In the previous chapter, you learned the exact steps you must perform to install an operating system from scratch, and how to upgrade an operating system. But installations and upgrades are time-consuming tasks. In this chapter, you'll learn how to automate installations and upgrades.

You've been asked to install Windows XP on 100 client computers. The installations need to be completed over a single weekend. You timed the installation on one of the computers, and it took almost two hours. Automating the installations will enable you to reduce the amount of time you need to complete the installations and meet your client's needs.

TOPIC A
Perform an Unattended Installation

Another technique you can use to automate the installation of computer operating systems is to perform unattended installations. In this topic, you'll learn how to create the files you need for an unattended installation along with how to perform the actual unattended installation.

Just as you saw with creating and deploying computer images, performing unattended installations can also save you hours of setup time. One reason is because you won't have to sit at each computer and respond to the prompts you see during a manual installation. Instead, the unattended installation process will use files you've configured with the answers to each of these prompts to automate the installation. This means that you can perform an unattended installation on several computers at once.

Given that performing an unattended installation requires more configuration on your part as compared to deploying a computer image, you might be wondering when you would choose to perform an unattended installation instead of imaging. Here are some reasons: First, you might choose to perform an unattended installation instead of deploying a computer image if the computers on which you want to install the operating system have significantly different hardware. Another reason why you might perform an unattended installation is if your company doesn't have money in its budget to purchase the necessary imaging software. In both scenarios, performing an unattended installation offers you a faster method for installing the operating system on multiple computers as compared to performing a manual installation.

Answer File

Definition:

An *answer file* is a setup file that provides the answers needed by the Windows Setup program during an unattended installation. An answer file is divided into sections that group together the settings that are required to complete the various phases of Windows Setup. An answer file must conform to the following general syntax:

```
[section name]
keyname = value
keyname = value
```

You can create an answer file by using the Setup Manager utility or any text editor (such as Notepad). You can save the answer file with the extension .sif or .txt. Table 22-1 lists the required sections in an answer file and the types of settings to specify in each section.

Table 22-1: *Required Sections in an Answer File*

Section Name	Contains Information For
[Unattended]	The text-mode portion of Setup, such as the installation folder, and the file system type. The Unattended mode key determines the level of user interaction permitted during the unattended installation.
[UserData]	System-specific information, including the name and organization, computer name, and product key. You must provide a computer name or configure Setup to automatically generate a name.
[GuiUnattended]	The GUI portion of Setup, including the time zone and administrator password.
[Display]	Display settings for the computer, such as the screen resolution and refresh rate.
[Networking]	Typical or custom networking settings. Required if you want to configure custom settings during the unattended installation.
[Identification]	The domain or workgroup this computer will join.

Example:

Figure 22-1 shows you an example of an answer file.

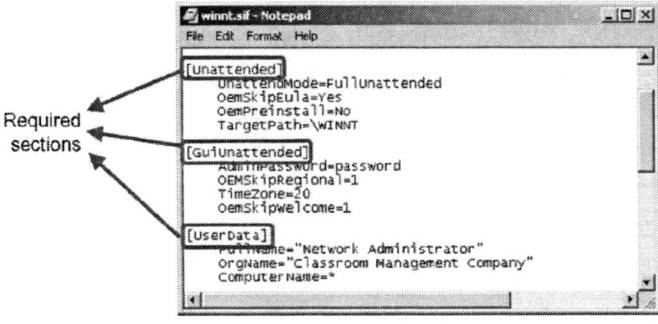

Figure 22-1: *An unattended answer file.*

Setup Command Syntax for Unattended Installations

When you're ready to perform an unattended installation, you begin the installation by using the appropriate Windows Setup program, followed by the option specifying the answer file you want to use. Here's the syntax:

`winnt32 /s:\\server\share /unattend:answer_file`

In this syntax, replace `\\server\share` with the name of the server and the shared folder name that contains the Windows installation files (you'll want to run an unattended installation using files on a network server so that you can install multiple computers at the same time). Replace `answer_file` with the name of the answer file you created.

Setup Batch Files

Instead of manually typing the commands to begin an unattended installation, you might choose to create a setup batch file to specify the appropriate commands for you. Inserting the correct command syntax in a file reduces the chance you might make a mistake in the command. You can then run the batch file yourself, or distribute it to users as a file so that they can launch the unattended setup.

How to Perform an Unattended Installation

Procedure Reference: Perform an Unattended Installation of Windows 2000

To perform an unattended installation of Windows 2000:

1. Use Setup Manager to create an unattended answer file.
   a. If you're using Windows XP, if necessary, install the Setup Manager Wizard (Setupmgr.exe).
      1. Create a folder in which to store Setup Manager.
      2. Access the Windows XP installation files (if necessary, insert the appropriate CD-ROM).
      3. Select the \Support\Tools folder.
      4. Double-click Deploy.cab.
      5. Copy the Setupmgr.exe and Setupmgx.dll files to a folder.
   b. If you're using Windows 2000, if necessary, install the Setup Manager Wizard (Setupmgr.exe).
      1. Create a folder in which to store Setup Manager.
      2. Access the Windows 2000 installation files (if necessary, insert the appropriate CD-ROM).
      3. Select the \Support\Tools folder.
      4. Double-click Deploy.cab.
      5. Copy the Setupmgr.exe and Setupmgr.chm files to a folder.
   c. Access the folder to which you copied the Setup Manager Wizard files and double-click Setupmgr.exe to run the wizard.

d. In the Windows Setup Manager Wizard, click Next.
e. Verify that Create A New Answer File is selected and click Next.
f. If you're using Windows 2000's Setup Manager, select Windows 2000 Unattended Installation and click Next.
g. If you're using Windows XP's Setup Manager, select Windows Unattended Installation and click Next.
h. On the Platform page, if you're using Windows 2000's Setup Manager, select one of the following:
   - Windows 2000 Professional
   - Windows 2000 Server
i. On the Platform page, if you're using Windows XP's Setup Manager, select one of the following:
   - Windows XP Home Edition
   - Windows XP Professional
   - Windows 2000 Server, Advanced Server, or Data Center
j. Click Next.
k. Select the level of user interaction you want during the unattended installation and click Next.
   - Provide Defaults—Answers you provide in the answer file are the default answers and Windows Setup prompts the user to review them. The user can change any answer.
   - Fully Automated—Windows Setup doesn't prompt the user for any answers during installation. You must provide all answers in the answer file.
   - Hide Pages—Hides the pages for which you have provided all answers in the answer file.
   - Read Only—If a page isn't hidden from the user, the user can't make any changes to the answers you supplied in the answer file.
   - GUI Attended—Automates only the text-mode portion of the installation. The user will be prompted to provide the necessary answers in the graphical portion of installation.
l. Follow the prompts to complete the information you want to include in the answer file. These prompts will vary depending on which user interaction level you select.
m. On the Computer names page, enter multiple computer names or check Automatically Generate Computer Names Based On Organization Name to have the unattended installation automatically name the computer for you.
n. Select the installation source. Use one of the following:
   - To copy the installation files from their current location to a shared distribution folder:
     a. Select Yes, Create Or Modify A Distribution Folder. Click Next.

b. Specify the current location of the installation files. The source folder, usually the \i386 folder, should contain the Dosnet.inf information file. Click Next.

c. Specify the target folder name and share name for the distribution folder. Click Next.

- To use an existing distribution folder, whether on a network share or on a CD-ROM:

  a. Select No, This Answer File Will Be Used To Install From A CD.

  b. Click Next.

o. When you have finished entering settings, select the Additional Commands page and click Finish.

p. Enter a path and file name for your answer file and click OK. The wizard will create the answer file and the associated UDF and setup batch files in this folder.

- If you will be installing directly from the Windows XP or Windows 2000 CD-ROM, you must save the answer file to a floppy disk as A:\Winnt.sif. Be sure that the [Data] section of the answer file contains the required parameters.

- For all other types of installations, you can name the answer file anything you like.

q. Close Setup Manager by clicking the Close box.

r. Open the answer file and setup batch file in a text editor to verify your custom settings.

2. If necessary, edit the setup batch file to provide the path to the network installation shared folder.

3. Perform an unattended installation. Use the following steps:

   a. Verify that the target computer's hardware meets the minimum Windows 2000 hardware requirements.

   b. If your answer file is on a floppy disk, insert the floppy disk.

   c. Launch the setup by using one of the following methods:

      - Boot the computer from the Windows 2000 installation CD-ROM. The Setup program will automatically locate and run the A:\Winnt.sif file (make sure you configure the computer to boot from the CD-ROM first).

      - Run the appropriate version of the Windows Setup program (Winnt.exe or Winnt32.exe) with the appropriate unattended setup switches.

      - Run a setup batch file. The batch file command syntax is `batch_file_name [ID]`, where [ID] is the appropriate ID code for this computer installation as defined in the [Unique IDs] section of the UDF.

   d. Respond to any prompts in Windows Setup to complete the installation.

Procedure Reference: Perform an Unattended Installation of Windows XP

To perform an unattended installation of Windows XP:

1. Use Setup Manager to create an unattended answer file.
   a. If you're using Windows XP, if necessary, install the Setup Manager Wizard (Setupmgr.exe).
      1. Create a folder in which to store Setup Manager.
      2. Access the Windows XP installation files (if necessary, insert the appropriate CD-ROM).
      3. Select the \Support\Tools folder.
      4. Double-click Deploy.cab.
      5. Copy the Setupmgr.exe and Setupmgr.chm files to the folder.
   b. Access the folder to which you copied the Setup Manager Wizard files and double-click Setupmgr.exe to run the wizard.
   c. In the Windows Setup Manager Wizard, click Next.
   d. Verify that Create A New Answer File is selected and click Next.
   e. Select Windows Unattended Installation and click Next.
   f. On the Platform page, select one of the following:
      - Windows XP Home Edition
      - Windows XP Professional
      - Windows 2000 Server, Advanced Server, or Data Center
   g. Click Next.
   h. Select the level of user interaction you want during the unattended installation and click Next.
      - Provide Defaults—Answers you provide in the answer file are the default answers and Windows Setup prompts the user to review them. The user can change any answer.
      - Fully Automated—Windows Setup doesn't prompt the user for any answers during installation. You must provide all answers in the answer file.
      - Hide Pages—Hides the pages for which you have provided all answers in the answer file.
      - Read Only—If a page isn't hidden from the user, the user can't make any changes to the answers you supplied in the answer file.
      - GUI Attended—Automates only the text-mode portion of the installation. The user will be prompted to provide the necessary answers in the graphical portion of installation.
   i. Select the installation source. Use one of the following:
      - To copy the installation files from their current location to a shared distribution folder:

- a. Select Yes, Create Or Modify A Distribution Folder. Click Next.
- b. Specify the current location of the installation files. The source folder, usually the \i386 folder, should contain the Dosnet.inf information file. Click Next.
- c. Specify the target folder name and share name for the distribution folder. Click Next.

- To use an existing distribution folder, whether on a network share or on a CD-ROM:
  - a. Select No, This Answer File Will Be Used To Install From A CD.
  - b. Click Next.

j. Check I Accept The Terms Of The License Agreement and click Next.

k. Complete the data required for each of the items listed in the left pane. For example, below General Settings, select Customize The Software. In the right pane, enter the Name and Organization for the user who will use the computer. Move to the next item in the left pane and complete the required information, and so on. When you have completed all required information, click Finish.

l. Enter a path and file name for your answer file and click OK. The wizard will create the answer file and the associated UDF and setup batch files in this folder.

- If you will be installing directly from the Windows XP or Windows 2000 CD-ROM, you must save the answer file to a floppy disk as A:\Winnt.sif. Be sure that the [Data] section of the answer file contains the required parameters.
- For all other types of installations, you can name the answer file anything you like.

m. Open the answer file and setup batch file in a text editor to verify your custom settings.

2. If necessary, edit the setup batch file to provide the path to the network installation shared folder.

3. Perform an unattended installation. Use the following steps:
   a. Verify that the target computer's hardware meets the minimum Windows XP hardware requirements.
   b. If your answer file is on a floppy disk, insert the floppy disk.
   c. Launch the setup by using one of the following methods:
      - Boot the computer from the Windows XP installation CD-ROM. The Setup program will automatically locate and run the A:\Winnt.sif file (make sure you configure the computer to boot from the CD-ROM first).
      - Run the appropriate version of the Windows Setup program (Winnt.exe or Winnt32.exe) with the appropriate unattended setup switches.
      - Run a setup batch file. The batch file command syntax is `batch_file_name [ID]`, where `[ID]` is the appropriate ID code for this computer installation as defined in the [Unique IDs] section of the UDF.

d. Respond to any prompts in Windows Setup to complete the installation.

Topic B
Create a Computer Image

In the last chapter, you learned how to perform a manual installation of an operating system. But what if you're responsible for installing an operating system along with all application software on 20 computers? One technique you can use to cut down on the amount of time you'll have to spend installing the operating system on these computers is to create an image of one computer and then install it on the remaining 19 computers. In this topic, you'll learn the first part of the imaging process by mastering the steps for creating a computer image.

Simply downloading a computer image is the fastest possible method for installing an operating system on a computer. Using a computer image to install an operating system on several computers also enables you to easily standardize their configuration. Because you'll be using a computer image over and over to install the operating system on so many computers, it's critical that you create a good image that contains everything you need. Configuring the image properly will help you avoid having to spend time recreating an image and then downloading it again to the computers for which you're responsible for installing.

Computer Image

For ease of installing multiple computers, you can "clone" a computer's hard disk onto a network server, and then download that clone onto other computers' hard disks. When you clone a computer's hard disk, you create an exact duplicate image of it. Installing this *computer image* onto other computers enables you to avoid having to install the operating system and all applications on each computer. Most companies use one of two tools for creating and downloading computer images: Symantec Ghost or Windows 2000/Windows XP Remote Installation Services (RIS). Because Symantec Ghost is so commonly used, you'll sometimes hear the process of imaging a computer referred to as *ghosting* a computer.

The Computer Image Deployment Process

The image-deployment process contains two main phases: the preparation phase and the deployment phase. First, you must prepare the image:

1. Prepare the computer of which you want to create an image:
   a. Install the operating system.
   b. Configure the operating system and applications while logged on as the user account you want to preserve in the image.
   c. Copy this user account's profile to the Default User profile.
   d. Test to verify the installation and configuration.

e. If you're creating an image of a Windows 2000 or Windows XP computer, prepare the computer with a system-preparation utility such as Sysprep. This utility enables each computer that receives the cloned image to have its own unique security identifier number (SID).

f. Shut down the computer.

2. Restart the computer by using a custom boot disk for your own network or by using a startup disk from the computer image utility (Ghost or RIS).

3. Run the computer image utility to duplicate the computer installation to a file.

4. Store the image on easily accessible media, such as a CD-ROM or a network share.

After you have prepared the image, you can deploy it to multiple computers:

1. Verify that the computer on which you want to install the image has identical hardware to the computer you cloned.

2. Start this computer by using a custom boot disk for your own network or by using a startup disk for the computer image utility.

3. Use the computer image utility to download the image onto the computer.

4. If you downloaded the image to a Windows 2000 or Windows XP computer, use the Sysprep mini-Setup routine to customize settings for the newly installed computer.

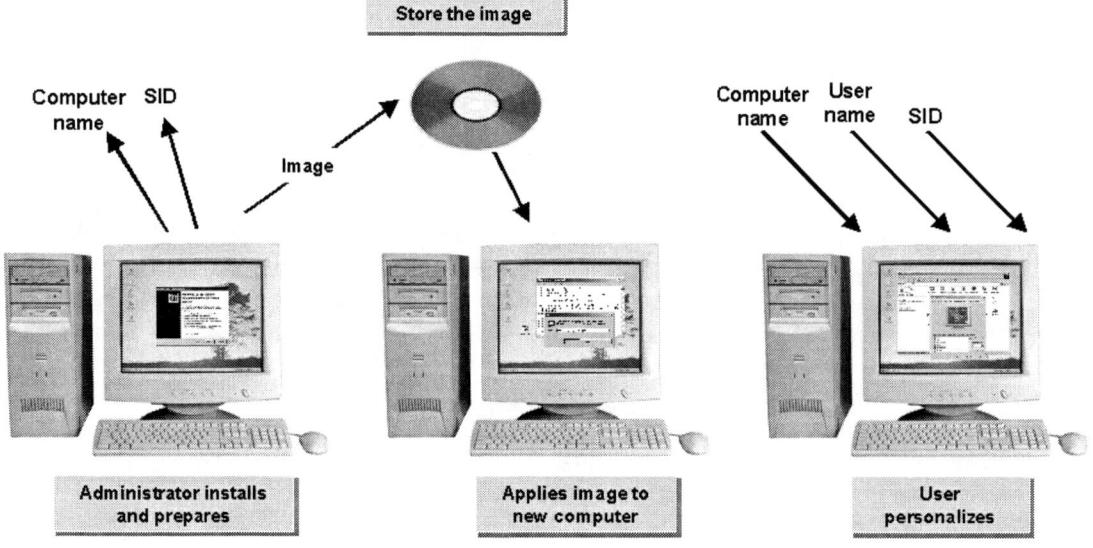

Figure 22-2: *Preparing and deploying a computer image.*

How to Create a Computer Image

Procedure Reference: Create a Computer Image and Store it on a Network Share

To create an image of a computer running Windows 2000, Windows XP, Windows NT, or Windows 98 and store it on a network share:

1. Install the Windows operating system.
2. Connect to the Windows Update Web site to update the operating system.
3. If you're using Windows 2000, Windows XP, or Windows NT, log on as a user account with administrative permissions and configure operating system settings. Install and configure all applications.
4. If necessary, install Ghost. (See the following procedure for how to install Ghost.)
5. Create a Ghost boot disk. (See the Create a Ghost Boot Disk procedure.)
6. Uninstall any applications you don't want to include in the computer image. For example, if you don't want to include the Ghost application on the image of the computer, uninstall Ghost.
7. If you're using Windows 2000, Windows XP, or Windows NT, copy this user's profile to the Default User profile.
    a. Log on as a local administrator.
    b. Open Windows Explorer.
    c. If you're using Windows 2000 or Windows XP, select the x:\Documents And Settings folder (replace x: with the drive letter on which Windows 2000 or Windows XP is installed). Configure this folder to display System and hidden files.

    If you're using Windows NT, select the x:\Winnt\Profiles folder (replace x: with the drive letter on which Windows 2000 or Windows XP is installed). Configure this folder to display System and hidden files.
    d. Close Windows Explorer.
    e. In Control Panel, double-click System.
    f. Select the User Profiles tab.
    g. In the Profiles Stored On This Computer list, select the profile you want to copy.
    h. Click Copy To.
    i. Below Copy Profile To, type or click Browse to enter the path x:\Documents And Settings\Default User. (replace x: with the drive letter on which Windows 2000 or Windows XP is installed).
    j. If you receive a warning stating that the Default User folder already exists, click Yes to overwrite the files.
    k. Below Permitted To Use, click Change.
    l. In the Name list, double-click Everyone.
    m. Click OK to copy the reference user's profile to the default user.

n. Click OK to close the System Properties dialog box.

o. Close Control Panel.

 If you use Setup Manager to create a Sysprep answer file, the mini-setup will automatically generate a unique name for the computer.

8. If you're using Windows 2000 or Windows XP and you want to automate the setup routine that will run after you deliver the computer to the user, use Setup Manager to create a Sysprep answer file. Save the file as \Sysprep\Sysprep.inf. The Sysprep answer file uses the same syntax as an unattended installation answer file, but supports only the necessary subset of sections and keys required by the mini-setup routine.

9. If you're using Windows 2000 or Windows XP, extract the Sysprep.exe and Setupcl.exe files from the \Support\Tools\Deploy.cab folder on the Windows XP or Windows 2000 installation CD-ROM to \Sysprep on the computer you want to image (the Sysprep and Setup Manager Wizard files must be in the same folder if you want to use an answer file to automate the mini-setup routine).

10. If you're cloning Windows XP, prepare the computer by running Sysprep with the appropriate parameters. See Table 22-2 for a list and description of the parameters you can use when preparing a computer for imaging. You can do either of the following:

- Run Sysprep at the command line with the appropriate switches. Use this syntax:
  sysprep [-switch]...[-switch]

- Run Sysprep.exe and make the appropriate selections in the System Preparation Tool graphical utility.

Table 22-2: *Windows XP Sysprep Parameters*

Switch	Graphical Equivalent	Purpose
–msoobe (default setting)	Leave MiniSetup unchecked	Uses Windows Welcome as the mini-setup routine.
–mini	Check MiniSetup	Runs an abbreviated version of the Windows XP Professional Setup Wizard as the mini-setup routine; detects and uses a Sysprep.inf file if present.
–quiet	None	Prevents the confirmation dialog boxes from being displayed.
–forceshutdown	From the Shutdown drop-down list, select Shutdown	Forces shutdown of the computer.
–reboot	From the Shutdown drop-down list, select Reboot	Forces a reboot of the computer after Sysprep is run.

Switch	Graphical Equivalent	Purpose
–pnp	Check PnP	Runs Plug and Play detection when the computer is restarted after the computer image is downloaded.

11. If you're cloning Windows 2000, prepare the computer by running Sysprep with the appropriate parameters. See Table 22-3 for a list and description of the parameters you can use when preparing a computer for imaging. You can Run Sysprep at the command line with the appropriate switches. Use this syntax: `sysprep [-switch]...[-switch]`.

Table 22-3: *Windows 2000 Sysprep Parameters*

Switch	Purpose
–quiet	Prevents the confirmation dialog boxes from being displayed.
–reboot	Forces a reboot of the computer after Sysprep is run.
–pnp	Runs Plug and Play detection when the computer is restarted after the computer image is downloaded.

12. Insert the Ghost boot disk and turn the computer on.
13. When prompted to log on, press Enter to log on as the user you specified when you created the boot disk.
14. When prompted, enter the user account's password.
15. Access the mapped network drive letter.
16. Enter `ghost` to run the Ghost utility.
17. On the License Agreement Warning page, press Enter to mark the computer's hard disk.
18. Press Enter again.
19. Verify that Local is selected and press Enter.
20. Verify that Disk is selected and press Enter.
21. Select To Image and press Enter.
22. Press Enter to select the computer's hard disk.
23. In the File Name text box, type a name for the computer image.
24. Press Alt+S to save the name.

25. Select a compression setting and press Enter.
    - Fast
    - High
26. Press Alt+Y to create the image.
27. Press Enter to continue.
28. Press Q to quit.
29. Press Y to quit.

Procedure Reference: Install Ghost

To install Ghost:

1. Insert the Norton Ghost installation CD-ROM or connect to a network share containing the installation files.
2. If necessary, double-click Ghost to start the installation.
3. In the InstallShield Wizard, click Next.
4. Select I Accept The Terms In The License Agreement and click Next.
5. If necessary, enter a name and company name in the User Name and Organization text boxes.
6. Click Next.
7. On the Destination Folder page, select the folder in which you want to install Ghost or click Next to accept the default path.
8. Click Install to begin the installation.
9. When the installation is complete, follow the pages in the wizard to register the software or click Skip to skip registration.
10. On the Installation Completed Successfully page, click Next.
11. Click Finish.

Procedure Reference: Create a Ghost Boot Disk

To create a Ghost boot disk:

1. If necessary, install Ghost (see the Install Ghost procedure).
2. Verify the driver used by the computer's network card. Use these steps:
    a. On the desktop, right-click My Computer and choose Properties.
    b. Select the Hardware tab.
    c. Click Device Manager.
    d. Expand Network Adapters.
    e. Record the name of the driver.

f. Close Device Manager.

g. Click OK to close the System Properties dialog box.

3. Run Norton Ghost (from the Start menu, choose Programs or All Programs→Norton Ghost 2003→Norton Ghost).

4. In the left pane, click Ghost Utilities.

5. Click Norton Ghost Boot Wizard.

6. Select Drive Mapping Boot Disk and click Next.

7. In the list of network card drivers, select the computer's network card driver if available (if the driver isn't available, click Add and follow the prompts to load the driver from the network card manufacturer's floppy disk or CD-ROM).

8. Click Next.

9. Verify that Use PC-DOS is selected and click Next.

10. In the Client Computer Name text box, type a name to use when you boot the computer from the boot disk. If you plan to run Ghost simultaneously on multiple computers, make sure that you configure each boot disk with a different computer name.

11. In the User Name text box, type a user name for the server on which you plan to store the computer image.

12. In the Domain text box, type the NetBIOS domain name for this server.

> Using G for this drive letter will make it easier for you to remember what letter to use when accessing the images.

13. Below Mapped Drive, from the Drive Letter drop-down list, select a drive letter.

14. In the Maps To text box, type the UNC share name for the folder in which you want to store the Ghost image.

15. Click Next.

16. Configure the TCP/IP addressing settings. Use one of the following:

    - Select DHCP Will Assign The IP Settings if you want to use a DHCP server to assign the IP address to the client when it boots from the boot disk.

    - Select The IP Address Settings Will Be Statically Defined if you want to manually assign the IP address, subnet mask, gateway, and DNS address to the client.

17. Click Next.

18. On the Destination Drive page, verify that the correct drive letter for the computer's floppy drive is specified.

19. Click Next.

20. On the Review page, click Next.

21. Click Start to format the floppy disk.
22. Click OK to confirm.
23. Click OK to close the Format Complete message box.
24. Click Close.
25. Click Finish.
26. Close Norton Ghost.
27. Remove the floppy disk and label it.
28. Copy Ghost.exe from the \Program Files\Symantec\Norton Ghost 2003 folder to the shared folder in which you plan to store the computer image.

Procedure Reference: Uninstall Ghost

To uninstall Ghost:

1. In Control Panel, double-click Add/Remove Programs.
2. In the list of currently installed programs, select Norton Ghost.
3. Click Remove.
4. Click Yes to remove Norton Ghost.
5. Close Add/Remove Programs and Control Panel.

Topic C
Install a Computer Image

In Topic 22B, you learned the skills necessary to create an image of a standard computer. Now you're ready to install that image on other computers. In this topic, you'll learn how to deploy an image onto a target computer.

Imagine the following scenario: You've been asked to install the Windows 2000 operating system, Microsoft Office, and the Lotus Notes client on 250 computers—all over the course of a single weekend. If it takes you three hours to install one computer's operating system and the applications, it will take you a total of 750 man hours to complete this task if you install all of the computers manually. Instead, you can dramatically reduce the amount of time you'll need to perform these installations by creating and then installing a computer image instead. Knowing how to create an image, as you saw in Topic 22B, and how to deploy an image will save you untold hours when you're responsible for installing and configuring a number of computers.

How to Install a Computer Image

Procedure Reference: Install a Computer Image

To install a computer image:

1. If necessary, create a Ghost boot disk (see the Create a Ghost Boot Disk procedure).
2. Insert the Ghost boot disk and turn the computer on.
3. When prompted to log on, press Enter to log on as the user you specified when you created the boot disk.
4. When prompted, enter the user account's password.
5. Access the mapped network drive letter.
6. Enter ghost to run the Ghost utility.
7. Press Enter.
8. Verify that Local is selected and press Enter.
9. Verify that Disk is selected and press Enter.
10. Select From Image and press Enter.
11. Use the arrow keys to highlight the image file you want to install and press Alt+O.
12. Press Enter to select the computer's hard disk.
13. If necessary, make any changes to the size of the computer's partitions.
14. Press Alt+O.
15. Press Alt+Y to install the image.
16. Press Enter to restart the computer.
17. Remove the boot disk.
18. If you used Sysprep to prepare the computer, complete the necessary pages in the mini-Setup wizard.
19. When prompted, log on to the computer. Verify that the computer is functioning correctly.

CHAPTER 22 FOLLOW-UP
Automating Client Operating System Installations

In this chapter, you learned how to automate installations by performing tasks such as an unattended installation, cloning a computer, and downloading the clone image to another computer. Because the process of installing an operating system is so time-consuming, using these techniques will help you to install computers much faster and save you quite a bit of work.

Essential Terms

- automated operating system installation
- client operating systems
- computer images
- imaging computers
- operating system images
- operating system installation
- operating systems
- unattended installation
- Windows operating systems

Review Questions

1. What is an answer file?
2. What two ways can you use to create an answer file?
3. An answer may be saved with either of what two file extensions?
4. There are six required sections in an answer file. What are they?
5. What is the section name that contains system-specific information?
6. What does the [identification] section of an answer file contain?
7. In Windows XP, what is the name of the file that installs the Setup Manager Wizard?
8. Which folder usually contains the Dosnet.inf information file?
9. You can select the level of user interaction during an unattended installation. What are the five levels?
10. What is the fastest possible method for installing an operating system?
11. What is cloning?
12. What are the two main phases of the image-deployment process?
13. If you're creating an image of a Windows 2000 or Windows XP computer, what system preparation tool should you use?
14. What is the purpose of the Sysprep utility?
15. Which Windows XP sysprep switch prevents the confirmation dialog from being displayed?
16. What is the purpose of the Windows XP Sysprep switch -msoobe?
17. Which Windows 2000 and Windows XP sysprep switch runs plug and play detection when the computer is restarted after the computer image is downloaded?
18. Which Windows 2000 and Windows XP sysprep switch prevents the confirmation dialog boxes from being displayed?

19. What are two reasons you'd perform unattended installs rather than image computers?
20. Where would you find the sysprep.exe and setupcl.exe folders?
21. You are preparing a computer for imaging. If you run sysprep from the command line, what is the correct syntax to use?
22. An answer file must conform to a general syntax. What does that syntax look like?
23. In Windows XP, what command do you enter at the run line to launch the Setup Manager Wizard?
24. You launch the Setup Manager Wizard in Windows XP. The second of the setup screens prompts you for the product the answer file is for. There are three options. What are they?
25. What are the two tools used by many companies to create and download computer images?

Review Projects

Project #1 Customizing Installations

In your readings you were introduced to the Sysprep utility. Sysprep, coupled with disk duplication software, is the most efficient installation method to use when you need to install Windows 2000 or Windows XP on a large number of computers. By creating a disk image of a Windows 2000 or XP installation, you can copy the image to destination computers and save valuable deployment time. Further, disk imaging provides you with a master copy of an installation which you can use to repair/recover systems later.

The Microsoft support article, "Customizing and Automating Installations," supplements the detailed step-by-step setup and configuration information in your readings. Access the article at the following location: **http://www.microsoft.com/windows2000/techinfo/reskit/en-us/default.asp?url=/windows2000/techinfo/reskit/en-us/prork/prbc_cai_gumy.asp**. This activity is split into two parts. First, read through the guide and note those areas that are new to you. If you have worked through the steps in your readings, go back and review them (or perform the steps again). In the second part of this activity, you'll watch a series of animations that show you how to perform specific actions using Symantec's Ghost imaging utility. View the six tutorials to see how Norton's ghost software works. Bookmark both sites for future reference. Also, under the support category on Symantec's site you can download the documentation for Ghost.

Project #2 Performing Unattended Installations

Performing an unattended installation is not a difficult process, but it can be intimidating if you have never performed one. In this activity, you'll work through a tutorial that will put a "GUI face" on the detailed step-by-step process presented in your readings. By employing both senses—by reading and seeing—you'll have a more complete understanding of the unattended install process.

The tutorial is avaialble on Hytek computer's Web site, which is located at **http://www.hytekcomputer.com/Articles/XPInstall/1.shtml**. When you reach the end of the tutorial (page 6) there are links located at the bottom of the page. Review the first three links which are:

- Deploying Windows XP Part I: Planning
- Deploying Windows XP Part II: Implementing
- Deploying Windows XP Using Windows Product Activation

The above articles are excellent white papers you can download for review later.

Project #3 Remote Installation Services (RIS)

Remote Installation Services was touched upon in your readings. RIS is a feature of Windows 2000 server that allows administrators to set up new client computers from a central location. RIS is server-based, which means that you create and dedicate a partition to store source files. In the following Microsoft article, you'll learn about RIS and the various services it employs to perform installations. The knowledge base article, "How To: Use Remote Installation Service to Install Windows 2000 Professional on Remote Computers," is located at **http://support.microsoft.com/?kbid=300483**. The objective of this activity is to read through the article and gain a general understanding of what RIS is and why it would be beneficial on larger networks. One of the clear benefits of this article is that you can see how these services—remote installation services—interact within a network environment. You should focus on understanding the interactions of those relationships rather than the specific steps involved in setting up and deploying RIS.

Reflective Questions

1. Have you ever performed an unattended installation? If yes, what was your experience with it?

2. Have you ever cloned a computer? If yes, how did it go? Were you able to successfully download the computer image to another computer? Why or why not?

Follow-up

In this course, you installed, removed, upgraded, maintained, and troubleshot computer hardware. You also performed operating systems management tasks in the Windows 98, Windows 2000, Windows NT, and Windows XP operating systems. Mastering the skills in this course will enable you to respond to any hardware or operating system technical support calls you encounter. By combining the class experience with review, study, and hands-on experience, you'll also be prepared to demonstrate your knowledge on the A+ certification examinations.

Reflective Questions

1. Will you be installing more internal or more external hardware?

2. What will be the most challenging hardware issues to troubleshoot?

3. What operating system(s) do you think you will be supporting?

4. Give some examples of operating system-related technical support calls you think you'll encounter.

Appendix A
A+ Certification Exam Objectives

A+ Core Hardware Exam Objectives

The following table lists the test domains and objectives for the A+ Core Hardware examination, and where they are covered in this course.

A+ Core Hardware Test Domains and Objectives	Chapter	Topic
Domain 1: Installation, Configuration, and Upgrading		
Objective 1.1: Identify the names, purpose, and characteristics of system modules. Recognize these modules by sight or definition.		
Examples of concepts and modules are:		
Motherboard	4	F
Firmware	4	D
Power Supply	4	E
Processor/CPU	4	B
Memory	4	A
Storage Devices	3	D
Adapter Cards	2	A
Ports	3	B
Cases	2	A
Riser Cards	4	F
Objective 1.2: Identify basic procedures for adding and removing field-replaceable modules for desktop systems. Given a replacement scenario, choose the appropriate sequences.		
Desktop components:		
Motherboard	4	F
Storage Devices	3	D
• FDD	3	D
• HDD	3	D
• CD/CDRW	3	D
• DVD/DVDRW	3	D

Appendix A: A+ Certification Exam Objectives

A+ Core Hardware Test Domains and Objectives	Chapter	Topic
• Tape Drive	3	D
• Removable Storage	3	D
Power Supply	4	E
• AC Adapter	4	E
• AT/ATX	4	F
Cooling Systems	4	B
• Fans	4	B
• Heat sinks	4	B
• Liquid cooling	8	F
Processor/CPU	4	B
Memory	4	A
Display device	2	A
Input devices	2	B
• Keyboard	2	B
• Mouse/pointer devices	2	B
• Touch screen	2	F
Adapters	3	B
• Network Interface Card (NIC)	3	C
• Sound card	2	E
• Video card	2	A
• Modem	2 3	D B
• SCSI	3	E, F
• IEEE 1394/FireWire	2	G
• USB	2	F
• Wireless	2	H
Objective 1.3: Identify basic procedures for adding and removing field-replaceable modules for portable systems. Given a replacement scenario, choose the appropriate sequences.		
Portable components:		
Storage Devices	5	B

A+ Core Hardware Test Domains and Objectives	Chapter	Topic
• FDD	5	B
• HDD	5	B
• CD/CD-RW	5	B
• DVD/DVD-RW	5	B
• Removable Storage	5	B
Power sources	5	A
• AC Adapter	5	A
• DC adapter	5	A
• Battery	5	A
Memory	5	E
Input devices	5	A
• Keyboard	5	A
• Mouse/pointer devices	5	A
• Touch screen	5	A
PCMCIA/Mini PCI Adapters	5	C, D
• Network Interface Card (NIC)	5	C, D
• Modem	5	C, D
• SCSI	5	C, D
• IEEE 1394/Firewire	5	C, D
• USB	5	C, D
• Storage (memory and hard drive)	5	C, D
Docking station / port replicators	5	A
LCD panel	5	A
Wireless	2	H
• Adapter / controller	2	H
• Antennae	2	H
Objective 1.4: Identify typical IRQs, DMAs, and I/O addresses, and procedures for altering these settings when installing and configuring devices. Choose the appropriate installation or configuration steps in a given scenario.		
Content may include the following:		

Appendix A: A+ Certification Exam Objectives

A+ Core Hardware Test Domains and Objectives	Chapter	Topic
Legacy devices (e.g. ISA sound card)	3	B
Specialized devices (e.g. CAD/CAM)	3	B
Internal modems	3	B
Floppy drive controllers	3	B
Hard drive controllers	3	B
Multimedia devices	3	B
NICs	3	B
I/O ports	3	B
• Serial	3	B
• Parallel	3	B
• USB ports	3	B
• IEEE 1394/FireWire	3	B
• Infrared	3	B
Objective 1.5: Identify the names, purposes, and performance characteristics of standardized/common peripheral ports, associated cabling, and their connectors. Recognize ports, cabling, and connectors by sight.		
Content may include the following:		
Port types	2	D, C, F, G, H
• Serial	2	D
• Parallel	2	C
• USB ports	2	F
• IEEE 1394/FireWire	2	G
• Infrared	2	H
Cable types	2	C, D, F
• Serial (straight through vs. null modem)	2	D
• Parallel	2	C
• USB	2	F
Connector types	2	B, C, D, F, G

A+ Core Hardware Test Domains and Objectives	Chapter	Topic
• Serial: — DB-9 — DB-25 — RJ-11 — RJ-45	2	D
• Parallel — DB-25 — Centronics (mini, 36)	2	C
• PS2/Mini-DIN	2	B
• USB	2	F
• IEE 1394	2	G
Objective 1.6: Identify proper procedures for installing and configuring common IDE devices. Choose the appropriate installation or configuration sequences in given scenarios. Recognize the associated cables.		
Content may include the following:		
IDE Interface Types	3	D
• EIDE	3	D
• ATA/ATAPI	3	D
• Serial ATA	3	D
• PIO	3	D
RAID (0, 1, and 5)	3	G
Master/Slave/Cable Select	3	D
Devices per channel	3	D
Primary/Secondary	3	D
Cable orientation/requirements	3	D
Objective 1.7: Identify proper procedures for installing and configuring common SCSI devices. Choose the appropriate installation or configuration sequences in given scenarios. Recognize the associated cables.		
Content may include the following:		
SCSI Interface Types	3	E
• Narrow	3	E
• Fast	3	E

A+ Core Hardware Test Domains and Objectives	Chapter	Topic
• Wide	3	E
• Ultra-wide	3	E
• LVD	3	E
• HVD	3	E
Internal versus external	3	E, F
SCSI IDs	3	E
• Jumper block/DIP switch settings (binary equivalents)	3	E
• Resolving ID conflicts	3	E
RAID (0, 1, and 5)	3	G
Cabling	3	E
• Length	3	E
• Type	3	E
• Termination requirements (active, passive, auto)	3	E
Objective 1.8: Identify proper procedures for installing and configuring common peripheral devices. Choose the appropriate installation or configuration sequences in given scenarios.		
Content may include the following:		
Modems and transceivers (dial-up, cable, DSL, ISDN)	2 3	D C
External storage	2 3	C, F, G F
Digital cameras	2	F
PDAs	2 5	H F
Infrared devices	2	H
Printers	2	C, D
UPS (Uninterruptable Power Supply) and supressors	6	B
Monitors	2	A
Objective 1.9: Identify procedures to optimize PC operations in specific situations. Predict the effects of specific procedures under given scenarios.		
Topics may include:		
Cooling systems	4 8	C F

A+ Core Hardware Test Domains and Objectives	Chapter	Topic
• Liquid	8	F
• Air	8	F
• Heat sink	4	C
• Thermal compound	4 8	C F
Disk subsystem enhancements	3	D, E
• Hard drives	3	D, E
• Controller cards (e.g. RAID, ATA-100, etc.)	3	D, E
• Cables	3	D, E
NICs	7	C
Specialized video cards	2 3	A B
Memory	4	A
Additional processors	4	C
Objective 1.10: Determine the issues that must be considered when upgrading a PC. In a given scenario, determine when and how to upgrade system components.		
Issues may include:		
Drivers for legacy devices	3	B
Bus types and characteristics	3	B
Cache in relationship to motherboards	4	A
Memory capacity and characteristics	4	A
Processor speed and compatibility	4	B
Hard drive capacity and characteristics	3	D, E
System/firmware limitations	4	G
Power supply output capacity	4	E
Components may include the following:		
Motherboards	4	F
Memory	4	A
Hard drives	3 4	D G
CPU	4	B
BIOS	4	D

Appendix A: A+ Certification Exam Objectives

A+ Core Hardware Test Domains and Objectives	Chapter	Topic
Adapter cards	3 4	B G
Laptop power sources	5	A
• Lithium ion	5	A
• NiMH	5	A
• Fuel cell	5	A
PCMCIA Type I, II, and III cards	5	C
Domain 2: Diagnosing and Troubleshooting		
Objective 2.1: Recognize common problems associated with each module and their symptoms, and identify steps to isolate and troubleshoot the problems. Given a problem situation, interpret the symptoms and infer the most likely cause.		
Content may include the following:		
I/O ports and cables	2 7 8	C, D, H B, C, G B
• Serial	2 8	D B
• Parallel	2 7	C G
• USB ports	7	B
• IEEE 1394/FireWire	7	C
• Infrared	2	H
• SCSI	7	C, D
Motherboards	7 8	D D
• CMOS/BIOS settings	8	D
• POST audible/visual error codes	7 8	D D
Peripherals	7	A, B
Computer case	7	C, E, F
• Power supply	8	C
• Slot covers	3	B
• Front cover alignment	7	E, F

A+ Core Hardware Test Domains and Objectives	Chapter	Topic
Storage devices and cables	7	D, E, F
• FDD	7	E
• HDD	7	D
• CD/CD-RW	7	F
• DVD/DVD-RW	7	F
• Tape drive	7	E
• Removable storage	7	E
Cooling systems	8	F
• Fans	8	F
• Heat sinks	8	F
• Liquid cooling	8	F
• Temperature sensors	8	F
Processor/CPU	8	F
Memory	8	E
Display device	7	A
Input devices	7	B
• Keyboard	7	B
• Mouse/pointer devices	7	B
• Touch screen	7	B
Adapters	7	C
• Network Interface Card (NIC)	7	C
• Sound card	7	C
• Video card	7	C
• Modem	7	C
• SCSI	7	C
• IEEE 1394/FireWire	7	C
• USB	7	C
Portable systems	8	G
• PCMCIA	8	G

Appendix A: A+ Certification Exam Objectives

A+ Core Hardware Test Domains and Objectives	Chapter	Topic
• Batteries	8	G
• Docking stations/Port replicators	8	G
• Portable unique storage	8	G
Objective 2.2: Identify basic troubleshooting procedures and tools, and how to elicit problem symptoms from customers. Justify asking particular questions in a given scenario.		
Content may include the following:		
Troubleshooting/isolation/problem determination procedures	7 8	A H
Determining whether a hardware or software problem	7 8	A H
Gathering information from user	8	H
• Customer environment	8	H
• Symptoms/error codes	8	H
• Situation when the problem occurred	8	H
Domain 3: PC Preventive Maintenance, Safety, and Environmental Issues		
Objective 3.1: Identify the various types of preventive maintenance measures, products, and procedures and when and how to use them.		
Content may include the following:		
Cleaning compounds	6	D
Types of materials to clean contacts and connections	6	E
Non-static vacuums (chassis, power supplies, fans)	6	B
Cleaning monitors	6	D
Cleaning removable media devices	6	E
Ventilation, dust and moisture control on the PC hardware interior	6	B, D, E
Hard disk maintenance (defragging, scan disk, CHKDSK)	6	A
Verifying UPS (Uninterruptible Power Supply) and suppressors	6	C
Objective 3.2: Identify various safety measures and procedures, and when/how to use them.		
Content may include the following:		
ESD (Electrostatic Discharge) precautions and procedures	3	A

A+ Core Hardware Test Domains and Objectives	Chapter	Topic
• What ESD can do, how it may be apparent or hidden	3	A
• Common ESD protection devices	3	A
• Situations that could present a danger or hazard	3	A
Potential hazards and proper safety procedures relating to:	3 6	A F
• High-voltage equipment	3 6	A F
• Power supply	3 6	A F
• CRTs	3 6	A F
Objective 3.3: Identify environmental protection measures and procedures, and when/how to use them.		
Content may include:		
Special disposal procedures that comply with environmental guidelines	6	F
• Batteries	6	F
• CRTs	6	F
• Chemical solvents and cans	6	F
• MSDS (Material Safety Data Sheet)	6	F
Domain 4: Motherboard/Processors/Memory		
Objective 4.1: Distinguish between the popular CPU chips in terms of their basic characteristics.		
Content may include the following:		
Popular CPU chips (Pentium class compatible)	4	B
Voltage	4	B
Speeds (actual vs. advertised)	4	B
Cache level I, II, III	3	A
Sockets/slots	4	B
VRM(s)	4	F
Objective 4.2: Identify the types of RAM (Random Access Memory), form factors, and operational characteristics. Determine banking and speed requirements under given scenarios.		
Content may include the following:		
Types	4	A

Appendix A: A+ Certification Exam Objectives

A+ Core Hardware Test Domains and Objectives	Chapter	Topic
• EDO RAM (Extended Data Output RAM)	4	A
• DRAM (Dynamic Random Access Memory)	4	A
• SRAM (Static RAM)	4	A
• VRAM (Video RAM)	4	A
• SDRAM (Synchronous Dynamic RAM)	4	A
• DDR (Double Data Rate)	4	A
• RAMBUS	4	A
Form factors (including pin count)	4	A
• SIMM (Single In-line Memory Module)	4	A
• DIMM (Dual In-line Memory Module)	4	A
• SoDIMM (Small outline DIMM)	4	A
• MicroDIMM	4	A
• RIMM (Rambus Inline Memory Module)	4	A
Operational characteristics	4	A
• Memory chips (8-bit, 16-bit, and 32-bit)	4	A
• Parity chips versus non-parity chips	4	A
• ECC vs. non-ECC	4	A
• Single-sided vs. double-sided	4	A
Objective 4.3: Identify the most popular types of motherboards, their components, and their architecture (bus structures).		
Content may include the following:		
Types of motherboards	4	F
• AT	4	F
• ATX	4	F
Components	4	F
Communications ports	2	C, D, F, G, H
• Serial	2	D
• USB	2	F
• Parallel	2	C

A+ Core Hardware Test Domains and Objectives	Chapter	Topic
• IEEE 1394/FireWire	2	G
• Infrared	2	H
Memory	4	A
• SIMM	4	A
• DIMM	4	A
• RIMM	4	A
• SoDIMM	4	A
• MicroDIMM	4	A
Processor sockets	4	B
• Slot 1	4	B
• Slot 2	4	B
• Slot A	4	B
• Socket A	4	B
• Socket 7	4	B
• Socket 8	4	B
• Socket 423	4	B
• Socket 478	4	B
• Socket 370	4	B
External cache memory (Level 2)	4	A
Bus Architecture	3	B
ISA	3	B
PCI	3	B
• PCI 32-bit	3	B
• PCI 64-bit	3	B
AGP	3	B
• 2X	3	B
• 4X	3	B
• 8X (Pro)	3	B
USB (Universal Serial Bus)	2	F

A+ Core Hardware Test Domains and Objectives	Chapter	Topic
AMR (audio modem riser) slots	4	F
CNR (communication network riser) slots	4	F
Basic compatibility guidelines	4	G
IDE (ATA, ATAPI, ULTRA-DMA, EIDE)	3	D
SCSI (Narrow, Wide, Fast, Ultra, HVD, LVD (Low Voltage Differential)	3	E, F
Chipsets	4	F
Objective 4.4: Identify the purpose of CMOS (Complementary Metal-Oxide Semiconductor) memory, what it contains, and how and when to change its parameters. Given a scenario involving CMOS, choose the appropriate course of action.		
CMOS Settings:		
Default settings	4	D
CPU settings	4	D
Printer parallel port—Uni, bi-directional, disable/ enable/ ECP, EPP	7	G
Com/serial port—memory address, interrupt request, disable	4	D
Floppy drive—enble/disable drive or boot, speed, density	4	D
Memory—speed, parity, non-parity	8	E
Boot sequence	8	D
Date/Time	4	D
Passwords	4	D
Plug & Play BIOS	4	D
Disabling on-board devices	4	D
Disabling virus protection	4	D
Power management	4	D
Infrared	4	D
Domain 5: Printers		
Objective 5.1: Identify printer technologies, interfaces, and options/upgrades.		
Technologies include:		
Laser	6	B
Ink dispersion (inkjet)	6	B
Dot matrix	6	B

A+ Core Hardware Test Domains and Objectives	Chapter	Topic
Solid ink	6	B
	7	G
Thermal	6	B
	7	G
Dye sublimation	6	B
	5	G
Interfaces include:		
Parallel	2	C
Network	3	C
SCSI	3	F
USB	2	F
Infrared	2	H
Serial	2	D
IEEE 1394/FireWire	2	G
Wireless	2	H
Options/Upgrades include:		
Memory	6	B
Hard drives	6	B
NICs	6	B
Trays and feeders	6	B
Finishers (e.g. stapling, etc)	6	B
Scanners/fax/copier	6	B
Objective 5.2: Recognize common printer problems and techniques used to resolve them.		
Content may include the following:		
Printer drivers	7	G
Firmware updates	7	G
Paper feed and output	7	G
Calibrations	7	G
Printing test pages	7	G
Errors (printed or displayed)	7	G
Memory	7	G
Configuration	7	G
Network connections	7	G
Connections	7	G

A+ Core Hardware Test Domains and Objectives	Chapter	Topic
Paper jam	7	G
Print quality	7	G
Safety precautions	7	G
Preventive maintenance	6	B
Consumables	6	F
Environment	6	F
Domain 6: Basic Networking		
Objective 6.1: Identify the common types of network cables, their characteristics and connectors.		
Cable types include:		
Coaxial	3	C
• RG6	3	C
• RG8	3	C
• RG58	3	C
• RG59	3	C
Plenum/PVC	3	C
UTP	3	C
• CAT3	3	C
• CAT 5/e	3	C
• CAT6	3	C
STP	3	C
Fiber	3	C
• Single-mode	3	C
• Multi-mode	3	C
Connector types include:		
BNC	3	C
RJ-45	2 3	D C
AUI	3	C
ST/SC	3	C
IDC/UDC	3	C
Objective 6.2: Identify basic networking concepts including how a network works.		
Concepts include:		

A+ Core Hardware Test Domains and Objectives	Chapter	Topic
Installing and configuring network cards	3	C
Addressing	3	C
Bandwidth	3	C
Status indicators	3	C
Protocols	3	C
• TCP/IP	3	C
• IPX/SPX (NWLink)	3	C
• AppleTalk	3	C
• NetBEUI/NetBIOS	3	C
Full-duplex, half-duplex	2	D
Cabling—Twisted Pair, Coaxial, Fiber Optic, RS-232	3	C
Networking models	3	C
• Peer-to-peer	3	C
• Client/server	3	C
Infrared	2 3	H C
Wireless	3	C
Objective 6.3: Identify common technologies available for establishing Internet connectivity and their characteristics.		
Technologies include:		
LAN	3	C
DSL	3	C
Cable	3	C
ISDN	3	C
Dial-up	3	C
Satellite	3	C
Wireless	3	C
Characteristics include:		
Definition	3	C
Speed	3	C
Connections	3	C

A+ Operating System Technologies Exam Objectives

The following table lists the test domains and objectives for the A+ Operating System Technologies examination, and where they are covered in this course.

A+ Operating System Technologies Exam Objectives	Chapter	Topic
Domain 1.0: Operating System Fundamentals		
Objective 1.1: Identify the major desktop components and interfaces, and their functions. Differentiate the characteristics of Windows 9x/ME, Windows NT 4.0 Workstation, Windows 2000 Professional, and Windows XP.		
Content may include the following:		
Contrasts between Windows 9x/ME, Windows NT 4.0 Workstation, Windows 2000 Professional, and Windows XP	21	A
Major operating system components	10 12	A, B D
• Registry	10	A
• Virtual memory	10	B
• File System	12	D
Major operating system interfaces	9	A, B
• Windows Explorer	9	A
• My Computer	9	A
• Control Panel	9	A
• Computer Management Console	9	A
• Accessories/System Tools	9	A
• Command Line	9	B
• Network Neighborhood/My Network Places	9	A
• Task Bar/systray	9	A
• Start Menu	9	A
• Device Manager	9	A
Objective 1.2: Identify the names, locations, purposes, and contents of major system files.		
Content may include the following:		

A+ Operating System Technologies Exam Objectives	Chapter	Topic
Windows 9x specific files	10 19	A, D A
• IO.SYS	19	A
• MSDOS.SYS	19	A
• AUTOEXEC.BAT	19	A
• COMMAND.COM	19	A
• CONFIG.SYS	19	A
• HIMEM.SYS	10	D
• EMM386.EXE	10	D
• WIN.COM	19	A
• SYSTEM.INI	19	A
• WIN.INI	19	A
• Registry data files — SYSTEM.DAT — USER.DAT	10	A
Windows NT-based specific files	10 19	A A
• BOOT.INI	19	A
• NTLDR	19	A
• NTDETECT.COM	19	A
• NTBOOTDD.SYS	19	A
• NTUSER.DAT	10	A
• Registry Data Files	10	A
Objective 1.3: Demonstrate the ability to use command-line functions and utilities to manage the operating system, including the proper syntax and switches.		
Command line functions and utilities include:		
Command/CMD	9	B
DIR	9	B
ATTRIB	9	B
VER	9	B

Appendix A: A+ Certification Exam Objectives

A+ Operating System Technologies Exam Objectives	Chapter	Topic
MEM	9	B
SCANDISK	9	B
DEFRAG	9	B
EDIT	9	B
XCOPY	9	B
COPY	9	B
FORMAT	9	B
FDISK	9	B
SETVER	9	B
SCANREG	19	E
MD/CD/RD	9	B
Delete/Rename	9	B
DELTREE	9	B
TYPE	9	B
ECHO	9	B
SET	9	B
PING	11	B
Objective 1.4: Identify basic concepts and procedures for creating, viewing, and managing disks, directories, and files. This includes procedures for changing file attributes and the ramifications of those changes (for example, security issues).		
Content may include the following:		
Disks	15	A
• Partitions — Active Partition — Primary Partition — Extended Partition — Logical Partition	15	A
• File Systems — FAT16 — FAT32 — NTFS4 — NTFS5.x	12	D

A+ Operating System Technologies Exam Objectives	Chapter	Topic
Directory Structures (root directory, subdirectory, etc.)	10	A
• Create folders	9	B
• Navigate the directory structure	9	A, B
• Maximum depth	9	A
Files	9 12 15	A D, E C
• Creating Files	9	A
• File naming conventions (most common extensions, 8.3, maximum length)	9	A
• File attributes—Read Only, Hidden, System, and Archive attributes	12	D
• File Compression	15	C
• File Encryption	12	E
• File Permissions	12	D
• File Types (text vs. binary file)	9	A
Objective 1.5: Identify the major operating system utilities, their purpose, location, and available switches.		
Disk Management Tools:		
DEFRAG.EXE	15	D
FDISK.EXE	15	1
Backup/Restore Utility (MSBackup, NTBackup, etc.)	19	D
ScanDisk	9	A
CHKDSK	9	B
Disk Cleanup	9	A
Format	9	B
System Management Tools:		
Device Manager	9	A
System Manager (System Monitor)	9	A
Computer Manager (Computer Management)	9	A

A+ Operating System Technologies Exam Objectives	Chapter	Topic
MSCONFIG.EXE	20	A
REGEDIT.EXE (View Information/Back up Registry)	10 19	A F
REGEDIT32.EXE	10	A
SYSEDIT.EXE	10	D
SCANREG	19	E
COMMAND/CMD	9	B
Event Viewer	9	A
Task Manager	20	A
File Management Tools:		
ATTRIB.EXE	9	B
EXTRACT.EXE	9	B
Edit.com	19	A
Windows Explorer	9	A
Domain 2: Installation, Configuration, and Upgrading		
Objective 2.1: Identify the procedures for installing Windows 9x, Windows ME, Windows NT 4.0 Workstation, Windows 2000 Professional, and Windows XP, and bringing the operating system to a basic operational level.		
Content may include the following:		
Verify hardware compatibility and minimum requirements	21	A
Determine OS installation options	21	A
• Installation type (typical, custom, other)	21	A
• Network configuration	21	A
• File system type	21	A
• Dual Boot Support	21	A
Disk preparation order (conceptual disk prepartion)	21	A
• Start the installation	21	A
• Partition	21	A
• Format drive	21	A
Run appropriate setup utility	21	A
• Setup	21	A

A+ Operating System Technologies Exam Objectives	Chapter	Topic
• Winnt	21	A
Installation methods	21	A
• Bootable CD	21	A
• Boot floppy	21	A
• Network installation	21	A
• Drive imaging	21	B
Device driver configuration	11	A
• Load default drivers	11	A
• Find updated drivers	11	A
Restore user data files (if applicable)	20 21	C B
Identify common symptoms and problems	21	C
Objective 2.2: Identify steps to perform an operating system upgrade from Windows 9x/ME, Windows NT 4.0 Workstation, Windows 2000 Professional, and Windows XP. Given an upgrade scenario, choose the appropriate steps.		
Content may include the following:		
Upgrade paths available	21 Appendix C Appendix D	B
Determine correct upgrade startup utility (e.g. WINNT32 vs. WINNT)	21	B
Verify hardware compatibility and minimum requirements	21	B
Verify application compatibility	21	B
Apply OS service packs, patches, and updates	21	A
Install additional Windows components	21	D
Objective 2.3: Identify the basic system boot sequences and boot methods, including the steps to create an emergency boot disk with utilities installed for Windows 9x/ME, Windows NT 4.0 Workstation, Windows 2000 Professional, and Windows XP.		
Content may include the following:		
Boot sequence	19	A
• Files required to boot	19	A
• Boot steps (9x, NT-based)	19	A

A+ Operating System Technologies Exam Objectives	Chapter	Topic
Alternative Boot Methods	19 20 21	A, C B, D A
• Using a Startup Disk	19	A
• Safe/VGA-only mode	20	B
• Last Known Good Configuration	20	B
• Command Prompt Mode	20	B
• Booting to a system restore point	20	D
• Recovery Console	19	C
• Boot.ini switches	19	A
• Dual Boot	21	A
Creating emergency disks with OS utilities	19	A
Creating an Emergency Repair Disk (ERD)	19	B
Objective 2.4: Identify procedures for installing/adding a device, including loading/adding/configuring device drivers and required software.		
Content may include the following:		
Device Driver Installation	11	A
• Plug-and-Play (PNP) and non-PNP devices	11	A
• Install and configure device drivers	11	A
• Install different device drivers	11	A
• Manually install a device driver	11	A
• Search the Internet for updated device drivers	11	A
• Using unsigned drivers (driver signing)	11	A
Install additional Windows components	21	D
Determine if permissions are adequate for performing the task	13	A
Objective 2.5: Identify procedures necessary to optimize the operating system and major operating system subsystems.		
Content may include the following:		
Virtual Memory Management	10	B
Disk Defragmentation	15	D

A+ Operating System Technologies Exam Objectives	Chapter	Topic
Files and Buffers	10	D
Caches	10 19	D A
Temporary file management	9	A
Domain 3: Diagnosing and Troubleshooting		
Objective 3.1: Recognize and interpret the meaning of common error codes and startup messages from the boot sequence, and identify steps to correct the problems.		
Content may include the following:		
Common Error Messages and Codes:		
Boot failure and errors	20	B
• Invalid boot disk	20	B
• Inaccessible boot device	20	B
• Missing NTLDR	20	B
• Bad or missing command interpreter	20	B
Startup messages	20	B
• Error in CONFIG.SYS line XX	20	B
• Himem.sys not loaded	20	B
• Missing or corrupt Himem.sys	20	B
• Device/service has failed to start	20	B
A device referenced in SYSTEM.INI, WIN.INI, Registry is not found	20	B
Event viewer — event log is full	20	A
Failure to start GUI	20	B
Windows Protection Error	20	A
User-modified settings cause improper operation at startup	20	A, B
Registry corruption	19	E
Using the correct utilities:		
Dr. Watson	20	A
Boot Disk	19	A
Event Viewer	9	A

A+ Operating System Technologies Exam Objectives	Chapter	Topic
Objective 3.2: Recognize when to use common diagnostic utilities and tools. Given a diagnostic scenario involving one of these utilities or tools, select the appropriate steps needed to resolve the problem.		
Utilities and tools may include the following:		
Startup disks	19	A
• Required files for a boot disk	19	A
• Boot disk with CD-ROM support	19	A
Startup modes	20	B
• Safe mode	20	B
• Safe mode with command prompt	20	B
• Safe mode with networking	20	B
• Step-by-Step/Single step mode	20	B
• Automatic Skip Driver (ASD.exe)	20	B
Diagnostic tools, utilities, and resources	9 13 14 19 20	B E E A A, B
• User/installation manuals	13 14	E E
• Internet/web resources	20	A
• Training materials	20	B
• Task Manager	20	A
• Dr. Watson	20	A
• Boot Disk	19	A
• Event Viewer	9	A
• Device Manager	9	A
• WinMSD	20	B
• MSD	9	B
• Recovery CD	20	B
• CONFIGSAFE	20	B

A+ Operating System Technologies Exam Objectives	Chapter	Topic
Eliciting problem symptoms from customers	20	A
Having customer reproduce error as part of the diagnostic process	20	A
Identifying recent changes to the computer environment from the user	20	A
Objective 3.3: Recognize common operational and usability problems and determine how to resolve them.		
Content may include the following:		
Troubleshooting Windows-specific printing problems	13	E
• Print spool is stalled	13	E
• Incorrect/incompatible driver for print	13	E
• Incorrect parameter	13	E
Other common problems	11 20	C A, B
• General Protection Faults	20	A
• Bluescreen error (BSOD)	20	A
• Illegal operation	20	A
• Invalid working directory	20	A
• System lock-up	20	A
• Option (Sound card, modem, input device) or will not function	20	B
• Application will not start or load	20	A
• Cannot log on to network (option — NIC not functioning)	11	C
• Applications don't install	20	A
• Network connection	11	C
Viruses and virus types	18	A
• What they are	18	A
• TSR (Terminate and Stay Resident) programs and viruses	18	A

A+ Operating System Technologies Exam Objectives	Chapter	Topic
• Sources (floppy, email, etc.)	18	A
• How to determine presence	18	A
Domain 4: Networks		
Objective 4.1: Identify the networking capabilities of Windows. Given configuration parameters, configure the operating system to connect to a network.		
Content may include the following:		
Configure protocols	11	A, B, D, E, G
• TCP/IP — Gateway — Subnet mask — DNS (and domain suffix) — WINS — Static address assignment — Automatic address assignment (APIPA, DHCP)	11	A, G
• IPX/SPX (NWLink)	11	E
• Appletalk	11	B
• NetBEUI/NetBIOS	11	D
Configure client options	11	F, G
• Microsoft	11 14	F A
• Novell	11	F, G
Verify the configuration	11	B, G
Understand the use of the following tools:	11	B, C, G
• IPCONFIG.EXE	11	B
• WINIPCFG.EXE	11	G
• PING	11	B
• TRACERT	11	C
• NSLOOKUP	11	C
Share resources (Understand the capabilities/ limitations with each OS version)	13 14	A, D C

A+ Operating System Technologies Exam Objectives	Chapter	Topic
Setting permissions to shared resources	13 14	A, D C
Network type and network card	11	A
Objective 4.2: Identify the basic Internet protocols and terminologies. Identify procedures for establishing Internet connectivity. In a given scenario, configure the operating system to connect to and use Internet resources.		
Content may include the following:		
Protocols and terminologies	11 17	B C, D
• ISP	11	B
• TCP/IP	11	B
• E-mail (POP, SMTP, IMAP)	17	D
• HTML	17	C
• HTTP	17	C
• HTTPS	17	C
• SSL	17	C
• Telnet	17	C
• FTP	17	C
• DNS	11	B
Connectivity technologies	17	A
• Dial-up networking	17	A
• DSL networking	17	A
• ISDN networking	17	A
• Cable	17	A
• Satellite	17	A
• Wireless	17	A
• LAN	17	A
Installing and Configuring Browsers	17	C
• Enable/disable script support	17	C
• Configure Proxy settings	17	C

A+ Operating System Technologies Exam Objectives	Chapter	Topic
• Configure security settings	17	C
Firewall protection under Windows XP	17	A

APPENDIX B
Basics of Electricity

Electrical Measurements

There are a number of different basic electrical terms that you might encounter as an A+ computer technician. Most of these terms have to do with measuring different aspects of electrical charge and flow.

Charge

An object's electrical *charge* is the difference between the number of electrons and protons in the object.

- If the object has accumulated extra electrons, it has a negative charge.
- If the object has lost some of its electrons, it has a positive charge.
- If the object has the same number of electrons and protons, it has a neutral charge.

Potential Energy

Potential energy is energy that is stored in a body as a result of the position or condition of the body. The energy can potentially be released, but only if the body changes its position or condition.

- A heavy rock at the top of a hill has energy that can be released if it falls.
- A coiled spring has energy that can be released if it is allowed to unwind. This potential energy is harnessed to drive spring-wound clocks and watches.
- A charged body has *electrical potential* energy, because it has the potential for electrons to flow towards it (if it has a positive charge) or away from it (if it has a negative charge).

Voltage

Voltage, or *potential difference*, is a measurement of the difference in electrical potential energy between two different objects. Voltage describes how many electrons could potentially move from one of the objects to the other, given a circuit over which the electrons can flow, and sufficient time. Voltage is like pressure pushing the electrons along. Voltage is one of the electrical values that is often measured directly. The unit of measure is the volt (V).

Computers work with voltages in the range of 12 volts (V) and lower. This voltage level is usually harmless for humans. Household electricity is 120 volts, which is enough to kill humans and completely destroy computers. The power supply in the computer acts as a transformer to convert the 120 volts from the electric outlet down to 12 volts or less for the computer. It also acts as a voltage regulator, breaking the voltage down to one of several different standard levels. A standard computer power supply puts out several voltages in this range, including, +12 volts, -12 volts, +5 volts, -5 volts, and zero volts. A negative voltage means the power supply is pushing electrons out, while a positive voltage means the supply is drawing electrons in. Zero volts is referred to as neutral, or ground, and is used as a basis for measuring the other voltages.

Voltage is usually determined by the power supply and is not something under your control. You can detect if a wire is connected to a +12 V or -5 V source, but you cannot easily bring the five volts down to three volts.

Current

Current is a measurement of how many electrons are passing a given point in a circuit over a given period of time. It describes the rate of transfer of electrons. In other words, if voltage measures the pressure or force pushing the electrons, then current measures how fast the electrons go.

The standard unit of measure of current is the ampere, or amp, (A), which is the number of electrons transferred per second. The electronics in a computer usually have electric current in the milli-ampere (one one-thousandth of an ampere) or micro-ampere (one one-millionth of an ampere) range. A bright light bulb has a current of one ampere, and an electric room heater might have a current of 10 amperes.

There are two major types of electric current.

- The current used by computers is *direct current (DC)*, which is electrical current that flows in only one direction and at a constant voltage. For example, the voltage output from a power supply remains constant at -12 V, so electrons always flow away from the output, never toward it.

- The current in a wall outlet is *alternating current (AC)*. The voltage in the wall outlet varies from +120 V to -120 V and back to +120 V sixty times a second. Electrons zoom back and forth through the wires, changing direction 120 times a second.

The power supply in a computer not only reduces the voltage of the electricity it receives from the wall outlet, but also switches it from alternating current to direct current.

Electrical Power and Electrical Energy

Electrical power describes the energy delivered by a flow of electrons in one second and is defined as voltage times current. Power is measured in watts (W). A light bulb connected to a 120 V power source that has 0.5 amps flowing through it uses 60 watts of power. An LED connected to a 2 V source with a current of 10 milli-amperes uses 20 milli-watts of power. A power supply rated at 500 W can deliver twice the electrical power as a 250 W power supply.

The term *electrical energy* is used to describe the total amount of electrical power delivered over any given time period. A high voltage with a high current supplies a great deal of energy. A low voltage with a low current delivers a small amount of energy. The total energy delivered can be spread over a long or short period of time.

Resistance

Resistance is the opposition to the flow of electric current through a material. Insulators like rubber and plastic have a very high resistance. Conductors like copper and silver have very low resistance. Resistance is measured in ohms. Electricians use the Greek letter *omega* (Ω) as a symbol for ohms.

Ohms are named for the German physicist Georg Simon Ohm, who formulated what is now known as Ohm's Law to show the relations between voltage, current, and resistance. Ohm's law states that you can compute resistance (R) in a circuit by dividing the voltage (V) by the current in amperes (I). With Ohm's law, if you know any two of the values, you can calculate the other. Therefore, Ohm's law may be written as an equation in three equivalent ways:

- R = V/I
- V = I*R
- I = V/R

If resistance remains the same in a material, higher voltages will produce higher currents and the power will go up. If the resistance remains the same, lower voltages will produce a lower current and the power goes down.

If the voltage source remains constant, which is the case in most computer circuits, higher resistances decrease current and lower resistances increase current. A volume control on a radio is a variable resistor that decreases in resistance as you turn the volume up so more current carrying more energy can get to the speaker and make more noise. A switch is a variable resistor that has zero resistance in the ON position and infinite resistance in the OFF position.

A transistor can be used as an electronic switch because it can change from acting as a conductor to acting as an insulator. Because of this, it is called a *semiconductor*.

Using A Multimeter

A *multimeter* is an electronic instrument used to measure voltage, current, and resistance. It usually has two wires, one red and one black, that are plugged into two sockets on the meter. Which socket you use will be determined by what you want to measure. Analog meters have a thin needle that swings in an arc and points to a number that indicates the value of what you are measuring. Digital meters have a screen that displays the numeric value of what you are measuring.

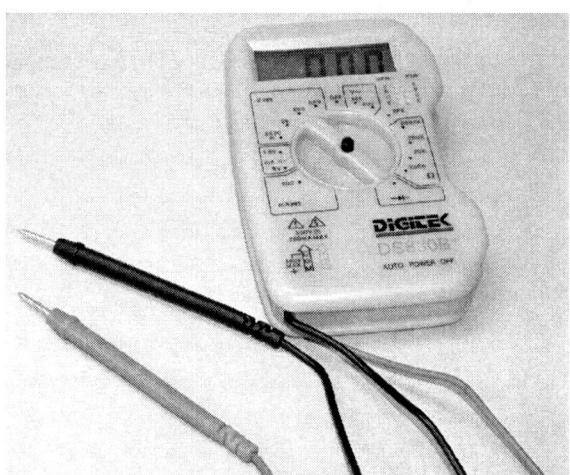

Figure B-1: *A digital multimeter.*

Figure B-2: *An analog multimeter.*

Measuring Voltage

Voltage measurement indicates the difference in electrical energy between two sources. Normally, you measure between an electrical source and a *ground*. A ground connection typically creates a circuit with the earth itself. The earth is so massive that, for all practical purposes, it can absorb and neutralize any electrical charge. Electrons on a grounded material have zero voltage because there are no forces trying to push them off or pull them onto the grounded item. The black wire from the multimeter is usually connected to a ground. In a computer, the metal case is an electric ground. A water pipe, or the screw on an electrical outlet cover are also commonly used as ground connections in other situations.

Before you touch the red probe to the electrical source you want to measure, you need to adjust the meter to the approximate voltage you expect to find. This may be done by turning a large, rotary switch, or by plugging the red probe into a special socket on the meter. If the meter is expecting to measure 2 V, and you touch a 120 V source, the extra voltage can damage the components in the meter. It is better to overestimate the voltage and reduce the settings later, than to underestimate the voltage and destroy the meter. Higher-end digital meters automatically detect the range for you.

If you are measuring direct current voltages, the black wire goes to the source of the electrons in the current, and the red wire goes to the destination for the electrons. If a wire has a +5 V applied to it, you would touch the red probe to the wire, and the black probe to ground (which has 0 V) because a positive voltage means the wire is drawing in electrons from the ground. If a wire has -5 V applied to it, you would touch the black probe to the wire because it is the source of the electrons, and the red wire to the ground because the ground is absorbing the electrons. Some digital multimeters automatically make this adjustment for you.

Measuring Resistance

A multimeter measures resistance by applying a small voltage to a material and seeing how much current flows through the material. A material with high resistance will let very little current flow, while a material with low resistance will let more current flow. The voltage the meter applies is small, but even a small voltage can damage electronic chips. So, you can measure the resistances of cables and wires and connections, but you should not measure the resistances between pins on a chip. If you try to measure the resistance of a component in a live circuit, the voltage in the circuit may be enough to damage the multimeter.

A good conductor will have close to 0 Ω resistance, while a wire with a break in it will have more than 100,000 Ω resistance. Resistance is measured most often to determine if the ends of a cable are making a good connection through the wire, and if a switch is really turning on and off.

Measuring Current

To measure an electrical current, you have to break the circuit and place a multimeter between the two ends of the break. This step is usually destructive and does not produce useful results, so, in most instances, you probably won't need to measure current.

Static Electricity

Static electricity is a build up of a stationary electrical charge on an object. It is called *static* because the charge cannot escape, but remains still. As soon as a circuit is created that permits the electrons to discharge, the static electricity is released with a spark. The spark can be as small as the ones that come off a dry blanket in the wintertime or as massive as a lightening strike, with its millions of volts.

Static electricity is often caused by friction; rubbing one object against another causes a transfer of electrons between the two. Using friction to create a static charge is called *triboelectric generation*. The amount of static that can be built up in this manner depends on various factors, including the types of materials, their surface area and texture, and the ambient humidity. If you have ever rubbed a balloon on your head and stuck it to the wall, you have used triboelectric generation.

Because air has very high resistance, static electric discharge usually requires contact with the statically-charged object. For a static discharge to arc through the air, it requires a very high voltage, and no other path to the ground with lower resistance. You can feel a static discharge starting at around 3,000 V. The drier the air, the greater the resistance, which is why static shocks on dry winter days can fall within the range of 10,000 to 20,000 volts. Keeping a room humidified is one way to reduce the risk of static electricity and ESD.

If 120 V from a household electrical outlet can kill you, why does a static spark of 20,000 V just startle you? Because, while the voltage might be high, the current is very low; very few total electrons are transferred in a static spark. All the energy of all the electrons in a spark added together cannot hurt you, even though it may surprise you. Each electron in a static discharge has extremely high energy, but the human body is just too big for the very small number of electrons involved in the spark to cause widespread damage. A few cells in your fingertip may be damaged, but they easily grow back.

On the other hand, voltages as low as 10 V can damage or destroy sensitive electronic circuits. This is why ESD is such an enemy of integrated circuits. Static charges can build up on both conductors and insulators, as well as in the human body. You can protect against ESD in your work environment by:

- Grounding conductive materials.
- Ionizing and humidifying the air to speed up static discharge from insulators.
- Grounding yourself before touching electronic equipment. To avoid a static shock, touch a grounded object made of a *dissipative material*. A dissipative material is a conductor, but with high resistance. It loses its electrical charge slowly, so, when you touch it, the electron flow is spread over time and you do not feel a shock.

APPENDIX C
Peripherals and Connector Types

The material in this course was organized by connector type. As new peripherals are developed, you will know how to install them by examining their connectors and referring to that section of this course. The following is a chart of common peripherals and the connectors they are found with.

Peripheral	Parallel	Serial	SCSI	USB	Firewire	Other
Cable modem				x		RJ-45
CD-ROM drive	x		x	x	x	
Digital camera		x		x	x	
DSL modem						RJ-45
DVD drive				x	x	
External hard drive	x		x	x	x	
External tape drive	x		x	x	x	
Flight controller		x		x		Game port
External floppy drive	x			x	x	
External cartridge drive	x		x	x	x	
Game controller pad		x		x		Game port
Joystick				x		Game port
Music keyboard						1/8-inch jack, MIDI, game port
Microphone						1/8-inch jack
MIDI device				x		Game port
Modem		x		x		
Monitor, CRT						VGA port

Peripheral	Parallel	Serial	SCSI	USB	Firewire	Other
Monitor, LCD flat panel						VGA or DVI port, depending on the monitor connector
Monitor, touchscreen		x		x		
Mouse		x				PS/2 cable
Network adapter						RJ-45
PDA		x		x		
Printer	x	x	x	x		
Scanner	x		x	x		
Speaker						1/8-inch jack
Steering wheel						Game port
Video display system						VGA
Video projector						VGA

APPENDIX D
Upgrade From Windows 95 to Windows 98

At some point you might be asked to upgrade a Windows 95 computer to Windows 98 to take advantage of Windows 98's larger set of features. Before you attempt to upgrade a Windows 95 computer to Windows 98, make sure that your computer's hardware meets the minimum requirements for Windows 98. In Table D-1, we list the hardware requirements your computer must meet.

Table D-1: *Windows 98 Hardware Requirements*

Hardware	Minimum Requirement
Processor	486DX 66 MHz
RAM	16 MB
Hard disk	At least 225 MB of free space
Video adapter	VGA
Installation source	CD-ROM or DVD-ROM (without one of these drives, you must install Windows 98 using floppy disks)
Pointing device	Mouse

To upgrade Windows 95 to Windows 98:

1. Verify that your hardware meets the hardware requirements for Windows 98 (use Table D-1).
2. Verify that any applications you're running on Windows 95 will work on Windows 98.
3. Back up the data files.
4. In Windows 95, close all programs, including any anti-virus programs.
5. Start the Windows 98 installation.
   - If you're installing from a CD-ROM, insert the CD-ROM. If you're prompted to upgrade, click Yes.
   - If you're installing from a network share and inserting the CD-ROM does not prompt you to upgrade, from the Start menu, choose Run. In the Open text box, type the command to start the installation.
     — Type $x:\setminus$`Setup` (where *x* is the drive letter assigned to your computer's CD-ROM drive). Click OK.
     — Type `\\computer\share_name\setup` to install from a shared network folder. Click OK.
6. The Windows 98 Setup Wizard starts. Complete the following tasks:

a. On the License Agreement page, select I Accept The Agreement and click Next.
b. Enter the Windows 98 product key and click Next.
c. On the Select Directory page, choose one of the following:
   - Select C:\WINDOWS to install Windows 98 in the default folder.
   - Select Other Directory if you want to choose a different folder in which to install Windows 98.
d. Click Next.
e. If you chose Other Directory, enter the path to the folder in which you want to install Windows 98, and then click Next.
f. On the Save System Files page, select the appropriate option.
   - Choose Yes if you want Setup to save your original Windows 95 installation so that you can later uninstall Windows 98 if necessary. Be aware that if you save your Windows 95 installation files, you will need an additional 110 MB of disk space to install Windows 98.
   - Choose No if you want to overwrite your Windows 95 installation.
g. Click Next.
h. If you have multiple hard disks or partitions in your computer, select the drive letter on which you want to store the uninstall files and click OK.
i. On the Setup Options page, select one of the following options:
   - Typical
   - Portable
   - Compact
   - Custom
j. Click Next.
k. On the User Information page, verify the user's name and the company name. Click Next.
l. On the Windows Components page, select one of the following:
   - Install The Most Common Components (Recommended).
   - Show Me The List Of Components So I Can Choose.
m. Click Next.
n. If you selected Show Me The List Of Components So I Can Choose, check the Windows components you want to install on the computer and then click Next.
o. Verify your country or region and click Next.
p. Click Next to create a Windows 98 Startup disk.
q. When prompted, insert a blank floppy disk and click OK.
r. When the Startup disk creation is complete, remove the floppy disk and label it. Click OK.
s. Click Next. Setup will now copy the Windows 98 files to your hard disk.

📌 The file copy process will take several minutes.

t. When the file copy is complete, click Restart Now.

📌 Setup will automatically restart the computer after 15 seconds.

7. After the computer restarts, Setup will attempt to detect the hardware. When hardware detection is complete, click Restart Now to restart the computer again.
8. Setup will automatically use your previously defined Windows 95 settings such as the computer name, workgroup name, and date/time properties.
9. When the installation is complete, click Restart Now.
10. If necessary, log on to Windows 98.
11. If necessary, install any hardware drivers that were not automatically installed during setup. For example, make sure that the drivers for devices such as sound cards, modems, and display adapters were installed correctly.
    a. If the Add New Hardware Wizard prompts you to install a new driver, click Next and follow the prompts to install the driver.
    b. Use Device Manager to view the status of these devices and to look for any devices for which Setup did not install the drivers.
    c. If you need new drivers, connect to the manufacturer's Web site to download the drivers for Windows 98.
    d. Use Add New Hardware in Control Panel to install the drivers. When prompted, do not have Windows 98 search for the device. Instead, select the driver from the files you downloaded.
12. Install any additional Windows 98 components. In Control Panel, open Add/Remove Programs and select the Windows Setup tab.
13. Install any operating system updates that are available on Microsoft's Web sites. These updates include patches and add-ons that increase functionality and make the operating system more secure.

APPENDIX E
Upgrade From Windows NT to Windows 2000 or Windows XP

Because Microsoft is phasing out Windows NT support, you might be asked to upgrade a Windows NT computer to Windows 2000 or Windows XP, Microsoft's newest operating systems in the Windows NT line. Before you upgrade Windows NT to Windows 2000 or Windows XP, you should make sure that your computer's hardware meets the requirements for the appropriate operating system. You'll find the hardware requirements for each operating system in Table E-1 and Table E-2.

Table E-1: *Windows 2000 Professional Hardware Requirements*

Hardware	Minimum Requirement
Processor	Pentium 133 MHz
RAM	32 MB (64 MB recommended)
Hard disk	2 GB with 1 GB free space
Video adapter	VGA
Installation source	12X CD-ROM
Pointing device	Mouse

Table E-2: *Windows XP Professional Hardware Requirements*

Hardware	Minimum Requirement
Processor	Pentium 233 MHz
RAM	64 MB
Available disk space	1.5 GB
Video adapter	Super VGA
Installation source	CD-ROM or DVD-ROM
Pointing device	Mouse

To upgrade from Windows NT to Windows 2000, complete the following steps:

1. Verify that the computer's hardware meets the requirements for Windows 2000 (see Table E-1).
2. Verify that any applications you're running on Windows NT will work on Windows 2000.
3. Back up the computer's data.
4. Start the installation.

- If the computer does not have a bootable CD-ROM drive, boot the computer from the first Setup disk. Use the following steps to create and use the Setup disks if you don't have them:
  a. Verify that you have three blank floppy disks.
  b. At a working computer, insert the Windows 2000 CD-ROM.
  c. Run \bootdisk\makebt32.exe from the Windows 2000 CD-ROM to create the Setup disks.
  d. Insert each disk when prompted.
  e. Label the disks.
  f. Insert the first Windows Setup disk and start the computer. When prompted, insert each additional disk as required.
- If the computer has a bootable CD-ROM drive, insert the Windows 2000 CD-ROM and start the computer. If prompted, press a key to boot from CD.
- If the installation files are on a network share, complete the following steps:
  a. Connect the computer to the network.
  b. Access the network share containing the installation files.
  c. Double-click winnt32.exe.

5. When prompted, click Yes to upgrade to Windows 2000.
6. On the Welcome page, select Upgrade To Windows 2000 (Recommended) and click Next.
7. When prompted, click Finish to restart the computer. At this point, Setup copies the files it needs to your computer. The file copy process will take several minutes.
8. Press Enter to restart your computer when the file copy process is complete.
9. Setup now detects and installs the device drivers it needs for your computer. This process will take several minutes.
10. When setup is complete, restart the computer.
11. Log on as a local administrator.
12. Uncheck Show This Screen At Startup and click Exit to close the Getting Started With Windows 2000 message box.
13. If necessary, configure the computer to connect to the Internet.
14. If necessary, install any hardware drivers that were not automatically installed during setup. For example, make sure that the drivers for devices such as sound cards, modems, and display adapters were installed correctly.
    a. Use Device Manager to view the status of these devices and to look for any devices for which Setup did not install the drivers.
    b. If you need new drivers, connect to the manufacturer's Web site to download the drivers for Windows 2000.
    c. Use Add New Hardware in Control Panel to install the drivers. When prompted, do not have Windows 2000 search for the device. Instead, select the driver from the files you downloaded.

15. Install any additional Windows 2000 components. In Control Panel, open Add/Remove Programs and click Add/Remove Windows Components.
16. Update Windows 2000.
    a. From the Start menu, choose Windows Update.
    b. Click Yes to install and run the Windows Update Control Package.
    c. If necessary, click Yes again.
    d. Click Scan For Updates.
    e. Click Review And Install Updates.
    f. Click Yes to continue.
    g. Follow the prompts to install the updates you want. You'll find that some of the updates are "exclusive," which means they can't be installed with other updates. If you choose to install an exclusive update, be sure to go back to the Windows Update Web site to check for other updates.
17. If necessary, restart the computer after the updates are installed.
18. Log back on to the computer.

You can upgrade Windows NT Workstation only to Windows XP Professional (not Windows XP Home Edition). To upgrade a computer from Windows NT Workstation to Windows XP Professional, complete the following steps:

1. Verify that the computer meets the hardware requirements for Windows XP (use Table E-2 or go to **www.microsoft.com/windowsxp/pro/evaluation/sysreqs.asp**).
2. Verify that any applications you're running on Windows NT will work on Windows XP.
3. Back up the computer's data.
4. Start the upgrade.
   - If the computer does not have a bootable CD-ROM drive, boot the computer from the first Setup disk. Use the following steps to create and use the Setup disks if you don't have them:
     a. Verify that you have three blank floppy disks.
     b. At a working computer, insert the Windows XP CD-ROM.
     c. If you're using Windows 9x or MS-DOS, run \bootdisk\makeboot.exe from the Windows XP CD-ROM to create the Setup disks.
     d. If you're using Windows 2000, Windows XP, or Windows NT, run \bootdisk\makebt32.exe from the Windows XP CD-ROM to create the Setup disks.
     e. Insert each disk when prompted.
     f. Label the disks.
     g. Insert the first Windows Setup disk and start the computer. When prompted, insert each additional disk as required.
   - If the computer has a bootable CD-ROM drive, insert the Windows XP CD-ROM and start the computer. If prompted, press a key to boot from CD.
   - If the installation files are on a network share, complete the following steps:

- a. Connect the computer to the network.
- b. Access the network share containing the installation files.
- c. Double-click winnt32.exe.

5. Click Install Windows XP.
6. On the Welcome To Windows Setup page, verify that Upgrade (Recommended) is selected and click Next.
7. Choose I Accept This Agreement and click Next.
8. Enter your product key and click Next.
9. When prompted, restart the computer.
10. Setup now copies some of the necessary files for the upgrade to your computer. This file copy process will take several minutes. When Setup completes the copying, your computer will automatically restart.
11. Setup now installs Windows XP using the configuration settings you selected for Windows NT. When the installation is complete, your computer will automatically restart.
12. On the Welcome To Microsoft Windows page, click Next.
13. If you want to register your copy of Windows XP with Microsoft, choose Yes, I'd Like To Register With Microsoft Now and click Next. Follow the prompts to register Windows XP. If not, choose No, Not At This Time and click Next.
14. If you want to use MSN to connect to the Internet, choose Get Online With MSN, click Next, and follow the prompts to establish an account. If you don't want to use MSN, choose Do Not Set Up An Internet Connection At This Time and click Next.
15. On the Who Will Use This Computer dialog box, use the text boxes to create any new user accounts you need and then click Next (if you don't want to create any new user accounts, click Skip).
16. Click Finish.
17. Log on as a local administrator.
18. If necessary, configure the computer to connect to the Internet.
19. If necessary, install any hardware drivers that were not automatically installed during setup. For example, make sure that the drivers for devices such as sound cards, modems, and display adapters were installed correctly.
    - a. Use Device Manager to view the status of these devices and to look for any devices for which Setup did not install the drivers.
    - b. If you need new drivers, connect to the manufacturer's Web site to download the drivers for Windows 2000.
    - c. Click Printers And Other Hardware in Control Panel. In the left pane, click Add Hardware to install the drivers. When prompted, do not have Windows XP search for the device. Instead, select the driver from the files you downloaded.
20. Install any additional Windows XP components. In Control Panel, open Add/Remove Programs and click Add/Remove Windows Components.

21. Update Windows XP.
    a. From the Start menu, choose Windows Update.
    b. Click Yes to install and run the Windows Update Control Package.
    c. If necessary, click Yes again.
    d. Click Scan For Updates.
    e. Click Review And Install Updates.
    f. Click Yes to continue.
    g. Follow the prompts to install the updates you want. You'll find that some of the updates are "exclusive," which means they can't be installed with other updates. If you choose to install an exclusive update, be sure to go back to the Windows Update Web site to check for other updates.
22. If necessary, restart the computer after the updates are installed.
23. Log back on to the computer.

APPENDIX F
Dynamic Disks

Windows 2000 and Windows XP support dynamic disks. In this appendix, you'll learn the procedures for:

- Converting a basic disk to a dynamic disk.
- Reverting to a basic disk.
- Creating a simple volume.
- Extending a simple volume.

Converting a basic disk to a dynamic disk enables you to take advantage of the advanced features of dynamic disks such as modifying the partitions on the disk without having to delete the disk's partitions and create new ones. For example, one feature of dynamic disks is that you can increase the available space in a partition—something you might do if a user is running out of space in a partition and there's free disk space available on the hard disk. The advantage to using a dynamic disk in this scenario is that the computer will use the same drive letter for the expanded partition and the user will simply see a larger partition. In contrast, if you have only a basic disk in the computer, your only choice is to create an additional partition with a different drive letter. This means that the user will have to get used to accessing two different drive letters in order to retrieve or save her files. To convert a basic disk to a dynamic disk, complete the following steps:

1. Log on as a local administrator.
2. Open Computer Management.
3. In the console tree, select the Disk Management folder.
4. Verify that you have at least 1 MB of free space on the disk.
5. If you're using Windows 2000, right-click the disk you want to convert and choose Upgrade To Dynamic Disk.

    If you're using Windows XP, right-click the disk you want to convert and choose Convert To Dynamic Disk.
6. Verify that the check box for the disk you want to convert is checked. Click OK.
7. The message box shows you a list of all the partitions on the disk that will be converted. Click Convert.
8. Click Yes twice to confirm the conversion.
9. Click OK to restart the computer and perform the conversion.
10. After the computer restarts, log on.
11. When prompted, click Yes to restart a second time (the system detects the converted disk as a new device; you need to reboot to install it).
12. After the computer restarts, log on.

13. In Disk Management, verify that the disk type is listed as Dynamic, and that all partitions on the original disk have been converted to simple volumes on the dynamic disk.

If you want to revert a dynamic disk to a basic disk, complete the following steps:

1. Log on as a local administrator.
2. Back up data in all volumes on the disk.
3. In Disk Management, delete all volumes on the disk.
4. Right-click the disk and choose Convert To Basic Disk.
5. After the conversion, create any partitions you need on the disk and restore your data.

Just as you saw earlier in the course with partitions, creating a volume makes a dynamic disk accessible to the user of the computer. As an A+ technician, there are several reasons why you might need to create volumes. For example, the user might have a dynamic disk with free space that you want to make accessible to the user. Another example might be if you need to redeploy an old computer for another user and you've determined that a dynamic disk is the best choice for the new user. In this scenario, you'll need to be able to create at least one volume within the dynamic disk to make it accessible to the new user. The bottom line? Without volumes in a dynamic disk, the hard disk might as well be considered an expensive paperweight because the user won't be able to store any data on the disk. To create a simple volume on a dynamic disk, complete the following steps:

1. Log on as a local administrator.
2. Open Computer Management (right-click My Computer and choose Manage).
3. In the console pane, select the Disk Management folder.
4. If you're using Windows 2000, right-click the available free space in the dynamic disk on which you want to create a new volume and choose Create Volume. The Create Volume Wizard starts.

   If you're using Windows XP, right-click the available free space in the disk on which you want to create a new partition and choose New Volume. The New Volume Wizard starts.
5. Click Next.
6. On the Select Partition Type page, select Primary Partition.
7. Click Next.
8. If you're using Windows 2000, in the Amount Of Disk Space To Use text box, type the size of the partition you want to create.

   If you're using Windows XP, in the Partition Size In MB text box, type the size of the partition you want to create.
9. Click Next.
10. On the Assign Drive Letter Or Path page, select one of the following:
    - If you want to assign a permanent drive letter to the new partition, choose a drive letter from the drop-down list.
    - If you want to mount the partition into an empty NTFS folder, enter the path to the folder or click Browse to select a folder.
    - If you do not want to assign a drive letter or mount path, select Do Not Assign A Drive Letter Or Drive Path.

11. Click Next.
12. Select whether or not to format this partition. If you choose to format the partition, you can select from the following options:
    - The file system to use (FAT, FAT32, or NTFS).
    - The allocation unit size. This is the size of the smallest available file-storage unit on the disk, and determines the size of the file clusters.
    - The volume label, a name that's assigned to the partition.
    - Check Perform A Quick Format if you want to perform a quick format instead of a full format.
    - Check Enable File And Folder Compression to enable compression on the entire partition.
13. Click Next.
14. Click Finish.
15. Close Computer Management.
16. Verify that the new partition is accessible by using a utility such as Windows Explorer or My Computer.

Imagine the following scenario: You've been called in as an A+ technician to support a Windows 2000 computer you didn't initially install; the user of this computer reports that he's running out of disk space. After some investigation, you determine that the original installer of the computer created a system volume that's 2 GB in size, a 4 GB data volume, and left over 12 GB of free disk space. You want to make all of this free space available to the user, but you don't want the user to have to learn to access a new drive letter (which is what would happen if you created a new volume). What's the best solution? Extend the existing data volume to include the 12 GB of free disk space. Extending the data volume enables the user to access the data volume using the same drive letter. In addition, you can extend the volume without having to worry about losing any of the existing files on the data volume. As you can see, extending a volume offers you a quick and painless solution to increasing the user's available disk space. To extend a simple volume, complete the following steps:

1. Log on as a local administrator.
2. Open Computer Management.
3. In the console tree, select the Disk Management folder.
4. In the details pane, right-click the volume you want to extend and choose Extend Volume.
5. In the Extend Volume Wizard, click Next.
6. Verify that the disk that contains the free space you want to use appears in the Selected list. If not, add it from the Available list.
7. In the Select The Amount Of Space In MB text box, enter the amount of free space you want to add. Click Next.
8. Click Finish. The two areas of space will appear with the same volume label. The total capacity of the volume appears in the list of volumes in the upper-right pane of Disk Management.

There are a few restrictions you should be aware of before attempting to extend a volume. You can extend a volume if:

Appendix F: Dynamic Disks

- You have administrative privileges.
- You have unallocated free space available.
- The volume is not formatted to FAT or FAT32 (you can extend NTFS volumes, or volumes that are not formatted).
- The volume does not contain the Windows 2000 or Windows XP Professional system files or the system boot information.

Glossary

8008
Introduced by Intel in 1972, the 8008 was the first microprocessor to be supported by a high-level language compiler.

abacus
An early calculating instrument that uses sliding beads in columns that are divided in two by a center bar.

AC
(alternating current) Electrical current that flows in two directions at variable voltages.

adapter card
Add-on boards or cards that provide special functions for customizing or extending a computer's capability.

AGP
(Accelerated Graphics Port) A bus architecture based on PCI and designed specifically to speed up 3D graphics.

ampere
Unit of measure for current. Also known as amps.

Analytical Engine
Charles Babbage's vision of a mechanical calculator that would follow programmed instructions to perform any mathematical operations. The engine could store results for use later, and look up values in tables and call on standard subroutines.

answer file
A setup file that provides the answers needed by the Windows Setup program during an unattended installation.

APIPA
(Automatic Private IP Addressing) The private IP address range from 169.254.0.1 to 169.254.255.254 used by Microsoft to provide temporary IP connectivity between Windows computers that are part of a single network segment and are not connected to the Internet.

application software
High-level programs that are written to run on specific operating systems and that provide specific functionality such as word processing, graphics creation, or database management.

ASR
(Automated System Recovery) A process that uses backup data and the Windows XP Professional installation source files to rebuild a failed computer.

asynchronous
A bit synchronization transmission technique that uses start and stop bits.

AT commands
The modem command set developed by the Hayes company for use on its modems and now used on most modems.

ATA
(Advanced Technology Attachment) The official ANSI term for IDE drives.

ATAPI
(AT Attachment Packet Interface) An extension to EIDE that enables support for CD-ROM, CD-R, CD-RW, DVD-ROM, DVD-R, and tape drives.

Autoexec.bat
A file used by the MS-DOS operating system to automatically load software whenever the computer boots.

backside bus
A bus connecting the CPU to L2 cache. It runs faster than the frontside bus. It connects the two chips at the same clock rate as the CPU itself as opposed to the frontside bus which runs at only a fraction of the CPU clock speed.

bank
Multiple rows of DRAM in a single system that can be accessed simultaneously.

basic disk
A physical hard disk that is divided logically into partitions. A basic hard disk can contain a maximum of four partitions, of which, a maximum of one can be extended.

binary number system
A numbering system based on two discrete states.

BIOS
(Basic Input Output System) Low-level software that acts as the interface between the hardware and the operating system in a computer.

bit
A single binary digit having a value of 0 or 1.

boolean
An expression where the results are either true or false. The expression uses AND, OR, and NOT functions to compare values.

boot partition
The hard disk partition that contains the \Windows or \Winnt folder.

boot sector
The reserved area on a hard disk or floppy disk where the information for booting the computer is stored.

boot sequence
The portion of the Windows 2000/NT/XP startup process where the computer physically starts up and the system hardware is initialized.

Bootsect.dos
A Windows 2000/NT/XP boot file that loads a non-Windows 2000, Windows XP, or Windows NT operating system on a dual-boot computer.

buffers
A configuration setting that enables you to specify how much memory is reserved for transferring temporary information between a non-Windows application in RAM and I/O devices.

built-in groups
The security groups created automatically when you install Windows 2000, Windows XP, or Window NT.

built-in user accounts
The user accounts created automatically when you install Windows 2000, Windows XP, or Windows NT.

bus
The collection of wires that connect an interface card and the microprocessor, and the rules that describe how data should be transferred through the connection. Examples include ISA, EISA, and PCI.

bus master
Takes control of the bus away from the CPU to transfer data directly to RAM or other devices.

bus topology
A physical topology where a single main cable called the bus or backbone carries all network data. Nodes connect directly to the bus.

byte
A group of 8 bits.

card services
Assigns resources of PC Cards and detects when a card is inserted or removed.

CardBus
A bus mastering technology used on PC Cards.

CAT5
(Category 5) A type of cabling that consists of four twisted-pairs of copper wire terminated by RJ-45 connectors. Can be used for Token Ring, 1000BaseT, 100BaseT, and 10BaseT networking.

channel
A communication path between components.

charge
The difference between the number of electrons and protons associated with a body.

chipset
The set of chips on the system board that support the CPU and other basic functions.

CIS
(Card Information Structure) A PC Card feature that passes information about the PC Card to the computer so that the card can be automatically configured for use.

client
A computer on a network that makes use of the resources managed by a server.

client-server network
A network where one or more computers act primarily as providers of network resources (servers), and one or more computers act primarily as consumers of network resources (clients).

cluster
The smallest unit of disk space used when the operating system writes to the hard disk.

CMOS
(Complimentary Metal Oxide Semiconductor) Pronounced see-moss. The most widely used type of integrated circuit for digital processors and memories. Virtually everything is configured through CMOS today.

CMOS RAM
(Complementary Metal Oxide Semiconductor RAM) A special type of memory that stores information about the computer's setup.

coaxial cable
A high-capacity cable used in communications and video, commonly called coax. It contains an insulated solid or stranded wire surrounded by a solid or braided metallic shield, wrapped in a plastic cover.

Command.com
An MS-DOS operating system file that provides the command line interface. Also called the command interpreter and the DOS shell.

computer image
An exact duplicate copy of a computer hard disk's information.

Config.sys
A file used by the MS-DOS operating system to perform tasks such as load device drivers, configuring the operating system environment, and optimizing memory management.

conventional memory
The first 640 KB of RAM in the computer. MS-DOS uses this portion of memory whenever you run an application such as the MS-DOS Edit program. If you run a DOS application within Windows, Windows uses some of the computer's memory to simulate conventional memory.

corona
An assembly within a laser printer that contains a wire (the corona wire) which is responsible for charging the paper.

CPU
(Central Processing Unit) The main chip on the system board, the CPU performs software instructions and mathematical and logical equations.

CPU cache
A type of high-speed RAM that is added directly to a processor to improve computing speed. Often referred to as onboard cache, primary cache, or L1 (Level 1) cache. Compare with L2 cache and RAM.

CRT
(Cathode Ray Tube) Displays images using phosphorous dots with a scanned electron beam.

current
The amount of electricity moving through a conductive material such as a wire. Current is measured in amps.

cylinder
The aggregate of all tracks that reside in the same location on every disk surface. On multiple-platter disks, the cylinder is the sum total of every track with the same track number on every surface. On a floppy disk, a cylinder comprises the top and corresponding bottom track.

data
The configuration information stored within a Registry value.

data bus
The connection between the CPU, memory, and peripheral devices.

DC
(direct current) Electrical current that flows in only one direction and at a constant voltage.

decimal number system
A numbering system based on 10 discrete states.

default gateway
An IP address used to identify a TCP/IP-based router that provides access to a remote network. When you configure a computer's default gateway, the computer forwards any communications for remote networks to the IP address of the default gateway.

degauss
Remove magnetism from a device.

device conflict
A conflict between devices that have been assigned the same resources.

device driver
Software that enables the operating system and a peripheral device to communicate with each other.

DHCP
(Dynamic Host Configuration Protocol) A protocol which enables a Windows NT or Windows 2000 server to dynamically assign IP addresses to clients.

dial-up connection
An outbound connection that uses WAN transmission media such as modems and phone lines to connect a client on one physical network to a Remote Access Server (RAS) on a remote network.

DIMM
(Dual In-line Memory Module) A group of memory chips that transfer information 64 bits at a time.

diode
An electronic component that acts like a one-way valve. Diodes are often used to change Alternating Current (AC) to Direct Current (DC), as temperature or light sensors, and as light emitters.

dip switch
Switches on hardware used to configure hardware settings. These are usually rocker switches (like light switches) to turn on or off.

dissipative material
A conductive material with high resistance that dissipates a charge slowly.

DMA
(Direct Memory Access) Specialized circuitry or a dedicated microprocessor that transfers data from adapters to memory without using the CPU.

DNS
(Domain Name System) A static, distributed, hierarchical database system used to map computer (host) names to IP addresses.

domain
A Microsoft network model that an administrator implements by grouping computers together for the purpose of sharing a centralized user account database. Sharing this user account database enables users to use these accounts to log on at any computer in the domain.

domain controller
A server that stores the user account database for the domain and is responsible for authenticating users when they log on to the domain.

dot-matrix printer
A printer that forms images out of dots on paper. Dot patterns are created by a set of pins that strike an inked ribbon.

DRAM
(Dynamic RAM) A type of RAM that needs to be refreshed.

drive controller
The circuitry that enables the drive and the CPU to communicate with each other.

drive interface
The collection of electrical and logical connections between a hard drive and a PC.

driver
Software that enables the operating system and a peripheral device to communicate with each other. Also referred to as device driver.

dynamic disk
A physical hard disk that is divided logically into volumes. A dynamic disk can contain an unlimited number of volumes.

ECC
(Error Correction Code) A type of memory that corrects errors on the fly.

ECP
(Extended Capability Port) Newer-generation parallel port standard that provides roughly 10 times faster throughput than the Centronics standard. Used by newer-generation printers and scanners.

EDO RAM
(Extended Data Output RAM) A type of DRAM that enables a memory address to hold data for multiple reads.

EDSAC
(Electronic Delay Storage Automatic Computer) A well-engineered machine built by Maurice Wilkes and colleagues at the University of Cambridge Mathematics Lab in 1949 and was a productive tool for mathematicians.

EDVAC
(Electronic Discrete Variable Automatic Computer) The first computer to use stored programs.

EEPROM
(Electrically Erasable Programmable Read-Only Memory) A memory chip that is programmed and erased electrically. When the EEPROM is programmed, it acts like a regular ROM chip.

EISA bus
(Extended Industry Standard Architecture bus) A PC bus standard that extends the 16-bit ISA bus (AT bus) to 32 bits and provides bus mastering.

electrical energy
The total amount of electrical power delivered in a given time period.

electrical potential
The potential energy stored in an electrically-charged body.

emm386.exe
A driver that must be loaded before DOS can access expanded memory. You load this driver by modifying the computer's config.sys file and adding the line `device = c:\dos\emm386.exe`. You can also use the emm386.exe driver to make the upper memory area accessible for storing TSRs by adding (or modifying) the line in config.sys to read `device = c:\dos\emm386.exe noems`.

EMS
(expanded RAM) The first technology that enabled computers and MS-DOS to access more than 1 MB of memory; this goal was accomplished by installing an expansion card in the computer with additional memory chips. MS-DOS accessed expanded RAM by swapping it in and out of the upper memory area, 64 KB at a time. This type of memory is also referred to as EMS, which is short for "expanded memory specification."

encryption
The process of using an encryption key to translate data into a coded version that cannot be read without access to the required decryption key.

ENIAC
(Electronic Numerical Integrator And Computer) Developed for the U.S. Army by J. Presper Eckert and John Mauchly at the University of Pennsylvania in Philadelphia. ENIAC was programmed by plugging in cords and setting thousands of switches to direct how 18,000 vacuum tubes would perform 5,000 calculations per second.

EPP
(Enhanced Parallel Port) Newer-generation parallel port standard that offers roughly 10 times faster throughput than the Centronics standard. Used mostly by non-printer peripherals such as CD-ROM drives and network adapters.

EPROM
(Erasable Programmable Read-Only Memory) A re-usable memory chip that is programmed electrically and erased by exposure to ultraviolet light. When the EPROM is programmed, it acts like a regular ROM chip.

ERD
(emergency repair disk) A disk that contains information about the current configuration of the operating system and that can be used to repair problems with the operating system.

ESD
(electrostatic discharge) Sparks (electrons) that jump from an electrically charged object to an approaching conductive object.

extended partition
A partition used simply for storing data. You cannot use an extended partition to boot a computer.

fastIrDA
Infrared standard that uses a transfer speed of 4 Mbps.

FAT32
A file system that provides support for disks larger than 2 GB on Windows 95 OSR2, Windows 98, and Windows ME systems.

files
A configuration setting that enables you to specify how much memory is reserved for the number of files opened by a DOS application.

FireWire
A high-speed serial bus developed by Apple and Texas Instruments that allows for the connection of up to 63 devices.

firmware
Software stored in memory chips that retains data whether or not power to the computer is on.

Flash memory
A special type of EEPROM that can be erased and written to in blocks instead of in bytes. When the flash memory is programmed, it acts like a regular ROM chip.

flash memory cards
A removable solid-state mass storage device that resides on a small card.

Flash ROM
Memory that stores data similarly to EEPROM, but uses a super-voltage charge to erase a block of data. Can only be erased and rewritten a few times.

form factor
The size and shape of a given component. Often used in terms of motherboard and drive characteristics.

FPM RAM
(Fast Page Mode RAM) Used in older 32-pin SIMMs.

fragmentation
The degree to which the pieces that make up files are spread across the hard disk.

frame type
Specifies the format in which the computer sends data and expects to receive data. Two computers must be using not only the NWLink IPX/SPX protocol but also the same frame type in order to communicate across a network.

full duplex
The ability to send and receive data simultaneously.

fusing assembly
A component in a laser printer that uses two rollers to heat toner particles, melting them into the paper.

geosynchronous
Maintains an orbit with a fixed relationship to Earth.

gigabyte
A means of measuring file or disk size, equivalent to 1,024 MB. Abbreviated as GB.

ground
Any conducting body with a potential of zero; usually, the earth itself or something connected to the earth.

group policy object
A collection of settings, applied within the Active Directory, that are used primarily to restrict users' actions on computers within an Active Directory domain.

GUI
(Graphical User Interface) A means of communicating with an operating system by using a mouse or other device to work with pictorial screen elements, instead of typing text commands at the keyboard.

Hal.dll
A Windows 2000/NT/XP driver that isolates the computer's hardware and device drivers from the operating system so that the same operating system can be used on a variety of hardware.

half duplex
The ability to send data in one direction at a time.

hazardous materials
Any materials that must be handled in a special way in order to prevent injury to people or damage to the environment.

heat sink
A device attached to a processor that addresses the problem of overheating processors. Cool air is blown by a fan onto the device's main elements, keeping the air around the processor cool.

hexadecimal number system
A numbering system based on 16 discrete states.

high memory area
The first 64 KB of RAM immediately after the first megabyte of RAM in the computer (this is the memory between 1024 KB and 1088 KB). In DOS, you can use the high memory area to store a single terminate-and-stay-resident (TSR) program, a device driver, or DOS itself. Windows does not simulate the high memory area when you run a non-Windows application.

himem.sys
A driver that must be loaded before DOS can access extended memory. You load this driver by modifying the computer's config.sys file and adding the line `device = c:\dos\himem.sys`.

hoax
Tricks users into believing there is a malicious code threat to their systems

hotswap
To change out a device without needing to power down the PC during installation or removal of the device.

HTML
(HyperText Markup Language) The authoring language used to create documents on the Web. HTML defines the structure and layout of a Web document as it should present itself in a Web browser.

hub
A central connecting device in a network that joins communication lines together in a star configuration.

HVD
(High Voltage Differential Signaling) A SCSI device that uses two wires, one for data and one for the inverse of data. These devices use high voltage and can't be used on a single-ended SCSI chain.

hybrid topology
A physical topology that uses two or more of the basic physical topologies, such as bus, ring, star, and mesh.

I/O address
A three-digit hexadecimal number (3F8, 278, and so on) used to identify and signal a peripheral device such as a parallel port, serial port, or sound card.

IDE
(Integrated Drive Electronics) A drive interface that provides inexpensive, high-speed data transfer between the IDE drive and the other components of the computer.

IEEE
(Institute of Electrical and Electronic Engineers) Pronounced "I-triple-E." An organization of scientists, engineers, and students of electronics and related fields whose technical and standards committees develop, publish, and revise computing and telecommunications standards.

inductance
Inductance is a circuit or device in which a change in the current generates an electromotive force.

infrared
Technology that uses a beam of light to transmit data, rather than cables, using line-of-sight technology.

inkjet printer
A printer that forms images by spraying ink on the paper.

instruction set
The collection of commands used by a CPU to perform calculations and other computing operations.

integrated circuit
An electronic component consisting of several transistors and resistors, connected together on a semiconductor chip.

interface card
A means of connecting devices to the system board so that they can communicate with the microprocessor.

interrupt
A signal that gets the attention of the CPU and is usually generated when I/O is required.

Io.sys
An MS-DOS operating system file that enables the operating system to access the computer's hardware.

Glossary

IP address
Four numbers that uniquely identify a computer on the network. This address is typically shown in the format 192.168.200.200. A portion of the IP address is used to identify the network on which the computer resides (similar to the street name in a mailing address); the remaining portion of the IP address is used to identify the computer itself (similar to the house number portion of a mailing address.)

IRQ
(Interrupt Request Line) A hardware interrupt on a PC. The interrupt lets the CPU know that the device needs attention from the CPU.

ISA bus
(Industry Standard Architecture bus) An expansion bus commonly used in PCs.

jumper
A small plug placed over pins (or removed from pins) to configure hardware settings. Metal contacts inside the plug complete an electrical circuit to specify the settings for the hardware.

key
A folder that appears in the left pane of the Registry Editor window. A key can contain other keys (also called subkeys) and values.

kilobyte
A means of measuring file or disk size, equivalent to 1,024 bytes. Abbreviated as KB.

L1 cache
See primary cache.

L2 cache
See secondary cache.

L2TP
(Layer Two Tunneling Protocol) An Internet standard VPN protocol for connecting a variety of VPN servers, including RRAS servers running L2TP.

L3 cache
Memory on the motherboard between the processor and RAM when there's a built-in L2 cache on the processor.

laser printer
A type of printer that produces images on paper by using a laser beam and an electrophotographic drum. Produces high-quality output.

latency
The time between when a message is sent and received by the other party.

LCD
(Liquid Crystal Display) A monitor constructed of a liquid crystal solution between two sheets of polarized material.

Li-Ion
Portable computer lithium battery with a long life.

Lithium Polymer
Portable computer battery using a jelly-like material.

load
Power consumption of a device. A load is calculated with inductance, capacitance, and other electrical characteristics.

load phases
The portion of the Windows 2000/NT/XP startup process where the operating system is loaded.

LVD
(Low Voltage Differential Signaling) A SCSI device that uses two wires, one for data and one for the inverse of data. These devices use a low voltage and can be used on a single-ended SCSI chain.

magnetic core memory
Memory that stores binary data (0 or 1) in the orientation of magnetic charges in ferrite cores about one-sixteenth-inch in diameter.

malicious code attack
A type of software-based attack where an attacker inserts malicious code into a user's system to disrupt or disable the operating system or an application.

Mark I
A programmable, electromechanical calculator that combined 78 adding machines to perform three calculations per second. It was designed by Howard Aiken, built by IBM, and installed at Harvard in 1944.

math coprocessor
A mathematical circuit that performs high-speed floating point operations. It is generally built into the CPU chip. In older PCs, such as the 386SX and 486SX, the math coprocessor was an optional and separate chip.

MBR
(Master Boot Record) Contains the instructions for finding and loading the computer's operating system.

media
In a network, the transmission media that links computers together in a network. Usually a cable, but could be a wireless medium. In drives, the storage object on which data is stored.

megabyte
A means of measuring file or disk size, equivalent to 1,024 KB. Abbreviated as MB.

memory
Internal storage areas of the computer.

memory address
An area of computer memory assigned to a device.

memory bank
The collection of memory expansion slots in a computer.

memory package
A circuit board design that holds the memory chips that are plugged into the memory expansion slots on the motherboard.

mesh topology
A physical topology in which each node has a direct connection to all other nodes on the network, providing dedicated, permanent point-to-point communication paths.

microprocessor
A complete central processing unit on a single chip, the microprocessor controls the operation of all the other computer components.

MIDI
(Musical Instrument Digital Interface) An interface that allows you to connect and control electronic musical devices such as electric keyboards (pianos), synthesizers, drum kits, and guitars.

MNP
(Microcom Networking Protocol) Five modem standards offering different levels of error correction and detection.

motherboard
The main circuit board in a personal computer. Also referred to as a system board.

Msdos.sys
An MS-DOS operating system file that enables the computer to access disks.

MSDS
(Material Safety Data Sheets) Technical bulletins designed to give users and emergency personnel information about the proper procedures of the storage and handling of a hazardous substance.

multimeter
Electronic test equipment that can perform multiple tasks, usually including measurement of voltage, current, and resistance.

Napier's Bones
A set of rectangular rods with numbers etched on them that let users do multiplication by adding the numbers on properly positioned rods. Precursor of the slide rule.

NetBEUI
A small network protocol, developed by Microsoft, that enables computers to communicate over a network. You can use NetBEUI in place of a network protocol such as TCP/IP as long as the computers on the network do not need to access the Internet.

network adapter
A printed circuit board that plugs into both the clients and servers and controls the exchange of data between them. Also referred to as network boards, network cards, and Network Interface Cards (NICs).

network client
A software component you install that enables a computer to access shared files and printers on another computer across the network. For example, if you want a Windows 2000 computer to access shared files on a Novell NetWare 4.12 server, you must install the Client Service For NetWare on the Windows 2000 computer first.

Glossary

network protocol
A special electronic language that enables network computers to communicate.

network-attached printer
A printer with an installed network card that is connected directly to the network cabling that you connect to by specifying its IP address.

nibble
A group of 4 bits. An 8-bit byte is written as 2 nibbles to make it easier to read.

NiCad
Portable computer battery made of nickel and cadmium with a three to four hour life.

NiMH
Environmentally friendly battery for portable computers.

node
Any of the devices that can be accessed on the network. This includes devices such as servers, clients, and printers.

non-routable
Refers to network protocols that cannot send data across routers.

Ntbootdd.sys
A Windows 2000/NT/XP boot file that initializes support for SCSI hard disks on which the BIOS is disabled.

Ntdetect.com
A Windows 2000/NT/XP boot file that performs hardware detection on the computer.

Ntldr
A Windows 2000/NT/XP boot file that loads the operating system.

Ntoskrnl.exe
A Windows 2000/NT/XP boot file that loads the basic Windows 2000, Windows NT, or Windows XP operating system.

NWLink IPX/SPX
Microsoft's version of Novell NetWare's proprietary network protocol, IPX/SPX. This protocol enables computers to communicate over a network (including across routers). The NWLink IPX/SPX protocol does not, however, enables computers to communicate on the Internet.

ohm
Unit of measure for resistance.

online UPS
A UPS that supplies power from a battery at all times. The battery is charged from the regular electrical supply.

operands
The values being compared in a logical or mathematical operation.

OS
(Operating System) A type of system software that provides the basic interface between the user and the computer components.

outbound connection
A network connection that connects clients on one physical network to resources on a remote network.

paging file
The file used by Windows to implement virtual memory. This file is also known as a swap file.

palmtop
Another name for a PDA.

parity
An error-checking method that uses a ninth bit or parity bit to validate the contents of memory.

partition
An area of hard disk that is treated logically as a single unit of storage.

Pascaline machine
A calculating machine that could add and subtract, developed in 1642 by Blaise Pascal.

path
An environment variable that enables you to specify the folders in which you want the operating system to search for executable files.

PC
(Personal Computer) Stand-alone, single-user desktop, or smaller, computers that can function independently. PC used to refer to any personal computer, but now refers to personal computers that follow the original design by IBM, use Intel or compatible chips, and usually have some version of Windows as an operating system. PCs are sometimes called IBM compatibles.

PC Card
The credit-card-sized devices which are used in portable instead of desktop expansion cards.

PCI bus
(Peripheral Component Interconnect bus) A peripheral bus commonly used in PCs that provides a high-speed data path between the CPU and peripheral devices.

PCMCIA
(Personal Computer Memory Card International Association) An association of organizations that establishes standards for PC Cards.

PDA
(Personal Digital Assistant) A very small computer that can be held in one hand. Often used to keep an electronic calendar and address book, get email, send faxes, and take notes on the go.

peer-to-peer network
A network where all computers connected to the network can act as a provider (server) or consumer (client) of network resources.

peripheral
Any computing device that is connected to the CPU and main memory.

PGA
(Pin Grid Array) A type of CPU packaging design on which pins are distributed evenly in parallel rows on the entire bottom of a square chip.

physical topology
The layout of networked computers in physical relationship to each other.

pixel
The smallest discrete element on a video display.

plenum
An air-handling space which is part of the heating and cooling system in a building and is often a convenient place to run cables.

plenum cable
Cable made of special materials in the insulation layers that make it fire resistant. When it burns, it produces a minimal amount of smoke and chemical fumes.

Plug and Play
A method in which the operating system automatically configures adapter settings. Also written as PnP.

port
A hardware connection interface on a computer system that enables devices to be connected to the system.

potential difference
A measurement of the difference in electrical potential energy between two different objects. Also called voltage.

potential energy
Energy that is stored in a body as a result of the position or condition of the body.

PPP
(Point-to-Point Protocol) A remote access protocol used to transmit data across phone lines.

PPTP
(Point-to-Point Tunneling Protocol) A Microsoft proprietary VPN protocol for connecting to Microsoft Routing and Remote Access Service (RRAS) servers running PPP.

primary cache
A type of high-speed RAM that is added directly to a processor to improve computing speed. Often referred to as onboard cache, CPU cache, or L1 (Level 1) cache. Compare with L2 cache and RAM.

primary network logon types
A configuration setting that determines how Windows 98 will attempt to log users on to the computer.

primary partition
A partition that can be used to boot the computer.

print driver
A software component you install in Windows to configure the operating system to communicate with a specific printer.

print spooler
The print process component that receives the job from the print driver and stores it until it can be produced on the printer.

processor
Another way to refer to the microprocessor, or CPU.

PROM
(Programmable Read-Only Memory) A memory chip that can be programmed once. After it's programmed, it acts like a regular ROM chip.

proprietary
A design that is unique to a specific manufacturer. The design has not been shared so there are no competing product lines making a component, so you are forced to purchase it directly from the manufacturer.

PS/2 interface
A round 6-pin port used to connect keyboards and mice to PCs.

RAM
(Random Access Memory) RAM chips are integrated circuit chips that act as the computer's primary temporary storage place for data.

RAM chip
An integrated circuit that acts as the computer's primary temporary storage place for data. RAM stands for Random Access Memory.

RAMDAC
(Random Access Memory Digital-Analog Converter) Component on the video card that reads the bytes of video data in the card's memory and converts the digital data in memory to continuous analog signals that tell the monitor what to display.

RDRAM
(Rambus Dynamic RAM) A new memory architecture by Rambus, Inc. that supports speeds up to 800 MHz.

Recovery Console
A command-line utility for repairing a computer.

register
A special high-speed storage area located within a processor.

Registry
A database of system and application configuration information.

remote connection
A network connection that connects clients on one physical network to resources on a remote network.

remote-access connection
A network connection that connects clients on one physical network to resources on a remote network.

resistance
Opposition to the flow of electrons.

resistor
An electronic component that resists the flow of electric current in an electronic circuit.

RIMM
(Rambus Inline Memory Module) A memory module for RDRAM. Supports from one to 16 direct RDRAM devices in a Rambus channel. Used primarily as main memory on a system board.

ring topology
A physical topology where all nodes are connected in a continuous loop, and nodes relay information around the loop in a round-robin manner.

riser card
A board that's plugged into the motherboard, it "rises" above the motherboard and is used to connect modems, audio cards, and network cards to the system.

ROM
(Read-Only Memory) A special type of memory that is permanent. It stores programs necessary to boot the computer and to diagnose problems.

SAM
(Sequential Access Memory) Used for memory where data can be stored in sequential order such as memory buffers.

SCSI
(Small Computer System Interface) A drive controller that provides high-performance data transfer between the SCSI device and the other components of the computer. Pronounced scuzzy.

SDRAM
(Synchronous DRAM) Memory that has a clock that is coordinated with the system clock to synchronize the memory chip's input and output signals.

SECC
(Single Edge Contact Cartridge) Type of CPU packaging that refers to a design where the processor is located on a circuit board that is inserted into a slot on the system board.

secondary cache
A type of high-speed RAM that is placed between the processor and conventional RAM to improve computing speed. Often referred to as L2 (Level 2) cache. Compare with CPU cache and RAM.

sector
The smallest unit of storage read or written on a disk.

semiconductor
A solid-state substance that can be electrically altered to act as either a conductor or an insulator.

server
A computer on a network that manages resources for other computers on the network.

share-level security
Enables you to set a password on each individual shared resource.

SIMM
(Single In-line Memory Module) A group of memory chips that transfer information 32 bits at a time.

single-ended device
SCSI device that uses a single wire for each bit of data.

SLIP
(Serial Line Internet Protocol) A remote access protocol used to transmit data across serial lines.

slowIrDA
Infrared standard that uses a transfer speed of 9.6 Kbps.

socket services
Device driver software for a PC Card.

SODIMM
(Small Outline Dual Inline Memory Module) A memory module standard used in some notebook and iMac systems.

soldered
A means of securing electronic components to a circuit board by using a combination of lead, tin, and silver (solder) and a tool called a soldering iron.

sound card
An internal card used to convert digital signals to sound waves. Includes several external ports for connecting electronic musical instruments, game controllers, speakers, and microphones. Usually also includes internal connections for playback of audio CDs.

SPGA
(Staggered Pin Grid Array) This CPU packaging design staggers pins so that more pins will fit on the same amount of surface.

spools
The process of storing a print job on a hard disk; this print job is then later sent to the printer.

SRAM
(Static RAM) A type of RAM that doesn't need to be refreshed.

Standby UPS
SUPSs are UPSs that supply power from a battery when power problems are detected. Also referred to as a Standby Power Supply (SPS).

star topology
A physical topology where all nodes individually connect to a central device such as a hub.

static IP address
An IP address that is configured manually, not using DHCP. Static IP addresses are not meant to change frequently.

Stepped Reckoner
A mechanical calculator developed by Gottfried von Leibniz that improved Pascal's design to include multiplication and division.

STP
(shielded twisted-pair) Twisted-pair cable that is wrapped in a metal sheath. This reduces the possibility of problems caused by electrical interference.

subnet mask
Four numbers used to distinguish the network portion of the IP address from that of the computer portion. For example, if a computer's IP address is 192.168.200.200 and the subnet mask is 255.255.255.0, this means that the network portion of the address is 192.168.200, and the computer portion is the remaining byte (200).

synchronous
Transmission of a bit stream of data where the transmitter and receiver are synchronized.

System
The Windows 2000/NT/XP Registry file that contains the system configuration information and a list of the device drivers to be loaded during the boot process.

system board
The main circuit board in a personal computer. Also referred to as a motherboard

system partition
The hard disk partition that contains the files necessary for booting the Windows 2000, Windows NT, or Windows XP operating system.

system policy
A collection of settings used to restrict users' actions on computers within a Windows NT domain. These settings are applied through the use of a system policy file on the domain controllers.

system software
Low-level programs that provide the most basic functionality, such as operating systems.

system state data
The Windows 2000 or Windows XP boot files, Registry, COM+ object registrations, and all files installed during the installation of Windows 2000 or Windows XP that have the .sys, .dll, .ttf, .fon, .ocx, and .exe extension.

System.ini
A Windows initialization (.ini) file that's used to configure specific parameters used by DOS and Windows 9x.

TCP/IP
(Transmission Control Protocol/Internet Protocol) A suite of protocols that enables computers to communicate across a network and over the Internet. This protocol suite consists of many different protocols, most notably, TCP and IP. In addition, it includes SNMP for sending email and HTTP for connecting to and downloading Web pages.

thermal compound
Used to attach a heat sink to a CPU. Manufactured to provide maximum heat transfer from the CPU to the heat sink.

throughput
The amount of data that can be processed from input through to output within a given time period.

toner
An electrically charged dry ink substance used in laser printers.

track
A storage channel on a disk or tape. On disks, tracks are concentric circles (hard and floppy disks) or spirals (CDs and video disks). On tapes, they are parallel lines.

transceiver
A device that has the circuitry to enable it to be both a transmitter and a receiver.

transistor
A device containing semiconductor material that can amplify a signal or open and close a circuit. In computers, transistors function as an electronic switch.

triboelectric generation
Using friction to create a static charge.

Trojan Horse
A piece of malicious code that masquerades as a harmless file.

TSR program
(terminate-and-stay-resident program) An MS-DOS program that remains in memory after you initially run it. A TSR stays in memory until you reboot the computer. You typically run TSR programs only on computers that are using MS-DOS as the operating system.

twisted-pair cable
A thin-diameter wire (22 to 26 gauge) commonly used for telephone and network cabling. The wires are twisted around each other to minimize interference from other twisted pairs in the cable.

Ultra DMA
A newer faster drive technology for data transfers on IDE drives. Also called Ultra ATA and Fast ATA-2. Provides for transfer speeds of up to 100 MBps.

UMB
(upper memory blocks) Blocks of memory that are not in use within the upper memory area.

UNIVAC
(Universal Automatic Computer) Completed in 1951 by Eckert and Mauchly for the U.S. Bureau of the Census. It was the first commercial computer in the United States and could handle both numerical and alphabetical information.

upper memory area
The 384 KB of RAM between 640 KB and 1 MB in a computer. This segment of RAM is reserved in MS-DOS for use by the computer's hardware devices. If you run a DOS application within Windows, Windows simulates the upper memory area for the application.

UPS
(Uninterruptible Power Supply) A battery-operated device that is intended to save computer components from damage due to power problems such as power failures, spikes, and sags.

USB
(Universal Serial Bus) A hardware interface for connecting up to 127 USB peripherals.

user-level security
Enables you to specify which users and groups have access to each individual shared resource.

UTP
(unshielded twisted-pair) Twisted-pair cable that has two unshielded wires twisted around each other. This type of cabling is inexpensive, but electrical interference can be a problem.

vacuum tube
A sealed glass or metal container that controls a flow of electrons through a vacuum.

value
An entry in the Registry database that contains configuration information. A value consists of three parts: a name, data type, and the data stored in the value.

video output device
A computer peripheral that enables users to view information on a computer system.

Virtual Device Driver
A type of device driver used in Windows 9x. You sometimes see virtual device drivers referred to as VxDs because their associated files have the extension .vxd.

virus
A piece of malicious code that spreads from one computer to another by attaching itself to other files.

volt
Unit of measurement for voltage.

voltage
Electric potential or potential difference, expressed in volts.

VPN connection
(Virtual Private Network connection) An outbound connection that uses existing local or outbound connection objects to connect a client on one physical network, through a private connection over a public network, to a VPN server on a remote network.

VRAM
(Video RAM) These chips have two access paths to a single memory address to improve performance. One path is used for reads, the other for writes.

VRM
(Voltage Regulator Module) A module on the system board that regulates the voltage that's passed to the CPU.

watt
Energy per second delivered by electric current. Unit of measurement for power.

Win.com
A file used by Windows 9x to start the operating system.

Win.ini
A Windows 9x initialization (.ini) file used to set environment parameters for older applications that were written for Windows 3.1.

Windows 9x share permission
A collection of defined rights that allow access to a shared resource.

WINS
(Windows Internet Naming System) A Windows NT or Windows 2000 service used to enable clients to obtain the IP address for a given computer name.

workgroup
A Microsoft network model that simply groups computers together for ease of finding shared resources such as folders and printers. A workgroup does not share a centralized user account database.

worm
A piece of malicious code that spreads from one computer to another on its own, not by attaching itself to another file.

WRAM
(Windows RAM) Developed by Samsung Electronics, this type of RAM is optimized for display adapters.

XIP
(Execute In Place) A PC Card feature that enables operating system and application code stored on the PC Card to run directly from the PC Card rather than executing in RAM.

XMS
(extended RAM) All of the memory in the computer after the first 1,088 KB. This segment of memory is also referred to as XMS, which is short for "extended memory specification."

ZIF socket
(Zero Insertion Force socket) A type of processor socket that uses a lever to tighten or loosen the pin connections between the processor chip and the socket.

Zinc Air
Portable computer battery that uses a carbon membrane that absorbs oxygen.

zoned-bit recording
A method of creating sectors on a hard disk so that there are more sectors on the outer tracks than on inner tracks.

ZV
(Zoomed Video) A connection between a PC Card and the host system that allows the card to write video data directly to the VGA controller.

INDEX

A

abacus, 2
AC power, 198, 229
Accelerated Graphics Port
  See: AGP
account management tools, 392
ACPI, 198
Active Matrix, 226
active termination, 153
actuator arms, 140
adapter cards, 96, 97, 98, 111, 311
  Also See: expansion cards
  identifying common problems, 312
  troubleshooting, 312, 315
  upgrading, 210
  using, 311
Add New Hardware Wizard, 41
address buses, 181
Advanced Power Management
  See: APM
Advanced Technology Attachment
  See: ATA
AGP, 103, 104
AGP cards, 104, 105
alternating current, 830
ALU, 175
American National Standards Institute
  See: ANSI
American Standard Code for Information Interchange
  See: ASCII
amperes, 91
AMR, 201
analog signals, 33
ANSI, 301
answer files, 778
aperture grills, 294
APIPA, 125, 445

APM, 198
AppleTalk protocol, 451
applications
  removing, 428
Archive file attribute, 680
Arithmetic and Logic Unit
  See: ALU
ASCII, 301
aspect ratios, 293
ASR, 698
  complete backup, 700
  preparing, 700
asynchronous mode, 63
AT Attachment Packet Interface
  See: ATAPI
AT commands, 66
ATA, 143
  -2, 145
  -3, 145
  -4, 145
  standards, 145
ATAPI, 143, 145
Attachment Unit Interface connectors
  See: AUI connectors
Attention commands
  See: AT commands
attributes, 502
ATX, 202, 206
Audio/Modem Riser
  See: AMR
AUI connectors, 119
Autoexec.bat, 664
Automated System Recovery
  See: ASR
Automatic Private IP Addressing
  See: APIPA
automatic termination, 153

B

Baby AT, 202
backbone cables, 119, 120
background logon authentication process, 403
backside bus, 169
backup media, 682
backup types, 681
banks, 169
basic disks, 562
Basic Input Output System
   See: BIOS
Basic Rate Interface
   See: BRI
batch/script files, 682
batteries, 230, 231, 283
Bayonet Nut Connector, 118
   Also See: British Naval Connector
   See: BNC connectors
Berg connectors, 195, 196
bidirectional ports, 49
binary digits, 53
binary number system, 52, 53, 105
BIOS, 191
  accessing system settings, 189
  defining, 189
  settings, 190
  upgrading, 210
  upgrading the system, 191
bits, 53
bits per second, 59
BNC connectors, 118
boolean, 175
boot disks, 650
boot partition, 669
boot process, 321, 361
  identifying common problems, 363
  troubleshooting, 363
boot sector, 665
boot sequence, 668
Boot.ini, 667, 670
Bootsect.dos, 667
branch prediction, 177
BRI, 131, 132
brightness, 36
British Naval Connector, 118
   Also See: Bayonet Nut Connector
   See: BNC connectors
buffers, 424
  configuring, 427
built-in groups, 483
built-in user accounts, 483
bus, 181
  defining, 98, 99, 100, 102, 103
  identifying the types, 99, 100, 102, 103
  upgrading, 210
bus masters, 236
bus topology, 125
bytes, 53

C

cable Internet connections, 131
cable modems, 65, 131, 597
cables, 114, 115, 117, 119, 120, 155, 223
cache, 169, 177, 179
captured print jobs
  viewing, 523
captured printer ports
  disconnecting, 524
Card Information Structure
   See: CIS
card services, 237
CardBus, 236
cartridge drives, 137
case component
  cleaning, 279
CAT5, 116
Category 5
   See: CAT5

Cathode Ray Tube
    See: CRT
CD and DVD drives, 134, 136
    identifying common problems, 331
    troubleshooting, 331, 332
Celeron, 179
Central Processing Unit
    See: CPU
Centronics standard, 48, 49
channels, 106
charge, 829
Check Disk tool, 258
chipsets, 199
Chkdsk switches, 259
Chkdsk tool, 320
Chkdsk.exe tool, 258
CIS, 237
CISC, 186
cleaning supplies, 276, 281
client-server networks, 127
clients, 113
clock speeds, 177, 179
clusters, 587
CMOS, 166, 295
CMOS Setup utility, 190
CNR, 201
coax cables, 117
coaxial cables, 117
    Also See: coax cables
coaxial connectors, 118
Collect phase, 290
Collect, Isolate, and Correct troubleshooting model, 370
    collecting information, 371
    correcting the problem, 374
    diagnosing system problems, 375
    isolating the problem, 372
color depth, 35
command-line tools, 392
    troubleshooting, 395

Command.com, 664
Communication and Networking Riser
    See: CNR
CompactFlash flash memory cards, 243, 245
Complex Instruction Set Computer
    See: CISC
Complimentary Metal Oxide Semiconductor
    See: CMOS
computer cases, 205, 206
computer images, 785
    creating and storing, 787
    deployment process, 785
    installing, 793
Computer Management, 387
computer peripherals
    video output devices, 31, 32
conductors, 93
Config.sys, 664
configuring, 427
connectors, 114, 115, 118, 119, 120, 155, 193, 194, 195, 196, 835
contrast, 36
Control Panel, 385
Control Unit, 175
conventional memory, 422
corona assembly, 262
Correct phase, 290
cost/benefit analysis, 212
CPU, 96, 174, 175, 181
    cooling, 176, 177
    identifying factors that affect performance, 177
    identifying the components, 175
    upgrading, 187
CPU cache, 169
    Also See: primary cache
    Also See: L1 cache
CPU packages, 184, 185, 186
CPU speeds, 180, 181
CRT, 32
    producing an image, 292, 293

current, 91, 830
cylinders, 141

D

data, 406
data bits, 59
data bus, 169, 179, 181
daughter boards, 199
DC power, 229
decimal number system, 105
decryption, 506
default gateway address, 443
default gateways, 123
degauss, 294
Device Bay, 81
device conflicts, 107
device drivers, 44, 45
 install using Device Manager, 436
Device Manager, 58, 59, 67, 107, 390, 435
 configuring driver signing options, 437
 identifying hardware devices, 435
 installing device drivers, 436
 verifying hardware device status, 435
device settings, 516
DHCP, 125, 445
dial-up connections, 132, 595
 creating, 599
 data encryption, 599
 private servers, 601
DIB, 177
digital signals, 33
Digital Subscriber Link Internet connection
 See: DSL
DIMM, 171
diode, 4
dip switches, 107
direct current, 830
Direct Memory Access
 See: DMA
Disk Defragmenter tool, 258, 320

disk drive geometry, 141
disk management tools, 391
display characteristics controlled by dialog boxes, 35
display characteristics controlled manually, 36
dissipative material, 834
distortion, 36
DMA, 106, 145
DNS, 124, 444
docking devices, 226, 227, 228
docking stations, 227, 233
domain, 494
 logging on, 541
domain controllers, 494
domain membership
 configuring, 496
Domain Name System
 See: DNS
DOS boot files, 664
DOS boot process, 665
DOS boot tools
 troubleshooting, 395
DOS memory segments, 422
 configuring, 424
 conventional memory, 422
 expanded memory, 422
 extended memory, 422
 high memory area, 422
 upper memory area, 422
dot pitch, 35
dot-matrix printers
 defining, 264, 265
 forming images, 340
 identifying common problems, 341
 maintaining, 270
 troubleshooting, 341
DRAM, 167
drive bay, 139
drive compression, 573
drive controllers, 146, 147

drive interfaces, 143, 144, 145, 146
drive partitions, 149
drive power connectors, 195, 196
driver signing options
  configuring with Device Manager, 437
drivers, 434
drives, 96, 134, 139, 141, 149, 233, 234
  cartridge, 137
  CD and DVD, 331
  floppy, 135, 279, 326, 329
  hard, 136, 140, 147, 149, 234, 317, 318, 320, 321, 322, 323, 324
  media, 279
  optical, 136
  tape, 138, 327
DSL Internet connection, 130
DSL modems, 65
Dual Independent Bus
  See: DIB
Dual Inline Memory Module
  See: DIMM
duplexing, 159
dust control, 95
dye sublimation printers, 342
  defining, 270
  maintaining, 272
dynamic disks, 562
Dynamic Host Configuration Protocol
  See: DHCP
Dynamic RAM
  See: DRAM

E

ECC, 173
ECP, 48, 49
editing a Registry, 408
EDO RAM, 167
EDSAC, 4
EDVAC, 4
EEPROM, 170

effective permissions process, 513
EISA bus, 100
EISA cards, 101
electrical energy, 830
electrical measurements, 829
electrical potential, 829
electrical power, 830
electrical process, 90
electrical safety, 357, 358
electrical safety hazards, 94
Electronically Erasable Programmable ROM
  See: EEPROM
electrostatic discharge
  See: ESD
email clients, 625
  common packages, 626
email protocol, 624
emergency repair disk
  See: ERD
emergency repair process, 676
emm386.exe, 422
enclosure styles, 206
encryption, 506
Enhanced Parallel Port
  See: EPP
ENIAC, 4
environment variables, 424
  configuring, 425
EPIC, 186
EPP, 48, 49
EPROM, 170
Epson Stylus Color 500 inkjet printers, 269
Erasable Programmable ROM
  See: EPROM
ERD, 675
  creating, 677
Error Correction Code
  See: ECC
error messages, 714

ESD process, 92
ESD safety equipment, 93, 94, 95
ESD-safe work area, 93, 94, 95
  establishing, 95
exam objectives, 799
eXecute In Place
  See: XIP
expanded memory, 422
expansion cards, 311
Explicitly Parallel Instruction Computing
  See: EPIC
Extended Capability Port
  See: ECP
Extended Data Output RAM
  See: EDO RAM
Extended Industry Standard Architecture bus
  See: EISA bus
extended memory, 422
extended partitions, 560
  creating, 566
  deleting, 570
external buses, 181

F

fast IrDA, 83
Fast Page Mode RAM
  See: FPM RAM
Fast SCSI, 154
Fast Wide SCSI, 154
FAT, 499
FAT partitions
  converting to NTFS; 571
FAT32, 499
FAT32 file systems, 580
FC-PGA, 185
FC-PGA2, 185
fiber-optic cables, 119, 120
file allocation table
  See: FAT
file and folder permissions
  assigning, 502
file attributes
  configuring, 505
file compression, 572
file system conversion, 571
file systems, 499
files, 424, 427
FireWire devices
  connecting to a system, 81
FireWire interfaces
  defining, 79, 80
firmware, 191
flash memory cards, 242, 243, 244, 245
Flash ROM, 170
flat connectors, 61
Flip Chip Pin Grid Array
  See: FC-PGA
floppy drives, 134, 135
  cleaning, 279
  troubleshooting, 329
  using, 326
flow control, 59
folders
  sharing, 514
fonts, 35
form factors, 202
formatting, 149
FPM RAM, 167
fragmentation, 258, 260, 261, 320, 574
frame type, 462
friction feed, 267
frontside buses, 181
    Also See: system buses
    Also See: local buses
full tower, 205
Full-size AT, 202
fusing assembly, 262

G

game devices, 70

Game Port, 68
genders, 35
geosynchronous, 128
Ghost
  creating a boot disk, 790
  installing, 790
  uninstalling, 792
ghosting, 785
graphical tools, 380
ground, 833
group memberships
  modifying, 491

H

Hal.dll, 667
hard disks, 258
  Also See: hard drives
  identifying maintenance tools
  checking for errors, 259, 260
  defragmenting, 260, 261, 574
hard drives, 134, 136, 140, 147
  formatting, 149
  identifying common problems, 318
  identifying reasons drives are slow, 320
  identifying the architecture, 140
  reading data from, 317
  troubleshooting, 318, 321, 322, 323, 324
  upgrading, 210
  using maintenance tools, 320
  writing to, 317
hardware devices
  identifying with Device Manager, 435
  verifying status with Device Manager, 435
hardware drivers, 434
hardware resources, 107
  defining, 106
  identifying typical settings, 107
hardware-based modems, 62
hazardous materials, 281, 283
  defining, 280, 281

disposing of, 284
heat sinks, 177
Help and Support Center utility, 351
hex memory addresses, 106
hexadecimal number systems, 105
Hibernation mode, 198
high memory area, 422
High Voltage Differential
  See: HVD
himem.sys, 422
hoax, 639
hotswap, 80
HP LaserJet 6P laser printers, 263
hubs, 125
Human Interface USB devices, 75
HVD signaling, 152
hybrid topology, 125

I

I/O addresses, 106
IDE, 143, 144, 145, 146
IDE drives, 147
  defining, 146
  installing, 148
  removing, 149
IEEE, 47, 80
image position, 36
Imaging USB devices, 75
inductance, 317
Industry Standard Architecture bus
  See: ISA bus
infrared devices, 82, 84
inkjet printers
  creating printed output, 339
  defining, 268, 269
  identifying common problems, 340
  maintaining, 271
inkjet technologies, 340
installation boot disks
  creating, 676

installation changes, 409
installation types, 765
installing a Windows application, 411
Institute of Electrical and Electronic Engineers
    See: IEEE
instruction sets, 186
insulators, 93
integrated circuits, 5, 96
Integrated Drive Electronics
    See: IDE
integrated keyboard and pointing devices, 43
integrated keyboards, 224
integrated monitors, 224
integrated peripherals, 223, 224, 225
integrated pointing devices, 225
Integrated Services Digital Network
    See: ISDN
Intel processors, 179, 180
internal adapter cards, 111
internal buses, 181
internal PC components, 96
  defining, 96
  installing, 111
internal removable media devices
  identifying problems, 328
  troubleshooting, 328
International Telecommunications Union
    See: ITU
Internet connections, 127, 128
  cable, 131
  dial-up, 132
  DSL, 130
  ISDN, 131, 132
  LAN, 128, 129, 130
  satellite, 132, 133
  setting up, 615
  wireless, 133
Internet Explorer
  configuring the Web browser, 620

Internet Service Provider
    See: ISP
Internet/intranet
  troubleshooting connection problems, 630
Interrupt Request Line
    See: IRQ
interrupts, 106
Io.sys, 664
Iomega software, 325
IP addresses, 121, 122, 123, 441, 443
ipconfig, 134, 351
  command, 446
  troubleshooting automatic TCP/IP configuration, 458
  troubleshooting TCP/IP connectivity, 458
IRQ, 106
ISA bus, 99
ISDN, 131, 132
Isolate phase, 290
ISP, 448
ITU, 63

J
jumpers, 107

K
key, 406
keyboards, 8, 43, 224
  cleaning, 278
  Dvorak, 43
  identifying common problems, 302
  identifying the components, 302
  Natural, 43
  Standard Windows, 43
  troubleshooting, 302, 303, 309
  using, 300, 301
  using scan codes, 301
Kodak Professional 8500 Digital Photo dye sublimation printers, 270

L

L1 cache, 169
   Also See: CPU cache
   Also See: primary cache
L2 cache, 169
   Also See: secondary cache
L3 cache, 169
LAN Internet connections, 128, 129, 130
large disk support, 580
laser printers, 262, 263, 282, 337
  identifying common problems, 338
  maintaining, 271
laser printing process, 337
latency, 132
Layer Two Tunneling Protocol
   See: L2TP
LCD, 32, 224, 226
Li-Ion, 232
Li-Ion batteries, 230
Line In, 68
liquid cleaning materials, 281
Liquid Crystal Display
   See: LCD
Lithium Polymer, 232
load phases, 668
loads, 102
local buses, 181
   Also See: system buses
   Also See: frontside buses
local printers
  installing, 525, 526, 547
local security, 482
local user accounts
  creating, 484
  deleting, 485
local user profiles
  deleting, 487
log files
  clearing, 713

Low Voltage Differential
   See: LVD
LPX, 202
LVD, 152
LVD signaling, 152

M

maintenance tools, 258, 320
Maintenance Wizard, 727
malicious code attacks, 638
Mass Storage USB devices, 75
Master Boot Record
   See: MBR
Material Safety Data Sheets
   See: MSDS
math coprocessors, 176
MBR, 665
McAfee AntiVirus Professional
  manually updating virus definitions, 655
McAfee VirusScan Professional 7.0
  configuring, 649
  creating an emergency disk, 653
  installing, 643
  removing a virus, 657
  system requirements, 640
media, 113
media drives, 279
memory, 175, 242
  defining, 166
  identifying common problems, 364
  identifying common symptoms, 364
  installing, 247
  troubleshooting, 364, 365
  upgrading, 210
memory addresses, 106
memory banks, 170
memory packages, 170, 171, 242
Memory Stick flash memory cards
   See: MS flash memory cards
mesh topology, 125

Mic In, 68
mice, 306
micro tower, 205
Micro-FCBGA, 186
Micro-FCPGA, 186
MicroDIMM, 171
Micronom Networking Protocol
    See: MNP
microphones, 70
mid tower, 205
MIDI, 72
Millions of Instructions Per Second
    See: MIPS
Mini-PCI cards, 240
  identifying the types, 239
  installing, 240
  removing or replacing, 241
MIPS, 177
mirroring, 159
MMX, 177
MNP, 64
modems, 62, 65
  class 5 MNP standard, 64
  commands, 66
  identifying common problems, 352
  transmission modes, 63
  troubleshooting, 352, 354
  V dot modem standards, 63
moisture control, 95
Molex connectors, 195, 196
monitors, 8, 224
  adjusting video settings, 39
  cleaning, 278
  controlling the positioning of electron beams, 294
  degaussing, 294
  identifying common problems, 295
  installing, 37
  troubleshooting, 295, 298

motherboards, 96, 199, 206, 199
    Also See: system boards
  identifying form factors, 202
mouse, 8
mouse ports, 43
MS flash memory cards, 245
MS-DOS boot disk
  creating, 671
MS-DOS mode, 581
Msdos.sys, 664
MSDS, 280
multimedia extensions
    See: MMX
multimeter, 831
multiple boot computer, 750
multiprocessing, 177
Musical Instrument Digital Interface
    See: MIDI
My Computer, 385
My Network Places, 388

N

name resolution
  troubleshooting using NSLookup, 457
  troubleshooting with ping, 457
name servers, 444
narrow SCSI, 154
    Also See: regular SCSI
NetBEUI, 459
  installing, 459
  removing, 459
NetBIOS names, 540
Netscape Navigator 7.01
  configuring, 622
  installing, 621
NetWare client
  installing, 469
  removing, 470
network adapters, 113
network architectures, 125

client-server, 127
peer-to-peer, 126
network cables, 114, 115, 117, 119, 120
network card drivers
　updating, 437
network cards
　installing, 133
　upgrading, 210
network client, 467
network commands, 134
network connections
　configuring, 473
　identifying common problems, 350
　troubleshooting, 350, 351
network connectors, 114, 115, 118, 119, 120
Network Neighborhood, 388
network printers
　connecting, 517
　installing, 548
network protocols, 113, 121, 125, 441
network troubleshooting utilities, 351
network-attached printer, 516
　connecting, 517
networks, 113, 121, 123, 124
　identifying common problems, 350
　identifying the components, 113, 114, 115, 117, 118, 119, 120
　troubleshooting, 350, 351
Ni-MH batteries, 230
NiCad, 231
Nickel Cadmium
　See: NiCad
Nickel Metal-Hydride
　See: NiMH
NiMH, 231
NLX, 202
nodes, 113
Non-MIDI electronic instruments, tape players/recorders, or radios, 70
non-routable, 459

non-Windows applications, 419
　installing with a setup program, 421
　installing without a setup program, 420
Norton AntiVirus
　creating an emergency disk set, 652
Norton AntiVirus 2003
　configuring, 649
　manually updating virus definitions, 654
　removing a virus, 656
notebook computers, 219, 221, 222, 223, 224, 225
NSLookup
　troubleshooting name resolution, 457
Ntbootdd.sys, 667
Ntdetect.com, 667
NTFS permissions, 501
Ntldr, 667
Ntoskrnl.exe, 667
null modem cables, 58
number systems, 105
　defining, 105
NWLink IPX/SPX, 461
　configuration settings, 462
　installing, 462
　removing, 463

O

ohms, 91
OkiData Microline 390 dot-matrix printers, 265
OLGA, 185
　Also See: OOI
omega, 831
online UPS, 274
OOI, 185
　Also See: OLGA
operands, 175
operating system components, 772
　adding, 772
　removing, 772
operating systems

replacing, 770
startup files, 422
troubleshooting installations, 771
optical drives, 136
optical mouse, 306
Organic Land Grid Array
  See: OLGA
out-of-order completion, 177
outbound connection, 594
Outlook Express
  adding a new account, 628
  configuring, 626

P

paging file, 415
Palm m130, 251
Palm V, 249
palmtops, 248
parallel interfaces, 47
parallel port devices
  defining, 51
  installing, 51
parallel ports, 47, 48, 49, 51, 106, 522
  configuring, 345
parity, 59, 172
partitions, 149, 560
Passive Matrix, 226
passive termination, 153
passwords
  changing, 490
path, 424
PC, 7
PC Cards, 236
  bus mastering, 236
  identifying the types, 236
  identifying the uses, 237
  installing, 238
  managing, 239
  using card and socket services, 237
  using CardBus, 236

using XIP, 236
using ZV, 236
PCI bus, 102
PCI cards, 102
PCI modem adapter cards, 98
PCMCIA, 236
PCMCIA cards, 210
PDA, 220, 248
  Also See: palmtops
  cleaning, 278
  connecting to a computer, 252
  identifying the types, 249, 251
peer-to-peer networks, 126
Pentium, 179
Pentium 4, 179
Pentium II, 179
Pentium III, 179
Pentium III with Xeon, 179
Pentium Pro, 179
Pentium with MMX, 179
Peripheral Component Interconnect bus
  See: PCI bus
peripheral devices, 30, 31, 835
  cleaning, 278
  parallel devices, 51
  video output devices, 37
Personal Computer Memory Card International Association
  See: PCMCIA
Personal Digital Assistant
  See: PDA
PGA, 185
physical topologies, 125
Piezoelectric technology, 269, 340
Pin Grid Array
  See: PGA
ping, 134, 351
  testing connectivity, 451
  troubleshooting TCP/IP connectivity, 456
  troubleshooting TCP/IP name resolution, 457

ping command, 447
pinouts, 42, 47, 55, 57, 195
PIO, 145
pixels, 35, 293
Plastic Pin Grid Array
   See: PPGA
platters, 140
plenum, 120
plenum cables, 121
Plug and Play, 435, 40
   Also See: PnP
PnP, 40, 41, 99
Point-to-Point Protocol
   See: PPP
Point-to-Point Tunneling Protocol
   See: PPTP
pointing devices, 226, 306
  2-button Microsoft mouse, 43
  3-button mouse, 43
  cleaning, 278
  identifying common problems, 306
  tablet and/or pen, 43
  touch pad, 43
  trackball, 43
  troubleshooting, 306, 309
  using, 304
Polyvinyl Chloride
   See: PVC
port capture, 523
port replicators, 227, 233
portable computer drives, 233, 234
  exchanging, 235
portable computing devices, 219, 242
  connecting to a docking station, 233
  connecting to a port replicator, 233
  connecting to a power source, 232
  defining, 218
  identifying common problems, 368
  identifying power sources, 229, 230

  identifying types, 220
  installing memory, 247
  troubleshooting, 368, 369
ports, 34, 42, 47, 48, 49, 51, 106
  defining, 34
potential difference, 829
potential energy, 829
power management, 295
power management standards, 198
power needs
  calculating, 196, 197
power supplies, 96, 192, 193, 194, 195
  identifying common problems, 356
  troubleshooting, 356, 359
  upgrading, 197, 210
power supply fans, 198
PPGA, 185
PPP, 597
PPTP, 608
PRI, 131, 132
primary cache, 169
   Also See: CPU cache
   Also See: L1 cache
primary network logon types, 472
primary partitions, 560
  creating, 564
  deleting, 569
Primary Rate Interface
   See: PRI
print components, 529
print drivers, 45, 516, 529
print permissions, 524
print problems, 530
print process, 530
print spooler, 529
Print Troubleshooter, 552
printer ports, 522
  capturing, 523
printer safety, 273

printers, 51
  affecting by the environment, 335
  dot-matrix, 264, 265, 270, 340, 341
  dye sublimation, 270, 272, 342
  identifying common problems, 335
  inkjet, 268, 269, 271, 339
  laser, 262, 263, 271, 337, 338
  solid ink, 270, 272, 342
  thermal wax, 342
  thermo autochrome, 342
  troubleshooting, 335, 338, 340, 341, 343, 531
processors, 179
  adding a second, 188
  removing a second, 188
  slot-based, 181, 183
  socket-based, 181, 182
  upgrading, 210
Programmable ROM
  See: PROM
PROM, 170
proprietary, 171
PS/2 devices
  identifying, 43
  installing, 46
PS/2 interfaces, 42, 43
  defining, 41, 42
PVC cables, 120

R

radio grades, 117
RAID, 158
RAID level 0, 159
  Also See: striping
RAID level 1, 159, 160
RAID level 5, 160
  Also See: striping with parity
RAM, 96, 139, 166, 167, 171, 177
  adding to a system, 173
RAM speeds, 168, 169

Rambus Dynamic RAM
  See: RDRAM
Rambus Inline Memory Module
  See: RIMM
RAMDAC, 292
Random Access Memory
  See: RAM
Random Access Memory Digital-Analog Converter
  See: RAMDAC
RAS, 597
RDRAM, 167
Read Only Memory
  See: ROM
read-write heads, 140
rechargeable batteries, 230
Recovery Console, 679
  installing, 679
Reduced Instruction Set Computer
  See: RISC
Redundant Array of Inexpensive Disks
  See: RAID
refresh rate, 35
register renaming, 177
registered jacks, 61
registers, 169
Registry, 404
  editing, 407
Registry Editor, 696
  backing up a Registry key, 696
Registry Editor backup
  restoring the Registry, 731
Registry entries, 406
regular SCSI, 154
  Also See: narrow SCSI
Remote Access Server
  See: RAS
remote connection, 594
remote-access connection, 594
removable cartridge drive software, 325

removable cartridge drives
  troubleshooting, 330
  using, 326
rendering, 530
resistance, 91, 831
resistor, 5
resolution, 35, 293
resource settings
  COM1, 109
  DMA, 107
  I/O Port, 107
  IRQ, 107
  memory addresses, 107
RIMM, 171
ring topology, 125
RISC, 186
riser cards, 201
RJ-11 cables, 61, 65
RJ-45 cables, 62
RJ-45 connectors, 115
ROM, 166, 170
ROM BIOS, 96

S

SAM, 166
satellite Internet connections, 132, 133
SC connectors, 120
scan codes, 301
Scan Disk tool, 258, 320
  running in Windows 98, 261
ScanDisk, 725
SCSI, 143, 150
  identifying the types, 154
  troubleshooting, 319
SCSI addresses, 151, 152
SCSI cables, 155
SCSI chains, 150
SCSI connectors, 155
SCSI devices
  accomplishing termination, 153

connecting an external device, 157
identifying by ID, 151, 152
identifying the characteristics, 150
installing an internal drive, 157
using signaling techniques, 152
SCSI interfaces, 155
SDRAM, 167
SE signaling, 152
SECC, 185
SECC2, 185
secondary cache, 169
  Also See: L2 cache
sectors, 141
Secure Digital (SD) and MultiMedia Cards
    MMC), 245
security cables, 223
security levels, 542
  configuring, 542
security slots, 223
semiconductor, 831
SEP, 185
Sequential Access Memory
  See: SAM
Serial ATA, 145
serial devices
  identifying, 53
  installing, 67
serial interfaces, 55, 57
  defining, 53, 54
  identifying settings, 58, 59, 67
Serial Line Internet Protocol
  See: SLIP
serial ports, 106, 522
  configuring settings, 67
serial transmissions, 53, 62
servers, 113
setup batch files, 780
setup command syntax, 780
shadow masks, 294
share permissions, 512

share-level security, 542
Shielded Twisted-Pair
   See: STP
signaling techniques, 152
SIMD, 177
SIMM, 171
Single Edge Contact Cartridge
   See: SECC
Single Edge Processor
   See: SEP
Single Ended
   See: SE
Single Inline Memory Module
   See: SIMM
Single Instruction Multiple Data
   See: SIMD
SLIP, 597
slots, 181, 183, 223
slotted masks, 294
slow IrDA, 83
Small Computer System Interface
   See: SCSI
Small Outline Dual Inline Memory Module
   See: SODIMM
SmartMedia flash memory cards, 244, 245
socket services, 237
sockets, 181, 182
SODIMM, 171
software-based modems, 62
solid ink printers, 342
  defining, 270
  maintaining, 272
sound cards, 69
  connecting sound devices, 73
  defining, 68
  identifying typical connections, 70
Speaker Out or Line Out, 68
speakers, 70
specialized video cards, 104, 105

speculative execution, 177
SPGA, 185
spindle motors, 140
spindles, 140
spools, 530
SPP, 49
SRAM, 167
ST connectors, 120
Staggered Pin Grid Array
   See: SPGA
Standard Parallel Port
   See: SPP
standby UPS, 275
star topology, 125
Start menu, 382
startup disks
  creating, 672
static, 834
static IP address, 445
Static RAM
   See: SRAM
stop bits, 59
STP, 115
straight through cables, 54
striping, 159
   Also See: RAID level 0
striping with parity, 160
   Also See: RAID level 5
subnet masks, 122, 123, 442
superpipelining, 177
superscalar, 177
support tools
  removing
surge protectors, 358
surge suppressors, 275
Suspend mode, 198
switches, 259
Symantec Norton AntiVirus 2003
  installing, 641

system requirements, 640
Synchronous DRAM
  See: SDRAM
synchronous mode, 63
System, 667
system boards, 199, 200, 199
  Also See: motherboards
  cleaning, 279
  identifying common problems, 366
  identifying other ports, 209
  identifying symptoms, 366
  replacing, 208
  troubleshooting, 366, 367
  upgrading, 210
system buses, 181
  Also See: frontside buses
  Also See: local buses
system partition, 669
system state data, 693
  backing up, 694
System.ini, 666

T

T-connectors, 118
tape drives, 134, 138, 327
taskbar, 381
TCP/IP, 123, 443
  automatic configuration methods, 445
  common connectivity problems, 454
  configuration process, 445
  configuring, 441, 448
  configuring automatically
  configuring manually
  configuring properties, 124, 125
  connectivity process, 453
  naming servers, 124
  testing connectivity with Winipcfg, 477
  troubleshooting automatic configuration with IPConfig, 458
  troubleshooting connectivity problems, 456
  troubleshooting connectivity using ping, 456
  troubleshooting connectivity with IPConfig, 458
  troubleshooting connectivity with tracert, 457
  troubleshooting name resolution with NSLookup, 457
  troubleshooting name resolution with ping, 457
  troubleshooting process, 452
  troubleshooting tools, 455
technician's toolkit, 110, 111
terminate and stay resident
  See: TSR
termination, 153
thermal compounds, 177
thermal wax printers, 342
thermo autochrome printers, 342
throughput, 49
toner, 262, 282
touch screen input devices, 77, 78
touch screens
  identifying common problems, 309
  troubleshooting, 309
  using, 308
tracert
  troubleshooting TCP/IP connectivity, 457
trackballs, 226, 306
trackpads, 226
  Also See: touchpads
  Also See: glide pads
trackpoints, 226
tracks, 141
tractor feed, 266
transceivers, 65
transistors, 5, 96
Transmission Control Protocol/Internet Protocol
  See: TCP/IP
triboelectric generation, 834
Trojan Horse, 639
troubleshooting, 290, 291, 292, 295
  adapter cards, 312, 315
  boot process, 363

booting the computer, 46
CD and DVD drives, 331, 332
checking for hard disk errors, 259
Collect, Isolate, and Correct model, 370, 371, 372, 374, 375
dot-matrix printers, 341
floppy drives, 329
hard drive boot problems, 321
hard drive data access problems, 323
hard drives, 318
inkjet printers, 340
internal removable media devices, 328
keyboards, 302, 303, 309
memory, 364, 365
modems, 352, 354
monitors, 295, 298
network connections, 134, 350, 351
networks, 350, 351
newly installed hard drives, 322
pointing devices, 306, 309
portable computing devices, 368, 369
power supplies, 356, 359
printers, 335, 338, 340, 343
removable cartridge drives, 330
SCSI, 319
system boards, 366, 367
system problems, 375
touch screens, 309
USB, 313
wrong drive size being reported, 324
troubleshooting resources, 373
troubleshooting tips, 291, 292
troubleshooting tools, 707
TSR, 422
twisted-pair cables, 115, 116
Type I Mini-PCI cards, 239
Type I PC Cards, 236
Type II Mini-PCI cards, 239
Type II PC Cards, 236
Type III Mini-PCI cards, 239

Type III PC Cards, 236

U

Ultra 320 SCSI, 155
Ultra DMA, 143, 145
Ultra SCSI, 154
Ultra Wide SCSI, 154
Ultra2 SCSI, 154
Ultra3 SCSI, 154
UMB, 422
unidirectional ports, 49
Uninterruptible Power Supply
   See: UPS
Universal Serial Bus
   See: USB
Unshielded Twisted-Pair
   See: UTP
upgrades
   deciding to upgrade, 211, 212
   identifying when to upgrade, 210
uplink, 132
   Also See: upstream data
upper memory area, 422
upper memory blocks
   See: UMB
UPS
   defining, 273, 274
   determining size needs, 275
   identifying types, 274, 275
   using and testing, 275
upstream data, 132
   Also See: uplink
USB, 74, 76
   identifying common problems, 313
   troubleshooting, 313
USB 2.0, 76
USB cables, 76
USB devices, 75
   connecting to a system, 79
USB hosts, 75

USB interconnects, 75
USB power, 78
user account properties, 489
  modifying, 492
user accounts
  renaming, 489
user data files, 693
user profile folders
  locations, 411
user profiles, 409, 553
  enabling, 554
  renaming, 490
user-level security, 542
UTP, 115

V

vacuum tube, 4
value, 406
ventilation control, 95
video cards, 210
video output devices, 31, 32, 37
Video RAM
  See: VRAM
Virtual Device Driver, 666
virtual memory, 415
  configuring, 415
Virtual Private Network connection
  See: VPN connection
virus, 638
virus protection software, 640
  common configuration properties, 645
virus removal options, 655
voice coil actuators, 140
voltage, 91, 193
Voltage Regulator Module
  See: VRM
volts, 91
VPN connections, 596
  creating, 609
VRAM, 167

VRM, 199

W

watts, 91, 193
Web browsers, 613
Web protocols, 614
Wide SCSI, 154
Win.com, 666
Win.ini, 666
Windows
  common problems, 770
Windows 2000
  assigning file and folder permissions, 502
  backing up data, 683
  backing up system state data, 694
  boot files, 667
  boot process, 668
  changing user passwords, 490
  Computer Management, 387
    Also See: Computer Management
  configuring domain membership, 496
  configuring environment variable, 425
  configuring file attributes, 505
  configuring files and buffers, 427
  configuring TCP/IP, 448
  configuring virtual memory, 416
  configuring workgroup membership, 495
  connecting to a network printer, 517
  connecting to a network-attached printer, 517
  converting FAT partitions, 571
  creating a boot disk, 673
  creating a VPN connection, 609
  creating an emergency repair disk, 677
  creating dial-up connections, 599
  creating extended partitions, 566
  creating installation boot disks, 676
  creating local user accounts, 484
  creating primary partitions, 564
  decrypting files and folders, 506
  defragmenting hard disks, 574

deleting extended partitions, 570
deleting local user accounts, 485
deleting local user profiles, 487
deleting primary partitions, 569
editing a Registry, 408
encrypting files and folders, 506
installing a Windows application, 411
installing local printers, 525
installing NetBEUI, 459
installing NetWare client, 469
installing NWLink IPX/SPX, 462
modifying group memberships, 491
modifying user account properties, 492
partition terminology, 669
performing an emergency repair, 736
performing an unattended installation, 780
removing an application, 428
removing NetBEUI, 459
removing NetWare client, 470
removing NWLink IPX/SPX, 463
removing support tools
renaming user accounts, 489
renaming user profiles, 490
restoring data, 728
restoring System State Data, 734
scheduling a backup, 684
setting up an Internet connection, 615
troubleshooting a hard disk, 716
updating network card drivers, 437
upgrading to Windows XP, 768
Windows 2000 Professional
  installing, 755
Windows 98
  backing up data, 691
  configuring environment variables, 426
  configuring files and buffers, 427
  configuring virtual memory, 418
  creating a Norton AntiVirus rescue disk set, 651
  creating a startup disk, 672
  creating an MS-DOS boot disk, 671
  creating dial-up connections, 606
  installing, 751
  installing a Windows application, 414
  removing an application, 429
  restoring data, 730
  restoring the Registry from a backup, 733
  system state data, 696
  troubleshooting a hard disk, 721
  updating a Norton AntiVirus 2003 rescue disk set, 652
  upgrading to Windows 2000, 766
Windows 98 Backup
  backing up the Registry, 698
Windows 9x
  boot files, 666
  boot process, 666
  configuring a network connection, 473
  configuring security levels, 542
  converting FAT to FAT32, 588
  creating partitions, 581
  creating VPN connections, 612
  defragmenting a hard disk, 589
  deleting partitions, 583
  drive compression, 584
  editing a Registry, 407
  enabling user profiles, 554
  FAT32 file systems, 580
  file conversion process, 586
  large disk support, 580
  MS-DOS mode, 581
  running ScanDisk, 725
  running the Maintenance Wizard, 727
  setting up an Internet connection, 618
  sharing folders using user-level security, 545
  sharing folders with share-level security, 544
  troubleshooting printers, 549
  uncompressing a drive, 586
  user profiles, 553
  Windows 9x share permissions, 543

Windows 9x users, 553
Windows applications
   installing, 402
Windows boot troubleshooting tools, 715
Windows Event Viewer, 713
Windows Explorer, 384
Windows graphical tools
   See: graphical tools
Windows installation requirements, 749
Windows Internet Naming System
   See: WINS
Windows NT
   assigning file and folder permissions, 504
   backing up data, 688
   boot files, 667
   boot process, 668
   changing user passwords, 490
   configuring domain membership, 498
   configuring environment variables, 426
   configuring file attributes, 505
   configuring files and buffers, 427
   configuring TCP/IP, 450
   configuring virtual memory, 417
   configuring workgroup membership, 498
   connecting to a network printer, 521
   converting FAT partitions, 571
   creating a boot disk, 673
   creating an emergency repair disk, 677
   creating dial-up connections, 604
   creating extended partitions, 568
   creating installation boot disks, 676
   creating local user accounts, 486
   creating primary partitions, 565
   creating VPN connections, 611
   deleting local user accounts, 487
   deleting local user profiles, 488
   deleting primary partitions, 569
   editing a Registry, 408
   installing a Windows application, 413
   installing local printers, 528
   installing NetBEUI, 460
   installing NetWare client, 471
   installing NWLink IPX/SPX, 465
   modifying group memberships, 491
   modifying user account properties, 492
   partiton terminology, 669
   performing an emergency repair, 737
   removing an application, 428
   removing NetBEUI, 460
   removing NetWare client, 472
   removing NWLink IPX/SPX, 466
   renaming user accounts, 489
   restoring data, 729
   restoring the Registry from a backup, 732
   scheduling a backup, 689
   setting up an Internet connection, 618
   troubleshooting a hard disk, 716
   updating network card drivers, 439
Windows NT Backup
   backing up the Registry, 697
Windows operating system features, 746
Windows print process, 336
Windows RAM
   See: WRAM
Windows setup programs, 750
Windows Update, 751
Windows upgrade paths, 751
Windows XP
   assigning file and folder permissions, 503
   backing up data, 685
   backing up system state data, 695
   boot files, 667
   boot process, 668
   changing user passwords, 490
   Computer Management, 387
   Also See: Computer Management
   configuring domain membership, 497
   configuring environment variables, 425

configuring file attributes, 505
configuring files and buffers, 427
configuring TCP/IP, 449
configuring virtual memory, 417
configuring workgroup membership, 496
connecting to a network printer, 519
connecting to a network-attached printer, 520
converting FAT partitions, 571
creating a boot disk, 673
creating an MS-DOS boot disk, 674
creating connections to private servers, 601
creating extended partitions, 566
creating local user accounts, 485
creating primary partitions, 564
creating VPN connections, 610
decrypting files and folders, 506
defragmenting hard disks, 574
deleting extended partitions, 570
deleting local user accounts, 486
deleting local user profiles, 488
deleting primary partitions, 569
editing a Registry, 408
encrypting files and folders, 506
installing a Windows application, 412
installing local printers, 526
installing NetWare client, 469
installing NWLink IPX/SPX, 464
modifying group memberships, 491
modifying user account properties, 492
partition terminology, 669
performing an unattended installation, 783
removing an application, 428
removing NetWare client, 470
removing NWLink IPX/SPX, 464
renaming user accounts, 489
renaming user profiles, 490
restoring data, 729
restoring System State Data, 735
scheduling a backup, 687

setting up an Internet connection, 617
troubleshooting a hard disk, 716
updating network card drivers, 438
using Recovery Console, 736
Windows XP Professional
  installing, 759
Winipcfg
  testing TCP/IP connectivity, 477
WINS, 124, 444
wire colors, 193
wireless connections, 82, 83
  connecting digital radio, 84
  connection infrared devices, 84
wireless Internet connection, 133
wizards
  Add New Hardware, 41
workgroup, 494
workgroup membership
  configuring, 495
workgroup or domain membership
  setting, 540
worm, 639
WRAM, 167

X

xD flash memory cards, 245
xD-Picture flash memory cards, 245
  Also See: xD flash memory cards
Xerox Phaser 8200B solid ink printers, 270
XIP, 236

Z

Zinc Air, 232
Zip drives, 325
ZIP sockets, 184
zoned-bit recording, 141
Zoomed Video
  See: ZV
ZV, 236